Digital Media Law

Digital Media Law

Second Edition

Ashley Packard

WILEY-BLACKWELL

A John Wiley & Sons, Ltd., Publication

This edition first published 2013
© 2013 John Wiley & Sons, Inc

Edition history: 1e (Wiley-Blackwell, 2010)

Wiley-Blackwell is an imprint of John Wiley & Sons, formed by the merger of Wiley's global Scientific, Technical and Medical business with Blackwell Publishing.

Registered Office
John Wiley & Sons Ltd, The Atrium, Southern Gate, Chichester, West Sussex, PO19 8SQ, UK

Editorial Offices
350 Main Street, Malden, MA 02148-5020, USA
9600 Garsington Road, Oxford, OX4 2DQ, UK
The Atrium, Southern Gate, Chichester, West Sussex, PO19 8SQ, UK

For details of our global editorial offices, for customer services, and for information about how to apply for permission to reuse the copyright material in this book please see our website at www.wiley.com/wiley-blackwell.

The right of Ashley Packard to be identified as the author of this work has been asserted in accordance with the UK Copyright, Designs and Patents Act 1988.

Library of Congress Cataloging-in-Publication Data

Packard, Ashley.
  Digital media law / Ashley Packard. – 2nd ed.
      p. cm.
  Includes bibliographical references and index.
    ISBN 978-1-118-29072-9 (pbk. : alk. paper)   1. Digital media–Law and legislation–United States.   2. Internet–Law and legislation–United States.   3. Telecommunication–Law and legislation–United States.   4. Freedom of expression–United States.   5. Digital media–Law and legislation.   I. Title.
  KF2750.P33 2012
  343.7309'9–dc23
                                2012015389

A catalogue record for this book is available from the British Library.

Cover images: background © Ozerina Anna/Shutterstock; tablet © pressureUA/Shutterstock
Cover design by Richard Boxall Design Associates based on an original concept by Kalan Lyra

Set in 10/13 pt Minion by Toppan Best-set Premedia Limited
Printed in Malaysia by Ho Printing (M) Sdn Bhd

2   2013

Brief Contents

Detailed Contents

List of Sidebars

Preface

It is time to stop thinking about media law as though it were the exclusive domain of traditional media organizations. Our global shift to digital media has precipitated a shift in information control. Meanwhile the affordability of digital media and their ease of use has democratized media production. With the right equipment, anyone can produce a website, listserv, blog or video with the potential to reach a mass audience. When *anyone* can become a media producer, *everyone* should know something about media law – both to protect their own rights and to avoid violating the rights of others.

This text focuses on digital media law, which like digital media, is characterized by its general applicability. The information presented here is applicable to professionals in fields such as publishing, public relations, advertising, marketing, e-commerce, graphic art, web design, animation, photography, video and audio production, game design, and instructional technology among others. But it is equally relevant to individuals who use digital media for personal interests – either to express themselves through social networking sites, blogs, and discussion boards or to engage in file trading or digital remixing.

As a field, digital media law is also characterized by its global impact. Digital media are borderless. Material uploaded to the Internet enters every country. Material broadcast via satellite reaches across entire continents. What does *not* travel internationally, however, is the First Amendment. American publishing companies and writers have been sued in courts all over the world for publishing information on the Internet that violated the laws of other countries. Foreign courts will apply their laws to material that is accessible within their borders through the Internet or via satellite if they perceive that material to have caused harm there. Producers of digital media need to understand how jurisdiction is determined and when foreign law can be applied to them.

Digital Media Law focuses on issues that are particularly relevant to the production and use of digital media. Its cases and controversies are based on freedom of expression, information access and protection, intellectual property, defamation, privacy, indecency, and commercial speech in the context of new media. This growing area of law also encompasses regulations imposed on the content and operation of telecommunications, such as broadcast, cable and satellite media, cellular communications, and the Internet. The material is framed to appeal to the broad audience of future media producers in communication and digital media disciplines. Current examples bring legal concepts to life. The text is also accompanied by a website (www.DigitalMediaLaw.us) that provides updated information about new court decisions and legislation, links to cases, and supplementary material. A little computer icon (⌨) appears in the text near cases and controversies that are still in progress. You can visit the "What's New" section on the website for new information about them.

Chapter 1 provides an introduction to the legal system and a guide to locate primary sources of law. Use it to gain a basic understanding of law before moving on to other topics.

Chapter 2 explores the First Amendment. Speech is presumed to be protected in the United States unless proven otherwise. This chapter addresses the extent of that protection and its limitations.

Chapter 3 covers telecommunications law, including regulations for broadcast media, cable, direct broadcast satellite, and phone service. It explores the varying levels of First Amendment protection that apply to different media and the Federal Communications Commission's efforts to adapt its rules to converging technologies.

Chapter 4 discusses the Internet's regulatory structure and explains the difference between domestic and international concepts of net neutrality. It describes legislative efforts to make the Internet more accessible to people with disabilities. It also details statutes in place to combat cybercrime and introduces the concept of virtual law.

Chapter 5 provides an introduction to the legal area of procedure called conflict of laws. It explains how jurisdiction, choice of law, and enforcement of foreign judgments applies to transnational conflicts involving digitally disseminated content.

Chapter 6 describes federal and state guarantees of access to information and protections for information sources. This area of law, which has always been of particular significance to traditional journalists, is now increasingly important to bloggers and podcasters.

Chapters 7 and 8 provide an overview of intellectual property law. Chapter 7 explains copyright law, a field that applies to every digital media producer's work. Chapter 8 describes patent law, trademark protection, trade secret protection, and cybersquatting legislation.

Chapter 9 addresses defamation law, which has always been the bane of traditional media, but is now increasingly applied to "average people" who post damaging accusations on websites, blogs, and listservs. It explains how U.S. libel law differs from that of other countries and the impact that difference has on the treatment of plaintiffs and defendants.

Chapter 10 explores protections for privacy, scattered among state and federal statutes, common law, and state constitutions. It addresses rights to privacy in the marketplace, work, home, and electronic communications.

Chapter 11 delves into the regulation of sex and violence. In particular, it explores varying protections accorded indecency v. obscenity and how states have tried to apply these theories to control violence in media.

Chapter 12 explains differences in First Amendment protection accorded to commercial speech. It describes the efforts of regulatory agencies to control deceptive advertisements, spam, and antitrust violations.

A glossary is provided at the back of the book for looking up key terms. After you've learned more about the law, you may be interested in doing some of your own research. Look in the appendix for a simplified guide to legal research. It will help you find different sources of law and understand how to read legal citations.

Acknowledgments

Without the dedicated editorial staff at Wiley-Blackwell, particularly Elizabeth Swayze and Julia Kirk, you would not be reading this book. Their experience and generosity guided me through its production. I also owe a debt of gratitude to the kind professors who reviewed the book for Wiley and, through their insightful comments, made the manuscript better. My deepest appreciation goes to my talented illustrator, Kalan Lyra, who took abstract ideas and turned them into something visually meaningful. I also want to thank three wonderful research assistants: Kyle Johnson, Jessica Casarez and Nick Pavlow. I remain indebted to William Fisch and Martha Dragich, my professors of constitutional law and legal research. Finally, my most sincere thanks goes to my husband, Chris, and daughter, Eliza, who supported me even when they realized how much time this book was taking away from them.

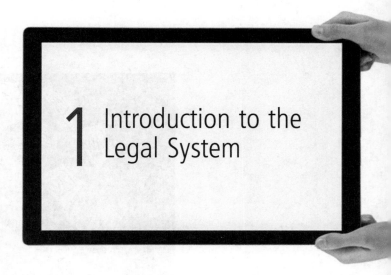

1 Introduction to the Legal System

It makes no sense to dive into a particular area of law without understanding the basic structure of the legal system and its terminology. This chapter describes the primary sources of law in the United States and how to find them. It explains the structure of the federal and state court systems, the basic differences between civil and criminal law, and the role of judicial review in the United States. It can be used to establish a foundation before proceeding to other chapters and as a reference later when you need to review a particular concept.

The Meaning of Law

Before discussing how law is made, it might be helpful to define it generally. Law is a system to guide behavior, both to protect the rights of individuals and to ensure public order. Although it may have a moral component, it differs from moral systems because the penalties for its violation are carried out by the state.

Digital media law encompasses all statutes, administrative rules, and court decisions that have an impact on digital technology. Because technology is always changing, digital media law is in a state of continuous adaptation. But its basic structure and principles are still grounded in the "brick-and-mortar" legal system.

Sources of Law in the United States

All students are taught in civics class that there are three branches of government and that each serves a unique function in relation to the law. The *legislative* branch makes

Digital Media Law, Second Edition. Ashley Packard.
© 2013 John Wiley & Sons, Inc. Published 2013 by John Wiley & Sons, Inc.

Figure 1.1   The legislative, executive and judicial branches of government make law.
Illustration: Kalan Lyra

law, the *judicial* branch interprets law, and the *executive* branch enforces law. Although this is true, it is also a little misleading because it suggests that each branch is completely compartmentalized. Actually, all three branches make law. The legislative branch produces statutory law. The executive branch issues executive orders and administrative rules. The judicial branch creates law through precedential decisions. In the United States, sources of law include constitutions, statutes, executive orders, administrative agencies, federal departments, and the common law and law of equity developed by the judiciary. The most important source of law, however, is the U.S. Constitution.

Constitutions

A political entity's constitution is the supreme law of the land because it is the foundation for government itself. The constitution specifies the organization, powers, and limits of government, as well as the rights guaranteed to citizens. Because the legislative, judicial, and executive branches of government draw their power from the U.S. Constitution, they cannot act in opposition to it. For this reason, federal courts will overturn statutes and administrative rules that exceed constitutional boundaries. They will also reverse lower courts when their decisions stray too far afield.

The *only* way to get around the Constitution is to alter the document. Ratification of an amendment requires approval from three-fourths of the states. Twenty-seven amendments have been ratified since the Constitution was signed. The first ten are known as the Bill of Rights.

In addition to the federal Constitution, there are 50 state constitutions. States are *sovereign* entities with the power to make their own laws. However, their laws must operate in accord with federal law. The U.S. Constitution includes a supremacy clause that requires state courts to follow federal law when conflicts arise between it and state constitutions or state law.[1] The federal constitution also requires that states give "full faith and credit" to other states' laws and judicial decisions.

> The U.S. Constitution declares its supremacy in Article XI: "This Constitution . . . shall be the supreme Law of the Land; and the Judges in every state shall be bound thereby, any Thing in the Constitution or Laws of any State to the Contrary notwithstanding."
>
> The Constitution Society provides links to the U.S. Constitution and all state constitutions at www.constitution.org/.

Statutes

When we think about the word "law," we generally have in mind the statutes passed by our elected representatives as part of city councils, county commissions, state legislatures, and the U.S. Congress. These laws, called *ordinances* at the city level and statutes at the state and federal level, are meant to serve as guidance to people before they act. Criminal law, in particular, must give people fair warning that an act is illegal before punishing them for violating it, so it is *always* statutory.

Statutes are intended to address potential social needs and problems, so they are written broadly to apply to a variety of circumstances. But their broad language sometimes creates confusion regarding the meaning of particular terms. In such cases, it falls to courts to interpret their meaning. Courts do this by looking at the statutory construction of laws, otherwise known as their *legislative history*. When laws are passed, they go through a series of committees. Each committee files a report, documenting its actions related to the law. This history of the legislative process usually includes the legislators' intent regarding the law's scope and interpretation. Judges may review the reports to find out what was discussed when legislators were hammering out the legislation and how they intended it to be applied.

As you read federal statutes, you will notice that many of them apply to activities carried out through "interstate or foreign commerce." For example, the federal stalking statute applies to anyone who uses "a facility of *interstate or foreign commerce* to engage in a course of conduct that causes substantial emotional distress." Likewise, federal law

> Federal statutes are found in the United States Code, available at http://uscode.house.gov/. State codes may be found at http://www.whpgs.org/f.htm.

---

[1] U.S. Const. art VI, § 2.

prohibits the transmission of obscene materials through *interstate and foreign commerce.* This phraseology is added to bring activities within the federal government's jurisdiction. The federal government does not have police power as states do. *Police power* – the right to legislate to protect the health, safety and welfare of citizens – is reserved for the states. So the federal government regulates activity related to these issues through its exclusive jurisdiction over interstate commerce. Article 1, Section 8 of the U.S. Constitution gives Congress the power "To regulate Commerce with foreign Nations, and among the several States . . . " Application of the term "commerce" does not mean that money must change hands. When the Constitution was written, commerce was also used in a non-economic context to refer to conduct. Congress applies the term loosely to conduct that crosses state and national borders. Activities carried on within a single state must be regulated under state law.

Executive orders

Within the executive branch of government, mayors, governors, and presidents have the power to issue *executive orders* that are legally binding. Some executive orders are issued to fill in the details of legislation passed by the legislative branch. For example, if Congress passes a bill requiring action on the part of federal agencies without providing sufficient information about how its mandate is to be implemented, the president may issue an executive order specifying procedure.

Executive orders may be found through the National Archives website at http:// www.archives.gov/federal-register/ executive-orders/.

In other cases, executives issue orders of their own accord to promote their policies. By directing federal agencies and officials to enforce their orders, presidents have created national parks, integrated the armed services, desegregated schools, funded and defunded stem cell research, and prohibited financial transactions with countries known for terrorism. Executive orders are also frequently used to regain order in the event of a threat to security. Following a natural disaster like a hurricane, for example, a governor may issue a state of emergency, which would empower him or her to make binding rules for a certain period of time.

Executive orders are passed without the legislature's consent, but the legislature may override them with enough votes. Congress can override a presidential executive order by passing legislation that contradicts it. If the president vetoes the legislation, Congress can override the veto with a two-thirds vote. Executive orders also may be challenged in court if they exceed the president's constitutional authority. For example, Harry Truman tried to avert a national strike of steel mill workers during the Korean War by issuing an executive order to the Commerce Department to seize control of private steel mills. The Supreme Court held the action unconstitutional.[2]

Administrative agencies and federal departments

Also within the executive branch, independent administrative agencies and federal departments are empowered to make *administrative rules* that carry the force of law.

[2]Youngstown Sheet & Tube Co. v. Sawyer, 343 U.S. 579 (1952).

Independent administrative agencies

Independent administrative agencies are so named because, although they are part of the executive branch of government, they carry out the mandates of the legislative branch in specific government-regulated industries. Agencies monitor technical areas of law thought to be better handled by specialists than members of Congress. Not only do they have the power to make rules and enforce them with fines and other retaliatory measures, but federal agencies also serve a quasi-judicial function. Their administrative courts are usually the first to hear cases related to violations of agency rules.

Congress provided the protocol for agency rule making and enforcement in the Administrative Procedures Act.[3] One of the Act's purposes is to keep agency rule making open to provide opportunities for public participation. To that end, the law requires agencies to publish notices of proposed rule making, opinions, and statements of policy in the *Federal Register*. Administrative rules are later codified in the *Code of Federal Regulations*.

Another purpose of the Administrative Procedures Act is to keep the process for rule making and adjudication across agencies relatively consistent by prescribing uniform standards and a mechanism for judicial oversight. A federal court may set aside an agency decision if the rule is "arbitrary and capricious, an abuse of discretion, or otherwise not in accordance with the law."[4] It is not the court's role to substitute its judgment for that of the agency, but to ensure that when an agency creates a new rule or modifies established policy that it articulates "a satisfactory explanation for its action including a 'rational connection between the facts found and the choice made.'"[5] A court may conclude that an agency action is arbitrary and capricious if the agency has:

- relied on factors Congress did not intend it to consider;
- failed to consider an important aspect of the problem;
- offered an explanation for its decision that contradicts evidence before the agency; or
- is too implausible to be ascribed to a difference in view or agency expertise.[6]

Independent agencies most likely to be involved with digital media law are the Federal Communications Commission and Federal Trade Commission. The Federal Communications Commission regulates interstate and international communication emanating from the United States. The Federal Trade Commission enforces fair advertising, consumer protection, and antitrust rules.

The Federal Register is a daily digest of proposed and final administrative regulations issued by federal executive departments and agencies in the United States. It is available online at http://www.gpo.gov/fdsys/.

After their initial publication in the Federal Register, U.S. agency and department rules are codified in the Code of Federal Regulations, available online at http://www.gpo.gov/fdsys/.

[3] 5 U.S.C. § 551 et seq. (2011).
[4] 5 U.S.C. § 706(2)(A) (2011).
[5] Motor Vehicle Mfrs. Ass'n of U.S., Inc. v. State Farm Mut. Auto. Ins. Co., 463 U.S. 29, 43 (1983) (citing Burlington Truck Lines, Inc. v. United States, 371 U.S. 156, 168 (1962)).
[6] *Id.*

Federal departments

Federal departments also make administrative rules, but do not act independently of the executive branch of government. Their leaders are appointed by the president and make up the president's cabinet.

The federal departments most likely to be involved with digital media law are the Departments of Commerce and Justice. The Department of Commerce fosters economic development and technological advancement. Among its many bureaus, the National Telecommunications and Information Administration, or NTIA, acts as the administrative branch's policy advisor for telecommunication issues. The Department of Justice, led by the Attorney General, supervises federal law enforcement. As such, it is involved in the prosecutions of crimes, such as incitement to violence, fraud, threats, and distribution of obscenity, that may be carried out through digital media. The Justice Department also represents the United States in suits against the government through the Office of the Solicitor General. Cases challenging U.S. law before the Supreme Court frequently include the Attorney General's name as one of the parties.

Common Law and Law of Equity

The role of courts in all legal systems is to determine whether law is applied appropriately in particular cases. But in common law legal systems – like those of the United Kingdom and its former colonies, such as the United States – courts also have the power to make law. There are two types of judge-made law: *common law* and *law of equity*.

Common law, also known as caselaw, is a body of legal precedent established through prior court decisions. Judges create common law when no statutory law covers the issue before them. Later judges rely on those precedents for guidance in future legal disputes based on similar circumstances.

The use of common law dates back to twelfth-century England. In order to wrest power for legal decision-making from local officials, King Henry II dispatched judges to travel in circuits around the country dispensing justice in the king's name. Because the king's judges had no knowledge of events that had taken place prior to their arrival, they assembled juries of local men to aid them in their decision-making. Jurors determined the facts of the case, while the judge determined the applicable law – a practice that is still in use today. These circuit judges adopted the customary rules they considered most appropriate and shared their decisions with each other. Their precedents eventually crystallized into a national common law dispensed by the Courts of the King's Bench, Common Pleas, and Exchequer – collectively known as the Common Law Courts.[7]

In a modern context, most common law is created in the areas of tort and contract law. *Torts* are civil wrongs that result in harm or injury and which act as grounds for lawsuits. *Contracts* are agreements between two or more parties that are enforceable by law. Within the context of digital media, for example, common law applies to such torts

There are a variety of sources for locating caselaw. A useful free resource is FindLaw, at www.findlaw.com/casecode. Additional sources are described in the Legal Research Appendix.

[7]William Searle Holdsworth, A History of English Law 204–31 (Little, Brown & Co. 1922) (1903).

as libel, invasion of privacy, intentional infliction of emotional distress and misappropriation of trade secrets, and to "click to sign" contracts connected with Internet and software use.

These types of cases are normally litigated at the state level, where most common law is made. At the federal level, common law has largely been supplanted by statute. However, federal courts still use it to delineate the boundaries of statutory and constitutional law. We see this occur when courts look back to previous decisions to determine the meaning of a particular term or phrase used in a statute in an effort to interpret the law.

When one party harms another through a practice prohibited by law, the wounded party can turn to the courts for redress. Under common law, a court can provide damages to compensate for that harm. However, this is not always what is needed to remedy a situation. Sometimes, what a plaintiff needs is for a court to act *before* the harm occurs, in order to prevent irreparable harm. Common law does not apply before the fact. However, law of equity, which serves as a supplement to common law, provides a mechanism for this.

Using law of equity, which also dates back to twelfth-century England, judges can create more flexible remedies for plaintiffs than those available under common law. Take, for example, a situation in which Apple learns that a disgruntled employee has stolen plans for its yet-to-be-released iMind – a device that transmits data directly into the human brain – and is threatening to upload them to the Internet. Once the plans have been published online, Apple will be able to sue the employee for misappropriation of it trade secrets under common law. It may even be able to collect a small portion of its damages. But, by that time, Apple's competitors will have access to its new product plans, and the potential damages incurred will far outweigh any damages the employee could repay. Equity fills the gap. Using the law of equity, a judge can issue a restraining order or injunction to prevent the thief from acting before the harm occurs.

Within the media context, equitable relief most often takes the form of *injunctions*, which are court orders that require someone to do something or not to do something. But courts grant other forms of equitable relief as well. Parties in doubt of their rights with regard to a particular legal issue may request a *declaratory judgment* from a court as a precursor to further legal action. This legally binding opinion sets out the rights and obligations of parties within a legal controversy. A party threatened with a lawsuit for engaging in a particular behavior, for example, might seek a declaratory judgment to assess his or her rights before acting.

Understanding precedents

The practice of following precedents under common law is known as *stare decisis* (pronounced "stair-ee da-sy-sis"), which literally means "to stand by that which is decided." The part of the case that sets the precedent is called the *holding*. This is the court's decision regarding the legal question presented. In some cases, a court will be very helpful by saying, "We hold that . . . ," but other times you have to sift though a lot of text to find the golden nugget.

Collateral statements made by judges are referred to as *obiter dictum* or "dicta." This is all the rest of the text in a judicial opinion. Dicta (which often encompass a lot of analogies, opinions, and explanation) can be interesting, but are not legally binding. Dicta may be used to understand a court's reasoning and provide an indication of how it might rule in the future.

In appellate court cases, a panel of judges – usually three, but sometimes as many as eleven – renders the decision. The opinion may be unanimous, but more commonly it is subdivided into a majority opinion with concurring and dissenting opinions. The *majority opinion*, so named because it is issued by a majority of the judges on the panel, includes the holding and the legal rationale to support it. To the extent that the opinion answers a new legal question or offers a new legal interpretation, it carries precedential value.

Judges who support the majority's conclusion based on an alternative rationale issue a *concurring opinion*, explaining the legal rule they would prefer to use. Judges who disagree with the majority's conclusion issue a *dissenting opinion*, explaining why they think the majority has misinterpreted the law. Concurring and dissenting opinions are published with the majority opinion, so someone reading the case can acquire a full understanding of the court's position on an issue.

In a small percentage of appellate cases, a majority of judges will reach consensus on a conclusion, without agreeing on a rationale or legal rule to support it. In these cases, the rationale that receives the most support is called the *plurality opinion*. Decisions in these cases are reached by combining coalitions of judges, citing different legal rules. A plurality decision in the Supreme Court, for example, might draw four justices supporting a conclusion with one rationale, two concurring with the decision, based on a different rationale, and three justices dissenting. In the end, the case will be resolved because six justices agree on a desired outcome, but its precedential value will be limited because no majority supported a legal rule to justify the outcome. Consequently, plurality opinions are narrowly interpreted. Only those aspects of the plurality opinion that draw support from concurring judges are binding.

A *binding precedent* is one that a court must follow. Whether a *precedent* is binding depends on the court's hierarchy and jurisdiction. Courts must follow decisions rendered by higher courts in their own jurisdictions. But even if a precedent is not binding, it still might be persuasive. A *persuasive precedent* is one that a court may use as guidance but also has the prerogative to reject. For example, a Georgia court is not bound by the decisions of other states. However, if the Georgia court is facing a new legal issue, with no precedent to follow from its own state, it will look to other states for guidance. If it finds that a Florida court has issued a well-reasoned opinion on the issue, the Georgia court may elect to adopt it as its own.

Modifying, distinguishing, and overruling precedents

The concept of stare decisis may lead to the assumption that courts are always bound by earlier precedents. In fact, they are not. The law is a lot like a coral reef. Precedents build upon one another in some areas, while in other areas they remain relatively consistent or may even be torn down.

Courts have the option of modifying, distinguishing, or overruling precedents.

Courts *modify* a precedent when they adapt it to fit a new situation. For example, courts had to modify "print-based" precedents to fit the first copyright cases related to the Internet. Courts *distinguish* a precedent when they determine that it does not fit the particular case or situation under analysis. For example, when the Supreme Court reviewed the Communications Decency Act, a law intended to control indecency on the Internet, the government tried to persuade the Court that the Act's restrictions on Internet speech were analogous to restrictions imposed on "dial-a-porn" that had already been upheld. The Court distinguished the dial-a-porn precedent from the Internet case because they dealt with different media. Courts *overrule* precedents when they decide that the precedents are no longer good law. For example, the Supreme Court decided in 1915 that films were public spectacles unworthy of First Amendment protection.[8] The Court reversed its opinion in 1952, deciding that films, like other media, are a form of protected expression.[9]

The Difference Between Common and Civil Law Legal Systems

Common law legal systems are unique to the United Kingdom and her former colonies. Civil law systems are actually more common. Civil law is used in most of Europe, all of Central and South America, parts of Asia and Africa, and in some states within common law countries, such as Louisiana in the United States and Quebec in Canada.[10] Judges do not make law in civil law systems. They rely exclusively on statutory law, usually set down in codes that are cohesively structured. Civil law is based on deductive logic. There is one rule of law and decisions for cases are drawn from the rule. In contrast, common law relies on inductive logic. The rule is based on a general conclusion from a number of cases.

Not only is civil law the dominant legal system, it is also the oldest. Its heritage can be traced back to the early Roman Empire. In the sixth century, the Emperor Justinian amassed all law into a unified code called the *Corpus Juris Civilis*. More commonly known as the Justinian code, it included a dictate that rejected precedent. It stated that "decisions should be rendered in accordance, not with examples, but with the law."[11] This policy can be traced back to Roman tradition, in which judges were appointed on a case-by-case basis and magistrates were appointed for no more than one year. As such, their individual decisions were not accorded much weight.[12]

As an alternative to stare decisis, civil law judges follow the doctrine of *jurisprudence constante*. The doctrine of jurisprudence constante does not require judges to follow earlier precedents; nevertheless, judicial deference to earlier decisions is commonplace. "Under civil law tradition, while a single decision is not binding on courts, when a series of decisions form a 'constant stream of uniform and homogenous rulings having the same reasoning,' jurisprudence constante applies and operates with 'considerable persuasive authority.'"[13]

[8] Mutual Film Corp. v. Industrial Comm'n of Ohio, 236 U.S. 230 (1915).

[9] Burstyn, Inc. v. Wilson, 343 U.S. 495 (1952).

[10] JAMES G. APPLE AND ROBERT P. DEYLING, A PRIMER ON THE CIVIL LAW SYSTEM 1 (Federal Judicial Center, 1995), *available at* www.fjc.gov/public/pdf.nsf/lookup/CivilLaw.pdf/$file/CivilLaw.pdf.

[11] *Id.* (citing JOHN P. DAWSON, ORACLES OF THE LAW 103, 123 (1968)).

[12] *Id.* at 5.

[13] Doerr v. Mobile Oil Co., 774 So.2d 119 (La. 2000) (citing Dennis, J. L., *Interpretation and Application of the Civil Code and the Evaluation of Judicial Precedent*, 54 LA. L. REV. 1, 15 (1993)).

The Structure of Court Systems

A court's jurisdiction and hierarchy determines whether the decision it renders will be a binding precedent. So a basic knowledge of the structure of court systems, along with their powers and limitations, is essential before reading particular cases. In the United States there are two court systems: the federal system and the state system.

In order for a court to consider a case, three conditions must apply:

- there must be a legitimate controversy that is ripe for review;
- the parties in the case must have standing, which is a direct interest in the case; and
- the case must fall within the court's jurisdiction or sphere of influence.

There are two types of jurisdiction, personal jurisdiction and subject matter jurisdiction. *Personal jurisdiction*, which is covered in greater detail in Chapter 5, refers to the court's right to exercise its control over the parties involved in a case, based on their residence in or contacts with a particular area. *Subject matter jurisdiction* refers to the particular issues that a court is empowered to decide.

The federal court system

The subject matter jurisdiction of federal courts is limited to actions described in Article III, Section II of the Constitution and federal statutes passed by Congress. Federal courts may consider:

- controversies arising under the Constitution, laws of the United States, and treaties;
- cases in which the United States is a party;
- cases between a state or its citizens and foreign states or their citizens;
- cases involving ambassadors and representatives from foreign states as parties;
- cases based on admiralty law (the law of the seas);
- copyright and patent cases;
- bankruptcy proceedings;
- lawsuits involving the military; and
- diversity cases, involving claims exceeding $75,000.

Diversity cases involve civil actions between citizens of different states.[14] For example, in 2011, actress Lindsay Lohan sued rapper Pitbull for defamation, intentional infliction

[14] 28 U.S.C. § 1332 (2010).

of emotional distress and the use of her name for commercial benefit, in a New York State court, for including the lyric "I got it locked up like Lindsay Lohan" in his popular song "Give Me Everything." The case was transferred to a federal court with diversity jurisdiction because Lohan was a resident of California, Pitbull was a resident of Florida, and the other defendants in the suit were residents of Georgia, New York, and the Netherlands.[15]

A federal court also may assume jurisdiction over a case that began in a state court if a constitutional or federal right is threatened during the course of litigation. For example, a federal court may prevent a state court from enforcing an unconstitutional state statute.

The federal court system includes the U.S. Supreme Court, U.S. Courts of Appeals, U.S. District Courts and bankruptcy courts. Congress has also created legislative courts with reduced powers. These include the U.S. Court of Military Appeals, U.S. Tax Court and U.S. Court of Veterans Appeals.

Federal court hierarchy

The point of entry for a case in the federal system is the *district court*. This is the trial level (that comes closest to television depictions of trials), where one judge sits on the bench, witnesses take the stand, and a jury examines the evidence to determine the facts of the case. The federal system is divided into 94 judicial districts, each staffed with multiple judges. Each state, along with the District of Columbia and U.S. territories, includes at least one district. Larger states, like California and Texas, include as many as four districts located in different parts of the state.

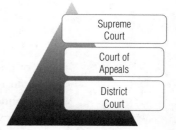

Figure 1.2

Above the trial level is the appellate level. Courts of appeals review lower court decisions to make sure the law was applied correctly. A panel of judges – usually three – examines the case to make sure judicial rules were followed, that proper witnesses were allowed, and that juries received correct instructions. A court of appeals normally does not re-examine the facts of a case. If, in the course of its review, an appellate court finds that a fact is still in dispute that could materially affect the outcome of the trial, it will send the case back (called *remanding* it) for a retrial to resolve the issue. Because there are no witnesses at the appellate level – only transcripts, lawyers, and judges – courtroom drama is considerably diminished.

Federal courts of appeals are divided into autonomous circuits. A decision from an appellate court is binding within its own circuit, but it does not bind courts in other circuits. There are 13 federal circuits within the United States. Eleven of them are drawn from clusters of states and U.S. territories.

[15] Lohan v. Perez, a/k/a Pitbull (filed Nov. 4, 2011, E.D.N.Y.) Notice of removal.

First Circuit	Maine, Massachusetts, New Hampshire, Puerto Rico, Rhode Island
Second Circuit	Connecticut, New York, Vermont
Third Circuit	Delaware, New Jersey, Pennsylvania, Virgin Islands
Fourth Circuit	Maryland, North Carolina, South Carolina, Virginia, West Virginia
Fifth Circuit	Louisiana, Mississippi, Texas
Sixth Circuit	Kentucky, Michigan, Ohio, Tennessee
Seventh Circuit	Illinois, Indiana, Wisconsin
Eighth Circuit	Arkansas, Iowa, Minnesota, Missouri, Nebraska, North Dakota, South Dakota
Ninth Circuit	Arizona, California, Guam, Hawaii, Idaho, Montana, Nevada, N. Mariana Islands, Oregon, Washington
Tenth Circuit	Colorado, Kansas, New Mexico, Utah, Oklahoma, Wyoming
Eleventh Circuit	Alabama, Florida, Georgia

The other two U.S. Courts of Appeals are located in Washington, D.C. The U.S. Court of Appeals for the District of Columbia Circuit hears appeals from administrative agencies in the nation's capital. The U.S. Court of Appeals for the Federal Circuit has nationwide jurisdiction for specialized cases. These include cases on patent law or cases that come from the Court of International Trade and the Court of Federal Claims.

In exceptional cases, the judges sitting on a circuit court of appeals may, at the request of one of the litigants or a circuit judge, vote to vacate a three-judge panel's decision and review the case *en banc*. In an en banc hearing, the full court sits to rehear and decide the case. Such reviews are rarely granted unless the panel's judgment was out of sync with the court's earlier decisions or the case involves a legal question of particular importance.

Decisions rendered by federal circuit courts may be appealed to the U.S. Supreme Court, which binds every lower court on constitutional and federal law. When the Supreme Court agrees to hear a case, it grants a *writ of certiorari*. The Court grants certiorari only to those cases that pose a significant legal issue. Of the approximately 10,000 petitions it receives each year, the Court reviews only 75–100 cases.[16]

The Supreme Court has original jurisdiction (the right to be the first to hear a case) in two types of cases: those involving ambassadors and those in which the United States is a party. In all other cases, it has appellate jurisdiction. As with courts of appeals, cases involve written briefs and oral arguments presented by attorneys, but no witnesses or juries. Court justices issue written opinions, explaining their decisions, months after hearing the case.

The Supreme Court has nine members – eight justices and a chief justice. They are, in order of seniority, Justices Antonin Scalia, Anthony Kennedy, Clarence Thomas, Ruth Bader Ginsburg, Stephen Breyer, John Roberts, Samuel Alito, Sonia Sotomayor, and

The Supreme Court issues a writ of certiorari when it accepts a case. The order requires a lower court to deliver its records of the case to the higher court for review. In Latin *certiorari* means "to be more fully informed."

If you aren't sure how to pronounce it, you are in good company. Justices on the Supreme Court all pronounce it differently, as "ser-shah-rair-eye," "ser-she-or-ary," and "ser-shah-rahr-ee."

[16] Supreme Court of the United States, Frequently Asked Questions, http://www.supremecourt.gov/faq.aspx.

Elena Kagan. John Roberts is chief justice. Occasionally, one of the justices will have a conflict of interest that makes it inappropriate to hear the case. For example, he or she may have a prior relationship with one of the parties. In such a case, the justice will voluntarily remove him or herself from the case, a process known as *recusal*. This would leave eight justices to decide the case. In the event of a tie, the lower court's decision would stand but would carry no precedential value beyond its own circuit.

The state court system

Although federal courts have produced more influential opinions regarding digital media law, most litigation takes place in state courts. In fact, 95 percent of all cases are filed there.[17] As sovereign entities, states courts are independent of the federal court system and independent of other states. They are the ultimate decision makers regarding their own laws and constitutions, even binding federal courts on interpretations of state law.

Like their federal counterparts, state courts are limited by personal and subject matter jurisdiction. There must be a connection between the litigants and the state to establish personal jurisdiction. A Florida court could not, for example, hear a case involving two residents of Mississippi about a matter that had nothing to do with Florida. State courts are also limited to particular subject areas. These include matters that involve state statutes, state constitutions or state common law. State courts handle most criminal cases, probate (wills and estates), contracts, torts (personal injuries), family law (marriages, divorce and adoptions) and juvenile justice.

Most states have two levels of trial courts: courts of limited jurisdiction or courts of general jurisdiction. *Courts of limited jurisdiction* handle cases involving misdemeanor behavior in criminal matters and sums under $10,000 in civil matters. Examples include municipal, justice of the peace, probate, family, juvenile and small claims courts.[18] More serious criminal and civil cases are tried in *courts of general jurisdiction*. These are commonly called district, circuit, or superior courts.

State court hierarchy

The decisions of these lower state courts may be appealed to intermediate appellate courts, usually called courts of appeals. Most states have one appellate court, but larger states like California have regional appellate courts. Because it is assumed that all cases deserve at least one appeal, intermediate appellate courts have little discretion over whether to accept cases from the trial level.

Each state also has a court of last resort, usually called its supreme court. However, in New York and Maryland, the highest courts are called court of appeals. These courts,

[17] National Center for State Courts, Examining the Work of State Courts, 2010, http://www.courtstatistics.org/.
[18] ROBERT A. CARP AND RONALD STIDHAM, JUDICIAL PROCESS IN AMERICA 67 (4th ed. 1998).

which range in size from three to nine judges (but most commonly have seven), are the final arbiters on state law. Most courts of last resort sit in states with intermediate appellate courts and therefore have the power to exercise discretion over the cases they choose to hear.[19] Like the U.S. Supreme Court, they generally elect to review only those cases that involve important policy issues.

Types of Law

Within the common law system, there are two different types of law: criminal law and civil law. The term civil law can be confusing because it has two meanings. As discussed earlier, civil law refers to a type of legal system that is distinct from the common law system. Within the United States, the term civil law more commonly refers to the body of law used to resolve disputes between private parties or organizations. In other areas of the world it is called private law, while its counterpart, criminal law, is called public law. Criminal law, prosecuted by the government, is probably more familiar to you because it is more commonly depicted in books, movies, and television. Unfortunately, these dramatic representations tend to gloss over the specifics.

Criminal law

Criminal law addresses violations against the state (government) that, even if directed toward an individual, are considered an offense to society as a whole. It may include the commission of an illegal act (like computer fraud or cyberstalking) or the omission of a duty (through negligent conduct, for example) that causes public harm. A state may sanction the violation of a criminal law using fines or imprisonment, as long as the punishment, like the crime, was clearly outlined in a statute passed by a legislative body before the act occurred.

Grand juries and preliminary hearings

Grand juries are distinct from trial juries. Grand juries determine whether there is enough evidence to charge a person with a crime. Trial juries determine whether a person has committed a crime.

The Fifth Amendment guarantees a *grand jury* hearing to anyone accused of a federal crime. Most grand juries consist of 16 to 23 citizens pulled from voter registration lists, who are empanelled for a period ranging from one month to one year. The federal prosecutor submits his or her evidence to the grand jurors, who determine whether there is probable cause to believe the accused committed a federal crime. The accused is not present at the time. If, after hearing the evidence, the grand jury is convinced there is probable cause to warrant a trial, it will issue a formal accusation of a felony,

[19]*Id.* at 71.

called an *indictment*, against the accused. Grand jury hearings and records are closed to the public. The Supreme Court has provided three justifications for this secrecy:

> (1) disclosure of pre-indictment proceedings would make many prospective witnesses "hesitant to come forward voluntarily, knowing that those against whom they testify would be aware of that testimony"; (2) witnesses who did appear "would be less likely to testify fully and frankly as they would be open to retribution as well as inducements"; and (3) there "would be the risk that those about to be indicted would flee or would try to influence individual grand jurors to vote against indictment."[20]

States have the option of using *preliminary hearings* led by a judge as an alternative to a grand jury hearing. The accused may be present at a preliminary hearing and may even present evidence in his or her favor, although most elect not to at that time. Preliminary hearings are also open to the public.

Arraignments

Once a grand jury or judge has determined there is probable cause for a trial, the accused goes before a judge, where he or she is read the formal charge and issues a plea in a proceeding called an *arraignment*. It is important to understand the distinction between an arrest and an arraignment to avoid publishing inaccurate information that could lead to a defamation suit. Only after an arraignment is it correct to publish that someone was "charged" with a crime. If the defendant's plea is "guilty," the judge may issue a sentence. If the plea is "not guilty," a trial date is set. Typically fewer than 10 percent of criminal cases make it to trial. Most are *plea-bargained* before trial, meaning the prosecutor and defendant agree to a deal that usually involves some form of leniency in exchange for a guilty plea.

The Sixth Amendment to the Constitution guarantees "a speedy and public trial" by an impartial jury in all criminal prosecutions. In the Speedy Trial Act of 1974, Congress interpreted the term "speedy" to mean that a trial must ensue within 100 days after criminal charges are filed or the case must be dismissed. States have enacted similar measures.

The jury

Potential trial jurors are subjected to a process called *voir dire* (pronounced "vwahr deer") to assess their suitability for jury service. During this period, the prosecution and defense ask potential jurors questions regarding their knowledge and attitudes about the case, as well as any relevant personal experiences or connections that might influence their decision. A common misperception is that potential jurors must not have heard anything about the case to be selected. That is not a requirement. It is only

---

[20] *In re* North (Omnibus Order), 16 F.3d 1234, 1242 (D.C. Cir. Spec. Div., 1994) (quoting Douglas Oil Co. v. Petrol Stops Northwest, 441 U.S. 211, 218–19 (1979)).

necessary that potential jurors believe themselves to be capable of impartiality. During the selection process, each side is given a number of peremptory challenges, which are opportunities to strike a person from the jury pool for no specific reason. These are useful when a potential juror displays no overt biases, but the attorney still has a bad feeling about the person. Peremptory challenges may not, however, be used to strike a juror on the basis of race or gender.[21] Strikes for cause are unlimited. Attorneys do not have to use one of their peremptory strikes to exclude a juror who displays an obvious bias regarding the case.

In a federal criminal trial, a jury must have twelve members who reach a unanimous decision. Most states also use twelve-member juries in criminal trials, but are permitted to use as few as six. A slight variation in votes is also permitted at the state level. The Supreme Court has held that a guilty verdict from nine members of a twelve-member jury is constitutionally permissible in state trials. However, a jury with only six members must be unanimous. Oregon and Louisiana are the only states that still permit nonunanimous juries in felony cases.

It is the jury's job to decide the facts of the case and render a verdict. It is the judge's job to make sure proper procedure is followed during the trial and to instruct the jurors about the meaning of the law and how it is to be applied. In most states, and at the federal level, the judge imposes the sentence.[22] However, some states place this responsibility on the jury.

Grounds for appeal

Approximately one-third of criminal verdicts are appealed. The appeal must be based on the contention that the law was misapplied, not that the facts were misinterpreted. Acceptable reasons might be that inadmissible evidence was allowed, jury selection was flawed, or the judge's instructions were incorrect. A successful appeal usually results in a new trial.

Civil law

Civil law seeks to resolve non-criminal disputes. These typically involve conflicts over contracts, the ownership or use of property, inheritance, domestic relations (involving marriage, divorce, child custody), and torts. These conflicts, between private people or organizations, emerge when one party alleges that the other has violated a civil statute or common law.

Civil cases are more common than criminal cases.[23] In civil trials, the court's role is to help settle the dispute. The proscribed remedy may be an injunction that requires someone to do something or prohibits someone from doing something, or the imposi-

---

[21] *See* Edmondson v. Leesville Concrete Co., 500 U.S. 614 (1991) and J.E.B. v. Alabama ex rel. T.B., 511 U.S. 127 (1994).
[22] DANIEL E. HALL, CRIMINAL LAW AND PROCEDURE 490 (5th ed. 2009).
[23] *Id.* at 184.

tion of a fine. Civil penalties do not involve imprisonment. On rare occasions, a state may be a party to a civil suit, but this is the exception rather than the rule.

Civil procedure

Civil procedure differs from criminal procedure in a number of respects. First, there is no prosecutor in civil cases. One party (the *plaintiff*) brings a suit against another party (the *defendant* or *respondent*). The plaintiff must have *standing* – a personal stake in the outcome of the case – in order to initiate the suit. Without standing, there is no real controversy between the parties for a court to settle. Second, the standard of proof required to win a civil case is less stringent than in criminal cases. It is usually sufficient for a plaintiff to show that the "preponderance of evidence" demonstrates the defendant's guilt. Plaintiffs are not required to demonstrate guilt beyond a reasonable doubt, the standard used in criminal trials. Third, due process protections are weaker in civil trials. The court is not required to provide an attorney for a defendant who cannot afford one, for example. Also, although the Seventh Amendment guarantees the right to a jury in a civil trial, the litigants have the right to waive that option in favor of a bench trial, in which the judge determines the facts of the case in addition to deciding questions of law.[24] When juries are used, they are frequently smaller than those used in criminal trials. Fewer than half the states require twelve-person juries, and about half permit nonunanimous verdicts.

To initiate a suit, the plaintiff or the plaintiff's attorney files a petition, called a *complaint*, outlining the circumstances that led to the dispute, the damages alleged and the compensation expected. After receiving a summons announcing the suit, the defendant or defendant's attorney may file a *motion* with the court to strike parts of the suit that are improper or irrelevant or to dismiss it entirely because it was improperly filed or because there is no sound basis for the suit.[25] If the court rejects the defendant's motions, the defendant will have to respond to the suit. The response, called the defendant's *answer*, may contain an admission, denial, defense, or counterclaim.[26]

At that point, the trial will enter a *discovery* phase in which the litigants gather and share information related to the dispute. Although surprises make good drama in television courtrooms, they are not appreciated in real trials. Opposing parties are obligated to disclose their evidence to each other before the trial. Pre-trial discovery, which is used in civil and criminal trials, gives each side the opportunity to search for new information to explain or rebut the opposing party's evidence, and minimizes opportunities to falsify evidence.[27] In civil trials, putting all of the evidence out on the table also encourages settlements before the case can go to trial. Litigants use a variety of tools for discovery.

[24] The Seventh Amendment is not deemed sufficiently fundamental to apply at the state level through the Fourteenth Amendment's due process clause. Thus defendants do not have a constitutional right to a jury in a state civil trial. *See* Curtis v. Loether, 415 U.S. 189, 198 (1974) and Dairy Queen v. Wood, 369 U.S. 469, 471–2 (1962).
[25] Curtis v. Loether, 415 U.S. 189, 196 (1974).
[26] *Id.*
[27] Comment, *Pre-Trial Disclosure in Criminal Cases*, 60 Yale L.J. 626–46 (1951).

One of the most common is the *deposition*. In a deposition, potential witnesses describe what they know, under oath, before the trial begins. Depositions normally occur in one of the attorney's offices. All parties are notified in advance so they can be present to hear the witness's testimony. The counsel for both the plaintiff and the defendant may question the witness during a deposition. Information is also gathered through *interrogatives*, which are questionnaires that the opposing party answers under oath. Each party is also entitled to request the opposition's list of witnesses to be called at trial, a summary of anticipated expert testimony, and any documents that may be used in the case as evidence.

Summary judgment

Either party in the trial may motion for a summary judgment in his or her favor. A *summary judgment* is a ruling that all factual issues have been discovered and the case can be decided on the facts without a trial. If, after considering the pleadings, depositions, answers to interrogatories, affidavits, and admissions on file, the judge determines that there is no genuine issue of material fact and that as a matter of law the motioning party is entitled to a judgment, the judge may render a summary judgment in the case.[28] If the court refuses to issue a summary judgment, the case will go to trial.

If the district court issues a summary judgment and the opposing party believes material facts remain that justify a full trial, he or she may appeal the summary judgment. An appellate court may choose to review *de novo* (anew) the evidence leading to the district court's summary judgment. If it does so, it will review the evidence in the light most favorable to the party who did not request summary judgment.

Remedies

Civil remedies usually come in the form of injunctions and/or fines, depending on the circumstances.

If a case involves an issue of *equity* (a problem that cannot be remedied after-the-fact by issuing damages), a judge may issue a *preliminary injunction* to prevent one party from doing something that harms the other party until the case can be considered fully at trial. Before granting a plaintiff a preliminary injunction, the court must be satisfied that (1) there is a substantial likelihood that the plaintiff would win a case against the defendant if it were to go to trial; (2) that the plaintiff would suffer "irreparable harm" without the injunction; (3) that the harm the plaintiff suffers would be worse than any harm the defendant would suffer from the injunction; and (4) that the injunction would not harm the public's interest.[29] If a trial later shows that the preliminary injunction was warranted, the court will replace it with a *permanent injunction*. If not, the preliminary injunction will be lifted.

[28] Fed. R. Civ. P. 56.
[29] *See* Johnson & Johnson Vision Care v. 1–800 Contacts, Inc., 299 F.3d 1242, 1246–47 (11th Cir. 2002).

If, on the other hand, the damage is already done and the judge or jury finds that the defendant is responsible, the defendant may be punished with a monetary fine. Civil juries issue two types of damage awards: compensatory and punitive. *Compensatory damages* compensate the victim for actual loss. *Punitive damages*, which may be awarded in addition to compensatory damages, serve as punishment and to set an example for future offenders.

Doctrine of respondeat superior

The civil liability doctrine of *respondeat superior* allows plaintiffs to sue not only the person directly responsible for a tort, but also those who may be tangentially responsible. Literally it comes from the ancient idea that the master is responsible for the servant. In modern times, it means the employer is responsible for the employee. People take advantage of the doctrine of respondeat superior when they are looking for deeper pockets. This means that if you harm someone in the context of your work, your company may also be liable for your actions. If you own a company, it means that you may be liable for your employees' actions and should have a good errors and omissions insurance policy.

Appeals

If the losing party feels that the court's judgment was reached in error because the law was somehow misapplied, he or she can ask the court to set aside its verdict. If the court refuses to do so, the losing party may appeal the decision. A losing party who is legally entitled to a review will become the *appellant*, while the opposing party becomes the *appellee*. If the higher court's review is discretionary – which is the case in appellate courts of last resort, usually called supreme courts – the losing party must petition the court for a writ of certiorari, a court order granting a review. The party requesting the review will be the *petitioner*. The opposing party will be the *respondent*. Case names are likely to change on appeal. A lawsuit brought by Jones against Smith will begin life as *Jones v. Smith*. If Smith loses and initiates an appeal, the case name will switch to *Smith v. Jones*.

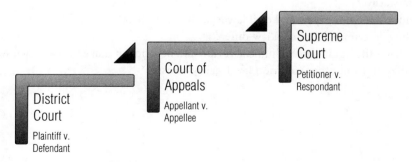

Figure 1.3   The terms used for parties in a case change as they move from one court level up to the next.

The Significance of Judicial Review

The power of *judicial review* refers to a court's authority to review the decisions of other branches of government. In the United States, judicial review gives federal courts the power to declare a law unconstitutional – in effect, to strike it down. Theoretically, any federal court in the United States has this power, but lower courts are reluctant to use it because it is guaranteed to lead to an appeal and embarrassment if the decision is overturned.

Although the framers of the Constitution never specifically granted the Supreme Court the power of judicial review, the Court nevertheless decided it must have that authority in *Marbury v. Madison* (1803).[30] The case involved a judicial appointment that President Adams made before leaving office following his loss to Thomas Jefferson. The Senate confirmed several of Adams' judicial appointees, but Adams' secretary of state did not have time to issue their commissions before leaving office. When Jefferson assumed the presidency, he asked his new secretary of state, James Madison, not to issue the commissions because he wanted to appoint his own judges to the bench.

William Marbury, who was in line for a federal judgeship, asked the Supreme Court to issue a *writ of mandamus*, a court order compelling a public official to do his duty, to force Madison to turn over the commission. Congress gave the Supreme Court the power to issue writs of mandamus in the Judiciary Act of 1789. But the Constitution does not give the Supreme Court original jurisdiction in such matters. Facing an untenable position, the Court concluded that the law must be unconstitutional and therefore invalid. In terms of constitutional law, the decision is the most important the Supreme Court has ever made. Shortly after, in *Martin v. Hunter's Lessee* (1816), the Court also held that it had the power to determine whether the decision of a state's legislature is constitutional.[31]

The Supreme Court's assertion of judicial review was controversial because it vested the one branch of government that is not democratically elected with the greatest power. However, the Court has used that power to protect minority rights that might otherwise have been trampled by the majority. Judicial review is particularly important to media law. Without it, courts would not have the power to strike down laws that impinge upon the First Amendment. Having that power over states also means that the Court can prevent 50 inconsistent laws.

Questions for Discussion

1. What are the different sources of law in the United States? Which is paramount and why?
2. How do hierarchy and jurisdiction determine whether a precedent is binding or persuasive?
3. How do common law and civil law legal systems differ?
4. How do criminal and civil law differ?
5. What is the significance of judicial review and how does it make the U.S. legal system different from other common law legal systems?

[30] 5 U.S. 137 (1803).
[31] 14 U.S. 304 (1816).

2 Freedom of Expression

No other country in the world is more protective of expression than the United States. In fact, some countries believe the United States takes speech protection too far, protecting expression at the expense of other equally important rights, such as personal rights to reputation and privacy. It should not be surprising that nations balance speech protections differently. Each nation forms concepts of what is acceptable in terms of expression based on its own cultural and political heritage. Countries such as France and Germany, for example, developed a particular sensitivity to the dangers of hate speech following their experiences with Nazism during the 1930s and 1940s. European countries in general are more sensitive to defamation. Their social structures grew out of feudalism during the Middle Ages and subsequent class divisions that extended through the nineteenth century. Historically, an accusation that marred the reputation of a member of the aristocracy was likely to result in a duel. Strict laws against defamation reduced violence. In contrast, American colonists represented a range of social strata, looking for religious, economic, and expressive freedom. The founding fathers incorporated these values into the U.S. Constitution.

This chapter will explore the First Amendment, the primary means through which expression is protected in the United States. It will consider the varying levels of protection accorded to different media; categories of speech without protection; and the legitimate scope of time, place, and manner restrictions. It will also address questions specifically related to Internet speech, such as whether the Internet is a public forum, computer code is considered speech, and student websites are protected.

The First Amendment

Protection for free expression in the United States draws its power from the First Amendment to the Constitution, which says:

Digital Media Law, Second Edition. Ashley Packard.
© 2013 John Wiley & Sons, Inc. Published 2013 by John Wiley & Sons, Inc.

Congress shall make no law respecting an establishment of religion, or prohibiting the free exercise thereof; or abridging the freedom of speech, or of the press; or the right of the people peaceably to assemble, and to petition the Government for a redress of grievances.

In those 45 words, the founding fathers integrated a number of rights: the right to freely exercise one's religious beliefs, protection against state establishment of religion, protection for freedom of speech and the press, the right to assemble freely and with it an implied freedom of association, and the right to petition for a redress of grievances.

The First Amendment's protection for speech and press is foundational to U.S. media law. It distinguishes our national approach to such issues as defamation, hate speech, and obscenity from those of other commonwealth and civil law countries. Other nations have included protections for expression in their constitutions, but no guarantee of speech and press freedom is as broadly stated as the First Amendment.

Ironically, the First Amendment's breadth is sometimes a source of confusion. The Supreme Court and Congress have struggled with its admonition "to make no law abridging freedom of speech."[1] On first reading the language seems clear enough, but it is actually quite open to interpretation. Judges and scholars have debated its meaning for two centuries. What exactly does freedom of speech mean? What does abridgement mean? How far can Congress go before it abridges freedom of speech? Advances in technology have also put the words "or of the press" in question. When the founding fathers wrote the First Amendment, the meaning of press was clear: books and newspapers. In the twentieth century, the meaning of press expanded to include radio, film, and television. In the twenty-first century, it encompasses websites, web logs, podcasts, videos, and even social networking sites. What will be next?

There is also the question of how closely the text should be followed. First Amendment absolutists, like Justices Hugo Black and William Douglas, interpreted the admonition to make "no law" respecting speech or the press to mean no law whatsoever.[2] Others have felt that the right of expression must be balanced against other rights and societal interests.

The First Amendment's Purpose

No matter how literally the First Amendment is interpreted, one thing is clear: it does not protect all expression. A common misconception is that the First Amendment protects anything we have to say, anywhere we want to say it. Actually, the First Amendment *only protects against government suppression* of expression. It does not prohibit private suppression of expression. If, in a fit of anger, you were to post a video on YouTube

---

[1] JUDICIAL REVIEW AND THE SUPREME COURT 141 (Leonard W. Levy ed., 1967).
[2] Konigsberg v. State Bar of California, 366 U.S. 36, 61 (1961) (Black, J., dissenting) ("[T]he First Amendment's unequivocal command that there shall be no abridgment of the rights of free speech and assembly shows that the men who drafted our Bill of Rights did all the 'balancing' that was to be done in this field.")

mocking your boss and later find yourself out of a job, you could not turn to the First Amendment for recourse.[3] Nor could you count on it to protect your expression on someone else's private property. This includes private onramps to the Internet like web hosts and social networking sites. If your posts venture into offensive territory, your web host is entitled to ask you to remove the speech. If you refuse to do so, the company may do it for you or close your account.

The situation gets trickier when government agencies retaliate against their employees for speech posted online. As government entities, public agencies must guard against suppression of speech. As employers, they also have "a legitimate interest in promoting the efficiency of their operations."[4] A public employee's speech, made in his or her capacity as an employee, is generally not protected if the speech is made "to further the employee's private interest."[5] However, speech made "as a citizen upon matters of public concern" is protected. When that speech causes a disruption at work, a court is required to balance the employee's right of free speech against the interest of the public employer.

The First Amendment protects speech from government suppression at the federal, state, and city level. This was not always thought to be the case. Because the First Amendment states "*Congress* shall make no law," the Supreme Court initially interpreted the First Amendment to apply only to the federal government.[6] Circumstances changed, however, when the Fourteenth Amendment was ratified in 1866. The Fourteenth Amendment says:

> No State shall make or enforce any law which shall abridge the privileges or immunities of citizens of the United States; nor shall any State deprive any person of life, liberty, or property, without due process of law; nor deny to any person within its jurisdiction the equal protection of the laws.

In 1925, the Supreme Court modified its position.[7] The Court determined that the Fourteenth Amendment's concept of liberty incorporates freedom of expression and that through the Fourteenth Amendment the First Amendment applies to the states. The Fourteenth Amendment binds the states to other guarantees in the Bill of Rights as well, under the theory that it incorporates the "fundamental principles of liberty and justice, which lie at the base of all our civil and political institutions."[8] This notion has

---

[3] However, the National Labor Relations Act does protect the rights of certain employees to engage in "protected concerted activity." The National Labor Relations Board describes this as when "two or more employees take action for their mutual aid or protection regarding terms and conditions of employment." In September 2011, an NLRB administrative judge found that a New York company had violated the Act by firing five employees who had been discussing job conditions on Facebook. *See* Administrative Law Judge Finds New York Nonprofit Unlawfully Discharged Employees Following Facebook Posts, National Labor Relations Board, Sept. 6, 2011, https://www.nlrb.gov/news/administrative-law-judge-finds-new-york-nonprofit-unlawfully-discharged-employees-following-fac.

[4] Mattingly v. Milligan, No. 4:11CV00215 (E.D. Ark Nov. 1, 2011).

[5] Sparr v. Ward, 306 F.3d 589, 594 (8th Cir. 2002).

[6] Barron v. The Mayor and City Council of Baltimore, 32 U.S. (7 Pet.) 243 (1933).

[7] Gitlow v. New York, 268 U.S. 652 (1925).

[8] Gideon v. Wainwright, 372 U.S. 335 (1963).

come to be known as the *incorporation doctrine*. In the landmark case *Gideon v. Wainwright* (1963), Justice Black outlined the amendment's scope:

> This Court has looked to the fundamental nature of original Bill of Rights guarantees to decide whether the Fourteenth Amendment makes them obligatory on the States. Explicitly recognized to be of this "fundamental nature" and therefore made immune from state invasion by the Fourteenth, or some part of it, are the First Amendment's freedoms of speech, press, religion, assembly, association, and petition for redress of grievances. For the same reason, though not always in precisely the same terminology, the Court has made obligatory on the States the Fifth Amendment's command that private property shall not be taken for public use without just compensation, the Fourth Amendment's prohibition of unreasonable searches and seizures, and the Eighth's ban on cruel and unusual punishment.[9]

Through the Fourteenth Amendment, the First Amendment also applies in U.S. territories, such as Puerto Rico and Guam,[10] and to aliens legally residing in the United States.[11] The Supreme Court has not incorporated the full Bill of Rights into the Fourteenth Amendment. Rights that the justices do not consider to be "fundamental" remain outside the amendment's reach. These include the Third Amendment's prohibition against quartering soldiers in private residences during peacetime, the Fifth Amendment's requirement of grand jury indictments, and the Seventh Amendment's right to a jury in civil trials.

Prohibition on prior restraint

Constitutional historians have noted that the founding fathers' understanding of press freedom when the Bill of Rights was written probably mirrored the English definition presented in the authoritative legal text used at the time, William Blackstone's *Commentaries on the Laws of England*.[12] Blackstone interpreted freedom of the press to mean freedom from *prior restraint*. In other words, he understood it to mean the freedom to publish without prior censorship, but not freedom from punishment after the fact. There is support for the contention that the founding fathers also understood freedom of the press as a limit on prior restraint. The First Amendment was ratified in 1791. Only seven years afterward, many of the same men who voted for it passed The Sedition Act of 1798. The Sedition Act made it a crime to "write, print, utter or publish . . . any false, scandalous and malicious writing or writings against the government of the United

Prior restraint is censorship before publication.

---

[9] *Id.* at 341–42.

[10] *See* Balzac v. Porto Rico, 258 U.S. 298, 313–14 (1922) and DeRoburt v. Gannett Co., 83 F.R.D. 574, 577–8 (D. Haw. 1979).

[11] *See* Kwong Hai Chew v. Colding, 344 U.S. 590 (1953) (holding that aliens who lawfully enter and are residing in the United States are entitled to rights guaranteed by the Constitution, including rights protected by the First Amendment) and Bridges v. Wixon, 326 U.S. 135 (1945) (holding that aliens residing in the United States are accorded freedom of speech and press).

[12] WILLIAM BLACKSTONE, COMMENTARIES ON THE LAWS OF ENGLAND (1769).

States, or either house of the Congress of the United States, or the President of the United States."[13] In the context of political discourse today, can you imagine it being illegal to criticize Congress or the president?

Although the meaning of the First Amendment was narrowly understood when it was first written, historian Leonard Levy observes that "it was boldly stated, and that the bold statement, the principle of unqualified free speech, was written into fundamental law and was meant to endure."[14] A broad libertarian theory of expression did emerge within a decade after the constitution's ratification – a contention supported by the fact that the Sedition Act was allowed to expire in 1801.[15]

However, it was not until the twentieth century that the power of the First Amendment began to take hold. In the years leading up to and immediately after World War I, the Supreme Court struggled with the question of just how far people should be allowed to go in their criticism of government, particularly in times of unrest. Political activists were thrown in jail for what we might consider today to be mild attempts to protest the war.[16] Part of this response was due to a natural propensity to tighten restrictions on freedoms when danger is present, a cycle that has played out through our legal history. But it is also helpful to understand that in the early part of the twentieth century, the prevailing view among social scientists (and no doubt many judges) was that the public was extremely vulnerable to political propaganda.[17]

A prohibition era case, divorced from the context of war, gave the Supreme Court an opportunity to consider the issue of government criticism in a different light. The Court confirmed that "The chief purpose of the guarantee of freedom of the press is to prevent previous restraint on publication" in the landmark case *Near v. Minnesota* (1931).[18] Jay Near, the petitioner in the case, was the editor of a scandal sheet called *The Saturday Press*, which vilified Jews and Catholics, among others. Shortly after the first edition was published, his co-editor, Howard Guilford, was shot. Near did not think authorities were doing enough to find his partner's assailant and used his paper to make his opinions known. He accused the chief of police of conspiring with Minneapolis gangsters and the local prosecutor of ignoring the matter. Minnesota had an abatement statute against "malicious, scandalous or defamatory newspapers, magazines or periodicals" and used it to enjoin publication of Near's paper. The Supreme Court's opinion, written by Justice Hughs, stated, "it has been generally, if not universally, considered that it is the chief purpose of the guaranty [of freedom of the press] to prevent previous restraints upon publication."[19] The Court overturned the state statute as a violation of

---

[13] An Act for the Punishment of Certain Crimes against the United States (Sedition Act), July 14, 1798 ch. 74, 1 Stat. 5.

[14] Levy, *supra* note 1, at 143.

[15] *Id.*

[16] Schenck v. United States, 249 U.S. 47 (1919); Debs v. United States, 249 U.S. 211 (1919); Frohwerk v. United States, 249 U.S. 204 (1919).

[17] Harold Laswell, *Theories of Political Propaganda*, 21 AM. POL. SCI. REV., 627–631 (Aug., 1927); WALTER LIPMANN, PUBLIC OPINION, 1922.

[18] 283 U.S. 697 (1931).

[19] *Id.* at 713.

the First Amendment, noting the seriousness of censoring charges of misconduct among public officers – which was a real concern during the Prohibition Era.

The Court concluded that prior restraint would only be allowed in four exceptional cases:

1. obstruction of military recruitment or the publication of sailing dates, the number or location of troops;
2. obscenity;
3. incitements to violent overthrow of government; and
4. protection of private rights according to equitable principles. (For example, prior restraints have been upheld in order to protect defendants' rights to a fair trail or plaintiffs' rights to protect their intellectual property.)

Courts have interpreted *Near* to mean that few circumstances other than national security can justify prior restraint on the press. In *New York Times Co. v. United States* (1971), the Supreme Court lifted an injunction barring *The New York Times* from printing the Pentagon's classified record of the Vietnam conflict (otherwise known as the "Pentagon Papers") because the government had not met the heavy burden required to warrant an injunction.[20] In a concurring opinion, Justice Stewart explained that publication would not clearly result in "direct, immediate, and irreparable damage to our Nation or its people."[21] But in *United States v. The Progressive* (1979), a federal district court concluded that the *Near* standard was met when it enjoined a magazine from publishing directions to make a hydrogen bomb.[22] Even though the information was available in the public domain in bits and pieces, the court believed that, when synthesized, it was too dangerous. The injunction was lifted later, however, when other publications printed the secret.

The Supreme Court declared that "prior restraints on speech and publication are the most serious and the least tolerable infringement on First Amendment rights" in *Nebraska Press Association v. Stuart* (1976).[23] The case involved a lower court's attempt to impose a gag order on the media to limit the potential damage of excessive press coverage on the defendant's right to a fair trail. The Supreme Court limited the circumstances in which a judge could issue a prior restraint to prevent excessive media coverage to situations in which no other alternative could curb the damaging effect of the publicity and a restraining order would actually be effective.[24]

Types of prior restraint orders

On those occasions when courts do issue prior restraint orders, they come in three forms: temporary restraining orders, preliminary injunctions, and permanent

[20] 403 U.S. 713 (1971).
[21] *Id.* at 730 (Stewart, J., concurring).
[22] United States v. The Progressive, 467 F. Supp. 990, 994 (1979).
[23] 437 U.S. 539 (1976).
[24] *Id.* at 562.

injunctions. A *temporary restraining order* is intended to supply immediate relief. An aggrieved party files a complaint with a court, applying for an order to stop someone from engaging in an action that if continued will result in "irreparable injury" before the matter can be heard in a formal court proceeding. Because the defendant is not present to defend his or her actions, the court may require the plaintiff to pay a bond to mitigate against any harm that may ensue to the defendant from the TRO if the plaintiff has misrepresented the circumstances. Along with the TRO, the court establishes a hearing date, so the defendant can come before the court to contest the order. At the hearing, the court may replace the TRO with a *preliminary injunction* if the plaintiff establishes both the potential for irreparable harm and the likelihood of winning a suit at trial. The court will also establish a trial date to determine whether issuing a permanent injunction is appropriate. A *permanent injunction*, established after a trial, is a court's final order to enjoin an action permanently.

Normally, the purpose of a temporary restraining order is to preserve the status quo until the court has time to give the matter due consideration. But, according to the U.S. Court of Appeals for the Sixth Circuit, a temporary restraining order "is a different beast in the First Amendment context."[25] In the context of press freedom, the status quo is to "publish news promptly that editors decide to publish. A restraining order disturbs the status quo and impinges on the exercise of editorial discretion."[26] Therefore, a court is obligated to deal with them on an emergency basis. Furthermore, while the criteria a court normally considers before issuing a restraining order include the potential for irreparable harm and the requesting party's likelihood for success on the merits of the suit, in a First Amendment context, "the hurdle is substantially higher: publication must threaten an interest more fundamental than the First Amendment itself."[27]

Are Restrictions on Political Funding a Prior Restraint?

In a representative democracy, people must be able to express their political views to effect change. Consequently, political speech is given the broadest protection under the First Amendment. The Supreme Court has even gone so far as to protect political spending on First Amendment grounds, reasoning that it is necessary to fund political speech, thus a restriction on political spending constitutes a prior restraint.

In 2010, the U.S. Supreme Court determined that restrictions on political speech by corporations and unions also counted as prior restraints in *Citizens United v. FEC*. In that case, the Supreme Court said that imposing limits on corporate spending to advocate for or against a particular candidate immediately before an election violated corporations' free speech rights. This holding unsettled more than 100 years of campaign finance restrictions intended to prohibit corruption or the appearance of corruption in the political process.

It may seem odd to think of corporations as having free speech rights. After all, they are not people. But in most legal

(Continued)

---

[25] Procter & Gamble Co. v. Banker's Trust Co., 78 F.3d 219, 226 (1996).
[26] *Id.* (citing *In re* Providence Journal Co., 820 F.2d 1342, 1351 (1st Cir. 1986)).
[27] *Id.* at 227.

systems, corporations are considered "legal persons." In legal parlance, a "person" is an entity subject to legal rights and duties. A *legal person* can own property, sue and be sued. Natural persons (people) are also legal persons to the extent that they are of sound mind and old enough to assume legal responsibilities.

The notion that corporations deserved equal protection under the Constitution entered American jurisprudence through an 1854 Supreme Court case about corporate property rights. During oral arguments, the Chief Justice remarked that the Court was of opinion that the Fourteenth Amendment, which forbids a state to deny equal protection of the laws to any person within its jurisdiction, applied to corporations. Although this statement was not part of the legal holding in the case, a clerk added it to the Court's printed opinion.[28] As later decisions incorporated the fiction of corporate personhood, corporate rights expanded. But Congress has long been wary of the influence of corporations on the political process. As early as 1907, it passed the Tillman Act barring corporations from making monetary contributions to national campaigns.

Following the Watergate scandal, Congress limited the amount of money individuals or organizations could donate to candidates for elections and required that donations above a certain threshold be disclosed to the Federal Election Commission, a regulatory agency it created to enforce the restrictions. Congress also limited the amount of money that candidates could spend on their campaigns.[29] The new rules were challenged as a violation of the First Amendment in *Buckley v. Valeo* (1976). The Supreme Court upheld campaign contribution limits and disclosure requirements, concluding that large contributions could lead people to believe there was some kind of quid pro quo arrangement between the contributor and candidate. But it struck down limits on campaign spending. The Court observed that "A restriction on the amount of money a person or group can spend on political

communication during a campaign necessarily reduces the quantity of expression by restricting the number of issues discussed, the depth of their exploration, and the size of the audience reached."[30] Further, it found no evidence that campaign spending led to corruption.

The Supreme Court did, however, accept limits on corporate spending in *Austin v. Michigan Chamber of Commerce* (1990). The Court upheld a Michigan law, challenged on First Amendment grounds, which prevented corporations from using their treasury funds for independent expenditures to support or oppose a candidate's election. The Court explained that, "Corporate wealth can unfairly influence elections when it is deployed in the form of independent expenditures, just as it can when it assumes the guise of political contributions."[31] It also noted that corporations still had an outlet for their political views because the law permitted them to support political action committees or to set up segregated funds to pay for political speech. What is the difference, you might ask? PACs and segregated funds are supported by individuals who are aware of and agree with the organization's political purpose. Speech funded by a corporation's treasury comes from stockholders who may not share the same political views.

In a continuing effort to combat the influence of "big money" in national politics, Congress passed the Bipartisan Campaign Reform Act in 1992. This law, better known as the McCain-Feingold Act, was intended to close loopholes left by earlier legislation. Among its many provisions, the law prevented corporations and unions from funding "electioneering communications."[32] This was defined as any "broadcast, cable, or satellite communication" that refers to "a clearly identified candidate for federal office" and that is made either 60 days before a general election or 30 days before a primary election. Print and Internet communications are exempt. The Court later interpreted electioneering communications as speech that expressly advocates for the election or defeat of a particular

[28] *Santa Clara County v. Southern Pacific R. Co.*, 118 U.S. 394, 396 (1886).
[29] Federal Election Campaign Act (FECA) of 1974. (P.L. No. 93–443).
[30] Buckley v. Valeo, 424 U.S. 1, 20 (1976).
[31] 494 U. S. 652 (1990).
[32] 2 U.S.C § 441b(c).

candidate, but not speech that refers to a candidate in the context of an issue ad.

The group Citizens United challenged the law when the Federal Election Commission prevented it from running a film on cable pay-per-view that disparaged Hilary Clinton's candidacy for president during the 2008 election cycle because the film was partially funded by a corporation. In a 5–4 decision, the Supreme Court struck down the provision that prevented corporations from funding political advocacy before an election, equating it to a prior restraint, and overruled its earlier holding in *Austin*. The Court pointed out "Laws that burden political speech are 'subject to strict scrutiny,' which requires the Government to prove that the restriction 'furthers a compelling interest and is narrowly tailored to achieve that interest.' "[33] In the majority's opinion, the government had not met that burden because it had not provided evidence that independent expenditures by corporations led to corruption or the appearance of corruption. Chief Justice Roberts asserted that the fact "[t]hat speakers have influence over or access to elected officials does not mean that those officials are corrupt. And the appearance of influence or access will not cause the electorate to lose faith in this democracy."[34]

Although it found the restriction on corporate speech to be facially overbroad, the Court refused to eliminate the law's disclaimer and disclosure previsions, based on the public's informational interest in knowing who is speaking. However, because print and Internet are not considered electioneering communications, the disclosure rules do not apply to them. Furthermore, Super PACs accept donations from organizations, like Crossroads GPS and Priority U.S.A. These 501(c)(4) groups (known by their number in the tax code) are allowed to maintain donor anonymity and participate in campaign activities, as long as campaigning is not their primary purpose.

Super PACs can raise and spend unlimited amounts of money on an election, as long as they don't coordinate their *spending* efforts with a candidate. They may be set up to support the campaigns of specific candidates and may even be started by associates of the candidate familiar with the candidate's messaging. Candidates are also free to ask supporters to contribute to their PACs. Although candidates may officially ask for no more than $5,000, donors are free to contribute as much as they like.

Some states have attempted to limit donor influence by publicly funding election campaigns. Arizona, for example, passed a campaign finance law called the Arizona Citizens Clean Elections Act that provided candidates for state elections with public funds if they promised to limit their personal spending to $500, participate in one debate, and return any unused funds at the end of the campaign. A unique aspect of the program was that candidates who entered the publicly funded program could get escalating funds to match money spent by privately financed candidates, or expenditures made on behalf of privately financed candidates by independent groups, that exceeded the initial grant for the publicly funded candidate's campaign. Matching funds maxed out at two times the initial grant to the publicly financed candidate. In *Arizona Free Enterprise Club v. Bennett* (2011), privately financed candidates and their support groups challenged the law's constitutionality, arguing that it penalized their speech and burdened their ability to fully exercise their First Amendment rights. The Supreme Court agreed. In a 5–4 decision, the Court concluded that the law diminished the effectiveness of the speech of those candidates willing to spend more by funding campaigns privately.[35] The majority considered the subsidy to be an unacceptable attempt by government to "level the playing field." The dissent considered it to be a reasonable attempt to combat corruption linked to special interests in a way that fostered more speech, not less.

---

[33] Citizens United v. Federal Election Comm'n, 130 S. Ct. 876, 898 (2010) (citing Wisconsin Right to Life, Inc., 551 U.S. 449, 464 (2007)).

[34] Citizens United v. Federal Election Comm'n, 130 S. Ct. at 884.

[35] Arizona Free Enterprise Club v. Bennett, 131 S. Ct. 2806 (2011).

Expanding the Meaning of the First Amendment

Throughout the twentieth century, protection for expression expanded beyond restrictions on prior restraint to protect against censorship *after* publication as well. Lawmakers began to understand that statutes could be applied in a variety of ways to restrict speech, and so they began to interpret the First Amendment as a protection against other barriers to expression. These included

The First Amendment now protects against suppression of expression before *and* after publication.

- undue burdens on expression, which make certain types of speech difficult to carry out;
- discriminatory applications of speech regulations, which treat expression differently depending on the speaker or the content of the speech; and
- censorship after the fact, which punishes speech that should have been protected.

First Amendment challenges to such restrictions may be based on the way they are applied or the way the law is written. An *applied challenge* is based on the argument that the law has not been applied fairly to a particular situation involving protected speech. A *facial challenge* is based on the argument that regardless of whether the litigant's speech is protected in the particular situation, the statute itself should be struck down because, as written, it has the potential to interfere with or "chill" the protected speech of others – either by limiting more speech than necessary to accomplish its purpose or by leaving people confused by ambiguous wording regarding what is prohibited.

Doctrines of overbreadth and vagueness

The Supreme Court has developed the doctrines of *overbreadth* and *vagueness* to address facial challenges to laws restricting speech. The *overbreadth doctrine* entitles a court to strike down a law that covers more protected speech or expressive conduct than necessary to accomplish its intended purpose. The Supreme Court explained the doctrine's purpose in *Virginia v. Hicks* (2003):

An overbroad law restricts more speech than necessary to accomplish its goal.

> We have provided this expansive remedy out of concern that the threat of enforcement of an overbroad law may deter or 'chill' constitutionally protected speech – especially when the overbroad statute imposes criminal sanctions . . . Many persons, rather than undertake the considerable burden (and sometimes risk) of vindicating their rights through case-by-case litigation, will choose simply to abstain from protected speech, . . . harming not only themselves but society as a whole, which is deprived of an uninhibited marketplace of ideas. Overbreadth adjudication, by suspending all enforcement of an over-inclusive law, reduces these social costs caused by the withholding of protected speech.[36]

A court will not invalidate a statute lightly, however. In *Broadrick v. Oklahoma* (1973), the Supreme Court explained that "the overbreadth of the statute must not only be real

[36] 539 U.S. 113, 119 (2003) (citations omitted).

but substantial as well, judged in relation to the statute's plainly legitimate sweep."[37] When overbreadth is not significant, the Court prefers to uphold the statute but narrow its interpretation.

Unlike the overbreadth doctrine, the *vagueness doctrine* is not specific to First Amendment cases. The Constitution's Fifth and Fourteenth Amendments include the right to due process of law. Due process requires that people be given fair warning regarding conduct that is deemed illegal. An ambiguously written law that fails to do that may be struck down as unconstitutionally vague. The Supreme Court has said that a law is unconstitutionally vague if persons of "common intelligence must necessarily guess at its meaning and differ as to its application."[38] When the challenged law concerns a fundamental right, like expression, the Court demands a higher degree of clarity. Aside from its potential to chill protected speech, a vague law is dangerous because it is subject to discriminatory enforcement by officials who interpret it as they see fit.

A vague law is one likely to require a person of common intelligence to guess at its meaning.

The vagueness doctrine is frequently coupled with the overbreadth doctrine in First Amendment cases. For example, in *Reno v. ACLU* (1997), the Supreme Court determined that a provision of the Communications Decency Act banning the Internet transmission of indecent and patently offensive materials to minors was both vague and overbroad.[39] It was vague because the terms *indecent* and *patently offensive* were not defined. It was overly broad because while it was meant to protect minors from indecent speech, it would also suppress speech that adults have the right to send and receive, when less restrictive options were available. Other provisions of the Act remain in place. Congress normally incorporates a severability clause in legislation that allows a court to sever parts of a law it finds unenforceable while retaining the rest of the statute.

Levels of judicial review

In First Amendment cases when courts suspect that the regulation challenged was put in place to restrict the expression of a particular idea or viewpoint, they subject the regulation to strict scrutiny, the highest level of judicial review. *Strict scrutiny* demands that content-based regulations be narrowly tailored to serve a compelling government interest. It is one of three levels of review that courts impose on government regulations and policies that burden speech. A mid-tier level of review known as *heightened* or *intermediate scrutiny* is generally applied to cases involving restrictions that burden speech, but which are not intended to target a particular idea or point of view. Under heightened scrutiny, a *content-neutral regulation* must serve an important government interest and restrict no more speech than necessary to achieve that interest. When legislative actions or agency regulations are challenged as arbitrary or capricious, courts impose a lower level of judicial scrutiny known as the *rational-basis test*. The test considers whether the government can supply a rational basis for the regulation and whether the regulation serves a legitimate state interest.

[37] Broadrick v. Oklahoma, 413 U.S. 601, 615 (1973).
[38] Connally v. General Construction Co., 269 U.S. 385, 391 (1926).
[39] 521 U.S. 844 (1997).

Limitations on Protection

Despite the First Amendment's broad application and wording, expression is not completely protected from government suppression. The level of protection for expression varies depending on the category of speech. For example, political speech is fully protected; commercial speech is protected as long as it is true; but other categories of speech, such as obscenity, are not protected. Protection of speech may vary depending on the medium used to convey the speech. The time, place, and manner of expression may be controlled when the expression occurs on government property, particularly if the expression does not comport with the intended use of the property. The government also has greater leeway to regulate expressive conduct and student speech.

Categorical speech limitation

A basic assumption in a liberal democracy is that government should not interfere with speech unless it poses a legitimate threat of harm. There are *categories of speech* that the Supreme Court considers unworthy of First Amendment protection because they carry this potential. These are areas of expression whose value appears to be so slight that they deserve no special consideration. Among them are incitement to violence, criminal solicitation, fighting words, true threats, obscenity, false commercial speech, and in some cases, libel. Restrictions related to these categories of speech are discussed in later chapters.

Medium specific protection

The Supreme Court does not grant equal First Amendment protection to all media. It bases the level of protection allotted to each form on its distinct characteristics. Print media, which require no special accommodations, get maximum protection from government intervention. Broadcast media, which require use of the public spectrum, operate under government constraints. They must be licensed to operate by the Federal Communications Commission and are subject to content restrictions based on their pervasiveness and accessibility to children. Cable, which relies on public rights of way for its lines, is obligated to carry signals from local broadcast stations, but as a subscription-based medium, it is generally free from content restrictions. Satellite, another subscription medium, must reserve some of its capacity for educational programming and local stations, but its own content is protected from censorship.

Initially the government was unsure about how to characterize the Internet. It is largely print-based, but it also carries audio and video and provides the immediacy of phone service. In reaction to a flawed Carnegie Mellon study spotlighted on the cover of *Time Magazine*, which suggested that 83 percent of the images on Usenet groups contained pornography, Congress imposed restrictions on the Internet that would be unconstitutional for print media.[40] It modified the Telecommunications Act to treat cyber porn like dial-a-porn, requiring websites with indecent content to verify that their users were adults via a credit card, debit account, or adult access code, as 900 numbers must do. In 1997, the Supreme Court struck down the legislation, observing that the government's comparison was flawed.[41] It concluded that like print, the Internet is worthy of full First Amendment protection.[42]

Time, place, and manner restrictions

As the trustee of public property, the government attempts to balance speech interests against its own interest in using public property for its intended purpose. When speech occurs on public property that is not reserved for speech purposes, the government may impose nondiscriminatory restrictions on the time, place, and manner in which the speech is conducted. The Supreme Court has indicated that the question to consider in assessing time, place, and manner restrictions is "whether the manner of expression is basically incompatible with the normal activity of a particular place at a particular time."

Forum analysis

The Supreme Court has adopted a forum analysis to assess the constitutionality of regulations that constrain speech on public property.[43] It identifies three forum tiers for public property: the traditional public forum, the designated public forum, and the nonpublic forum.[44]

Traditional public forums include public spaces that have traditionally been open for speech – like parks, street corners, sidewalks, and the steps of city hall. According to Justice Owen Roberts, these places "have immemorially been held in trust for the use of the public and, time out of mind, have been used for purposes of assembly, communicating thoughts between citizens, and discussing public questions."[45] In a traditional public forum, government restrictions on speech are subject to strict scrutiny.

Designated or limited public forums are public places like fairgrounds, town halls, and some public school facilities that government entities have opened to the public as a place for expressive activity.[46] Once public property has been intentionally opened for expressive activity, the government must make it available on a nondiscriminatory basis. But it may still impose reasonable time, place, and manner restrictions in keeping with the property's primary use.

---

[40] Martin Rimm, *Marketing Pornography on the Information Superhighway*, 83 GEORGETOWN L. J. 1849 (1995). *See also* Philip Elmer-DeWitt, *On a Screen Near You: Cyberporn*, TIME, July 3, 1995. The original study is at http://www.sics.se/~psm/kr9512-001.html.

[41] Reno v. American Civil Liberties Union, 521 U.S. 844 (1997).

[42] *Id.* at 864–85.

[43] Ark. Educ. Television Comm'n v. Forbes, 523 U.S. 666, 677 (1998).

[44] Perry Education Ass'n v. Perry Local Educators' Ass'n, 460 U.S. 37 (1983).

[45] Hague v. CIO, 307 U.S. 496, 515 (1939).

[46] Perry Education Ass'n v. Perry Local Educators' Ass'n, 460 U.S. at 45.

Courts subject "time, place, and manner" restrictions on speech in limited public forums to intermediate scrutiny. They assume that the government may enforce certain restrictions if the following conditions are met:[47]

- The law must be content neutral, both on its face and in the manner in which it is applied.
- The law must not constitute a complete ban on communication. Alternative options must be available to the speaker.
- The law must be narrowly tailored to further a substantial state interest and restrain no more expression than necessary to further that interest.

Consider, for example, a regulation that limits demonstrations in a neighborhood park to the hours in which it is open to the public, but requires demonstrators to leave when the park closes for the night. The time constraint may have the unintended effect of limiting expression, but it is not intended to target particular expression, so the regulation would be considered content neutral. It does not impose a complete ban on speech, because groups are free to demonstrate during daylight hours. It also serves an important purpose – ensuring people who live around the park a peaceful period in which to sleep – that is both unrelated to suppression of speech and narrowly tailored to accomplish that goal.

Nonpublic forums include public areas designated for purposes other than expression, such as airport concourses, polling places, subway stations, prisons, and military bases, which have never been opened for speech purposes. Government has the right to restrict speech in these areas.

Case study: Occupy Wall Street

Occupy Wall Street, a social movement that spread from New York to more than 100 cities across the United States, illustrates the application of time, place and manner restrictions to speech in public places. Protestors, angry at Wall Street for its role in precipitating a global economic recession, demonstrated against corporate greed and influence that they contended had influenced the democratic process, contributing to a growing disparity of wealth. The first protest was stationed in Manhattan's Financial District in a park that was privately owned. Because the property management company that owned the park waited three weeks to complain, police initially took no action to remove protesters who were encamped there. Police eventually removed them after a two-month stay. Police also arrested more than 700 protesters who blocked the Brooklyn Bridge by moving from the sidewalks into the street and cited them for disorderly conduct.

"Occupy" protesters were arrested or cited in public parks in Atlanta, Chicago, Cincinnati, Denver, Phoenix, Tucson, Arizona, Oakland, California, and Portland,

---

[47] United States v. Grace, 461 U.S. 171 (1983).

Figure 2.1   Protesters on day 14 of their occupation of Zuccotti Park in Manhattan, Sept. 30, 2011.
Source: David Shankbone, http://www.flickr.com/photos/shankbone/

Oregon. Limp demonstrators were dragged out of a city park in Portland, after it had closed for the night. In Oakland, California, protestors camped in a city park and a courthouse plaza for two weeks were treated more roughly. Police, who arrived after midnight, used tear gas to remove them. Protestors in the parks were reduced substantially in subsequent days by the city's decision to use the sprinkler system in the park continuously.

Is the Internet a public forum?

The question of whether the Internet constitutes a public forum is open for debate. Many message boards, blogs and social media sites serve as "spaces" open to the public where ideas are expressed and information is exchanged. However, most Internet service providers and social networking sites are privately owned. As private owners, they are not bound by the First Amendment to protect their users' speech. An Internet service provider, like Verizon, is well within its rights to withdraw service from any subscriber who violates its rules. Likewise, Facebook may delete your account if your speech violates its terms of service.

Despite its conviction that the Internet is entitled to full First Amendment protection, the Supreme Court has been reluctant to recognize the Internet as a public forum. In *United States v. American Library Association* (2003), the Supreme Court rejected a district court's use of public forum analysis to justify a right of access to public library computers, and through them, to the Internet.[48] The case concerned the

[48]United States v. Am. Library Ass'n, Inc., 539 U.S. 194, 199 (2003).

Figure 2.2 Illustration: Kalan Lyra

constitutionality of the Children's Internet Protection Act, which Congress enacted in 2000 to require libraries that receive public funding to install software on their computer terminals to block indecent speech. The Supreme Court did not consider the Internet to be a traditional public forum and would not recognize library terminals as a designated public forum without the government's express intent to transform them into such.

In fact, the Supreme Court has resisted applying forum analysis to any medium. In *Denver Area Educational Telecommunications Consortium v. FCC* (1996), it refused to apply forum analysis to public access cable channels. In the case, which concerned a First Amendment challenge to restrictions on indecency, Justice David Souter said "As broadcast, cable, and the cybertechnology of the Internet and World Wide Web approach the day of using a common receiver, we can hardly assume that standards for judging the regulation of one of them will not have immense, but now unknown and unknowable, effects on the others."[49] The justices were reluctant to apply forum analysis to a "new and changing area."

In his dissent, Justice Anthony Kennedy countered that forum analysis was appropriate despite the newness of the medium because, "Minds are not changed in streets and parks as they once were. To an increasing degree, the more significant interchanges of ideas and shaping of public consciousness occur in mass and electronic media."[50]

---

[49] 518 U.S. 727, 776–77 (1996) (Souter, J., concurring).

[50] Id. at 802–03 (Kennedy, J., concurring in part, concurring in judgment in part, dissenting in part).

Following Supreme Court precedent, federal appellate courts have rejected public forum analysis applied to city websites. In *Putnam Pit v. City of Cookeville* (1998), the Sixth Circuit weighed the question of whether a local publisher was entitled to a link from the city's website to his publication. Geoffrey Davidian, the publisher of *The Putnam Pit*, argued that by granting links to anyone who requested one on the city website, the city of Cookeville, Tennessee, had created a designated public forum. After reviewing Supreme Court forum analysis, the court stated that a public forum was a place "which by long tradition or by government fiat has been devoted to assembly and debate . . ."[51] It concluded that the city website did not allow for "open communication or the free exchange of ideas between members of the public" and therefore was a non-public forum.[52] The court based its determination on a two-part test that considered whether the city made the website available to an entire class of speakers and whether it was legitimate to limit speech occurring on the website to "that which is compatible with the forum's purpose."[53] The court observed that links had been granted on a case-by-case basis and deferred to the city administrator's contention that the site's purpose was to provide information about jobs, taxes, and other municipal news.

While states may not violate the First Amendment, they have the prerogative to supplement their citizens' rights to free expression within their own constitutions and statutory codes. California courts have interpreted the Internet to be a public forum. One appellate court found a Yahoo! message board to be a public forum. The court reasoned that "The term 'public forum' includes forms of public communication other than those occurring in a physical setting. Thus the electronic communication media may constitute public forums. Web sites that are accessible free of charge to any member of the public where members of the public may read the views and information posted, and post their own opinions, meet the definition of a public forum" under California law.[54]

Must a forum be a place?

The conceptual relationship between the Internet and forum analysis is complicated by the traditional assumption that a forum is a place defined in the sense of real property. This is usually the case. However, it is not axiomatic. A forum also may be a publication

---

[51] Putnam Pit v. City of Cookeville, 221 F.3d 834 (6th Cir. 2000) (quoting Perry Educ. Ass'n v. Perry Local Educators' Ass'n, 460 U.S. 37, 45 (1983)). *See also* Sutliffe v. Epping School District, 584 F.3d 314 (2009) (rejecting the argument that a city website was a designated public forum) and Loving v. Boren, 133 F.3d 771 (10th Cir. 1998) (holding that University of Oklahoma's computers and Internet services did not constitute a public forum.)

[52] Putnam Pit v. City of Cookeville, at 843.

[53] *Id.* at 843–44.

[54] Ampex Corp. v. Cargle, 128 Cal. App. 4th 1569, 1571 (2005). *See also*, New.net, Inc. v. Lavasoft, 356 F. Supp. 2d 1090, 1107 (C.D. Cal. 2004) (citing Global Telemedia Intern., Inc. v. Doe 1, 132 F. Supp. 2d 1261, 1264 (C.D. Cal. 2001) and MCSi, Inc. v. Woods, 290 F. Supp. 2d 1030, 2003 (N.D. Cal. 2003) (holding that a web chat room is a public forum).

or a program that fosters expression (like a mail system, a charitable contribution program, or a Student Activities Fund).[55] For example, in *Rosenburger v. Rector and Visitors of the University of Virginia* (1995), the Supreme Court described the university's Student Activities Fund as "a forum more in a metaphysical than in a spatial or geographic sense, but the same principles are applicable."[56]

Of course, the Internet is not a place. It is a collection of wires and routers and computer servers that transfer bits of data back and forth. Nevertheless, people conceive of it as a place when they refer to it as "cyberspace," a term coined by William Gibson in his 1984 novel *Neuromancer*. This metaphor has a powerful hold on the Internet. When we go online, we visit websites, chat rooms, home pages, simulated worlds, and online communities.[57] Justice O'Connor made this observation in *Reno v. ACLU* when she said, "cyberspace undeniably reflects some form of geography; chat rooms and Web sites, for example, exist at fixed 'locations' on the Internet."[58]

Expressive conduct

Although we normally think of communication as verbal, communication can also be nonverbal. Sit-ins and flag burning, for example, are both forms of expressive conduct meant to communicate a message. So was the 1996 decision by thousands of website operators to blacken their home pages in protest of the Communications Decency Act. But, at the same time, it cannot be assumed that all acts are intended to communicate a message. The act must be evaluated in context. The Supreme Court developed a test for symbolic speech in 1974. Courts are required to consider *whether the intent to convey a particularized message was present, and whether the likelihood was great that the message would be understood by those who viewed it.*[59] The test has since been modified. After reviewing a case that involved a homosexual group's denial of entrance into a parade, the Court pointed out that although there is no particular message in a parade, parading is certainly a "form of expression." A "narrow, succinctly articulable message is not a condition of constitutional protection."[60]

The government has more leeway to regulate symbolic speech than pure speech. The landmark case on expressive conduct is *United States v. O'Brien* (1968).[61] In that case, David O'Brien and three of his friends were arrested and convicted for violating an amendment to the Selective Service Act that prohibited the mutilation or destruction of a draft card. The defendants argued that burning their draft cards was a gesture meant to show their disgust for the Vietnam War and that the true purpose of the law was to

---

[55] *See* Perry Educ. Ass'n. v. Perry Local Educators' Assn., 460 U.S. at 46; Cornelius v. NAACP Legal Defense & Ed. Fund, Inc., 473 U.S. 788, 806 (1985).

[56] Rosenburger v. Rector and Visitors of the Univ. of Virginia, 515 U.S. 819, 830 (1995).

[57] Dan Hunter, *Cyberspace as Place and the Tragedy of the Digital Anticommons*, 91 CAL. L. REV. 439, 491 (2003).

[58] 521 U.S. 844, 890 (O'Connor, J., concurring in the judgment in part and dissenting in part).

[59] Spence v. Washington, 418 U.S. 405, 410–11 (1974).

[60] Hurley v. Irish-American Gay, Lesbian & Bisexual Group of Boston, 515 U.S. 557, 569 (1995).

[61] 391 U.S. 367, 377 (1968).

prohibit that form of political expression. The government argued that the law was drafted to improve the administration and operation of the selective service system, an important government objective that had no relationship to suppression of particular expression. The Supreme Court devised a test for regulations suppressing symbolic speech, which relies on an alternatively phrased version of intermediate scrutiny. If the following questions can be answered in the affirmative, the regulation can stand:

1. Did Congress have the constitutional authority to enact the regulation?
2. Does the regulation further a substantial government interest?
3. Is the government interest served by the regulation unrelated to the suppression of free expression?
4. Is the incidental restriction on free expression no greater than what is essential to the furtherance of that interest?

Is computer code speech or conduct?

Some forms of expressive speech contain *both* speech and nonspeech elements. The U.S. Court of Appeals for the Second Circuit has classified the posting and linking of computer code as expressive conduct rather than pure speech in *Universal City Studios, Inc. v. Corley* (2001).[62] The appellants, Eric Corley and his company 2600 Enterprises, published a magazine and website targeted to computer hackers. On the website, Corley posted a copy of the computer program "DeCSS" that can be used to circumvent the "CSS" encryption technology that movie studios like Universal have placed on DVDs to prevent unauthorized viewing and copying. When Universal got a preliminary injunction requiring Corley to take the program down, he complied but linked to another site with the program. Universal got a permanent injunction that also barred Corley from linking to other sites with DeCSS. The injunction was based on the anti-trafficking provisions of the Digital Millennium Copyright Act, which make it illegal to circumvent technologies designed to prevent access to a copyrighted work.[63]

Corley challenged the injunction and the DMCA as a violation of the First Amendment. The court acknowledged that computer code and computer programs are forms of speech covered by the First Amendment. However, because a program can function without additional human action, the court concluded that it contains both speech and nonspeech components:

> Computer programs are not exempted from the category of First Amendment speech simply because their instructions require use of a computer. A recipe is no less "speech" because it calls for the use of an oven, and a musical score is no less "speech" because it specifies performance on an electric guitar. Arguably distinguishing computer programs from conventional language instructions is the fact that programs are executable on a computer.[64]

[62] 273 F.3d 429 (2nd Cir. 2001).
[63] 17 U.S.C. §§ 1201(a)(2), (b)(1) (2010).
[64] Universal City Studios, Inc. v. Corley, 273 F.3d 429, 447 (2nd Cir. 2001).

The *Corley* court noted that the scope of protection for speech generally depends on whether the restriction is "content based" or "content neutral" and that the government's motive is usually the controlling factor in making that determination. It concluded that the DMCA and injunction were not motivated by DeCSS's capacity to convey information, but rather its capacity to instruct a computer to decrypt CSS. The court applied the same reasoning to hyperlinks, concluding that they have both a speech and non-speech component. The hyperlink conveys information that is protected speech, but it also has the functional capacity to bring the content of the linked page to the user's computer screen.

Student speech

Students once limited to sharing their thoughts about school with each other or on the bathroom wall now share them on the Web. This has created a new challenge for schools and courts. While it is clear that student speech on campus may be restricted and that speech off campus is protected, Internet posts – made off school property but accessible on campus – fall into a gray area in between on- and off-campus speech. How courts interpret student online speech depends on how they view its relationship to the line of cases the Supreme Court has decided concerning other forms of expression. The Supreme Court has stated that the "constitutional rights of students in public school are not automatically coextensive with the rights of adults in other settings."[65] While students in grades kindergarten through 12 are on campus or at school-sanctioned events, their speech rights may be curtailed if the speech:

- materially and substantially interferes with the requirements of appropriate discipline in the operation of the school;
- is "vulgar and offensive" based on the words used rather than the viewpoint expressed; or
- would be interpreted by a reasonable observer as advocating illegal drug use without commenting on any political or social issue.

The Court first considered the issue of student speech rights in *Tinker v. Des Moines Independent School District* (1969), a case brought by three students who were suspended from school for wearing black armbands in silent protest of the Vietnam War. In its opinion, the Court famously declared that students do not "shed their constitutional rights to freedom of speech or expression at the schoolhouse gate."[66] It held that student speech would be protected unless it "materially disrupts classwork or involves substantial disorder or invasion of the rights of others."[67]

---

[65] Bethel School Dist. No. 403 v. Fraser, 478 U.S. 675, 682 (1986).
[66] 393 U.S. 503, 506 (1969).
[67] *Id.* at 513.

However, the Court was considerably less deferential to student rights when the speech in question was "lewd and indecent."[68] In *Bethel School District v. Fraser* (1986), it considered the rights of a student suspended from school for delivering a speech at a school assembly that was laced with sexual innuendo. The speech that petitioner Matthew Fraser delivered in support of a friend's candidacy for student government to a captive audience of 600 high school students, made the following promise:

> I know a man who is firm – he's firm in his pants, he's firm in his shirt, his character is firm – but most . . . of all, his belief in you, the students of Bethel, is firm. Jeff Kuhlman is a man who takes his point and pounds it in. If necessary, he'll take an issue and nail it to the wall. He doesn't attack things in spurts – he drives hard, pushing and pushing until finally – he succeeds. Jeff is a man who will go to the very end – even the climax, for each and every one of you. So vote for Jeff for A. S. B. vice-president – he'll never come between you and the best our high school can be.[69]

The school suspended Fraser for violating its disruptive conduct rule – obviously crafted in response to *Tinker* – which "prohibited conduct that substantially interfered with the educational process, including the use of obscene, profane language or gestures." Frasier challenged the suspension as a violation of his First Amendment rights, but lost.

The Court did not find Fraser's speech to be substantially disruptive under *Tinker*. Rather it concluded that teaching civility is the work of the schools and the district was under no obligation to tolerate speech that conflicted with that purpose. "The schools, as instruments of the state, may determine that the essential lessons of civil, mature conduct cannot be conveyed in a school that tolerates lewd, indecent, or offensive speech and conduct. . . ."[70]

In *Morse v. Frederick* (2007), the Court indicated that schools are also tasked with the responsibility of educating students about the dangers of illegal drug use and therefore are not required to tolerate speech that appears to promote it.[71] The case involved a student's First Amendment challenge to his suspension for displaying a banner that read "BONG HiTS 4 JESUS" during an Olympic torch rally that passed in front of his high school. The student, Joseph Frederick, argued that his case did not concern school speech because he was standing across the street from the school rather than on school grounds when he held the banner. The Court rejected the argument because the event was school-sanctioned; it took place during school hours, at the school's behest, and under faculty supervision.

In the decision, Chief Justice Roberts was careful to point out that neither *Bethel* nor *Frederick* should be interpreted as allowing schools to restrict speech merely because it

---

[68] Bethel School District No. 403 v. Fraser, 478 U.S. at 685.

[69] *Id.* at 687 (Brennan J., concurring).

[70] *Id.* at 683.

[71] Morse v. Frederick, 551 U.S. 393 (2007).

is offensive. Political and religious speech is often offensive but would nevertheless be protected. Although Bethel's expression was in part a campaign speech, it clearly was not taken as serious political speech by the Court, and Frederick asserted that his banner was only meant as a joke with no intended meaning.

The previous three cases have all concerned speech in public schools, but the student press is also limited. In *Hazelwood v. Kulhmeier* (1988), the Court held that "educators do not offend the First Amendment by exercising editorial control over the style and content of student speech in school-sponsored expressive activities so long as their actions are reasonably related to legitimate pedagogical concerns."[72] If a publication is school sponsored, part of the curriculum, and not a public forum, administrators can censor content that might be interpreted to "bear the imprimatur of the school."[73] The U.S. Court of Appeals panel applied *Hazelwood* to college students in *Kincaid v. Gibson* (1999), when it held that the university yearbook was a school-sponsored expressive activity and university officials could regulate its content in any reasonable manner. However, the case was subsequently reversed in 2001 by the Sixth Circuit sitting *en banc*, on the basis that the university's actions should be reviewed with greater scrutiny than *Hazelwood*'s reasonableness test.[74]

An en banc decision is rendered by the full appellate court rather than the usual three-judge panel.

Although the Supreme Court has not considered whether the First Amendment precludes schools from punishing online speech, the Second, Third and Fourth Circuits have and reached different decisions on the issue. In each of these cases, decided in 2011, the losing party petitioned the Supreme Court for review and was denied certiorari, leaving the decisions in place.

The U.S. Court of Appeals for the Third Circuit concluded that school discipline of students who had created parodies of their principals on MySpace violated the First Amendment. The court considered the issue *en banc* to resolve two conflicting panel decisions reached in cases with similar fact patterns, *J.S. v. Blue Mountain School District* and *Layshock v. Hermitage School District*.[75] While the appellate court did not go so far as to conclude that off-campus speech could not be regulated under *Tinker*, it held that in the cases before it there was no evidence that the student speech would have satisfied the *Tinker* standard of "substantial disruption." The court agreed that the speech was lewd and offensive – particularly J. S.'s speech, which implied that her principal had engaged in sexual misconduct. However it refused to apply *Bethel*, because the speech was made off campus. The Second Circuit reached a different conclusion. In *Doninger v. Niehoff*, the court held that officials did not violate a student's First Amendment rights by preventing her from running for senior class secretary in response to a

---

[72] 484 U. S. 260, 273 (1988).
[73] *Id.* at 271.
[74] Kincaid v. Gibson, 236 F.3d 342 (6th Cir. 2001)(en banc).
[75] Layshock v. Hermitage Sch. Dist. 650 F.3d 205 (3rd Cir. 2011); J.S. v. Blue Mountain Sch. Dist. 650 F.3d 915 (3rd Cir. 2011). See also Beussink v. Woodland R-IV School District (in which a federal district court in the Eighth Circuit ruled similarly).

blog written from home that was critical of school officials.[76] In her blog, Doninger complained about a concert that had been postponed and invited readers to respond by contacting school officials, which did in fact occur. The court concluded that Doninger should have known that her call to action would have disruptive consequences on her campus.

The Fourth Circuit upheld a school's disciplinary action against a West Virginia high school student who created a MySpace page titled "S.A.S.H." ("Students Against Sluts Herpes"), on which she made disparaging remarks about another student and invited other students to comment. In *Kowalski v. Berkeley County Schools*, the appellate court concluded that a school suspension did not violate the student's First Amendment rights because school officials could reasonably forecast that her speech would be disruptive on campus and lead to more serious harassment.[77] Of the four cases, Kowalski is the most far reaching because the speech was not directed at the school. Punishing a student for off-campus speech seems overreaching, but at the same time, schools don't want to cast a blind eye to cyberbullying.

When students cross the line into threatening speech it is easier for courts to assume that their conduct is materially disruptive to the school or invades the rights of others. For example, in *J.S. v. Bethlehem Area School District* (2000) a student's website with a teacher's severed head dripping blood and an animation of the teacher's face morphing into a picture of Adolf Hitler, combined with a request for funds to cover a hit man, was deemed to have been substantially disruptive.[78] In fact, the teacher took medical leave for the rest of the year. Concluding that the speech was not protected, the Pennsylvania Supreme Court upheld the student's permanent expulsion.

No Compelled Speech

Freedom of expression includes another element that receives less attention but is just as important – the right not to speak. The Supreme Court has said that "Since all speech inherently involves choices of what to say and what to leave unsaid, one important manifestation of the principle of free speech is that one who chooses to speak may also decide 'what not to say.'"[79] Government may not compel individuals to convey messages with which they disagree or associate individuals or groups with unwanted messages.[80]

---

[76]Doninger v. Niehoff, 2011 WL 1532289 (2rd Cir. Apr. 25, 2011).

[77]Kowalski v. Berkeley County Schools, 652 F.3d 565 (4th Cir. 2011).

[78]569 Pa. 638, 807 A.2d 847 (Pa. 2002).

[79]Hurley v. Irish-American Gay, Lesbian and Bisexual Group of Boston, 515 U.S. 557, 573 (1995) (quoting Pacific Gas & Electric Co. v. Public Utilities Comm'n of Cal., 475 U.S. 1, 16 (1986)).

[80]*See* West Virginia Bd. of Ed. v. Barnette, 319 U.S. 624, 633–4 (1943), Wooley v. Maynard, 430 U.S. 705, 713–17, (1977), and BSA v. Dale, 530 U.S. 640, 653 (2000).

First Amendment Theories

The Constitution does not link protection of expression to any particular objective and the Supreme Court has not reached a consensus on a unified legal theory upon which to determine what should be protected. Various political theories have emerged to explain the purpose of the First Amendment. Some focus on the collective process and the benefits to society as a whole. Others focus on individual rights.

One powerful theory suggests that freedom of expression is required for self-government. The democratic process is dependent upon free expression, both for the purpose of participatory democracy and to ensure people have the information they need to vote intelligently. Alexander Meiklejohn argued that because government derives its power from the consent of the governed, political speech – above all other types of expression – should be protected absolutely.[81] A related idea is that free expression serves as a check on government abuse of power. Vincent Blasi theorized that fear of public exposure deters government officials from going astray.[82] When that is not sufficient, information about the abuse empowers voters to fight it at the ballot box.

Americans also believe that freedom of expression serves as a safety valve of sorts – a very important function in a period plagued by terrorism. Justice Louis Brandeis expressed this idea in the now-famous metaphor: "sunlight is the most powerful of all disinfectants."[83] He warned that

it is hazardous to discourage thought, hope and imagination; that fear breeds repression; that repression breeds hate; that hate menaces stable government; that the path to safety lies in the opportunity to discuss freely supposed grievances and proposed remedies; and that the fitting remedy for evil counsels is good ones.[84]

In other words, although we may not like to hear what some people have to say, allowing people to express their views gets them out in the open where we can address them. Silencing people with whom we disagree does not make them change their views. It just increases their resentment.

Freedom of expression is also required for "individual self-fulfillment"[85] Through communication we relate to others, express our thoughts and emotions, and develop our personalities. Conversing with others is instrumental in developing our mental faculties.[86] It helps us form our own beliefs and opinions, promoting autonomous decision-making.[87] When others listen to what we have to say, we develop self-respect. Limits placed on what we can say undermine our sense of dignity.[88]

The most common justification for freedom of expression is the search for truth. In *On Liberty*, John Stuart Mill argued that the particular danger of government suppression of speech is its potential to suppress ideas that are true. Moreover, even if a statement is clearly wrong, suppression denies the public the opportunity to reexamine and reaffirm what is true. Mill assumed that freedom of expression would result in the communication of good and bad information, but he also believed that if left unfettered society could, over time, sort out the truth. This theory of truth discovery is called the marketplace of ideas rationale. It was reiterated by Justice Oliver

[81] ALEXANDER MEIKLEJOHN, FREE SPEECH AND ITS RELATION TO SELF-GOVERNMENT (The Lawbook Exchange, Ltd. 2004) (1948).

[82] Vincent Blasi, *The Checking Value in First Amendment Theory*, 2 AM. B. FOUND. RES. J. 521 (1977).

[83] LOUIS D. BRANDEIS, OTHER PEOPLE'S MONEY AND HOW THE BANKER'S USE IT 92 (1914).

[84] Whitney v. California, 274 U.S. 357, 375 (1927) (Brandeis, J., concurring).

[85] See C. Edwin Baker, *Scope of the First Amendment Freedom of Speech*, 25 UCLA L. REV. 964, 965–91 (1978) and THOMAS I. EMERSON, THE SYSTEM OF FREEDOM OF EXPRESSION 6 (1970).

[86] See M. Redish, *Self-Realization, Democracy and Freedom of Expression: A Reply to Professor Baker*, 130 U. PA. L. REV. 678, 684 (1982).

[87] See Thomas I. Emerson, *Towards a General Theory of the First Amendment*, 72 YALE L. J. 877, 879–80 (1963).

[88] See Kent Greenawalt, *Free Speech Justifications*, 89 COLUM. L. REV. 119, 145–6 (1987).

Wendell Holmes in his dissenting opinion in *Abrams v. United States* (1919).[89] Focusing on the collective search for truth, Holmes wrote:

> [W]hen men have realized that time has upset many fighting faiths, they may come to believe even more than they believe the very foundation of their own beliefs that the ultimate good desired is better reached by free trade of ideas — that the best test of truth is the power of the thought to get itself accepted in the competition of the market, and that truth is the only ground upon which their wishes safely can be carried out. That at any rate is the theory of our constitution. It is an experiment, as all life is an experiment.[90]

Aside from the existential question of whether truth exists, the primary criticism of the marketplace of ideas theory is that the marketplace is not equally open to everyone. The voices that dominate the marketplace are those that belong to people with enough power and money to demand access to the press, making it difficult for alternative views to be heard. To a certain extent, this criticism is valid. A man like Rupert Murdoch, who runs News Corporation with Fox Broadcasting, Twentieth Century Fox, and now MySpace, certainly has more power to be heard than the average person on the street. However, digital media have lowered the cost of entry into the marketplace of ideas. The online encyclopedia Wikipedia is an example of the marketplace theory in action. Anyone with Internet access can edit Wikipedia entries, which makes them vulnerable to bias and error. But, by the same token, biased or deceptive entries are usually corrected by other users. For example, the night before John McCain announced that Alaska Governor Sarah Palin would be his running mate in the 2008 presidential election, someone made 30 changes to Palin's Wikipedia entry, adding favorable references, including a description of her as a politician of "eye-popping integrity," while downplaying references that might be perceived as negative.[91] Within a day most of the changes had been reversed or toned down. Aside from Wikipedia, many blogs can boast audiences that are at least as big as those drawn by mainstream media. Celebrity gossip blog Perez Hilton attracts 100 million monthly readers — as many as *Forbes Magazine*. Matt Drudge claims his Drudge Report gets 17 million hits a day.

Questions for Discussion

1. How is the Fourteenth Amendment used to make the First Amendment applicable to the states and why is it necessary?
2. In what ways are First Amendment protections limited?
3. What is the difference between a content-neutral restriction and a content-based restriction? How do levels of judicial review differ for each?
4. How does First Amendment protection for student speech differ from First Amendment protection for adult speech?

---

[89] Abrams v. United States, 250 U.S. 616 (1919).

[90] *Id.* at 630 (Holmes, J., dissenting).

[91] Noam Cohen, *Don't Like Palin's Wikipedia Story? Change It*, N.Y. TIMES, Sept. 1, 2008, at C3.

3 Telecommunications Regulation

The modern smart phone can handle mobile calls and Internet use, enabling the user to download books, access streaming audio and video from broadcast stations, watch cable shows on sites like Hulu, or enjoy films on Netflix – all delivered via satellite. This seamless flow of content through one device could naturally lead to the assumption that everything on it would be similarly regulated, but that is not the case. The regulatory framework for telecommunications has not kept pace with convergent technology. As a result, services and content offered through such multimedia devices may be regulated differently.

This chapter describes the regulations and First Amendment protections applicable to broadcast, cable, satellite, and phone companies. These traditional telecommunications media, now offered in digital and convergent form, are positioned for new regulatory changes in Congress and the courts.

A Bird's Eye View

Telecommunications media are more heavily regulated than print media. Government regulations applicable to telecommunications dictate their terms of ownership, the physical operation of their facilities and, in some respects, even the content transmitted through them. This intrusion is justified under the theory that wireless media, such as broadcast and satellite, benefit from the use of a public resource – the electromagnetic spectrum – and, as trustees of that resource, should operate in the public interest. Wired media, such as cable and telephone systems, on the other hand, are subject to government regulation because their lines are strung along public rights of way.

Digital Media Law, Second Edition. Ashley Packard.
© 2013 John Wiley & Sons, Inc. Published 2013 by John Wiley & Sons, Inc.

The Federal Communications Commission regulates most telecommunications media in the United States. The FCC exerts control over broadcast media through its right to grant, renew, or revoke stations' licenses and over satellite media through its right to license construction and operation of direct broadcast satellite systems. Other forms of telecommunications, including cable and telephone service, fall within its sphere of influence, although it does not have exclusive control of them. State and municipal governments grant cable companies franchises to operate in particular areas, and therefore play an important role in cable regulation. State public utility commissions regulate aspects of telephony.

The Internet does not fall within the FCC's jurisdiction. However, the FCC has developed a network neutrality policy for broadband access to it, based on its oversight of cable, satellite and phone services. This policy and other regulatory efforts applicable to the Internet are discussed in Chapter 4.

Establishing a Regulatory Framework

Before cyberspace, the frontier media most wanted to conquer was the electromagnetic spectrum, a continuum of electromagnetic energy that carries radio waves and microwaves. The U.S. government was the predominant user of the spectrum until 1912 when it began to license private radio operators to use it. However, because it offered no guidance on the use of frequencies, radio operators were soon broadcasting over one another. In 1927, Congress created the Federal Radio Commission to allocate specific frequencies and assign permission to use them based on the operator's agreement to operate in the "public interest, convenience and necessity." Another federal agency, the Interstate Commerce Commission, regulated communications through telephone and telegraph carriers.

Congress consolidated regulatory responsibilities for all communications under one agency – the Federal Communications Commission – through its passage of the Communications Act of 1934.

The statute is divided into sections called titles, which enumerate the agency's responsibilities and powers with respect to different forms of media.

A common carrier, such as a phone service provider, acts as a nondiscriminatory conduit for others' communications rather than its own.

- Title I outlines the purposes of the law, the FCC's jurisdiction, and its organizational structure.
- Title II authorizes the FCC to develop rules for the regulation of *common carriers*.
- Title III establishes the Commission's responsibility to license and regulate radio communications that use the electromagnetic spectrum.
- Title IV outlines the procedures for due process in FCC decision-making.
- Title V describes the range of civil and criminal penalties in force for violation of the Communications Act or rules developed by the Commission.
- Title VI sets out general provisions for ownership and operation of cable stations.
- Title VII contains miscellaneous provisions, such as requirements for communication services to establish reasonable access for the disabled.

As new media have evolved, new titles have been added to bring them under the Act's regulatory umbrella. The FCC now has the power to make and enforce rules related to use of the spectrum by broadcast, satellite, Wi-Fi and cellular media. It also imposes regulations on wireline communications through telephones, digital subscriber lines – *DSL*, cable, or anything related to the development of broadband technology.

Federal Communications Commission structure

The FCC is directed by a five-member board of commissioners, appointed by the president and confirmed by the Senate. The president selects one member to serve as chair. The chair sets the agenda for the agency and designates the leaders of agency bureaus and departments. To ensure that the Commission remains relatively nonpartisan, the president is allowed to appoint no more than three commissioners from the same party. Normally, the president sways the balance by ensuring that the majority belongs to his party. Commissioners serve five-year terms that are staggered so their terms expire in different years.

Commissioners have final decision-making authority on all FCC matters, but the day-to-day functions of the agency are divided among seven policy-making bureaus that handle the agency's workload:

- The *Media Bureau* develops and administers rules for cable television, broadcast television, radio, and satellite.
- The *Wireline Competition Bureau* develops policies and rules for phone companies.
- The *Wireless Telecommunications Bureau* oversees mobile phones, personal communications services, pagers, and two-way radios.
- The *International Bureau* oversees satellite and policy matters related to international telecommunications services.
- The *Consumer and Government Affairs Bureau* informs consumers about telecommunication products and services, coordinates telecommunications policy with other government agencies, and handles matters related to disability rights.
- The *Enforcement Bureau* enforces the Communications Act and the Commission's rules.
- The *Public Safety and Homeland Security Bureau* recommends and administers telecommunications policy related to public safety and emergency management.[1]

The FCC also has an Office of Administrative Law Judges that serves a judicial function within the agency. In cases involving alleged violations of FCC regulations, administrative law judges conduct administrative hearings in which they act as fact finders and issue initial decisions that may be appealed to the Commission and ultimately in the federal court system.

[1] Federal Communications Commission, About the FCC, http://www.fcc.gov/aboutus.html (last visited Jan. 24, 2012).

FCC rulemaking

The FCC's primary role is to implement provisions of the Communications Act, but it is also empowered to make rules of its own that carry the force of law. Its initiatives might result from Congressional legislation that requires the FCC to fulfill its mandates by enacting specific rules, a judicial order that requires the agency to reconsider a course of action, or the agency's convictions that a change would improve telecommunications policy.

The agency acts through a notice and comment procedure that is standard among government regulatory agencies. When an FCC bureau proposes to change or implement a rule, it publishes a *Notice of Proposed Rulemaking* in the Federal Register, the government's daily digest of administrative actions. The public is given a minimum of 30 days to comment on the proposed rule before the FCC acts. For example, in 2011, the FCC proposed rules to implement the Commercial Advertisement Loudness Mitigation Act, passed by Congress to end those annoying spikes in the volume of television commercials compared to their adjacent programming.[2] The FCC's Notice of Proposed Rulemaking on the CALM Act described the regulations the agency planned to impose on providers of video programming and gave them an opportunity to comment. Had the FCC wanted feedback on the issue before proposing specific rules, it could have taken an alternative track by publishing a *Notice of Inquiry* to solicit general comments first.

After assessing public comments, the agency may choose to revise and reissue its proposal as a *Further Notice of Proposed Rulemaking*. Alternatively, it may move forward to the next step by issuing a *Report and Order* containing its final decision. The FCC's Report and Order on the CALM Act, released six months after its Notice of Proposed Rulemaking, described the means stations would use to control advertising volume and clarified that the regulations would apply to digital programming from broadcast, cable and satellite distributors.[3]

A Report and Order is generally accompanied by a detailed justification of the agency's policy to avoid accusations that the change was *arbitrary and capricious*. Because the Administrative Procedures Act requires federal agencies to articulate a rational basis for the choices they make, plaintiffs who challenge agency rules frequently do so on the principle that they are arbitrary and capricious.

Parties that object to an FCC decision may file a *Petition for Reconsideration* within 30 days of the decision's publication in the Federal Register. After considering the petition, the Commission will respond with a *Memorandum and Order*. If the Commission denies the petition, the party may challenge the FCC order in a federal court of appeals.

---

[2] Implementation of the Commercial Advertisement Loudness Mitigation (CALM) Act, 76 FR 32116, (proposed May 27, 2011) (to be codified at 47 CFR 73.682(e) and 76.607.

[3] Implementation of Implementation of the Commercial Advertisement Loudness Mitigation (CALM) Act, 76 FR 77830, FCC Report and Order (Dec. 13, 2011)(to be codified at 47 CFR §73.682(e) and § 76.607).

The first digital media law

Congress changed the regulatory structure for telecommunications drastically in 1996 when it overhauled the Communications Act to prepare the way for digital convergence.[4] The omnibus legislation, called the Telecommunications Act of 1996, was arguably the first "digital media law." Through it, Congress eliminated ownership rules that prevented communication companies from offering services in more than one sector. The Act opened up new possibilities for digital communication by allowing phone companies to supply video and information services, cable companies to supply telecommunications services, broadcasters to own cable systems, regional telephone companies to offer long distance service, and long distance companies to offer regional service.

The Telecommunications Act also pushed analog media in a digital direction. Congress allocated additional spectrum to full-powered television stations so they could transition from analog to digital programming. This provision, which took effect in 2009, brought the quality of broadcast programming up to that of satellite and cable, which were already transmitting digital as well as analog signals. Because radio stations require less bandwidth, they can simulcast digital signals on either side of the frequency used for analog programming.

While the Telecommunications Act reduced barriers to technological convergence and transitioned electronic media from analog to digital, it did nothing to address the fact that the policies designed for separate media remained in effect, despite their convergence.

—————— Broadcast Regulation

Among electronic media, broadcast radio and television have traditionally received the most government oversight. As the eldest child of the electronic media family, broadcast was forced to operate under stricter rules than its younger siblings, cable and satellite, which benefited from a looser regulatory structure.

The Federal Communications Commission has imposed licensing and ownership restrictions, as well as content requirements, on broadcast media, based on the theory that

Figure 3.1   Illustration: Kalan Lyra

[4]Pub. L. 104-104, 110 Stat. 56 (codified in various sections of 47 U.S.C.).

the electromagnetic spectrum is a scarce public resource and that those entitled to use it should be required to operate in the public interest. FCC powers to impose regulations "in the public interest" were challenged by the networks and upheld by the Supreme Court in *National Broadcasting Company v. United States* (1943).[5] Writing for the Court, Justice Felix Frankfurter cited scarcity as a justification, pointing out that:

> Freedom of utterance is abridged to many who wish to use the limited facilities of radio. Unlike other modes of expression, radio inherently is not available to all. That is its unique characteristic, and that is why, unlike other modes of expression, it is subject to governmental regulation.[6]

In the mid-1980s, the FCC acknowledged that the spectrum scarcity theory was no longer valid. Nevertheless, the theory dictated the FCC's policies for broadcast up until that point and in some respects still does.

One of those policies was to ensure the fair representation of all viewpoints in the media. This policy reflected the concern that broadcasters might use their stations to advocate for a singular perspective. The FCC's Fairness Doctrine, initiated in 1949, required broadcasters to devote adequate time to the discussion of controversial issues of public importance in news and public affairs coverage and to ensure that opposing points of view were represented in that coverage. In an effort to promote fairness, the FCC also required broadcasters to offer anyone subjected to a personal attack during the station's programming an opportunity to respond. Broadcasters who endorsed political candidates were required to invite other candidates on air to respond. Further, the agency required stations that offered airtime to any candidate for office to make an "equal opportunity" available to any other qualified candidate competing in the same election.

In the 1970s, the FCC referred to the Fairness Doctrine as the "single most important requirement of operation in the public interest – the sine qua non for grant of a renewal of license."[7] But journalists were disturbed by government efforts to take discretion for programming away from them. A Pennsylvania radio station challenged the constitutionality of the fairness doctrine in *Red Lion Broadcasting Co. v. FCC* (1969).[8] It argued that the FCC rule violated the First Amendment because it treated broadcast media differently than print media. But the Supreme Court upheld the constitutionality of the Fairness Doctrine, noting that differences in the character of broadcast media justified differences in the First Amendment standards applied to them.[9]

---

[5] 319 U.S. 190 (1943).
[6] *Id.* at 226–27.
[7] Dan Fletcher, *The Fairness Doctrine*, TIME, Feb. 20, 2009, http://www.time.com/time/nation/article/0,8599,1880786,00.html.
[8] 395 U.S. 367 (1969).
[9] *Id.* at 387.

The Court found the FCC's argument that the doctrine promoted the First Amendment rights of listeners by ensuring greater access to information persuasive. In upholding the Fairness Doctrine, Justice White explained:

> Because of the scarcity of radio frequencies, the government is permitted to put restraints on licenses in favor of others whose views should be expressed in this unique medium. But the people as a whole retain their interest in free speech by radio and their collective right to have the medium function consistently with the ends and purposes of the First Amendment. It is the right of the viewers and listeners, not the right of the broadcasters, which is paramount. . . . It is the right of the public to receive suitable access to social, political, esthetic, moral and other ideas and experiences which is crucial here.[10]

This was a new idea – that the First Amendment protected not only speakers' rights to convey information, but also listeners' rights to have information. However, it is not a theory that has thrived in Supreme Court doctrine. In later cases, the Supreme Court denied a right of access to print and broadcast media to petitioners who argued that access was necessary to preserve the public's right to information, preferencing instead the media's right to convey information without government interference.[11] Nevertheless, the enduring significance of the Supreme Court's *Red Lion* decision is its affirmation of the government's power to impose regulations on broadcast media that serve the public interest in exchange for exclusive licenses to use the public airwaves.

The FCC abandoned enforcement of Fairness Doctrine in 1987, under the theory that market forces reduced the need for such control, but waited until 2011 to discard the rule officially. In 1999, the agency rescinded its personal attack rules.[12] The U.S. Court of Appeals for the D.C. Circuit held that the rules "interfere[d] with editorial judgment of professional journalists and entangle[d] the government in day-to-day operations of the media."[13] It ordered the FCC to justify or repeal them. When the FCC did not act, the appeals court ordered the Commission to repeal the rules the following year.[14]

Although the scarcity rationale has fallen out of favor as a justification for interference in broadcast content, the Supreme Court's *Red Lion* decision, upholding the FCC's right to impose regulations in the public interest, is still in force. In an effort to pursue

---

[10] *Id.* at 390.

[11] *See* Miami Herald Publishing Co. v. Tornillo, 418 U.S. 241, 248 (1974) and CBS v. Democratic National Committee, 412 U.S. 94, 121–31 (1973).

[12] In the matter of Repeal or Modification of the Personal Attack and Political Editorial Rules, 15 F.C.C.R. 20697 (2000).

[13] Radio-Television News Dirs. Ass'n v. Federal Communications Commission, 184 F.3d 872, 881 (D.C. Cir. 1999).

[14] Radio-Television News Dirs. Ass'n v. Federal Communications Commission, 229 F.3d 269 (D.C. Cir. 2000).

policy objectives to foster localism, competition and diversity in broadcasting, the agency still imposes some restrictions on ownership and content. Some of its policies have been extended to cable and satellite when they serve as originators of programming within their exclusive control.

Broadcast Station Licensing

FCC power over broadcasters comes from the agency's ability to grant and take away station licenses, which literally means the difference between broadcasting life or death. A station cannot operate without a license.

Until 1993, the FCC allocated licenses through a competitive process – essentially evaluating two or more stations vying for the same license and basing its decision on which would be more likely to serve in the public interest, convenience and necessity. The U.S. Court of Appeals for the D.C. Circuit effectively banned that process in *Bechtel v. FCC* (1993).[15] The FCC now issues licenses by auction. The FCC's auction of spectrum freed up by broadcasters' transition to digital programming netted $19.6 billion in 2008.[16]

The Commission will only award licenses to American applicants. It is barred by the Communications Act from granting a broadcast or common carrier license to a person who is not a citizen of the United States, a foreign company, any company of which more than one-fifth of the stock is owned by foreigners, or any company directed by another company of which one-fourth of the stock is foreign-owned.[17] The rule applies to radio and television stations and telephone companies that use a radio, satellite or microwave link, but it does not apply to cable. In order to acquire the television stations in the Fox network, Rupert Murdoch, a native Australian, had to change his citizenship.

Stations are licensed for periods up to eight years and must apply for renewal before their terms expire. In their renewal applications they must show that they are in compliance with federal laws and FCC regulations and that they have operated in the public's interest.

Failure to comply with FCC regulations can result in sanctions. The Commission has the authority to (1) issue cease and desist orders, (2) impose monetary forfeitures (fines), (3) grant a short-term license renewal, (4) deny renewal, or (5) revoke a station's license. If a station's license is revoked, it may appeal the decision before an administrative law judge within the FCC. If the decision is upheld, it may appeal to the U.S. Court of Appeals for the D.C. Circuit and, eventually, the Supreme Court. Aside from licensing, the FCC regulates technical aspects of operation, including station location, classification, call letters, frequencies, power, times of operation, and ownership restrictions.

Media Ownership Rules

To further its policies of fostering localism, competition and diversity in media, the FCC has imposed restrictions on ownership of media operations. Over the years these restrictions have been reduced significantly by Congress through the Telecommunications Act, FCC rulemaking, and courts in challenges based on the First Amendment. However, the following rules remain in place to encourage a healthy marketplace of ideas:

---

[15] 10 F.3d 875 (D.C. Cir. 1993).
[16] Anne Broache, *FCC's Wireless Airwaves Sale Raises $19.6 Billion*, CNET, March 18, 2008, at http://news.cnet.com/8301-10784_3-9897297-7.html.
[17] 47 U.S.C. § 310 (2010).

National television ownership: There is no particular limit on the number of television broadcast stations that one person or company can own, but the aggregate national reach of stations owned cannot exceed 39 percent of U.S. households. UHF stations are factored into the equation at only 50 percent of their audience reach. The U.S. Court of Appeals of the D.C. Circuit struck down an FCC rule limiting the aggregate national reach of cable stations owned by one party to 30 percent in 2009.[18] No limits are imposed on satellite or fiber optic providers.

Duopolies: One party may own two television stations in the same market if eight full-power independent television stations (commercial and noncommercial) will remain after the merger and one of them is not among the top-four ranked stations based on its audience share. This has come to be known as the "voices test" because it is supposed to guarantee that adequate voices remain in the market to ensure a diversity of views and news. Co-ownership is also allowed in markets in which the licensee is the only reasonably available buyer and the station purchased is failing. The FCC also may waive the rule for a licensee that plans to build a new station.

Broadcast/cable cross ownership: One party may own a television station and a cable television service in the same market, as long as the cable operator faces effective competition in the market.

Dual network ownership: One party may own a major VHF network like ABC, CBS, Fox, or NBC and a UHF network like UPN or WB. Viacom, for example, owns CBS and a large portion of UPN. However, the rule prohibits a merger between ABC, CBS, FOX or NBC.

Broadcast/newspaper cross ownership: Media companies have been prevented from owning both the newspaper and a television station in the same media market since 1975. The FCC attempted to lift the restraint on cross-ownership in limited markets in 2007. Its stated purpose was to help struggling newspapers in those markets, which if allowed to purchase more profitable television stations could shore up their bottom lines. However, preservation of the newspaper industry is not the FCC's responsibility. In 2011, the Third Circuit reinstated the ban in *Prometheus Radio Project v. FCC.*[19] The court was responding to the concern that the public was not given adequate notice and opportunity to comment.

Television/radio co-ownership: One party that owns a television station (or two under the duopoly rule) may own:
- up to four radio stations in any market where at least 10 independent voices would remain post-merger;
- up to six radio stations in any market where at least 20 independent voices would remain post-merger; or

[18] Comcast v. Federal Communications Commission, 579 F.3d 1 (D.C. Cir. 2009).
[19] 652 F.3d 431 (2011).

- one radio station (AM or FM) regardless of the number of other stations in the market.

National radio ownership: There is no national cap on the number of radio stations one party can own. But there are restrictions on the number of stations owned in one market. One party may own, operate, or control:
- up to 8 commercial radio stations in a market with 45 or more commercial radio stations, provided that no more than 5 of the stations are in the same service (AM or FM);
- up to 7 commercial radio stations in a market with between 30 and 44 commercial radio stations, provided that no more than 4 are in the same service (AM or FM);
- up to 6 commercial radio stations in a market with between 15 and 29 commercial radio stations, provided that no more than 4 are in the same service (AM or FM); and
- up to 5 commercial radio stations in a market with 14 or fewer commercial radio stations, provided that no more than 3 are in the same service (AM or FM), with the exception that one party may not own more than 50 percent of the stations in a market.

The Telecommunications Act was particularly criticized for its drastic deregulation of radio ownership. Before the Act was passed, one party could own no more than 20 AM stations and 20 FM stations. At one point after it was passed, Clear Channel amassed 1,200 stations.

Broadcast content requirements

In addition to its ownership rules, the FCC imposes some content requirements on broadcasters. For example, it still requires broadcasters to give candidates in an election equal opportunities for access to their audiences. Stations are also required to identify their sponsors, provide quarterly reports demonstrating that their programming meets the needs of their community, and offer programming specifically for children.

Equal opportunity (equal time) provision

In general, there is no First Amendment right of access to broadcast stations. The Supreme Court held that neither the Communications Act nor the First Amendment is violated when radio stations refuse to sell time to groups that want to air their editorial views in *CBS v. Democratic National Committee* (1973).[20] However, there is one excep-

---

[20]Columbia Broadcasting Sys. v. Democratic National Comm., 412 U.S. 94 (1973).

tion. FCC rules mandate a certain amount of access to broadcast and satellite media for candidates in *federal* elections.[21]

Broadcasters and satellite providers are not obligated to provide free airtime to federal candidates who cannot afford to advertise. But they are required to offer such candidates the "lowest unit charge" or, the lowest rate charged to other advertisers for comparable time, during the 45 days preceding a primary election and 60 days preceding a general election. The Communications Act provides that a broadcast station's license may be revoked for "willful or repeated failure to allow reasonable access to or to permit purchase of reasonable amounts of time for the use of a broadcasting station by a legally qualified candidate for Federal elective office."[22]

During the 2012 election cycle, anti-abortion activist Randall Terry, declared himself a nominee for president of the United States with the goal of running a campaign commercial that featured aborted fetuses during the Super Bowl. Two days before the game, the FCC's Media Bureau ruled that WMAQ-TV, NBC's Chicago affiliate, was not obligated to run the ad. The FCC concluded that Terry did not make a substantial showing of candidacy, and even if he had, the station's denial was not unreasonable. It stipulated that even if Terry were a legally qualified federal candidate, he would not be entitled to place his ads on a particular program on a station's broadcast schedule.[23]

Broadcast, cable, and satellite programmers must give other political candidates equal opportunities to use their facilities if they decide to open their facilities to them.[24] A company that sells or gives away advertising space to one candidate must grant the same opportunity to the opposing candidate. This rule, codified in Section 315 of the Communications Act, is intended to keep broadcasters from trying to manipulate elections by controlling the amount of media coverage candidates receive.

Concerned that news organizations might avoid covering political candidates because such coverage would obligate them to provide equal time to the candidate's opponent, Congress provided four exceptions to the rule. A candidate's appearance will not trigger the equal access rule if it occurs during:

- bona fide newscasts;
- news interviews;
- on-the-spot news events (including political conventions); and
- news documentaries (assuming they are not based on the candidate).

The FCC's interpretation of what constitutes a newscast is pretty broad. It includes "Entertainment Tonight." The agency has also classified talk show appearances on such shows as "The Tonight Show with Jay Leno," "The 700 Club," and "Howard Stern," as

---

[21] Reasonable access, 47 C.F.R. § 73.1944.

[22] 47 U.S.C. § 312(a)(7).

[23] In re Complaint of Randall Terry Against Station WMAQ-TV, Chicago, Illinois, DA12–145, Rel. Feb. 3, 2012 (Memorandum and Order).

[24] *See* 47 C.F.R. § 73.1941 (for broadcast rules), 47 C.F.R. § 76.205 (for cable rules) and 47 C.F.R. § 25.701 (for DBS rules).

news interviews. It has interpreted political debates to be on-the-spot news coverage, which allows stations to arrange debates involving some rather than all of the candidates in an election. Documentaries will not trigger the equal time rule if the candidate's appearance is incidental rather than the principle focus. Television appearances that have nothing to do with news, however, will trigger the equal opportunity provision. During President Ronald Reagan's campaigns, television stations were careful to avoid showing movies from his earlier acting career.

The Communications Act also prohibits broadcast, cable, and satellite programmers from censoring candidates' on-air statements.[25] In another case involving an anti-abortion candidate, the FCC ruled in favor of a Georgia station that tried to restrict a graphic advertisement showing an abortion in progress, but the U.S. Court of Appeals for the District of Columbia Circuit overruled the FCC's decision. Daniel Becker, a candidate for Congress, submitted the 30-minute political advertisement to an Atlanta TV station, requesting that the ad appear immediately after a National Football League broadcast of a game between the Falcons and the Rams. The station considered the videotape indecent, but editing the footage was not an option, so it scheduled the ad to run during the middle of the night. The FCC issued a Memorandum Opinion and Order indicating that stations were entitled to make good faith editorial judgments in such matters. But the D.C. Circuit reversed the decision on the theory that the ruling encouraged candidates to engage in self-censorship.[26] The court said the FCC rule put candidates in the position of sacrificing what they wanted to say to the audience they wanted to reach and allowed broadcasters to discriminate against them. Stations are now limited to pre-ad disclaimers warning viewers of the graphic nature of the ads.

The Supreme Court has ruled that because broadcasters are not allowed to censor candidates' messages, they cannot be held responsible for them. In *Farmers Educational Cooperative Union v. WDAY*, Inc. (1943), it held that broadcasters cannot be liable for defamatory remarks made by candidates.[27]

Sponsor identification and underwriting

The Communications Act and FCC rules require broadcasters and cable operators that offer original programming to identify sponsors that have given them money or some other consideration in exchange for the transmission of particular content in a program.[28] This rule is intended to protect the public's right to know the identity of program sponsors so they can evaluate the creditability of that material.

Stations face two issues related to sponsor identification. One is the practice of pay for play, otherwise known as *payola*. The other is the practice of accepting programming

---

[25] 47 U.S.C. § 315 (2011).

[26] Becker v. FCC, 95 F.3d 75 (D.C. Cir. 1996).

[27] 319 U.S. 190 (1943).

[28] 47 U.S.C. § 317; 47 C.F.R. §§ 73.1212 and 76.1615.

content for free from parties with a vested interest in influencing the station's audience without acknowledging the source of that content.

Accepting payola is not illegal, *but not disclosing it is*. Further, the obligation to disclose is not limited to the station. Under the Communications Act, it is crime for a person or company to provide money or some other service to a station employee in exchange for the inclusion of material in a broadcast without disclosing that exchange to the station airing the broadcast.[29] Violations may be punished by a fine or imprisonment for up to one year.

Payola is classically associated with music companies that pay radio station personnel to play their songs, but it is increasingly used in television. In 2005, the FCC learned that conservative commentator Armstrong Williams had accepted $240,000 from the Department of Education to promote the "No Child Left Behind" initiative in programs he produced or appeared in without disclosing that payment to viewers or the stations that aired the shows.[30] The FCC fined two broadcasters, Sonshine Family Television, Inc. and Sinclair Broadcasting Group, for running the programs and warned Armstrong that if it happened again he would be cited too.[31]

A station's decision to air material supplied by outside sources, without acknowledging the source of that content, will also trigger sponsorship rules. In the age of declining resources and the 24-hour news cycle, stations are increasingly willing to air video news releases created by companies and other organizations that may have an agenda. However, they rarely admit to their viewers that what they are offering as news is really public relations. A Fox television station in Minneapolis was fined in 2011 for airing a video news release or VNR produced by General Motors as a news segment.[32] The VNR, which showed twelve different shots of GM convertibles, "reported on" the desirability of convertibles in summer. Although GM didn't pay for the placement, its provision of content free of charge triggered sponsorship identification rules, which stipulate that:

A video news release is a video segment produced in a newscast format that is used for public relations purposes to promote a company, product or service, and distributed to the media free of charge.

> a disclosure is required for material furnished without charge or at nominal charge when the use of the material involves "an identification of any person, product, service, trademark or brand name beyond an identification reasonably related to the use of such service or property on the broadcast.[33]

In the context of any political broadcast or any broadcast involving the discussion of a controversial issue of public importance, "any film, record, transcription, talent, script, or other material . . . furnished, directly or indirectly, to a station as an inducement for broadcasting such matter" must be acknowledged at the beginning and conclusion of the broadcast. If the segment is less than five minutes, one announcement, either at the beginning or end will suffice.

---

[29] 47 U.S.C. § 507.

[30] Fox Television Stations, 26 FCC Rcd. 3964, Enf. Bur. 2011 (Notice of Apparent Liability for Forfeiture).

[31] *Morning Show Payola*, On the Media (National Public Radio broadcast, Dec. 16, 2011).

[32] Fox Television Stations, 26 FCC Rcd. 3964, Enf. Bur. 2011 (Notice of Apparent Liability for Forfeiture).

[33] 47 U.S.C. 317(a)(1), as implemented in 47 C.F.R. § 73.1212(a)

When advertising is embedded in programming, advertisers are usually listed at the end of the show, among the credits. Identification is not required "when it is clear that the mention of the name of the product constitutes a sponsorship identification."[34]

Programming reports

All radio and television broadcast stations are required to document their public services efforts. Stations compile quarterly reports, detailing the important issues facing their communities and the programs aired in the previous three months that addressed those issues, and make those files available for public inspection. The FCC is moving toward rules that would require those reports to go online. It is also considering requiring television stations to post online information about the sponsors of political advertisements.

Children's programming

Congress passed the Children's Television Act in 1990 to increase educational and informational programming for children and to limit their exposure to advertising. Broadcast television stations – both commercial and noncommercial – are required to serve the needs of children by offering at least three hours of core children's programming per channel per week. The FCC defines "educational and informational" programming as that which "in any respect furthers the educational and informational needs of children 16 years old and under (this includes their intellectual/cognitive or social/emotional needs)."[35] A program is specifically designed to serve children's educational and information needs if:

- it is designed to be informative;
- it is aired between 7 a.m. and 10 p.m.;
- it is a regularly scheduled weekly program; and
- it is at least 30 minutes in length.[36]

Commercial television stations are required to identify core educational/informational programming by displaying the "E/I" symbol throughout the program.

In addition, broadcaster, cable operators and satellite providers are required to limit advertising targeted at children age 12 and under to 10.5 minutes per hour on weekends and 12 minutes per hour on weekdays.

---

[34] 47 C.F.R. § 73.1212(f).

[35] FCC Media Bureau, The Public and Broadcasting (July 1999), at http://www.fcc.gov/mb/audio/decdoc/public_and_broadcasting.html#OBSCENE.

[36] 47 C.F.R. § 73.671.

Content restrictions for broadcasters

The FCC also imposes content restrictions on broadcasters and in some cases on cable and satellite providers who supply original programming. For example, it prevents any electronic medium under its jurisdiction from airing cigarette commercials. It also prevents broadcasters from airing surreptitiously recorded phone conversations or hoaxes. Most notoriously, the FCC has limited indecency in broadcast media.

Cigarette Advertising

Advertisements for cigarettes, little cigars, and smokeless tobacco products are prohibited on broadcast, cable and satellite media. Congress enacted the ban in 1970 with the FCC's support. The agency had asserted that smoking is a controversial topic and, under the Fairness Doctrine, stations should not be allowed to air commercials for cigarettes without supplying the opposing view that they were dangerous. The Fairness Doctrine is no longer enforced, but the ban remains in place.

Broadcast of telephone conversations

Although it is legal in some states to record a conversation over the phone without obtaining permission from the other party, broadcasting a conversation recorded without permission is a violation of FCC rules.[37] The rule – put in place to protect individuals' expectation of privacy – applies equally to private individuals and public officials.[38]

The FCC issued forfeiture notices (fines) of $25,000 to a licensee for two stations in Puerto Rico for broadcasting telephone conversations without giving prior notice in connection with prank calls during a comedy segment called "You Fell For It."[39] In the first prank, the caller pretended to be an intruder hiding under the bed. In the second, the caller pretended to be a loan shark attempting to collect on a debt.

Some stations initiate prank calls and then ask the "victim's" permission to air the call, but this practice is technically a violation as well. The Commission has stated that the "recording of such [a] conversation with the intention of informing the other party later – whether during the conversation or after it is completed but before it is broadcast – does not comply with the Rule . . ."[40] In 2004, the FCC fined a Miami radio station $3,500 for broadcasting a crank call made to Cuban President Fidel Castro.[41] DJs Joe

---

[37] Broadcast of telephone conversations, 47 C.F.R. § 73.1206.

[38] In the matter of Rejoynetwork, LLC, File Nos. EB-06-IH-1772 and EB-06-IH-1748, ¶ 12, Rel. Oct. 16, 2008 (Forfeiture Order).

[39] In the matter of Spanish Broadcasting System Holding Co., Inc., File No. EB-06-IH-2171, Rel. Feb. 16, 2011 (Forfeiture Order).

[40] Station-Initiated Telephone Calls which Fail to Comply with Section 73.1206 of the Rules, Public Notice, 35 F.C.C.2d 940, 941 (1972).

[41] In the matter of WXDJ Licensing, File No. EB-03-IH-0275, Rel. Nov. 24, 2004 (Forfeiture Order).

Ferrero and Enrique Santos of WXDJ telephoned the Cuban Ministry of Foreign Relations and convinced several Cuban officials that President Hugo Chavez of Venezuela was waiting on the line to speak to President Castro about a matter of state business. When Castro answered the phone, the DJs admitted the call was a joke. The FCC said that it did not matter that Castro was informed before the actual broadcast that the conversation had been recorded.

The FCC rule does not apply to cable and satellite. The Comedy Central show *Crank Yankers* was built around the prank call concept.[42]

On-air hoaxes

FCC rules prohibit on-air hoaxes that include the broadcast of a false distress signal or the report of a crime or catastrophe. A station may be punished if the licensee knows the information is false, it is foreseeable that the broadcast of the information will cause substantial public harm, and the broadcast does in fact cause substantial public harm.[43] Harm is interpreted as damage to property or the health and safety of the public or a distraction of emergency workers from their duties.

The FCC revoked a station's license in 1980, following its decision to stage the kidnapping of one of its disc jockeys. In 1974, the station manager of KIKX-FM in Tucson, Arizona, concocted a promotion centered on the disappearance of DJ Arthur Gropen. The station released details about the vehicle used in the abduction and the suspected kidnapper. It even incorporated a fake sound bite from the police. Worried listeners clogged police phone lines. Five days passed before the station admitted that the kidnapping was a hoax. When the FCC conducted a renewal hearing, the station was admonished for a number of violations, but the most serious charge was related to the hoax.

Revoking a station's license is rare, however. More commonly, the FCC issues a fine. For example, in 1990, it fined a Crestwood, Missouri, radio station $25,000 after one of its DJs interrupted regular programming with an air raid siren and the announcement "Attention, attention. This is an official civil defense warning. This is not a test. The United States is under nuclear attack." Although the station apologized repeatedly for the hoax, the FCC punished it because Section 325(a) of the Communications Act prohibits broadcasters from issuing false distress signals.

In the same year, three Los Angeles DJ's broadcast a false murder confession on a morning call-in show on KROQ. The Los Angeles County Sheriff's Department spent 10 months investigating the confession before learning from an anonymous tip that it was a hoax. Because the station required the DJs to compensate the Sheriff's Department for the cost of the investigation and to perform 149 hours each of community service, the station got off with a public admonishment.

[42] Mel Idato, *Tough call pays off for cranks*, THE AGE, July 24, 2003, at 19.
[43] Broadcast hoaxes, 47 C.F.R. 73.1217.

FCC efforts to regulate indecency

The FCC's most controversial actions have been associated with its attempts to regulate indecency in broadcast media. The Communications Act specifically restricts the FCC from engaging in censorship. Section 326 of Title III provides that:

> [n]othing in this chapter shall be understood or construed to give the Commission the power of censorship over the radio communications or signals transmitted by any radio [or television] station, and no regulation or condition shall be promulgated or fixed by the Commission which shall interfere with the right of free speech by means of radio communication.

However, a contradictory mandate has put the agency in a difficult position. Federal law prohibits the transmission of obscenity or indecency over the airwaves. Title 18 of the United States Code, Section 1464, bans the utterance of "any obscene, indecent or profane language by means of radio communication."

The Supreme Court has said that, although obscenity may be constitutionally restricted, indecency is protected speech.[44] Consequently, the FCC has had to walk a very fine line. In *FCC v. Pacifica* (1978), the Supreme Court upheld the FCC's right to regulate indecency under narrow circumstances. The case concerned a Pacifica radio station's broadcast of a satiric monologue by George Carlin entitled "Filthy Words." In it, the comedian rattled off the seven dirty words that "you couldn't say on the public, ah, airwaves, um, the ones you definitely wouldn't say, ever" over and over in a variety of contexts. After receiving a complaint about the broadcast, the Commission reviewed it and characterized it as "patently indecent."

The FCC did not fine the station but issued a declaratory statement indicating that Pacifica "could have been the subject of administrative sanctions" and would be if subsequent complaints were received.[45] Pacifica sued, arguing that because the recording was not obscene, prohibiting its broadcast was an abridgement of the First Amendment. The Supreme Court upheld the FCC's right to regulate broadcast indecency based on the medium's unique characteristics. Justice John Paul Stevens pointed out that of all media, broadcasting received the most limited form of First Amendment protection because they were a "uniquely pervasive presence in the lives of all Americans" and were "uniquely accessible to children, even those too young to read."[46]

The decision allowed the FCC to channel indecency in broadcast media into a period when children were less likely to be in the audience. This block of time, between 10 p.m. and 6 a.m., is known as the safe harbor period.

The FCC has defined indecency as speech that "depicts or describes sexual or excretory organs or activities in terms patently offensive as measured by contemporary community standards." It determined patent offensiveness from three factors:

---

[44] Cohen v. California, 403 U.S. 15 (1971) (finding that the message "F**k the Draft" on the defendant's jacket was protected speech).

[45] 56 F.C.C.2d 94, 99 (1975).

[46] Federal Communications Commission v. Pacifica Foundation, 438 U.S. 726, 748-49 (1978).

- whether the description or depiction was explicit or graphic;
- whether the material dwelled on or repeated at length descriptions or depictions of sexual or excretory organs; and
- whether the material appeared to pander or is used to titillate or shock.[47]

For 30 years following *FCC v. Pacifica,* the FCC ignored "fleeting expletives," reserving punitive action for indecency so "pervasive as to amount to 'shock treatment' for the audience," as in Carlin's broadcast.[48] But in 2004, the FCC indicated that policy was "no longer good law."[49] The Commission put broadcasters on notice that sustained use of profanity would no longer be required to find that material was patently offensive. The Commission's about-face came after NBC's broadcast of the 2003 Golden Globe Awards, when U2 singer Bono described his award as "f***ing brilliant." Fox was in the hot seat over two fleeting uses of expletives by Cher and Nicole Richie during the 2002 and 2003 Billboard Music Awards. The FCC admonished the broadcasters for indecency, but it did not fine them because that would have involved retroactive punishment for a policy change that had not yet occurred before the broadcasts. However, in a 2004 Memorandum Opinion and Order, commonly called the Golden Globe Awards Order, the Commission indicated that henceforth even isolated uses of profanity outside the safe harbor period could be considered a violation punishable by fines. Repeated violations could lead to the revocation of a station's license.

Several networks petitioned the FCC to withdraw the Golden Globe Awards order. When it did not, Fox, CBS, and NBC petitioned the U.S. Court of Appeals for the Second Circuit to review the order. In *Fox Television Stations, Inc. v. Federal Communications Commission* (2007), the Second Circuit struck down the "fleeting expletive" policy as arbitrary and capricious under the Administrative Procedures Act.[50] The court concluded that the FCC had not presented a reasoned analysis for the change. Because it found the policy to be a violation of the Administrative Procedures Act, the appellate court did not decide whether it was also a violation of the First Amendment (although it suggested that it might be). Courts that are able to resolve a legal question without reaching a constitutional issue will do so as part of their prudential mandate to decide constitutional questions only out of *strict necessity.*

> The Doctrine of Strict Necessity is a prudential rule courts follow to decide constitutional issues only when it is absolutely necessary. If the record presents a narrower ground upon which to decide the case, a court will follow that path as a way of minimizing its impact on the governmental process.

By a narrow margin, the Supreme Court reversed the Second Circuit decision. Writing for the Court, Justice Scalia indicated that although an agency must show good reasons for a new policy, "it need not demonstrate to a court's satisfaction that the reasons for the new policy are better than the reasons for the old one."[51] It is sufficient "that the new policy is permissible under the statute, that there are good reasons for it, and that the agency believes it to be better . . ."[52]

---

[47] In the Matter of Industry Guidance on the Commission's Case Law Interpreting 18 U.S.C. § 1464 and Enforcement Policies Regarding Broadcast Indecency, 16 F.C.C.R. 7999, 8003, ¶ 10, April 6, 2001.

[48] CBS Corp. v. Federal Communications Commission, 535 F.3d 167, 174 (2008).

[49] *In re* Complaints Against Various Broadcast Licensees Regarding Their Airing of the "Golden Globe Awards" Program, 19 F.C.C.R. 4975, 4977, Rel. March 18, 2004 (Memorandum Opinion and Order).

[50] 489 F.3d 444 (2nd Cir. 2007).

[51] Federal Communications Commission v. Fox Television Stations, 129 S. Ct. 1800 (2009).

[52] *Id.* at 1804.

Figure 3.2   Illustration: Kalan Lyra

The Supreme Court decision only addressed the adequacy of the FCC's *explanation* for the policy change under the Administrative Procedures Act, which is subject to the *rational basis test*, a very deferential standard of review. It left open the possibility that the policy itself might implicate the First Amendment. Several justices expressed their concern about the FCC's stricter regulation of broadcast programming now that most people get it bundled with cable and satellite services that fall under a different regulatory structure. The Court remanded the case back to the Second Circuit for further analysis of the policy's potential impact on broadcasters' speech. The Second Circuit struck the policy down again, this time on First Amendment grounds.[53] The court was confused by the FCC's inconsistent application of the new rule. For example, the agency provided no specific news exception to its indecency rules, yet it disregarded the use of indecency in news stories or interviews.[54] Consequently, a clip of Bono's acceptance

The rational basis test, applied in cases in which no fundamental right appears to be threatened, calls for the lowest level of judicial scrutiny. To withstand the review, the government must show that the restriction is a reasonable means of achieving a legitimate government goal.

[53] Fox v. Federal Communications Comm'n, 613 F.3d 317 (2nd Cir. 2010).
[54] C-SPAN persuaded the judges to allow cameras to film the court in session. The video is on YouTube at http://youtube.com/watch?v=QdCsup3zqyA&feature=user.

The Supreme Court reviewed the case again in early 2012, but did not release its opinion before this book went to press. Go to www.digitalmedialaw.us and click on What's New: Chapter 3 for its decision.

speech would not have been considered indecent as background material in a news story. The Commission also allowed the repeated use of expletives in films, such as *Saving Private Ryan*, when raw language was central to the artistic integrity of the work, but denied it in other cases that seemed plausible. It determined that the FCC's policy was unconstitutionally vague and, therefore, open to discriminatory application. The FCC appealed the decision to the Supreme Court.

The FCC's crackdown on indecency followed CBS's broadcast of the 2004 Super Bowl, when singer Justin Timberlake ripped Janet Jackson's bodice, exposing her left breast to 90 million viewers during the half-time show. Following the incident, Congress passed the Broadcast Decency Enforcement Act, raising the maximum fine for a single violation of indecency rules from $32,500 to $325,000 with a $3 million cap for continuing violation.[55] Although the FCC had also allowed fleeting images for the last 30 years, it fined CBS $550,000 for the broadcast.[56] CBS appealed the fine in *CBS Corporation v. FCC* (2008).[57] The U.S. Court of Appeals for the Third Circuit held that the FCC had "acted arbitrarily and capriciously" by fining CBS for a half-second of nudity. In light of its *FCC v. Fox* holding, the Supreme Court ordered the Third Circuit to reexamine its ruling.[58] But after re-examining the case, the Third Circuit reached the same conclusion. The appellate court observed that the Supreme Court's decision had focused on the adequacy of the FCC's *explanation* for its policy change, while its own had examined the adequacy of the FCC's *notice* of the change. The Administrative Procedures Act requires that agencies supply both a notice and explanation before altering a well-established policy. The FCC had fined CBS for a broadcast that occurred before its policy change, so notice was absent. In *Fox*, the Supreme Court had indicated that "assessing penalties based on violations of previously unannounced policies would amount to arbitrarily punishing parties without notice of the potential consequences of their actions."[59] Writing for the Third Circuit, Judge Rendell stated. "We conclude that, if anything, *Fox* confirms our previous ruling in this case and that we should readopt our earlier analysis and holding that the Commission acted arbitrarily in this case."[60]

Multi-Channel Video Program Distributors

As the Supreme Court pointed out in *FCC v. Fox*, the irony of discussing regulations imposed specifically on broadcast media is that most American households now get broadcast programming bundled with cable and satellite. These content providers, known as *multi-channel video programming distributors* (MVPDs), sell programming

---

[55] 47 U.S.C. § 503 (2006).

[56] *In re* Complaints Against Various Television Licensees Concerning Their February 1, 2004 Broadcast of the Super Bowl XXXVIII Halftime Show, 21 F.C.C.R. 2760 (2006) (Forfeiture Order).

[57] 535 F.3d 167 (2008).

[58] Federal Communications Commission v. Fox Television Stations, 556 U.S. 502 (2009).

[59] CBS Corp. v. Federal Communications Commission, 663 F.3d 122, 129 (3rd Cir 2011).

[60] *Id.* at 124.

for a price and operate under a separate regulatory scheme. MVPDs, which also include phone companies that deliver programming, provide television service to 90 percent of American homes.[61]

Although some public service obligations have been imposed upon cable and satellite, including a requirement to carry broadcast channels, they have traditionally received more First Amendment protection than broadcast media. Because consumers subscribe to them – presumably with knowledge of their content – courts have deemed them less pervasive and accessible than broadcast. However, now that 90 percent of television viewers watch broadcast programming through paid programming services, it is increasingly difficult to argue that one channel should be more heavily regulated than another.

Cable television

Because cable does not use the public airwaves to distribute programming, it was not initially placed under the FCC's jurisdiction. The FCC was reluctant to attempt to regulate it until the Commission realized that, left unchecked, cable could undermine free broadcast television programming.

Approximately 50 percent of U.S. households rely on cable for their programming needs.[62] In comparison, fewer than 10 percent still rely on over-the-air broadcasting. This represents a dramatic audience gain since the 1940s when cable television was developed to import broadcast signals into rural and mountainous areas without local stations. As cable moved into areas with television stations, local broadcasters worried that viewers would prefer cable programming drawn from larger cities and pleaded with the FCC to regulate it.

In 1965, the FCC did just that by requiring cable systems to carry local channels and prohibiting them from importing signals that duplicated local programming. The cable industry challenged the FCC's authority to enact the regulations in *United States v. Southwestern Cable Co.* (1968). But the Supreme Court upheld them, concluding that the Communications Act empowered the FCC to regulate "all interstate and foreign communication by wire or radio," including cable.[63]

Must carry rules

Cable companies considered the "must carry" rule to be a form of compelled speech that infringed upon their First Amendment rights. When the rule was enacted most cable systems offered fewer than 20 channels. Carrying broadcast signals required them to give up channel capacity they would have preferred to use for something else. Congress agreed and repealed the must carry rule in the Cable Act of 1984, when it deregulated the industry. With the must carry rule out of the way, cable systems began to drop independent local stations as the FCC had predicted.

Although most American homes get their programming through cable, its penetration has dropped substantially in the last 10 years due to increasing competition from other multi-channel video programmers and Internet sites like Hulu and Netflix. In fact, the popularity of Internet video has precipitated a decline in television ownership. According to Nielsen, 96.7 percent of American households owned TV sets in 2011, down from 98.9 percent previously.

---

[61] NIELSON, STATE OF THE MEDIA: THE CROSS-PLATFORM REPORT, QUARTER 1 (2011) at 8.
[62] *Id.*
[63] United States v. Southwestern Cable Co., 392 U.S. 157, 158 (1968).

In the early 1990s, 40 percent of American households still relied on over-the-air signals for programming. Congress began to realize that if local broadcasters lost more than half of their viewers as cable stations dropped them, they would also lose a significant percentage of their advertising revenue. The loss might make it impossible to continue to provide free programming to their remaining viewers. So it reinstated the must carry provision in the 1992 Cable Television Consumer Protection and Competition Act.[64] The law gives local broadcast stations the right to demand retransmission on local cable systems. Cable providers must carry their video and audio in full, without changes or deletions.

Cable mogul Ted Turner, who feared his networks would be dropped from cable systems forced to carry local broadcasters instead, challenged the must carry provision as a violation of the First Amendment. The Supreme Court considered the case three times before narrowly upholding the provision. The Court acknowledged that the First Amendment protects cable and that the FCC's rule burdened programmers' speech. But because the provision did not distinguish between favored and disfavored speech on the basis of views expressed, the Court classified it as a content-neutral regulation subject to intermediate rather than strict scrutiny.[65] It concluded that the must carry provision serves an important government interest (the preservation of free programming) without substantially burdening more speech than necessary to further that interest.[66]

> Under *intermediate scrutiny*, a content-neutral regulation will be upheld if it advances important governmental interests unrelated to the suppression of free speech and does not burden substantially more speech than necessary to further those interests.

Inclusion is at the local broadcast station's discretion. The 1992 Cable Act includes a *retransmission consent provision* that entitles local broadcast stations to negotiate compensation for their retransmission over a cable system. Now that cable companies (and broadcasters) understand that cable subscribers expect to have access to local channels on their cable systems, broadcasters have begun to negotiate more aggressively with cable providers for higher retransmission fees. In 2010, broadcasters in five states withheld their signals until their demands were met. Fox blocked access to its stations during the baseball playoffs and World Series, affecting 3 million households that subscribed to cable in the New York and Philadelphia markets.[67] Networks that negotiate on behalf of local affiliates increase the bargaining power of local stations and take a cut of the retransmission consent fees in the process.

Broadcasters are also protected by network nonduplication, syndicated program exclusivity, and sports blackout rules that apply to cable. The *network non-duplication rule* guarantees local affiliates' exclusive right to distribute network programming on local cable systems. This rule protects the local affiliate's ratings, which would be harmed if the cable provider carried other network affiliates, offering the same shows, on different channels. The *syndicated program exclusivity rule* protects local stations' exclusive right to distribute syndicated programming on local cable systems. Broadcast stations

---

[64] Public Law 102-385, 106 Stat. 1460 (1992) (codified in scattered sections of 47 U.S.C.).

[65] Turner Broadcasting System, Inc. v. FCC, 512 U.S. 622, 643 (1994) ("Turner I").

[66] Turner Broadcasting System, Inc. v. FCC, 520 U.S. 180, 189 (1997) ("Turner II") (citing United States v. O'Brien, 391 U.S. 367, 377 (1968)).

[67] Jack Fields, *Fix broken broadcast retransmission consent system*, THE HILL, Nov. 15, 2010, http://thehill.com/blogs/congress-blog/technology/129157-fix-broken-broadcast-retransmission-consent-system.

may demand that the local cable system blackout duplicate networked or syndicated programs on competing channels, even if the local TV station's signal is not carried by the cable system in question. The *sports blackout rule* protects the rights of entities that have negotiated the exclusive right to disseminate a particular sports program. If a local station does not have permission to broadcast the sports program, a local cable system may not import another broadcast signal carrying the game from another market.

Franchising authorities

The FCC does not issue licenses to cable companies as it does broadcast stations. Cable companies must have a franchise to operate in a local market. These are essentially contracts to build and operate a cable system in a particular area. The county commissions and city councils that enter into contracts with cable companies and regulate them locally are known as "local franchising authorities." Without permission to operate from a franchising authority, cable companies would not be able to lay their lines through public rights of way.

Franchising authorities are responsible for regulating rates for basic cable services. Rates for cable programming services beyond the basic tier and pay-per-view channels are not regulated. Because cable is expensive, it is tempting to steal it. Stealing cable TV is a crime. The 1984 Cable Act provides penalties of up to two years in prison and/or $50,000 in fines for illegally intercepting cable or manufacturing or selling equipment used for interception.[68]

Access channels

Congress authorized franchising authorities to require cable systems to set aside channels for public, educational, or government use as part of their franchise contracts. These are known as PEG stations. To further its goal of encouraging local programming, the FCC also requires cable companies to set aside some channel capacity that organizations can lease in order to provide their own programming. A system with 36 to 54 channels must set aside 10 percent of its capacity for leased access, while a system with 55 channels or more must set aside 15 percent.

Cable companies may not censor or alter content delivered on PEG stations, but they may impose minimum, content-neutral standards on production quality. The 1992 Cable Act gave cable operators the right to refuse to transmit sexually explicit programming on leased or public access channels. In 1996, the Supreme Court upheld cable operators' rights to control indecency on leased access stations, but not on public access stations.[69]

In fact, the local franchises that require cable companies to provide public access channels are not able to censor them either. Some towns have opted to drop their public

---

[68] 47 U.S.C. § 553 (2010).
[69] Denver Area Educational Telecommunications Consortium, Inc. v. Federal Communication Comm'n, 518 U.S. 727 (1996).

access stations from their cable contracts rather than allow groups with extremist views, such as the Ku Klux Klan or the Aryan Nation, to use them.[70]

Content regulation

The FCC has not attempted to control indecency on cable programming. Because cable viewers subscribe to the service, it is harder to argue that indecency sneaks up on them with no warning. In fact, some subscribers want channels that offer sexually oriented programming.

The Supreme Court reasoned in *Turner Inc. v. FCC.* (1994) that cable, unlike broadcast, is not limited to a select number of speakers licensed to use radio frequency, so it should not be subject to the same level of technical regulation.[71] However, it fractured over whether cable was entitled to full First Amendment protection with respect to content regulation. In *Denver Area Educational Telecommunications Consortium, Inc. v. FCC.* (1996), the Court upheld a content-based restriction in the 1992 Cable Act that permitted cable operators to prohibit indecent material on access channels they leased to other programmers.[72] Writing for the Court, Justice Breyer analogized indecency on leased access channels to the indecent radio broadcasts at issue in *FCC v. Pacifica Foundation.* He observed that cable television "is as 'accessible to children' as over-the-air broadcasting, if not more so . . . [Cable has] 'established a uniquely pervasive presence in the lives of all Americans,'" and can "'confron[t] the citizen' in the 'privacy of the home,' with little or no prior warning."[73] A plurality of the Court agreed that the need to protect children from indecent speech is compelling, but there was broad disagreement over whether the provision did this in the least restrictive way. Dissenting justices thought the Court should have applied *strict scrutiny*, the appropriate standard of review for a content-based restriction affecting a fully protected medium.

The Court finally asserted cable's full First Amendment in *United States v. Playboy Entertainment Group* (2000).[74] As originally written, the Telecommunications Act required cable companies to block all non-subscribers' access to video and audio on sexually explicit channels completely, whether requested to do so or not. Blocking a station that is digital is no problem; nothing shows. But analog signals are difficult to block without some seepage of audio or video. Consequently, while this provision was active, cable companies had to restrict sexually oriented channels to safe harbor hours. Playboy challenged the provision and the Supreme Court overturned it. Not only did the provision target particular types of speech, but also particular types of speakers. The Court determined that the provision failed the strict scrutiny test because a

Under *strict scrutiny*, a content-based regulation will be upheld only if it is narrowly tailored to serve a compelling government interest.

The Supreme Court acknowledged cable's full First Amendment protection in United States v. Playboy Entertainment Group (2000).

---

[70]David Kaplan, *TV View: Is the Klan Entitled to Access?* July 31, 1988, NY TIMES; Steve Farnsworth, *Kansas City Plan Seeks to Cut Klan's Cable Access,* CHI. TRIBUNE, May 10, 1988.
[71]512 U.S. 622 (1994).
[72]518 U.S. 727 (1996).
[73]*Id.* at 744–45.
[74]529 U.S. 803 (2000).

less restrictive option was available to protect consumers. Another section of the Telecommunication Act requires cable companies to provide blocking devices to subscribers who request them.

Direct broadcast satellite service

Direct broadcast satellite service is the second most popular paid programming option, capturing approximately 30 percent of U.S. households. Congress vested the FCC with regulatory authority over direct broadcast satellite service through the Communications Satellite Act of 1962. But classification of DBS for regulatory purposes has been a little tricky. The FCC sees DBS as something of a hybrid between broadcasters and common carriers. Communication satellites, like broadcasters, require the use of the electromagnetic spectrum to disseminate video programming. On the other hand, they are also subscription-based services like cable.

When the FCC decided it would not subject DBS to the same regulations broadcasters had to follow, broadcasters challenged the decision in federal court. The U.S. Court of Appeals for the D.C. Circuit upheld the FCC's decision that DBS operators could be excused from broadcast obligations. But it remanded the case back to the FCC with instructions to clarify the distinction between DBS operators and broadcasters.[75] On remand, the FCC focused its definition of broadcasting on whether or not a programmer scrambled its signals. Broadcasting is made available "to the general public."[76] A programming provider's decision to scramble a signal that would be sold by subscription indicated a lack of intent to send a signal "to all alike, without charge or restriction to any listener." The appellate court upheld the FCC's categorization.[77]

Satellite content regulation

The Supreme Court has not yet considered whether direct broadcast satellite programmers are entitled to full First Amendment protection. Two federal circuit courts have come to opposite conclusions on the issue. The U.S. Court of Appeals for the District of Columbia Circuit concluded that DBS providers, like broadcasters, are afforded lesser First Amendment protections because they are both beneficiaries of limited spectrum.[78] In contrast, the Fourth Circuit concluded that "both satellite carriers and cable operators engage in speech protected by the First Amendment when they exercise editorial discretion over the menu of channels they offer to their subscribers."[79]

U.S. Courts of Appeals have split on the question of whether satellite is entitled to full First Amendment protection. The Supreme Court has not yet ruled on the matter, but the FCC treats satellite like cable.

[75] National Ass'n of Broadcasters v. Federal Communications Comm'n, 740 F.2d 1190 (D.C. Cir. 1984).

[76] Subscription Video, 2 F.C.C.R. 1001 (1987) (Report and Order).

[77] National Ass'n for Better Broadcasting v. Federal Communications Comm'n, 849 F.2d 665, 667–68 (D.C. Cir. 1988).

[78] Time Warner Entertainment v. Federal Communications Comm'n, 93 F.3d 957, 975 (D.C. Cir. 1996).

[79] Satellite Broadcasting and Communications Ass'n v. Federal Communications Comm'n, 275 F.3d 337, 353 (4th Cir. 2001).

Regardless of these conflicting decisions, the FCC has made it clear that it plans to regulate satellite content like cable content. In 2008, former FCC Chairman Kevin Martin said the Commission strived for regulatory parity between the two.[80] Satellite programmers are also required to meet some of the same public interest obligations that cable providers do. For example, DBS providers must set aside some channel capacity for public use and carry local broadcast channels equally.

Channel set-asides

Congress required DBS providers to set aside at least 4 percent of their channel capacity for noncommercial educational or informational programming in the 1992 Cable Act.[81] DBS services may apply minimal technical standards to channels set aside for public interest use, but they have no editorial control over program content on them. They may not pre-screen or refuse to air programming unless they believe, in good faith, that the programming does not meet the noncommercial educational or informational requirement. However, if DBS providers have more demand from potential educational programmers than channel capacity to offer, they may select programmers from the overall pool based on factors such as the programmer's experience, reliability, and reputation for quality programming.

Carry one, carry all provision

The must-carry provision cable companies fought against initially put them in a stronger position than DBS providers because they were able to supply local programming to their customers while satellite subscribers had to pay an additional fee for local programs. In 1999, Congress passed the Satellite Home Viewer Improvement Act, which created a statutory license that allowed satellite carriers to transmit local broadcast signals without getting special permission from the copyright holders. A "carry one, carry all" provision in the Act obligated satellite carriers that wanted to take advantage of the license to carry one station, to carry all requesting stations within the same market in order to preserve free broadcast programming. The Act also instructed the FCC to develop rules for mandatory carriage of broadcast signals, retransmission consent, network non-duplication, syndicated exclusivity, and sports blackout to put satellite television carriers on a level playing field with cable.[82] Satellite providers challenged the carry one, carry all provision as a violation of the First Amendment in *Satellite Broadcasting and Communications Association v. FCC* (2001). Citing *Turner v. FCC*, the Fourth Circuit upheld the provision as a content-neutral regulation that served an important

---

[80] John Eggerton, *FCC Allows Satellite-TV Providers to Phase In HD*, BROADCASTING & CABLE, March 27, 2008.
[81] 47 U.S.C. § 335(b)(1) (2006).
[82] Commission Implements Satellite Home Viewer Improvement Act Sports Blackout and Program Exclusivity Rule Provisions for Satellite Carriers [FCC news release], Oct. 27, 2000, at http://www.fcc.gov/mb/shva/.

government purpose.[83] Now, like cable providers, DBS providers must negotiate with broadcasters to get the local content their subscribers have come to expect.

Phone Companies

The FCC also has regulatory authority over telephony. Traditional local exchange carriers (local phone companies) fall under the supervision of the FCC's Wireline Bureau, while its Wireless Telecommunications Bureau regulates commercial mobile services.

As telecommunications services, phone companies have traditionally been considered common carriers because they act as a nondiscriminatory conduit for others' communications rather than their own. Telephone companies don't try to dictate who can use their lines to make phone calls or what can be said over them. They are prohibited from censoring what travels through their lines or treating one type of message differently than another.

By the end of 2010, 96 percent of Americans carried mobile phones.[84] More than 26 percent of homes had dropped their wired carriers and were relying exclusively on mobile phones or Voice over Internet Protocol (VOIP) companies like Skype for their telecommunications needs. The FCC has mandated number portability. Wireless phone services must allow their customers who change service providers in the same local area to keep their local numbers. Customers may also move a wired telephone number to a mobile phone in some cases.

In Europe, mobile devices work with all carriers, creating more content options for wireless consumers. For the first time, in 2008, the FCC moved in that direction by requiring that the auction winner for the 700 MHz spectrum vacated by analog TV stations open its service to all devices. As the winner, Verizon has to provide service to any wireless phone or personal communication device.

Mobile phones will likely be a driving force behind the continued growth of the Internet, particularly at the international level, because more people can afford wireless phones than personal computers. In the United States, mobile devices, like smart phones, are increasingly used for information and entertainment purposes. According to Neilson, 43 percent of mobile subscribers have streamed music over their phones, while 35 percent have reported watching video on their phones. More than 28 million mobile subscribers watched video on their phones in 2011, representing a 41 percent increase from the year before. This content is delivered to users through mobile broadband.

Broadband service offered by phone, cable, and satellite companies is regulated differently. Its regulatory structure and impact on the Internet and network neutrality is discussed in Chapter 4.

---

[83] 275 F.3d 337, 353 (4th Cir. 2001).
[84] CTIA-The Wireless Association, Semi-Annual Wireless Industry Survey, 2010, http://files.ctia.org.

What is the Electromagnetic Spectrum?

To understand government regulation of media based on their use of the public spectrum, it is helpful to understand what the electromagnetic spectrum is and how it works.

The electromagnetic spectrum is a band of radiation made up of oscillating electric and magnetic fields. The interaction of these two fields produces waves of energy of different lengths. These wavelengths correspond to unique frequencies assigned to electronic media. Frequency measures the number of times a wave moves up and down, or oscillates, per second. The unit of measurement employed to calculate frequency is the hertz (Hz). One hertz equals one oscillation per second. One hundred waves per second would be noted as 100 hertz (Hz). Kilohertz represents thousands of cycles per second, megahertz represents millions of cycles per second, and gigahertz represents billions.

We divide the electromagnetic spectrum into frequency bands that can be used for different purposes, such as radio, television, satellites, mobile phones, and personal communication devices. The mid-range frequencies of the electromagnetic spectrum, those between 300 to 3,000 kHz, are used for radio broadcasts. The very high frequency (VHF) region, between 30 to 300 MHz, is used for television and FM radio broadcasts. The ultra-high-frequency (UHF) region, between 300 to 3,000 MHz, is also used for television, while satellites use bands near 4 and 6 GHz and between 11 and 13 GHz.

The 700 MHz band that analog television vacated was the last big corridor up for grabs. It is especially desirable because signals at this frequency penetrate walls so well.

Because transmissions cannot share the same frequency, the government manages spectrum use closely. While the Federal Communications Commission coordinates public, state, and municipal use of the electromagnetic spectrum, the National Telecommunications and Information Administration, a bureau of the Commerce Department, coordinates federal use of the spectrum. The NTIA develops policies for government use of the spectrum for public safety operations, government satellite networks, and federal agency radio communications.

Use of the electromagnetic spectrum is very competitive. Within the private sector, there has been an explosive growth in telecommunications – in satellite television, Wi-Fi, ultra wideband, third- and fourth-generation advanced services (otherwise known as 3G and 4G) for high-speed wireless broadband, and global position satellite systems. Within the public sector, demand is also rising among public safety agencies and the armed forces for radio, radars, and defense systems. View a color illustration of the electromagnetic spectrum at www.ntia.doc.gov/osmhome/allochrt.pdf.

Questions for Discussion

1. Should media be regulated differently based on their use of the electromagnetic spectrum?
2. What content requirements do broadcast and multi-channel program distributors have in common? What requirements are specific to broadcast?
3. How have media ownership restrictions changed since the Telecommunications Act of 1996 was passed and what impact has that had on the media industry?
4. Why are cable programmers required to carry broadcast programming? Should they be?

4 Internet Regulation

In contrast to the telecommunications discussed in Chapter 3, the Internet is more informally regulated. There is no broad political oversight of the Internet – no agency is in charge of licensing service providers, ensuring universal access, regulating prices, or controlling content. The Internet's global reach and distributed architecture makes it impossible for one agency to control it effectively.

That does not mean, however, that the Internet is beyond regulation. Although no international body controls Internet content or service, the network receives technical oversight through the Internet Corporation for Assigned Names and Numbers, a non-profit corporation in charge of maintaining the Internet's functionality. To varying degrees, individual governments have also attempted to impose restraints on Internet content or service within their own borders.

This chapter discusses the managerial role that ICANN plays in the Internet's functionality, the political influence the United States wields through its contract with ICANN, and the larger participatory role other nations desire in the Internet's governance. It explains the difference between global and domestic concepts of net neutrality. It describes rules applied by the U.S. government to make the Internet more accessible to those with disabilities. It also provides an overview of legislative efforts to control cybercrime and introduces the concept of virtual law.

ICANN, the Internet's Manager

The Internet Corporation for Assigned Names and Numbers coordinates the Internet's technical function, essentially serving as its manager. The nonprofit corporation, located in California, was created in 1998 under the auspices of the U.S. Department of Commerce to assume control of the Internet domain name system. The DNS is a global,

Digital Media Law, Second Edition. Ashley Packard.
© 2013 John Wiley & Sons, Inc. Published 2013 by John Wiley & Sons, Inc.

Figure 4.1 Illustration: Kalan Lyra

distributed database that translates easy-to-remember mnemonic addresses, like www.digitalmedialaw.us, into numerical identifiers, like 213.86.83.116, that computers can use to locate websites and deliver e-mail.[1] Each numerical identifier – called an Internet Protocol address – leads to one computer, the way a telephone number points to one phone. ICANN ensures that domain names and their corresponding IP addresses are globally unique, so the same address always leads to the same location.

ICANN is also responsible for the delegation of top-level domain names, or TLDs. These include the 22 generic top-level domains – such as .edu, .com, .net, .org, .gov, and .mil – and 250 top-level domains with country codes, like .us or .uk. It accredits the *registry operators* assigned to manage particular top-level domains (like VeriSign, which is responsible for domains ending in .com, .net, and .gov). These companies maintain a registry of all domains within their TLD and certify individual *registrars* that help customers find out if particular domain names are available and then register domain names for them with the appropriate registry operator.

ICANN decided in 2011 to launch a new program that could add hundreds of new generic TLDs to the domain name system. Organizations can apply for TLDs based on their own brand names (like .Coke or .Pepsi), generic products or services (like .bank or .beer), or geographic locations (like .NYC or .Tokyo). Applicants will effectively

---

[1] The InterNic website provides a helpful explanation of the domain name system's organization and function at http://www.internic.net/faqs/authoritative-dns.html.

become registry operators for every site under their TLD. The application fee alone is $185,000.

In 2009, the United States gave up unilateral control of ICANN, transitioning it to multinational oversight.[2] In place of an annual review conducted by the Commerce Department, ICANN is subject to three-year reviews by a multi-national advisory committee. The U.S. participates as one of the nations on that committee.

Internet Assigned Numbers Authority

Although ICANN is now technically independent, the U.S. government still asserts political oversight over ICANN through another mechanism. It has awarded the corporation a government contract to manage the Internet Assigned Numbers Authority – which is the body that actually controls the Internet's key traffic management functions. The IANA is the original organization founded by Internet pioneer Jon Postal to perform technical functions needed to keep the Internet running smoothly. When Postal died in 1998, its contract with University of Southern California, where he taught, was transferred to ICANN. When the U.S. released ICANN, it did not release the IANA contract.

IANA responsibilities include:

- coordinating the assignment of technical parameters used in Internet protocols – the set of rules used to exchange messages with other Internet points at the information packet level and to send and receive messages at the Internet address level;
- allocating blocks of addresses to regional registries that, in turn, allocate them through Internet service providers to Internet end users; and
- administering functions related to the management of the root zone of the domain name system.[3]

The third responsibility is, perhaps, the IANA's most important function, at least from the perspective of other countries. It edits the root zone file, which is the apex of the DNS hierarchical distributed database. The root zone file lists the names and numeric IP addresses of the authoritative DNS servers for all top-level domains such as .org, .com, and .us. The root zone file is stored on 13 distributed root server networks. IANA does not control the root servers; various corporations, professional associations and government organizations do. But IANA has the power to change the file stored on the root servers, which contains the information the servers need to direct queries to the TLD registries that can supply the location of all web addresses stored by them.[4]

---

[2] Affirmation of Commitments by the U.S. Department of Commerce and the Internet Corporation for Assigned Names and Numbers, Sept. 30, 2009, at http://www.icann.org/en/announcements/announcement-30sep09-en.htm#affirmation.

[3] Introducing IANA, http://www.iana.org/about (last visited Feb. 3, 2012).

[4] Daniel Karrenberg, *Root Name Services Explained for NonExperts*, Internet Society (Sept. 2007). http://www.isoc.org/briefings/019/.

Here's how it works. TLD registry locations are stored on the root servers. Internet traffic does not travel through them. Instead, root servers answer questions from other servers regarding the location of TLDs. Other DNS servers cache the information on root servers, querying them periodically for updates. When you search for a domain like www.digitalmedialaw.us for the first time, your computer works on the address from right to left. It consults one of the DNS servers with cached root server information to locate the registry that manages the top-level domain in your address. Once it finds the right TLD registry, in this case NeuStar, Inc., it queries the registry for the IP address corresponding to the rest of the website.

ICANN exerts control over the root zone file through the IANA contract in connection with its overall management of the domain name system. It was assumed that the United States would relinquish control over the root zone file when it freed ICANN. However, in 2005, the National Telecommunications and Information Administration, the Commerce Department branch that works with ICANN, asserted permanent control over the root zone file.[5] In 2006, the Commerce Department made it clear that the IANA contract is not inextricably tied to ICANN and could be given to another operator. The implication was that regardless of ICANN's independence, the U.S. would hold onto control of that aspect of Internet function. In early 2012, the U.S. surprised ICANN by rejecting its bid for the next IANA contract.[6] Citing a need for a greater separation between policy making and implemenation, the Commerce Department gave ICANN a six-month contract extension to come up with a new proposal. Although the Commerce Department did not cite particular ICANN policies that were problematic, it had earlier expressed dissatisfaction with ICANN's plan to add generic top-level domains, which might create trademark problems for some companies.

Alternatives to U.S. control of Internet functionality

From the point at which ICANN was created, the Commerce Department maintained that its eventual goal was to release ICANN from government supervision as soon as it was ready to stand on its own. The original target date for independence was 2000. But it took nine more years and considerable pressure from the United Nations before the U.S. government kept that promise.

The Commerce Department's decision to transition ICANN to international oversight was a political one. Although the United States developed the Internet, it is no longer the Internet's majority user. The United States accounts for less than 13 percent of the Internet's use.[7] Other countries as heavily invested in the Internet's stability, or

---

[5] National Telecommunications and Information Administration, U.S. Principles on the Internet's Domain Name and Addressing System, http://www.ntia.doc.gov/ntiahome/domainname (follow "II. U.S. Principles" hyperlink).

[6] National Telecommunications and Information Administration, Notice – Cancelled Internet Assigned Numbers Authority (IANA) Functions – Request for Proposal (RFP) SA1301-12-RP-IANA, March 10, 2012,http://www.ntia.doc.gov/other-publication/2012/notice-internet-assigned-numbers-authority-iana-functions-request-proposal-rf.

[7] Internet World Stats, Usage and Population Statistics, March 31, 2011, http://www.internetworldstats.com/stats.htm.

more so, felt uncomfortable with the United States' unilateral control of the network. They expressed a preference for ICANN's independence or an alternative governing body that would be more inclusive.

In response to its members' concerns, the United Nations sponsored two international summits devoted to the subject of Internet governance. World Summit on the Information Society meetings, held in 2003 and 2005, addressed dissatisfaction with the Internet's management with regard to transparency, network security, protection of private information, and the proliferation of spam. Member nations with non-Roman alphabets also wanted an internationalized domain system with domain names that incorporated their own characters.

Developing countries, in particular, wanted decision-making regarding the Internet to be more inclusive and still do. The Internet has more than two billion users and is expected to gain another billion in the next decade.[8] Most of that growth will come from developing countries. Even in places where computers are in short supply, web-enabled cell phones will bring millions of new users to the Internet, particularly in countries with burgeoning populations like India and China.[9]

Delegates to the U.N. summits considered what a new structure for Internet governance might look like but were unable to agree on a particular model. As a compromise, they settled on the implementation of a nonbinding organization called the Internet Governance Forum. The role of the IGF is to make policy recommendations on Internet governance drawn from a range of stakeholders, including governments, civil society, and businesses, to the international community.[10] It has no policy-making authority, but is able to communicate the will of its stakeholders to ICANN.

In response to pressure from the international community, ICANN changed significantly. In 2008, it developed privacy policies for information collected through the domain name registration process and stored in its database, *Whois* (pronounced "who is"). In 2009, it allowed countries that used non-Roman characters to register top-level domains incorporating characters from their own alphabets. The U.S. also gave the international community what it wanted most – ICANN's freedom, although transitioning ICANN to independence while retaining exclusive control over the IANA was a little like presenting the gift of an empty box.

The National Telecommunications and Information Administration explained its purpose in holding on to the IANA as a matter of security "given the Internet's importance to the world economy."[11] However, it also allows the United States to exert pressure on ICANN policies through its yearly negotiation of the IANA contract.

ICANN requires registrars of domain names to log information about domain name registrants in the publicly available database Whois. Information collected includes the domain name, the date the domain was created, the date it will expire, the registrar, the name of the domain owner and the domain owner's contact information. If the registrar offers private registration, contact information is supplied for the registrar instead. Privacy advocates complain that anyone can search through Whois to find the source of information of Internet speech, interfering with anonymity.

---

[8] *Id.*

[9] Jay Baage, *IGF: The future of the Internet is in Asia, on Cell Phones*, Digital Media Wire, Oct. 30, 2006, http://www.dmwmedia.com/news/2006/10/30/igf-the-future-of-the-internet-is-in-asia-on-cell-phones.

[10] Internet Governance Forum, Internet Governance Forum Mandate, http://www.intgovforum.org/mandate.htm.

[11] Internet Assigned Numbers Authority (IANA) Functions Further Notice of Inquiry, 76 FR 34658 (June 14, 2011).

Network Neutrality

The Internet governance movement describes freedom of expression as one of its primary goals but conceptualizes the issue in terms of network neutrality. Network neutrality is the principle that all content flowing through the Internet should be treated equally. Applied as policy, however, the term can be confusing because it actually has two meanings. Internationally, network neutrality refers to the idea that end-to-end Internet use should be unimpeded, regardless of content, application, or sender. International advocates of net neutrality want to eliminate barriers to Internet access. Domestically, the term network neutrality refers to the notion that high-speed Internet, or broadband, access providers should not be allowed to show preference to certain providers of content or types of content by supplying them with faster service. Advocates of net neutrality as end-to-end access would prefer that Americans not use the term network neutrality in relation to bandwidth management. From their perspective, it trivializes a much larger issue – universal access to the Internet generally and more specifically to its content. Both ideas are discussed in the next section.

Net neutrality as end-to-end access

Although it has grown exponentially, more than doubling in the last five years, the Internet is still used by a minority of the world's population. Worldwide, Internet penetration is roughly 30 percent and unequally distributed. Among developed countries, 71 percent of the population uses the Internet, but in developing countries that number falls to 21 percent.[12]

Many developing countries provide their citizens with Internet access that is slow or expensive, or in some regions, no access at all. Consequently, populations in underdeveloped countries are deprived of informational and economic resources that could improve their standard of living. Barriers to overcome include: inadequate communications infrastructure, unreliable electrical power, limited access to equipment, and substandard educational systems that cannot produce the human capital needed to build and operate a national network. In some countries, unstable governments compound the problem. Africa is, by far, the least connected part of the world. According to the International Telecommunications Union, fewer than 10 percent of Africans have Internet access.[13]

In other places around the world, cultural barriers deprive individuals of full access to the Internet. Countries such as China and Iran, for example, provide their citizens with access to the latest technology, but censor the content that comes through it. Iran's Directorate of Management and Support of the Information Technology Network, for example, has boasted that various government agencies in his country have blocked up

---

[12] INTERNATIONAL TELECOMMUNICATIONS UNION, THE WORLD IN 2010: ICT FACTS AND FIGURES, 4, http://www.itu.int.

[13] Id.

to 10 million Internet sites using filtering techniques. During Egypt's revolutionary protests in 2011, the Egyptian government shut down Internet access and cell phone services across the country for five days, a tactic employed in Myanmar during 2007 protests and in Nepal in 2005.[14]

The Open Net Initiative has monitored government censorship of the Internet since 2001. The organization has found that filtering is most prevalent in Central Asia, East Asia, Northern Africa, and the Middle East. Governments use it to block websites and social media networks with content they consider controversial, such as pornography, gambling, political or religious information, or popular culture deemed offensive. Occasionally, Internet applications, such as Voice over Internet Protocol, are targeted. But censorship is more commonly carried out by Internet Service Providers who are either licensed to operate on the condition that they filter objectionable content or made legally liable for it. Some filter URLs or websites that contain keywords. Others filter specific sites known to contain particular kinds of content.

A particular irony is that U.S. companies have participated directly in censorship efforts. In 2010, an Iranian political activist sued Nokia Siemens Networks in a U.S. federal district court for its role in selling Iran the surveillance equipment used to monitor his cellphone use before his arrest.[15] Yahoo!, Microsoft, and Skype have censored sites for China, either at its direct request or as a self-protective measure to avoid being filtered by the government.[16] Cisco supplied equipment Chinese authorities used for censorship. Yahoo!, in particular, was criticized for turning over the e-mail records of four Chinese dissidents to the Chinese government in 2004, which resulted in their imprisonment.[17]

Internet censorship is not limited to non-democratic countries. Worldwide, it is common to prohibit content that is considered obscene. European countries prohibit hate speech. Germany, in particular, prohibits "propaganda against the democratic constitutional order," incitement to hatred, denial of the holocaust, glorified depictions of human violence, depictions that instigate or incite the commission of certain crimes or violation of human dignity through the depiction of human death or mortal suffering.[18] The United States prohibits online gambling, discussed later in the chapter.

---

[14] Dubai School of Government, Dubai Social Media Report, Vol. 1, No. 2, May 11, at www.dsg.ae/NEWSANDEVENTS/.../ASMRHome.aspx; See also Christopher Rhoads and Geoffrey Fowler, Government Shuts Down Internet, Cellphone Services, Wall Street J., Jan. 29, 2011 at A11.

[15] Sarah Fitzpatrick, Nokia Siemens Networks Sued for Selling Spy Kit to Iran, Cellular News, Aug. 17, 2010, http://www.cellular-news.com/story/44882.php.

[16] Race to the bottom, Human Rights Watch, Vol. 18, No. 8(c), August 2006, yaleglobal.yale.edu/sites/default/files/pdf/china-web.pdf.

[17] A corporate struggle to do the right thing in China. Judgment call. Four professionals offer expert advice, Financial Times (London), Nov. 7, 2007 at 18.

[18] See § 86 of the German Criminal Code and § 4(1) JMStV (The Interstate Treaty for the protection of human dignity and the protection of minors in the media) (cited in Jonathan L. Zittrain and John G. Palfrey Jr., Internet Filtering: The Politics and Mechanisms of Control, in Ronald J. Deibert et al. ed., Access Denied: The Practice and Policy of Internet Filtering 7 (2007), http://opennet.net/node/957 (follow "Chapter 2: Internet Filtering" hyperlink).

Net neutrality as broadband management

In the United States, the term network neutrality refers to restrictions that may or may not be imposed on content that travels through an Internet broadband service. Broadband revolutionized Internet use by providing the capacity and speed required for large-scale data transmission, streaming video, phone service and real-time gaming. Advocates of network neutrality believe broadband service providers should not be allowed to impose limits on the type or speed of data that travels through broadband connections. In contrast, broadband providers want the flexibility to prioritize certain types of data flowing through their networks and to charge higher fees to subscribers who use more bandwidth.

Before broadband service was available, people relied on dial-up services for their Internet connections. Dial-up services connect computer users to the Internet over traditional phone lines, with a maximum speed of 56 kilobits per second. This is very slow compared to broadband, which operates at speeds equal to or faster than 256Kbps. Because dial-up services operate over traditional phone lines, they benefit from common carrier regulations that prevent phone companies from discriminating against them. Any company that wants to offer dial-up service over a phone line may do so. The same is not true for broadband services. Because common carrier rules do not apply to them, they may deny use of their lines to potential competitors.

The Federal Communications Commission freed broadband service providers of common carrier obligations in 2002. The FCC's decision to deregulate broadband was precipitated by a change in the Telecommunications Act of 1996. In it, Congress distinguished a "telecommunications service" from "information service." A telecommunications service is a common carrier. It provides for "the transmission, between or among points specified by the user, of information of the user's choosing, without change in the form or content of the information as sent and received."[19] In contrast, an information service is not a common carrier. It provides users with the "capability for generating, acquiring, storing, transforming, processing, retrieving, utilizing, or making available information via telecommunications . . ." but does not include any use of any such capability for the operation of a telecommunications service.[20]

The FCC issued a declaratory ruling that broadband service provided through cable qualifies as an information service rather than a telecommunications service. It did this on the theory that deregulation of broadband would encourage more investment and innovation. In earlier precedents, the FCC had classified companies that provided data over other carriers' lines as information services and companies that carried data over their own lines as telecommunications services subject to common carrier regulations. Under this classification, broadband supplied by cable companies would be considered a telecommunications service because it was transmitted over cable lines. Upon reconsideration, the FCC determined that cable's broadband service, examined in isolation from its other services, was essentially no different than that offered by Internet service

---

[19]47 U.S.C. § 153 (43).
[20]47 U.S.C. § 153 (20).

providers that do not transmit data over their own lines. Freed of common carrier burdens, cable could deny use of its lines to other Internet service providers.

Rival Internet service providers challenged the FCC's new interpretation. The Ninth Circuit held that the FCC had misinterpreted definitions in the Telecommunications Act of 1996 and vacated the agency's ruling.[21] The Supreme Court reversed the decision. In *National Cable & Telecommunications Association v. Brand X* (2005), the Court upheld the FCC's regulatory scheme to spare cable from common carrier rules.[22]

One month after the Supreme Court's *Brand X* ruling, the FCC issued another declaratory ruling categorizing digital subscriber line, or DSL, suppliers as information service providers, outside the boundaries of common carrier regulation as well. While creating a uniform regulatory scheme for broadband access, the decision represented another policy reversal. The FCC had previously characterized DSL broadband as a telecommunications service subject to common-carrier provisions. The FCC's about-face gave phone companies the right to deny competing Internet service providers access to their DSL lines.

Broadband management and censorship

The notion that telecom companies will be deciding what will and will not go through their networks and at what rate of speed is unsettling to the Internet community. Critics of the *Brand X* decision worried that it also gave broadband providers the power to censor content and applications moving through their lines or to provide more favorable conditions for their own content and applications.

Broadband companies use a technology called deep packet inspection to manage bandwidth. DPI is a computer network packet filtering technique that can be used to detect the type of material transmitted in Internet packets, e.g., an e-mail, VoIP, or peer-to-peer download, and prioritize or delay its transmission. Time Warner and AT&T use DPI to meter usage in some U.S. markets. Customers who go over a set gigabyte allowance have to pay overage fees like customers who use too many cell phone minutes.

In August of 2008, the FCC sanctioned Comcast for discriminatory broadband network management practices when it became clear that the company was secretly blocking the peer-to-peer, or *P2P*, application BitTorrent.[23] With 160 million registered users, BitTorrent is the largest P2P and is widely used to distribute large data files, like video, that take up a lot of bandwidth. Comcast denied blocking BitTorrent until it couldn't anymore. The Associated Press conducted nationwide tests using the King James Bible that demonstrated that Comcast was preventing users from uploading even relatively small files on BitTorrent by sending messages to their computers that ended the connection. The FCC did not fine Comcast, but demanded that it stop discriminating against particular applications, disclose the extent and manner in which it engaged

---

[21] Brand X Internet Servs. v. Federal Communications Commission, 345 F.3d 1120, 1132 (9th Cir. 2003).

[22] 545 U.S. 967 (2005).

[23] Declan McCullagh, *FCC Probably Can't Police Comcast's BitTorrent Throttling*, CNET, July 28, 2008, at http://news.cnet.com/8301-13578_3-10000821-38.html.

in blocking, and publicly disclose its broadband management policies. The FCC's policy on broadband management was pretty vague at the time. A statement issued in 2005 indicated that "consumers are entitled to run applications and services of their choice . . . subject to reasonable network management." Comcast challenged the FCC's enforcement order and in 2010, the U.S. Court of Appeals for the D.C. Circuit overturned it.[24] The court found that the FCC had no authority over Comcast's broadband service.

The court observed that the FCC had classified broadband Internet service as an unregulated "information service" under the Communications Act, placing broadband outside of FCC jurisdiction. Now with the Comcast order, the FCC seemed to be asserting authority to regulate it. The court had a point. The FCC's shift in position did seem a little bizarre. It is helpful to remember that the FCC that deregulated broadband under the Bush administration was not the same Commission striving to protect network neutrality under the Obama administration. Its political structure had changed.

The FCC argued that it should be allowed to impose neutrality on broadband under an ancillary theory that the Communications Act gave the FCC the right to "perform any and all acts, make such rules and regulations, and issue such orders . . . as may be necessary in the execution of its functions."[25] But the court interpreted that ancillary authority to apply to the FCC's *statutory* functions, which no longer included broadband. The court did not foreclose the possibility of FCC broadband regulation, but indicated that the Commission would have to come up with a better theory to support it.

The FCC's Network Neutrality Policy

After *Comcast*, the FCC went back to the drawing board to develop a new network neutrality policy. The FCC now asserts that it has the right to promote network neutrality on several fronts, which include:

The Communications Act is divided into sections called titles, which enumerate the agency's responsibilities and powers with respect to different forms of media. The FCC asserts that under titles 1, 2, 3 and 6 of the Act it has the right to promote network neutrality.

- Title I ancillary jurisdiction to regulate interstate and foreign communications;
- Title II authority to protect competition and consumers of telecommunications services, which now include Voice over Internet Protocol;
- Title III authority to license spectrum used to provide fixed and mobile wireless services;
- Title VI authority to protect competition in video services, including Internet video; and
- authority under Section 706 of the Telecommunications Act of 1996 to "take immediate action" to remove barriers to investment and competition if advanced telecommunications were not being deployed rapidly enough to U.S. citizens. [Six months before issuing the policy, the FCC decided that this was the case.]

---

[24]Comcast v. Federal Communications Commission, 600 F.3d 642 (D.C. Cir. 2010).
[25]47 U.S.C. § 154(i).

The new policy relied heavily on one put forth by Google and Verizon several months earlier. It supported a structure in which wired broadband would be prevented from discriminating against content, but in which wireless broadband would remain relatively free to do so.

The policy has three basic principles: transparency, no blocking and no unreasonable discrimination:[26]

Rule 1: Transparency

Broadband providers are required to disclose accurate information regarding their network management practices, performance, and commercial terms of their broadband Internet access services so consumers can make an informed choice regarding use of their services.

Rule 2: No Blocking

Providers of fixed broadband service (as opposed to mobile broadband) are not allowed to block lawful content, applications or services, "subject to reasonable network management."

Mobile broadband providers may not block consumers from accessing lawful websites or applications that compete with the provider's voice or video services, "subject to reasonable network management."

Rule 3: No Unreasonable Discrimination

Providers of fixed broadband service cannot unreasonably discriminate against lawful network traffic, subject to reasonable network management. This section does not appear to apply to mobile broadband.

The FCC justifies a different regulatory structure for mobile broadband by pointing out that the technology is in an earlier stage of development than fixed broadband and experiencing rapid change and development; mobile broadband speeds are typically slower than those of fixed broadband, and consumers have more choices among mobile broadband providers.

An obvious question is what constitutes "reasonable network management practices." The FCC says that legitimate network management practices include: "ensuring network security and integrity, including by addressing traffic that is harmful to the network; addressing traffic that is unwanted by users . . . consistent with a user's choices regarding parental controls or security capabilities; and by reducing or mitigating the effects of congestion on the network."[27]

The commission warned broadband providers that accepting payment from third-party content providers to prioritize their service would be "unlikely to satisfy the 'no

---

[26] 47 C.F.R. §§ 8.1–8.17

[27] Preserving the Open Internet, 76 FR 59192 (Sept. 23, 2011)(Order to be codified at 47 CFR Parts 0 and 8).

unreasonable discrimination rule.'"[28] This arrangement would disadvantage noncommercial Internet users. It could also provide an incentive to broadband providers to limit the quality of nonprioritized traffic. The FCC also warned broadband providers (like Comcast, which offers video on demand) against prioritizing their own content and applications over that of their competitors.

It is still not clear whether the FCC really has the authority to enforce the policy without a congressional mandate to do so. If not, it could theoretically revoke its earlier decision to classify broadband providers as information services and reclassify them as telecommunications services subject to common carrier regulation. Of course, that decision would represent a policy change that would have "significant implications for the heretofore-unregulated Internet."[29] A legal challenge would be inevitable and congressional action would be likely to follow.

It is likely that one will follow anyway. Five groups filed suit against the FCC after it announced the new policy. Verizon, which helped propose the policy, was among them. It now argues that the policy is beyond the FCC's authority. Other groups, like Free Press, argue that the policy does not go far enough because it provides fewer protections against wireless companies.[30]

Municipal efforts to offer broadband

Some communities have responded to the telecom/cable lock on broadband by offering to provide wireless broadband as a municipal service. But that effort has not gone unopposed. Broadband providers have lobbied for legislation to stop municipalities from offering competing services. State governments that have prevented municipalities from offering telecommunications services have usually done so on the theory that government ownership is likely to impede progress that market competition would encourage.

When Missouri enacted a statute that barred political subdivisions within the state from offering telecommunications services, municipal utilities sued. They argued that the Telecommunications Act barred state or local laws "prohibiting the ability of *any entity* to provide any interstate or intrastate telecommunications service."[31] However, in *Nixon v. Municipal Missouri League et al.* (2004), the Supreme Court ruled that Congress did not mean to include in the words "any entity" a state's own political subdivisions.[32] The Court asserted that "any entity" refers only to private entities. Under that conclusion, states have the power to prevent municipalities from offering such services. At least

---

[28] *Id.*

[29] Marc Martin and Martin Stern, *Court Overturns FCC's Net Neutrality Based Decision Against Comcast: What Happens Next?*, TMT LAW WATCH, April 8, 2010, at http://www.tmtlawwatch.com/2010/04/articles/court-overturns-fccs-net-neutralitybased-decision-against-comcast-what-happens-next/.

[30] Josh Smith, *D.C. Court Will Hear Net Neutrality Lawsuits*, NAT'L J., Oct. 6, 2011, available at http://techdailydose.nationaljournal.com/2011/10/dc-court-will-hear-net-neutral.php.

[31] *See* 47 U.S.C.S. §§ 253(a) and (d) (2011).

[32] 541 U.S. § 125 (2004).

15 states – Arkansas, Florida, Iowa, Minnesota, Missouri, Nebraska, Nevada, Pennsylvania, South Carolina, Tennessee, Texas, Utah, Virginia, Washington, and Wisconsin – have passed bills restricting the implementation of new publicly funded broadband projects, although existing initiatives are allowed to operate.[33] Other states, like New Jersey and Vermont, have passed bills that authorize communities to provide broadband infrastructure and service.[34]

Voice over Internet Protocol

One of the most popular uses for broadband technology is Voice over Internet Protocol. VoIP allows computer users to make phone calls over the Internet rather than through traditional telephone systems. VoIP converts analog voice or facsimile transmissions into digital signals. These signals can then be carried in data packets over the Internet, like any other file, as long as subscribers have a broadband connection and an analog telephone adapter to take advantage of the service. From the consumer's perspective, it functions like a telecommunications service. But in reality it works more like a software application.

The FCC has yet to classify VoIP as either an information or telecommunications service. In comparison to wireline or mobile telephony, VoIP is minimally regulated, but it is subject to certain laws imposed on telecommunications providers.[35] For example, in 2007, the FCC imposed disability access requirements on VoIP that require the service to assist people with speech and hearing disabilities. In 2005, the FCC required VoIP providers that offer interconnected service to phones on switched networks to support 911 calls.[36] It also required VoIP operators to comply with the Communications Assistance for Law Enforcement Act of 1994, which compels telecommunications carriers to assist law enforcement in electronic surveillance pursuant to a court order or other lawful authorization, and to contribute to the Universal Service Fund, as other telecommunications companies do, to support telecommunications access in high-cost areas.

Internet-based phone companies offer an interstate service, so the FCC has barred individual states from attempting to regulate them. In 2007, a federal court upheld an FCC order preventing Minnesota from applying its telephone company regulations, including state tariffs and rate regulations, to Vonage.[37]

---

[33] AR Code § 23-17-409; CO SB 05–152, FL SB 1322, IA Statute § 388.10, MN Stat. Ann § 237.19, Revised Statutes of MO § 392.410(7), NE LB 645, NV Statutes § 268.086, PA House Bill 30, SC Code § 58-9-2600, TN HB 1403, TX Pub. Util. Code §§ 54.201 et seq, UT Code § 10–18, VA Code § 15.2–2160, VA Code § 56–265.4: 4, Revised Code of WA § 54.16.330, Wis. Stat. Ann. § 66.0422(2)(a).

[34] VT Act 79; NJ ACS 804.

[35] Voice over Internet Protocol, Federal Communications Commission, http://www.fcc.gov/voip/ (last visited Jan. 26, 2012).

[36] E911 Service, 47 C.F.R. § 9.5.

[37] Minnesota PUC v. Federal Communications Comm'n, 483 F.3d 570 (8th Cir. 2007).

eAccessibility

The Internet has the potential to reduce or raise barriers for people with disabilities, depending on the design of websites and the availability of interfaces that make the Web accessible. Producers of websites intended for private use have no legal obligations to make their sites accessible, but producers of websites for federal, state and local government and public educational institutions do. The Americans with Disabilities Act requires state and local governments to make information accessible if they accept federal funding. Section 508 of the Rehabilitation Act of 1973 describes technical requirements for federal agencies that provide information available in an electronic format.[38] All states have codified the legislation into their own statutes, either in whole or in part. Requirements focus on accessibility for those with impairments of vision, hearing or fine motor skills. The following provisions apply to the design of government websites, unless they would pose an undue burden:

Georgia Tech provides a convenient list of state eAccessibility statutes at http://accessibility.gtri.gatech.edu/sitid/stateLawAtGlance.php.

"Longdesc" is a shortened form of long description.

(A) A text equivalent for every non-text element shall be provided (e.g., via "alt", "longdesc", or in element content);

(B) Equivalent alternatives for any multimedia presentation shall be synchronized with the presentation.

(C) Web pages shall be designed so that all information conveyed with color is also available without color, for example from context or markup.

(D) Documents shall be organized so they are readable without requiring an associated style sheet.

(E) Redundant text links shall be provided for each active region of a server-side image map.

(F) Client-side image maps shall be provided instead of server-side image maps except where the regions cannot be defined with an available geometric shape.

(G) Row and column headers shall be identified for data tables.

(H) Markup shall be used to associate data cells and header cells for data tables that have two or more logical levels of row or column headers.

(I) Frames shall be titled with text that facilitates frame identification and navigation.

(J) Pages shall be designed to avoid causing the screen to flicker with a frequency greater than 2 Hz and lower than 55 Hz.

(K) A text-only page, with equivalent information or functionality, shall be provided to make a website comply with the provisions of these standards, when compliance cannot be accomplished in any other way. The content of the text-only page shall be updated whenever the primary page changes.

(L) When pages utilize scripting languages to display content, or to create interface elements, the information provided by the script shall be identified with functional text that can be read by assistive technology.

---

[38] 29 U.S.C. § 794 (d).

(M) When a web page requires that an applet, plug-in or other application be present on the client system to interpret page content, the page must provide a link to a plug-in or applet that complies with § 1194.21(a) through (l).

(N) When electronic forms are designed for completion online, the form shall allow people using assistive technology to access the information, field elements, and functionality required for completion and submission of the form, including all directions and cues.

(O) A method shall be provided that permits users to skip repetitive navigation links.

(P) When a timed response is required, the user shall be alerted and given sufficient time to indicate more time is required.[39]

In 2010, Congress passed the Twenty-First Century Communications and Video Accessibility Act to improve accessibility to advanced communications. The law requires the FCC to develop rules for captioning television programs delivered on the Internet. It also mandates hearing aid compatibility for Internet telephones and requires providers of smart phones with web browsers to provide an Interface that allows people with visual impairments to use them.[40]

The World Wide Web Consortium (W3C), the main international standards organization for the Web, founded by Tim Berners Lee, also offers Web accessibility standards at http://www.w3.org/WAI/.

Cybercrime

As the Internet has opened up new avenues for communication, it has also opened up new avenues for illegal behavior. Some crimes and torts – like dissemination of pornography, copyright infringement, and defamation – are simply made more expedient by virtue of the Internet, and therefore not an issue for this chapter. But other activities – like computer hacking and misuse – are practically defined by Internet use. Meanwhile activities like gambling and hate speech are complicated by the Internet because they are illegal in some countries but not in others. Regulating any illegal behavior on the Internet is always a challenge because, while the effects of the activity may be felt locally, the actual crime may be initiated halfway across the world.

Computer hacking – viruses, worms, and Trojan horses

The U.S. Pentagon admitted that its computers had been hacked in 2011. According to the deputy secretary of defence, a foreign intelligence service stole 24,000 Defense Department files.[41] The files held aircraft avionics, surveillance technologies, satellite

---

[39] Access Board, web-based Intranet and Internet Information and Applications, June 21, 2001, http://www.access-board.gov/sec508/guide/1194.22.htm (last visited Feb. 18, 2012).

[40] Pub. L. 111–260, 124 Stat. 2771, OCT. 8, 2010.

[41] Kevin Baron, *Cyber Strategy: Take a More Active Role in Preventing Attacks*, STARS AND STRIPES, July 14, 2011; Thom Shanker and Elisabeth Bumiller, *After Suffering Damaging Cyberattack, the Pentagon Takes Offensive Action*, NY TIMES, July 15, 2011, at A6.

communications systems, and network security protocols.[42] Other sites that have been hacked include government agencies like the Central Intelligence Agency, the U.S. Senate, and Britain's Serious and Organised Crime Agency, and companies such as defense contractor Lockheed Martin and Computer Security Vendor RSA, a security firm that protects other computers including those used by the U.S. government and major banks.

Following the hacks, the Pentagon announced that it might consider computer sabotage that caused extensive damage an act of war, leaving an opening for a military attack in such a case.[43] It also initiated a program to help defense contractors improve their security that, among other things, involved sharing top secret information about Internet threats with those companies.[44] The Department of Homeland Security may extend the program to other sectors, if Congress gives it the authority to do so. Power plants, electrical grids, pipelines, transportation systems, telecommunications, and the financial sector are all tied into computer networks. Ninety percent of that critical infrastructure is privately owned with security systems that vary in strength. When this book was in press, Congress was considering five cyber-security bills but could not agree on the role of government in regulating Internet security.

Most hacks are carried out through malware – software maliciously designed to steal or harm other computers. The most common forms of malware are worms and viruses. A *computer virus* is a parasitic program that attaches itself to another application. When it is activated, it self replicates and spreads throughout a computer system and then, via shared files, to other computers. *Computer worms* engage in the same malicious behavior, but do so independently. The essential difference between them is that worms do not need a host application. Viruses and worms are most commonly spread through e-mail attachments, links to infected websites, P2P file sharing, and free software downloads from the Internet.

One of the most sophisticated hacks to date involved a worm called Stuxnet. It was designed to burrow through the Internet and attack only one kind of computer – the kind that controlled Iranian centrifuges used to process uranium for bomb making.[45] Released in mid-2009, the worm caused the centrifuges in Iranian nuclear facilities to spin so quickly they destroyed themselves. At the same time, it transmitted a signal to nuclear plant operators simulating normal operations to avoid arousing suspicion before the damage was done. The worm destroyed 984 computers, setting Iran's nuclear program back an estimated three to five years. German cyber security expert Ralph Langner, who first figured out how it worked, has suggested that only one country in the world had the technological sophistication to construct such a superworm,

---

[42] Michael Riley and Ashlee Vance, *The Code War*, Bloomsberg Bus. Wk., July 25–31, 2011, at 53; William Broad et al., *Israeli Tests Called Crucial in Iran Nuclear Setback*, NY Times, Jan. 16, 2011, at A1.

[43] Siobhan Gorman and Julian Barnes, *Cyber Combat: Act of War*, Wall St. J., May 21, 2011, at A1; Eleanor Hall, *When is Computer Hacking an Act of War?* The World Today (ABC broadcast June 2, 2011).

[44] Lolita Baldor, *Pentagon extends program to defend cyber networks*, Associated Press, Sept. 26, 2011.

[45] Michael Riley and Ashlee Vance, *The Code War*, Bloomsberg Bus. Wk., July 25–31, 2011, at 53; William Broad et al., A1, *Israeli Tests Called Crucial in Iran Nuclear Setback*, NY Times, Jan. 16, 2011, at A1.

combined with the intelligence needed to penetrate Iran's nuclear facilities, the United States.[46] U.S. officials would neither confirm nor deny the charge. But Langner pointed out that the danger of releasing a worm like that is that once it was out on the Internet others could modify it and use it against its maker.

There have been other instances of politically motivated malware use. Google, for example, was hacked from China in 2009 and again in 2011. The sophistication of the attacks and the fact that the Gmail accounts of Chinese dissidents and human rights activists were targeted, led the company to believe it was organized by the Chinese government.[47] Georgian government sites were hacked during the country's weeklong war with Russia.[48]

Trojan horses – software programs that appear friendly, but actually carry malware, frequently deliver viruses and worms. Sometimes the malware is used to create *botnets*. These are collections of thousands, even millions, of computers infected with a malicious code that can be commandeered without their owner's knowledge. At a set point in time, the computers can be triggered for a coordinated attack on a particular site. In 2009, Twitter was taken down when thousands of computers tried to communicate with its servers at the same time overwhelming its computers. The attack was thought to be a targeted attempt to silence a particular Twitter user, Georgian blogger Georgy Jakhaia, who was known as a critic of the Russian government.[49]

Beyond the cloak and dagger hacks are those meant to defraud companies for financial gain or to harm them for revenge. In 2011, Citibank announced that a hacker had stolen the names, account numbers and e-mail addresses of approximately 200,000 of its customers. When Sony went after users for modifying its PlayStation 3 operating system to accept other software, its website was hacked at least three times in 2011. The perpetrators breached more than 1 million accounts, accessing names, passwords, e-mail addresses, home addresses and dates of birth for many of its users and then publicly dumping the information for others to use.[50]

Protection from computer misuse exists through a number of statutes, but is most commonly identified with the Computer Fraud and Abuse Act. Under this statute (found at 18 U.S.C. 1030) it is a felony offense to hack into a protected computer, transmit a virus, or traffic in computer passwords. A protected computer is one used in interstate or foreign commerce, located in or outside the United States, or one used by the U.S. government or a financial institution. Specifically, the statute prohibits

---

[46] Siobhan Gorman and Julian Barnes, *Cyber Combat: Act of War*, WALL ST. J., May 21, 2011, at A1; Tom Gjelten, *Security Expert: U.S. "leading force" behind Stuxnet*, NPR, April 26, 2011, audio and transcript available at http://www.npr.org/2011/09/26/140789306/security-expert-u-s-leading-force-behind-stuxnet.

[47] Dominic Rushe, *Google Accuses Beijing of Sabotaging with Email Service*, THE GUARDIAN, March 21, 2011, at 14.

[48] Matthew Clayfield, *Cyber Attack Preceded Russian Tank Invasion – War in Georgia*, THE AUSTRALIAN, Aug. 15, 2008, at 19.

[49] Joel Schectman, *Computer hacking made easy*, BLOOMSBERG BUS. WK., Aug. 13, 2009, http://www.businessweek.com/magazine/content/09_34/b4144036807250.htm.

[50] Julianne Pepitone, *Group claims fresh hack of 1 million Sony accounts*, CNNMoney.com, June 2, 2011, http://money.cnn.com/2011/06/02/technology/sony_lulz_hack/index.htm.

intentionally *accessing* a computer without authorization or exceeding authorized access to obtain information from any protected computer if the conduct involves an interstate or foreign communication. It also criminalizes knowingly *transmitting* "a program, information, code, or command" that intentionally causes damage to a protected computer or "*trafficking* in any password or similar information through which a computer may be accessed without authorization."

The punishment for unauthorized access is normally a fine or up to one year in prison. It increases to five years if the unauthorized access is for commercial advantage, furthers another tortious act, or the value of the information obtained exceeds $5,000. If the information protected for national defense reasons is accessed and transmitted to anyone not entitled to receive it, the perpetrator may be sentenced to 10 years in prison. The statue also entitles those who suffer damage or loss due to behavior prohibited by the Act to file a civil suit against the violator.

Identity theft

Before 2009, cyber security was more closely tied to concerns about *identity theft*. Identity theft occurs when an imposter captures a victim's personal information, such as a Social Security number or credit card number, and uses it for fraudulent purposes. The Federal Trade Commission estimates that as many as 9 million U.S. citizens are victims of identity theft each year.[51]

Phishing and pharming are common ploys used to gather information. *Phishing* involves schemes to trick people into revealing their personal identifying information or financial data, generally through e-mails masking the identity of the user's financial institution. *Pharming*, a related scam, involves domain spoofing. Pharmers redirect users from legitimate commercial websites to malicious ones that look identical. The cloned sites are used to steal Social Security numbers, bank account numbers, credit card numbers, debit card pins, mothers' maiden names, and passwords.[52] When users enter their identifying information, the hackers who run the site capture it for their own use.[53] PayPal and eBay are the companies most often spoofed.[54] Pharmers also plant spyware on computers to steal private information, frequently through the use of Trojan horses.

Pharmers may use Trojan horses to attack a computer user's browser, redirecting it to a spoofed site, or a more sophisticated technique, known as domain name system poisoning, that manipulates the Internet server. DNS poisoning, also known as cache poisoning, corrupts the server's domain name system table by substituting a

---

[51] Federal Trade Commission, About Identity Theft, http://www.ftc.gov/bcp/edu/microsites/idtheft/consumers/about-identity-theft.html (last visited Jan. 26, 2012).

[52] Jonathan J. Rusch, *Phishing and Federal Law Enforcement*, U.S. Department of Justice, Aug. 6, 2004, http://www.abanet.org/adminlaw/annual2004/Phishing/PhishingABAAug2004Rusch.ppt.

[53] Michelle Dello, *Pharming Out-Scams Phishing*, Wired.com, March 14, 2005, http://www.wired.com/techbiz/it/news/2005/03/66853.

[54] OpenDNS, PhishTank Annual Report 4 (Oct. 9, 2007), www.phishtank.com/images/PhishTank_Annual_Report_10-9-07.pdf.

legitimate site's Internet protocol address with the IP address for a phony site. When users type in the correct URL for the site they are trying to reach, they are redirected to another site designed to look like the original. If the spoof is done well, they won't be able to tell the difference.

Protection from identity theft also exists through a number of statutes, including the Identity Theft and Assumption Deterrence Act, the Wire Fraud statute and the CAN-SPAM Act.

The Identity Theft and Assumption Deterrence Act outlaws fraud related to identity theft and falsification of documents. Specifically, the statute prohibits the knowing transfer, possession, or use of another person's means of identification without authorization to commit a crime.[55] The term "means of identification" can include: name, Social Security number, date of birth, driver's license or identification number, alien registration number, government passport number, or employer or taxpayer identification number. It also applies to electronic identification numbers, addresses, or routing codes and to telecommunication identifying information or access devices.

The statute criminalizes falsification of identifying documents, particularly those that would be issued by the federal government, such as birth certificates; driver's licenses; personal identification cards; or authentication features like holograms, watermarks, certifications, symbols, codes, images, or sequences of numbers or letters. The statute also prohibits the production, transfer, or possession of document-making implements, such as templates, computer files, computer discs, electronic devices, or computer hardware or software, specifically configured or primarily used for making identification documents.

An offense related to identification theft or the production of fraudulent documents is punishable by a fine or up to five years imprisonment, or both. The punishment may increase to 15 years if, as a result of the offense, any individual involved obtains something of value worth $1,000 or the fraudulent identification appears to be issued by the United States. Penalties can reach 20–30 years if the fraud is committed in conjunction with another crime that involves drug trafficking, violence, or domestic terrorism.

The CAN-SPAM Act criminalizes e-mail fraud, which may be associated with identity theft, particularly in the case of phishing.[56] The statute criminalizes both the transmission of multiple commercial e-mail messages through a protected computer with the intent to deceive recipients and the use of false header information on multiple commercial e-mails. Maximum penalties can reach five years if the offense is conducted in conjunction with a felony or the offender has been previously convicted of sending spam. This provision is discussed in greater depth in Chapter 12 in conjunction with the CAN-SPAM Act's restrictions on commercial speech.

Computer misuse or identity theft may also be targeted with the federal wire fraud statute.[57] *Wire fraud* involves any scheme to defraud or obtain money or property under false pretenses by a means of wire, radio, or television communication in interstate or

---

[55] 18 U.S.C. § 1028(a)(7).
[56] 18 U.S.C. § 1037.
[57] 18 U.S.C. § 1343.

foreign commerce. The offense is punishable by fines of up to $250,000 or 20 years in prison. Maximum penalties include fines up to $1 million or 30 years imprisonment if the wire fraud affects a financial institution or disbursement paid in connection with a national disaster or emergency.

Cybersquatting

Cybersquatting involves the registration of a domain name with the intent to profit from it in a way that shows "bad faith." Usually, this involves trying to sell the domain name back to the person or company that rightfully owns the trademarked name in the domain address. But it may also be done to divert others from the trademark owner's site, either for commercial gain or with the intent to tarnish or disparage the mark.

Cybersquatting is prohibited by the Anticybersquatting Consumer Protection Act.[58] The statute allows trademark owners to sue a person who has registered, trafficked in, or used a domain name that is identical or confusingly similar to the owner's trademark, if that conduct was undertaken in bad faith. If the site owner is found guilty of cybersquatting the domain may be cancelled or forfeited. If, on the other hand, the court finds that the site owner had reasonable grounds to believe that the use of the domain name was a fair use or otherwise lawful, no liability will be found.

If the domain owner cannot be found, the law also empowers a trademark owner to file an *in rem* civil action against a domain name in the judicial district in which the domain name registrar or registry is located. "In rem" refers to a lawsuit or legal action directed toward property that is in dispute, rather than a particular person.

In some circumstances, the matter may be settled through arbitration instead of a lawsuit. Although many people who register a domain ending in .com, .net, and .org are not aware of it, their contracts stipulate that they must submit to an arbitration proceeding if a trademark owner files a complaint against them for cybersquatting. ICANN has developed a Uniform Domain Name Resolution Policy that is used in arbitration proceedings to settle these disputes. Cybersquatting is discussed in greater detail in Chapter 8 in conjunction with trademark law.

"Trespassing" on websites

Spiders, robots, and web crawlers are all names for the same idea – an automated program that visits websites to gather information from them. Without them, search engines like Google or Yahoo would never be able to keep track of the growing and changing content offered online. Some companies also use web crawlers to monitor their competition. When a web crawler's visits become excessive, however, its search queries can tie up valuable server time.

In some jurisdictions, companies have successfully sued competitors for web crawler invasions under the common law tort of *trespass to chattels*. Unlike trespass, which involves unauthorized access to real property (land), trespass to chattels refers to inter-

---

[58] 15 U.S.C. § 1125(d).

ference with possession of personal property (things) that causes damage or prevents the owner from using it. This theory was applied to web crawlers by a federal district court in *eBay, Inc. v. Bidder's Edge* (2000). The defendant, Bidder's Edge, ran Auction-Watch.com, which aggregated data from auction sites so its users could keep track of multiple auctions of a particular product on the same screen. EBay sued Bidder's Edge because its web crawlers were accessing eBay's server more than 100,000 times a day. To prevail on a claim for trespass to chattels, involving unauthorized access to a computer system, the plaintiff must show that the defendant (1) intentionally and without authorization interfered with the plaintiff's computer system and that (2) the use directly resulted in damage to the plaintiff.[59]

Although no particular damage resulted to eBay's system, the court enjoined Bidder's Edge from using its web crawler on eBay's server. It did so on the slippery slope theory that if Bidder's Edge were allowed to continue to use eBay's system in such a way, other web crawlers would do so as well, and eBay's system eventually would be overwhelmed.

A federal district court in New York similarly held in *Register.com v. Verio* (2000), that a competing web hosting company's repeated use of a web crawler to query Register.com's Whois database to look for potential customers amounted to trespass to chattels.[60] The court concluded that Register.com had a legitimate fear that its servers would be "flooded by search robots."[61]

Some legal scholars have argued that the application of a trespass theory to websites suggests that, for legal purposes, courts really do think of them as spaces to be protected.[62] Neither Verio nor Bidder's Edge harmed the plaintiffs' property with their queries. Traditionally, the trespass to chattels tort has required significant harm, while trespass to real property has not. Moreover, courts have defined chattel as the computer, bandwidth, capacity, processing power, or network. With the exception of the computer, none of these are chattels because there is no private property right in bandwidth, processing power, or network.[63]

The California Supreme Court rejected the notion of extending trespass law to websites and servers in *Intel v. Hamidi* (2003), reasoning that

> [c]reating an absolute property right to exclude undesired communications from one's e-mail and web servers might help force spammers to internalize the costs they impose on ISPs and their customers. But such a property rule might also create substantial new costs, to e-mail and e-commerce users and to society generally, in lost ease and openness of communication and in lost network benefits.[64]

---

[59] eBay Inc. v. Bidder's Edge, Inc., 100 F. Supp. 2d 1058, 1069–70 (N.D. Cal. 2000).

[60] Register.com, Inc. v. Verio, Inc., 126 F. Supp. 2d 238, 248–51 (S.D.N.Y. 2000).

[61] *Id.* at 251.

[62] Dan Hunter, *Cyberspace as Place and the Tragedy of the Digital Anticommons*, 91 Cal. L. Rev. 439 (2003); Mark A. Lemley, *Place and Cyberspace*, 91 Cal. L. Rev. 521 (2003).

[63] Hunter, 91 Cal. L. Rev., at 486.

[64] Intel Corp. v. Hamidi, 30 Cal. 4th 1342, 1363 (2003).

The court clarified that under California law, the trespass to chattels tort "does not encompass, and should not be extended to encompass, an electronic communication that neither damages the recipient computer system nor impairs its functioning."[65] It reversed an injunction against the defendant, a disgruntled employee who used Intel's e-mail system to send critical messages to employees about the company's employment practices, because Intel's e-mail system was never impaired. It added that while a private entity's refusal to transmit another's electronic mail messages does not implicate the First Amendment, because no governmental action is involved, the issuance of an injunction in a private lawsuit is an application of state power that must comply with First Amendment limits.[66]

Internet Gambling

While at least 50 countries consider gambling on the Internet to be a legal activity, the United States does not.[67] In the past decade, the industry has grown considerably. There are now approximately 2,000 online gambling sites, operating overseas, particularly in the Caribbean, Europe and the Asian/Pacific rim. Ironically, their customer base is largely drawn from the United States. Americans are estimated to spend more than $100 billion annually with offshore Internet gambling organizations.[68]

Although federal law does not directly prohibit U.S. citizens from gambling online, Congress has attempted to curtail the practice by passing legislation that prohibits businesses from taking bets online and banks from accepting payments from online gambling operations. In 2006, it passed the Unlawful Internet Gambling Enforcement Act, which applied to Internet wagers on sporting events as well as bets through online casinos. The statute prohibits gambling businesses from accepting credit cards, electronic fund transfers, checks, or drafts from Internet customers. It also directs the Federal Reserve, in consultation with the Attorney General, to prescribe regulations to require banks to identify and block financial transactions associated with Internet gambling.[69]

The Wire Communications Act is also used to control Internet gambling. It prohibits gambling businesses from "knowingly us[ing] a wire communication facility for the transmission in interstate or foreign commerce of bets or wagers or information assisting in the placing of bets or wagers on any sporting event or contest."[70] It also prohibits wire communications that entitle the recipient to receive money or credit as a result of bets or wagers or provide information to assist in the placing of bets or wagers. Because

---

[65] *Id.* at 1347.

[66] *Id.* at 1364.

[67] Panel Report, United States – Measures Affecting the Cross-Border Supply of Gambling and Betting Services: Recourse to Article 21.5 of the DSU by Antigua and Barbuda, WT/DS285/R (April 20, 2005), as modified by Appellate Body Report, WT/DS285/AB/R, DSR 2005:XII, 5797.

[68] Michelle Hirsch, *Internet gambling: Betting on new tax revenue*, THE FISCAL TIMES, May 20, 2010, at http://www.thefiscaltimes.com/Articles/2010/05/20/Internet-Gambling-Betting-on-New-Tax-Revenue.Aspx#page1.

[69] 109 Pub. L. 109–347, Title VIII (Oct. 13, 2006) (codified at 31 U.S.C. §§ 5301, 5361–7).

[70] 18 U.S.C. § 1084 (a) (2011).

the statute bars "information assisting in the placing of bets or wagers on any sporting event or contest," the statute has been interpreted by some courts as applying only to sporting events and not to online casinos. But the Department of Justice disagrees with this interpretation.

Two other statutes used to curtail gambling are the Travel Act and the Illegal Gambling Business Act. The Travel Act prohibits the distribution of proceeds from any unlawful activity, including any enterprise involving gambling, in interstate or foreign commerce.[71] The Illegal Gambling Business Act makes it a crime to operate a gambling business prohibited by state law, involving five or more people, in operation more than 30 days or grossing more than $2,000 in one day. Congress passed the law in 1970 to target illegal gambling used to finance organized crime, an activity that affected interstate commerce.[72]

There is a domestic exception to Internet gambling, however. Congress included a specific exemption for horse racing in the Unlawful Internet Gambling Enforcement Act because a number of states allow pari-mutuel wagering on horse races.[73] In pari-mutuel wagers, gamblers bet against one another rather than against the house. Their money is pooled and most is distributed to the winner. A percentage is reserved for the racetrack, jockeys, and government.

Another exemption, for all practical purposes, is fantasy sports, which have become a $1.5 billion Internet industry. Participants in fantasy sports leagues manage virtual teams in a competition to get the best statistical outcome. Colorado attorney Charles Humphrey challenged the legality of fantasy sports in a suit against Viacom, CBS, ESPN, Inc., Sportsline.com Inc., and Vulcan Sports Media filed under anti-gambling and gambling loss recovery laws in New Jersey and several other states. The federal district court dismissed the suit, holding that the activities did not constitute online gambling because: "(1) the entry fees are paid unconditionally, (2) the prizes offered to fantasy sports contestants are for amounts certain and are guaranteed to be awarded, and (3) defendants do not compete for the prizes."[74]

The United States imposes its gambling laws outside its borders. A foreign site that accepts a bet from a U.S. citizen through the Internet violates the Wire Act. One that accepts payment from a U.S. citizen via credit, bank transfer, or check violates the Unlawful Internet Gambling Enforcement Act. Sites that accept bets from residents of states in which gambling is illegal also violate the Travel Act and the Illegal Gambling Business Act.

---

[71] 18 U.S.C. §§ 1952, 1955 (2011).

[72] *See* United States v. Sacco, 491 F.2d 995, 998–1001 (9th Cir. 1974) and United States v. Lee, 173 F.3d 809, 810–11 (11th Cir. 1999) ("if Congress, or a committee thereof, makes legislative findings that a statute regulates activities with a substantial effect on commerce, a court may not override those findings unless they lack a rational basis").

[73] Panel Report, United States – Measures Affecting the Cross-Border Supply of Gambling and Betting Services: Recourse to Article 21.5 of the DSU by Antigua and Barbuda, WT/DS285/RW (Mar. 30, 2007).

[74] Humphrey v. Viacom, Inc., No. 06–2768 (DMC), 2007 WL 1797648 (D.N.J. June 20, 2007).

The World Trade Organization censured the United States for violating its General Agreement on Trade in Services obligations by preventing other nations from offering Internet gambling services to U.S. citizens. Antigua, a Caribbean nation that earns substantial profits from online gambling, filed a complaint with the WTO, claiming that a combination of the Wire Act, the Travel Act, and the Illegal Gambling Business Act blocked all gambling exchanges between the United States and Antigua. The WTO sided with Antigua in 2004 and the decision was upheld on appeal in 2005.[75] The WTO focused on the disconnect between banning international gambling sites from serving U.S. citizens while allowing domestic Internet gambling on horse races. The WTO ruled that the United States could either ban all forms of gambling or allow Americans to do business with offshore sites. When the U.S. ignored the ruling, the WTO awarded Antigua an annual $21 million credit on trade sanctions.[76] The credit would allow Antigua to violate U.S. copyrights up to that value.

At the time this book was written, three bills were before Congress that would legalize Internet gambling.[77] Their sponsors observed that the United States is giving up billions each year in tax revenue. Even states that were formerly opposed to Internet gambling, either because they thought it to be a danger to their citizens or to their own in-state gambling operations, have flipped on the issue. Several have lobbied Congress to repeal the Unlawful Internet Gambling Enforcement Act and the Justice Department to change its position that Internet gambling is illegal.

Virtual Law

One area of digital law with growth potential concerns property and relationships that take place in virtual worlds but are litigated in the real world. Virtual worlds, like Second Life and other simulations (commonly known as sims), are used for gaming, social networking, business, education, and entertainment. In these massively multi-player online role-playing games, computer users inhabit virtual worlds through graphic representations of themselves called avatars. In many MMORPGs, users exchange virtual currency to buy and sell "property" online. Some games also allow users to convert virtual currency into real currency. A key issue is whether "virtual property" is real and deserving of protection in the real world, or whether it is just a service provided at the discretion of the company.

In the United States suits inspired by virtual relationships have not yet answered that question. For example, in 2007, Marc Bragg sued Linden Lab, the company behind

---

[75] Panel Report, United States – Measures Affecting the Cross-Border Supply of Gambling and Betting Services: Recourse to Article 21.5 of the DSU by Antigua and Barbuda, WT/DS285/R (April 20, 2005), as modified by Appellate Body Report, WT/DS285/AB/R, DSR 2005:XII, 5797.

[76] James Kanter and Gary Rivlin, *Antigua Wins Freedom to Violate U.S. Copyrights*, INT'L HERALD TRIB., Dec. 22, 2007, at 13.

[77] H.R. 1174, H.R. 2230 and H.R. 2366 112th Cong. (2011–2012).

Figure 4.2   Illustration: Kalan Lyra

Second Life, for violating the company's terms of service by suspending his account and confiscating online property that he used for business purposes "in world." Bragg inundated the court with press releases and articles in which the game's originator, Philip Rosedale, claimed that Second Life users "owned" the virtual property they purchased in the game. Linden also charged users taxes on that land paid in real currency.[78] Linden asserted that its terms of service, to which Bragg agreed, described what he got as a "limited license" to use the service. Bragg argued that the terms were changed without his consent. The case was settled, so no precedent emerged from the conflict.

In 2012, Linden still faced a *class action lawsuit* in California for suspending user accounts and denying them access to the property they believed they owned.[79] These users agreed to Second Life's terms of service which stipulated they were getting a "limited license" to use the service, that the "Linden dollars" used in the game are not real currency, and that Linden is entitled to *disable any user's access to the Service without notice or liability*.[80] The question is whether users would have understood the distinction

[78] Bragg v. Linden Research, Inc., 487 F. Supp. 2d 593 (E.D. Pa. 2007).
[79] Evans v. Linden Research, 11-cv-01078-DMR (E.D. Pa. and N.D. Cal. 2010).
[80] Terms of Service, Second Life, http://secondlife.com/corporate/tos.php (last visited Jan. 26, 2012).

between the company's terms to which they assented when they clicked "I agree" and the marketing rhetoric of the company that promised users ownership in property in Second Life.

The terms of service for Entropia Universe, a MMORPG owned by Swedish software developer MindArk, remind users that virtual items are fictional, that users are licensed to use them, and that MindArk retains the title to everything in the game and all intellectual property rights to any virtual items users create. Nevertheless, Entropia has fostered a real-cash economy. Entropia's in-world currency may be exchanged for U.S. dollars at a set rate of 10:1. One player paid the equivalent of $635,000 for a virtual nightclub. Another purchased a space station for $330,000.[81]

Virtual crime is taken seriously in other countries. A British hacker was sentenced to two years in prison for stealing 400 billion virtual poker chips from Zynga's Poker application on Facebook, and then selling them for real currency on eBay for $85,870.[82] Game players purchase chips directly from Zynga for use at the virtual tables every day. The virtual chips would have been worth $12 million had Zynga sold them. The court found that although virtual currency is technically in infinite supply (the company can always make more), it is nevertheless still worth protecting.

In Holland, two 14-year-old boys were convicted of virtual property theft after they forced another boy to transfer virtual items from his account to theirs. Although the teens coerced their victim to transfer virtual items and currency he had won in the game by threatening him with a knife, the court focused on the property theft rather than the assault. Finding that "virtual goods are goods" under Dutch law, the court sentenced the boys to community service and probation for the theft.[83] In a second case, a Dutch teenager was arrested for theft and computer hacking because he hacked into other users' accounts to steal the equivalent of $6,000 in virtual furniture in the online game Habbo Hotel.[84]

In China, Li Hongchen successfully sued the manufacturer of the game Red Moon after another avatar exploited a programming weakness to steal his online treasure and weapons. The Beijing Chaoyang District People's Court recognized the value of Hongchen's labor and awarded him a sum equal to the real-world value of the items.[85]

---

[81] Daniel Bates, *Internet Estate Agent Sells Virtual Nightclub on an Asteroid in Online Game for £400,000*, THE DAILY MAIL, Nov.18, 2010, http://www.dailymail.co.uk/sciencetech/article-1330552/Jon-Jacobs-sells-virtual-nightclub-Club-Neverdie-online-Entropia-game-400k.html.

[82] Steven Morris, *Hacker Jailed for £7m Virtual Game Chips Scam*, THE GUARDIAN, March 18, 2011, at 25; Jas Purewell, *The first virtual currency crime: hacker jailed after $12 Zynga theft*, GAMER/LAW, http://www.gamerlaw.co.uk/2011/02/first-virtual-currency-crime-hacker.html.

[83] *Dutch Court Convicts 2 of Stealing Virtual Items*, MSNBC.com, Oct. 21, 2008.

[84] Emma Thomasson, *Dutch police Arrest Teenage Online Furniture Thief*, Reuters UK, Nov. 14, 2007, http://uk.reuters.com/article/oddlyEnoughNews/idUKL1453844620071114.

[85] Jeff W. Le Blanc, *The Pursuit of Virtual Life, Liberty, and Happiness and its Economic and Legal Recognition in the Real World*, 9 FLA. COASTAL L. REV. 255 (2008).

Both China and South Korea also consider profits made through virtual currency taxable.[86]

Finally, even in the virtual world, there are crimes of passion. A Japanese woman was arrested for computer hacking in 2008 after she "killed" another player's avatar.[87] When her virtual husband divorced her in the anime-style game Maple Story, she logged into his account and terminated his license, effectively terminating him as well.

The First International Treaty on Cybercrime

Computer misuse laws vary considerably at the international level. Some countries have yet to enact them. A virus dubbed the "Love Bug" traveled through 45 million computers in 2000, destroying data as it went. It got its name from the "I love you" subject line of the e-mails that carried it. When a victim opened one of the infected e-mails, the virus replicated by sending itself to everyone listed in the victim's contacts file. All told, it is estimated that it caused $10 billion in damages. Filipino hacker Onel de Guzman admitted responsibility for the attack but was never punished because the Philippines had no law criminalizing misuse of computers.

The following year, the Council of Europe drafted the Convention on Cybercrime.[88] The treaty stipulates that all signatories will adopt legislation that criminalizes illegal access to a computer system, illegal interception of nonpublic data transmissions, data interference, system interference, misuse of devices for transmission of malware, computer-related forgery, and computer-related fraud. The convention also applies to traditional crimes committed via a computer, such as offenses related to child pornography, copyright infringement, or aiding and abetting another's criminal activities. Only 32 nations, including the United States, have ratified the treaty.[89]

All countries are not in agreement on what constitutes cybercrime. After the Council of Europe's Convention on Cybercrime went into effect, an additional protocol was added to prevent the dissemination of hate speech. The protocol entered into force in January of 2006.[90] The 35 nations that signed the protocol agreed to "establish as criminal offences under its domestic law, when committed intentionally and without right," the act of "distributing, or otherwise making available, racist and xenophobic material to the public through a computer system" (Additional Protocol, 2002, p. 14). Although the United States signed the larger cybercrime convention, it did not sign the protocol because it conflicted with the First Amendment.

---

[86] *Real Taxes for Real Money Made by Online Game Players*, WALL STREET J., Oct. 31, 2008, http://blogs.wsj.com/chinarealtime/2008/10/31/real-taxes-for-real-money-made-by-online-game-players/; *South Korea allows the trading of cyber money*, Virtual Judgment, Jan. 13, 2010, www.virtualjudgment.com/index.php?option=com_mojo&Itemid=26&p=27.

[87] Mari Yamaguchi, *Angry Online Divorcee 'Kills' Virtual Ex-Hubby*, MSNBC.com, Oct. 23, 2008, http://www.msnbc.msn.com/id/27337812/.

[88] Council of Europe, Convention on Cybercrime, Budapest, Nov. 23, 2001, CETS No. 185, http://conventions.coe.int/Treaty/en/Treaties/Html/185.htm.

[89] Council of Europe, Convention on Cybercrime, CETS No. 185, http://conventions.coe.int/Treaty/Commun/ChercheSig.asp?NT=185&CM=&DF=&CL=ENG (last visited Jan. 26, 2012).

[90] Additional Protocol to the Convention on cybercrime concerning the criminalization of acts of a racist and xenophobic nature committed through computer systems (Nov. 7, 2002). Council of Europe Treaty Office, Strasbourg, Jan. 28, 2003, CETS No. 189, http://conventions.coe.int/Treaty/en/Treaties/Html/189.htm.

Questions for Discussion

1. What role does ICANN play in the Internet's management? Does ICANN regulate content?
2. What is the United States' role in the management of Internet functions?
3. What is the difference between the domestic and international concepts of network neutrality?
4. What federal statutes are in place to combat computer misuse? What is the challenge that lawmakers face regarding international computer crimes?
5. What is virtual law? Should it be litigated in "real world" courts?

5 Conflict of Laws

From a technology perspective, we've never been closer to Marshall McLuhan's vision of a global village. Internet content can be accessed anywhere. Mobile phones and VoIP numbers cross borders as easily as the people who carry them. The footprint of a geostationary satellite can span multiple continents at once, and broadcast signals cross all borders within their area of reception. But from a legal perspective, our villages are still quite distinct. The world is made up of sovereign territories that do not always agree about the suitability of content that crosses their borders. Although they may praise digital media's power to extend science, art, and commerce, they also worry about its ability to exacerbate defamation, obscenity, hate speech, and fraud.

One might assume that nations and states have no recourse to battle content that is published elsewhere in the world – particularly through a medium like the Internet that goes everywhere. But it does occur and with greater frequency. States will prosecute publishers in other countries who disseminate content they consider illegal. They will allow their citizens to sue content producers in other countries for material perceived to cause harm. In some cases, they will even allow nonresidents to sue other nonresidents in their courts for online content received within their borders.

Internet publishers have been summoned to courts all over the world for content posted online that was legal in their home countries, but which was alleged to violate the law somewhere else. For example, Dow Jones was sued in Australia and the UK for material accessible through its *Barron's* magazine and *Wall Street Journal* websites. *The Washington Post* was sued in Canada for a story about an African UN worker. Two Russian citizens sued Forbes in the UK. A French court found Yahoo! guilty of listing Nazi paraphernalia on its website. Germany tried and convicted an Australian for operating an English-language holocaust denial website.

These controversies highlight the increasing importance of an area of procedural law called *conflict of laws*, which is used to determine where conflicts between litigants from

Digital Media Law, Second Edition. Ashley Packard.
© 2013 John Wiley & Sons, Inc. Published 2013 by John Wiley & Sons, Inc.

different places will be resolved and which nation or state's laws will apply. *Procedural law* is the body of legal rules that control access to the legal system. It is generally given less attention than *substantive law*, which defines a person's rights and limitations in a civil society. But it is an area of law that no one in digital media can afford to ignore.

This chapter explains how three areas of procedural law – jurisdiction, choice of law, and enforcement of foreign judgments – are determined in domestic and international transborder conflicts. Specifically it focuses on how these procedural rules are evolving to address material published on the Internet and the impact of those changes on digital media. It also discusses potential strategies to deal with these changes, such as geolocation filtering and online dispute resolution.

Jurisdiction, Choice of Law, and Enforcement of Judgments

In the United States, conflicts law has three distinct branches: jurisdiction, choice of law, and enforcement of judgments. *Jurisdiction* refers to a court's prerogative to hear and adjudicate a case. A court with jurisdiction to decide a case is known as the forum court. *Choice of law* refers to the law that will apply in the case. In criminal cases, the applicable law will always be the law of the forum, *lex fori*. But in civil cases involving parties from different states, the applicable law is normally that of the state with the closest connection to the conflict. If the case involves a tortious act committed elsewhere, the law of the place of the harm, *lex loci*, usually applies. *Enforcement of judgments* refers to the state's power to put a court's judgment into effect. A state is powerless to enforce a judgment outside of its own jurisdiction. A plaintiff who wins a judgment in a forum court against a defendant who resides in another state will be forced to petition a court within the defendant's jurisdiction to enforce the foreign judgment.

Jurisdiction

Subject matter jurisdiction refers to a court's authority to hear cases related to particular issues.

Personal jurisdiction refers to a court's right to exercise its control over the parties involved in a case. There are two types of personal jurisdiction: general and specific.

A state's sovereign power to make and enforce law is limited by its *jurisdiction*. There are two ways to think of jurisdiction. It literally refers to the "geographic region" in which a government may operate. But it also refers to a state's "purview," the subject matter and people over which a government may impose its authority. *Subject matter jurisdiction* was discussed in Chapter 1. This chapter will focus on *personal jurisdiction*.

Personal jurisdiction may be based on one or more of three criteria: nationality, territory, and effects. A state's courts may exercise *general jurisdiction* over its own citizens, regardless of their location; nonresidents in its territory; activities that take place within its territory; or people who have consented to jurisdiction in its territory (normally through a contract). It also may assert *specific jurisdiction* over nonresidents outside its borders, if their conduct precipitates harmful or damaging effects within its territory and asserting jurisdiction over them does not violate their rights of due process.

Due process refers to the fair application of legal procedures. The concept can be traced to thirteenth-century England. After years of enduring King John's absolute rule,

English barons turned on him and extracted a promise that from then forward he would act only in accordance with the "law of the land." His promises were incorporated into the Magna Carta, the forerunner of modern constitutions. In the United States, due process rights are guaranteed in the Constitution's Fifth and Fourteenth Amendments, which stipulate that no person may be deprived of "life, liberty, or property, without due process of law."

The Supreme Court originally interpreted the right of due process to prohibit states from asserting jurisdiction over people who were not present within their territory.[1] It has since reversed itself on that point, but still limits states' assertion of jurisdiction over nonresidents to cases in which the defendant has established "minimum contacts with [the forum] such that the maintenance of the suit does not offend traditional notions of fair play and substantial justice."[2] A court will not assert jurisdiction over an out-of-state defendant based on the court's connection to the plaintiff. The court must have a connection to the defendant.

General jurisdiction

A court may exercise general jurisdiction over a defendant if the defendant's contacts with the state have been continuous and systematic.[3] This would, of course, include residents or businesses operating within a state's territory. But it may also apply to nonresidents who do business within a state on a regular basis.

Specific jurisdiction

If a state does not have the right to assert general jurisdiction over a nonresident defendant, it may still assert specific jurisdiction over the nonresident without violating due process if the controversy before the court is related to or "arises out of" the defendant's contacts with the forum state.[4] In other words, the defendant must have established minimum contacts with the state and the claim must be related to the effects of those contacts. In *Keeton v. Hustler Magazine* (1984), a New York resident sued an Ohio publisher in New Hampshire because it was the only state left in which the statute of limitations for a defamation action had not expired.[5] The Supreme Court held that the defendant's circulation of the magazine in the state established minimum contacts sufficient to justify New Hampshire's personal jurisdiction over the case, considering that the cause of action stemmed from the magazine's publication.[6]

---

[1] Pennoyer v. Neff, 95 U.S. 714 (1878).
[2] Int'l Shoe Co. v. Washington, 326 U.S. 310, 316 (1945).
[3] Helicopteros Nacionales de Columbia v. Hall, 466 U.S. at 415.
[4] Id. at 427.
[5] 465 U.S. 770 (1984).
[6] *Id.* at 780.

The critical question a court will consider in assessing its right to assert specific jurisdiction over a nonresident is whether the defendant "purposely avail[ed] . . . of the privilege of conducting activities within the forum State, thus invoking the benefits and protections of its laws,"[7] and consequently "should reasonably anticipate being haled into court there."[8]

On occasion, states do claim jurisdiction over defendants who have had little to no contact with the forum, but whose actions have nonetheless caused injury there. In order to satisfy due process in such situations, courts look for indicators of the defendant's intent to harm within the jurisdiction. In *Calder v. Jones* (1984) actress Shirley Jones, a resident of California, sued the *National Enquirer* and members of its staff for defamation.[9] The *Enquirer* is a weekly magazine published in Florida and Calder, its editor, was a Florida resident who had been to California on only two occasions unrelated to the article. The Supreme Court concluded that California's jurisdiction over the defendants was reasonable under the circumstances because the defendants *purposely aimed their actions toward a resident of the state, knowing that the brunt of the injury would be felt there.*[10]

Jurisdictional Analysis

A state may assert personal jurisdiction over:

- its citizens or legal residents, regardless of their location;
- businesses operating within its territory;
- nonresidents currently within its territory;
- nonresidents who have consented to its jurisdiction; or
- nonresidents outside its territory who have caused harm within its territory, if specific or general jurisdiction applies.

Criteria for general jurisdiction

1. The defendant's contacts with the state, if unrelated to the cause of action, must be continuous and systematic.

Criteria for specific jurisdiction

1. The defendant must have purposely availed of the forum state's benefits.
2. The claim must arise out of the defendant's contacts with the forum.
3. The exercise of jurisdiction must be consistent with due process notions of "fair play" and "substantial justice."

Long-arm statutes

Following the Supreme Court's decision in *International Shoe Co. v. Washington* (1945) to allow states to assert jurisdiction over nonresidents, states began to pass *long-arm*

---

[7] Hanson v. Denckla, 357 U.S. 235, 253 (1958).
[8] World-Wide Volkswagen v. Woodson, 444 U.S. 286, 297 (1980).
[9] 465 U.S. 783 (1984).
[10] *Id.* at 789–90.

statutes specifying the conditions under which courts could serve process to out-of-state defendants. Many modeled their statutes on the Uniform Interstate and International Procedures Act, which suggests jurisdiction over out-of-state defendants is appropriate when they:

- own or possess real estate within the state;
- transact business within the state;
- perform a tortious act within the state;
- insure a person or property within the state; or
- engage in an activity outside the state that causes injury within the state.

Most long-arm statutes permit personal jurisdiction to the full extent allowed by the Constitution. Consequently, a court's consideration of whether it may lawfully claim jurisdiction over a nonresident defendant is a two-part process. It must first examine its state's long-arm statute to determine whether its assertion of jurisdiction would be consistent with state law. If so, it moves to the second phase of analysis, determining whether personal jurisdiction would be consistent with the defendant's right to due process.

Forum non conveniens

Once a court has determined that it has the right to exercise jurisdiction over an out-of-state defendant, it must decide whether it should. In common law systems, defendants may petition a court to stay (suspend) an action under the doctrine of *forum non conveniens* (a Latin term that means inconvenient forum) if litigating the case in the plaintiff's chosen jurisdiction would pose a particular hardship to other parties in the case and a competent alternative forum exists. The court may oblige if it believes that the interests of justice and the parties involved would be better served elsewhere.[11]

In a trial involving foreign citizens and residents of the United States, the Supreme Court has made it clear that one factor that would *not* apply to a decision of forum non conveniens is "whether the substantive law that would be applied in the alternative forum is less favorable to the plaintiffs than that of the present forum."[12] The Court reiterated that the central issue in a forum non conveniens decision is convenience. It recognized that there would be exceptions, however, adding that "if the remedy provided by the alternative forum is so clearly inadequate or unsatisfactory that it is no remedy at all, the unfavorable change in law may be given substantial weight . . ."[13]

The Supreme Court also noted that although courts normally defer to the plaintiff in choice of forum, less deference would be granted when the plaintiff is foreign. It justified the distinction by pointing out, "[A] plaintiff's choice of forum is entitled to greater

---

[11] In the United States, this principle is codified at 28 U.S.C. § 1404(a) ("For the convenience of parties and witnesses, in the interest of justice, a district court may transfer any civil action to any other district or division where it might have been brought.").

[12] Piper Aircraft Co. v. Reyno, 454 U.S. 235, 247 (1981).

[13] *Id.* at 254.

deference when the plaintiff has chosen the home forum. When the home forum has been chosen, it is reasonable to assume that this choice is convenient. When the plaintiff is foreign, however, this assumption is much less reasonable."[14]

Evolution of jurisdiction in light of the Internet

The United States – with 50 separate jurisdictions – has more experience with Internet jurisdiction than any other country in the world. Over the last two decades, its philosophy has evolved considerably. Originally, courts based jurisdiction on whether or not the site was accessible within the forum. In 1996, for example, a Connecticut federal court claimed jurisdiction over a Massachusetts defendant in a trademark infringement case. The court concluded the defendant could reasonably anticipate being haled into Connecticut because its Internet advertisements were directed toward all states, including Connecticut.[15]

As courts' understanding of the Internet became more sophisticated, they began to reject the proposition that jurisdiction could be based on Internet access alone. A federal court in Pennsylvania developed an alternative test in *Zippo Manufacturing Company v. Zippo Dot Com, Inc.* (1997). The court concluded that a website operator's contacts with a forum should be assessed on a sliding scale, based on the website's level of commercial activity and interactive ability. At one end of the spectrum are websites that do business over the Internet. If the defendant regularly exchanges files and enters into contracts with customers, personal jurisdiction is appropriate. At the other end are passive websites. If the defendant simply posts information for anyone to read, jurisdiction is not appropriate. In between are interactive websites. In these cases, courts must consider "the level of interactivity and commercial nature of the exchange of information that occurs on the Web site."[16]

The *Zippo* test: The *Zippo* test is widely used among federal and state courts to establish a defendant's personal availment of a forum's benefits in an Internet context.[17] Its application is particularly appropriate in commercial cases. For example, the California Supreme Court used the *Zippo* test to establish personal availment in *Snowney v. Harrah's Entertainment, Inc.* (2005)[18] A California resident sued Harrah's hotel in Las Vegas for overcharging him. When the defendant moved to have the summons quashed for lack of personal jurisdiction, the trial court granted the

---

[14]*Id.* at 255–56 (citations omitted).
[15]Inset Systems, Inc. v. Instruction Set, Inc., 937 F. Supp. 161, 165 (D. Conn. 1996).
[16]Zippo Mfg. Co. v. Zippo Dot Com, Inc., 952 F. Supp. 1119, 1124 (W.D. Pa. 1997).
[17]*See, e.g.,* Toys "R" Us, Inc. v. Step Two, S.A., 318 F.3d 446, 453 (3rd Cir. 2003) (describing it as the "seminal authority regarding personal jurisdiction" involving websites); ALS Scan, Inc. v. Digital Serv. Consultants, Inc., 293 F.3d 707, 713–14 (4th Cir. 2002); Cybersell, Inc. v. Cybersell, Inc., 130 F.3d 414, 418 (9th Cir. 1997).
[18]5 Cal. 4th 1054 (2005).

motion. But a California appellate court reversed, and the California Supreme Court upheld the decision. The California Supreme Court observed that the defendant's website, which quoted rates and accepted reservations, was interactive, putting it in the middle of the *Zippo* sliding scale. Also, by advertising in California and supplying directions to the hotel from California, the defendants targeted the state. Many of their hotel's guests were from California, so the hotel benefited from the state – indicating that they personally availed themselves of conducting business there.

Zippo is not recognized in all jurisdictions. The U.S. Court of Appeals for the Seventh Circuit has rejected the test, concluding that merely operating a website, even a highly interactive one, accessible from the forum is not sufficient to justify asserting jurisdiction over a nonresident defendant. Instead, it looks for evidence that the defendant *targeted* the forum. Meanwhile jurisdictions that apply *Zippo* without reservation in commercial cases involving issues such as trademark infringement or dilution, unfair competition, or false advertising, have observed that the test is insufficient in other contexts. Defamation is one example. The *Zippo* test focuses on the character of the website rather than the character of the statement. However, a libelous statement posted on a passive, noncommercial website may be just as harmful as one made on an interactive, commercial site.

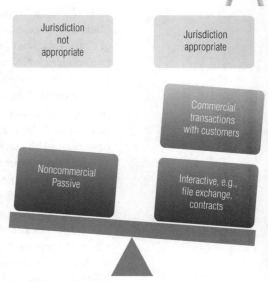

Figure 5.1 Zippo test

Targeting test: The targeting test, from *Calder v. Jones*, is now commonly used to assess specific jurisdiction in Internet cases. It is not sufficient that the plaintiff, who resides in the forum, merely feels the effects of the defendant's actions there. The test requires courts to look for evidence that the defendant *targeted its actions at a particular state knowing that harm was likely to occur there*. The U.S. Court of Appeals for the Fourth Circuit applied the *Calder* test in *Young v. New Haven Advocate* (2002).[19] The case involved a Virginia prison warden who sued two Connecticut newspapers in Virginia for libel in response to newspaper articles published on their websites. He believed the articles, which concerned Connecticut prisoners housed in a Virginia prison under his care, suggested that the prisoners were being mistreated. Applying the *Calder* test, the Fourth Circuit reached the conclusion that jurisdiction in Virginia would not be reasonable. Although the articles were accessible in Virginia via the Internet, they were targeted at Connecticut readers. The court took into account that the newspapers had no offices in Virginia or personnel who worked there, and that most of their subscribers lived in Connecticut.

---

[19] 315 F. 3d 256 (4th Cir. 2002).

However, a New Jersey appellate court found that targeting was apparent in the Internet libel case *Goldhaber v. Kohlenberg* (2007).[20] The defendant in the case, a resident of California, was alleged to have made disparaging remarks on an Internet forum about two residents of New Jersey. It was clear that the author of the remarks, which involved accusations of incest and bestiality, knew where the plaintiff resided, because his references extended beyond the plaintiffs to their town, its police department, and the plaintiffs' neighbors. Applying *Calder*, the court concluded that the defendant had in fact targeted the plaintiff in New Jersey and that his conduct was such that he should have reasonably anticipated being haled into court there.

The Ohio Supreme Court also found evidence of targeting in *Kauffman Racing Equip., L.L.C., v. Roberts* (2010). Kauffman, a company that manufactured parts for racing cars sued a former customer from Virginia in Ohio for making allegedly defamatory remarks on several online forums for racing aficionados. The defendant purchased an engine block from Kauffman and then complained that it was defective. Kauffman offered to replace it but then retracted the offer after concluding that the part had been modified. The defendant's subsequent posts reflected his anger toward the company. Dissenting judges in the case pointed out that the online forums had no connection to Ohio and Kauffmann could only point to five people in Ohio who had read the defendant's comments. But the majority found evidence of targeting. Roberts posted his comments on multiple sites, for audiences in the racing community, and his posts suggested a vendetta. For example, two of the posts read:

> Now, I have and have had since the day the block was delivered, a USELESS BLOCK. I didn't say worthless! I plan to get a lot of mileage out of it[.] And when i'm [sic] done Steve Kauffman will be able to attest to its worth.
>
> I did send it back. They still have it. Steve Kauffman admitted on the phone that he got similar numbers on the sonic test as i [sic] did but he won't take it back because I did some work to it and have had it to [sic] long. I guess it doesn't matter that the day I got it all of the **defects** exsisted [sic] andnothing I have done caused them. But don't worry about that. What I loose [sic] in dollars I will make up in entertainment at their expence [sic].[21]

Where speech is at issue, courts generally have concluded that defendants who post messages on websites, listservs, and newsgroups accessible in another state do not establish minimum contacts with the state sufficient to justify personal jurisdiction, unless they avail themselves of the state's benefits in some way or engage in a specific action to target the state, knowing harm will result there.[22]

[20] 395 N.J. Super. 380, 387 (App. Div. 2007).

[21] Kaufmann Racing Equip., LLC v. Roberts, 126 Ohio St.3d 81, 2010-Ohio-2551.

[22] *See, e.g.,* Bible and Gospel Trust v. Wyman, 354 F. Supp. 2d 1025 (D. Minn. 2005); Medinah Mining, Inc. v. Amunategui, 237 F. Supp. 2d 1132 (D. Nev. 2002); Burleson v. Toback, 391 F. Supp. 2d 401 (M.D. N.C. 2005); Barrett v. Catacombs Press, 44 F. Supp. 2d 717 (E.D. Pa. 1999); Novak v. Benn, 896 So.2d 513 (Ala. Civ. App. 2004).

However, it is not particularly difficult to find contradictory decisions regarding jurisdiction in Internet cases because courts disagree over what constitutes targeting. The Tenth Circuit found that a gripe site about an investment bank in New Mexico created by a Florida resident showed evidence of targeting because the defendant: intended to damage the plaintiff's reputation via the gripe site, expressly aimed his site at the state of New Mexico, the site complained about a New Mexico resident and company; it complained about a deal gone sour in New Mexico; the site was available in New Mexico; and the defendant knew the brunt of the harm would be felt there.[23] These characteristics are common with all gripe sites. It may also have been a factor, however, that the defendant used the threat of posting the blog to try to exact a refund from the plaintiff. The name of the site was also "DavidSilverSantaFe.com."

Choice of law

Intuitively one would assume that the court that handles a case would apply its own law, but this is not always true. In conflicts law, *jurisdiction* and *choice of law* are two separate issues. It is standard practice for courts to apply their own procedural law to determine jurisdiction and how process will be served. But in cases involving litigants from different places, the forum court may decide that justice would be better served by applying another state or nation's substantive law to the matter at issue in the case. Criminal cases are an exception. The law of the forum always applies in criminal trials, for procedural and substantive decisions.

Until the mid-twentieth century, U.S. courts primarily based choice-of-law decisions on territorial considerations. In tort cases, in which plaintiffs claimed that a foreign defendant had injured them in some way (physically, emotionally, or financially), U.S. courts applied the substantive law of the place where the injury occurred (*lex loci delicti commissi*). In this respect, U.S. conflicts law was aligned with the practices of other common law and civil laws systems, which also favored lex loci.

But in the latter half of the twentieth century, a philosophical movement called legal realism took hold in the United States. Legal realists questioned the practice of applying other states' or nations' laws rather than applying the law of the forum, which would further its social policies. As an alternative to basing choice of law on the place of the wrong, they suggested basing choice of law on government interests, functional analysis, or the better law for the particular case. Their theories had the effect of promoting local law. Other areas of the world considered the approach more parochial than revolutionary. This period of change in the United States has come to be known as the "conflicts revolution."

Seeking a compromise between the two perspectives on choice of law, the American Law Institute published the Restatement (Second) of the Conflict of Laws, which applies the laws of the state with "the *most significant relationship* to the occurrence and the

---

[23] Silver v. Brown, 2010 WL 2354123 (10th Cir. 2010).

parties."[24] To determine which state has the most significant relationship, the forum court must consider a range of factors, including:

- the needs of the interstate or international system;
- policies of the forum and interested states;
- protection of the parties' expectations;
- general policies underlying the particular area of law;
- the need for certainty, predictability, and uniformity of result;
- ease in determining and applying the law;
- the place where the harm occurred and the conduct causing the injury;
- nationalities of the parties, their residence or place of incorporation; and
- where the relationship between the parties, if any, exists.[25]

The process of balancing these factors is often referred to as interest analysis. American courts like the approach because it gives them flexibility. Consequently, most jurisdictions in the United States have adopted it. But the sacrifice for flexibility has been the consistency and predictability that other nations prize.

Enforcement of judgments

In general, states are obligated to enforce one another's judgments, even if they would not be able to render the same judgment under their own laws. Article 4, Section 1 of the Constitution stipulates that states must give "full faith and credit" to the laws and proceedings of other states in the nation.

However, if the court asked to enforce the out-of-state judgment is not convinced that the original court had jurisdiction over the defendant when the judgment was rendered, it may refuse. The Supreme Court of Minnesota rejected an Alabama judgment based on lack of jurisdiction in *Griffis v. Luban* (2002). A University of Alabama professor of Egyptology brought a libel action against a Minnesota resident who disparaged her academic credentials on an Internet archaeology newsgroup. When the defendant did not answer the suit, the Alabama court entered a default judgment against her. The defendant fought the plaintiff's attempts to enforce the judgment up to Minnesota's Supreme Court. It concluded that Alabama's jurisdiction was not proper because the defendant had not "expressly aimed the allegedly tortious conduct" at Alabama and refused to enforce the judgment.[26]

Private International Law

Beyond U.S. borders, conflicts law is more commonly called *private international law*. The term private international law can be somewhat misleading because it suggests there

---

[24] Restatement (Second) of Conflict of Laws § 145 (1971).

[25] *Id.* at §§ 6, 145.

[26] Griffis v. Luban, 646 N.W.2d 527, 535 (Minn. 2002).

is an international body of law that applies to transborder conflicts when, in fact, there is not. The word *private* characterizes the type of litigants involved in civil cases – individuals, corporations, or organizations, while the word *international* reflects the fact that they come from different countries. Private international law is, in fact, a domestic branch of law. Each country (or state, in the case of federations like the United States) establishes its own conflicts rules. There are, however, many similarities among the approaches taken by sovereign nations that share common legal systems.

International law, the body of law governing the legal relationships between nations rather than individuals, is distinguished from private international law by most countries as *public international law*. Public international law includes treaties, decisions of the International Court of Justice, United Nations resolutions, and criminal law.

International jurisdiction takes three forms: (a) jurisdiction to adjudicate, (b) jurisdiction to prescribe, and (c) jurisdiction to enforce. These legal terms correspond to personal jurisdiction, choice of law, and enforcement of foreign judgments in the United States.[27]

Jurisdiction to adjudicate

Jurisdiction to adjudicate, also called adjudicative or judicial jurisdiction, refers to a nation's authority to subject persons or things to the process of its courts or administrative tribunals.[28] Before a court may adjudicate a case, it must have jurisdiction over the parties and the subject matter involved. Although nations address due process concerns differently, most follow procedural standards to ensure that jurisdiction is reasonable, based on factors such as whether:

- there is a link between one of the parties and the state;
- the party has consented to exercise of jurisdiction;
- the party regularly does business in the state; or
- the party engaged in an activity outside the state that had a substantial and foreseeable effect within the state.[29]

Transnational conflicts involving the Internet are often based on the last factor.

Foreseeable effects

The international approach to personal jurisdiction based on the effects of Internet content differs from that of the United States with respect to what is required to satisfy due process concerns. Before asserting jurisdiction over a foreign defendant, a U.S. court would have to be satisfied that the defendant had established a connection to the forum.

---

[27]Restatement (Third) of the Foreign Relations Law of the United States § 401 cmt. a (1987).
[28]*Id.* at § 401(b).
[29]*Id.* at § 421(2).

If the defendant's contacts were not continuous and systematic, but rather minimal in scope, he or she must have targeted the forum or at least personally availed of its benefits before jurisdiction would be considered reasonable. In contrast, most nations do not demand a specific connection between the defendant and the forum to satisfy due process. It is sufficient that the defendant could have reasonably foreseen that his actions would cause harm in the forum and that his actions did, in fact, cause harm there.[30]

The legacy of foreseeable effects

Internationally, the most significant transnational case to consider jurisdiction based on the foreseeable effects of Internet material is *Dow Jones v. Gutnick* (2001).[31] As the first of such cases to reach a nation's highest court, it has been widely cited by other courts around the world. The case involved a libel suit filed by Joseph Gutnick, an Australian entrepreneur, against Dow Jones, the U.S. publisher of *Barron's* magazine, in response to a *Barron's* article that implied he was involved in money laundering. Although the article was published in New Jersey, it could be accessed via an online subscription in Victoria, Australia, where Gutnick resided and filed the suit.

Dow Jones filed a motion for forum non conveniens, arguing that Victoria was an inconvenient forum because its editorial offices and servers were located in the United States, along with 95 percent of its subscribers. But the company conceded that it had 1,700 subscribers in Australia and that several hundred of them resided in Victoria. The trial court concluded that Victoria was the more appropriate forum for the suit because any harm to Gutnick's reputation was likely to have occurred there.

Dow Jones appealed to Australia's High Court, which upheld the lower court's decision. In its appeal, Dow Jones argued that the action should be litigated in New Jersey, where the article was published. But the High Court distinguished between publication as an *act* and publication as a *fact*. While acknowledging that the article was uploaded to a server in New Jersey, the court contended that publication actually takes place when the material is downloaded. It reasoned that "[h]arm to reputation is done when a defamatory publication is comprehended by the reader, the listener, or the observer . . . This being so it would be wrong to treat publication as if it were a unilateral act on the part of the publisher alone."[32]

In fact, the court explained, it is "the bilateral nature of publication [that] underpins the long-established common law rule that every communication of defamatory matter founds a separate cause of action."[33] Australia, like many other countries around the world, allows plaintiffs to sue for multiple causes of action, meaning they can file suit

[30] Ronald Brand, *Community Competence for Matters of Judicial Cooperation at The Hague Conference on Private International Law: A View From the United States*, 21 J. L. & COM. 191, 199–205 (2002).

[31] Dow Jones & Co., Inc. v. Gutnick, [2002] HCA 56 ¶ 9 (Austl.) at http://www.austlii.edu.au/ (enter Dow Jones v. Gutnick in search operator; then follow hyperlink for "Dow Jones & Company Inc v. Gutnick, [2002] HCA 56").

[32] *Id.* at ¶ 26.

[33] *Id.* at ¶ 27.

in every jurisdiction in which they experience injury. For example, a plaintiff libeled in a book published in Australia and Canada could sue the defendant in both places.

Dow Jones contended that the court's theory that publication takes place at the point of reception, combined with its policy of allowing multiple causes of action, would expose a publisher to litigation wherever the material is accessible. However, the High Court considered this unlikely. It reasoned that plaintiffs would only be likely to sue in places where they had a reputation to protect and a judgment would be of value to them, and that a judgment's value would depend on whether the defendant had assets there. Nevertheless, the court clearly considered it "foreseeable" to defendants who publish on the Internet that harm could occur anywhere. It said "However broad may be the reach of any particular means of communication, those who post information on the World Wide Web do so knowing that the information they make available is available to all and sundry without any geographic restriction."[34]

The Supreme Court of Judicature in the UK cited this passage from *Gutnick* when it upheld a lower court's assertion of jurisdiction over an Internet libel case in which both the plaintiff and defendants were U.S. residents and the websites carrying the disputed material were based in California. This practice of filing libel suits in countries that are especially plaintiff friendly is known as "*libel tourism*." American boxing promoter Don King filed suit against boxer Lennox Lewis (who is an English citizen, but a resident of New York), his promoter, and his attorney, in the UK where libel laws are much more favorable to plaintiffs than those in the United States. When the suit was filed, all parties resided in the United States and were involved in a separate suit that had generated heated public comments. By the time it reached trial, the defendants in *Lewis and others v. King* had dwindled down to one, Lewis's attorney, Judd Burstein, who had described King as anti-Semitic in interviews published on two California websites for boxing enthusiasts. The case seemingly had no connection to the UK other than the fact that the websites were accessible there. But the UK court that claimed jurisdiction observed that King was well known in the UK (and therefore considered to have had a reputation there to protect). King also provided evidence that UK boxing fans had read the websites and were aware of the accusation. The justices dismissed Burstein's argument that the appropriate forum should be the one targeted by the publisher. The court said "it makes little sense to distinguish between one jurisdiction and another in order to decide which the defendant has 'targeted,' when in truth he has 'targeted' every jurisdiction where his text may be downloaded."[35]

The English House of Lords affirmed a lower court's decision to allow two Russian citizens to sue *Forbes* magazine in the United Kingdom in *Berezovsky v. Michaels* (2000).[36] The plaintiffs sued the magazine after it published an exposé, in print and on its website,

[34] Lewis and others v. King, [2004] EWCA Civ. 1329, ¶ 29 (Eng.) (quoting Dow Jones & Co. Inc. v. Gutnick, [2002] HCA 56 ¶ 39).

[35] *Id.* at ¶ 34.

[36] Berezovsky v. Michaels, [2001] EWCA Civ. 409; Berezovsky v. Michaels, [2000] 2 All ER 986 (affirming Berezovsky v. Michaels, [1999] EMLR 278 (Eng.) at http://www.publications.parliament.uk/pa/ld199900/ldjudgmt/jd000511/bere-1.htm.

Figure 5.2   Illustration: Kalan Lyra

suggesting that they were involved in organized crime. The article, titled "Godfather of the Kremlin?" described the plaintiffs as "criminals on an outrageous scale" and suggested Berezovsky was involved in the murder of a Russian television personality. The article was based on police reports and interviews with dozens of witness, but Berezovsky was never charged with the crime. *Forbes* motioned for forum non conveniens, arguing that the case would be better tried in the United States, where the magazine is published, or in Russia, where the plaintiffs resided. But the court refused. The plaintiffs engaged in business in London, so the court considered the UK an appropriate forum for the suit despite *Forbes'* limited circulation there. Forbes was forced to issue an apology and a retraction. Four years later the *Forbes* reporter who wrote the article was murdered in Russia.[37] The case remains unsolved.

Canada also bases jurisdiction on foreseeability. In *Burke v. NYP Holdings, Inc.* (2005), a British Columbia court asserted jurisdiction over the *New York Post* in an Internet defamation case.[38] The plaintiff, Vancouver Canucks' ex-manager Brian Burke, sued the newspaper for publishing a column that suggested he had challenged his players to harm a member of an opposing team in a hockey game. The *Post* did not deliver the paper to British Columbia, but the column was accessible there via the Web. The newspaper could not tell how many people had accessed the site in British Columbia, but it was clear that at least one person had. A Canadian radio host read the article on his show. The court asserted that the defendant should have reasonably foreseen that the article would be republished in Canada.

[37] Michael Freedman, *Dark Force*, Forbes.com, May 21, 2007, http://www.forbes.com/business/forbes/2007/0521/130.html.
[38] Burke v. NYP Holdings, Inc., 2005 BCSC 1287 (Can.).

But foreseeability has its limits. The Ontario Court of Appeals reversed a lower court's decision to claim jurisdiction over *The Washington Post* in a libel suit based on articles it had published about the plaintiff while he lived in Africa.[39] Cheickh Bangoura worked for the United Nations as a regional director for its U.N. Drug Control Program. While he was working in Kenya, *The Washington Post* reported that his colleagues had accused him of "sexual harassment, financial improprieties and nepotism."[40] Bangoura subsequently lost his job and moved to Montreal, then three years later to Ontario, where he filed the suit after three more years. The articles were accessible in Ontario through the newspaper's Internet archive, but only one person had accessed them – Bangoura's attorney. The court said *The Washington Post* could not have foreseen that Bangoura would move to Canada. "To hold otherwise would mean that a defendant could be sued almost anywhere in the world based upon where a plaintiff may decide to establish his or her residence long after the publication of the defamation."

The basic principle of assuming jurisdiction where the harm occurs applies to all media, including broadcast. In *Jenner v. Sun Oil Company Limited et al.*, an Ontario court claimed jurisdiction over two U.S. broadcasters and a New York radio station because their New York broadcast about the plaintiff could be heard in Ontario.[41]

Jurisdiction to prescribe

Jurisdiction to prescribe, also called prescriptive or legislative jurisdiction, is the international analog to choice of law. It refers to a nation's authority to apply its law to particular individuals and circumstances.[42] A nation or state may apply its laws to a conflict or controversy as long as there is a sufficient nexus between it and the conduct at issue to justify state action.[43] Prescriptive jurisdiction may be based on four principles: territory, nationality, effects, and protection. A state may prescribe its laws to:

1. (a) conduct that, wholly or in substantial part, takes place within its territory;
   (b) the status of persons, or interests in things, present within its territory;
   (c) conduct outside its territory that has or is intended to have substantial effect within its territory;
2. the activities, interests, status, or relations of its nationals outside as well as within its territory; and
3. certain conduct outside its territory by persons not its nationals that is directed against the security of the state or against a limited class of other state interests.[44]

---

[39] Bangoura v. Washington Post, [2005] O.J. No. 3849 (Can).

[40] *Id.* at ¶ 5 and for next quote ¶ 25.

[41] Jenner v. Sun Oil Co. Ltd. et al., [1952] O.R. 240 (Ont. H.C.) (Can.).

[42] RESTATEMENT (THIRD) OF THE FOREIGN RELATIONS LAW OF THE UNITED STATES § 401(a) (1987).

[43] David J. Gerber, *Symposium: Prescriptive Authority: Global Markets as a Challenge to National Regulatory Systems*, 26 HOUS. J. INT'L L. 287, 290 (2004).

[44] RESTATEMENT (THIRD) OF THE FOREIGN RELATIONS LAW OF THE UNITED STATES § 402 (1987).

There is one other principle upon which prescriptive jurisdiction may be based – universality.[45] States may prescribe punishment for certain offenses that are recognized among nations as of universal concern, even when none of the other bases for jurisdiction indicated is present. These include piracy, slave trade, attacks on or hijacking of aircraft, genocide, war crimes, and certain acts of terrorism.

Comity

A nation or state exercising prescriptive jurisdiction is obligated to consider the interests of other states that might have a connection to the controversy. This practice is known as *comity*. "The doctrine of comity asserts that the courts of each country should exercise their judicial powers in a manner that takes into consideration the aims and interests of other states in order to further cooperation, reciprocity and international courtesy."[46] Most courts equate comity with reasonableness.[47]

Jurisdiction to enforce

Jurisdiction to enforce, also called executive jurisdiction, refers to a state's abilities to enforce judgments rendered against a defendant. Although a court that claims jurisdiction over a defendant may render a judgment against the party, the court is powerless to enforce the judgment outside of its own jurisdiction. Consequently, if the defendant has no assets in the jurisdiction and resides elsewhere, the plaintiff is forced to take the judgment to a court within the defendant's jurisdiction to request that it enforce the foreign judgment.

The doctrine of comity suggests that unless there is an overwhelming reason not to honor the foreign judgment, a court should do so. However, there are occasions when enforcing a foreign judgment may be seen as inappropriate. For example, a court may refuse to enforce a foreign judgment if it believes (1) the judicial system that rendered it does not provide impartial tribunals; (2) the judgment was obtained fraudulently; (3) a valid, earlier judgment is in effect that contradicts it; or (4) that the forum court exercised exorbitant jurisdiction by accepting a case when it had no real connection to the claim.[48]

---

[45] *Id.* at § 404.

[46] Ayelet Ben-Ezer and Ariel L. Bendor, *Conceptualizing Yahoo! v. L.C.R.A.: Private Law, Constitutional Review and International Conflict of Laws*, 25 CARDOZO L. REV. 2089, 2109 (2004).

[47] RESTATEMENT (THIRD) OF THE FOREIGN RELATIONS LAW OF THE UNITED STATES § 403 cmt. a (1987).

[48] *See* Uniform Foreign-Country Money Judgments Recognition Act § 4 (2005) (updating the Uniform Foreign Money Judgments Recognition Act of 1962, which codified prevalent common law rules regarding the recognition of money judgments).

The public policy exception and the SPEECH Act

Courts are also within their rights to refuse judgments that contradict their deeply rooted public policies. American courts have used the *public policy exception* to reject judgments that would undermine First Amendment protections.[49]

In 2010, Congress passed the Securing the Protection of our Enduring and Established Constitutional Heritage Act (better known as the SPEECH Act) to uphold U.S. policies of extending greater leeway for speech in defamation cases. The law was meant to discourage libel tourism, the practice of shopping for the friendliest forum in which to file a libel suit. Specifically, it prohibits a U.S. court from enforcing a foreign judgment for defamation unless the domestic court determines that (1) the judgment would satisfy First Amendment or state constitutional protections for expression and (2) that exercise of personal jurisdiction by the court that rendered the judgment comported with the due process requirements imposed on domestic courts. It was first used in *Pontigon v. Lord* (2011) to shield a Missouri woman from a Canadian libel judgment connected to a book she self-published on the Internet.[50]

The SPEECH Act was modeled after a New York law, inspired by the plight of New York author Rachel Ehrenfeld.[51] Dr. Ehrenfeld, a recognized authority on financing international terrorism, was sued for libel in the UK by Saudi banker Khalid bin Mahfouz after she accused him of funding Osama bin Laden in her book *Funding Evil: How Terrorism Is Financed and How to Stop It*. Only 23 copies of the book found their way to the UK – all through Internet orders. Nevertheless a UK court issued a default judgment against her for £225,000 and demanded that she destroy all remaining copies of her book. Ehrenfeld countersued Mahfouz in New York, requesting a *declaratory judgment* that the UK judgment violated her rights under the First Amendment. However, she wasn't able to get it because the American court decided it had no jurisdiction over Mahfouz. The New York Assembly responded to the case by passing the Libel Terrorism Protection Act in 2008, also known as "Rachel's Law."

Several states, including New York, Illinois and Florida, now require their courts to refuse to enforce libel judgments against their residents if the judgments were rendered by foreign courts that lack the same speech protections guaranteed by the U.S. Constitution and their state constitutions.

However, these laws only apply to cases that concern libel. The now famous case *Yahoo! Inc. v. La Ligue Contre Le Racisme et L'Antisemitisme* would not have been affected by the SPEECH Act.[52] In that case, Yahoo! sought confirmation that an American court's

> Courts issue *declaratory judgments* to clarify the rights and obligations of parties in cases that present an actual controversy. The court's declaration then carries the effect of a final judgment.

---

[49] *See, e.g.*, Telnikoff v. Matusevitch, 347 M.D. 561, 702 A.2d 230 (Md. 1997) (in which the Maryland Court of Appeals determined that enforcing a foreign libel judgment that lacked the same speech protections the U.S. gives plaintiffs in libel cases would effectively chill protected speech) *aff'd* Matusevitch v. Telnikoff, 877 F. Supp. 1 (D.D.C. 1995).

[50] Pontigon v. Lord, 340 SW 3d 315 (Mo. Ct. App. 2011).

[51] Libel Terrorism Protection Act, ch. 66, § 3, 2008 N.Y. Laws 66 (codified as amended at N.Y. C.P.L.R. 302(d) (McKinney Supp. 2009)).

[52] 433 F.3d 1199 (9th Cir. 2006) (en banc), cert denied, 126 S.Ct. 2332, 164 L. Ed. 2d 841 (2006).

enforcement of a French judgment against it would violate the First Amendment.[53] A French court ordered Yahoo! to block French citizens' access to its auction site, which displayed Nazi memorabilia for sale, because the sale or display of racist material in France is a crime.[54] Failure to block the site would result in fines amounting to approximately $14,000 a day. A California federal district court held that enforcement of the order would violate Yahoo!'s First Amendment rights because the display of Nazi paraphernalia is legal in the United States. However, the Ninth Circuit reversed. The court of appeals did not disagree with the district court on the First Amendment issue, but concluded that the case was not ripe for adjudication because the French plaintiffs had not yet moved to enforce the judgment in the United States.[55] U.S. courts prefer to wait until a controversy is "ripe" before adjudicating the matter, not only to conserve judicial resources, but also to avoid setting a bad precedent in a situation that is too abstract.

Criminal judgments

Comity does not extend to the enforcement of foreign criminal judgments. However, to assist a foreign court that has rendered a penal judgment against a defendant, another country may agree to cooperate in extradition proceedings, by surrendering the defendant to the state with jurisdiction.

Alternatively, the court that rendered the judgment will have to wait to enforce it until the defendant enters the country. This is what happened to Fredrick Tobin, an Australian citizen, prosecuted in absentia in Germany, for dissemination of hate speech. Tobin, who was born in Germany, operated a website in Australia that questioned Holocaust history. Although the documents were printed in English and posted on an Australian server, the court observed that the website was accessible in Germany where people might read the text and recirculate it. When Tobin visited Germany, he was arrested and jailed for seven months.[56] Germany is the first country to prosecute someone from another country for disseminating hate speech on the Internet.

An Italian Court convicted three Google executives in absentia (giving them six-month suspended sentences) for the company's action of hosting a video that showed four boys bullying another who was mentally disabled.[57] By the time Italian police brought the video to the company's attention, it had been viewed 12,000 times. Google

---

[53] Yahoo! Inc. v. La Ligue Contre Le Racisme et L'Antisemitisme, 145 F. Supp. 2d 1168 (N.D. Cal. 2001).

[54] Association Union des Etudiants Juifs de France v. Yahoo!, Inc, High Court of Paris, May 22, 2000, Interim Court Order No. 00/05308, 00/05309, translated at http://www.juriscom.net/txt/jurisfr/cti/yauctions 20000522.htm.

[55] Yahoo! Inc. v. La Ligue Contre le Racisme et L'Antisemitisme, 433 F.3d 1199, 1205 (9th Cir. 2006) (en banc).

[56] BGHZ 46, 212 (Case Az.: 1 StR 184/00) decided on Dec.12, 2000.

[57] *Google bosses convicted in Italy*, BBC News, Feb. 24, 2010, http://news.bbc.co.uk/2/hi/8533695.stm.

not only removed it but also helped the police locate the person who posted it. Nevertheless, the Google executives were charged and convicted of failing to protect the privacy of the bullied teen. Prosecutors argued that Google should have had consent from all parties in the video before it was allowed to go online.

In contrast, a French court acquitted a New York University professor tried in Paris for criminal defamation over a book review he published on a U.S. website. As editor of the European Journal of International Law and its associated book review website, Joseph Weiler commissioned a book review of a legal treatise on the International Criminal Court written by an Israeli academic. The reviewer, a German professor, criticized the author's coverage of the subject. The author demanded that Weiler remove the review, and when he refused to do so, offering instead to post her response alongside it, she filed a criminal complaint against him in a Paris court. Although the author lived and worked is Israel, she held dual citizenship in France. Aside from her dual nationality, there was no other apparent connection to France. The defendant lived in New York, the review was published on an American website, the reviewer was German, the book's publisher was Dutch, and both the review and the book were written in English.

Professor Weiler might have ignored the trial, having no assets in France to lose, but that would have led to a default judgment against him and complications when he tried to visit the country. The SPEECH Act would not have helped him. While it prevents U.S. courts from enforcing foreign judgments that appear unconstitutional, it can do nothing to expunge criminal convictions in other countries. Weiler went to France to defend himself and won. The French court found its jurisdiction to be improper because there was no evidence that the review had been accessed in France. It also found the claim to be an abuse of process because the complaint was an example of forum shopping and the tone of the review "merely expresse[d], in terms which are in fact restrained, a scientific opinion of a work."[58]

However, this is another case in which procedural law made all the difference. France takes defamation very seriously, viewing it as a form of assault. Referral to a court for a criminal libel complaint is granted automatically. There was no prior review by a prosecutor or preliminary hearing to ensure that the evidence was sufficient for a trial. Moreover, the state rather than the complainant absorbs the costs of litigation because it is a criminal matter. The impact of this procedure is mitigated, in part, by the different role the prosecutor plays in French trials. France uses an inquisitorial system in which the role of prosecutor or investigating magistrate is to get to the truth by questioning all parties during the trial, and then to make recommendations to the court. In contrast, the U.S. uses an adversarial system in which the prosecutor's role is to fight for conviction on behalf of the state. In inquisitorial systems, judges also have the opportunity to interview the parties.

---

[58]Public Prosecutor v. Weiler, Case No. 0718523043, Tribunal de Grand Instance de Paris, March 3, 2011, An unofficial English translation of the court's opinion can be found at http://www.ejiltalk.org/in-the-dock-in-paris-%E2%80%93-the-judgment-by-joseph-weiler-2/.

Choice of Forum/Choice of Law Agreements

It has become common among companies engaged in business to include clauses within their contracts specifying the jurisdiction and law that would apply should a legal dispute occur. Usually the two clauses are side by side. If the parties to a contract have not made a specific choice regarding the law to be applied in the event of a legal clash, the court will infer a choice based on the law of the place with the closest connection to the contract. This is usually either where the contract was signed or executed.

Most Internet users are parties to *choice of forum* and *choice of court* agreements whether they realize it or not. These clauses are buried in the terms of use agreements that users must accept by clicking "OK" or "I accept" before registering to use a commercial site like Facebook or eBay. For example, eBay's terms of service include the following language:

> This Agreement shall be governed in all respects by the laws of the State of California as they apply to agreements entered into and to be performed entirely within California between California residents, without regard to conflict of law provisions. . . . You agree to submit to the personal jurisdiction of the courts located within Santa Clara County, California for the purpose of litigating all such claims or disputes.

American courts enforce these contracts, regardless of whether the party who clicked assent to the terms actually read them first. They are not, however, enforceable in all countries.

European Union Directives

The European Union will not enforce choice of forum clauses. Its refusal to do so is intended to protect online consumers, so they can litigate conflicts at home rather than traveling to a retailer's jurisdiction. The policy is balanced, however, by the EU's *E-Commerce Directive*, which dictates that choice of law in e-commerce cases is that of the country of origination rather than the country of reception.[59] So while an EU plaintiff from France might be able to sue an online retailer from Germany in France, German law would apply. The directive only applies to commercial messages. It is not applicable to personal torts like defamation or invasion of privacy. The directive also preferences EU states. If a defendant like Yahoo! operates a website outside the EU, choice of law reverts back to the member state. Consequently, a French plaintiff could sue in France under French law.

The European Union's *Audiovisual Media Services Directive*, which applies to video on demand, mobile TV, and audiovisual services on digital TV, assigns jurisdiction in cases

---

[59] Directive 2000/31/EC of the European Parliament and of the Council of 8 June 2000 on certain legal aspects of information society services, in particular electronic commerce, in the Internal Market, O.J. L 178/4, 17/07/2000 p. 0001–0016, http://eurlex.europa.eu/LexUriServ/site/en/oj/2000/l_178/l_17820000717en0001 0016.pdf.

involving programming to the country of origin. The directive applies only to commercial "television-like" mass media services. Its application to the Internet is limited. It is not intended to apply to text-based online communications or audio programming, but it does apply to video programs that are streamed, webcast, or downloaded from the Internet. The policy does not mention privacy or defamation explicitly for jurisdictional purposes, but it includes a provision for a right of reply in cases in which someone's reputation is harmed by a television program that uses incorrect information.[60]

Treaties on Jurisdiction and Choice of Law

Various courts have suggested that the conflict of laws problem is intransigent and that the only real solution will have to come through diplomatic negotiations at the international level. The Hague Conference on Private International Law took up the challenge of developing an international treaty on recognition of jurisdiction and foreign judgments in the late 1990s but did not succeed.[61] The treaty finally negotiated was a dramatically scaled-down version of the original goal that addressed business-to-business choice of court agreements.

In contrast, the European Union has successfully negotiated treaties on jurisdiction and choice of law with its member states. The EU's treaty governing jurisdiction is called the Brussels Regulation.[62] In general, it establishes jurisdiction in the state where the defendant resides. But in cases involving torts like defamation or invasion of privacy, it assigns jurisdiction to the place where the harmful event occurred or may occur. In the case of multi-jurisdictional publication, this could mean anywhere the plaintiff feels he or she has a reputation worth protecting and the material was accessed.

The world's largest treaty on choice of law agreements is the European Union's Rome Convention.[63] The treaty, signed in Rome in 1980, indicates that choice of law in cases arising from contract disputes will be the law of the state specified in the terms of the contract. In 2007, members of the European Union also finalized a treaty on choice of law in noncontractual obligations – including torts – called Rome II. Although member nations seemed to be in agreement on jurisdiction, choice of law was another issue. Negotiating the treaty took four years and the members were never able to reach a consensus on the applicable law in defamation and privacy actions, particularly where the Internet is concerned.

---

[60] Directive of the European Parliament and of the Council Amending Council Directive on the coordination of certain provisions laid down by law, regulation or administrative action in Member States concerning the pursuit of television broadcasting activities, 89/552/EEC, COM (2007) 170; 2005/0260 (COD), Final (May 22, 2007).

[61] Hague Conference on Private International Law, Summary of the outcome of the discussion in Commission II of the first part of the diplomatic conference (June 2001), www.uspto.gov/go/dcom/olia/interimhague_508.pdf.

[62] Council Regulation (EC) No. 44/2001 on Jurisdiction and the Recognition and Enforcement of Judgments in Civil and Commercial Matters, O.J. L 12/1, Art. 5, 16 (Dec. 22, 2000).

[63] Convention on the Law Applicable to Contractual Obligations (June 19, 1980), O.J. L 266 (Sept. 10, 1980).

For updates, visit www.
digitalmedialaw.us. Click on "What's
New: Chapter 5.

"The problem is clear," said EU Vice President of Parliament Diana Wallis, "They don't want to be subject to each other's laws. The UK media will tell you that they don't want to be subject to French privacy laws. Look at it from the French side; they are scared silly about damage awards in the UK."[64]

Violations of privacy and rights relating to personality, including defamation, were excluded from the treaty that went into effect in 2009. But the issue has not gone away. Debates to revise the treaty to include privacy and libel have refaced, along with a recommendation from Parliament to create a center for the voluntary settlement of cross-border disputes through alternative dispute resolution.

Alternative Dispute Resolution

In the absence of a multinational agreement, parties in transborder conflicts may have to seek out their own diplomacy through private dispute resolution specialists. As an alternative to litigation through the traditional legal system, more digital content providers are turning to arbitration and mediation.

Arbitration is a dispute resolution process in which a legally trained, neutral third person or panel of experts hears a dispute between two or more parties in conflict and, after considering the evidence, renders a verdict based on law in favor of one party. In essence, the arbitrator takes the place of judge and jury. Arbitration offers the same range of legal remedies that courts offer, but opportunities for appeal are limited. If the parties opt for binding arbitration, the arbitrator's decision will be legally enforceable. If the disputing parties opt for nonbinding arbitration, they will still have the opportunity to pursue litigation following the arbitration if they are not satisfied with its outcome. Many of the click-through contracts that commercial websites employ now require consumers to submit to binding arbitration.

Mediation is an alternative dispute resolution process in which disputing parties volunteer to work together with a neutral mediator to find a mutually agreeable solution. The resulting solution is negotiated rather than imposed on the parties involved. It may be legally enforced if the parties agree to turn it into a binding settlement agreement.

Alternative dispute resolution has gained popularity because disputes are generally settled faster and less expensively than they would be in a traditional court system. Dispute resolution services are also available online, using web-based technology such as VoIP, e-mail, chat rooms, instant messaging, video conferencing, and wikis, which is much more convenient for people who cannot afford the cost of travel or the time that goes into traditional litigation.[65] In an international dispute, online dispute resolution also bypasses the issue of whether a particular court has jurisdiction over a dispute.

---

[64]Telephone interview with Diane Wallis, Vice President, European Union Parliament, June 21, 2007.
[65]Joseph W. Goodman, *The Pros and Cons of Online Dispute Resolution: An Assessment of Cyber-Mediation Websites*, 2003 DUKE L. & TECH. REV. 4, ¶ 18.

Geolocation Filtering: Code v. Law

Computer code is also used as an alternative to litigation with mixed results. Because publishers are not sure where they may be liable for the content they publish, some are experimenting with geolocation software that restricts access to readers from particular countries.

The New York Times, for example, prevented British readers from accessing an article it published about a foiled terrorism plot in London. In 2006, London police arrested more than 20 people for plotting to detonate explosives on trans-Atlantic flights between the UK and the United States. One week later, The New York Times published a front-page article titled "In Tapes, Receipts and a Diary, Details of the British Terror Case Emerge," which detailed all that had been learned since the arrest. The story posed no problems under U.S. laws. However, The New York Times editorial staff was concerned that it might violate the UK's Contempt of Court Act, which prohibits media organizations from publishing anything about a suspect arrested for a criminal act that might bias a jury pool. Editors who violate the Act risk jail. The UK has demonstrated its willingness to assert jurisdiction in other circumstances involving Internet material published in the United States. With this in mind, editors at the Times blocked English readers' access with the same software it uses to direct advertisements to readers in particular geographic locations.

The New York Times hasn't attempted to block a story since and doesn't have an official policy on it. "Whether we would do something similar again would depend on the circumstances," said George Freeman, vice president and assistant general counsel of The New York Times.[66] "The law is, from our perspective, very strict. There were some who argued that we ought to oppose it. But it is tough to fight a battle like that not on your home turf. It would also put us in the position of telling another country what's appropriate, and that's not a good position to be in."

Geolocation technology works by blocking Internet Protocol addresses – the unique numerical identifiers that allow computers to communicate with one another on the Internet.

When a computer user requests access to a file online, like a particular article in an online publication for example, the user's browser supplies the file server with an IP address that tells it where to send the information. A server programmed to consider the user's location before granting access to a file will forward the request to a geolocation service first to see if it should grant access to the information.

Other online content providers, like the popular photo-sharing site Flickr, also use geolocation filtering. Flickr blocks Internet users in Germany, Hong Kong, India, Korea, Romania and Singapore from accessing particular types of imagery to avoid litigation. The photo site, which carries millions of images that range from innocent to indecent, categorizes its content as safe, moderate, and restricted based on its suitability for varying types of audiences. The site's SafeSearch filter restricts access to safe images, unless web users register for a membership. Members who are 18 or older can adjust the filter for access to all content if they like, unless they reside in one of these six countries.

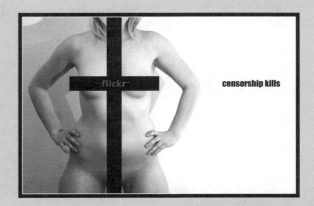

Figure 5.3 Flickr users in certain countries received filtered content to avoid violating local laws restricting indecency.
Source: Hannes Trapp, http://www.flickr.com/photos/ht82/564962375/

(Continued)

---

[66] E-mail from George Freeman, Asst. General Counsel, N.Y. TIMES (July 31, 2007) (on file with the author).

As geolocation technology becomes more prevalent, courts may be more likely to expect websites to use it. In *Yahoo! v. LICRA*, Yahoo! was ordered to block French users' access to its U.S. website with Nazi paraphernalia. In *Dow Jones v. Gutnick*, the publishing company's attorney threatened that if Australia claimed jurisdiction over American publishing companies, they might just find it cheaper to deny Australians access to U.S. content than contend with potential legal fees. To the attorney's surprise, one of the justices replied "It is inconceivable to me that that has not been done."[67]

Geolocation technology is not that precise though. Users with the incentive and know-how to get around geolocation filtering can, usually by using proxy sites that mask their IP addresses. Even if geolocation were completely accurate, it would still be time consuming and difficult to filter content for particular audiences. There are at least 190 libel laws to consider, apart from other national laws regarding trademark, copyright, obscenity, and privacy that vary by jurisdiction.[68] Realistically, it would be simpler to block everyone but domestic readers. Kurt Wimmer, senior vice president and general counsel for Gannett Co., says the company would be hesitant to use geolocation technology for editorial purposes. "The true value of the Internet as a means of fostering free expression beyond borders is the ability of people in potentially restrictive countries to have full access to information. Once we start erecting border-crossings on the Internet and block access for countries where content might be seen as inappropriate, we've lost that potential value."[69]

Questions for Discussion

1. What is due process? How does the American concept of due process lead it to treat jurisdiction differently than other parts of the world?
2. What is personal jurisdiction? How do the criteria for special and general jurisdiction differ?
3. How has the treatment of jurisdiction evolved due to the Internet?
4. Is geolocation filtering a suitable substitute for a treaty on conflict of laws?

[67] Dow Jones & Company, Inc. v. Gutnick M3/2002 (May 28, 2002) at 70, http://www.austlii.edu.au/au/other/hca/transcripts/2002/M3/2.html.

[68] Editorial, *A Blow to Online Freedom*, N.Y. TIMES, Dec. 11, 2002, at A34.

[69] E-mail from Kurt Wimmer, Senior Vice President and Counsel, Gannett Co. (July 24, 2007) (on file with the author).

6 Information Gathering

Digital media have expanded the concept of freedom of expression by making information and the means to share it more accessible. Easier access to information has not only benefited traditional media, but also precipitated new levels of civic engagement in the form of blogs, podcasts, webcasts and even social media. In fact, some blogs get more than 1 million visitors a month, attracting larger audiences than many traditional media sources.[1] Companies, professional associations, and special interest groups also supply news related to particular industries and causes through e-publications that serve a quasi-journalistic role. This democratization of information raises legal questions addressed in this chapter about the kind of information we're entitled to have, as well as the kind of information we're entitled to protect. It questions what it means to be a journalist and who should qualify for the privileges and protections traditionally extended to journalists regarding access to information and protection for their sources.

Access to Information

Access to information is a basic human right recognized by more than 80 countries in two international treaties – the American Convention on Human Rights (1978) and the International Covenant on Civil and Political Rights (1966). At least 80 nations, including the United States, have also enacted laws to protect the right to receive information.[2] Moreover, 53 have expressly guaranteed that right in their constitutions.[3] The U.S.

---

[1] eBizMBA, 30 Most Popular Blogs (August 2008) http://www.ebizmba.com/articles/popular-blogs.

[2] Roger Vleugels, *Overview of all FOIA*, 2010, http://right2info.org/resources/publications/Fringe%20Special%20-%20Overview%20FOIA%20-%20sep%2020%202010.pdf/view.

[3] Good Law & Practice, *Constitutional Protections of the Right to Information*, Right2Info.org, http://right2info.org/constitutional-protections-of-the-right-to.

Digital Media Law, Second Edition. Ashley Packard.
© 2013 John Wiley & Sons, Inc. Published 2013 by John Wiley & Sons, Inc.

Supreme Court has also stated that the "right to receive information and ideas" is encompassed in the First Amendment.[4]

At the most basic level, access to information is necessary for self-preservation. Harvard economist and Nobel Prize winner Amartya Sen has observed, for example, that there has never been a famine in a country with a free press.[5] Information is also the means by which people govern themselves in a democracy. Digital media have not only armed people with information, according to researcher Christopher Kedzie, they have been instrumental in the spread of democracy. Kedzie found that computer network connectivity proved to be the "single predictor, dominant over economic development, schooling, ethnic homogeneity, life expectancy and population size" in the spread of democracy.[6]

The Freedom of Information Act

In the United States, the Freedom of Information Act facilitates access to government information.[7] Congress passed the law in 1966 to open records in the executive branch to public inspection. Although it does not extend to the legislative or judicial branches, its reach is significant. It provides access to every federal department, military branch, independent regulatory agency, government-controlled corporation, and the Executive Office of the President.[8] Together, 90 agencies fall within its purview.

An agency is any executive department, military department, government controlled corporation, or other establishment in the executive branch (including the Executive Office of the President), or any independent regulatory agency.

The FOIA does not require agencies to answer specific questions or to create documents. It requires them to produce records they already have in their possession. These include rules, opinions, orders, files, and proceedings they have created or control that exist in any format – as paper, photographs, film, digital bits, or even three-dimensional objects. In contrast, personal notes, papers, and calendars are not public documents.

To distinguish between public and personal records for purposes of the Act, the U.S. Court of Appeals for the District of Columbia developed a four-part test. A court will consider:

1. the intent of the document's creator to retain or relinquish control over the records;
2. the ability of the agency to use and dispose of the record as it sees fit;
3. the extent to which agency personnel have read or relied upon the document; and
4. the degree to which the document was integrated into the agency's record system or files.[9]

[4] Kleindienst v. Mandel, 408 U.S. 753, 762 (1972).
[5] ARTICLE 19, ACCESS TO INFORMATION: AN INSTRUMENTAL RIGHT FOR EMPOWERMENT 9 (2007, July), www.article19.org/pdfs/publications/ati-empowerment-right.pdf.
[6] Christopher Kedzie, The third waves, in B. Kahin and C. Nesson eds., BORDERS IN CYBERSPACE 115 (1997).
[7] 5 U.S.C. § 552 (2007).
[8] Id. at § 552(f)(1).
[9] Tax Analysts v. U.S. Dep't of Justice, 845 F.2d 1060, 1069 (D.C. Cir. 1988) aff'd 492 U.S. 136 (1989).

Requesting information

Anyone can request information from the government using the Freedom of Information Act. The requester's identity and purpose are irrelevant.[10] The Supreme Court has stated "when documents are within FOIA's disclosure provisions, citizens should not be required to explain why they seek the information. A person requesting the information needs no preconceived idea of the uses the data might serve. The information belongs to citizens to do with as they choose."[11]

The Justice Department maintains an FOIA site that provides contact information for all federal agencies at http://www.foia.gov/report-makerequest.html. All requests for information must be submitted in writing. The more detailed the request, the more likely the information officer will be able to fulfill it. But the request does not need to precisely name the document. A description that enables an agency employee familiar with the subject area of the request to locate the information with a reasonable amount of effort is sufficient.[12] Agencies are entitled to charge reasonable fees for search time and duplication costs, but favored requesters – from educational and noncommercial scientific institutions and representatives of the media – receive two hours of search time and their first 100 pages free.

The Act defines "a representative of the news media" as "any person or entity that gathers information of potential interest to a segment of the public, uses its editorial skills to turn the raw materials into a distinct work, and distributes that work to an audience."[13] It defines "news" as "information that is about current events or that would be of current interest to the public."[14] Nonexclusive examples of news media entities include "television or radio stations broadcasting to the public at large and publishers of periodicals (but only if such entities qualify as disseminators of 'news') who make their products available for purchase by or subscriptions by or free distribution to the general public."[15] The Act recognizes that news delivery has evolved and includes electronic media delivered via telecommunications services. It also recognizes that the definition of journalist has evolved and includes freelance journalists. But it doesn't leave the door wide open for anyone to claim to be a freelance journalist. It says a freelancer "shall be regarded as working for a news media entity if the journalist can demonstrate a solid basis for expecting publication through that entity, whether or not the journalist is actually employed by that entity."[16] It suggests that a publication contract or record of past publication could be used to establish that basis. It is not clear whether the expanded definition would include bloggers. However, those who plan to publish the information on their sites should request the exemption because agencies have the

The Freedom of Information Act opens records to citizens and noncitizens alike, as well as organizations.

The Reporters Committee for Freedom of the Press offers an FOIA letter generator for requests for information at http://www.rcfp.org/foi_letter/generate.php.

---

[10] Dep't of Defense v. Fed. Labor Relations Auth., 510 U.S. 487 (1994).

[11] Nat. Archives and Records Admin. v. Favish, 541 U.S. 157, 171–2 (2004) (citation omitted).

[12] Marks v. United States (Dep't of Justice), 578 F.2d 261 (9th Cir. 1978).

[13] 5 U.S.C. § 552(a)(4)(A)(ii) (2007).

[14] *Id.*

[15] *Id.*

[16] *Id.* at § 552(a)(6)(C)(iii).

discretion to waive fees entirely if the information sought is likely to "contribute significantly to public understanding of the operations or activities of the government and is not primarily in the commercial interest of the requester."[17]

An agency has 20 business days to fulfill the request. The clock starts ticking when the request is first received by the appropriate component of the agency (and no later than 10 days after the request is received by any component of the agency). If the agency must ask for clarification on some point regarding the request, for example its proposed fee assessment, the clock may stop while it is waiting for an answer.

Individuals who demonstrate a compelling need for rapid access to the information may request expedited processing. A compelling need includes imminent threat to life or safety or, in the case of media representatives, urgency to inform the public about an actual or alleged government activity.[18] The agency must provide notice of its determination regarding requests for expedited processing within 10 days.

If the agency fails to comply with the time limit on the request, and there are no unusual or exceptional circumstances to justify the delay, it may not assess search fees or in the case of a favored requester (e.g., a representative of the news media or someone from an educational institution) duplication fees. *Unusual circumstances* refer to delays caused when records are stored off-site, when the number of records that must be searched is voluminous, or the agency is required to consult with another agency that also may have an interest in the request. If the agency encounters any of the three unusual circumstances, it is obligated to contact the requester to inform him or her of the expected delay and to offer the requester an opportunity to limit the scope of the request so it can be processed in time or arrange an alternative time frame. A person's refusal to do either would be considered a factor in determining whether an *exceptional circumstance* existed. An exceptional circumstance does not, however, include "a delay that results from a predictable agency workload of requests . . . unless the agency demonstrates reasonable progress in reducing its backlog of pending requests."[19]

Electronic Freedom of Information Act

Congress amended the FOIA in 1996 to apply to electronic records. The Electronic Freedom of Information Act requires agencies to publish online indexes of the documents they possess. Many of these indexes include full-text documents for download. The amendment also required agencies to provide records in electronic form to requesters who prefer that format if the records are computerized. This makes it easier for media operations to do database comparisons that would be too expensive to manage with paper records. For example, the *St. Louis Post Dispatch* used electronic records to uncover voter fraud in East St. Louis, Illinois. By merging voter and death records, its reporters discovered that deceased residents of East St. Louis were still voting.[20]

---

[17] *Id.* at § 552(4)(iii).
[18] *Id.* § 552(a)(6)(E)(v).
[19] *Id.* § 552(a)(6)(C)(ii).
[20] George Landau, *Quantum leaps: Computer Journalism Takes Off*, 31 COLUM. JOURNALISM REV. 61 (1992).

FOIA Exemptions

Agencies have the discretion, although not the duty, to deny a request for information if it falls within the boundaries of nine exemptions provided by the Act.[21] These include:

1. **National security**

   Agencies may protect matters "specifically authorized under criteria established by an Executive order to be kept secret in the interest of national defense or foreign policy and . . . properly classified pursuant to such Executive order."

2. **Internal agency personnel rules and practices**

   In *Milner v. Department of Navy* (2011) the Supreme Court clarified that this exemption refers to "conditions of employment in federal agencies – such matters as hiring and firing, work rules and discipline, compensation and benefits."[22] It is not meant to be applied generally to materials that are "predominantly internal," but construed narrowly to focus on human resource matters.

3. **Information exempted from disclosure by other statutes**

   Agencies may shield information that is protected by other statutes. For example, Congress included an Exemption 3 provision in the Homeland Security Act that protects information about "critical infrastructure" given to the Department of Homeland Security by members of the private sector. This can be used to shield details about power plants, bridges, ports, or chemical plants. Intelligence agencies are usually protected by statutes such as the National Security Act, which exempts "the names, titles, salaries or number of persons employed by" the agency from FOIA disclosure.[23] Personal information accumulated for tax and census purposes is also protected from public disclosure.

4. **Trade secrets and commercial or financial information that is privileged or confidential**

   The only way to protect a trade secret is to keep it secret, so government agencies, like the Food and Drug Administration for example, are careful not to release secret processes and formulas that could give an unfair advantage to a business's competitors.

5. **Inter-agency or intra-agency memos or letters that would not be available by law to a party other than an agency in litigation with the agency**

   As explained by the Court of Appeals for the District of Columbia Circuit, the "exemption was intended to encourage the free exchange of ideas during the process of deliberation and policymaking; accordingly, it has been held to protect internal communications consisting of advice, recommendations, opinions, and other material reflecting deliberative or policy-making processes, but not purely factual or investigatory reports."[24] It is also used to protect the attorney–client privilege.

[21] Chrysler Corp. v. Brown, 441 U.S. 281, 293 (1979).
[22] Milner v. Dep't of Navy, 131 S. Ct. 1259, 1261 (2011).
[23] 50 U.S.C. § 402.
[24] Soucie v. David, 448 F.2d 1067, 1077 (D.C. Cir. 1971).

6. **Personnel and medical files or similar files that would involve an unwarranted invasion of privacy to individuals**

The exemption applies to individuals only. Corporations and business associations possess no protectable privacy interests.[25] Congress explained in the legislative history of the Act that the phrase "unwarranted invasion of personal privacy" demands a "balancing of interests between the protection of an individual's private affairs from unnecessary public scrutiny, and the preservation of the public's right to governmental information."[26] If an individual's privacy rights are implicated, the requester bears the burden of establishing that the disclosure would serve the public interest. Moreover, that should be the type of public interest for which the Act was created – "shedding light on an agency's performance of its statutory duties."[27]

7. **Investigatory records of law enforcement**

Agency protection is warranted if the information might be expected to interfere in law enforcement proceedings or provide information about law enforcement techniques that would enable someone to circumvent the law. Information is also protected if its release could endanger the life or safety of any individual, deprive a person of the right to a fair trial, disclose a confidential source, or violate someone's right of privacy.

8. **Reports prepared on behalf of agencies that regulate or supervise financial institutions**

The exemption is intended to promote the candor of bank officials regarding conditions that affect their institution's condition and lending policies. Financial institutions are given extra consideration because of their unique role in the economy, their vulnerability to rumors and speculation, and the government's obligation to protect the federal deposit insurance fund.[28]

9. **Geological and geophysical information**

Agencies protect information, such as geological maps concerning wells, which would lead to prospecting.

Redaction

Information covered by one of the exemptions may be deleted or blacked out through *redaction* so that the remaining parts of a record may be released to the requester. An agency may only withhold an entire record if its exempt and nonexempt parts are "'inextricably intertwined,' such that the excision of exempt information would impose significant costs on the agency and produce an edited document with little informational value."[29] When releasing documents that have been redacted, the agency should

---

[25] Fed. Communications Comm'n v. AT&T, 131 S. Ct. 1177 (2011)(holding that the FOIA's personal privacy exemption does not apply to corporations as legal persons).

[26] S. Rep. No. 813, 89th Cong., 1st Sess. 9 (1965).

[27] Dep't of Justice v. Reporters Committee for Freedom of the Press, 489 U.S. 749, 773 (1989).

[28] Roy A. Schotland, *Re-Examining the Freedom of Information Act's Exemption 8: Does It Give an Unduly "Full Service" Exemption for Bank Examination Reports and Related Materials*, 9 ADMIN. L.J. AM. U. 43 (1995).

[29] Mays v. Drug Enforcement Admin., 234 F.3d 1324, 1327 (D.C. Cir. 2000).

specify the amount of information that has been deleted and where, along with the exemption under which the deletion is made.

In some cases involving national security or privacy, agencies refuse to acknowledge whether or not the requested information exists. This is known as the *Glomar response*. The name comes from a case challenging the CIA's refusal to confirm or deny records in an FOIA request regarding its ties to Howard Hughes's experimental ship, the Glomar Explorer.[30] The ship was supposedly designed for undersea mining, but alleged to have been a CIA project to recover sunken Soviet submarines. Courts allow agencies to use the Glomar response in national security exemption cases.[31] The Justice Department also applies it in privacy exemption cases. Its policy is that the "'Glomar' response can be justified only when the confirmation or denial of the existence of responsive records would, in and of itself, reveal exempt information."[32]

FOIA appeals

An agency that denies a FOIA request must cite the appropriate exemption within 20 days and provide information regarding its procedure to appeal the decision. Requesters who appeal a decision and are denied at the administrative level may ask a federal court to review the decision – either in the federal district in which they reside or operate a place of business, in the federal district in which the records are located, or in the District of Columbia.

FOIA appeals are not easy to win. Technically, the agency bears the burden of proving that the documents should be withheld, but courts are under obligation to afford "substantial weight" to agency affidavits explaining their justification for withholding the information. Because plaintiffs have not seen the documents, it may be impossible to rebut the agency's argument. Courts have the authority to examine the documents in camera, meaning in the judge's chambers, to determine whether they were properly withheld, but they rarely do so.

However, if the court finds evidence that agency personnel arbitrarily or capriciously withheld documents from the requester, it will direct a special counsel to initiate an investigation to determine whether disciplinary action is warranted against the individual or individuals responsible for the decision. If disciplinary action is warranted, the special prosecutor will inform the head of the agency responsible for administering it. If the agency reverses its position after the suit commences, the court may assess the agency fees and court costs. If a court grants relief to a requester and the agency continues to withhold the information sought, the court may order agency personnel in contempt.

---

[30] Phillippi v. Central Intelligence Agency, 546 F.2d 1009, 1013 (D.C. Cir. 1976).

[31] People for Am. Way Found. v. Nat. Security Agency, 462 F. Supp. 2d 21(D.D.C. 2006) (finding the National Security Agency's refusal to confirm or deny the existence of national security documents sought by a non-profit organization proper because doing either would cause harm under the Freedom of Information exception.).

[32] Robert H. Moll, Department of Justice Memorandum, "Glomar" responses to Freedom of Information Act (FOIA) requests (Sept. 4, 1998), http://www.doi.gov/foia/glomar.htm.

Prying OPEN Government

Although the Supreme Court has clearly stated that the Freedom of Information Act establishes a "strong presumption in favor of disclosure" and that its dominant objective is "disclosure, not secrecy," federal agencies have not always been that forthcoming.[33] In fact, in 2010, the federal government spent $201 creating and securing old secrets for every tax dollar spent declassifying in 2010. Moreover, while the cost to maintain secrecy ($10.17 billion) increased 13 percent, agencies declassified only 1 percent more pages than were declassified in 2009.[34]

Following the terrorist attacks on Sept. 11, 2001, there appeared to be a presumption in favor of withholding information. In 2001, Attorney General John Ashcroft authorized federal agencies "to disclose information protected under the FOIA . . . only after full and deliberate consideration of the institutional, commercial, and personal privacy interests that could be implicated by disclosure of the information."[35] He promised that the Justice Department would defend decisions "to withhold records, in whole or in part . . . unless they lack[ed] a sound legal basis or present[ed] an unwarranted risk of adverse impact on the ability of other agencies to protect other important records."[36]

Congress addressed the problem in 2007 by passing the Open Government Act.[37] The amendment made federal agencies more accountable to FOIA requesters. It required agencies to assign tracking numbers to requests that take more than 10 days to process and establish a phone or Internet system requesters could use to check on the status of their requests. Agencies must provide a public liaison to assist in the resolution of disputes between the agency and the FOIA requester. The Act established an office in the National Archives and Records Administration to review agency compliance with FOIA policies and procedures, and to offer mediation services to resolve disputes between requesters and agencies as a nonexclusive alternative to litigation. Federal agencies were also required to submit annual reports to Congress detailing their FOIA activities. Nevertheless, processing of requests remained slow. Some agencies had FOIA requests pending that were more than a decade old.

The Open Government Initiative, set in motion by the Obama administration in 2009, pushed agencies further to be more transparent and collaborative. The White House directed agencies to update FOIA guidance and training materials, to develop uniform guidelines for handling sensitive but nonclassified information to reduce over-classification, to devote adequate resources to responding to FOIA requests promptly,

---

[33] See Department of State v. Ray, 502 U.S. 164 (1991); Department of Air Force v. Rose, 425 U.S. 352 (1976).

[34] Patrice McDermott, Amy Bennett and Abby Paulson, Secrecy Report 2011 OpenTheGovernment.Org 11 (2011), www.openthegovernment.org/sites/default/files/SRC_2011.pdf.

[35] U.S. Department of Justice Office of Information and Privacy FOIA Post, Memorandum from John Ashcroft, Attorney General, to Heads of All Federal Departments and Agencies ¶ 10 (Oct. 12, 2001).

[36] Id. at ¶ 11.

[37] Openness Promotes Effectiveness in our National (OPEN) Government Act, Pub L. No. 110–175, 121 Stat. 2524 (2007).

and to open websites outlining their own open government plans.[38] A National Declassification Center was also developed to streamline the declassification process for records of historical value.[39] As a result, backlogged FOIA requests dropped by 10 percent.

Public access to agency information improved. The Justice Department launched FOIA.gov, a website to provide FOIA information consolidated from top government agencies in one place. The Consumer Product Safety Commission finally agreed to share its consumer complaints database – dealing with product defects in baby cribs, drywall, etc. The Administration also developed Data.gov, a website to make government data sets available for everyone's use, and the IT Dashboard, a site that enables the public to track federal technology investment projects. On its first day up, the IT Dashboard showed that $27 billion of IT projects were over budget or behind schedule. Modifications or cancellations of those projects led to an estimated $3 billion savings.[40]

Government records are now consolidated on two websites, FOIA.gov and DATA.gov.

But there is still much improvement needed to change an ingrained culture. The 2011 Knight Open Government Survey found that two years after the president's executive order only half of federal agencies had responded with meaningful changes.[41] ProPublica also found that federal agencies were using 240 different laws in conjunction with exemption 3 to deny access to information.[42] Some of those laws, like protecting access to medical or tax records, were entirely reasonable. Others – like the one that withholds lists of watermelon growers under the Watermelon Research and Promotion Act – were obviously put in place by Congress in response to special interest groups.

Executive privilege

The FOIA applies to the Executive Office of the President, but not to the president or his immediate staff. The Conference Report for the 1974 FOIA Amendments indicates that "the President's immediate personal staff or units in the Executive Office whose sole function is to advise and assist the President" are not included within the term "agency" under the FOIA.[43] Offices of the Chief of Staff or the President's Counsel are considered to serve an advisory role.

The law is less clear concerning the White House's executive privilege to withhold documents or refuse to testify before a court or Congress. In 2007, Congress subpoenaed former White House Counsel Harriet Miers to testify about her role in the firing of nine

---

[38] White House Open Government Directive, Dec. 8, 2009, http://www.whitehouse.gov/open/documents/open-government-directive.

[39] Controlled Unclassified Information Office Notice 75 FR 68675; National Declassification Center, Vol. 75 FR 108 (2010).

[40] Vivek Kundra, *White House White Board: The IT Dashboard & the Value of Transparency*, Mar 16, 2011, http://youtu.be/I8sBAXile9c.

[41] NATIONAL SECURITY ARCHIVE, GLASS HALF FULL: 2011 KNIGHT OPEN GOVERNMENT SURVEY, 2011, http://www.gwu.edu/~nsarchiv/NSAEBB/NSAEBB338/index.htm.

[42] Jennifer LaFleur, Al Shaw, and Jeff Larson, *FOIA Eyes Only: How Buried Statutes Are Keeping Information Secret*, ProPublica, March 10, 2010, http://projects.propublica.org/foia-exemptions/.

[43] Kissinger v. Reporters Committee for Freedom of the Press, 445 U.S. 136, 156 (1980).

U.S. attorneys. The Senate Judiciary and House Judiciary Committees launched investigations into allegations that the decisions were politically motivated when it became clear that seven attorneys were fired on the same day. Ultimately, Attorney General Alberto Gonzales resigned over the affair. Congress also subpoenaed White House documents and e-mails related to the investigation. The Bush administration invoked executive privilege, submitting neither Miers nor the documents.

The law is gray in this area. There are precedents from earlier administrations in which presidential aides – from the Nixon, Carter, Reagan, and Clinton administrations – testified before Congress, some under threat of subpoena.[44] In 1974, the Supreme Court prohibited the Nixon administration from withholding the Watergate tapes from federal prosecutors. But the Court would not address the larger issue of whether presidents may refuse Congressional demands for testimony from White House staff. In 2008, the House of Representatives cited Miers and White House Chief of Staff Joshua Bolton for contempt of Congress.[45] It was the first time that a White House official had been cited for contempt. However the Justice Department refused to act on the contempt order because the White House refused to cooperate based on the Justice Department's ruling that executive privilege applied in the case. Having no other recourse, the House Judiciary Committee filed a civil lawsuit in federal court to compel Miers and Bolton to submit to its requests. The federal district court denied Miers' claim to absolute immunity from compelled compliance with the subpoena. It concluded that she must appear before the committee where she might invoke executive privilege to specific questions, which could be analyzed later.[46]

Presidential Records Act of 1978

Documents concerning particular presidential administrations can be accessed through the Presidential Records Act. The Act gives the United States ownership and control of presidential and vice presidential records and requires the president to take the necessary steps to assure "that the activities, deliberations, decisions, and policies that reflect the performance of his constitutional, statutory, or other official or ceremonial duties are adequately documented" and maintained as Presidential records.[47]

The Presidential Records Act applies to documentary materials created by the president and his immediate staff. The term documentary materials includes "books, correspondence, memorandums, documents, papers, pamphlets, works of art, models, pictures, photographs, plats, maps, films, and motion pictures, including, but not limited

---

[44] Louis Fisher, *Politics and Policy: Executive Privilege and the Bush Administration: Essay: Congressional Access to Information: Using Legislative Will and Leverage*, 52 DUKE L.J. 323 (2002).

[45] Paul Kane, *West Wing Aides Cited for Contempt; Refusal to Testify Prompts House Action*, WASHINGTON POST, Feb. 15, 2008, at A4.

[46] Committee on the Judiciary, U.S. House of Representatives v. Harriet Miers, Civil Action No. 08-0409 (JDB) 156 (D.D.C. 2008); 2008 U.S. Dist. LEXIS 58050.

[47] 44 U.S.C. § 2203(a) (2006).

to, audio, audiovisual, or other electronic or mechanical recordations" created in the course of activities that relate to the president's responsibilities.[48] The Act does not apply to personal records, such as notes or diaries that have nothing to do with presidential duties, or to information strictly related to the president's election campaign.

At the end of a president's term in office, the National Archivist assumes custody of the presidential records. The president may claim executive privilege to withhold the information, but his power to do so is not absolute. President Barack Obama passed a resolution on his first day in office giving the Attorney General and White House Counsel discretion to determine that invocation of executive privilege is not justified.[49] The order also revoked the right of former presidents to withhold their records. The president may dispose of records that have no more administrative, historical, informational, or evidentiary value after first consulting with the National Archivist.

The National Security Archive

The National Security Archive is an independent repository for documents obtained under the Freedom of Information Act. The archive, housed at George Washington University in Washington, D.C., has won access to thousands of classified documents containing intelligence from major national events ranging from the Cuban Missile Crisis in 1962 to the terrorist attacks of 2001.

It is accustomed to refusals and doggedly tracks the records of agencies that do not comply with the law. Each year it gives the Rosemary Award to the agency with the worst FOIA record. The award is named after President Nixon's secretary, Rosemary Woods, who testified to erasing 18.5 minutes of the White House tapes containing conversations about Watergate. The 2009 award went to the FBI for responding to no FOIA requests that year and the 2010 award went to the Federal Chief Information Officers Council for its failure to create an e-mail preservation system for the government.

The National Security Archive filed suit against the White House in 2007 when it learned that the White House was missing key e-mails from the Bush administration.[50] The loss of documents was first noticed on January 23, 2006, during a trial against Lewis "Scooter" Libby, the chief of staff for former Vice President Dick Cheney, for perjury and obstruction of justice. Prosecutors informed Libby's counsel that they were unable to find e-mails the defense requested. The White House later admitted that 5 million e-mails were missing and that it had been recycling e-mail storage tapes. Actually, the number was closer to 22 million, or at least that is what the White House said it had recovered in 2009 with the help of computer experts at a cost of more than $10 million. The first of the e-mails, now on file with the National Archive, will be available in 2014.

The National Security Archive collects and publishes declassified documents acquired through the Freedom of Information Act at http://www.gwu.edu/~nsarchiv/.

---

[48] *Id.* § 2201(1).

[49] Exec. Order No. 13489, Presidential Records, 74 Fed. Reg. 4667 (Jan. 21, 2009).

[50] A history of the missing e-mails and resulting litigation is documented on the National Security Archive site at http://www.gwu.edu/~nsarchiv/news/20080417/chron.htm (last visited Feb. 1, 2012).

State Freedom of Information Laws

All states have statutes giving the public access to state records. Ten states also include a right of access to government records in their constitutions.[51] Like the federal Freedom of Information Act, state public information acts apply to the executive branch of government. However, some states, like Texas for example, provide access to records from the legislative branch as well.

Public information acts vary from state to state in their comprehensiveness. More than half of the states list computer records in their definition of public documents or provide that a public record can be any recorded information, regardless of form. Some also specifically mention e-mail in their definitions. At least 22 states direct public bodies to make records available to the public in an electronic format or through a database if the record is already available in a digitized form.[52]

Links to all state public information laws, provided by the National Freedom of Information Coalition, can be found at http://www.nfoic.org/state-foi-laws.

In general, state public records are open to anyone who requests them. A few states have attempted to limit access to the citizens of their states. But federal courts have overturned those laws.[53] Pennsylvania, however, limits access to its records to residents of the United States, while Louisiana limits access to requesters who have reached the age of majority. It is not necessary to explain why the records are needed; the purpose of the request is irrelevant. However, some states do require requesters to provide identification.

Most states also provide civil penalties for public records officers who violate the law. Fines normally reach $1,000, or may include monetary damages to individuals who incurred a loss due to the inaccessibility of the records.

Access to Public Officials

Although individuals have every right to use their state open records acts to gather information from public officials, they do not have a right to interview them. Courts have distinguished between access to public records, events, and facilities and access to individuals for interviews. In general, journalists are not entitled to information that is not ordinarily available to the public. In a series of cases, courts have sided with government officials who issued "no comment" directives after being offended by press

---

[51] California, Florida, Louisiana, Michigan, Mississippi, Montana, New Hampshire, North Dakota, Ohio, and Rhode Island.

[52] Arkansas, California, Connecticut, District of Columbia, Florida, Georgia, Idaho, Indiana, Iowa, Mississippi, Montana, Nebraska, Nevada, New Jersey, North Carolina, Ohio, Rhode Island, Texas, Utah, Vermont, Virginia, and West Virginia.

[53] Lee v. Minor, 458 F.3d 194 (3rd Cir. 2006)(overturning Deleware's law limiting access to state records to its own citizens. The ruling also applies to Arkansas, New Jersey, Pennsylvania, and Virginia.).

coverage, concluding that journalists are not entitled to one-on-one interviews "not otherwise available to the public."[54]

In *Baltimore Sun Company v. Ehrlich* (2006), the U.S. Court of Appeals for the Fourth Circuit ruled that Maryland Governor Robert Ehrlich's decision to ban state executive branch employees from speaking to two *Baltimore Sun* reporters did not violate the journalists' First Amendment rights. The governor felt the journalists were biased against him. The *Sun* argued that the order was a form of retaliation against the paper for exercising its First Amendment rights and that it chilled the *Sun's* right to free expression. Since the reporters continued to write regularly, the court concluded that any chilling effect on report was *de minimis*. The court assumed that just as an elected official had the right to reward an exclusive interview to one reporter, the official could deny an interview to another. "Having access to relatively less information than other reporters on account of one's reporting is so commonplace that to allow the *Sun* to proceed on its retaliation claim addressing that condition would 'plant the seed of a constitutional case' in 'virtually every' interchange between public official and press."[55]

Access to Legislative Information

The Freedom of Information Act does not apply to the legislative branch, but it is possible to track federal legislative information through various digital sources. The primary access point for citizens who want to follow legislation is the Thomas database. The database includes the text of all bills currently under consideration in Congress and their status. The information includes sponsors, co-sponsors, short and official titles, floor and executive actions, legislative history, Congressional Record references, and committee and subcommittee referrals. The full text of bills going back to the 101st Congress is also available. The site also includes committee reports, treaties, information about activities taking place on the floor of Congress, and a daily digest from the Congressional Record.

The Government Printing Office also disseminates legislative information, along with information from the executive and judicial branches of government. Its website includes conference reports, congressional hearing transcripts, congressional bills, the Congressional Record, public and private laws, and the U.S. Code.

Legislative information is posted on the Thomas database at http://thomas.loc.gov/.

Access to Judicial Information

The Freedom of Information Act does not apply to the judicial branch of government either, but judicial information is accessible though a variety of sources. The U.S. Judiciary supplies case information in real time from the federal appellate, district, and

[54] *See* Raycom National, Inc. v. Campbell, 361 F. Supp. 2d 679 (N.D. Ohio 2004); Baltimore Sun Co. v. Ehrlich, 356 F. Supp. 2d 577 (D. Md. 2005); Snyder v. Ringgold, No. 97–1358 (4th Cir. 1998); Snyder v. Ringgold, 40 F. Supp.2d 714 (D. Md. 1999) (Snyder II).

[55] Baltimore Sun Co. v. Robert Erlich, Jr. 437 F.3d 410, 418 (4th Cir. 2005).

bankruptcy courts through the Public Access to Court Electronic Records (PACER) database. Through an Internet connection, anyone can access civil and bankruptcy case information, including the names of case litigants, judges, attorneys, and trustees; the nature of a suit or cause of action; a chronology of case events; a listing of daily cases; appellate court opinions; judgments; and copies of documents filed for certain cases. In addition, most federal courts post selected published and unpublished decisions and dockets on their websites.

The Judicial Conference of the United States, the principal policy-making body for the U.S. Federal Courts, adopted privacy policies to protect some personal information in court documents. Upon the request of the litigants, personal data identifiers, such as Social Security numbers, dates of birth, financial account numbers, and names of minor children, which might appear in civil or bankruptcy files, will be modified or partially redacted.

The Judicial Conference has not approved unfettered public remote electronic access to criminal case files. It has justified its decision by pointing out that routine access to criminal files would expose defendants' cooperation with law enforcement in some government cases, which might subject them or their families to greater risk of intimidation or harm. The judiciary was also concerned that electronic public access to criminal files might "inadvertently increase the risk of unauthorized public access to pre-indictment information, such as unexecuted arrest and search warrants," which might put law enforcement personnel in danger. The policy gives judges the discretion to disseminate criminal documents through PACER and court websites, but does not require them to do so. Many states, however, do provide websites that provide remote access for criminal history record checks.

Courtrooms are also open to the public. The Supreme Court held that the right to attend criminal trials was implicitly guaranteed by the First Amendment right to receive information and ideas in *Richmond Newspapers, Inc. v. Virginia* (1980).[56] This is true even when the defendant has waived his or her Sixth Amendment right to a public trial. Keeping the courtroom open helps to ensure that the judicial process is carried on fairly. That right can only be overcome if there is a compelling justification addressed through narrow tailoring. For example, a judge might consider closing a portion of the trial in which a minor recounted sexual abuse. Jury selection is also open to the public.[57]

In contrast, grand jury proceedings have historically been conducted in secret. The grand jury is the body that hears the prosecutor's evidence to determine whether an indictment is warranted. Since the evidence has not been tested at trial and the defendant is unable to defend himself at the time, the process is assumed to be prejudicial to a potential jury. Rules determining access to judicial proceedings involving minors depend on the jurisdiction. Minors have traditionally been afforded greater protection from public scrutiny under the theory that they should not be permanently stigmatized

Case and docket information from federal appellate, district and bankruptcy courts is available from the PACER database at http://www.pacer.gov.

---

[56] 448 U.S. 555, 557 (1980).

[57] Press Enterprise Co. v. Riverside County Superior Court, 468 U.S. 501 (1984); Presley v. Georgia, 130 S. Ct. 721 (2010).

for youthful indiscretions. However, as minors have been accused of more significant crimes, and even tried as adults, attitudes regarding access have changed.

Most civil trials are open to the public, based either on the theory that the same reasoning used in *Richmond Newspapers* regarding a right of access to judicial proceedings should apply in civil proceedings or on state common law, which has traditionally recognized a right of access. In general, courts also recognize a common law right of access to court records, pretrial motions, discovery documents once a trial has begun, and trial transcripts. In some cases, courts will make audiovisual records used as evidence available, but this right is not absolute.

Courts have had mixed reactions to observers' use of electronic devices in a courtroom to blog or tweet about trials as they happen. Participants in the trial, such as attorneys, witnesses and jurors are generally prohibited from doing so. Some judges are concerned that real-time posts from a trial could influence witnesses' testimony, prejudicing a defendant's right to a fair trial. Others have interpreted the rules of civil and criminal procedure to prohibit such activity. For example, a federal district court in Georgia interpreted Rule 53 of the Federal Rules of Criminal Procedure, which prohibits "the taking of photographs in the courtroom during judicial proceedings or the broadcasting of judicial proceedings" to bar tweeting.[58] Some judges are simply put off by the distracting clicking of keys. In contrast, there are also judges who feel that blogging and tweeting add to the trial's transparency. Rules vary by jurisdiction and by presiding judge. Normally they are found on courthouse websites.[59]

Protection of Information

In addition to the many publicly available sources of information, it is inevitable that those who report on issues of public concern – either through traditional or nontraditional media – will gain access to information that is proprietary, confidential, or illegally obtained. From a legal perspective, access to such information raises two questions: (1) whether the information can be reported and (2) whether the source of the information can be protected.

Reporting on illegally obtained information

The Supreme Court has determined that the First Amendment protects media disclosure of illegally intercepted information, as long as the information concerns an issue of public importance and the media do not participate in the illegal interception. The extent to which this protection applies to nontraditional media sources or the publication of classified documents is, however, still unclear.

---

[58] United States v. Shelnutt, 2009 U.S. Dist. LEXIS 101427 (M.D. Ga., Nov. 2, 2009).
[59] Citizen Media Law Project, Live Blogging and Tweeting from Court, http://www.citmedialaw.org/legal-guide/live-blogging-and-tweeting-from-court (last visited Feb. 1, 2012).

In *Bartnicki v. Vopper* (2001), the Supreme Court considered whether the broadcast of an illegally intercepted cellular telephone conversation violated federal and state wiretapping laws.[60] Gloria Bartnicki, the petitioner in the case, was the chief negotiator in a looming teacher strike in Pennsylvania, whose cell phone call to the president of the teacher's union was intercepted and later broadcast on a local radio station. Frederick Vopper, the respondent, was a radio commentator who received a tape of the conversation from a man who claimed to have found it in his mailbox. Vopper played the tape on the radio in conjunction with news coverage regarding the strike.

The Court acknowledged that the respondents in the case violated the Wiretapping and Electronic Surveillance statute, which not only prohibits the interception but also the disclosure of wire, electronic, and oral communications.[61] But under the circumstances, it decided that application of the statute violated the First Amendment. Three factors weighed in the decision: the respondents played no part in the illegal interception of the material; their access to it was lawfully obtained; and it concerned a matter of public interest.

The government, which stepped in to protect the statute from the constitutional challenge, raised two issues: that it served as a deterrent against illegal wiretapping and that it protected the privacy interests of others. The Court dismissed the deterrent argument since Vopper had nothing to do with the actual interception. But it took the privacy argument seriously. Writing for the Court, Justice Stevens noted that "some intrusions on privacy are more offensive than others, and that the disclosure of the contents of a private conversation can be an even greater intrusion on privacy than the interception itself."[62] Nevertheless, the Court chose to balance the interests of privacy and speech, and in this case found that "privacy concerns give way when balanced against the interest in publishing matters of public importance."[63]

Although *Bartnicki* was very important with respect to privacy, it did not relate to the more serious matter of national security. The legality of publishing classified government information remains unresolved. Under the Espionage Act of 1917 it is a crime not only to *take* information relating to the national defense, which the possessor has reason to believe could be used to harm the United States, but also to *receive* or *communicate* that information, knowing it was taken without authorization.[64] Technically, the statute could be used to punish the media for publishing sensitive information, but so far it has not been used to do so.

In the famous Pentagon Papers case, *New York Times Co. v. United States* (1971), the Supreme Court refused to enjoin *The New York Times* and *The Washington Post* from publishing information from stolen government documents because the government had not met the "heavy burden" necessary to justify prior restraint.[65] In coming to its decision, the Court focused on the character of the information and the risk of publication to national security. The documents, which described the secret history leading up

---

[60] 532 U.S. 514 (2001).
[61] 18 U.S.C. § 2511(1)(c) (2007).
[62] Bartnicki, 532 U.S. at 533.
[63] *Id.* at 534.
[64] 18 U.S.C. § 793(d)(e).
[65] 403 U.S. 713 (1971).

to the Vietnam War, contained sensitive information, but their publication did not seem likely to bring about irreparable national harm. It refused the government's request for an injunction. But the Court left open the question of whether, under other circumstances, a medium could be prosecuted for publishing classified documents.

Daniel Ellsberg, the analyst who gave the documents to *The New York Times* and 18 other papers, because he believed they demonstrated that President Johnson had misled Americans about the war, was prosecuted under the Espionage Act. But the trial never reached a conclusion. The judge dismissed the case for governmental misconduct when it came to light that White House aides had broken into Ellsberg's doctor's office in an attempt to steal his psychiatric records. The aides, who called themselves "the Plumbers", because they were tasked with fixing White House leaks, were also caught breaking into the Watergate hotel to bug the Democratic National Committee office, precipitating the Watergate scandal that led to President Nixon's resignation.

The Pentagon Papers leak was miniscule in comparison to the scope of WikiLeaks' publication of secret government files. The international whistle-blowing organization, which accepts documents from anonymous contributors and then posts them on its website, has been a particular challenge to the U.S. government. In 2010, the attorney general announced the organization was under criminal investigation for its part in releasing classified government documents on its website – a violation of the Espionage Act. Most of the documents were alleged to have come from a U.S. Army intelligence analyst in Iraq with top-secret security clearance. The leak included two videos of helicopter attacks in Iraq and Afghanistan that killed civilians; the Afghan War Diary, a compendium of 92,000 Army logs detailing military action in Afghanistan – 76,000 of which were published, and more than 250,000 diplomatic cables from the State Department.

Despite the exorbitant number of classified documents now available through its website, the government has not indicted WikiLeaks' leader Julian Assange or any other member of the group. Assange has made it difficult to do so. On at least two occasions, he shared the documents with *The New York Times*, *The Guardian* in the UK and *Der Spiegel* in Germany, aligning his organization with traditional news sources and effectively implicating them as well. This puts the government back in the uncomfortable position of deciding whether it could or *should* prosecute media for printing the truth.

New York Times journalist Eric Schmitt, who was sent to London to review the WikiLeaks documents Assange presented, said that *The New York Times* was very aware of the dangerous position it faced in printing the documents and approached them with caution. "We went to the government and told them what we had and what we intended to do with it," Schmitt said. Editors at the *Times* redacted the names of foreign sources to U.S. intelligence agencies who might be threatened by publication of the documents and then asked the government if they had missed anything else that was a threat to national security.[66] "We didn't give them any guarantees, but we gave them a chance to push back," Schmitt said. He believes that decision, along with the fact that publications outside the U.S. had access to the same sources, prevented the government from going after the *Times*.

---

[66]Eric Schmit, Reporter, N.Y. Times, Address at the Houston Bar Association Law & the Media Seminar (Jan. 28, 2012).

Assange took measures to protect himself as well. In addition to the files published on the WikiLeaks site in readable form, Assange has published a huge encrypted file labeled "Insurance" that has been downloaded more than 100,000 times. He has said, "All we have to do is release the password to that material and it is instantly available."[67] It is likely that the Justice Department has inferred from that statement that actions on its part may prompt the release of additional classified information.

Efforts to suppress an organization like WikiLeaks highlight a particular characteristic of the Internet that makes censorship ineffective. The phenomenon is known as the *Streisand Effect*. The term refers to the likelihood that efforts to censor information will draw greater attention to it. Coined by Mike Masnick, the CEO of TechDirt, the Streisand Effect alludes to a lawsuit Barbra Streisand launched against an amateur photographer who inadvertently posted a picture of her home on the Web. The defendant, Kenneth Adelman, photographed the California coastline from a helicopter for an environmental project to document coastal erosion. He took 12,000 aerial photos in all. When he put them on the Web, he was not aware that Streisand's house was visible in image 3,850. She sued for $10 million for violating a California "anti paparazzi" law and her privacy rights. The media attention from the case peaked the interest of Internet users who downloaded the image en masse.[68] A Los Angeles Superior Court Judge dismissed the suit because it restricted Adelman's speech rights on a matter of public concern. The image is still accessible and now labeled as the Streisand Estate.[69]

Figure 6.1

Source: copyright © 2002–2012 Kenneth & Gabrielle Adelman, California Coastal Records Project, www.californiacoastline.org

---

[67] Chris Vallance, *WikiLeaks Encryption Use Offers "Legal Challenge,"* BBC News, Aug. 10, 2010, http://www.bbc.co.uk/news/technology-11026659.

[68] Mike Masnick, *Photo of Streisand Home Becomes an Internet Hit,* Techdirt, June 24, 2003, http://www.techdirt.com/articles/20030624/1231228.shtml.

[69] California Coastal Records Project, Streisand Estate, Malibu (Sept. 23, 2002). http://www.californiacoastline.org/cgi-bin/image.cgi?image=3850&mode=sequential&flags=0.

Subpoenaing Evidence and eDiscovery

Information considered potentially useful in a criminal or civil case may be subpoenaed by law enforcement or demanded through discovery. Digital data is well suited to investigation because it is both searchable and hard to destroy. Common targets for subpoenas include electronic documents, e-mails, text messages, posts and photos on social networking sites, voicemail, audio, video, and even browsing histories.

Parties who are involved in litigation or expect to be involved in litigation have a legal obligation to preserve electronic data that may be relevant to the case.[70] Courts may sanction parties who fail to preserve evidence, even if that failure predates the official commencement of a case, if a legal proceeding was reasonably anticipated.

In criminal cases, government authorities may gather evidence from individuals under investigation or third parties, such as their Internet service providers. The Stored Communications Act allows authorities with a court order to access electronic files and messages that Internet service providers store for their subscribers. Courts vary widely in their interpretation of what the statute allows, however. As written, it requires authorities to get a *warrant* to access information that has been stored on the ISP's server for fewer than 180 days and a *subpoena* for anything stored longer than that. The Sixth Circuit has held that a warrant is always required.[71]

If the government investigation involves espionage or potential terrorism, authorities can subpoena the information with a national security letter, under the U.S.A. PATRIOT Act. These letters are generally accompanied by gag orders to prevent the subject under investigation from knowing about the subpoena. In its investigation of WikiLeaks, the government subpoenaed Twitter to get files related to Julian Assange and other WikiLeaks activists. The court order to release the files was accompanied by a gag order preventing Twitter from informing the targets of the government's request. Twitter challenged the gag order and got permission to disclose the subpoena's existence to the targets, so they would be able to challenge it on their own behalf. A federal court rejected the appeal by the three account holders and required Twitter to give up the data. The judge reasoned that Twitter users voluntarily gave Twitter their IP addresses when they signed up for the service and agreed to Twitter's terms and conditions, which state that Twitter "may disclose information about an account if Twitter believes it is reasonably necessary to comply with a law, regulation or legal request."[72]

The rules of Federal Criminal Procedure require the government to share evidence gathered with a person accused of a crime. Specifically "the government must permit

Discovery is a pre-trial procedure in which one party may demand evidence possessed by the adverse party for the purpose of preparing a case.

To obtain a warrant authorizing access to private information, officials must demonstrate to a court that there is probable cause to believe the evidence sought is needed for the investigation of a specific crime.

A subpoena may be issued if there is a possibility that the information sought will be relevant to an ongoing investigation.

---

[70] *See* 18 U.S.C. 1512(c)(imposing imposes criminal penalties on anyone who corruptly "alters, destroys, mutilates, or conceals a record, document, or other object, or attempts to do so, with the intent to impair the object's integrity or availability for use in an official proceeding"); USCS Fed Rules Civ Proc R 37 (specifying penalties for anyone who hides evidence in a civil trial); The duty to preserve evidence before a suit is based in common law.

[71] United States v. Warshak, 631 F.3d 266, 288 (6th Cir. 2010).

[72] *In re* Application of the United States of America for an order pursuant to 18 U.S.C § 2703(d), Case 1:11-dm-00003-TCB-LO (filed Nov. 11, 2011 E.D. Va.).

the defendant to inspect and to copy or photograph books, papers, documents, data, photographs, tangible objects, buildings or places, or copies or portions of any of these items" if the item is material to the preparation of a defense, the government plans to use it in the trial, or the item belongs to the defendant.[73]

In civil cases, one party may compel electronically stored information from the adverse party in the form of electronic files, e-mails, texts, voicemail and social networking posts, if the material is relevant to the case, the discovery request is narrowly tailored, and the information is sought directly from the user. A civil litigant, may not, however, subpoena stored electronic information from a third party, such as an Internet Service Provider. The Stored Communications Act provides an exception for civil subpoenas. Where social networking sites are concerned, courts have interpreted the Act to allow third parties to turn over information that is publicly accessible, but to safeguard information protected by privacy settings.[74]

Journalist's privilege

Rules of evidence afford protections for information communicated in certain types of relationships. Collectively, these rules comprise the law of privilege.[75] For example, a privilege exists between attorneys and their clients, doctors and their patients, clergy and penitents, and husbands and wives. Courts and legislatures have implemented these privileges because they think that other policy considerations outweigh the interests that may be served by the evidence the person could provide. Most jurisdictions also recognize a *journalist's privilege* to protect confidential sources of information and even nonconfidential sources in some instances. However, the privilege is generally qualified, meaning that it can be overcome if a court sees the need.

For a variety of reasons, journalists do not like to share the names of sources or documentary materials with law enforcement. Journalists worry that if they are perceived to be tools of law enforcement, sources will be less likely to share information. They argue that the First Amendment should provide the privilege to keep sources of information confidential in order to preserve channels of information that ultimately benefit the public. Journalists also want to protect their sources from retribution. Sources who share information about criminal activities may be harassed or harmed by criminals who want to keep their activities secret. Sources who blow the whistle on their employers for engaging in illegal or unethical actions may be punished or fired by their employers for sharing information with the media. Government employees, in particular, get practically no whistleblower protection if they share information related to their jobs. Although the False Claims Act protects federal employees who report

[73]Fed. R. Crim. P. 16(a)(1)(E).
[74]Crispin v. Audigier, 717 F.Supp. 2d 965 (C.D. Cal. 2010).
[75]Karl H. Schmid, *Journalist's Privilege in Criminal Proceedings: An Analysis of United States Courts of Appeals' Decisions from 1973 to 1999*, 39 Am. Crim. L. Rev. 1441, 1448 (2002).

government fraud, it does not protect them from retribution following reports of waste, mismanagement or other illegalities.[76] The Supreme Court in *Garcetti v. Ceballos* (2006) held that the First Amendment does not protect disclosures made by public employees within the scope of their employees' duties.[77] If the information is classified, the government employee may face criminal prosecution. Thomas Drake, a National Security Agency employee, who revealed to *The New York Times* that the NSA was conducting a warrantless surveillance program of Americans' digital communications on a massive scale, was prosecuted under the Espionage Act for leaking information to the media. Drake expressed his concerns about the legality of the program to NSA's lead counsel and a congressional subcommittee on intelligence oversight first. It was only after he was ignored that he went to the press.[78] The government dropped felony charges after a judge in the case ruled that Drake would not be able to defend himself unless the government revealed details about its telecommunications collection program.[79]

Of course, sources want journalists to protect their identities, not only to avoid retribution, but because they may be involved in illegal activities or simply want to protect their privacy. On several occasions sources have sued media organizations for revealing their identities. Sources who were promised confidentiality and later betrayed have earned courts' sympathy. The Supreme Court held that a source may sue a reporter who violates a promise of confidentiality for *promissory estoppel* (a tort analogous to violating an oral contract) without infringing on the First Amendment.[80] Sources who are guilty of crimes do not receive the same sympathy. The Sixth Circuit dismissed a lawsuit against a *Cincinnati Enquirer* reporter who identified his source to a grand jury investigating the reporter's illegal access to a company's phone mail system. The Sixth Circuit found no breach of contract because the source aided the reporter by supplying him with access codes, and public policy "precludes enforcements of agreements to conceal a crime."[81]

Finally, journalists know that if they are perceived as tools of law enforcement, they are more likely to be harmed as they search for information. *Wall Street Journal* Asia Bureau Chief Daniel Pearl was murdered in 2002 by terrorists in Pakistan who assumed he was connected with the CIA. The CIA purported to ban the use of journalists as spies in 1977, but a 1996 Council on Foreign Relations task force report showed that the agency continued to cloak agents as journalists.[82] In 1996, Congress passed an Intelligence Authorization Act that supposedly prohibited the use of journalists

---

[76] 31 USC § 3729 (2011).

[77] Garcetti v. Ceballos, 547 U.S. 410 (2006).

[78] Jane Mayer, *The Secret Sharer*, New Yorker, May 23, 2011, at 46.

[79] Marcy Wheeler, *Government Case Against Whistleblower Thomas Drake Collapses*, The Nation, June 13, 2011.

[80] Cohen v. Cowles Media Co., 501 U.S. 663 (1991).

[81] Ventura v. Cincinnati Enquirer, 396 F.3d 784, 791 (2005).

[82] Alicia Upano, *Will a History of Government Using Journalists Repeat Itself Under the Department of Homeland Security?* 27 The News Media & the Law 10 (Winter, 2003).

for intelligence gathering, but in effect through its exemptions, authorized the president or the CIA director to waive the restriction by notifying the House and Senate Intelligence oversight committees. It also exempted the use of willing participants as spies.

The media are not alone in believing that journalist's privilege is important. Most Americans support the idea as well. A poll conducted by the First Amendment Center in 2011 found that 75 percent of Americans agree with the statement: "Journalists should be allowed to keep a news source confidential."[83] States also support the privilege. Forty-nine states and the District of Columbia offer some level of protection for a journalist's sources.[84] (Wyoming is the exception.) There is very little uniformity among them, however.

Mechanisms for journalist's privilege

Journalist's privilege comes from three sources: shield laws, common law and constitutions. Protection varies considerably by jurisdiction, depending on the type of case, the role of the journalist in the case, and the type of information sought.

Journalist's privilege most commonly comes from *shield laws*. These are statutes that entitle journalists to protect the identities of their sources or other information collected. There is no national shield law, although a bill to provide one has been introduced in the last three congressional sessions. However, forty states have shield laws that offer journalists varying levels of protection. These include Alabama, Alaska, Arizona, Arkansas, California, Colorado, Connecticut, Delaware, District of Columbia, Florida, Georgia, Hawaii, Illinois, Indiana, Kansas, Kentucky, Louisiana, Maine, Maryland, Michigan, Minnesota, Montana, Nebraska, Nevada, New Jersey, New Mexico, New York, North Carolina, North Dakota, Ohio, Oklahoma, Oregon, Pennsylvania, Rhode Island, South Carolina, Tennessee, Texas, Utah, Washington, West Virginia, and Wisconsin.

Where legislatures have not acted, courts have – by finding a qualified privilege within state *common law* or adopting it within their own rules of procedure. Courts in 18 states offer varying protections for journalists' sources. These are Hawaii, Idaho, Iowa, Kansas, Maine, Massachusetts, Mississippi, Missouri, New Hampshire, New Mexico, South Dakota, Texas, Utah, Vermont, Virginia, West Virginia, Washington, and Wisconsin. Courts in these states employ a balancing test. In order to compel a journalist to disclose sources of information, the other party must establish that the public benefit brought by disclosure of the information outweighs the inhibiting effect of forced disclosure on the free flow of information.

---

[83] First Amendment Center, 2011 State of the First Amendment National Survey, http://www.firstamendmentcenter.org/ (follow State of the First Amendment hyperlink; then follow "See the reports").

[84] *In re* Grand Jury Subpoena, Judith Miller, 397 F.3d 964, 993 (D.C. Cir. 2005) (Tatel, J., concurring).

Two states – California and New York – have included provisions recognizing journalist's privilege in their constitutions.[85]

Journalist's privilege and the First Amendment

The question of whether journalist's privilege is protected under the U.S. Constitution is debatable. Although journalists argue that the First Amendment protects journalist's privilege, courts are not unanimously convinced that it does. The Supreme Court rejected the notion that the First Amendment protects journalists from having to testify before a grand jury in *Branzburg v. Hayes* (1972).[86] Nevertheless, many lower courts believe it can be applied in other circumstances.

The Supreme Court's landmark ruling in *Branzburg v. Hayes* has confused journalists and lower courts. In it, the Court consolidated three cases, each involving the question of whether a reporter could choose to ignore a grand jury summons. Lower courts that had examined the cases were split on the issue.

The Supreme Court rejected a First Amendment privilege to refuse to testify before a grand jury hearing. It clarified that grand juries serve an essential role in the carriage of justice and, like all citizens, the petitioners had a duty to cooperate with grand jury investigations. The Court observed that media have the right not to publish information, but "the right to withhold news is not equivalent to a First Amendment exemption from an ordinary duty of all other citizens to furnish relevant information to a grand jury performing an important public function."[87]

Writing for the Court, Justice White pointed out that "the only testimonial privilege for unofficial witnesses that is rooted in the Federal Constitution is the Fifth Amendment privilege against compelled self-incrimination."[88] The Court had no intention of creating a new one, even to secure channels of information regarding criminal activity. Justice White reasoned that when a confidential source has committed a crime, the Court could not "seriously entertain the notion that the First Amendment protects a newsman's agreement to conceal the criminal conduct of his source, or evidence thereof, on the theory that it is better to write about a crime than to do something about it."[89] When a confidential source has not committed a crime, but may be aware of criminal activity, the Court could not "accept the argument that the public interest in possible future news about crime from undisclosed, unverified sources must take precedence over the public interest in pursuing and prosecuting those crimes reported to the press by informants and in thus deterring the commission of such crimes in the future."[90] The majority determined that no privilege existed unless the recipient could demonstrate

---

[85] CAL. CONST. art. I, § 2.; O'Neill v. Oakgrove Construction Inc., 71 N.Y.S.2d 521, 529 n. 3 (1988)(noting that the New York Constitution may provide more protection than that available under the First Amendment).

[86] 408 U.S. 665 (1972).

[87] *Id.* at 697.

[88] *Id.* at 690.

[89] *Id.* at 692.

[90] *Id.* at 695.

that the subpoena was issued by the grand jury in bad faith or as a means of harassment – the same exception that would apply to anyone summoned to testify.

Four justices dissented from the majority opinion. Justice Douglas argued that journalist's privilege not only existed but should be absolute unless the journalist was the one being investigated for the criminal act. Justice Stewart, joined by Justices Brennan and Marshall, took a more measured approach. Justice Stewart suggested that journalist's privilege should be evaluated objectively based on its relevance to the outcome of the trial and the potential availability of the information from other sources.[91]

In a Court divided on the issue, Justice Powell broke the tie by agreeing with the majority's decision, but submitted a concurring opinion with his own reasoning. In it he suggested that while no constitutional protection existed to refuse to testify before grand juries, reporters may be entitled to a qualified protection in other areas. He wrote "The asserted claim to privilege should be judged on its facts by the striking of a proper balance between freedom of the press and the obligation of all citizens to give relevant testimony with respect to criminal conduct."[92] He added if the journalist "is called upon to give information bearing only on a remote and tenuous relationship to the subject of the investigation, or if he has some other reason to believe that his testimony implicates confidential source relationships without a legitimate need of law enforcement, he will have access to the court on a motion to quash and an appropriate protective order may be entered."[93] A concurring opinion, like Justice Powell's, is not part of the authoritative precedent set by the majority. Nevertheless, many lower courts have assumed that some kind of qualified privilege based on the First Amendment must exist for journalists in cases that do *not* involve grand jury testimony, the specific circumstance addressed in *Branzburg*.

Among the 13 U.S. Courts of Appeals, eleven recognize a qualified privilege for journalists against forced disclosure of their sources. The Sixth Circuit has refused to recognize the privilege until the Supreme Court forces it to do so. The Seventh Circuit has not ruled on the issue directly, but its opinions suggest that it is skeptical of the privilege.[94] The Eighth Circuit considers the question "open," but the privilege is extended in some of its districts.[95]

Although circuits may disagree over whether and in what context the First Amendment protects journalistic privilege, most agree that a qualified privilege has developed through federal common law. Three years after *Branzburg* was decided, Congress delegated power to federal courts to develop rules on evidentiary privileges, including privileges accorded to witnesses.[96] Federal courts are also required to apply state rules

---

[91] *Id.* at 743 (Stewart, J., dissenting).

[92] *Id.* at 710 (Powell, J., concurring).

[93] *Id.* at 710.

[94] McKevitt v. Pallasch, 339 F.3d 530, 531–2 (7th Cir. 2003) ("A large number of cases conclude, rather surprisingly in light of Branzburg, that there is a reporter's privilege, though they do not agree on its scope. A few cases refuse to recognize the privilege . . . Our court has not taken sides.").

[95] *In re* Grand Jury Subpoena Duces Tecum, 112 F.3d 910, 918 (8th Cir. 1997).

[96] Fed. R. Evid. 501 (2011).

on journalist's privilege in civil cases that arise under state law but which are brought into the federal court system.

Journalist's privilege in criminal cases

Courts are least likely to recognize journalist's privilege when sources could provide information relevant to a criminal case. Individuals facing prosecution have a Sixth Amendment right to compel testimony from witnesses that may be used to prove their innocence. Courts often make this determination by following the balancing approach suggested by Justice Powell in his concurring opinion in *Branzburg*. Using Justice Powell's approach, courts balance the defendant's Sixth Amendment right to a fair trial against the public's interest in preserving the free flow of information. In some cases, the court may also determine that the public's greater interest is better served by compelling disclosure of evidence that can resolve a crime.

Alternatively, courts may resolve the issue by applying a three-pronged approach suggested by Justice Stewart in his dissenting opinion in *Branzburg v. Hayes*. Justice Stewart suggested that in order to compel a journalist to testify in a criminal proceeding, the prosecution must establish that:

Figure 6.2 Illustration: Kalan Lyra

1. the information is clearly relevant to the specific violation of law;
2. the information cannot be obtained by alternative means less destructive of First Amendment rights; and
3. there is compelling and overriding need for the information.[97]

A need for information is *compelling* if it is likely to affect the outcome of the case.

Perhaps the most famous confidential source in the United States is Deep Throat, later identified as Mark Felt, the FBI's second in command during the Nixon administration. Felt's revelations were instrumental in bringing down the Nixon presidency during the Watergate scandal. For 33 years *The Washington Post* and its reporters, Bob Woodward and Carl Bernstein, protected Felt's secret until 2005 when he and his family chose to reveal it.[98] It is highly unlikely that, under the same circumstances, the journalists would be allowed to protect the secret today.

Although protections for journalists' sources have expanded, the quality of the protection seems to have declined. Within the last 10 years, U.S. Courts of Appeals have affirmed contempt citations resulting in harsher sentences than any previously experienced in American history against reporters who refused to reveal their sources.[99]

When a journalist ignores a subpoena to testify in a judicial proceeding, he or she may be held in *contempt of court*. A court may attempt to compel compliance by fining or incarcerating the journalist until he or she cooperates. A court may jail an individual for civil contempt up to 18 months or until the subpoenaed materials are relinquished.[100] If the court finds that the journalist has interfered with its ability to function, it may issue a finding of criminal contempt, which may also result in a fine or incarceration. However, in this case, the journalist no longer holds the key to the door. Revocation of the penalty is not tied to the journalist's decision to cooperate.

One of the most prominent contempt cases involved a journalist from *The New York Times* who was held in jail for 12 weeks when she refused to reveal the source of a White House leak without his permission. In the 2003 State of the Union address, leading up to the invasion of Iraq, President George Bush implied that former Iraqi leader Saddam Hussein had been searching in Africa for a source of uranium, a key ingredient for nuclear weapons. At the time, it was the administration's contention that Iraq was making weapons of mass destruction. Former U.S. Ambassador Joseph Wilson wrote an op-ed article published by *The New York Times* six months later that cast doubt on the president's statement.[101] Wilson claimed to have been sent by the CIA to Niger in 2002 to answer Vice President Cheney's inquiry regarding whether Saddam Hussein had

---

[97] 408 U.S. 665, 743 (1972) (Stewart, J., dissenting).

[98] David Von Drehle, *FBI's No. 2 Was 'Deep Throat': Mark Felt Ends 30-Year Mystery of The Post's Watergate Source*, WASH. POST, June 1, 2005, at A1.

[99] Assembly Joint Resolution No. 24, at 4 (adopted Aug. 30, 2007), info.sen.ca.gov/pub/07-08/bill/asm/ab_0001-0050/ajr_24_bill_20070904_enrolled.pdf.

[100] 28 U.S.C. § 1826(a) (2011).

[101] Joseph Wilson, *What I Didn't Find in Africa*, N.Y. TIMES, July 6, 2003, at Sec. 4, 9.

tried to purchase uranium from the country. Wilson said he conducted an investigation and found no evidence that Iraq had approached Niger for uranium. A week after Wilson's op-ed appeared, Robert Novak, a *Chicago Sun-Times* columnist, wrote that two senior administration officials had told him that Wilson was not sent to Niger on the recommendation of the CIA director, but on that of Wilson's wife, Valerie Plame, who was a CIA "operative on weapons of mass destruction."[102] Wilson accused Novak's sources of divulging his wife's secret identity as payback for embarrassing the president. Following his assertion, other reporters claimed to have been contacted by administration officials who offered the same information. The unauthorized disclosure of the identity of a CIA agent is a federal crime.[103]

The Justice Department launched an investigation to determine whether someone in the White House had violated the law. Its own guidelines specify that before issuing a subpoena to the media, the department should believe that "information sought is essential to a successful investigation – particularly with reference to establishing guilt or innocence" and that "all reasonable efforts should be made to obtain the desired information from alternative sources."[104] They also assert that whenever possible subpoenas should be targeted toward a narrow topic and period of time and that the Justice Department should be willing to negotiate with the media to find a solution that accommodates both of their interests.

Two of the reporters subpoenaed to testify in a grand jury investigation of the leak were Matthew Cooper of *Time Magazine* and Judith Miller of *The New York Times*. Both had been given Plame's name by White House leakers, but neither had taken the bait to write a story. The journalists moved to quash the subpoenas based on a First Amendment privilege to protect media sources. When their motions were denied and they failed to comply, the district court held them in civil contempt. The U.S. Court of Appeals for the D.C. Circuit upheld the decision based on *Branzburg* and the Supreme Court denied certiorari.[105] It is instructive, however, that attorneys general from 34 states and the District of Columbia encouraged the Court to reverse the opinion stating: "A federal policy that allows journalists to be imprisoned for engaging in the same conduct that these State privileges encourage and protect 'buck(s) that clear policy of virtually all states,' and undermines both the purpose of the shield laws, and the policy determinations of the State courts and legislatures that adopted them."[106]

The night before Cooper was to go to jail, the president's deputy chief of staff released him from his promise of confidentiality. Twelve weeks into her confinement, Miller claimed that the vice president's chief of staff, Scooter Libby, absolved her of her promise, although he claimed to have done it a year earlier. However, the decision to

---

[102] Robert Novak, *The Mission to Niger*, CHI. SUN-TIMES, July 14, 2003, at 3.

[103] 50 U.S.C. § 421 (criminalizing disclosure of the identity of a covert agent by anyone with authorized access to classified information).

[104] Policy with regard to the issuance of subpoenas to members of the news media, 28 C.F.R. § 50.10.

[105] *In re* Grand Jury Subpoena (Miller), 397 F.3d 964 (2005).

[106] Brief for the States of Okla. et al. as Amici Curiae Supporting Petitioners at 7, Miller v. United States, 545 U.S. 1150 (2005) (Nos. 04–1507 and 04–1508), 2005 WL 1317523, at 7.

waive the promise of anonymity belongs to the journalist, not the source. Judge Tatel explained in his concurring opinion that "a source's waiver is irrelevant to the reasons for the privilege. Because the government could demand waivers – perhaps even before any leak occurs – as a condition of employment, a privilege subject to waiver may, again, amount to no privilege at all, even in those leak cases where protecting the confidential source is most compelling."[107] He also pointed out that while a source's interest "is limited to the particular case, the reporter's interest aligns with the public, for journalists must cultivate relationships with other sources who might keep mum if waiving confidentiality at the government's behest could lead to their exposure."[108]

Journalist's privilege in civil cases

Courts are more willing to recognize journalist's privilege in the context of civil cases, where the Supreme Court's *Branzburg* decision is not considered controlling. In fact, the Fifth and Tenth Circuits recognize journalist's privilege exclusively in civil cases. In criminal cases, courts have to balance the public benefit of First Amendment protection of information against the public benefit of justice served through compelled disclosure. Although justice is still the issue in civil cases, the balance shifts. Courts weigh the public interest in protecting the journalist's sources against the plaintiff's private interest in compelling the journalist's testimony.

Tests used for journalist's privilege in civil trials are similar to those used in criminal trials. Some courts apply a version of Justice Powell's balancing test. Others apply a version of Justice Stewart's three-part test that looks for relevance, a compelling interest in the information, and evidence that the information cannot be obtained by other means.[109]

A court's willingness to extend the qualified privilege depends on the position of the journalist and the type of information sought. Journalist's privilege is strongest when the reporter is not a party to the suit and when the source protected has been promised confidentiality.

Who is a journalist?

When *Branzburg* was decided, the Supreme Court was reluctant to create a special privilege for journalists, because it would require courts to determine who would qualify for it. Justice White pointed out that this would be a questionable procedure in light of the traditional doctrine that "liberty of the press is the right of the lonely pamphleteer who uses carbon paper or a mimeograph just as much as of the large metropolitan publisher who utilizes the latest photocomposition methods."[110] In the 1970s it was still relatively easy to distinguish journalists. Still the court acknowledged "freedom of the

---

[107] *In re* Grand Jury Subpoena (Miller), 397 F.3d at 1000 (Tatel, J., concurring).
[108] *Id.*
[109] *See, e.g.,* Miller v. Transamerican Press, 621 F.2d 721, 725 (5th Cir. 1980).
[110] Branzburg v. Hayes, 408 U.S. 665, 704 (1972).

press is a 'fundamental personal right . . . not confined to newspapers and periodicals. It necessarily embraces pamphlets and leaflets . . . The press in its historic connotation comprehends every sort of publication which affords a vehicle of information and opinion.'"[111] Today, the definition of "journalist" is much more complicated.

Changes in technology have redefined news organizations and the people who disseminate news. In addition to traditional journalism, which appears in a broader array of forms, companies and associations are now using the Internet to disseminate industry news to their constituents as a form of public relations. More individuals are also taking advantage of digital technology by circulating information through blogs and podcasts. According to a 2010 study by the Pew Research Center, one-in-ten online adults maintains a blog.[112]

Judge Sentelle of the D.C. Circuit Court mulled the distinction between blogger and journalist in his concurring opinion in the Judith Miller case, asking:

> Are we then to create a privilege that protects only those reporters employed by *Time Magazine*, *The New York Times*, and other media giants, or do we extend that protection as well to the owner of a desktop printer producing a weekly newsletter to inform his neighbors, lodge brothers, co-religionists, or co-conspirators? Perhaps more to the point today, does the privilege also protect the proprietor of a web log: the stereotypical "blogger" sitting in his pajamas at his personal computer posting on the World Wide Web his best product to inform whoever happens to browse his way? If not, why not? How could one draw a distinction consistent with the court's vision of a broadly granted personal right?[113]

The use of social networking sites blurs the distinction even further. More than two-thirds of the world's Internet population uses social networking sites.[114] Increasingly sites like Facebook and Twitter are used to report on political affairs. Their influence in political revolutions in Egypt, Libya, and Tunisia, and in protest movements in Iran, Syria, and Yemen cannot be denied.[115] Citizens used them to organize demonstrations and exchange information.

And then of course, there are organizations like WikiLeaks that profess to be engaging in journalism. This site, and other whistle-blower sites like it, are provided with information that they publish. Documents are not edited, but appear in their raw form. WikiLeaks volunteers do, however, pick and choose what appears on the site. Does this selection process qualify as editing?

---

[111] *Id.* at 703 (quoting Lovell v. Griffin, 303 U.S. 444, 450 (1938)).

[112] Amanda Lenhart, Kristen Purcell, Aaron Smith and Kathryn Zickuhr, *Social Media and Mobile Internet Use Among Teens and Young Adults*, Pew Internet & American Life Project (Feb. 3, 2010), http://pewinternet.org/Reports/2010/Social-Media-and-Young-Adults.aspx.

[113] *In re* Grand Jury Subpoena, 397 F.3d 964, 968–72, 979 (D.C.C. 2005) (Sentelle, J., concurring).

[114] NIELSON, GLOBAL FACES AND NETWORKED PLACES: A NIELSEN REPORT ON SOCIAL NETWORKING'S NEW GLOBAL FOOTPRINT, March 2009, 1.

[115] DUBAI SCHOOL OF GOVERNMENT, DUBAI SOCIAL MEDIA REPORT, Vol. 1, No. 2, May 11, at www.dsg.ae/NEWSANDEVENTS/.../ASMRHome.aspx.

So how is a journalist defined in the twenty-first century? The Ninth Circuit has said that "what makes journalism is not its format but its content" and "the critical question for deciding whether a person may invoke the journalist's privilege is whether she is gathering news for dissemination to the public."[116] The Third Circuit has concluded that a journalist is someone who is engaged in news gathering and who possessed the intent at the beginning of the news gathering process to disseminate the information to the public.[117] The Second Circuit has said that an important factor is collecting information for the purpose of independent reporting and commentary.[118] Based on these criteria, many bloggers, filmmakers and information providers qualify for that title.

Privileges for bloggers

More states are now offering privileges to nontraditional journalists and bloggers. Some base the protection on the function the person serves, others on the regularity of publication, and still others on the person's financial remuneration for the activity.

In cases in which there is no reference to online activities in state shield laws, courts have had to look for applicable language to suggest one is appropriate. A California appellate court was one of the first to conclude that online journalists enjoy the same rights to protect sources that offline journalists do.[119] When Apple realized that two websites were carrying information about a new product it had not yet disclosed, the company attempted to identify the source of the leaks by subpoenaing e-mail records from their Internet service provider.[120] The site's publisher, Jason O'Grady motioned for a protective order to block Apple's discovery, and was rejected by a lower court. But a state appellate court reversed the decision in *O'Grady v. Superior Court of Santa Clara County* (2006).

The appellate court rejected Apple's argument that the websites were not legitimate journalists entitled to protect their sources. O'Grady, was no pajama-clad blogger. He operated a news site with a staff of nine editors and reporters and an average circulation of 300,000 visitors per month. California's constitution states "A publisher, editor, reporter, or other person connected with or employed upon a newspaper, magazine, or other periodical publication . . . shall not be adjudged in contempt . . . for refusing to disclose the source of any information procured while so connected or employed for publication in a newspaper, magazine or other periodical publication, or for refusing to disclose any unpublished information obtained or prepared in gathering, receiving or processing of information for communication to the public."[121]

[116] Shoen v. Shoen, 5 F.3d 1289, 1293 (1993).

[117] *In re* Madden, Titan Sports v. Turner Broadcasting Systems, 151 F.3d 125 (3rd Cir. 1998).

[118] Chevron Corp. v. Berlinger, 629 F.3d 297, 307 (2nd Cir. 2011).

[119] O'Grady v. Superior Court of Santa Clara County, 139 Cal. App. 4th 1423 (2006).

[120] Apple Computer, Inc. v. Doe 1, 74 U.S.P.Q.2d (BNA) 1191, 33 Media L. Rep. (BNA) 1449 (Cal. Santa Clara County Super. Ct. Mar. 11, 2005), petition for appeal filed sub nom. O'Grady, et al. v. Apple Computer, Inc., No. H028579 (Sixth App. Dist. filed March 22, 2005).

[121] Cal. Const. art. I, § 2(b).

The court considered whether journalist's privilege applied to the petitioners on the basis of First Amendment protection and concluded that it must. It stated "we can see no sustainable basis to distinguish petitioners from the reporters, editors, and publishers who provide news to the public through traditional print and broadcast media. It is established without contradiction that they gather, select, and prepare, for purposes of publication to a mass audience, information about current events of interest and concern to that audience."[122]

In another case, the New Hampshire Supreme Court held that an informational website that reported on the mortgage industry was entitled to assert journalist's privilege to protect the identity of its sources in a defamation suit, which the court would then balance against the plaintiff's rights.[123] The court observed that "The informative function asserted by representatives of the organized press . . . is also performed by lecturers, political pollsters, novelists, academic researchers, and dramatists. Almost any author may quite accurately assert that he is contributing to the flow of information to the public, that he relies on confidential sources of information, and that these sources will be silenced if he is forced to make disclosures."

The New Jersey Supreme Court also acknowledged the legitimacy of nontraditional media under the state's shield law, but denied that protection to a "self-described journalist who posted comments on an Internet message board." In *Too Much Media LLC. V. Hale* (2011), the defendant, who posted inflammatory messages on message boards accusing the adult entertainment industry of corruption, argued that she was engaged in investigative reporting and intended to publish her findings eventually on her own website.[124] The court rejected the "intent" test applied by several federal circuits, indicating that if the legislature had wanted to base the shield law on intent to publish it would have done so. As a message board poster, her link to the media was too tenuous.

An Oregon court denied a blogger source protection, pointing out that she was not affiliated with any medium. But the larger issue in that case was that the defendant was attempting to use journalist's privilege to protect the identity of her source, while at the same time using the existence of the source as evidence that she did not act with negligence in making her blog post.[125] Most courts reject the use of unidentified sources as evidence for a defense. Despite the judge's reference to the blogger's lack of affiliation with a professional organization, Oregon law provides shield protection to those "employed by or engaged in any medium of communication . . . [which] includes, *but is not limited to*, any newspaper, magazine or other periodical, book, pamphlet, news service, wire service, news or feature syndicate, broadcast station or network, or cable television system."[126] The law gave the judge the wiggle room he would have needed to protect the defendant had she had a stronger case.

---

[122] O'Grady v. Superior Court of Santa Clara County, 139 Cal. App. 4th at 1467.

[123] The Mortgage Specialists, Inc. v. Implode-Explode Heavy Industries, Inc., 160 N.H. 227 (N.H. 2010).

[124] Too Much Media v. Hale, 20 A.3d 364 (N.J. 2011).

[125] Obsidian Finance Group, LLC v. Cox, No. CV-11-57-H (D. Or. Nov. 30, 2011).

[126] Ore. Rev. Stat. 44.510(2).

States are most likely to apply journalist privilege to bloggers who show evidence of professionalism. In some states, like Texas, for example, shield laws specifically require that bloggers' journalistic activities amount to "a substantial portion" of their livelihoods or "substantial financial gain" to qualify for the privilege.[127]

Bloggers in federal courts have not fared as well. Blogger and videographer Josh Wolf served eight months in jail in 2006 for refusing to turn over video footage that he shot during a San Francisco protest of a Group of Eight (G8) summit in Scotland. The FBI subpoenaed the tape because it suspected that Wolf might have documented an attack on a police officer during the protest and an attempt to set fire to a police car. The federal agency claimed jurisdiction over the case because part of the car was purchased with federal funds.

Because the case concerned a criminal matter in a federal court, California's shield law did not protect Wolf as it had the bloggers in the Apple case. When Wolf refused to give up the video, a federal district court held him in civil contempt. Not only was Wolf the first blogger to go to jail for refusing to share information with the government, he served the longest sentence ever given a journalist. He was released when he finally agreed to give up the tape but did not have to testify before the grand jury.

Wolf's incarceration was only slightly longer than Vanessa Leggett's. Another "questionable journalist," Leggett was a part-time lecturer at a Houston university, who spent five and a half months in jail for contempt of court because she refused to give a federal grand jury her notes and tapes of interviews with confidential sources for a book she said she planned to write about the 1997 murder of a Houston socialite. A federal grand jury was considering whether there was enough evidence to indict the victim's husband, who had been acquitted of the murder charge in state court. The Fifth Circuit, which recognizes no journalist's privilege in criminal cases, upheld Leggett's contempt citation. It stated, "Even assuming that Leggett, a virtually unpublished free-lance writer operating without an employer or a contract for publication, qualifies as a journalist under the law, the journalist's privilege is ineffectual against a grand jury subpoena absent evidence of government harassment or oppression."[128]

Leggett never revealed the information to the grand jury. She was released after 168 days because its term expired. The next grand jury empanelled returned an indictment without her notes or testimony. She did, however, get a book contract from a division of Random House after her release.

Privacy Protection Act of 1980

Another point to be debated in relation to bloggers is whether the Privacy Protection Act of 1980 applies to them. Congress passed the Act in 1980 in reaction to the Supreme Court decision in *Zurcher v. Stanford Daily* (1978), finding that the Fourth Amendment

---

[127] Texas Free Flow of Information Act, Tex. Civ. Prac. & Rem. Code § 22.021, Tex. Code Crim. Proc. art. 38.11 (2009).

[128] *In re* Grand Jury Subpoenas (Vanessa Leggett), 29 Media L. Rep. 2301 (BNA) (5th Cir. 2001) (unpublished).

did not prohibit police searches of documentary evidence held by third parties like journalists.[129] The Act was meant to shield journalists' work products and documentary materials from newsroom searches used to skirt delays normally associated with a subpoena.[130] But the law's wording does not specifically refer to newsrooms, and if interpreted plainly should apply to bloggers. It says:

> Notwithstanding any other law, it shall be unlawful for a government officer or employee, in connection with the investigation or prosecution of a criminal offense, to search for or seize any work product materials *possessed by a person reasonably believed to have a purpose to disseminate to the public a newspaper, book, broadcast, or other similar form of public communication, in or affecting interstate or foreign commerce* . . . [131]

The same standards and exceptions apply to documentary materials (like notes, photographs, or tapes) used in connection with the dissemination of information to the public. Exceptions would apply if:

- there is probable cause to believe the person possessing the materials is committing the criminal offense under investigation;
- immediate seizure of the materials is necessary to prevent bodily harm to someone;
- there is reason to believe that issuing a subpoena first would result in the destruction, alteration, or concealment of the materials; or
- the materials have not been produced in response to a court order directing compliance with a subpoena, all appellate remedies have been exhausted, and there is reason to believe that further delay would threaten justice.

A federal district court in Texas concluded that the U.S. Secret Service violated the Privacy Protection Act by raiding the office of Steve Jackson Games and confiscating its computing equipment. The Austin-based company publishes fantasy books and computer games and formerly operated a bulletin board service for gamers called Illuminati. In 1990, the Secret Service incorrectly believed that one of Jackson's employees possessed information about a hacker who had broken into Bell South's computer system. It not only raided the employee's home, but confiscated Jackson's equipment for four months. During that period, Jackson's company nearly went out of business. It closed the Illuminati BBS, missed publishing deadlines, and laid-off half the workers. When the computers were returned, data was missing. The court awarded Jackson $51,000 for damages under the Privacy Protection Act.[132]

---

[129] Zurcher v. Stanford Daily, 436 U.S. 547 (1978).

[130] S. Rep. No. 96–874, at 4 (1980), reprinted in 1980 U.S.C.C.A.N. 3950 (explaining that Congress meant the Act to provide "the press and certain other persons not suspected of committing a crime with protections not provided currently by the Fourth Amendment").

[131] 42 U.S.C. § 2000aa (2006) (emphasis added).

[132] *See* Steve Jackson Games v. United States, 816 F. Supp. 432 (W.D. Tex. 1993), appeal filed on other grounds, 36 F.3d 457 (5th Cir. 1993).

Questions for Discussion

1. What does the Freedom of Information Act do? What is an "agency" under the Freedom of Information Act?
2. How can people get information about the legislative and judicial branches?
3. Does the First Amendment protect journalist's privilege?
4. Are bloggers protected by journalist's privilege? Does the Privacy Protection Act of 1980 apply to them?

7 Intellectual Property: Copyright

No area of law has been more affected by digital media than intellectual property. The ease with which digital works can be reproduced, manipulated, and shared has transformed copyright law, in particular, from the realm of the obscure into a subject that lay people genuinely want to understand. And if they have difficulty understanding, it is no wonder. The law is very much still in transition as lawmakers struggle to adapt copyright protection to a fluid medium while maintaining a balance between the rights of copyright holders and copyright users.

The struggle has met with mixed success. Efforts to protect copyright holders against digital piracy have changed assumptions about fair use and criminalized some forms of conduct that were formerly protected. Changes in the law to make it more consistent with copyright in other countries have provided better international protection for U.S. works, but also kept millions of works out of the public domain. Meanwhile, although courts are reaching a greater consensus on how copyright protection applies online, there are still areas of litigation, particularly regarding file sharing, that have produced contradictory opinions.

This chapter will discuss what can and cannot be copyrighted, what constitutes infringement and how to avoid it, fair use, file trading, sampling, and the First Amendment implications of copyright law.

Source and Purpose of Intellectual Property Protection

The Constitution's copyright and patent clause empowers Congress "To promote the Progress of Science and useful Arts, by securing for limited Times to Authors and Inventors the exclusive Right to their respective Writings and Discoveries." Implicit is the assumption that people will produce more creative work if they are guaranteed

Digital Media Law, Second Edition. Ashley Packard.
© 2013 John Wiley & Sons, Inc. Published 2013 by John Wiley & Sons, Inc.

protection for the fruits of their labors. If others can exploit their work for personal benefit without contributing to its production, creators have less of an incentive to produce.

Intellectual property protection is not unlimited, however. It is counterbalanced by the notion that after a certain period of time the work should move into the public domain, where it will be accessible to others who also may use it to contribute to the body of knowledge. Although we may speak of intellectual property *owners*, copyrights and patents are not permanent property rights in the traditional sense. They are actually limited monopoly rights.

What Can Be Copyrighted?

Of all forms of intellectual property protection, copyright is the most directly applicable to digital media products. It protects all forms of art, literature, music, video, imagery, and software that a digital artist or producer is likely to create. Specifically, copyright law protects "original works of authorship fixed in any tangible medium of expression."[1] The Supreme Court has clarified that "[o]riginality does not signify novelty."[2] In fact, should two artists miraculously create the same piece, each without knowing of the work of the other, both works would be copyrightable. Instead, it means that the work must be a product of the author's labor, rather than borrowed from some other source.

Figure 7.1 Illustration: Kalan Lyra

[1] 17 U.S.C. § 102(a) (2011).
[2] Feist Publications, Inc. v. Rural Telephone Service Co., 499 U.S. 340, 345 (1991).

For purposes of copyright, a work is considered fixed in a tangible medium if it is "sufficiently permanent or stable to permit it to be perceived, reproduced, or otherwise communicated for a period of more than transitory duration."[3] The fixation requirement is technologically neutral. In 1976, Congress amended copyright law to apply to works in any medium of expression "now known or later developed, from which they can be perceived, reproduced, or otherwise communicated, either directly or with the aid of a machine or device."[4] Fixation has been interpreted to include paper, film, video, computer discs, read-only memory, and random access memory – essentially anything that can retain information. It is the difference between a speech saved in a file on a computer, for example, and a speaker's impromptu remarks that evaporate when spoken.

To qualify for protection, a work also must display "some minimal level of *creativity*."[5] Creativity is not judged by the caliber of the work. In fact, the Supreme Court has acknowledged that the level of creativity required is "extremely low." Most works qualify for copyright "no matter how crude, humble or obvious" they might be as long as there is some sign of "intellectual production, of thought, and conception."[6] To earn copyright protection, a work must be:

1. original;
2. fixed in a tangible medium of expression; and
3. moderately creative.

The Copyright Act places "original works of authorship" eligible for protection into the following categories:

*   literary works, including computer programs;
*   musical works;
*   dramatic works;
*   pantomimes and choreographic works;
*   pictorial, graphic, and sculptural works;
*   motion pictures and other audiovisual works;
*   sound recordings; and
*   architectural works.

Copyright protection for architectural works is intended to prohibit the unauthorized duplication of a building or its architectural blueprints. It does not prevent others from making, distributing, or publicly displaying paintings, photographs, or other pictorial representations of a building in public view.[7]

Copyright also applies to *collected works*, which are collections of individually copyrighted works amassed into larger works, such as anthologies. In such cases, the copyright for the collected work is separate from the copyright for the individual

---

[3] 17 U.S.C. § 101 (2011).

[4] *Id.* § 102(a).

[5] Feist Publications, Inc. v. Rural Telephone Service Co., 499 U.S. at 358.

[6] *Id.* at 362 (citing 1 M. Nimmer and D. Nimmer, Copyright 1.08[C]1 (1990) and Burrow-Giles Lithographic Co. v. Sarony, 111 U.S. 53, 59–60 (1884)).

[7] 17 U.S.C. § 120(a) (2011).

work. The owner of the copyright to the collected work has the right to reproduce the work as a whole, but not to reproduce its individual parts. Copyright also protects *compilations* of facts, as long as they possess the requisite level of originality.

What Cannot Be Copyrighted?

Facts and ideas

Because the primary purpose behind copyright protection is the creation of knowledge, copyright law does not protect facts or ideas. It only protects the unique way that facts or ideas are expressed. Others may use the same information, as long as they express it in a different way. Courts refer to this distinction between what is, and is not, protected as the idea/expression or fact/expression dichotomy. In practice, it means that a CNN news piece about the president would receive protection for the way the information is conveyed – the words chosen, the arrangement of the facts and selection of imagery to go with them – but not the actual information conveyed. If the contrary were true, we would all have to watch CNN to get the information in CNN's control.[8] The same guidelines apply to creative material. For example, copyright protects the particular lyrics and arrangement of a song, but not the underlying idea expressed through the music. If a songwriter were entitled to control an idea, we might be limited to one song about falling in love and another about breaking up. The Top 40 would look more like the Top 2.

Facts are not protected because "[n]o one may claim originality as to facts."[9] Facts are not authored; they are discovered. In contrast, a compilation of facts may be sufficiently original to justify protection. Writing for the Supreme Court in *Feist Publications, Inc. v. Rural Telephone Service Co.* (1991), Justice O'Connor explained:

> The compilation author typically chooses which facts to include, in what order to place them, and how to arrange the collected data so that they may be used effectively by readers. These choices as to selection and arrangement, so long as they are made independently by the compiler and entail a minimal degree of creativity, are sufficiently original that Congress may protect such compilations through the copyright laws.[10]

Still, in a compilation, copyright subsists only in the parts of the work that are original, not in the facts themselves. If there is nothing distinctive about the arrangement of the data, no amount of work invested in its assembly will justify copyright protection.

---

[8] *See, e.g.,* Int'l News Service v. Associated Press, 248 U.S. 215, 234 (1918) (indicating that "the news element – the information respecting current events contained in the literary production – is not the creation of the writer, but is a report of matters that ordinarily are publici juris; it is the history of the day.").
[9] Feist Publications, Inc. v. Rural Telephone Service Co., 499 U.S. 340, 347 (1991).
[10] *Id.* at 348.

The Supreme Court illustrated this point in *Feist Publications* when it rejected the "sweat of the brow" theory that a compiler's hard work put toward collecting facts deserved protection.[11] Rural Telephone Service Company sued Feist Publications for republishing parts of its alphabetized telephone directory and was granted summary judgment on its copyright claim in district court. The Court of Appeals affirmed the judgment, but the Supreme Court reversed, finding that Rural Telephone's alphabetical listings displayed no originality worth protection. Acknowledging that it may seem unfair for others to benefit from a compiler's labor, the Court explained that the "primary objective of copyright is not to reward the labor of authors, but '[t]o promote the Progress of Science and useful Arts.' To this end, copyright assures authors the right to their original expression, but encourages others to build freely upon the ideas and information conveyed by a work."[12]

However, the European Union does protect databases. In 1996, the EU passed the Database Directive[13] to harmonize levels of protection for databases among member states, some of which protected databases under copyright rules and some of which did not. The directive defines a database as a "collection of independent works, data or other materials arranged in a systematic or methodical way and individually accessible by electronic or other means." It requires member states to recognize a *sui generis* (meaning unique or different) right to protect a database when there has been "qualitatively and/or quantitatively a substantial investment in either the obtaining, verification or presentation of the contents."[14] The right allows a database owner to prevent the unauthorized extraction or reuse of all or a substantial part of the contents of a database.

Procedures, processes, systems, or methods of operation

Copyright does not protect procedures, processes, systems or methods of operation. However, works that fall into these categories may receive protection under patent law.

Scenes à faire

Copyright does not protect *scenes à faire*, which are stock or standard expressions of an idea customary to a particular genre. Some incidents, characters, and settings are indispensable to the treatment of a topic and therefore expected to be used repeatedly.[15] In *Data East USA, Inc. v. EPYX, Inc.* (1988), the copyright holder for the electronic game "Karate Champ" won a judgment against the distributor of "World Karate

---

[11] *Id.* at 353.

[12] *Id.* at 350 (citations omitted).

[13] Directive 96/9/EC of the European Parliament and of the Council of 11 March 1996 on the legal protection of databases, OJ L 077, 27/03/1996 p. 0020–0028 at http://eur-lex.europa.eu/LexUriServ/LexUriServ.do?uri=CELEX:31996L0009:EN:HTML.

[14] *Id.* at ch. 3, art. 7(1).

[15] Atari, Inc. v. N. Am. Philips Consumer Elecs. Corp., 672 F.2d 607, 616 (7th Cir. 1982).

Championship" for copyright infringement. Both games included karate matches in which there were two opponents, one wearing white and the other wearing red, using similar karate moves. The Ninth Circuit reversed the judgment because both games incorporated *scenes à faire*.[16] The appellate court determined that the common features were necessary to the idea of a karate game. Likewise, in 2011, a New Jersey court dismissed a copyright suit against rapper 50 Cent, ruling that thematic similarities between his film and the plaintiff's book, which involved depictions of a young man from the inner city who gets caught up in a life of crime, were *scenes à faire* common to rap and "gangsta" movies.[17]

The *scenes à faire* exemption has also been used in the context of computer software to exclude certain elements of a work from copyright protection that are dictated by external constraints on the work's production. The Tenth Circuit explained that "[f]or computer-related applications, these external factors include hardware standards and mechanical specifications, software standards, and compatibility requirements, computer manufacturer design standards, industry programming practices, and practices and demands of the industry being serviced."[18]

Titles and names

Titles and names cannot be copyrighted, which is why so many works carry the same name. However, some titles and names receive protection under trademark law, discussed in Chapter 8, or laws related to unfair competition.

Typefaces

The word "font" refers to a complete set of characters in a typeface. Fonts are not copyrightable. However, the word "font" also may be used to describe the software programs that render specific typefaces. The programs are copyrightable.

A typeface, which is the actual shape of the letters and characters used to create a font like Helvetica, is not copyrighted.[19] However, the computer program that enables a computer to represent the typeface on the screen, alter its size and style, and then send it to a printer, is copyrightable. Font software is usually licensed using end-user agreements. Users are charged a fee for the right to use the software. The license agreement may also come with certain restrictions on the font's use, so it should be read carefully before using the font to create commercial products. Web designers who embed font data into their websites so visitors can view the pages with the same fonts also need to make sure to get a license to use that font on the Web first.

U.S. government documents

Copyright protection does not apply to U.S. government works. These are items produced by federal employees in the course of their official duties. Most reports produced

---

[16] Data East USA, Inc. v. EPYX, Inc., 862 F.2d 204 (1988).

[17] Charles Toutant, *Copyright Suit Against Rapper 50 Cent Fails Under "Scenes a Faire" Doctrine*, New Jersey Law Journal, Sept. 22, 2011, http://www.law.com/jsp/nj/PubArticleNJ.jsp?id=1202516581321.

[18] Mitel, Inc. v. Iqtel, Inc., 124 F.3d 1366, 1375 (10th Cir. 1997).

[19] 37 CFR 202.1.

by government agencies belong in the public domain and may be used without restrictions. C-SPAN video of House and Senate floor proceedings is also part of the public domain. Its video of other federal government events, like Congressional committee hearings and White House briefings is not, but the network permits public Internet sites to make noncommercial use of it.[20]

Although the U.S. government cannot copyright its own work in the United States, U.S. agencies outside the United States may obtain protection for government works through foreign copyright laws. The U.S. government also may own copyrighted material that is transferred or bequeathed to it.[21] Work prepared for the U.S. government by private contractors may be copyrighted. The owner of the work depends on the terms of the contract. A privately prepared work that includes material from government documents may be copyrighted, but the copyright would not extend to the government work in the document, only to the original material added by the author.

Works produced by state or municipal governments do not necessarily fall into the public domain. As sovereign entities, states and municipalities are responsible for setting their own policies regarding the use of their documents. Sometimes they assert a copyright interest in them.

Works in the public domain

The *public domain* is a conceptual category of works that never had or no longer have copyright protection and therefore are freely available for anyone to use at any time for any purpose. All works enter the public domain when their copyright protection expires. Others are there because their copyright was abandoned or not properly registered or renewed when copyright registration and renewal were required. In 2004, for example, Ludlow Music, Inc. demanded that JibJab Media, the creator of a widely circulated web animation parodying George Bush and John Kerry to "This Land is Your Land," remove the animation from the Internet and compensate the company for the unlicensed use of its copyrighted song. JibJab enlisted the Electronic Frontier Foundation's help to file for a declaratory judgment, requesting judicial confirmation that its use of the song was fair.[22] While preparing for the case, EFF discovered that the song had been in the public domain since 1973. Woody Guthrie, the composer, filed the original copyright for the song when copyright protection lasted 28 years, with the option to renew for another 28 years. Ludlow acquired the copyright from Guthrie, but failed to renew it.

---

[20] C-SPAN policies on use of its video can be found on its website at http://www.c-spanvideo.org/rights (last visited Feb. 3, 2012).

[21] 17 U.S.C. § 105 (2007).

[22] Fred von Lohmann, *This Song Belongs to You and Me*, Electronic Frontier Foundation, Aug. 24, 2004, https://www.eff.org/deeplinks/2004/08/song-belongs-you-and-me, and JibJab Media v. Ludlow Music ("This Land" Parody), Electronic Frontier Foundation, http://www.eff.org/cases/jibjab-media-inc-v-ludlow-music-inc.

Who Qualifies for Copyright Protection?

Copyright protection vests in the creator of a work the moment the work is produced. If two or more people produce a work, they are considered to be joint owners of the copyright.

Works prepared by an employee in the scope of his or her employment are considered *works for hire* and belong to the employer. A graphic artist, writer, or web designer employed by a company to create a work for the company has no right to authorize others to use the work without the permission of his or her employer. A work commissioned by an organization from a freelancer also may be considered a work for hire. But both parties must agree in a signed document before the work commences that it will constitute a work for hire.[23]

In *New York Times Co. v. Tasini* (2001), the Supreme Court held that *The New York Times* violated its freelance writers' distribution rights by making their work available in computer databases that sell access to articles divorced from the newspaper. *The New York Times* owned the compilation right to the particular issues that contained the freelancers' articles, but it did not have the right to use the articles individually for other purposes.[24] The win was short-lived for the freelancers. After its loss, the *Times* simply required them to sign over the electronic rights to their work before the paper would publish it.

Occasionally, it is not clear whether a work's creator is an employee producing a work for hire or an independent contractor who may retain the copyright. The Supreme Court considered the issue in *Community for Creative Non-Violence v. Reid* (1989).[25] Community for Creative Non-Violence, an organization that aids the homeless, commissioned a sculpture depicting their plight and then fought the artist for the copyright to it. The artist who produced the work created it in his studio, where the organization's representatives visited on several occasions to check on its progress and provide suggestions regarding its size and configuration. When the statue was delivered, the organization paid the artist for the work and installed it. Subsequently, both parties filed competing copyright claims. When CCNV sued to determine copyright ownership, the district court found in its favor, concluding that the statue was a work for hire. But the D.C. Court of Appeals reversed, because the statue was not "prepared by an employee within the scope of his or her employment" and the parties had not agreed in writing that it was a work for hire. The Supreme Court developed criteria to determine whether a party hired for a particular job may be categorized as an employee within the meaning of the Copyright Act's work for hire provision. Factors to consider include:

- the hiring party's right to control the manner by which the work is done;
- the skill required to complete the work;

[23] 17 U.S.C. § 101(2) (2007).
[24] 533 U.S. 438 (2001).
[25] 490 U.S. 730 (1989).

- the source of the instruments or tools used to produce the work;
- the location of the work;
- the duration of the business relationship between the parties;
- whether the hiring party may assign additional projects to the hired party;
- the hired party's discretion over when and how long to work;
- the method of payment;
- the hired party's role in hiring and paying assistants;
- whether the work is part of the hiring party's regular business;
- whether the hiring party is in business;
- the provision of employee benefits; and
- the tax treatment of the hired party.[26]

Basing its analysis on these factors, the Supreme Court concluded that Reid was an independent contractor who retained ownership of the copyright.

What Are a Copyright Holder's Exclusive Rights?

Although the word *copyright* implies the right to reproduce a work, copyright law actually encompasses a bundle of individual rights, which are listed in Section 106 of the Copyright Act. Copyright holders have the exclusive right to do or authorize someone else to do any of the following:

1. to reproduce the copyrighted work in copies or *phonorecords*;
2. to prepare *derivative* works based upon the copyrighted work;
3. to distribute copies or phonorecords of the copyrighted work to the public by sale or other transfer of ownership, or by rental, lease, or lending;
4. in the case of literary, musical, dramatic, and choreographic works, pantomimes, motion pictures, and other audiovisual works, to perform the copyrighted work publicly;
5. in the case of literary, musical, dramatic, and choreographic works, pantomimes, and pictorial, graphic, or sculptural works, including the individual images of a motion picture or other audiovisual work, to display the copyrighted work publicly; and
6. in the case of sound recordings, to perform the copyrighted work publicly by means of a digital audio transmission.

"Phonorecords" sounds like an antiquated term but actually encompasses any modern sound recording.

A derivative work is one that has been "recast, transformed, or adapted" from the original. It may include newly edited editions, translations, dramatizations, abridgments, adaptations, compilations, and works republished with new matter added.

Copyrights are separable. Copyright holders may transfer all or some of the rights to a copyrighted work to others, either through sale or bequeathal in a will. Consequently, the rights to one work may be controlled by more than one person or organization. To be valid the transfer must be in writing and signed by the copyright holder.

[26] *Id.* at 751–52.

The Copyright Act also provides a limited right of attribution and integrity to visual artists. It gives authors of visual works of art, whether or not they are the copyright owners of the work, the right to claim authorship of their works, or alternatively, the right to prevent the association of their names with works they did not create or which have been distorted, mutilated or modified.[27] It also entitles the author of a visual work, subject to some restrictions, to prevent any intentional "distortion, mutilation, or other modification of that work which would be prejudicial to his or her honor or reputation" or "to prevent the destruction of a work of recognized stature."[28]

First sale doctrine

Generally, however, copyright holders have no right to control the physical product embodying their expression once it has been sold. The Copyright Act distinguishes between expressive content, such as a movie, which is exclusively controlled by a copyright holder, and the physical object containing the expression, such as a DVD, which anyone may own.[29] A provision of the Act known as the *first sale doctrine*, entitles the lawful owner of a copyrighted work to sell, transfer or dispose of the physical work without infringing on the copyright owner's distribution right.[30] The provision assumes, however, that once that transfer is complete, the owner will no longer possess the work. So for example, the owner of a DVD may sell or give it away, but may not burn a second copy for a friend and keep the original.

The first sale doctrine is the source of secondary markets for books, CDs and DVDs, but its boundaries have been constrained by recent court decisions. One of these concerned the application of the first sale doctrine to software. The U.S. Court of Appeals for the Ninth Circuit held in *Vernor v. Autodesk* (2010) that the purchaser of a copy of AutoCAD software was not entitled to resell it under the first sale doctrine, because he was not its legal owner, but rather a licensee.[31] When Autodesk, the software's manufacturer, prevented Timothy Vernor from selling used copies of AutoCAD on eBay, he sought a declaratory judgment that the sale was protected by the first sale doctrine. The district court granted Vernor summary judgment, but the Ninth Circuit reversed. The shrinkwrap agreement on the software stated that the user was granted a license to use it. Citing earlier precedent, the court stated that "where a transferee receives a particular copy of a copyrighted work pursuant to a written agreement, [the court] consider[s] all of the provisions of the agreement to determine whether the transferee became an owner of the copy or received a license."[32] Since the original buyer was only a licensee, Autodesk retained the rights to all copies of the software.

[27] 17 U.S.C. § 106A(a) (2007).
[28] *Id.*
[29] *Id.* § 202.
[30] 17 U.S.C. 109(a).
[31] Vernor v. Autodesk, 621 F.3d 1102 (2010).
[32] *Id.* at 1109.

The Ninth Circuit also interpreted the first sale doctrine to apply exclusively to items produced and distributed in the United States. In *Costco Wholesale Corp. v. Omega* (2008) the court considered whether a discount retailer was entitled to buy Swiss watches abroad, where they were sold less expensively, and resell them in the U.S. at a price that undercut the manufacturer's.[33] The Ninth Circuit concluded that the first sale doctrine did not apply under these circumstances because Copyright law provides that the unauthorized importation of a work violates the copyright owner's distribution right.[34] Normally copyright law would not apply to a watch. Omega, the watch manufacturer, based its case on the unauthorized distribution of the copyrighted crown symbol on the watch – an unusual assertion that the Ninth Circuit accepted. The Supreme Court reviewed the decision but issued no opinion of its own.[35] One member of the Court recused herself from the case, leaving eight left who divided four to four on whether the first sale doctrine applied. In such cases, the lower court's decision is allowed to stand, but does not become a national precedent.

In a case more directly related to copyrighted material, the Second Circuit offered an even narrower interpretation of the first sale doctrine. It held in *John Wiley & Sons, Inc. v. Kirtsaeng* (2011), that the first sale doctrine is only applicable to domestically produced works. The defendant in the case, a doctoral student from Thailand, subsidized his American education by importing foreign editions of U.S. textbooks sold at discounted prices in Asia, and then reselling them on sites like eBay at prices that undercut those the publishers charged for domestic editions of the books sold in the United States.[36] When Wiley sued Kirtsaeng for selling foreign editions of its textbooks in the U.S., Kirtsaeng argued that the practice was legal under the first sale doctrine. The court agreed that the first sale doctrine applies to the lawful owner of a book, but did not think that Kirtsaeng had acquired the books lawfully. The Copyright Act also states that "Importation into the United States, *without the authority of the owner of copyright under this title*, of copies . . . of a work that have been acquired outside the United States is an infringement of the exclusive right to distribute copies" of the work.[37] It concluded from this provision that the first sale doctrine must only apply to copies manufactured domestically. The broad scope of the holding is worrisome because so many books – including this one – are printed outside the United States. If taken at face value, the Second Circuit's interpretation could allow publishers to sidestep the first sale doctrine by manufacturing their goods abroad and then importing them for sale in the U.S.[38]

The Supreme Court has agreed to review this case.

---

[33] Omega S.A. v. Costco Wholesale Corp., v (2008).

[34] 17 U.S.C. 602(a)(1).

[35] Costco Wholesale Corp. v. Omega, 131 S. Ct. 565 (2010).

[36] John Wiley & Sons, Inc. v. Kirtsaeng, 654 F.3d 210 (2nd Cir. 2011).

[37] 17 U.S.C. § 602(a)(1) (emphasis added).

[38] John Wiley & Sons, Inc. v. Kirtsaeng, 654 F.3d. at 222, n. 44 ("Kirtsaeng argues that this holding is undesirable as a matter of public policy because it may permit a plaintiff to vitiate the first sale doctrine by 'manufactur[ing] *all* of its volumes overseas only to then ship them into the U.S. for domestic sales.' . . . The result might be that American manufacturing would contract along with the protections of the first sale doctrine. Kirtsaeng argues that this could not possibly have been Congress's intent. We acknowledge the force of this concern, but it does not affect or alter our interpretation of the Copyright Act.").

Registering and Protecting Works

Copyright, once protected through state and common law, is now exclusively protected through federal law. It is no longer necessary, however, to register a work officially through the Copyright Office to acquire copyright in it.[39] All works created from 1978 on have been protected upon creation. The United States made this concession in order to join the Berne Convention for the Protection of Literary and Artistic Works. The treaty, originally signed in Berne, Switzerland, in 1886, has 164 member nations who recognize the international validity of each other's copyrights.[40]

Although copyright registration is not required in the United States, certain conveniences and rights accrue from it that make the extra effort and expense worthwhile. To sue for copyright infringement, for example, the work must be registered. It is possible to register a work after the infringement has taken place, but doing so poses a delay and the copyright holder may be limited to an award of *actual damages*. A copyright holder who registers a work within three months of publication or prior to the infringement of the work may be awarded statutory damages and attorney's fees.

Although registration is not required for copyright protection in the United States, it is advantageous for many reasons.

To register a work, the copyright owner must submit a completed application form and $45 fee to the Copyright Office along with two copies of a published work or one copy of an unpublished work to be deposited in the Library of Congress. The Register of Copyrights will issue a certificate of registration to the copyright holder. A certificate issued before, or within five years after, a work is first published constitutes *prima facie* evidence of a valid copyright that may be used later in a judicial proceeding should someone else use the work illegally.[41]

Affixing a notice of copyright to a published work is not required for copyright protection but is advisable. It may later serve as evidence in a copyright suit that the alleged infringer's use was not innocent. A copyright notice consists of three elements:

1. the letter "c" in a circle (©) or the word "Copyright," written in its entirety or abbreviated as Copr.;
2. the year the work was first published; and
3. the name of the copyright owner.

If the copyrighted work is a "phonorecord," then the letter c is replaced with the letter p in a circle accompanied by the year of publication and the copyright holder's name. A copyright notice also may be placed on an unpublished work, as in the following example: Unpublished work © 2012 Ashley Packard.

Because the copyright notice is not required, it is never safe to assume that its absence means a work may be freely used. In general, unless a work is very old, you should assume that it is copyrighted and permission to use it is required. However, identifying

---

[39] 17 U.S.C. § 408 (2011).
[40] Berne Convention Implementation Act of 1988, Pub. L. 100–568, 102 Stat. 2853.
[41] 17 U.S.C. § 410 (2007).

the copyright holder for a work is not always easy. Some works are not only missing the copyright information, but also published anonymously or under a pseudonym. The name accompanying the copyright notice published with the work may no longer be valid if the copyright has changed hands. Also, the copyright holders responsible for individual parts of a collected work may not be listed. The best place to begin a search for a copyright holder is through Copyright Office records, which include registration information.

Copyright Office records for more recently copyrighted works are accessible through their website at www.copyright.gov/records and searchable by the author, copyright notice, or title.

How long does copyright protection last?

Copyright in a work created since 1978 lasts for the life of the author plus 70 years, expiring at the end of the calendar year.[42] If two or more people jointly own the work, copyright endures 70 years beyond the life of the last surviving author. A work for hire, or a work that is anonymous or pseudonymous, is protected for 95 years after the date of publication or 120 years after the work is created, whichever comes first.

Determining the term of protection for a work created before January 1, 1978, is more complicated. At that time, copyrights were protected for 28 years, with the option to renew another 28 years. But changes in the law extended the renewal period on the second term from 28 to 67 years. As of January of 2012, any work published or copyrighted prior to 1923 has expired.

Congress extended copyright protection prospectively and retrospectively by 20 years in 1998 with the passage of the Copyright Term Extension Act.[43] The extension made American copyright terms consistent with those in the European Union. The EU's Council of Ministers passed a directive in 1993 requiring all EU members to protect their own copyrights for a term equal to the life of the author plus 70 years and foreign copyrights for a term equal to that guaranteed by their own countries.[44] At the time, the duration of U.S. copyright protection complied with the minimum standard required by the Berne Convention – 50 years beyond the life of the author. Congress passed the 20-year extension to ensure that EU countries protected American works as long as their own.

The extension was also politically motivated. Disney lobbied hard for it because the copyrights on its characters Mickey Mouse, Goofy, and Pluto were about to expire and

Myth of the Poor Man's Copyright

It is commonly asserted that in lieu of official registration through the U.S. Copyright Office, a creator can protect a work using something called the "poor man's copyright." The theory is that if the creator places the work in a sealed envelope and mails it to him or herself, the postmarked letter will stand in place of official registration. This is not true. While this type of an action might be useful in establishing ownership of the work on the date the envelope was postmarked – thus helping the creator register the work after an infringement takes place – it would not take the place of the official registration required to file a copyright suit in federal court. A creator denied access to the statutory damages and attorney's fees limited to those who register a work before it is infringed would, however, come out of a copyright suit a poorer man. Even if he won the suit, he would be limited to actual damages, which rarely cover the cost of going to trial.

Authors whose works fell into the public domain in 2012 under the "life plus 70 years" term include James Joyce, Virginia Wolfe, and Johan Wagenaar.

---

[42] *Id.* §§ 302, 305.

[43] Sonny Bono Copyright Term Extension Act. See Pub. L. 105–298 (October 27, 1998).

[44] *See* Jenny Dixon, *The Copyright Term Extension Act: Is Life Plus Seventy Too Much?* 18 HASTINGS COMM. ENT. L.J. 945, 968 (1996) (citing Council Directive 93/98, 1993 O.J. (L 290)).

move into the public domain.[45] In that event, others could have used the characters for creative purposes. Disney itself has been a tremendous beneficiary of public domain works. It has generated millions in revenue reinterpreting folk tales in the public domain, such as Cinderella and Snow White, and literature in the public domain, such as Victor Hugo's *The Hunchback of Notre Dame* and the Grimm brothers' fairy tales.

Eric Eldred, the publisher of an online repository of public domain works, challenged the constitutionality of the Copyright Term Extension Act in *Eldred v. Ashcroft* (2003).[46] Eldred argued that the law (which extended copyright's duration for the eleventh time) violated the constitutional mandate to protect works for *limited times.* He also argued that, by giving retroactive protection to copyrighted works destined for the public domain, the law violated the First Amendment rights of others entitled to use them. However, the Supreme Court upheld the extension. It concluded that extending copyright terms to meet the EU standard was a rational exercise of Congressional authority.

In *Golan v. Holder* (2012), the Supreme Court considered whether it was constitutional to restore copyright protection to works that had already been in the public domain and whether doing so violated the First Amendment rights of people who were no longer allowed to use them.[47] The case involved a challenge to a 1994 law that Congress passed to implement a global trade agreement negotiated in Uruguay. The treaty required members of the Berne Convention to protect foreign works – even those that had fallen into the public domain – if the works were still protected in their home countries, or risk penalties imposed by the World Trade Organization. The affect of the law, called the Uruguay Round Agreements Act, was to restore protection to works such as Prokofiev's *Peter and the Wolf* and Alfred Hitchcock's film *Number 17*. Petitioners in the case were orchestra conductors, educators, performers, publishers, archivists, and motion picture distributors who had grown to rely on these and others works that the Act removed from the public domain.

As in *Eldred*, the Supreme Court concluded that Congress had not exceeded its constitutional authority through its retroactive application of copyright protection. Writing for the Court, Justice Ginsberg stated that the Constitution does not "render the public domain untouchable by Congress."[48] She cited historical examples of Congress adjusting copyright law to protect categories of works once outside its reach, such as dramatic works, photographs, motion pictures, sound recordings and architectural works. The majority viewed the law as a rational restriction that "ensured that most works, whether foreign or domestic, would be governed by the same legal regime."[49] It did not consider the law to be a violation of the First Amendment. The petitioners had no "vested rights"

---

[45] *See* Christina Gifford, *Note: The Sonny Bono Copyright Term Extension Act*, 30 U. Mem L. Rev. 363, 398 (2000) (indicating that 10 of 13 sponsors for the House bill and eight of 12 sponsors for the Senate bill received contributions from Disney.).

[46] 537 U.S. 186 (2003).

[47] Golan v. Holder, No. 10–545, 2012 U.S. LEXIS 907 (Oct. 5, 2011).

[48] *Id.* at 51.

[49] *Id.* at 57.

in the works because they were in the public domain. Moreover, the law did not deny petitioners' access to the works. Petitioners could still make fair use of parts of the work or complete use of the works by licensing them.

What is Copyright Infringement?

Reproducing, distributing, publicly displaying, publicly performing, or producing a derivative version of a copyrighted work without the copyright holder's permission constitutes copyright infringement. To succeed in a copyright infringement case, plaintiffs must prove their ownership of the work and that the defendant violated one or more of their exclusive rights. Because there is rarely direct evidence that a person copied a work, courts will settle for circumstantial evidence that the defendant had access to the copyrighted work prior to the creation of his or her own and that there is substantial similarity between them, both in ideas and expression. An exact reproduction is not required.

Those involved in the production of digital media particularly need to understand that a series of steps taken with regard to one work may violate more than one right. For example, making an unauthorized copy of someone else's copyrighted work, altering it, and then distributing it without permission, would violate three of the copyright holder's exclusive rights, each punishable separately.

Misconceptions regarding the derivative right are common. Copyright holders possess the exclusive right to make alternative versions of their work. Finding an image on the Internet and altering it does not create a new work; it creates a derivative work that violates the copyright holder's exclusive right. Although urban myths suggest that altering a work by 20 percent or changing it a certain number of times can protect against suits for copyright infringement, no such formula exists. A good rule of thumb is that if the original work is still recognizable, it can still be considered a derivative version.

Copyright liability

Copyright infringement is a strict liability offense, meaning that intent to infringe has no bearing on a determination of guilt. In *Pinkham v. Sara Lee Corp.* (1992), the Eighth Circuit explained that:

> Once a plaintiff has proven that he or she owns the copyright on a particular work, and that the defendant has infringed upon those "exclusive rights," the defendant is liable for the infringement and this liability is absolute. The defendant's intent is simply not relevant: The defendant is liable even for "innocent" or "accidental" infringements.[50]

[50]Pinkham v. Sara Lee Corp., 983 F.2d 824, 828 (1992).

An *indemnity agreement* is a contract in which one party agrees to accept financial responsibility for any loss or damage that might result from a particular action taken.

An *errors and omissions policy* insures professionals for the costs of negligent actions made in service to others.

A court may dispose of a case without a trial, using summary judgment, if it is convinced that there is no dispute regarding the material facts of the case and a party is entitled to judgment.

The application of *strict liability* proceeds from the assumption that the infringer, unlike the copyright owner, "has an opportunity to guard against liability for infringement by diligent inquiry, or at least the ability to guard against liability for infringement by an indemnity agreement from his supplier or by an 'errors and omissions' insurance policy."[51]

There are three levels of copyright liability: direct liability, contributory liability, and vicarious liability. Individuals who infringe upon the exclusive rights guaranteed to copyright holders in Section 106 of the Copyright Act are *directly liable* for copyright infringement, whether they were aware of the infringement or not.

Although not part of the Copyright statute, courts have also developed doctrines for contributory liability for copyright infringement. Individuals who "knowingly" induce, cause, or materially contribute to the infringing conduct of others, but who have not actually committed the copyright infringement themselves, may be *contributorily liable* for copyright infringement.[52] A court also may impose liability for contributory infringement on individuals who aid an infringer without knowledge of the infringement, but who should "have reason to know" they are aiding an infringer. For example, in *Religious Technology Center v. Netcom On-Line Communication Services* (1995), a California district judge denied *summary judgment* to an Internet service provider that was sued for copyright infringement based on its subscriber's activities.[53] The subscriber was a disgruntled former minister of the Church of Scientology who began posting the church's secret texts online so others could read and comment on them. Netcom, the ISP, claimed no knowledge of copyright infringement on the part of its subscriber, specifically because it didn't review the posts. However, because the plaintiff, the church's publisher, had notified Netcom of the infringement prior to the suit and copyright notices were still present on the documents posted, the court believed there was a legitimate question as to whether the ISP knew or should have known about the subscriber's activity, implicating contributory liability on its part.

Individuals may be *vicariously liable* for copyright infringement if they have the right and ability to supervise the infringing conduct of others, as well as a direct financial interest in the infringement. Knowledge of the infringement is not required. Vicarious liability, which applies to other areas of tort law as well, evolved from the doctrine of respondeat superior, which dictates that the master (employer) is responsible for the actions of the servant (employee). However, it no longer requires an employer–employee relationship, as long as some level of control and financial remuneration is involved.

File Sharing

Cases involving illegal file sharing can be used to illustrate all three levels of liability. Courts have made it clear that sharing copyrighted music, games, and videos is a form of direct copyright infringement. Over a five-year period, the Recording Industry

---

[51] *Id.* at 829 (quoting Melville B. Nimmer and David Nimmer, 3 Nimmer on Copyright § 13.08 at 139 (1992)).
[52] Gershwin Publishing Corp. v. Columbia Artists Management, Inc., 443 F.2d 1159, 1162 (2d Cir. 1971).
[53] 907 F. Supp. 1361 (N.D. Cal. 1995).

Association of America filed suit against more than 30,000 file traders. Most of these actions ended in out-of-court settlements, but a few went to trial.

The most renowned of these cases involved Jammie Thomas-Rasset, who was fined $1.5 million in 2009 for willfully infringing 24 songs, which the judge later reduced to $54,000.[54] Thomas-Rasset, whom the RIAA alleged traded as many as 1,700 songs on the file-sharing network Kazaa, lost her case three times. In 2007, a jury issued a $222,000 verdict against her. After learning that he had given the jury inaccurate instructions, the judge set aside the verdict and ordered a new trial.[55] The judge had instructed the jury that the act of making sound recordings available for electronic distribution without authorization violated the copyright owner's distribution right even without evidence that the file was ever downloaded. He had been unaware of an earlier precedent within its circuit that infringement of the distribution right requires an *actual* distribution of a copyrighted work.[56] Courts in different jurisdictions disagree on whether making a copyrighted work available for download constitutes an actual distribution or merely an offer to distribute.[57] However, there is no question that the unauthorized act of uploading or downloading copyrighted music violates the reproduction right.

A second jury found Thomas-Rasset guilty of both uploading and downloading music and issued a $1.92 million judgment against her. The judge reduced the fine to $54,000 or $2,250 per song, which is three times the statutory minimum. The RIAA offered Thomas-Rasset a $25K settlement to vacate the ruling reducing the settlement (and negate a precedent for a reduced judgment), but she refused. She insisted on a third trial to reevaluate damages owed to the RIAA. The third jury, tasked only with determining an appropriate judgment for the liability decided in the second trial, imposed a penalty of $1.5 million, which amounted to $62,500 per song for the RIAA. Calling the original fee "appalling" and "oppressive" the judge reduced the judgment again to $54,000, which he stated was the maximum consistent with due process.[58] The RIAA has appealed the reduction to the Eighth Circuit. It is clear from the defendant's modest income that she probably could not afford the $54,000 fine, much less one of $1.5 million, but the RIAA is interested in the precedent the case will set.

[54]Virgin Records Am., Inc. v. Thomas (formerly Capitol Records v. Thomas), CV-06-1497 (MJD/RLE) (D. Minn. 2009).

[55]Capitol Records v. Thomas, CV-06-1497 (MJD/RLE) (D. Minn. 2007).

[56]National Car Rental System, Inc. v. Computer Associates Int'l, Inc., 991 F.2d 426, 434 (8th Cir. 1993) (citing 2 Nimmer on Copyright §8.11[A], at 8–124.1).

[57]*See* Atlantic Recording Corp. v. Howell, 554 F. Supp. 2d 976 (D. Ariz. 2008) (finding that "making available" recordings for distribution is not actionable under copyright law); London-Sire v. Doe, 542 F. Supp. 2d 153 (D. Mass. 2008) (holding that "merely exposing music files to the internet is not copyright infringement"). *But see* Elektra v. Barker, 551 F. Supp. 2d 234 (S.D. N.Y. 2008) (finding that offering to distribute files on a file sharing network can implicate the distribution right.); Warner Bros. Records, Inc. v. Payne, Civil Action No. W-06-CA-051, 2006 WL 2844415, at *3–4 (W.D. Tex. July 17, 2006) ("Listing unauthorized copies of sound recordings using an online file-sharing system constitutes an offer to distribute those works, thereby violating a copyright owner's exclusive right of distribution.").

[58]Capital Records v. Jammie Thomas Rasset, CASE 0:06-cv-01497-MJD-LIB Document 457(filed July 22, 2011).

In December of 2008, the RIAA announced its intention to abandon new lawsuits against individual file sharers, which had become a public relations fiasco. Instead it planned to work with ISPs to discontinue service to repeat offenders.[59]

Courts consider the provision of file trading services or software to be a form of contributory infringement, if the software provider is aware of the infringement. In *A&M Records v. Napster, Inc.* (2001), the Ninth Circuit found Napster's action of providing a centralized website, where subscribers could find the titles of the music they wanted to download, a contributory and vicarious copyright infringement, even though subscribers downloaded the actual songs from other customer's computers.[60] It was clear to the Ninth Circuit that Napster was not only aware of the infringing activity but facilitated it by channeling subscribers to the music. It was also apparent that, although Napster could have taken actions to restrict the infringement, it did not and that it profited from the service.

Grokster, a West Indies-based software company, was found to have contributorily and vicariously infringed upon MGM Studios' copyrights by supplying software that enabled Internet users to engage in illegal file trading. Grokster attempted to rely on *Sony Corp. of America v. Universal City Studios, Inc.* (1984) to defeat the claim of contributory infringement. In *Sony*, the Supreme Court held that the distribution of a commercial product, like Sony's video recorder, which was capable of substantial noninfringing uses, would not result in contributory liability for infringement.[61] Although video recorders could be used to make unauthorized copies of televised programs, the court focused on a more common noninfringing use – time shifting.

In *MGM Studios v. Grokster*, however, the Court found that the software was primarily used for infringing purposes and that its distributors had *induced* direct infringement among its users. Distinguishing between the two cases, Justice Souter explained:

> Evidence of active steps . . . taken to encourage direct infringement, such as advertising an infringing use or instructing how to engage in an infringing use, shows an affirmative intent that the product be used to infringe, and overcomes the law's reluctance to find liability when a defendant merely sells a commercial product suitable for some lawful use.[62]

The Supreme Court also pointed to evidence of vicarious infringement, when it noted that Grokster's profits from advertising increased with the number of users drawn to the service and that the company could have used filtering tools to diminish infringing activity, but did not do so.

Aside from legal differences, *Sony* and *Grokster* also can be distinguished by their real-world economic ramifications. By the time the Court heard *Sony*, videocassette recorders were common in American homes. It would have been difficult to suddenly

---

[59] Sarah McBride, *Music Industry to Abandon Mass Suits*, WALL ST. J., Dec. 18, 2008, at B1.

[60] 239 F.3d 1004, 1011–14 (2001); *See also* Hotaling v. Church of Jesus Christ of Latter-Day Saints, 118 F.3d 199 (4th Cir. 1997) (holding that making a work available online violates its owner's distribution right).

[61] 464 U.S. 417 (1984).

[62] MGM Studios v. Grokster, 545 U.S. 913, 936 (2005) (citations omitted).

"outlaw" them. Moreover, Universal Studios had no data indicating that the recorders had caused it direct harm. The software Grokster supplied for peer-to-peer (P2P) file trading was free. Users had not invested hundreds of dollars in the technology. Film studios and music publishers also provided data regarding actual damages caused by file trading.

Digital Millennium Copyright Act

Digital media have posed a significant challenge for copyright law because they make it almost effortless to infringe upon others' rights. Lawmakers have responded by passing a series of measures to tighten protection on digital works, the most significant being the Digital Millennium Copyright Act.[63] The DMCA makes it illegal to circumvent digital rights management technology directly or to "import, offer to the public, provide, or otherwise traffic" in any technology, product, or service that can circumvent technological measures used to control access to copyrighted works.[64]

Courts take violations of the DMCA very seriously. In 2010, Blizzard Entertainment, the company behind the game World of Warcraft, won an $88 million default judgment against a defendant who enabled users to circumvent its authentication software. The defendant used a private server that hosted a community of 427,393 members who played WoW there instead of on Blizzard's servers. The court multiplied the number of users by the statutory minimum of $200 per act. That amounted to statutory damages of $85,478,600, plus profits made on the service and legal fees. The judge added, "To the extent that this figure appears unreasonably large, Congress has mandated this approach and the Court is unable to deviate from it."[65]

A default judgment is one that is rendered without the defendant's participation in the trial.

Certain circumventions of digital rights management software are allowed under the DMCA. Schools and libraries may circumvent copyright technology to see whether they want to purchase a legitimate copy of a work. Individuals may break the defensive code in a software program in order to reverse engineer it for the purpose of creating another program that works with it. Encryption researchers may circumvent copyright locks "to identify and analyze flaws and vulnerabilities in encryption technologies," as long as the code breaking and any information disseminated regarding it is done for the purpose of advancing the technology rather than facilitating infringement.[66] Exemptions are also provided for those who do security testing for computer networks. Computer users are also allowed to disable technologies used to collect and disseminate personally identifying information about them.

Congress incorporated a "fail safe" provision into the Act to deal with the DMCA's unanticipated impact on legitimate uses of particular categories of copyrighted works.

---

[63] Pub. L. No. 105–304, 112 Stat. 2860 (Oct. 28, 1998), codified at 17 U.S.C. § 1201, et seq.
[64] 17 U.S.C. §§ 1201(a)(b) (2007).
[65] Blizzard Entm't, Inc. v. Reeves, 2010 U.S. Dist. LEXIS 85560, at 9 (C.D. Cal., Aug. 10, 2010).
[66] 17 U.S.C. § 1201(g).

The DMCA authorizes the Librarian of Congress to create limited exemptions to the anti-circumvention provision every three years to spare individuals whose fair use of some copyrighted materials otherwise would be adversely affected. Some of the exemptions created by the Librarian of Congress and the Copyright Office in 2010 permitted people to:

- "jailbreak" smart phones, like the iPhone, by circumventing DRM software that prevents users from installing lawful applications that may not have been approved by the manufacturer;
- unlock phones for use with other wireless providers;
- disable controls on electronic books that prevent the read-aloud function or use of screen readers; and
- circumvent DRM software on lawfully purchased DVDs to incorporate short portions of motion pictures into new works for criticism or comment in documentary filmmaking, educational purposes and other noncommercial uses.[67]

The right to circumvent digital rights management software on DVDs would also protect amateur creators of mashups on sites like YouTube.

The DMCA brought the United States into compliance with the World Intellectual Property Organization Copyright Treaty ("WIPO Treaty"), which requires signatories to "provide adequate legal protection and effective legal remedies against the circumvention of effective technological measures" used by copyright holders to restrict unauthorized use of their work.[68] However, its anti-circumvention provision has been controversial because it arguably alters the balance between the rights of copyright holders and copyright users. Critics have claimed that it effectively creates a new right to control access to copyrighted works by prohibiting the circumvention of digital rights management technology used to restrict access to digital works.

Exemption for Internet service providers

The Digital Millennium Copyright Act created an exemption to shield Internet service providers from liability for the infringing actions of their subscribers or for linking to sites that contain infringing information. The DMCA's safe harbor for service providers shields ISPs from liability for "(1) transitory digital network communications; (2) system caching; (3) information residing on systems or networks at the direction of users; and (4) information location tools."[69] The exemption applies as long as the service provider takes no part in editing the material or selecting its audience, has no actual knowledge of the infringement or awareness of "facts and circumstances from which

---

[67]Copyright Office, Library of Congress, Final Rule: Exemption to Prohibition on Circumvention of Copyright Protection Systems for Access Control Technologies, https://www.eff.org/files/filenode/dmca_2009/RM-2008-8.pdf.
[68]WIPO Copyright Treaty, Apr. 12, 1997, art. 11, S. Treaty Doc. No. 105–17 (1997), 1997 WL 447232.
[69]17 U.S.C. §§ 512(a)(b)(c)(d) (2011).

infringing activity is apparent," and gains no financial benefit from the infringing activity. Once service providers learn from copyright holders that material accessible through their systems is infringing, they are required to remove or disable access to it expeditiously. The exemption has consequently come to be known as the DMCA "take-down" provision.

An ISP that disables access to material on the good-faith belief that the content is infringing will not be held liable for any damages that might be caused by the material's removal, even if it later proves not to be infringing. But the service provider is obligated to notify the subscriber that the material has been removed. If the subscriber supplies a counter notification indicating that the material is not infringing, the ISP must forward it to the person who submitted the original notice requesting its removal, informing him or her that access to the material will be restored in 10 days. If the recipient wishes to pursue the matter, he or she must then seek a court order to restrain the subscriber from further infringing the work.

A party who knowingly and materially misrepresents that a document published on an ISP's system is infringing may later be held liable for any damages or legal fees incurred by the alleged infringer or the ISP for the removal of the work.[70] The term *materially* means that the misrepresentation affected the ISP's actions. Such was the case in *Online Policy Group v. Diebold* (2004), when a California federal district court found Diebold Election Systems, a manufacturer of electronic voting machines, guilty of misusing the DMCA to squelch speech.[71] The case began when two Swarthmore College students gained access to Diebold employees' e-mails, acknowledging faults in Diebold voting machines and bugs that made its software vulnerable to hackers, and posted them on various websites. IndyMedia, an online news source, published an article about the e-mails and links to them. Diebold sent cease and desist letters to Swarthmore College, which provided the students' Internet access, and to IndyMedia's access provider, advising them that they would be shielded from a copyright suit by Diebold under the DMCA safe harbor provision as long as they removed the material from their systems. Swarthmore responded to the threat by requiring the students to take the e-mails down. But Online Policy Group, which provided Internet access for IndyMedia, filed for a declaratory judgment that the material was not infringing and monetary relief based on Diebold's misrepresentation of its copyright claim. Diebold, which never followed through with the suit, told the court that it would not send anymore cease and desist letters regarding the e-mails, so the only question left was whether the plaintiffs had a claim for damages regarding its misrepresentation. Judge Jeremy Fogel believed they did. Pointing out that it would be hard to find a subject more worthy of public interest than memos suggesting that votes might be calculated incorrectly, he concluded that use of the memos was fair. He added that the fact that Diebold never filed a copyright suit against the students suggested that it had tried to use the DMCA "as a sword to suppress publication of embarrassing content rather than as a shield to protect its

---

[70] *Id.* § 512(f).
[71] 337 F. Supp. 2d 1195 (2004).

intellectual property." In a later case, the Ninth Circuit made explicit what was implicit in Judge Fogel's decision, that "there must be a demonstration of some actual knowledge of misrepresentation on the part of the copyright owner" for the provision to apply.[72]

Courts are now beginning to consider the extent to which the DMCA's safe harbor provision applies to other Web 2.0 technologies that allow users to upload content. In 2010, a federal district court threw out a copyright infringement suit Viacom had filed against Google, YouTube's corporate parent, holding that the DMCA shielded the video sharing site from liability for its users' infringements. Viacom appealed, arguing that the safe harbor provision should not protect YouTube because it was generally aware that infringement was taking place on its site. Google defended YouTube's good-faith efforts to remove infringing content when notified about it, but maintained that YouTube has no legal obligation to act on general, non-particularized knowledge that copyright infringements are occurring on its site. In 2012, the Second Circuit agreed, holding that Google is protected by the DMCA, unless Viacom could show that YouTube has been "willfully blind" or exerted "substantial influence" on its users' infringing activities.[73]

In a factually similar case, the Ninth Circuit also applied the DMCA to a video sharing site and held that the site's general knowledge that its service could be used to post infringing material was insufficient to override safe harbor protection. In *UMG Recordings, Inc. v. Shelter Capital Partners* (2010), the appellate court upheld a lower court decision granting summary judgment to Veoh Networks in UMG's copyright suit against it.[74] The court determined that the copyright holder is in the best position to recognize infringing material on a site and to respond to it through the DMCA's notice and takedown provision. Unfortunately, Veoh's victory was hollow. Although vindicated, its legal bills forced the company to file for bankruptcy.

The National Music Publishers Association, which was a plaintiff in a companion suit against YouTube, settled with the company in 2011 after working out a licensing agreement for music videos loaded on the site.[75] Legal commentators speculate that Viacom's suit against YouTube will eventually end in a settlement as well because neither party would benefit from an either-or solution when an arrangement to license the content would benefit both.[76]

---

[72] Rossi v. Motion Picture Association of America, 391 F.3d 1000, 1005 (9th Cir. 2004).

[73] Viacom Int'l, Inc. v. YouTube, Inc., 718 F. Supp. 2d 514 (S.D.N.Y. 2010); Viacom v. YouTube, 10-03270 (2nd Cir. April 15, 2012). To follow the case's progression, go to http://news.justia.com/cases/featured/new-york/nysdce/1:2007cv02103/302164/.

[74] UMG Recordings, Inc. v. Shelter Capital Partners Veoh Networks, Inc., 2011 U.S. App. LEXIS 25168 (9th Cir. Dec. 20, 2011).

[75] Don Jeffrey, *Music Publishing Group Drops Appeal of YouTube Copyright Infringement Case*, Bloomberg, Aug. 17, 2011, http://www.bloomberg.com/news/2011-08-17/music-publishing-group-drops-appeal-of-youtube-copyright-infringement-case.html.

[76] *See, e.g.*, Erika Morphy, *Viacom v. Google Wends Its Way Through Legal Fog*, Tech. News World, May 28, 2008, http://www.technewsworld.com/story/63187.html?welcome=1212698989.

Remedies for Copyright Infringement

Because copyright is a federal law, all infringement claims are litigated in federal court. A copyright holder has three years from the date of the infringement to file a civil suit under the Act. If the infringement is ongoing, a court may issue a temporary restraining order followed by an injunction to stop it. Courts may also impose civil remedies on infringers that include either (a) the copyright holder's actual damages, along with any profits the infringer may have accrued from the illegal use of the work, or (b) statutory damages that range from $750 to $30,000.[77] If the copyright holder can prove that the infringer's actions were willful, the court may increase statutory damages to a maximum of $150,000 per infringing act. One sign of willfulness is providing false contact information to a domain registry in connection with the infringement.

If the infringer can prove that he or she did not know and further had no reason to know that the material taken was copyrighted, a court may reduce statutory damages to as little as $200.[78] The choice to pursue statutory damages as an alternative to the actual damages belongs to the copyright holder and must be made before the court enters its final judgment.

Criminal infringement

Copyright infringement may also be prosecuted as a criminal offense if the infringement was willful and was committed

(A) for purposes of commercial advantage or private financial gain;
(B) by the reproduction or distribution, including by electronic means, during any 180–day period, of 1 or more copies or phonorecords of 1 or more copyrighted works, which have a total retail value of more than $1,000; or
(C) by the distribution of a work being prepared for commercial distribution, by making it available on a computer network accessible to members of the public, if such person knew or should have known that the work was intended for commercial distribution.[79]

A work prepared for commercial distribution would include computer software, motion pictures, music, or other audiovisual works reasonably expected to generate a commercial gain for the copyright holder.

Other actions associated with criminal infringement include placing a fraudulent notice of copyright on someone else's work, fraudulently removing a copyright notice from a copyrighted work, or making false representations in an application for copyright registration. These actions may result in a fine of up to $2,500, along with the destruction of infringing copies of a work and any equipment used to produce them.

---

[77] 17 U.S.C. § 504(a), (c)(1) (2007).
[78] Id. § 504(c)(2).
[79] Id. § 506(a)(1).

Willful circumvention of copyright protection systems for commercial or private financial gain will result in the most severe penalties. A person may be fined up to $500,000 or imprisoned for up to five years for a first offense. For a subsequent offense, a person may be fined up to $1 million or imprisoned for up to 10 years. The statute of limitations on a criminal offense is five years.

Operation in Our Sites

The Department of Homeland Security's Immigration and Customs Enforcement division began seizing domains used for copyright infringement in 2010 as part of a program called "Operation in Our Sites." Warrants are issued based on the government's assertion of probable cause to believe that the domain names were used to commit criminal violations of copyright law. The domain names were seized under 18 U.S.C § 2323(a) as property used or intended to be used to commit or facilitate the commission of criminal copyright infringement – a copyright analogue to the law that allows the government to confiscate materials used for counterfeiting. At least 125 sites have been seized without notice or first having a hearing to determine whether the material on the sites was indeed infringing. What is particularly surprising about this move is that a number of the sites included pure speech; others simply linked to other sites. The *in rem* seizure of pure speech, accomplished because it may be infringing, potentially violates procedural safeguards instituted by the First Amendment.[80]

During an in rem proceeding a court exercises its power to determine the legal status of property.

In 2011, a federal court held that the government did not have to return two domains seized from the plaintiff because the seizure did not pose a significant hardship. The plaintiff in the case was Puerto 80, a Spanish company that operated the popular sports streaming sites Rojadirecta.com and Rojadirecta.org. The U.S. government seized the sites, even though a Spanish court had earlier ruled that their content was not infringing.[81] The court concluded that the plaintiff could simply use another domain.

Balancing the Rights of Copyright Owners and Users

Although copyright protects original works of authorship, it has long since been understood that few works are truly original. Therefore it is necessary to find a balance between an author's right to protect expression in a work and the rights of others to draw inspiration from it. "Recognizing that science and art generally rely on works that came before them and rarely spring forth in a vacuum," the Copyright Act limits the rights of a copyright owner regarding works that build upon, reinterpret, and reconceive existing works."[82] It also protects the public's right to use them as the basis for social criticism and political debate.

[80] Andrew Sellars, *Seized Sites: The In Rem Forfeiture of Copyright-Infringing Domain Names* (May 8, 2011). Available at SSRN: http://ssrn.com/abstract=1835604 or doi:10.2139/ssrn.1835604.

[81] Puerto 80 Projects v. Dept. of Homeland Security, Immigration and Customs Enforcement, 11 Civ. 4139 (S.D.N.Y. filed Aug. 4, 2011).

[82] Mattel v. Walking Mountain Productions, 353 F.3d 792 (2003).

Copyright and freedom of expression

The Supreme Court has described copyright as "the engine of free expression," adding that "[b]y establishing a marketable right to the use of one's expression, copyright supplies the economic incentive to create and disseminate ideas."[83] As a general rule, courts have not recognized a conflict between copyright protection and First Amendment rights. They base this assumption on two factors: the idea/expression dichotomy and fair use. The idea/expression dichotomy "strike[s] a definitional balance between the First Amendment and the Copyright Act by permitting free communication of facts while still protecting an author's expression."[84] In other words, it assumes that because facts and ideas are not protected the basic tenor of an idea can always be phrased another way. Fair use allows the public to make limited use of others' expression.

Fair use

The Copyright Act provides the right to make *fair use* of a work, even without permission, under certain circumstances. Favored uses include "criticism, comment, news reporting, teaching (including multiple copies for classroom use), scholarship, or research."[85] But, beyond these generalizations, fair use is hard to pin down. There is no predetermined list of what is and is not acceptable to take. Courts determine what constitutes fair use on a case-by-case basis by assessing four factors:

1. the purpose and character of the use, including whether such use is of a commercial nature or is for nonprofit educational purposes;
2. the nature of the copyrighted work;
3. the amount and substantiality of the portion used in relation to the copyrighted work as a whole; and
4. the effect of the use upon the potential market for or value of the copyrighted work.[86]

Courts do not consider the potential impact of criticism on the market value of a work. They are concerned with whether the junior work could take the place of the original work in the market.

No one factor is determinative of the outcome. The results of the analysis are weighed together in light of copyright's goals.[87]

In analyzing the first factor, the purpose and character of the use, a court will consider how the protected work was used and whether the use was for commercial or nonprofit purposes. The use of a work is more likely to be considered fair if it is noncommercial. Another important consideration is the degree to which the work is transformative.[88]

---

[83] Harper & Row Publishers, Inc., v. Nation Enterprises, 471 U.S. 539, 558 (1985).
[84] *Id.* at 556 (quoting appellate decision at 723 F.2d 195, 203 (1983)).
[85] 17 U.S.C. § 107 (2007).
[86] *Id.*
[87] Campbell v. Acuff-Rose Music, Inc., 510 U.S. 569, 578 (1994).
[88] *Id.* at 584.

Keeping in mind that the purpose of copyright law is to foster new knowledge, the work should add "something new, with a further purpose or different character, altering the first with new expression, meaning, or message."[89] If the new work merely supplants the original or contributes nothing to society, it is less apt to be viewed as fair. Transformation is not essential to a finding of fair use, but "the more transformative the new work, the less will be the significance of other factors, like commercialism, that may weigh against a finding of fair use."[90] For example, the Ninth Circuit held that the use of "screen shots" taken from a computer game for the purpose of comparative advertising was fair because it was socially useful.[91]

The second factor, the nature of the copyrighted work, considers the characteristics of the work itself, for example whether the work is factual or creative, published or unpublished. Courts are more sympathetic to the use of factual works, which serve as building blocks for other factual works, than the unauthorized use of fictional works. Likewise, fair use applies more readily to published works than to unpublished works, based on the assumption that their creators were ready to expose them to the public.[92]

Courts consider the extent of the unauthorized use when they analyze the third factor, the amount and substantiality of the portion of the work used in relation to the whole. Copyright law includes no formula upon which users may rely, no number of words or percentage that it is acceptable to take. In general, the smaller the use, the more likely it is to be considered fair. But even a small use may be problematic if it constitutes the "heart of the work." For example, the copyright case *Harper & Row, Publishers, Inc. v. Nation Enterprises* (1985) concerned *The Nation* magazine's verbatim use of 300–400 words from former President Gerald Ford's unpublished manuscript.[93] That isn't very much in relation to an entire book. However the section taken constituted the heart of the work – Ford's explanation for pardoning Richard Nixon following the Watergate scandal. Ford's publisher, Harper & Row, sued *The Nation*'s publisher for copyright infringement and won at the district level, but the Second Circuit reversed, finding that *The Nation*'s quotation of Ford's work was a fair use. The Supreme Court disagreed and reversed the decision, pointing to the significance of the particular passages taken, the work's unpublished status and the economic impact of the use on the value of the work.

The actual effect of the unauthorized use on the market value of the work is the fourth and most important factor that courts consider in a fair use analysis. A commercial use that directly impairs the market for a work mitigates against fair use. So does a commercial use that interferes with a copyright holder's ability to capitalize on derivative rights. For example, Harry Potter novelist J. K. Rowling won a permanent injunction against the publisher of the Harry Potter Lexicon, preventing him from publishing an encyclopedia modeled after his successful website based on her novels.

---

[89] *Id.* at 579.
[90] *Id.* at 579.
[91] Sony Computer Entertainment America, Inc. v. Bleem, 214 F.3d 1022 (9th Cir. 2000).
[92] Salinger v. Random House, Inc., 811 F.2d 90, 97 (2nd Cir. 1987).
[93] 471 U.S. 539 (1985).

Rowling had supported the website but contended that the book would interfere with her plans to pursue a similar project.[94]

Even a noncommercial use can weigh against fair use if it deprives the copyright holder of the work's value. File trading, for example, may not appear to be "commercial" because those engaging in file exchanges are not selling music files. However, file trading allows those who otherwise might have bought the work to avoid paying for it, so it does damage the copyright holder's ability to exploit the market value of the work. The Supreme Court has said that for a noncommercial use to negate fair use "one need only show that if the challenged use should become widespread, it would adversely affect the potential market for the copyrighted work."[95]

News and fair use

The Nation tried to assert a fair use exception to copyright for matters of public concern without success when it tried to publish part of President Ford's memoirs in advance of the book's publication. In *Harper & Row, Publishers, Inc. v. Nation Enterprises*, the Court pointed out that an exception for matters of public concern "would expand fair use to effectively destroy any expectation of copyright protection in the work of a public figure. Absent such protection, and there would be little incentive to create or profit in financing such memoirs, and the public would be denied an important source of significant historical information."[96]

The Supreme Court also refused to create an exception for news based on the First Amendment in *Zacchini v. Scripps Howard Broadcasting Co.* (1977).[97] Hugo Zacchini performed a 15-second "human cannonball" act in an Ohio county fair. Against his wishes, a freelance reporter for a local television station filmed the act and broadcast it as part of a story about the fair. Zacchini sued. His cause of action was based on the "right to publicity" value of his performance. *Right of publicity* is a proprietary right protected through state law. Instead of protecting the commercial value of expression in one's work, it protects the commercial value of one's name and likeness. The Supreme Court agreed to review the case, which normally would have been a state matter, because the Ohio Supreme Court based an exception to the right of publicity on the First Amendment right to report matters of public interest. The Ohio court said the media

must be accorded broad latitude in its choice of how much it presents of each story or incident, and of the emphasis to be given to such presentation. No fixed standard which would bar the press from reporting or depicting either an entire occurrence or an entire discrete part of a public performance can be formulated which would not unduly restrict the "breathing room" in reporting which freedom of the press requires.[98]

---

[94]Warner Bros. Entertainment, Inc. v. RDR Books, O7 Civ. 9667 (RPP) (S.D. N.Y. 2008).
[95]Sony Corp. of America v. Universal City Studios, Inc., 464 U.S. 417, 451 (1984).
[96]*Id.* at 557.
[97]433 U.S. 562 (1977).
[98]Zacchini v. Scripps Howard Broadcasting Co., 47 Ohio St. 2d 224, 235 (1976).

The U.S. Supreme Court believed the Ohio court had misapplied constitutional law. It said, "Wherever the line in particular situations is to be drawn between media reports that are protected and those that are not, we are quite sure that the First and Fourteenth Amendments do not immunize the media when they broadcast a performer's entire act without his consent."[99] The case would have been very different, the Court said, if the television station had simply described the act rather than showing it in its entirety. It focused on the market value of the work, observing that if people could see it on television, they had no incentive to pay to see it at the fair.

Parodies and fair use

Parodies, which imitate "the characteristic style of an author or a work for comic effect or ridicule," are normally considered a fair use because they are intended as social or literary criticism. No one listening to Luther Campbell singing "Oh hairy woman, you better shave that stuff," would assume that his mocking parody of "Oh Pretty Woman" was meant to supplant Roy Orbison's work. Yet a lower court did rule against Campbell in a copyright suit because his parody was intended for commercial use. In *Campbell v. Acuff-Rose* (1994) the Supreme Court reversed the decision. It held that a work's commercial purpose should not automatically disqualify it from a finding of fair use when it is unlikely to be taken as a substitute for the original. It has also rejected the argument that a parody's criticism could harm the future derivative value of a work.

For a parody to enjoy fair use, however, it must be perceived as such.[100] The copyrighted work must be the "target" of the satire. An imitation of the copyrighted work's style to spear something else won't do. In *Dr. Seuss Enterprises v. Penguin Books USA, Inc.*, the defendant's poem about O. J. Simpson's trial, titled "Cat NOT in the HAT," did not qualify as a parody of Dr. Seuss's work. Although its stanzas imitated the familiar cadence of "Cat in the Hat," the poem commented on Simpson.[101]

In contrast, the photographs artist Tom Forsyth displayed on his website, depicting Barbie in compromising positions among various kitchen implements, were clearly meant to mock the gender stereotype the iconic doll has come to embody. In a series titled "Food Chain Barbie," Forsyth juxtaposed Barbie against the dangers of domesticity by photographing her nude and under attack by kitchen appliances. Barbie's corporate parent, Mattel, was not amused. The company sued the artist for copyright and trademark infringement. The Ninth Circuit Court of Appeals observed that Forsyth's use of Barbie for social criticism was fair. The character and purpose of the use was transformative; although Barbie is a creative work, parodies are generally based on creative works; Forsyth's use of the entire work was not considered excessive because any less would have required him to sever Barbie; and although his series was intended for sale, its commercial purpose did not harm Barbie's market value.[102]

---

[99] Zacchini v. Scripps Howard Broadcasting Co., 433 U.S. at 575.

[100] Campbell v. Acuff-Rose Music, Inc., 510 U.S. 569, 582 (1994).

[101] Dr. Seuss Enterprises, L.P. v. Penguin Books USA, Inc., 109 F.3d 1394, 1401 (9th Cir. 1997).

[102] Mattel v. Walking Mountain Productions, 353 F.3d 792 (9th Cir. 2003).

The Eleventh Circuit described a lower court's injunction of *The Wind Done Gone*, a parody of Margaret Mitchell's *Gone With the Wind* written from a slave's perspective, as "at odds with the shared principles of the First Amendment" and "a prior restraint on speech."[103] Mitchell's heirs convinced a Georgia court that the parody would interfere with the market for the original work. The Eleventh Circuit lifted the injunction in *SunTrust Bank v. Houghton Mifflin Co.* (2001), declaring it improbable that fans of Mitchell's romanticized view of the South would be confused by Randall's parody, written to undermine the original book's stereotypes.

Linking and fair use

The act of linking by itself is generally not considered an infringement. Courts have followed the reasoning expressed in *Ticketmaster v. Tickets.com* (2000) that "hyperlinking does not itself involve a violation of the Copyright Act (whatever it may do for other claims) since no copying is involved."[104] However, there are different types and levels of linking.

Deep linking, the practice of bypassing a website's homepage to link to an internal page is legal. However, most sites – particularly news sites – would prefer links to pages that include their identifying information and advertising.

Inline linking involves the placement of a html link for an image on one website into the code of another website, creating the illusion that the image is part of the second site. It is also legal – at least in the Ninth Circuit. However, many content owners would rather their work not be linked to in this fashion, because the image not only appears without source information but also may be connected to a site of spurious reputation. Inline linking, also known as hotlinking, was challenged in *Perfect 10 v. Amazon* (2007).[105] Perfect 10 sued Amazon and Google for directly infringing its display and distribution rights by linking to thumbnails and full-size images of its subscription photos of nude models. The district court had concluded that the question of infringement in inline linking cases hung on whether the linker stored a copy of the protected work on its server or simply directed others to the original stored on another server via the link.[106] The Court of Appeals agreed. Based on the district court's "server test," Google did not directly infringe on the full-size images, because it simply linked to other pages without storing the images on its servers. It did cache copies of the thumbnails, but this was determined to be a fair use because their use for information retrieval was deemed to be transformative.

It is now common for Internet users to embed videos from video sharing sites like YouTube into their own websites using inline links. In their terms of service, YouTube and Vimeo require that posters agree to let other users use their content in this way, so

On the popular social media site Pinterest, users "pin" images from other websites to their virtual boards using inline links. Pinterest also caches low resolution copies of those images on its servers for repinning. Is this a transformative use?

---

[103] SunTrust Bank v. Houghton Mifflin Co., 268 F.3d 1257, 1276 (11th Cir. 2001).

[104] Ticketmaster Corp. v. Tickets.com, Inc., 2000 U.S. Dist. LEXIS 4553, 6 (C.D. Cal., March 27, 2000) (unpublished opinion).

[105] 487 F.3d 701 (2007).

[106] Perfect 10 v. Google, Inc, 416 F. Supp. 2d 828, 843–5 (C.D. Cal. 2006)).

embedding content from these sites is legal as long as the original poster owned the content. (YouTube also pays licensing fees to the American Society of Composers, Authors, and Publishers that cover public performances of ASCAP music in YouTube videos from YouTube's servers all the way through to the end user embeds.) Until the matter of embedding videos has been litigated it would be wise to carefully read a site's terms of service to see if posters are required to license their work for embedding. However, even when a site's terms require posters to allow embedding, those terms only apply to posters who own the content. Embedding a video posted on a video sharing site by a user who did not own the content rights might be considered a contributory infringement if it was clear that the content was likely infringing.

Courts are less respectful of linking when it is clear that the linker knows that the link connects to a site that aids infringers or carries infringing material. The first case in which a defendant was prohibited from linking was *Universal City Studios v. Corley* (2001).[107] Eric Corley, the publisher of *2600*, a magazine for hackers, wrote an article about the development of "DeCSS," a computer program created to circumvent the CSS encryption technology used in DVDs, and posted the article on his magazine's website with a copy of the program. Eight film studios sued him for violating the anti-trafficking provision of the DMCA, which makes it illegal to traffic in technology that can circumvent a technological measure used to protect a copyrighted work. A federal district judge issued a preliminary injunction barring Corley from publishing the computer program or knowingly linking to any other website that posted it. Corley removed the program, but not the links. Challenging the constitutionality of the DMCA, he argued that computer programs are speech protected by the First Amendment. He defended his action of posting the code, saying "in a journalistic world, . . . you have to show your evidence . . . and particularly in the magazine that I work for, people want to see specifically what it is that we are referring to . . . "[108] The district court judge agreed that computer programs constitute protected speech. But he said the DMCA was targeting the "functional" aspect of that speech rather than its content. The Court of Appeals for the Second Circuit upheld the lower court's injunction. It agreed that computer programs, which include code and operational instructions, are protected speech. But it distinguished them from other sets of instructions because computers execute them.

> Unlike a blueprint or a recipe, which cannot yield any functional result without human comprehension of its content, human decision-making, and human action, computer code can instantly cause a computer to accomplish tasks and instantly render the results of those tasks available throughout the world via the Internet. The only human action required to achieve these results can be as limited and instantaneous as a single click of a mouse. These realities of what code is and what its normal functions are require a First Amendment analysis that treats code as combining nonspeech and speech elements, i.e., functional and expressive elements.[109]

[107] 273 F.3d 429 (2001).
[108] *Id.* at 339 (citing trial transcript).
[109] *Id.* at 451.

The court concluded that the "government interest in preventing unauthorized access to encrypted copyrighted material is unquestionably substantial" and regulating DeCSS served that interest.[110]

Corley argued that 1201(c)(1) of the DMCA, which provides that "nothing in this section shall affect rights, remedies, limitations or defenses to copyright infringement, including fair use" should be read to allow the circumvention of encryption technology protecting copyrighted material when the material would be put to "fair use." The Court of Appeals rejected that interpretation, indicating instead that the DMCA targets circumvention and is not concerned with the use made of the materials afterward. It also rejected Corley's argument that the DMCA unconstitutionally restricts fair use, noting that there is no constitutional entitlement to fair use.

Since *Corley*, the law has been amended to allow confiscation of equipment used for infringement. The Immigration and Customs Enforcement branch of Homeland Security has interpreted the law to allow the confiscation of Internet domains that contain infringing content or link to sites that promote copyright infringement.

Social networking and fair use

Social networking sites thrive on the exchange of information. As of yet, there have been no cases of users suing each other for copyright infringement for either forwarding or altering posts or tweets without permission. It is conceivable that a post could meet copyright criteria, but highly unlikely that anyone would be willing to register one in order to sue. However, it is possible that a series of posts might be copyrighted as a compilation. Steve Martin announced in 2011 that he was turning his tweets into a book.

Twitter allows users to establish post streams by placing a hash symbol in front of a keyword, e.g. #DigitalMediaLaw, used in a tweet. Users who search for that hashtag will pull up tweets in that stream.

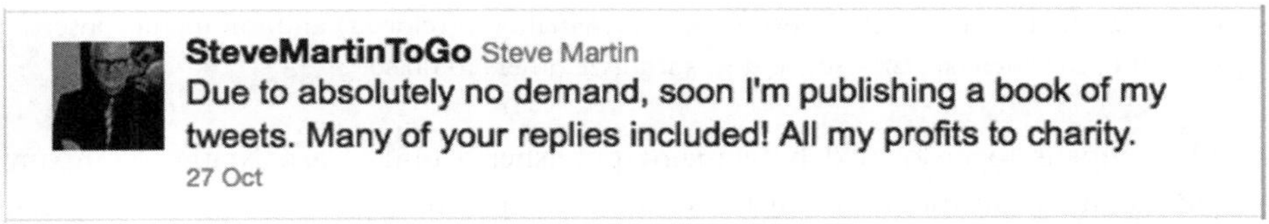

SteveMartinToGo Steve Martin
Due to absolutely no demand, soon I'm publishing a book of my tweets. Many of your replies included! All my profits to charity.
27 Oct

Figure 7.2

Apparently, Martin is assuming that incorporating others' tweets in his book would be a fair use, and it probably is. It is now common practice to republish tweets in other venues, such as blogs and on television shows that solicit comments through Twitter *hashtags*.

In contrast, posters who upload photos, videos and articles to social networking sites have a stronger claim to their intellectual property and have sued others for taking them without permission. Photographer Daniel Morel posted photos he had taken in Haiti following the 2010 Haitian earthquake on Twitpic and linked them to Twitter. Shortly after, another Twitter user copied the photos and uploaded them to his Twitpic account. Agence France Presse obtained the photos from this user's Twitpic account and shared

---

[110] *Id.* at 454.

them with Getty images, crediting the Twitter user who took Morel's photos without his permission.[111] Morel sued for copyright infringement. In its terms of service, Twitter requires its users to give it a worldwide license to use content posted on its service. Agence France Presse argued that, as a Twitter user, the license entitled it to use Morel's photos as well. Refusing to dismiss the suit, a federal court pointed out that the license applied to Twitter, not its users. As a general guideline, it is better to link to an interesting article or photo than to copy and repost it.

Morel's case highlights an important point that most social networking users overlook when they register for these services. In most cases, the terms of service to which they agree grant the company a *non-exclusive, transferable, sub-licensable, royalty-free, worldwide license* to use intellectual property uploaded by subscribers for any purpose. That means that sites like Twitter and Facebook not only have a legal right to use the content you upload on their services but to sublicense the use of that content to others – like their advertisers – as well.

Author James Erwin learned this the hard way after posting his time-travel story "Rome, Sweet Rome" onto the social networking site, Reddit.com in the hope of attracting a movie studio's attention. Warner Brothers liked the story and bought the film rights for it. Only afterward did the author realize that he had given Reddit an unlimited right to use his work.[112] In fact, this is specifically what he agreed to (no doubt without reading the terms first):

> you agree that by posting messages, uploading files, inputting data, or engaging in any other form of communication with or through the Website, you grant us a royalty-free, perpetual, non-exclusive, unrestricted, worldwide license to use, reproduce, modify, adapt, translate, enhance, transmit, distribute, publicly perform, display, or sublicense any such communication in any medium (now in existence or hereinafter developed) and for any purpose, including commercial purposes, and to authorize others to do so.

Reddit happens to be owned by a major publisher, Condé Nast. Neither company would comment on the license at the time of this printing. But these broad licenses, intended to encourage free exchange of information on social networking sites, may present potential problems for copyright holders who want to share, but not give away their work.

Fair use and sampling

Sampling involves the incorporation of a portion of a sound recording, video, or photograph into a new work. Opinions vary on this practice. Some view it as a way to reference earlier works or invest them with new meaning. Others see it as theft. The music and motion picture industries definitely fall into the second camp and have made

---

[111] Agence France Presse v. Morel, No. 769 F. Supp. 2d 295 (S.D.N.Y. 2011).

[112] *Does Warner Bros. Really Have Exclusive Movie Rights to a Story Posted on Reddit?* Hollywood Reporter, Oct. 20, 2011, http://www.hollywoodreporter.com/thr-esq/does-warner-bros-have-movie-250726.

it especially difficult to sample their copyrighted works by incorporating digital rights management software into CDs and DVDs.

The Copyright Office decided in 2010 that removing DRM software on DVDs to incorporate small portions of a motion picture in a video for noncommercial purposes associated with education, commentary or criticism is not an infringement. This laid the groundwork for protection of some of the amazingly creative mashups users have posted on YouTube and other video sites.

The right to incorporate others' music into videos and other songs, on the other hand, is still quite limited. Fair use is most likely to apply when the product is noncommercial and includes a small portion of the copyrighted work rather than the entire song. YouTube is handling the problem in a creative way that not only provides flexibility for its users, but also generates revenue for copyright holders. In 2007, the video sharing site agreed to pay licensing fees to music labels and publishers on behalf of its users. As part of the arrangement, YouTube launched a technology called Content ID that scans user-posted videos for copyrighted content. When copyrighted content is detected, YouTube applies a predetermined protocol put in place by the rights holder. It blocks the content, monetizes it by placing advertisements with the video, or adds links to buy the song in Apple's iTunes, sharing revenue with the rights holder. Most rights holders elect to monetize the content instead of taking it down. In 2011, between one-third and one-half of the money YouTube paid copyright holders came from revenue generated by user-posted content rather than videos posted by rights holders themselves.[113] One of the most famous is the viral video "JK Wedding Entrance Dance" featuring Chris Brown's *Forever*, which has been viewed more than 70 million times.[114]

When music is incorporated into a commercial product, there is practically no leeway for sampling without the copyright holder's permission. Two circuit courts have considered the issue of music sampling, and although they reached separate conclusions, neither welcomed more than *de minimis* use. A use is considered de minimis if the average audience is unlikely to recognize its appropriation.

In *Newton v. Diamond* (2003), the Ninth Circuit found the Beastie Boys' de minimis incorporation of a six-second, three-note segment of James Newton's jazz composition into one of their songs to be too trivial to trigger a copyright violation.[115] To sample part of a song, a musician must acquire a license to use both the sound recording and the composition because they are distinct works. The Beastie Boys licensed use of the sound recording from EMC Records, but did not license use of the composition from Newton, who retained all rights to it. Newton sued the group for copyright infringement. Although the plaintiff's sound is distinctive, it was not relevant to the court's inquiry because the recording was licensed. The court focused exclusively on the notes taken from the composition, which were less likely to be recognized by the average audience. The Beastie Boys looped the segment repeatedly throughout their song "Pass

[113]Antony Bruno, Partnering Against Piracy, Grammy.com, Aug. 12, 2011, http://www.grammy.com/news/partnering-against-piracy.

[114]TheKheinz, JK Wedding Entrance Dance, July 19, 2009, http://www.youtube.com/watch?v=4-94JhLEiN0.

[115]Newton v. Diamond, 388 F.3d 1189 (2003).

the Mic," but the relevant question was not the extent to which they used the copied segment, but how much of the original work was taken. The court also considered whether the portion taken was a trivial or substantial element in the original work. It found that the three-note sequence, which appeared only once in Newton's work, was not qualitatively original or quantitatively significant enough to implicate copyright.

In contrast, the Sixth Circuit ruled that any sample used in a work – even if unrecognizable – should be licensed in *Bridgeport Music, Inc. v. Dimension Films* (2005).[116] NWA, the defendant in the case, sampled a three-note, two-second guitar riff from Funkadelic's "Get Off Your Ass and Jam" for its song "100 Miles and Runnin." The group did not have a license to use the music or composition. The district court granted summary judgment on the case in favor of the defendant because it did not believe the defendant's de minimis use constituted infringement. The two-second sample, which was looped and extended to 16 beats, was used five times in the new song. The Court of Appeals reversed. Its decision established a "bright line" rule regarding sampling that where no authorization exists, infringement is established.

In a later case, *Bridgeport Music, Inc., et al v UMG Recordings, Inc., et al.* (2009), the Sixth Circuit affirmed a jury's finding of willful infringement against Public Announcement for its unlicensed used bits of George Clinton's "Atomic Dog" in its own song "D.O.G. in Me." The infringement was based on the use of the phrase "Bow wow wow, yippie yo, yippie yea," repetition of the word "dog," and the sound of panting. The court concluded that copyright infringement could occur from the unlicensed use of a single common word such as "dog," if the use in the new composition followed the same pattern of use in the original musical composition.[117]

Licensing and music

The best way to avoid a copyright suit for the unauthorized use of a musical work is to license the song before incorporating it into another work. There are two categories of works protected by musical licenses: musical works and sound recordings. The *musical work* is the composition of music and lyrics, generally owned by the songwriter or a music publisher. The *sound recording* is the final product produced in a studio by musicians, producers, and sound engineers, which is generally owned by the record company. The license required will depend on its intended use for the music.

A *performance license* is required to play a musical work. These licenses are paid by television and radio broadcasters; musicians or bands that perform other artists' music; and venues, such as restaurants and nightclubs, that play music or hire bands that use cover songs. A performance license may be negotiated directly with a copyright owner or indirectly through a performing rights organization that represents the copyright owner. Performing rights organizations keep track of musical performances, collect royalties from them, and redistribute the royalties to the copyright holders they represent. Trade groups such as the American Society of Composers, Authors, and Publishers,

[116] 410 F.3d 792 (6th Cir. 2005).
[117] Bridgeport Music, Inc. v. UMG Recordings, Inc., 585 F.3d 267 (6th Cir. 2009).

Broadcast Music, Inc. (also known as BMI), and SESAC license the performance of compositions and collect royalties for their members who are songwriters, composers, and publishers.

Broadcasters or venue owners may pay to license songs individually, but most choose to pay a *blanket license* fee in return for the right to use any music from the performing rights organization's repertoire. To keep track of the particular songs performed under a blanket license, ASCAP conducts sample and census surveys of networks, stations, and Internet sites that license its music. The licensing fees it collects from bars and restaurants are lumped into a general licensing fund, and copyright holders are paid from the fund at a rate proportional to their featured performances on radio and television.[118]

A performance of a "dramatic" musical work, such as a musical comedy, opera or ballet, or the use of such a work as a part of a story or plot, requires a *grand license*. A grand license must be obtained from the composer or publisher of the work, rather than a performing rights organization.

Until 1995, copyright owners of sound recordings could not collect licensing fees for the performance of their music. With the passage of the Sound Recordings Act of 1995 and the Digital Millennium Copyright Act, Congress created a performance right in sound recordings that are digitally transmitted through noninteractive services. Consequently, webcasters and broadcasters who simulcast on the Web now need a *sound recording license* as well as a public performance license.

Congress opted to deter potential monopolistic behavior related to sound recordings by including a statutory (compulsory) license in the Copyright Act that entitles parties who satisfy certain conditions to exercise some of a copyright holder's exclusive rights without permission, as long as they pay the copyright holder a predetermined licensing fee. Section 114 of the Copyright Act provides a compulsory license to perform sound recordings publicly by digital audio transmission, without the permission of the copyright holder, for a licensing fee. The statutory license applies to simulcasters, noninteractive webcasters (like Pandora), satellite radio, and subscription services that provide music over digital cable or satellite television. There is no licensing scheme for podcasters, because they are considered interactive. Sound Exchange has been designated as the performance rights organization to distribute licensing fees.

Individuals who wish to incorporate a musical work into a video need a *synchronization license* from the songwriter or publisher before associating the work with something else. A sound recording license from the label is needed as well, if they desire to include the artist's rendition of the song.

A *mechanical license* is required to reproduce a sound recording, for a CD compilation or digital download. The reproduction right in a sound recording must be licensed from the record label, which may license a work at its discretion. But the right

---

[118] In 1998, Congress drastically reduced the amount of licensing fees collected from restaurants and other small businesses that use radio or television to supply music for their customers when it passed the Fairness in Music Licensing Act. The Act exempted approximately 70 percent of food and drinking establishments from paying licensing fees, as long as the establishment is less than 3,750 square feet and does not retransmit the music.

to reproduce the musical composition (by covering the song, for example) is subject to a statutory license under Section 115 of the Copyright Act. Once a song has been commercially released, others may re-record it without the copyright holder's permission, as long as they pay the copyright holder a licensing fee and their primary purpose is to distribute the music to the public for private use.[119]

The Copyright Royalty Board, a three-judge panel employed by the Library of Congress, sets the royalty fees for statutory licensing. In order to take advantage of a statutory license, the user must first file a "Notice of Use" with the Copyright Office. If the copyright holder is known, the user must send the license fee to him or her directly. If the copyright holder is not known, the licensing fee is paid to the Register of Copyrights in the Copyright Office.

Licensing fees are paid for music regardless of whether any revenue is accrued from use of the music or whether a fraction of the song or the whole song is played. The Copyright Royalty Board made this determination based on the assumption that a station's inability to generate revenue had no relationship to the market value of a copyrighted work. However noncommercial rates are available to webcasters operated by tax-exempt organizations and government entities.

The Creative Commons

Although copyright provides a bundle of exclusive rights, the copyright holder may not want to exercise them all. In fact, some copyright holders want to share their work with others in order to draw wider exposure to it or to foster the spirit of intellectual creativity.

The nonprofit organization Creative Commons provides a mechanism to allow copyright holders to license certain uses of their work that they consider acceptable, while retaining control over other uses. Some artists license others to reproduce, remix, and distribute their work for noncommercial uses, as long as they receive credit for the original. Others license their work for reproduction and distribution but restrict users from making derivatives from the original. Still others allow their works to be used for derivatives as long as users share alike with others by licensing their derivatives similarly. Finally, some CC copyright holders allow unlimited use of their work.

The Creative Commons website provides directions for licensing and a search function to locate music, video, photos, and art that can be modified, adapted, and built upon or that can be used for commercial purposes. Creative Commons licenses – expressed as a "cc" within a circle – are free. They are not meant to serve as a substitute for official registration, but they are legally enforceable and will terminate if abused.

Creative Commons was established in 2001, following the loss of *Eldred v. Ashcroft*, the case that challenged the legitimacy of copyright extensions that kept millions of works out of the public domain for another 20 years. Eric Eldred and his attorney, Harvard law professor Lawrence Lessig, helped to found the organization, along with experts in

---

[119] 17 U.S.C. § 115(a)(2) (2007).

Figure 7.3   *Big Buck Bunny*, a 3D animated film, debuted under a Creative Commons license to demonstrate Blender, open-source 3D animation software. Source: http://creativecommons.org/weblog/entry/8223

copyright and computer science. The name alludes to land held in common for cultivation in Northwestern Europe that was privatized during the Enclosure Movement between the fifteenth and nineteenth centuries at tremendous cost to the common people who had relied on it for their survival.[120] The reference suggests that creative works do not spring wholly formed from the minds of their creators, but that all works are in some way inspired by earlier works that must be protected from further enclosure.

The Difference between Copyright Permission and a Model Release

A photographer may license the use of his or her work under a Creative Commons license. But permission to use the *subject's* image for commercial purposes must come from the person photographed.

A 16-year-old Texas girl and her family sued Virgin Mobile Australia for using her image in its advertisements without her permission. Her church youth counselor included her image among photos from a church event that he posted on the photosharing site Flickr under a Creative Commons license. The CC license gave Virgin Mobile unrestricted use of the photo, but it did not give the company the right to appropriate the girl's image for commercial use (a privacy tort

discussed in Chapter 10). Virgin used her image in a national campaign with the mocking slogans, "Dump your Pen Friend" and "Free Text Virgin to Virgin."

There is no forum selection or choice of law clause in Creative Commons licenses, so the license was not tied to Texas. The federal district court in Texas in which the family filed suit would not assert juristiction over the Australian defendant. After learning they would have to fight the case in Australia, the family dropped the suit. Nevertheless, the case is a warning not only to acquire copyright permission but also a model release before using a photo for commercial purposes.

---

[120] *See* James Boyle, *The Second Enclosure Movement and the Construction of the Public Domain, Law and Contemporary Problems*, 66 LAW & CONTEMP. PROBS. 33 (Winter/Spring 2003) (analogizing copyright's impact on the public domain to the English Enclosure Movement). Professor Boyle is also a founding member of the Creative Commons.

Questions for Discussion

1. What does a work need to acquire copyright protection in the United States?
2. What cannot be copyrighted? Why?
3. Is it necessary to register a work? What are the benefits of doing so?
4. What is the relationship between copyright law and freedom of expression?
5. What is fair use? Why is it hard to know if fair use will apply in any particular instance?

8 Intellectual Property: Patents, Trademarks, and Trade Secrets

Intellectual property is commonly divided into two categories: copyright and industrial property. Copyright, discussed in the previous chapter, protects literary or artistic works. Patent, trademark, and trade secret law protect industrial property, a category that encompasses all digital media devices and products, as well as the words and symbols used to market them.

Although copyright, patent, trademark, and trade secret laws are lumped together within the category of intellectual property, they are all very different. As Richard Stallman, who pioneered the free software movement, has pointed out, they "originated separately, evolved differently, cover different activities, have different rules, and raise different public policy issues."[1] What they do have in common, however, is the challenge they face adapting to the acceleration of technology. All are "in flux" to some extent.

This chapter discusses the application and reach of patent, trademark, and trade secret law. It pays attention to areas that are still in transition, such as the use of trademarks in contextual advertising, metatags, and cybersquatting. It also discusses the fair use of trademarks in social commentary, parodies, and gripe sites.

Patents

Patent law protects inventions, processes, devices, and methods. In the context of digital media, it applies to digital media devices like computers, flash drives, DVD players, and MP3 players, and to some software.

[1] Richard Stallman, *Did You Say "Intellectual Property"? It's a Seductive Mirage*, GNU Operating System, http://www.gnu.org/philosophy/not-ipr.html (last visited Feb. 3, 2012).

Digital Media Law, Second Edition. Ashley Packard.
© 2013 John Wiley & Sons, Inc. Published 2013 by John Wiley & Sons, Inc.

The same section of the U.S. Constitution that directs Congress to protect copyright also empowers it to protect patents by securing inventors' exclusive rights to inventions and discoveries for a limited period of time.[2] Unlike copyright law, however, its duration of protection is much more limited. While copyright protects a work for the life of the creator plus 70 years, patent protection lasts 20 years from the date of application.

Types of patents

There are three types of patents: utility, design, and plant patents.

1. Utility patents apply to the invention or discovery of "any new and useful process, machine, article of manufacture, or composition of matter," or improvement thereof.[3] An iPhone or Kindle would be protected by utility patents.
2. Design patents apply to "new, original and ornamental design for an article of manufacture."[4] The unique design of a Movado watch would be protected by a design patent.
3. Plant patents apply to the invention or discovery and asexual reproduction of new kinds of plants.[5] An example would be those seedless watermelons that are so much easier to eat.

Some subject matter cannot be patented. The U.S. Patent and Trademark Office will not grant patents for laws of nature, natural phenomena, or abstract ideas. Albert Einstein could not have patented the formula $e = mc^2$, for example.

The PTO used to include business methods within the category of abstract ideas. However, the U.S. Court of Appeals for the Federal Circuit reversed that rule. Courts now interpret utility patents to cover business methods as long as they are computerized, a factor likely to become increasingly important to companies involved in e-commerce.[6]

Congress has given the U.S. Court of Appeals for the Federal Circuit exclusive appellate jurisdiction over patent cases arising from the federal district courts.

Registering and protecting patents

Protection for patents, unlike copyrights, is not automatic. Patents must be registered through the PTO to acquire protection. The application must include a sufficiently detailed description of the invention and its use to allow a PTO examiner to determine whether it qualifies for patent protection.

The requirements for patent protection are also a bit more stringent than for copyright protection. Assuming the invention or discovery qualifies for patent protection, the creator must show that it meets three criteria: it must be *novel*, *useful*, and *not obvious*. To preserve its novelty, an inventor must make sure that the invention is not described anywhere in print before the date of the invention or within one year before

---

[2] U.S. Const., art. 1, § 8.
[3] 35 U.S.C. §101 (2011).
[4] *Id.* § 171.
[5] *Id.* § 161.
[6] *See* State Street Bank & Trust v. Signature Financial Group, Inc., 149 F.3d 1368 (Fed. Cir. 1998).

the application date of the patent. To meet the utility requirement, the invention or discovery must serve a purpose. To be nonobvious, the invention must display some ingenuity. It cannot be something that is simply a common sense solution to a person of ordinary skill.

Applications for patent protection are limited to natural persons. But once the person has acquired the patent, he or she may assign the rights to a corporation or license the patent for use by someone else. A patent registered in the United States will only be effective in the U.S. and U.S. territories.

The America Invents Act

The most significant reform of patent law since 1952 occurred in 2011 when Congress passed the America Invents Act.[7] The legislation harmonized the American patent process with that of other countries by awarding patents on a first-to-file basis instead of a first-to-invent basis. The change was intended to encourage inventors to seek patent protection in other countries and market their inventions abroad. The law also created a fast-track option for new companies that could reduce the patent processing wait from an average of three years to twelve months. New resources were provided to the Patent and Trademark Office to help it reduce a backlog of 700,000 applications. To reduce patent litigation, the law clarified and tightened standards for issuing patents and created a post-grant review system to weed out bad patents.

Patent infringement and remedies

Patent infringement applies to "whoever without authority makes, uses, offers to sell, or sells any patented invention, within the United States, or imports into the United States any patented invention during the term of the patent."[8] It also applies to anyone who actively induces infringement.[9]

Patent law offers no statutory provision for fair use.[10] A common law exception for patent infringement has developed for experimental use and research.[11] But the U.S. Court of Appeals for the Federal Circuit has taken a narrow view of it, saying that the "slightest commercial implication" or "any conduct that is in keeping with the alleged infringer's legitimate business, regardless of commercial implications" is enough to defeat it.[12] It considers the defense "limited to actions performed 'for amusement, to satisfy idle curiosity, or for strictly philosophical inquiry.' "[13]

---

[7] Pub.L. No. 11–29 § 16(b)(4), 125 Stat. 284, 329 (2011).

[8] 35 U.S.C. § 271(a) (2011).

[9] *Id.* § 271(b).

[10] *Id.* § 271(e).

[11] *See* Lorelei R. De Larena, *What Copyright Teaches Patent Law About "Fair Use" and Why Universities Are Ignoring the Lesson*, 84 ORE. L. REV. 779, 790 (2005).

[12] Madey v. Duke University, 307 F.3d 1351, 1362 (Fed. Cir. 2002) (quoting Embrex, Inc. v. Serv. Eng'g Corp., 216 F.3d 1343, 1353 (Fed. Cir. 2000) (Rader, J., concurring)).

[13] *Id.* (quoting Embrex, 216 F.3d at 1349).

Patent infringement is a civil violation tried in federal court. It can be remedied by an injunction to stop the infringement or damages if the plaintiff has been harmed. Actual damages are normally equal to a reasonable royalty for the use made of the invention, along with interest and court costs.[14] If the plaintiff can show that the infringement was willful (committed with knowledge of the patent), the court may triple the damages.

Trolling for patents

In recent years, patent litigation has spiraled out of control. A business model has emerged in which companies that make nothing of their own acquire the patents of others, specifically for the purpose of collecting licensing fees on those patents or penalties from lawsuits they file for patent infringement. These companies – known as patent

Figure 8.1   Illustration: Kalan Lyra

[14] 35 U.S.C. § 274.

trolls – may acquire portfolios with tens of thousands of patents, particularly on software, that make it virtually impossible to invent new technology without paying them first. Take smartphones, for example. On average, 250,000 patents cover the technology behind them and the components that make them work.[15] If a court finds that even one of those patents has been infringed, it can restrict the sale of the product.

In addition, patent litigation can cost millions. For example, Internet phone carrier Vonage was sued by Verizon, Sprint Nextel, and AT&T for infringing patents related to Voice over Internet Protocol (known as "VoIP") services, including one for technology that linked the Internet telephone network with ordinary telephones. The combined total to settle the suits, $199 million, nearly drove the company into bankruptcy.[16]

As a hedge against being sued, tech companies are buying up as many patents as they can, regardless of whether they need any one in particular. When Nortel put its 6,000 patents up for auction, they sold for three times their value at auction – $4.5 billion – to a consortium of companies that included Apple, Microsoft, RIM, EMC, Ericsson and Sony.[17] Naturally, this cost is eventually passed on to consumers.

Challenging bad patents

One of the functions of the America Invents Act is to create a post-grant review system to challenge bad patents. Although the PTO investigates patent applications before approving them, it has not had the resources to investigate all of the applications that it receives thoroughly. As a result, some processes and devices are patented that really should not be. One the most egregious examples is U.S. patent #5,443,036 for "Method of exercising a cat," described as "directing a beam of invisible light produced by a handheld laser apparatus onto the floor or wall or other opaque surface in the vicinity of the cat, then moving the laser so as to cause the bright pattern of light to move in an irregular way fascinating to cats."[18] But even that runs second place to patent #6,080,436 granted in 2000, for the "Bread Refreshing Method," more commonly known as making toast.

Aside from the ridiculous, a more common problem is that multiple patents may be issued for the same idea. Among the many patents for processes to back up computer files, there are three that even use the same title: "System and method for backing up computer files over a wide area computer network." Or, patents may be too broad or issued for things that have been invented already.

The Electronic Frontier Foundation has organized a Patent Busting Program to combat software patents that are not novel. The foundation searches for "prior art," the

---

[15]Eric Savitz, *Turn the Tables on Patent Trolls*, FORBES, Aug. 9, 2011, http://www.forbes.com/sites/ciocentral/2011/08/09/turn-the-tables-on-patent-trolls/.

[16]Verizon Services Corp. v. Vonage Holdings Corp. 503 F.3d 1295 (Fed. Cir. 2007); Amol Sharma, *Vonage Says Patent Suits Could Lead to Bankruptcy*, WALL ST. J., April 18, 2007, at A2.

[17]Nadia Damouni, *Dealtalk: Google Bid "pi" for Nortel Patents and Lost*, Reuters, July 1, 2011, http://www.reuters.com/article/2011/07/02/us-dealtalk-nortel-google-idUSTRE76104L20110702.

[18]*See* U.S. Patent No. 5,443,036 (issued Aug. 22, 1995).

PTO's term for technology that predates the patent, and asks the PTO to reexamine patents that appear to overreach. One of its requests prompted the PTO to revoke a patent owned by Live Nation for a method to capture, mix, and burn music from live concerts on a CD for immediate purchase following the show. The patent locked music groups into reliance on the company for the all-in-one service. EFF discovered that another company had produced a similar technology a year before the patent application for Live Nation's method was filed.[19]

Trademarks

Trademark law protects consumers from misleading packaging and advertisements that could confuse them about the source of the products and services they buy.[20] In doing so, it promotes economic efficiencies by reducing consumer search costs and providing incentives among manufacturers to produce quality products and services that consumers will remember.[21] Unlike copyright and patent law, which stimulate the marketplace of ideas by promoting writings and discoveries, trademark law stimulates the economic marketplace by promoting competition.

Types of marks

Trademark law protects the different *marks* companies use to identify their products and services and distinguish them from competitors. A mark may be a name, word, slogan, symbol, picture, or combination of any of these elements. *Trademarks* identify goods already in or intended for commerce. Coca-Cola, for example, is distinguished from its competitors not only by its name, but also by its trademarked script, contour bottle, and slogans, such as "Have a Coke and a smile." *Service marks* identify businesses in the service industry. NBC's colorful peacock and three-note chime are examples of registered service marks. *Collective marks*, like the block R used by the National Association of Realtors, identify membership organizations. A related mark intended for use by someone other than the mark's owner, is the *certification mark*. It is used to certify "origin, material, mode of manufacture, quality, accuracy, or other characteristics" of the person's good or service. For example, Wi-Fi® is a registered certification mark of the Wi-Fi Alliance.

Distinctiveness

To acquire trademark protection, a mark must be *distinctive*. Marks considered to be *inherently distinctive* are fanciful, arbitrary, or suggestive:

---

[19] Max Hefflinger, *U.S. Patent Office to Revoke Instant Live Concert CD Patent*, Digital Media Wire, March 12, 2007, http://www.dmwmedia.com/news/2007/03/13/u-s-patent-office-to-revoke-instant-live-concert-cd-patent.
[20] Margreth Barrett, *Internet Trademark Suits and the Demise of "Trademark Use,"* 39 U.C. Davis L. Rev. 371, 376 (2006).
[21] *Id.*

1. A *fanciful* mark, like Google, is invented specifically for the product or service and is the easiest mark to protect because the name is not associated with anything else
2. An *arbitrary* mark, like Apple, Inc., is one that has no relationship to the purpose or characteristics of the product or service it represents. There is no obvious connection, for example, between computers and fruit.
3. A *suggestive* mark, like YouTube or Microsoft, hints at the product's function, but is still abstract enough to require some imagination.

Assuming the mark is not already in use or misleadingly similar to another in use, it will qualify for trademark protection if it is inherently distinctive.

Marks that incorporate the name or characteristic of a product or service, like International Business Machines, or the geographic region in which they are sold, like Saint Louis Bread Company, are considered to be merely *descriptive*. A descriptive mark must develop a secondary meaning to earn trademark status. It must conjure up the particular company, not just one that makes business machines sold internationally or bread in St. Louis, in the minds of consumers. Marks based on surnames are also treated as descriptive marks until they acquire secondary meaning. That occurs when people begin to think of the business before the person, such as Dell, Ford, or McDonald's. Courts look for three factors when they are deciding whether a product has acquired secondary meaning: the extent to which the mark has been promoted through advertising, the product's sales and, most importantly, the length of time the mark has been used. Under Section 1052(f) of the Trademark Act, exclusive and continuous use of a mark for five years is prima facie evidence that it is distinctive.

Some marks will not qualify for registration even if they do achieve a secondary meaning. These include words or images that are "immoral, deceptive or scandalous" or which may "disparage or falsely suggest a connection with persons, living or dead, institutions, beliefs, or national symbols."[22] For example, an application to register the mark "Khoran" for wine was rejected on the basis of disparagement because of its similarity to the holy text of Islam, the Koran, which prohibits alcohol.[23] Generic words, like computer or camera, cannot be trademarked because they are part of the public domain and must remain available for others to use to identify their products and services.

Trade dress

Other aspects of a brand's "total image and overall appearance," such as its packaging, color, size and shape, may acquire protection under trademark law if their imitation is likely to result in consumer confusion regarding the source of the product or service.[24] Protection for these distinctive characteristics is known as *trade dress*.[25] Originally

---

[22] 15 U.S.C. § 1052(a) (2011).
[23] *In re* Lebanese Arak Corporation, 94 U.S.P.Q.2d 1215 (TTAB 2010).
[24] See Blue Bell Bio-Medical v. Cin-Bad, Inc., 864 F.2d 1253, 1256 (5th Cir. 1989); John J. Harland Co. v. Clarke Checks, Inc., 711 F.2d 966, 980 (11th Cir. 1983).
[25] Section 43(a) of the Lanham Act, codified at 15 U.S.C. § 1125(a)(3).

intended to apply to product packaging, trade dress has evolved to include other characteristics of a product or marketing effort that are inherently distinctive or that have acquired distinctiveness through a "secondary meaning." Examples include the red wax seal on a bottle of Maker's Mark whiskey, the décor of a restaurant, the layout of a kiosk display or the distinctive format of a magazine cover.[26]

Trade dress protection does not extend to functional aspects of a product's packaging or design or other elements that make it particularly useful. An element is functional if it is essential to the purpose of the product or affects its quality or cost.[27] An element is also considered functional if its exclusive use would put competitors at a disadvantage. For example, a court would not recognize the use of frames on a website as a protected element under trade dress, but it might recognize the distinctive look and feel of a site.

In a trade dress case brought by Conference Companion against its former partner-turned-competitor Sound Images, the U.S. District Court for the Western District of Pennsylvania held that trade dress applies to websites, explaining

> Like the famed Coca-Cola classic dynamic ribbon, or the iconic Apple logo, on the Internet, the appearance of a web site is essential to a firm's standing in the market. The simple layout of Google's home page, the listing of tweets on Twitter.com, or the organization of photographs and status updates on Facebook.com are all integral to the recognition of their brands, and consequently the firm's reputation.[28]

The court said there were two critical layers to consider when comparing "look and feel" of the sites: "visual design" and the "interface design." Static elements, such as photos, colors, orientation, borders, and frames, contribute to the look of the site; interactive elements create the overall mood, style or impression of the site.[29]

Acquiring trademark protection

One can acquire common law trademark protection by being the first to use a particular trademark in commerce. However, protection for the mark will be limited to the geographic area in which the product is sold. So, for example, the owner of Bayou Design Company in Louisiana may be able to establish the legitimacy of the trademark there, but would not be able to prevent another person from starting a company with the same name in Florida. To acquire protection for the mark nationwide, it must be officially registered through the Patent and Trademark Office.

Registration confers other benefits as well. It makes it easier for others to research the trademark to avoid infringement. It serves as notice to potential infringers that the

---

[26] Two Pesos, Inc. v. Taco Cabana, Inc., 505 U.S. 763 (1992); Butterick Co. v. McCall Pattern Co. 222 U.S.P.Q. 314, 317 (S.D.N.Y. 1984); Time Inc. v. Globe Communications Corp., 712 F.Supp. 1103 (S.D.N.Y. 1989).
[27] *See* TrafFix Devices, Inc. v. Mktg. Displays, Inc., 532 U.S. 23 (2001).
[28] Conference Archives, Inc. v. Sound Images, Inc., Civil No. 3: 2006-76, 51, 2010 WL 1626072 (W.D. Pa. Mar. 31, 2010).
[29] *Id.* at 47.

mark is taken, eliminating the potential for "innocent" infringement. In the event of an infringement, it entitles the mark's owner to sue for trademark infringement in federal court, while providing prima facie evidence of ownership and the exclusive right to use the mark. Certain remedies, such as treble damages for willful infringement and attorney's fees, are also tied to registration.

To avoid wasted time and effort on a mark that is already taken, the application process should begin with a search of existing trademarks. The Patent and Trademark Office offers an electronic search service called Trademark Electronic Search System (TESS), available through its website. If the mark is available, registration can be filed electronically for a $325 application fee.

Search the Trademark Electronic Search System at tess2.uspto.gov/.

It takes the Patent and Trademark Office about 15 to 18 months to issue a certificate of registration. A party who claims ownership of a mark may use the TM for trademarks or SM for service marks that are not registered or pending registration. Once the certificate of registration arrives, the mark should be changed to an R enclosed in a circle, ®.

The certificate is good for 10 years, but the trademark owner must file a form in the fifth year asserting its continuous use of the mark. After that, protection is renewable every 10 years and, as long as registration is maintained, may last indefinitely. The trademark for Singer sewing machines, for example, was registered in 1880. Löwenbräu beer first used its lion mark in 1383.

Products sold outside the United States must be trademarked in each country in which they are distributed. However, the owner of a trademark registered or pending registration in the United States is entitled to register the trademark in any of the 84 countries that are members of the Madrid Protocol by filing one "international application" with the International Bureau of the World Property Intellectual Organization, through the U.S. Patent and Trademark Office, and paying the registration fee required by each.

Losing trademark protection

A trademark is considered abandoned when the owner discontinues its use. If the mark has not been used for three consecutive years, its abandonment is inferred. Once a mark is lost, it cannot be re-registered by another party. The mark moves into the public domain.

A trademark also may be lost if its owner allows the trademark to become a generic name for a good or service. A mark must maintain its *distinctiveness* to preserve its protection. Names like aspirin, corn flakes, zipper, thermos, yo-yo and shredded wheat are products that lost their distinctiveness, and by extension their trademark status, in the United States because they were used as nouns rather than adjectives. However, some of these products, such as aspirin and thermos, still retain their trademarks in other countries. Finally, a mark will be lost if it was fraudulently registered in the first place. The law defines "fraud" as a knowing misrepresentation or concealment of a material fact.

Trademark Act of 1946

Although some aspects of trademark are protected through state and common law, trademark is primarily secured through federal law under the Trademark Act of 1946, also known as the Lanham Act. The statute protects trademark owners against trademark infringement, false designation of origin, and trademark dilution.

Trademark infringement

Trademark infringement occurs when a registered mark is used, without the permission of the mark's owner, on a product or in an advertisement for a product or service in a manner that is likely to confuse consumers about the source of the product or service. Specifically, Section 1114 of the Trademark Act prohibits the

> use in commerce [of] any reproduction, counterfeit, copy, or colorable imitation of a registered mark in connection with the sale, offering for sale, distribution, or advertising of any goods or services on or in connection with which such use is likely to cause confusion, or to cause mistake, or to deceive.[30]

False designation of origin

Section 1125 of the Trademark Act protects competitors against false designation of origin *and* false advertising.

Unregistered marks and trade dress also receive protection under a section of the Act that prohibits false designations of origin. Section 1125 imposes liability on anyone who:

> on or in connection with any goods or services, or any container for goods, uses in commerce any word, term, name, symbol, or device, or any combination thereof, or any false designation of origin, false or misleading description of fact, or false or misleading representation of fact, which –
> (A) is likely to cause confusion, or to cause mistake, or to deceive as to the affiliation, connection, or association of such person with another person, or as to the origin, sponsorship, or approval of his or her goods, services, or commercial activities by another person . . . [31]

Essentially, in cases involving allegations of trademark infringement or false designation of origin, plaintiffs are required to prove five things:

1. that they possess a valid mark;
2. that the defendant used the mark;
3. that the defendant's use of the mark occurred "in commerce";

---

[30] 15 U.S.C. § 1114(1) (2011).
[31] *Id.* § 1125(a)(1)(A).

4. that the defendant used the mark "in connection with the sale . . . or advertising of any goods"; and
5. that the defendant used the mark in a manner likely to confuse consumers.[32]

A court will consider each of these factors in order. It will first ask if the plaintiff owns the mark. If the mark is not registered to the plaintiff, the plaintiff will have to demonstrate that he or she has acquired possession of the mark through first use and that the mark is distinctive or has acquired a secondary meaning associated with the plaintiff. Only then will the court consider whether the defendant has used the mark and, if so, whether the use was "in commerce."

Circuits differ regarding their interpretation of *commerce*. The definition provided in the Lanham Act is circular, stating "The word 'commerce' means all commerce which may lawfully be regulated by Congress."[33] Some circuits have chosen to interpret "in commerce" as commercial activity, and therefore assume that trademark infringement and false designation of origin only apply to *commercial speech*. Other circuits have chosen to interpret "in commerce" to refer to activities that fall within the purview of congressional jurisdiction. This interpretation acknowledges Congress's authority to legislate interstate activity based on the Constitution's commerce clause, which gives it the exclusive right "To regulate commerce with foreign nations, and among the several states . . ." These courts have observed that in other sections of the Act Congress has prohibited the "commercial use in commerce of a mark," concluding that trademark infringement and false designation of origin may also apply to noncommercial speech.

The court will then decide whether the mark was used "in connection with a sale, distribution or advertisement of goods and services" (in the case of trademark infringement) or "in connection with any goods or services" (in the case of false designation of origin). If the plaintiff is able to establish each of these factors, the court will consider whether the fraudulent use was likely to cause confusion among consumers.

Trademark infringement and false designation of origin are illegal because the fraudulent use of a mark is likely to confuse consumers, not because it harms the mark or its owner.

To assess the *likelihood of confusion*, courts consider the following factors:

1. the strength of the plaintiff's mark;
2. the similarity between the plaintiff's mark and the allegedly infringing mark;
3. the similarity between the products and services offered by the plaintiff and defendant;
4. the similarity of the sales methods;
5. the similarity of advertising methods;
6. the defendant's intent, e.g., whether the defendant hopes to gain competitive advantage by associating his product with the plaintiff's established mark; and
7. actual confusion.[34]

---

[32] *See* North American Medical Corp. v. Axiom Worldwide, Inc., 522 F.3d 1211, 1218 (11th Cir. 2008) (citing 1–800 Contacts, Inc. v. WhenU.com, Inc., 414 F.3d 400, 406–7 (2nd Cir. 2005)); People for Ethical Treatment of Animals v. Doughney, 263 F.3d 359, 364 (4th Cir. 2001).

[33] 15 U.S.C. § 1127 (2011).

[34] Alliance Metals, Inc. of Atlanta v. Hinely Indus., Inc., 222 F.3d 895, 907 (11th Cir. 2000).

Trademark dilution

The Trademark Act has protected consumers from confusion resulting from trademark misuse since 1945, but in 1995, Congress added a layer of protection for trademark owners by amending the Act to prohibit trademark dilution.[35] *Trademark dilution* is "the lessening of the capacity of a famous mark to identify and distinguish goods or services." The Trademark Dilution Act gives owners of famous trademarks the right to prevent others from using them commercially if the use is likely to dilute the distinctive quality of the marks by blurring or tarnishing them. A mark may be *blurred* if its association with a dissimilar product weakens the unique identity of the original. The amendment's legislative history gives "DUPONT shoes, BUICK aspirin, and KODAK pianos" as examples of uses that would be actionable under the legislation.[36] A mark may be *tarnished* if it is associated with an inferior or disreputable product.

Trademark dilution is illegal because it harms a famous mark, lessening the mark's capacity to distinguish goods and services, either through blurring or tarnishment.

A dispute involving the famous Victoria's Secret trademark led to a landmark decision by the Supreme Court's on trademark dilution and Congress's subsequent efforts to overturn it. In *Moseley v. V Secret Catalogue, Inc.* (2003), the retail chain sued the owners of an adult novelty shop called Victor's Secret for trademark infringement and dilution. When a recipient of the novelty shop's ad alerted Victoria's Secret to the mark's use, the corporation contacted the store's owners, Victor and Cathy Moseley, requesting that they change its name. The Moseleys changed the name to Victor's Little Secret. Victoria's Secret wasn't satisfied and filed for an injunction to prevent the Moseleys from using the name. Finding no likelihood of consumer confusion, the district court granted summary judgment in favor of the Moseleys on the trademark infringement action and proceeded to the trademark dilution claim. The district court concluded that Victor's Little Secret diluted the Victoria's Secret mark by tarnishing it and enjoined the Moseleys from further use of the mark. The Sixth Circuit affirmed the decision, but the Supreme Court reversed, holding that unlike trademark infringement, which requires the *likelihood* of harm, trademark dilution required *actual* harm.

Congress responded by passing the Trademark Dilution Revision Act, in essence, overruling the Supreme Court's decision.[37] The Act asserts that concrete proof of blurring or tarnishing is not required for an action to succeed; likelihood of dilution will suffice. Reexamining the Victoria's Secret case against Victor Moseley under the Trademark Dilution Revision Act, the Sixth Circuit upheld an injunction barring use of the name "Victor's Little Secret." The court concluded that the use of a junior mark to sell sex-related products creates a strong inference of dilution by tarnishment of a famous mark.[38]

---

[35] 15 U.S.C. §§ 1125(c), 1127 (2011).
[36] Victor Moseley v. V. Secret Catalogue, 537 U.S. 418, 431 (2003) (citing H. R. Rep. No. 104–374, 1030 (1995)).
[37] 15 U.S.C. § 1125(c).
[38] V. Secret Catalogue v. Victor Moseley, 605 F.3d 382 (6th Cir. 2010).

Remedies

Trademark infringement and false designation of origin

Remedies for trademark infringement and false designation of origin include injunctive relief, fines, and the seizure and destruction of infringing articles that include the mark. Plaintiffs are most likely to request injunctive relief to stop the defendant from further use of the mark without permission. When an infringement is committed innocently by third parties printing or publishing a mark for someone else, plaintiffs are only entitled to injunctive relief.[39]

Courts may award plaintiffs the defendant's profits from the use of the mark, actual damages sustained from the infringement and court costs associated with pursuing the case. In assessing damages, a court may render a judgment for as much as three times the actual damages. In exceptional cases, it may also award attorney's fees to the winning party.[40]

Trademark dilution

Mark owners who sue for trademark dilution are only entitled to injunctive relief if the dilution is willful. In that case, the plaintiff will also be entitled to the infringement remedies described above.

State trademark protection

Trademark protection is also available through state law. Many states have adopted most or all of the International Trademark Association's model state trademark bill. The legislation, which prohibits infringement and dilution, is similar to federal trademark law but recommends a five-year renewal period. It also does not restrict suits for trademark dilution to famous marks.

State trademark laws are useful to small businesses that do not sell products or services in interstate or foreign commerce.

Trademark owners who file suit for trademark infringement or dilution usually also assert claims under state unfair competition laws. "Unfair competition" refers to the tort of engaging in business practices meant to confuse consumers. Some states have adopted the Uniform Deceptive Trade Practices Act, a model law to deal with fraudulent business practices related to misidentification of goods and services and false advertising. But most have varying definitions of unfair business practices. Trademarks are also protected at the state level through common law that prohibits "passing off" goods and services as those of another.

Trademark and free speech

Congress never meant trademark infringement and dilution claims to be used to inhibit free speech. In the case of trademark infringement, claims can only succeed if use of the

[39] 15 U.S.C. § 1114(1)(b)(2) (2011).
[40] *Id.* § 1117.

trademark is likely to confuse consumers regarding the source of a product or service. To succeed in a trademark dilution claim, a plaintiff must show that the mark was used commercially and likely diluted by the use. Congress was particularly concerned about protecting speech that might be critical of a product or service when it amended the Trademark Act to prohibit trademark dilution. So it precluded liability for fair uses of trademarks in comparative advertising, parodies, criticism, and commentary, along with references to trademarks in news reporting and commentary.[41]

The incorporation of Playboy's trademarks into a former Playboy Playmate's website was considered a fair use by the Ninth Circuit. Playboy sued Terry Welles for using the "Playboy," "Playmate," and "Playmate of the Year 1981" marks on her website. The district court granted summary judgment in favor of Welles on Playboy's claims of trademark infringement and dilution, false designation of origin, and unfair competition. The Court of Appeals upheld the ruling, concluding that most of Welles's uses constituted a *nominative fair use* of Playboy's marks that served to identify her as a former Playmate without suggesting Playboy's sponsorship of the website.[42] A nominative fair use of a trademark occurs when (1) no term other than the trademark could adequately identify the subject, (2) the trademark is used no more than necessary to identify the subject, and (3) the use does not suggest the trademark holder's sponsorship or endorsement.

A federal district court held that trademark dilution does not apply to the noncommercial expression of political views in *Lucasfilm Ltd. v. High Frontier* (1985).[43] *Star Wars* creator George Lucas filed a trademark dilution suit against political groups that adopted the term "Star Wars" to identify the Reagan Administration's Strategic Defense Initiative. The court dismissed the complaint because the defendants were not using the plaintiff's mark in connection with the sale of goods or services in commerce. It said the defendants were "not engaged in selling anything but ideas . . . Purveying points of view is not a service."[44]

More recently, a U.S. district judge denied Fox News's request for an injunction to prevent Penguin Books from using its trademarked slogan "fair and balanced" on Al Franken's book *Lies and the Lying Liars Who Tell Them: A Fair and Balanced Look at the Right.* Fox argued that use of the slogan and its commentator Bill O'Reilly's picture on the cover of the book might trick consumers into believing it was a Fox product. It also argued that the Fox trademark would be tarnished through its association with Franken on the book's cover. The judge said the case had no merit and that the network was "trying to undermine the First Amendment." He also said "fair and balanced" was "unlikely a valid trademark" because it was weak as trademarks go.[45] Fox withdrew the suit.

---

[41] *Id.* § 1125 (c)(4).

[42] Playboy Enterprises, Inc. v. Terri Welles, Inc., 279 F.3d 796 (9th Cir. 2002).

[43] 622 F. Supp. 931 (D.D.C. 1985).

[44] *Id.* at 934.

[45] Susan Saulny, *In Courtroom, Laughter at Fox and a Victory for Al Franken*, N.Y. Times, Aug. 23, 2003, at B1.

In most cases, parodies are also protected from trademark dilution claims. In *L.L. Bean v. Drake Publishers* (1987), the First Circuit reversed a ruling against a pornographic magazine that spoofed Bean's catalog with an article called the "Back-to-School-Sex-Catalog."[46] The article, which included bawdy advertisements for new products, was labeled "humor" and "parody" in the table of contents. A district court granted summary judgment to the clothing company on its trademark dilution claim because it thought the piece tarnished Bean's reputation, but the First Circuit reversed. It said "Denying parodists the opportunity to poke fun at symbols and names which have become woven into the fabric of our daily life would constitute a serious curtailment of a protected form of expression."[47]

But in *Mutual of Omaha v. Novak* (1987), an artist's parody of Mutual of Omaha's Indian head logo was considered a trademark infringement.[48] Franklyn Novak produced shirts and mugs advertising nuclear holocaust insurance, which depicted the profile of an emaciated human head wearing a feathered headdress above text that read "Mutant of Omaha." In reference to *Wild Kingdom*, the television show the company sponsored, some of the items showed a one-eyed tiger accompanied by the title "Mutant of Omaha's Mutant Kingdom." There was no evidence that Novak intended to pass off his goods as Mutual of Omaha's. His art was intended as political commentary on the potential for nuclear war. Surprisingly, however, the company was able to demonstrate consumer confusion regarding the source of the products. Mutual of Omaha submitted a survey as evidence that 40 out of 400 people from several cities believed that Mutual of Omaha had approved the T-shirts and other paraphernalia "to help make people aware of the nuclear war problem." The court's injunction prevented Novak from marketing Mutant of Omaha products, but left other avenues open for his parody in books, magazines, or films.

Our consumer culture is increasingly tied to brand names that appear in songs, movies, and art. Restrictions on their use for commentary and art are bound to raise First Amendment concerns. Kembrew McLeod, the author of *Owning Culture*, wanted to make a statement about the increasing power of intellectual property law to influence discourse, so in 1998 he trademarked the phrase "Freedom of Expression." He submitted the registration as a joke and was very surprised when the Patent and Trademark Office allowed him to register it. McLeod lost the mark because he didn't renew in time. Because a trademark cannot be re-registered by another person, "Freedom of Expression" is appropriately back in the public domain.

Contextual advertising

Contextual advertising, also called keyword advertising, has become a multi-billion dollar marketing tool on the Internet. Advertisers pay search engines to show their ads

---

[46] L.L. Bean, Inc. v. Drake Publishers, Inc., 811 F.2d 26 (1st Cir. 1987).

[47] *Id*. at 34.

[48] 836 F.2d 397 (8th Cir. 1987).

or sponsored links when computer users search for particular "keywords." For example, using Google's AdWords program, a digital media studies program can select the keywords "digital," "interactive," and "new media" to trigger its ad. Users who type in any of these terms would see the program's sponsored link among their search results. Some businesses select keywords that include the names of competitors' trademarks to trigger their ads or sponsored links. Courts have grappled with two questions to determine whether this practice constitutes trademark infringement: whether the practice is a "use in commerce" – the first step in finding a trademark violation – and, if so, whether it is likely to confuse consumers.

Keywords are used within the search engine's code, rather than displayed on a good or in an advertisement for a good or service. So they fall outside the traditional understanding of a "use in commerce . . . in connection with the sale, offering for sale, distribution, or advertising of any goods or services." Nevertheless, when trademarks are bought and sold for use as keywords without the trademark holder's permission, they are being traded commercially. Courts have generally come to the conclusion that selling them is a use in commerce.[49]

The second area of disagreement is whether their use is likely to confuse consumers who never see the keywords in the code. Assuming the competitor's sponsored link or ad does not actually incorporate the plaintiff's trademark, people will see it as one of many links or ads among search results. Search engine users are accustomed to selecting the links they want to open from a list of search results. Placing a competitor's link or ad near the plaintiff's link is no more likely to confuse them than placing two competing products side by side on a shelf.

Nevertheless, some federal circuits have found the practice to constitute trademark infringement based on a theory called *initial interest confusion*. The theory assumes that by using the plaintiff's trademark to divert people looking for the plaintiff's website, the defendant improperly benefited from good will associated with the plaintiff's mark. This reasoning has been criticized because the purpose of the Trademark Act is not to secure the trademark owner's good will, but to avoid confusion among consumers.

The theory was first applied to web searches through a line of trademark challenges based on the use of *metatags*. These are words or phrases embedded in a website's code, which search engines use to provide short descriptions of the information included on the site. At one point, metatags were influential to search rankings, but search engines now use other criteria.

Several circuits found the use of metatags to be infringing based on initial interest confusion. The Ninth Circuit, for example, used this theory to deem metatag use a

---

[49] Playboy Enterprises v. Netscape Communications Corp., 354 F.3d 1020 (9th Cir. 2004); Government Employees Insurance Co. v. Google, Inc., 330 F. Supp. 2d 700 (E.D. Va. 2004); 800-JR Cigar, Inc. v. GoTo.com, Inc. (2006); Google v. American Blind and Wallpaper Factory, Case No. C03-05340-F (N.D. Cal., March 30, 2005, settled Aug. 31, 2007); Int'l Profit Associates v. Paisola, 461 F. Supp. 2d 672 (N.D. Ill. 2006) (finding trademark use in keywords likely to cause confusion); Edina Realty, Inc. v. TheMLSOnline.Com, 2006 U.S. Dist. LEXIS 13775 (D. Minn. 2006); J.G. Wentworth, S.S.C. v. Settlement Funding LLC, 2007 U.S. Dist. LEXIS 288 (E.D. Pa. 2007); Rescue.Com Corp. v. Google, Inc., 562 F.3d 123 (2nd Cir. 2009).

trademark infringement in *Brookfield Communications v. West Coast Entertainment Corp.* (1999).[50] The defendant, a video rental chain, used the plaintiff's "Movie Buff" trademark as a metatag in the coding for its website to affect search results. The court understood that a search engine user would be able to distinguish the website he or she sought from a list of search results that included the competitor's site, and that even if the user chose to look at the competitor's site it was not likely that he or she would be confused about its source. Yet it based its decision on consumers' "initial interest confusion."

The Seventh Circuit adopted the same theory in *Promatek Industries Ltd. v. Equitrac Corp.* (2002), when it upheld an injunction that barred a company from using a competitor's trademark as a metatag. It explained that initial interest confusion occurs "when a customer is lured to a product by the similarity of the mark, even if the customer realizes the true source of the goods before the sale is consummated."[51] The Tenth Circuit concluded that a defendant's use of metatags containing the plaintiff's trademark resulted in initial interest confusion despite the defendant's use of a disclaimer on its website. In *Australian Gold, Inc. v. Hatfield* (2006), the court reasoned that "a defendant's website disclaimer, disavowing any connection with its competitor, cannot prevent the damage of initial interest confusion, which will already have been done by the misdirection of consumers looking for the plaintiff's websites."[52]

The Eleventh Circuit also held in 2008 that the unauthorized use of a trademark as a metatag could be an infringement, but its decision could be distinguished from those of the Seventh, Ninth, and Tenth Circuits because the defendant used the plaintiff's mark in a description of its website that accompanied its link, so the mark was no longer hidden in the code.[53]

Search engines no longer rely on metatags to prioritize sites in natural searches, so the use of trademarks in metatags has declined. However, keyword advertising has never been more popular. Google, for example, makes 95 percent of its revenue from keyword advertising. Many of those keywords are competitor trademarks. Noting the increasing sophistication of Internet users, courts are beginning to take a more nuanced approach to deciding whether keyword advertising is confusing. In *Network Automation, Inc. v. Advanced Systems Concepts, Inc.* (2011), the Ninth Circuit showed new skepticism regarding initial interest confusion.[54] It concluded that a software company's purchase of a competitor's trademark as a keyword was not likely to cause consumer confusion. Sending the case back to the lower court for further analysis, the Ninth Circuit stated that a trademark owner "must demonstrate likely confusion, not mere diversion" to win a trademark suit. It directed courts to consider such factors as (1) the strength of the mark; (2) evidence of actual confusion; (3) the degree of care the search engine user would be likely to exercise; and (4) the labeling, appearance and context of surrounding

[50] 174 F.3d 1036 (9th Cir. 1999).
[51] Promatek Industries Ltd. v. Equitrac Corp., 300 F.3d 808 (7th Cir. 2002).
[52] 436 F.3d 1228, 1240 (2006).
[53] North American Medical Corp. v. Axiom Worldwide, Inc., 522 F.3d 1211 (11th Cir. 2008).
[54] Network Automation, Inc. v. Advanced Systems Concepts Inc. (9th Cir. 2011).

content displayed in the search results. The Fifth Circuit also affirmed a jury's decision that a defendant's keyword purchases, absent other action, did not compel a finding of likelihood of confusion and trademark infringement.[55]

Companies that advertise on Google will find it especially hard to mount a trademark claim against Google for selling their trademarks through its AdWords program. In their contracts with Google, advertisers now grant Google "a non-exclusive, worldwide, perpetual, and royalty-free license to . . . (c) use all trademarks and trade names included in the Product Information." In *Video Professor v. Amazon.com* (2010), a Colorado court found that Amazon.com had not committed trademark infringement by using Video Professor's trademarked name to trigger a sponsored link because Video Professor had authorized Google to use its trademark for any purpose, not just for the purpose of advertising Video Professor's products.[56]

The European Union's highest court gave Google the go-ahead to sell trademarked names in a case Louis Vuitton brought against it. The European Court of Justice determined in 2010 that the search engine would not be required to block sales of brand names as advertising keywords, as long as it removed ads when brand owners complained that rivals had violated their marks and avoided questionable practices, such as suggesting trademarked names in conjunction with suspicious searches like "imitation handbags." The court warned, however, that individual advertisers could be held liable for keyword advertising if their ads were found to mislead consumers.[57]

The Federal Court of Australia reached a similar conclusion. The court held that Google's sale of trade names for sponsored links was neither misleading nor deceptive because a "sponsored link" is understood to be an advertisement and the identity of the advertiser would usually be apparent from the website address displayed beneath the headline.[58]

Cybersquatting

Entrepreneurial types frequently register domain names with the intent of selling them at a profit. It is legal to register and sell a domain that incorporates a generic term that cannot be trademarked, a distinctive term that has not yet been trademarked (through official registration or regular use), or a term that was formerly trademarked, but that has fallen into the public domain. However, registering a domain that incorporates someone else's trademark, or a term that is confusingly similar to the trademark, with the intent to sell it back to the trademark owner or to profit from the trademark owner's good will is illegal. This practice, known as *cybersquatting*, has become an international

---

[55]College Network, Inc. v. Moore Educational Publishers, Inc., 2010 WL 1923763 (5th Cir. May 12, 2010) (unpublished).

[56]Video Professor, Inc. v. Amazon.com, Inc. 2010 WL 1644630 (D. Colo. 2010).

[57]Eric Pfanner, *Europe Lets Google Sell Brand Advertising*, N.Y. TIMES, March 24, 2010, at B9.

[58]Australian Competition and Consumer Commission v. Trading Post Australia Pty Ltd [2011] FCA 1086 (Sept. 22, 2011).

Figure 8.2 Illustration: Kalan Lyra

problem. In 2010, the World International Property Organization heard complaints against cybersquatters in 57 countries.

Congress amended the Trademark Act to prevent cybersquatting in 1999. The Anti-Cybersquatting Consumer Protection Act – or ACPA – imposes liability on anyone who "registers, traffics in, or uses a domain name" that is identical or confusingly similar to a mark that was distinctive at the time of registration or identical or confusingly similar to a mark that was a famous mark at the time of registration with a "bad faith intent to profit from the mark."[59]

To determine whether someone is operating in bad faith, a court may consider a variety of factors, including:

- the user's trademark rights in the domain name;
- the extent to which the domain includes the legal name of the person or another commonly used to identify the person;
- the person's prior use of the domain name in connection with the legitimate commerce;
- the person's bona fide noncommercial or fair use of the mark in a site that uses the domain name;
- the person's intent to divert traffic from the mark owner's site, either for commercial gain or with the intent to tarnish or disparage the mark, by creating a likelihood of confusion regarding the source of the site;

---

[59] 15 U.S.C. § 1125(d)(1)(A) (2011).

- the person's offer to transfer, sell, or otherwise assign the domain name to the mark owner or any third party for financial gain or the person's prior pattern of such conduct;
- the person's provision of false contact information when applying for the registration of the domain name or failure to maintain accurate information with the registrar;
- the person's registration or acquisition of multiple domain names which the person knows are identical or confusingly similar to marks of others or dilutive of famous marks; and
- the extent to which the mark incorporated into the domain name is distinctive or famous.[60]

If a court determines that a defendant has violated the ACPA, it may order the defendant to forfeit the domain and transfer it to the rightful owner of the trademark. It also may impose actual or statutory damages, ranging from $1,000 to $100,000.[61] If the violator knowingly provided false contact information to register the site, a court may assume the violation is willful.[62]

One cybersquatter, John Zuccarini, was fined $500,000 for five domains registered in bad faith that were confusingly similar to service marks used by Electronics Boutique, a video games and software retailer.[63] Zuccarini registered domain names that included typos users might make while entering the address for a site – a practice nicknamed typosquatting – and filled them with pay-per-click advertising. Users who stumbled into the sites were forced to click through a plethora of ads before they could escape, each earning Zuccarini 10 to 25 cents per click. He earned between $800,000 and $1 million annually from the thousands of domain names he registered.[64]

The Internet Corporation of Assigned Names and Numbers, the organization responsible for the management of the Internet domain name system, has established an arbitration procedure for victims of cybersquatters who would rather avoid the expense and delays associated with trial. Domain registrants agree to standard conditions imposed by ICANN when they register a domain name. Among these is the requirement that the registrant submit to an arbitration proceeding initiated by a trademark holder who believes the domain is confusingly similar to his or her trademark.

Using trademarks for gripe sites

Some people register domains that incorporate company trademarks to criticize a company rather than to profit from it. Gripe sites have received mixed receptions from

---

[60] *Id.* § 1125(d)(1)(B)(i).
[61] *Id.* § 1117(d).
[62] *Id.* § 1117.
[63] Electronics Boutique Holdings Corp. v. Zuccarini, No. 00–4055, 2000 U.S. Dist. LEXIS 15719 (E.D. Pa. 2000).
[64] *See* Shields v. Zuccarini, No.00–494, 2000 U.S. Dist. LEXIS 15223 (E.D. Pa. 2000).

courts, depending on their interpretation of whether the sites were used "in connection with goods or services," a factor considered in determining "bad faith."

Most gripe sites are informational. However, in *United We Stand America v. United We Stand America New York, Inc.* (1997), the Second Circuit reached the surprising conclusion that the nonprofit dissemination of information or opinion could be considered a "service" for purposes of the Trademark Act.[65] The case involved a trademark infringement suit against a breakaway chapter of Ross Perot's campaign organization that continued to use the United We Stand name.

The Second Circuit suggested that liability for the unauthorized use of a mark should depend on whether it is likely to cause confusion, not whether it is commercial. The defendant argued that its political use of the plaintiff's mark was protected, referencing the *Lucasfilm* decision regarding the use of "Star Wars" in a political context. The Second Circuit said that while it agreed with the outcome of that case, it disagreed with the *Lucasfilm* court's reasoning. "[I]f the court were right that communicating ideas and purveying points of view is not a service, subject to the controls established by trademark law, then one who established a learning center would be free to call it Harvard or Yale University."[66]

The Fourth Circuit has also accepted the position that "services" may be interpreted to include "dissemination of information, including purely ideological information."[67] In *People for the Ethical Treatment of Animals v. Doughney* (2001), the appellate court upheld a lower court's grant of summary judgment in favor of an animal rights organization on trademark infringement and cybersquatting claims. The defendant used PETA's mark to create a parody site based on the acronym "People Eating Tasty Animals." The court concluded that

> To use PETA's Mark "in connection with" goods or services, Doughney need not have actually sold or advertised goods or services on the www.peta.org website. Rather, Doughney need only have prevented users from obtaining or using PETA's goods or services, or need only have connected the website to other's goods or services.[68]

It concluded the defendant's use of the mark was likely to prevent some users from reaching PETA's site because upon failing to find it after typing in PETA.org, they may be angry, frustrated, or under the impression that PETA's site didn't exist.

This argument that the use of a mark that diverts traffic from a plaintiff's site, potentially causing commercial harm, constitutes a use "in connection with" the sale of

[65] 128 F.3d 86 (2nd Cir. 1997).
[66] *Id.* at 91.
[67] People for the Ethical Treatment of Animals, Inc., v. Doughney, 263 F.3d 359 (4th Cir. 2001).
[68] *Id.* at 365.

products and services for purposes of the Lanham Act has also been accepted by the Third Circuit,[69] but rejected by the First,[70] Sixth,[71] and Ninth Circuits.[72]

The Fourth Circuit found evidence that Doughney's site was used in connection with goods and services because it included links to other sites that sold animal-based products. This argument, which invests the linking site with the characteristics of the linked site, is also accepted in the Sixth Circuit.[73]

The appellate court found the use of PETA's mark in the domain likely to cause confusion on the part of consumers. It rejected the defendant's parody defense because the domain *name* did not indicate a parody. The parody was not apparent until the user clicked on the website and read its content. The court asserted that "A parody must 'convey two simultaneous – and contradictory – messages: that it is the original, but also that it is not the original and is instead a parody.'"[74] The appellate court faulted Doughney for not conveying the messages "simultaneously" in the domain name.

It is likely that the court took such a hard line because the defendant had a history of registering company trademarks as domain names and had allegedly offered to sell the domain to PETA. Doughney also acquired the plaintiff's domain by providing false information to his Internet service provider. The court considered this evidence of bad faith for purposes of the Anti-Cybersquatting Act.

In another case involving a gripe site against Jerry Falwell, the Fourth Circuit acknowledged that a criticism site could be protected. In *Lamparello v. Falwell Ministries* (2005), the Fourth Circuit ruled in favor of the defendant who registered a gripe site, using a domain that was confusingly similar to one owned by Rev. Jerry Falwell, to dispute the minister's claims that gays and lesbians were sinners who could change their ways.[75] The court noted that the defendant's site carried a prominent disclaimer that the site did not belong to Falwell and a link to Falwell's site for those who still wanted it. Lamparello did not use the site to sell goods or services. His links to other organizations included one to a book on Amazon.com, but the link did "not diminish the communicative function of this site."[76]

---

[69] See Jews for Jesus v. Brodsky, 993 F. Supp. 282, 309 (D. N.J. 1998) ("The conduct of the Defendant is not only designed to, but is likely to, prevent some Internet users from reaching the Internet site of the Plaintiff Organization . . . As such, the conduct of the Defendant is 'in connection with goods and services' as that term is used in Section 1125(a)."), *aff'd*, 159 F.3d 1351; 1998 U.S. App. LEXIS 18889 (3rd Cir. 1998) (decision without published opinion).

[70] See Int'l Ass'n of Machinists & Aerospace Workers v. Winship Green Nursing Home, 103 F.3d 196 (1st Cir. 1996) (rejecting the argument that defendant's use of the mark in manner that impedes plaintiff's sale or offering of services constitutes use "in connection with any goods or services").

[71] See Taubman Co. v. Webfeats, 319 F.3d 770, 777 (6th Cir. 2003) (questioning reasoning in Planned Parenthood).

[72] See Nissan Motor Co. v. Nissan Computer Corp., 378 F.3d 1002 (9th Cir. 2004) (rejecting "effect on commerce" test for commercial use) and Bosley Medical Institute, Inc. v. Steven Kremer, 403 F.3d 672, 674 (2005).

[73] Taubman Co. v. Webfeats, 319 F.3d at 775 (finding that, although defendant's linking was "extremely minimal," it was sufficient to constitute a use "in connection with the sale or advertising of a good or service.").

[74] People for the Ethical Treatment of Animals v. Doughney, 263 F.3d at 366 (citing Cliffs Notes, Inc. v. Bantam Doubleday Dell Publ. Group, Inc., 886 F.2d 490, 494 (2nd Cir. 1989)).

[75] 420 F.3d 309 (4th Cir. 2005).

[76] *Id.* at 320.

The Fifth, Sixth, and Ninth Circuits have endorsed the view that the noncommercial use of a trademark as a domain name does not violate the Lanham Act. In *Taubman Co. v. Webfeats* (2003), the Sixth Circuit held that a gripe site that contained no commercial content, advertisements, or links to other commercial sites was a protected form of expression:[77]

> [T]he First Amendment protects critical commentary when there is no confusion as to source, even when it involves the criticism of a business. Such use is not subject to scrutiny under the Lanham Act. In fact, Taubman concedes that [the defendant] is "free to shout 'Taubman Sucks!' from the rooftops . . . " Essentially, this is what he has done in his domain name. The rooftops of our past have evolved into the Internet domain names of our present. We find that the domain name is a type of public expression, no different in scope than a billboard or a pulpit, and [the defendant] has a First Amendment right to express his opinion about Taubman, and as long as his speech is not commercially misleading, the Lanham Act cannot be summoned to prevent it.[78]

The Fifth Circuit held in *TMI v. Maxwell* (2004) that a gripe site which mixed noncommercial content and commercial content by including a recommendation for one contractor, could still be considered noncommercial because it accepted no payment for advertising, carried no links to other sites, and did not sell products, services, or domain names.[79]

Coming to the same conclusion, the Ninth Circuit warned that the *PETA* court's theory that use of a trademark as a domain name satisfies the Lanham Act by deterring customers from reaching the plaintiff's site "would place most critical, otherwise protected consumer commentary under the restrictions of the Lanham Act."[80]

Trade Secrets

A trade secret is a confidential formula, pattern, compilation, program, device, method, technique, or process that offers its owner an economic advantage over competitors who do not know it. An example would be the "Colonel's secret chicken recipe", proprietary research, product development plans, or an invention that has not yet been patented. Protecting trade secrets is thought to encourage research and development that supplements the patent system.[81]

Protecting a trade secret

The best way to protect a trade secret is by keeping it secret. Trade secrets, unlike copyrights, patents, and trademarks, are never registered. Registration requires public

---

[77] 319 F.3d 770, 774 (6th Cir. 2003).
[78] *Id.* at 778.
[79] 368 F.3d 433, 438 (5th Cir. 2004).
[80] Bosley Medical Institute v. Kramer, 403 F.3d 672, 679 (2005).
[81] *See* Ford Motor Co. v. Lane, 67 F. Supp. 2d 745, 749 (E.D. Mich. 1999).

Figure 8.3   Coca-Cola keeps its trade secret formula locked in a vault.
Source: Coca-Cola

disclosure of the information, which would expose the secret. Once a trade secret is divulged to the public, its protection ends.

Some companies expend great effort protecting their trade secrets. Coca-Cola, for example, locks its formula, which dates back to 1886, in a 10-foot vault at the World of Coca-Cola museum that can only be opened by a resolution from its board of directors. No more than two employees ever know the secret at one time and they are not allowed to fly on the same plane together.[82]

But such extreme measures are not necessary to acquire legal protection. Reasonable precautions for maintaining secrecy include advising employees who work with the information of its trade secret status to prevent them from inadvertently sharing it, limiting access to the information to those who need it, labeling materials "confidential," locking up files when not in use, and maintaining proper computer security.

Companies also commonly require their employees to sign non-disclosure agreements, which are legally enforceable contracts that prevent them from revealing confidential information to third parties. Some firms also require employees to sign

[82] *See* Coca-Cola Bottling Co. v. Coca-Cola Co., 107 F.R.D. 288 (Del. 1995).

non-compete clauses that prevent them from working for direct competitors for a speci-fied period of time after leaving the company.

How long does a trade secret last?

The distinct advantage of trade secret protection is that it is perpetual. So a formula or method that would only be protected for 20 years if it were patented can be held indefi-nitely. The disadvantage is that once the information is made available to the public, the protection ends.

What legal rights does the trade secret owner have?

Most states have enacted civil legislation that prohibits misappropriation of trade secrets. *Misappropriation* is the acquisition or disclosure of a trade secret by someone who knows or has reason to know that it was acquired improperly and its use is unauthorized.

Trade secret protection applies if:

- the information derives independent economic value, actual or potential, from not being known to the public or people who could benefit from its disclosure; and
- the owner has made reasonable efforts under the circumstances to maintain its secrecy.

Misappropriation claims do not apply to people who learn about trade secrets inde-pendently through separate invention or reverse engineering. In fact, because two parties can own a trade secret separately, a person or company that invests heavily in the reverse engineering of a product or formula may also protect the information it has discovered as a trade secret.

A person damaged by misappropriation of a trade secret may sue for compensation. The statute of limitations for misappropriation is normally three years. If the plaintiff establishes his or her case, the court may issue an award for actual damages for losses incurred that include compensation for the defendant's unjust enrichment from the trade secret. Alternatively, the court can order the defendant to pay a sum equal to reasonable royalties on the use of the information. If the defendant's misappropriation was willful, the court may double the damages.

If the trade secret has not yet been disclosed, the trade secret owner can file for an injunction to prevent it. Courts are empowered to enjoin actual or threatened disclosure of trade secrets for as long as the trade secret remains valid. During the course of the litigation, the court will act to preserve secrecy of the information by granting protective orders, holding in-camera hearings (closed to the public), and sealing records.

The intentional theft of a trade secret is a criminal offense under the Economic Espio-nage Act of 1996.[83] An individual acting for economic benefit, who steals a trade secret

---

[83] 18 U.S.C. § 1831.

related to or included in a product meant for interstate or foreign commerce, or who accepts one knowing it was taken without authorization, may be fined or imprisoned for as much as 10 years. A company may be fined as much as $5,000,000.[84] If the trade secret was stolen for the benefit of a foreign government, an individual may be fined as much as $500,000 or imprisoned up to 15 years. A corporation may be fined up to $10,000,000.[85]

Trade secrets and the Internet

Increasingly, cases filed for misappropriation of trade secrets involve information published on the Internet by bloggers. Apple, Inc. and Ford Motor Company have each sued college students for revealing information about company products on their websites. In both cases, the information was provided to the websites anonymously. Both plaintiffs and defendants assumed that it came from company employees who were bound by confidentiality agreements.

Apple experienced a backlash when it sued the publisher of Think Secret, a Mac enthusiast site that ran news about products in development, for misappropriation of trade secrets.[86] The site had developed a loyal following among Mac users who accused the company of censorship. Apple eventually settled the suit for an unknown sum to get the Harvard student who ran the site to shut it down.

Ford's legal battle with the publisher of an enthusiast site that disclosed its secrets was not resolved so easily. Robert Lane published information about quality issues concerning the Cobra engine, fuel efficiency strategies for the year 2010, and engineering blueprints on his website BlueOvalNews.com. Ford asked the court to enjoin Lane from further publication of its secrets, but the court refused.

The court held that restraining Lane from publishing Ford's trade secrets "would constitute an invalid prior restraint of free speech in violation of the First Amendment."[87] It cited a Sixth Circuit decision in *Procter & Gamble Co. v. Bankers Trust Co.* (1996) that overturned an injunction on publication of trade secrets. The Court of Appeals decision directed courts to consider, in cases involving prior restraint of pure speech, whether publication "threaten[s] an interest more fundamental than the First Amendment itself."[88] It explained that "private litigants' interest in protecting their vanity or their commercial self-interest simply does not qualify as grounds for imposing a prior restraint."[89]

The court would not impose an injunction on Lane in the absence of a confidentiality agreement or fiduciary duty between the parties. However, it did enjoin Lane from posting Ford's copyrighted documents and required him to divulge any information he had about the sources of the proprietary information.

---

[84] *Id.* § 1832.
[85] *Id.* § 1831.
[86] Apple Computer, Inc. v. DePlume, et al., Case No. 1-05-CV-033341 (Cal. Santa Clara County Super. Ct. filed Jan. 4, 2005).
[87] Ford Motor Co. v. Lane, 67 F. Supp. 2d 745, 746 (E.D. Mich. 1999).
[88] 78 F.3d 219, 227 (6th Cir. 1996).
[89] *Id.* at 225.

Questions for Discussion

1. What is required to get patent, trademark, and trade secret protection?
2. What kinds of marks are inherently distinctive? How does a mark earn distinctiveness if it is not inherently distinctive?
3. What is the difference between trademark infringement and trademark dilution?
4. How can you post a gripe site without being accused of cybersquatting?

9 Defamation

Around the world, countries balance protections for freedom of expression and reputation differently. The United States, which protects freedom of speech and press in the Constitution, tips the balance in favor of expression. Reputation is still considered worthy of protection but must give way if society's need for information is more pressing. This policy choice is evident in the Supreme Court's decision to impose First Amendment constraints on state defamation laws.

Unlike other nations, the United States no longer imposes strict liability upon libel defendants. The Supreme Court has created "a zone of protection for errors of fact" that inevitably occur in publication.[1] Plaintiffs who sue for defamation regarding a matter of public concern must prove negligence or malice on the part of the defendant, as well as the falsity of the defendant's statements. The United States is also unique in allowing plaintiffs to sue defendants for libel in only one jurisdiction, regardless of how widely the defamation was published. As a result, media have more protection against defamation in the United States than any other country in the world.

This chapter discusses the elements required to establish a libel claim and defenses that apply in libel suits. It describes how U.S. defamation law differs from that of other countries and the impact that difference has had on the way various types of plaintiffs are treated. Just as importantly, it explains how libel laws apply to traditional media defendants v. nontraditional or non-media defendants in a period in which we are all producing digital media products. Finally, it considers the tort of infliction of emotional distress and its relationship to defamation law.

[1] Time, Inc. v. Pape, 401 U.S. 279 (1971).

Digital Media Law, Second Edition. Ashley Packard.
© 2013 John Wiley & Sons, Inc. Published 2013 by John Wiley & Sons, Inc.

What is Defamation?

A tort is an intentional or negligent act that injures another, resulting in civil liability.

Respondeat superior is a common-law doctrine that employers are responsible for the actions or omissions of their employees resulting from their employment.

Defamation is a *tort* regulated through state law that involves harm to someone's reputation. It occurs when a false communication exposes a person to hatred, contempt, or ridicule, or lowers a person's stature in the community.[2] The communication may take a variety of forms. It might be a verbal statement in front of a group, an article printed in a publication, an advertisement broadcast on air, a video circulated on YouTube, or a cartoon distributed through e-mail.

Defamation is one of the more serious torts to plague media professionals. People do not dismiss harm to their reputations easily and will sue for vindication even when they know their chances of winning are slim. Defamation suits are also very costly. The average jury award against media defendants is around $2.8 million. Under the *doctrine of respondeat superior*, a plaintiff can sue a media company for a defamatory statement made by its employee and generally will because the company is the one with deeper pockets. Juries are empowered to decide the facts of the case, and their decisions occasionally reflect a bias against the media.

The largest jury award for libel was $223 million, rendered in Texas in 1997. The plaintiff was a Houston brokerage firm that sued *The Wall Street Journal* for libel after it published an article that alleged the company had been involved in criminal activity.[3] When a former employee of the brokerage firm came forward with a tape recording of the firm's executives supporting the *Journal*'s accusations, the verdict was set aside.[4] Many media awards in libel suits are vacated or reduced on appeal. In the interim, however, defendants lose time and money defending themselves.

Fortunately, defamation suits against journalists are on the decline. The Media Law Resource Center found that libel trials against traditional media organizations have dropped substantially in the last three decades. There were 266 trials in the 1980s, 192 in the 1990s, and 124 in the 2000s.[5] (Of course, that data doesn't account for the number of suits filed and either dismissed or settled before trial.) There are likely to be several reasons for the decline. One is that the Internet gives publications a quick way to make corrections and potential plaintiffs a way to respond that may quell the urge to litigate. Another is the fact that libel suits are not only expensive to litigate but hard to win. Even when the media lose at the trial level, they usually win on appeal. The "Streisand effect," discussed in Chapter 6, is also a factor. Lawsuits generate publicity, which encourages people to search for the offending material. Finally, and sadly, in the current economic environment, the media don't have the same budgets for investigative reporting, which means there are fewer opportunities to "afflict the comfortable."

---

[2] RESTATEMENT (SECOND) OF TORTS § 581A cmt. f (1977).

[3] MMAR Group, Inc. v. Dow Jones & Co., Civ. No. H-95-1262 (S.D. Tex. 1997).

[4] MMAR Group, Inc. v. Dow Jones & Co., 187 F.R.D. 282; 1999 U.S. Dist. LEXIS 14941 (1999).

[5] John Koblin, *The End of Libel?* N.Y. OBSERVER, June 9, 2010, http://www.observer.com/2010/media/end-libel.

Unfortunately, the number of libel suits against bloggers and users of social media is on the rise. The Media Law Resource Center, which tracks lawsuits against bloggers, logged 109 libel suits between the years of 2005 and 2009.[6] In fact, bloggers have faced $47 million in defamation judgments.[7]

Types of Defamation

Defamation can be subdivided into two categories: libel and slander. *Libel* is defamation in printed or broadcast form. *Slander* refers to spoken words of limited reach. Of the two, libel is considered more damaging because it is fixed and can be circulated broadly. A slanderous statement is transitory in nature, so its potential for damage is presumed to be less severe.

Who Can Be Defamed?

Individuals, as well as corporations and nonprofit organizations, can sue for damage to their reputations. While individuals are considered "natural persons" under the law, a corporation is treated as a "legal person" with standing to sue apart from its officials and stockholders. Some torts, like defamation, apply to natural as well as legal persons; others, like invasion of privacy, apply only to natural persons.

Government entities may not sue for defamation under the theory that the government should not be permitted to use public funds to prevent the public from criticizing it.[8] But government officials are entitled to sue on their own behalf. By necessity, public officials are subject to greater scrutiny than private citizens, so courts require them to meet a higher standard of proof in defamation cases.

On rare occasions plaintiffs find they cannot sue for defamation because they have no reputation left to protect. In a case fought by archrivals of porn, Penthouse publisher Robert Guccione sued Larry Flynt, the publisher of *Hustler*, for libel because Flynt printed that Guccione "is married and also has a live-in girlfriend." Because adultery was technically illegal in New York, where the suit was filed, and Guccione had been divorced four years, a jury awarded him a $1.6 million judgment. Observing that while Guccione was divorced when the article was published, he had in fact lived with his

---

[6] Eric P. Robinson, *Lawsuits Against Bloggers: MLRC's Data on Blog Suits*, 2009, www.medialaw.org/.../MLRC.../LawsuitsAgainstBloggers_ER.pdf.

[7] Dan Springer, *A $2.5 Million Libel Judgment Brings the Question: Are Bloggers Journalists*, Fox.com, Dec. 22, 2011, http://www.foxnews.com/us/2011/12/22/bloggers-not-journalists/#ixzz1icqtRjda.

[8] *See* New York Times v. Sullivan, 376 U.S. 254, 291 (1964) (holding that prosecutions for libel against the government have no place in the American system of jurisprudence); Klein v. Port Arthur Independent School District, 92 S.W.3d 889; 2002 Tex. App. LEXIS 8966 (2002) (affirming summary judgment in favor of a blogger sued by the Port Arthur School District for writing about a gang fight at a local prom because government entities cannot sue for defamation).

girlfriend while married for 13 of the 17 years prior to its publication, the Second Circuit reversed the judgment. It found Guccione "libel proof" with respect to the issue of adultery because numerous articles had already mentioned his infidelity.[9] Few individuals are libel proof for all purposes, however. Courts usually reserve that designation for notorious criminals.[10]

Once we die, we also lose our rights to protect our reputations. Under common law, both in the United States and the United Kingdom, libel claims cannot be made on behalf of the dead. We cannot protect our reputations in perpetuity. Some states have statutes that prohibit libeling the dead, usually in conjunction with criminal libel laws. But courts no longer recognize claims under them.[11]

Trade libel

A subcategory of defamation known as *trade libel* protects the market for particular products that may be harmed by false allegations. Oprah Winfrey, for example, was sued for disparaging beef. A guest on a "dangerous food" segment of her show suggested that mad cow disease could make AIDS look like the common cold and that the United States was doing too little to protect consumers from tainted beef. Other guests refuted the danger, but when the show was edited for time, some of their assurances were removed. Following a drastic drop in cattle prices after the show, Texas cattle ranchers sued Winfrey for violating the state's False Disparagement of Perishable Food Products Act. The jury ruled in Winfrey's favor because the cattlemen could not prove she had made "knowingly false statements" about them.[12]

SLAPP suits

Companies have been known to use the threat of a prolonged legal battle to intimidate legitimate critics. Libel suits filed for this purpose are known as Strategic Lawsuit Against Public Participation or, more commonly, *SLAPP suits*.

SLAPP suits are now being used to silence posters on Internet review sites. When San Francisco marketing manager Jennifer Batoon vented about a dental procedure on Yelp, her dentist filed a libel suit against her. She had posted "Don't go here, unless u like mouth torture," then described her experience.[13] California Anti-SLAPP Project, a

---

[9] Guccione v. Hustler Magazine, 800 F.2d 298 (1986).

[10] *See, e.g.,* Thomas v. Telegraph Publishing Company, 155 N.H. 314 (N.H. 2007) (in which the New Hampshire Supreme Court found that a repeat criminal was not libel proof because he had not been made notorious through prior publicity of his crimes).

[11] Colorado Revised Statute Section 18-13-105, Idaho Code § 18–4801, Georgia Code – Crimes and Offenses – Title 16, Section 16-11-40, Louisiana Revised Statute § 14:47, and Nevada Revised Statutes § 200.510 all include a prohibition against defaming the dead in their criminal libel statutes. Texas and Utah also prohibit libeling the dead through civil statutes (Tex. Civ. Prac. & Rem. Code § 73.001 (2012); (Utah Code Ann. § 45-2-2 (2012)).

[12] Texas Beef Group v. Winfrey, 11 F. Supp. 2d 858 (1998), aff'd, 201 F.3d 680 (5th Cir. 2000).

[13] *Editorial, Want to complain online? Look out. You might be sued,* USA TODAY, June 8, 2010, at 8A.

public interest law firm and policy organization, defended her. The judge in the case threw out the suit and ordered the dentist to pay more than $40,000 in Batoon's legal fees. Batoon's case is one of several involving doctors pursuing patients for poor reviews.

At least 27 states have passed anti-SLAPP statutes that empower courts to dismiss SLAPP suits intended to chill protected expression and award attorneys' fees to the victim. They are Arizona, Arkansas, California, Delaware, Florida, Georgia, Hawaii, Illinois, Indiana, Louisiana, Maine, Maryland, Massachusetts, Minnesota, Missouri, Nebraska, Nevada, New Mexico, New York, Oklahoma, Oregon, Pennsylvania, Rhode Island, Tennessee, Texas, Utah and Washington. Courts in Colorado and West Virginia have created analogous common law defenses that individuals may use if they are targeted for libel suits based on their petitions to government for action on issues of public importance.[14]

Elements of Libel

Libel is a combination of six elements: publication, identification, defamation, falsity, fault, and damage. Before an allegation can be considered defamatory, a judge or jury must be convinced that the statement was of or concerning the plaintiff, that it was harmful to reputation and untrue, that the defendant was at fault, and that the statement resulted in damage to the plaintiff.

Publication

An accusation must be made public before it can harm someone's reputation. So the first thing a libel plaintiff must establish in a claim is that the statement in question was published. An article that appears in a printed or online news source is considered published; so is a story distributed via broadcast, cable or satellite. But publication is not exclusive to the mass media. Information may be "published" on a personal website or blog, a social networking site like Facebook or Twitter, or through an e-mail or fax circulated among colleagues. Technically, the requirement for publication is met when a third person sees the information.

Identification

Next, the plaintiff must prove the he or she was the subject of the offensive remark. A statement that cannot be shown to be "of or concerning" the plaintiff will not be considered harmful to the plaintiff's reputation.

Identification may occur in a variety of ways. A plaintiff who is named is obviously identified, but a name is not required for identification. Any information or depiction

---

[14]Responding to Strategic Lawsuits Against Public Participation (SLAPPs), Citizen's Media Law Project, http://www.citmedialaw.org/legal-guide/responding-strategic-lawsuits-against-public-participation-slapps. (Last updated on July 7th, 2011).

in which the plaintiff is recognizable will do. This could be accomplished through a picture, cartoon, video, or a sufficiently detailed description. For example, a reference to "a Scientologist, married to Katie Holmes, who starred in the *Mission Impossible* films series" should bring Tom Cruise to mind without using his name.

Group membership is not a sufficient basis for identification, unless a reference to a group could reasonably be interpreted as referring to specific individuals. Under the *group libel doctrine*, a plaintiff will not be considered identified if he or she is referenced solely as a member of a group.[15] For example, a libel suit filed by 67 members of the religious group Falun Gong was dismissed because they could not prove that articles written by the defendants about "New York-based Falun Gong practitioners" referenced any of them specifically.[16] In general, courts have been reluctant to acknowledge "group libel," particularly for groups of 25 or more.

Defamation

After a court is satisfied that the statement in question was published and that the plaintiff has been identified as its subject, it will consider whether the words themselves could be considered damaging to reputation. The court or jury will look at the words in light of their ordinary meaning.

In all but three states (Arkansas, Kansas, and Missouri), libel can also be subdivided into two categories: libel per se and libel per quod.

Libel per se is a statement that is obviously damaging to one's reputation (or as courts say, libelous on its face). Suggesting that someone is guilty of a crime, disreputable in business, sexually promiscuous, or suffers from a communicable disease would be considered libel per se. *Libel per quod* is not obvious. Its negative implication depends on innuendo or knowledge of extraneous facts. For example, a California newspaper published a photo of a police officer sitting in his squad car, tilting his head to one side. The accompanying caption described him prowling for traffic violations on a lightly traveled street, adding "his tilted head may suggest something." Readers assumed he was sleeping on duty. Actually, he was writing a citation, a fact the editors knew when they published the caption. Other cases of libel per quod appear completely innocent unless readers happen to have additional information. For example, a meat market advertisement that included bacon wouldn't raise an eyebrow among readers, unless they happened to know that the butcher was a kosher meat dealer.

A common misconception is that qualifying words like "alleged" or "reportedly" will prevent libel suits. In *Time, Inc. v. Pape* (1971), the Supreme Court said the word "alleged" should not be construed as "a superfluity in published reports of information damaging to reputation."[17] Qualifying words may offer some protection when used as verbs, such as *Police alleged that Smith was the murderer*. But they should never be used

---

[15] *See* Church of Scientology Int'l v. Time Warner, 806 F. Supp. 1157, 1160 (S.D. N.Y. 1992).

[16] Friends of Falun Gong v. Pacific Cultural Enterprise, Inc., 288 F. Supp. 2d 273, aff'd, 2004 U.S. App. LEXIS 16419 (2nd Cir. N.Y., Aug. 9, 2004).

[17] 401 U.S. 279, 292 (1971).

as adjectives: *Smith is the alleged murderer*. Ultimately, however, it is safer and more accurate to use a verifiable statement of fact, such as *Police arrested Smith in connection with the murder*.

Another misconception is that quotation marks will protect a writer from liability for a source's defamatory comments. They will not. Repeating a defamatory remark made by someone else is known as *republication of libel*. The person republishing the libel also bears responsibility for it. It is not enough to quote a source accurately.[18] Before publishing information that could be contentious, it is important to check more than one source.

Falsity

No matter how much harm a statement does to a plaintiff's reputation, it is only libelous if it is *false*. Assessments of falsity are based on the substance of the accusation. Minor inaccuracies that bear no relationship to the statement's "sting" are not taken into account. The falsity also must be believable. A statement that cannot be taken seriously is presumed to cause no real damage.

In the United States, the plaintiff is responsible for proving an accusation's falsity if he or she is a *public figure* or the statement involves a matter of public concern. An exception to this rule is provided when proving the falsity of the statement would require the plaintiff to prove a negative – for example, that he or she never cheated or lied. In other common law legal systems, it is the defendant's obligation to prove the statement's truth.

As fact finder, the jury (or judge in a bench trial) will determine whether a statement is true or false. However, on appeal, the appellate court has an obligation to examine the evidence as well to make sure that "the judgment does not constitute a forbidden intrusion on the field of free expression."[19]

Fault

If the defamation concerns a matter of public interest, the plaintiff must not only prove falsity but also some level of fault on the part of the defendant. The level of fault depends on whether the plaintiff is a public or private figure.

A *public figure* is one who willingly assumes a position in the public arena and has ready access to the media to refute false accusations. Certain individuals are considered to be public figures for all purposes. These include celebrities with "pervasive fame and notoriety" and public officials. A *public official* includes a candidate for public office, an elected official, or an appointed official with substantial responsibility for or control

---

[18] *See, e.g.,* Little v. Consolidated Publishing, 2011 Ala. Civ. App. LEXIS 125 (Ala. Civ. App. May 13, 2011) (holding that a story that quoted a libelous statement correctly, pointed out that the rumor was unverified, and included the subject's denial could still constitute republication of libel.)

[19] Bose Corp. v. Consumers Union of United States, Inc., 466 U.S. 485, 499 (1984) (quoting New York Times v. Sullivan, 376 U.S. 254, 284–6 (1964)).

over governmental affairs.[20] Public officials need not be people in high places. Some states consider police officers to be public figures, for example.

A *limited-purpose public figure* is someone who voluntarily thrusts him or herself into the spotlight in regard to a public issue or controversy and who has effective access to the media to rebut false statements made in relation to that controversy. This would include individuals like the leaders of "Occupy Wall Street" or Cindy Sheehan, the mother of a soldier killed in Iraq, who garnered national attention for protesting the war outside former president George Bush's Texas ranch. There is also limited support for an *involuntary limited-purpose public figure* category that would include people who are unwitting subjects of media coverage related to events of public interest, such as an air traffic controller on duty during a plane crash.[21] However, while courts have acknowledged this category, its use is exceedingly rare.

Most of us fall into the private figure category. A *private figure* is a person who has not voluntarily exposed him or herself to the increased risk of defamation by seeking media attention and who has no special access to the media to challenge an accusation. Courts consider private plaintiffs to be disadvantaged by their lack of influence over the media and therefore less able to defend themselves against malicious attacks.

Because public figures have more venues in which to counter damaging statements than private figures, courts have subjected them to a higher standard of proof in libel suits. Public figures must prove with clear and convincing evidence that the defendant acted with actual malice. The term *actual malice* is defined as either knowledge of falsity or reckless disregard for the truth. To prove actual malice, a plaintiff must demonstrate that the defendant made the statement knowing that it was false at the time or "entertained serious doubts" about its truth.[22]

Proving actual malice is very difficult. It requires substantially more than a showing of "extreme departure from professional standards."[23] The first case in which the Supreme Court affirmed a finding of actual malice against a media defendant was *Harte-Hanks Communications v. Connaughton* (1989). The plaintiff was a candidate for a municipal judge position in Hamilton, Ohio, who lost the election after the local newspaper suggested he had used "dirty tricks" to unseat his opponent. The article suggested Connaughton had bribed a woman who witnessed improprieties in his opponent's office to cooperate in an investigation to discredit the incumbent judge. The paper's editors, who endorsed Connaughton's opponent, reported accusations made against him by a source whose veracity was questionable while ignoring Connaughton's denial and contradictory evidence from five other sources. No one from the paper attempted to interview the witness Connaughton was accused of bribing. Nor did anyone listen to the recording Connaughton provided of his meeting with the witness in which she

---

[20] *See* Rosenblatt v. Baer, 383 U.S. 75 (1966).

[21] *See* Dameron v. Washington Magazine, Inc., 779 F.2d 736, 737 (D.C. Cir. 1985) (concerning an air traffic controller who became an involuntary, limited-purpose public figure due to his role in a major public occurrence). *But see* Wells v. Liddy, 186 F.3d 505 (4th Cir. 1999) (setting a higher standard to ensure that involuntary limited public figures are "exceedingly rare").

[22] *See* Time, Inc. v. Pape, 401 U.S. 279, 292 (1971).

[23] Harte-Hanks Communications v. Connaughton, 491 U.S. 657, 664 (1989).

described what she had seen. The Supreme Court concluded that the editors' actions amounted to a "purposeful avoidance of truth" that constituted reckless disregard under the actual malice standard.[24] The case could be read as checklist of behaviors that might support a finding of actual malice: relying on questionable sources, failing to interview relevant sources, ignoring contradictory evidence and denials, accepting improbable notions, and exhibiting obvious prejudice.[25]

Limited-purpose public figures are required to prove actual malice on the part of a defendant if the statement alleged to be libelous was made in relation to the public issue or controversy for which the plaintiff sought media attention. In any other circumstance, the plaintiff would be treated like a private figure.

Private figure plaintiffs are not required to prove actual malice in cases involving a matter of public concern, but they are required to establish negligence on the part of the defendant. *Negligence* equates to a dereliction of duty. A negligent person either does something that a reasonable person would not do, or fails to do something that a reasonable person would do. Professional negligence amounts to a failure to follow accepted professional practices. Applied to a journalist, this might include failure to check public records, verify information through other sources, or contact the person defamed before running the story. It would not include the failure to verify facts from a wire service, because wire services are normally trustworthy. A court will also consider the degree to which the story in question was "hot news."[26] Time-sensitive stories offer a narrower window for fact checking.

The Supreme Court has not ruled on whether a private figure is required to prove fault in a libel case that has no public relevance. Some jurisdictions require private plaintiffs to prove some level of fault regardless of the issue. Others require them to prove fault only in matters of public interest.[27]

> In matters of public interest, a plaintiff who is a public figure or official must prove the defendant acted with actual malice. A private person plaintiff is normally required to show that the defendant's actions were negligent.

Damage

In a libel suit, plaintiffs are required to prove damages that go beyond mere embarrassment. These might include loss of income, denial of employment, suffering from documented depression or anxiety, or being shunned by one's colleagues.

Damages may be presumed for public figures who establish actual malice on the part of the defendant in cases of libel per se, but not in libel per quod. Public figure plaintiffs who allege libel per quod must show actual damages because the impact in libel per quod cases is presumed to be limited to the small group of readers or viewers aware of the extraneous facts that make the remark libelous.

Private figures who sue for libel in a case involving a matter of public interest are always expected to prove damages. If they seek actual damages in recompense for their

---

[24] *Id.* at 684–5.

[25] *Id.* at 691–2.

[26] *See* Curtis Publishing Co. v. Butts, 388 U.S. 130 (1967).

[27] *See* Lyrissa Barnett Lidsky and R. George Wright, Freedom of the Press: A Reference Guide to the United States Constitution 73–75 (2004).

loss, they will have to prove negligence. If they seek punitive damages, they will have to prove actual malice. In contrast, a private figure plaintiff suing over a matter that does not concern the public interest, may be entitled to an award of presumed and punitive damages without showing actual malice in cases of libel per se.

Defenses to Libel

Truth

Truth is an absolute defense against libel claims. A story need not be accurate in every detail, though. Courts expect minor inaccuracies to occur during reporting and, therefore, look for "substantial truth." *Bustos v. A & E Television Networks* (2011) illustrates this point. When cable network A&E aired footage from a Colorado prison on its show *Gangland: Aryan Brotherhood* with narration that mistakenly identified inmate Jerry Bustos as a member of the Aryan Brotherhood gang, he sued for libel. Bustos found himself in a "world of trouble" after the show aired. He was threatened by prisoners who now believed he was a clandestine member of the Aryan Brotherhood, and Brotherhood members who were upset that he appeared as part of their gang without an invitation. The U.S. Court of Appeals for the Tenth Circuit agreed that the statement was damaging but nevertheless accepted A&E's defense that the story was substantially true.[28] Although not a member of the gang, Bustos had, in fact, conspired with members of the gang to smuggle drugs into the prison. The court didn't think the challenged statement that Bustos was a member of the gang would cause a reasonable juror to think significantly less of him than the truth that he associated with Aryan members and aided them in committing a crime.

By the same token, a truth defense will not stand if the individual facts are correct but combined in a manner that creates a false impression. In *Richardson v. State-Record Co.* (1998), a South Carolina woman sued a newspaper for publishing an article that, while technically true, libeled her through the omission of information.[29] The plaintiff, Nora Richardson, hit the police chief of Eastover, S.C., with her car. He died one year later. The State Record reported his death in an article titled "Eastover chief dies a year after being hit by car." The article correctly stated that Richardson had seriously injured the chief in the accident and that he had never fully recovered. A follow-up story, titled "Chief's death won't bring new charges against driver," indicated that Richardson would face no more charges because she had already pled guilty and could not be charged twice for the same crime. Each sentence was true, but what the paper neglected to mention was that the chief died of rectal cancer. The court pointed out that the truth defense "must substantially cover the 'gist' or the 'sting' of the defamatory statement."[30]

---

[28] Bustos v. A & E Television Networks, 646 F.3d 762 (2011).
[29] 330 S.C. 562, 499 S.E.2d 822 (Ct. App. 1998).
[30] *Id.* at 566.

Opinion

The Supreme Court has not created a separate constitutional protection for *opinion* in defamation cases. But it has asserted that "a statement of opinion relating to matters of public concern, which does not contain a provably false factual connotation, will receive full constitutional protection."[31] In other words, a statement of opinion that cannot be proved true or false will be protected. This protection, according to the Court, is simply an extension of its policy that "a statement on matters of public concern must be provable as false before there can be liability under state defamation law."[32]

The Supreme Court considered the contours of opinion as a libel defense in *Milkovich v. Lorain Journal Co.* (1990). The petitioner in the case was a high school wrestling coach whose team had been punished following an altercation with another team in which several people were injured. The Ohio High School Athletic Association placed the team on probation for one year. Several of the wrestlers' parents filed suit, asking for an injunction preventing enforcement of the association's decision. Milkovich testified during the proceeding. The following day a local columnist implied that Milkovich had lied under oath. The trial court granted summary judgment to the paper on the grounds that the article was opinion. The Supreme Court reversed.

It stated that protection does not extend to verifiable statements couched as opinions. A statement like "In my opinion, Jones is a liar," for example, would *not* qualify as a genuine opinion because a reasonable listener could interpret its essence – Jones is a liar – as a fact subject to verification.[33] In contrast, a statement like "Jones is a fool" would be protected because it is subjective. (A fool by whose measure?) The question to consider is not whether evidence for the statement exists, but whether it is "susceptible of being proved true or false."[34]

In statements, discount introductory phrases like "I think" or "In my opinion." If what remains is *potentially provable*, the statement is not a protected opinion.

Fair comment and criticism

Statements of opinion on matters of public interest also may be protected under the common law defense of fair comment and criticism. The protection applies to comments, supported by facts and made without malice, which convey an honest expression of the writer's opinion. The defense, adopted from English common law, was explained by a New York court in *Hoeppner v. Dunkirk* (1930):

> Everyone has a right to comment on matters of public interest and concern, provided they do so fairly and with an honest purpose. Such comments or criticism are not libelous, however severe in their terms, unless they are written maliciously. Thus it has been held that books, prints, pictures, and statuary publicly exhibited, and the architecture or public

[31] Milkovich v. Lorain Journal Co., 497 U.S. 1, 20 (1990).

[32] *Id.* at 20–21.

[33] *Id.* at 19.

[34] *Id.* at 21–22.

buildings, and actors and exhibitors, are all the legitimate subjects of newspapers' criticism, and such criticism fairly and honestly made is not libelous, however strong the terms of censure may be.[35]

Fair comment and criticism protected a Louisiana food critic who described a restaurant's "hideous sauces" as "yellow death on duck" and "trout a la green plague."[36] The court ruled that the critic's comments about the sauces reflected his expertise on the subject and that his colorful descriptions were merely hyperbole.

Rhetorical hyperbole

Rhetorical *hyperbole* – or exaggeration for effect – is protected under common law on the theory that a false statement must be believable before it can be considered defamatory.[37] Rhetorical hyperbole applies to statements so extreme and overstated that no reader or listener could seriously consider them to imply factual charges.[38] Take, for example, the title "Director of Butt Licking." Virginia Tech's student newspaper printed the appellation under a pull-quote by the university's Vice President of Student Affairs, which accompanied an article about her efforts to promote a state fellowship program. She sued the paper for libel, claiming she had been accused of "moral turpitude." While acknowledging that the term was "in extremely bad taste," the Virginia Supreme Court upheld a lower court's dismissal of the suit, finding that as a matter of law the phrase could not be defamatory because it was "void of literal meaning" and no reasonable person would accept it as a factual statement about the plaintiff.[39] Although the designation is generally associated with sycophantic behavior, the court found nothing in the article to support the conclusion that the plaintiff's behavior was in any way unprofessional.

In determining whether speech is protected as rhetorical hyperbole, courts consider the context in which it appears. For example, in an emotional debate over the murder of abortion providers, talk show host Geraldo Rivera described Neal Horsley, the creator of the Nuremberg Files website (discussed in Chapter 11) that listed the names and addresses of abortion providers and classified them as working, wounded, or deceased, as "an accomplice to homicide." Horsley sued Rivera for libel. A district court in Georgia determined that the First Amendment did not protect Rivera's statement. The U.S. Court of Appeals for the Eleventh Circuit reversed, concluding that the statement was rhetorical hyperbole.[40] It said a reasonable viewer would have understood that Rivera's

---

[35] Hoeppner v. Dunkirk Printing Co., 254 N.Y. 95 (1930).

[36] Mashburn v. Collin, 355 So.2d 879 (La. 1977).

[37] *See* Greenbelt Cooperative Publishing Assn. v. Bresler, 398 U.S. 6, 15 (1970) (finding that a plaintiff characterized as blackmailing the city during a zoning negotiation was not libeled because the term was rhetorical hyperbole); Underwager v. Channel 9 Australia, 69 F.3d 361, 366–7 (9th Cir. 1995).

[38] *See* Milkovich v. Lorain Journal Co., 497 U.S. 1, 20 (1990).

[39] Yeagle v. Collegiate Times, 497 S.E.2d 136 (Va. 1998).

[40] Horsley v. Rivera, 292 F.3d 695, 698, 702 (11th Cir. 2002).

comment was meant to suggest that Horsley was morally culpable for one of the murders, not that he had committed a felony.

The rhetorical hyperbole defense applies to music as well. Former record producer Armen Boladian lost a libel suit against musician George Clinton, when the Sixth Circuit held that Clinton's rap lyrics referring to the "sorrows and horrors of Armen's abuse," and describing him as a "disgrace to the species," were rhetorical hyperbole and puerile taunts.[41] Ultimately, the test is whether the audience would take the accusation seriously.

Privilege

The law also acknowledges a certain level of privilege to make defamatory statements in pursuit of a legal, moral, or social duty. There are three kinds of privileges that serve as protection against libel suits: absolute, fair reporting, and neutral reportage.

Absolute privilege immunizes people in certain positions from liability for defamation. The U.S. Constitution, for example, provides that members of Congress are privileged from suits based on their remarks on the floor of either house.[42] Courts have extended absolute privilege to other officials engaged in public proceedings, such as judges on the bench or city council members during official meetings. The guarantee is intended to provide these officials with a safe zone in which to speak their minds on important public issues. Absolute privilege also applies to public records from government agencies, legislative committee reports, and trial transcripts.[43]

Absolute privilege does not, however, serve as a free pass to say or print anything "off the job." Its protection applies only to officials engaged in their official duties. The case *Hutchinson v. Proxmire* (1979) illustrates this caveat.[44] Senator William Proxmire invented the Golden Fleece Award to shame people who he believed had fleeced the American public. One of its recipients – a researcher given a federal grant to study aggression in monkeys – sued Proxmire for defamation after Proxmire distributed a news release and newsletters that accused the researcher of making a monkey out of tax payers. While Proxmire's comments on the floor of the Senate and to his staff were protected, his comments in the press releases and newsletters were not because they were not part of the legislative "deliberative process."

The *fair reporting privilege* is a common law defense against libel that protects those who report information from public records or proceedings later alleged to be defamatory. The justification for the privilege is two-fold. First, the public needs access to information regarding the workings of government. Second, information taken from public sources would already have been available to any citizen who could have attended the proceeding or read the public document. However, fair reporting is a qualified

---

[41] Boladian v. UMG Recordings, Inc., 123 F. App'x 165, 2005, U.S. App. LEXIS 68 (6th Cir. 2005).
[42] U.S. Const., art. 1, § 6.
[43] *See* Doe v. McMillan, 412 U.S. 306, 307–10 (1973) and Brown & Williamson v. Jacobson, 713 F.2d 262 (7th Cir. 1983).
[44] 443 U.S. 111 (1979).

privilege that can be overcome. *Time Magazine* was denied the privilege for an inaccurate report of a judicial proceeding.[45] To secure the fair reporting privilege, editors and writers must report information fairly and accurately.

Some jurisdictions also recognize the privilege of *neutral reportage*, which acknowledges that accusations made by one prominent organization or public figure against another may qualify as a matter of public interest. The U.S. Court of Appeals for the Second Circuit accepted neutral reportage as a First Amendment defense against republication of libel in *Edwards v. National Audubon Society* (1977). Plaintiffs in the case were scientists, who supported the use of DDT as a pesticide. The National Audubon Society accused them of being "paid liars." When *The New York Times* reported the accusation, the scientists sued it for libel. The court dismissed the defamation suit, noting that such reports are immunized if four conditions are met:

- The accusation is made by a responsible, prominent organization or individual;
- It involves a serious charge on a matter of public interest;
- The accusation is made against another public figure or organization; and
- The charge is accurately and disinterestedly reported.[46]

Because the neutral reportage privilege is based on the assumption that the accusation itself is newsworthy, regardless of whether it is likely to be true, it is controversial. Some courts have flatly rejected the defense because it provides no exception for actual malice and has never been recognized by the Supreme Court.[47] Jurisdictions that do recognize neutral reportage require that the reports be based on a "good faith" belief that the charges have been accurately conveyed and compiled without additional commentary.

Mitigation of Damages

Printing or broadcasting an apology or a retraction will not serve as a defense to libel, but it may mitigate libel damages and serve as an indication to a court or jury that malice was not intended. However, if the defamatory statement appeared at the beginning of a broadcast, the retraction cannot appear at the end. It must be as conspicuous and prominent as the earlier statement.

Under the *mitigation of damages doctrine*, plaintiffs who are harmed by a tort are expected to take reasonable steps, following the harmful act, to minimize their damages. In libel cases, plaintiffs are expected to notify defendants of the libel so the defendant can issue a correction or retract the article. Many states have retraction statutes that shield media defendants who issue a retraction for a libelous statement from punitive damages. Other states bar plaintiffs from seeking punitive damages if they fail to notify

---

[45]Time, Inc. v. Firestone, 424 U.S. 448 (1976).

[46]556 F.2d 113 (2nd Cir. 1977).

[47]*See* Kyu Ho Youm, *Recent Rulings Weaken Neutral Reportage Defense*, 27 NEWSPAPER RES. J. 58 (2006).

defendants about problem material before filing suit.[48] For example, a Georgia court denied punitive damages in a libel suit against an electronic message board owner because the plaintiff failed to seek a retraction before filing suit.[49]

However, the applicability of retraction statutes is not always clear-cut. In many states retraction statutes are specific to certain media, such as newspapers, broadcasts, and periodicals. Courts do not always consider an online publication or website to be a "periodical." A California Court of Appeals held that the term applied to "all ongoing, recurring news publications," including online magazines.[50] But a Wisconsin appellate court would not apply the state's retraction statute to an interactive bulletin board service because communication of messages on the site did not appear at regular intervals.[51]

How Has Defamation Changed?

Before 1964, the U.S. approach to libel was like that of other common law countries. A plaintiff bringing a libel suit was required to show that the defendant's statement was published and that it was defamatory in nature. The plaintiff was not required to prove that the defendant's statement was false or that the defendant had acted with malice. If the defendant could not prove the statement's truth, malice was inferred. The plaintiff was not required to show that the statement damaged his or her reputation. Damages were presumed. A defendant could avoid strict liability for defamation by proving that the statement was either true or privileged. A defendant who could show the statement was privileged rebutted the presumption of malice, obligating the plaintiff to prove that the defendant had abused the privilege defense by acting in bad faith or with actual malice.[52]

The Supreme Court overturned 200 years of settled law when it decided to subject state libel claims to constitutional review in *New York Times v. Sullivan* (1964) and its progeny.[53] It did so on the theory that a court judgment, even one applying common law, constitutes an exercise of state action. In other areas of law, state action imposing content-based restrictions on speech is presumed to violate the First Amendment unless the government can establish that it is justified under strict scrutiny (the requirement that the regulation serve a compelling interest). In *New York Times v. Sullivan*, the Court applied what is essentially the same level of scrutiny to a libel claim, but required the plaintiff to bear the burden of showing that the restriction on speech was justified.[54]

New York Times v. Sullivan (1964) is the case that set U.S. libel law apart from that of other countries.

---

[48] *See* Edward Seaton, *The Uniform Corrections Act: A Way Out of the Libel Litigation Nightmare*, THE AMERICAN EDITOR, Am. Soc. of Newspaper Editors, July 17, 1998, http://asne.org/kiosk/editor/98.april/seaton1.htm.

[49] Mathis v. Cannon, 276 Ga. 16; 573 S.E.2d 376 (Ga. 2002).

[50] O'Grady v. Superior Court of Santa Clara County, 139 Cal. App. 4th 1423 (Cal. App. 2006).

[51] It's in the Cards, Inc. v. Fuschetto, 535 N.W.2d 11 (Wis. Ct. App. 1995).

[52] *See* Steven W. Workman, *Note: Reports on Public Proceedings and Documents: Absolutely Protected by Constitutional Privilege*, 1985 U. ILL. L. REV. 1059 (1985).

[53] Dun & Bradstreet, Inc. v. Greenmoss Builders, Inc., 472 U.S. 749, 766 (1985) (White, J., concurring).

[54] *See* David A. Anderson, First Amendment Limitations on Tort Law, 69 BROOKLYN L. REV. 755, 767, 771 (2004).

The plaintiff in *New York Times v. Sullivan* was a Montgomery, Ala., police commissioner who alleged that a political ad in *The New York Times* had libeled him. The ad – placed by a group of African American ministers active in the civil rights movement – described police action taken against students during a protest at Alabama State College and, on other occasions, against Martin Luther King, the leader of the civil rights movement. The plaintiff was not named in the ad, but he claimed it referred to him because he supervised the police department alleged to have been responsible for a "wave of terror."[55] The ad contained minor inaccuracies. For example, it claimed police had ringed the campus when, in fact, they had only been there in large numbers. It also stated that King had been arrested seven times; it was actually four. Under common law, false statements of fact were unworthy of protection. The Supreme Court established a new framework for libel when it observed that errors in reporting are inevitable and that a policy of strict liability might discourage the media from covering public issues if they could not guarantee complete accuracy.[56]

The Court wanted to provide "breathing room" for debate, particularly where the actions of public officials were concerned. To that end, it required public officials who sue for libel to prove that the offensive statement is false and that the defendant made it with actual malice – either knowledge of its falsity or reckless disregard of the truth. This standard of proof is exceedingly difficult to meet because, in essence, it requires the plaintiff to probe the defendant's state of mind.[57]

New York Times v. Sullivan not only revolutionized libel law; it also had an unexpected impact on commercial speech. Advertisements were not constitutionally protected in 1964. But the ad in *Sullivan* concerned political speech, which has traditionally been accorded the highest level of protection. Consequently, the case was the first to put advertising under the umbrella of the First Amendment.

The Supreme Court extended the actual malice requirement to public figures in *Curtis Publishing Co. v. Butts* (1967), a case involving a well-known athletic director accused of fixing football games.[58] The Court defined public figures as individuals who are "intimately involved in the resolution of important public questions or, by reason of their fame, shape events in areas of concern to society at large."[59] In his concurring opinion, Chief Justice Warren explained, "[o]ur citizenry has a legitimate and substantial interest in the conduct of such persons, and freedom of the press to engage in uninhibited debate about their involvement in public issues and events is as crucial as it is in the case of public officials . . ."[60] In an accompanying case, the Supreme Court concluded that a plaintiff also could be classified as a public figure by "thrusting . . . his personality into the 'vortex' of an important public controversy."[61] The Court later clari-

---

[55] New York Times v. Sullivan, 376 U.S. 254, 258 (1964).

[56] *Id.* at 270–72 (1964).

[57] *See* Herbert v. Lando, 441 U.S. 153 (1979).

[58] 388 U.S. 130 (1967).

[59] *Id.* at 167 (Warren, C. J., concurring).

[60] *Id.* at 164 (Warren, C. J., concurring).

[61] *Id.* at 155.

fied the distinction between general-purpose and limited-purpose public figures. It explained that people who hold positions of pervasive fame or power may be deemed public figures for all purposes. Individuals who voluntarily inject themselves or are drawn into a particular public controversy become public figures for a limited range of issues.[62]

For a short time, the actual malice standard was extended to private figure plaintiffs in libel cases involving "matters of general or public concern."[63] In *Rosenbloom v. Metromedia, Inc.* (1971), a plurality of the Court held that the context of the defamation rather than the notoriety of the plaintiff should determine whether actual malice applied. The decision to impose the actual malice requirement on public officials and figures was intended to prevent holdings that might chill public debate on important issues, so extending the standard to all cases involving matters of public interest seemed to make sense at the time. But the new theory imposed a particular burden on private plaintiffs who were less equipped to fight defamatory accusations than public figures.

The Court reversed itself three years later in *Gertz v. Robert Welch, Inc.* (1974).[64] It held that private figure plaintiffs should not be compelled to prove actual malice in libel cases. Private figures are more vulnerable than public figures. They have not voluntarily assumed a position in the public eye and do not have ready access to the media to refute defamatory statements. However, if the case concerns a matter of public interest, the plaintiff is still expected to prove some level of fault, generally negligence, on the part of the defendant. If the plaintiff seeks punitive damages, the level of fault rises to actual malice.

Finally, in *Dun & Bradstreet, Inc. v. Greenmoss Builders, Inc.* (1985), the Supreme Court considered how libel should be handled in cases involving private figure plaintiffs who sue over statements that do *not* involve a matter of public interest. The case concerned a construction company's suit against a credit agency that issued false credit reports to five of its subscribers stating that the builder had declared bankruptcy. The Court reasoned "not all speech is of equal First Amendment importance."[65] When the speech concerns a private issue, there "is no threat to the free and robust debate of public issues; there is no potential interference with a meaningful dialogue of ideas concerning self-government; and there is no threat of liability causing a reaction of self-censorship by the press."[66] Consequently, the First Amendment interest in protecting speech is deemed less important and the balance shifts toward protection of the plaintiff's interests.

The Court distinguished this case from *Gertz v. Welch*, which required private plaintiffs to prove actual malice to get punitive damages in libel cases involving matters of public interest. In *Dun & Bradstreet*, the Court held that in libel cases involving *private* interests punitive damages may be awarded without demonstrating "actual malice." The

A *plurality opinion* is the controlling opinion when no clear majority exists. It describes a situation in which a majority of justices can reach a conclusion necessary to dispose of a case, but cannot agree on a rationale for that conclusion. The precedential value of the decision is limited to those points on which a majority is able to agree.

[62] Gertz v. Robert Welch, Inc., 418 U.S. 323, 351 (1974).
[63] Rosenbloom v. Metromedia, Inc., 403 U.S. 29, 48 (1971).
[64] 418 U.S. 323 (1974).
[65] Dun & Bradstreet, Inc. v. Greenmoss Builders, Inc., 472 U.S. 749, 758 (1985).
[66] *Id.* at 760.

decision invoked the common law standard that had applied prior to the Court's application of First Amendment principles to libel.

The Court did not resolve whether a private figure plaintiff suing over a private matter should be required to prove falsity and fault. Concurring statements by Chief Justice Burger and Justice White suggested that the Court intended to follow traditional common law principles with respect to those factors as well, in which case, the plaintiff would not bear that burden. In *Obsidian Finance v. Cox* (2011), a federal district judge in Oregon applied traditional common law standards to a blogger sued for libel. The court focused on three points: that the plaintiff, an attorney, was not a public figure; that the statements at issue, accusing him of fraud, were not on matters of public concern; and that the defendant was not a journalist. He concluded there were no First Amendment implications associated with the case.[67] Because the case was so unusual, it is likely to be appealed.

The Single Publication Rule

The U.S. approach to defamation differs from other countries in another important respect. Under traditional common and civil law principles, every distribution of a libelous statement constitutes a separate publication and a libel plaintiff is entitled to sue for each one of them. The United States has adopted a *single publication rule*, which allows plaintiffs to sue for libel only once, eliminating the possibility of multiple libel suits for the same defamatory statement.

The borderless nature of the Internet has highlighted this difference. In Europe, a plaintiff who is defamed in an Internet publication may sue in every country in which the publication may be downloaded, as long as the plaintiff can convince a court that he or she has a reputation there to protect. In the United States, the plaintiff may sue in only one jurisdiction, even if the defamatory statement was published on the Internet or broadcast via satellite and accessible in every state.

Statutes of Limitation

A statute of limitations establishes the maximum time after an event that legal proceedings may be initiated.

All states impose a *statute of limitations* on defamation claims. Depending on the jurisdiction, this period in which a person may file a libel suit ranges from one to three years after the date of publication. The statute of limitations is shorter in some states if the claim is filed against a government entity. California, for example, requires claims against state agencies to be filed within six months.

Courts have rejected the claim that publication on the Web constitutes continuous publication.[68] The statute of limitations on Internet material begins when the informa-

---

[67] Obsidian Finance v. Cox, 2011 U.S. Dist. LEXIS 137548; 40 Media L. Rep. 1084 (Ore. Filed Nov. 30, 2011).
[68] *See* Nationwide Biweekly Administration, Inc., v. Belo Corp., 512 F.3d 137 (5th Cir. 2007); Oja v. U.S. Army Corp. of Engineers, 440 F.3d 1122 (9th Cir. 2006); Van Buskirk v. N.Y. Times Co., 325 F.3d 87 (2nd Cir. 2003).

tion is first published. Updating the website will not affect that unless the particular article alleged to be defamatory is altered.[69]

Criminal Libel

Although they are rarely enforced, statutes criminalizing the communication of a libelous statement are still on the books in one-third of the states.[70] Criminal libel is subject to the same constitutional restraints imposed on civil libel. Before a state could successfully prosecute a libel on behalf of a public figure, for example, it would have to prove that the defendant acted with actual malice.[71]

Criminal libel is rarely applied to formal media operations. In 2002, a jury convicted journalists of criminal libel for the first time in 30 years. Criminal charges were filed against the publisher and editor of the *Kansas City News Observer* after they ran an article during the middle of the plaintiff's reelection for a mayoral position in Wyandotte County, Kansas, which implied that she did not meet the residency requirement for the office.[72] The *Observer*'s publisher, David Carson, and editor, Edward Powers – both disbarred attorneys – were known for using the publication to irritate local officials. In fact, the Kansas Supreme Court had to assign a judge from a neighboring county to preside over the trial because all the Wyandotte County judges recused themselves. A special prosecutor was appointed to replace the one who brought charges against Carson and Powers because he too had a contentious history with the paper. Carson and Powers claimed to have obtained their information from unnamed sources, but later admitted to knowing that the mayor lived in the county. A Kansas Court of Appeals upheld the criminal libel verdict in 2004 and the Supreme Court refused to review the decision. Each received a $700 fine and one year of probation.

Criminal libel statutes are more commonly applied to individuals operating websites than journalists. Unfortunately, some cases have involved students who used the Internet to express their frustrations with school. Utah, for example, applied its 1876 criminal libel statute in a case against Ian Lake, a 16-year-old high school student who disparaged

---

[69] *See, e.g.,* Firth v. State, 98 N.Y.2d 365, 371 (2002) (finding that an unrelated modification to a website did not constitute republication).

[70] Ala. Code § 13A-11-160; Colo. Rev. Stat § 18-13-105 (2005); Fla. Stat. Ann. §836.01 (West 2000); Ga. Code Ann. § 16-11-40 (2005) (declared partially unconstitutional); Idaho Code §18–4801 (Michie 2002); Kan. Stat. Ann. § 21–4004 (2001); La. Stat. Ann. § 14:47 (2010); Ann. Laws Mass. § 98C; Mich. Comp. Laws Ann. § 750.370 (West 2002); Minn. Stat. Ann. § 609.765 (West 2002); Miss. Code Ann. § 97-3-55 (not enforced); Mont. Code Ann. § 45-8-212 (2005) (declared unconstitutional); Nev. Rev. Stat. § 200.510 (declared unconstitutional); N.H. Rev. Stat. Ann. § 644:11 (2002); New Mexico Statute Annotated, §30-11-1 (declared partially unconstitutional); N.C. Gen. Stat. §14–47 (2003); N.D. Cent. Code §12.1-15-01 (2001); Okla. Stat. Ann. tit. 21 § 771 (West 1996); Utah Code Ann. § 76-9-404 (2003); Va. Code Ann. § 18.2–417 (Michie 2002); Wis. Stat. Ann. § 942.01 (West 2001).

[71] *See* Garrison v. Louisiana, 379 U.S. 64 (1964).

[72] Felicity Barringer, *A Criminal Defamation Verdict Roils Politics in Kansas City, Kan.*, N.Y. TIMES, July 29, 2002, at C7.

his teachers, principal, and schoolmates on his website. Lake described his principal as a drunk who was having an affair with the school secretary and suggested that one of his teachers was a homosexual leading a double life. Although there were no threats or references to violence on the website, the Beaver County Sheriff's Department arrested Lake and held him in juvenile detention for a week to avoid a "Columbine"-type of incident. When the juvenile court would not dismiss the case, Lake appealed. The Utah Supreme Court held that the statute was unconstitutional because it covered protected speech and included no standard for actual malice. It presumed malice from the act of making a libelous statement and provided no immunity for truth.[73] However a 1973 criminal defamation law that does incorporate actual malice remains in place.

A Colorado judge threw out a case against a University of North Colorado student who doctored a photograph of a finance professor and published it on a satirical website about the university. Thomas Mink, the editor of *The Howling Pig*, digitally altered a photo of Professor Junius Peake to resemble KISS singer Gene Simmons with an Adolf Hitler mustache and added a caption describing its subject as "Junius Puke," a KISS roadie who made a fortune by riding "the tech bubble of the nineties like a $20 whore." Police confiscated Mink's computer and launched an investigation against him for violating Colorado's criminal libel law, which makes it a crime to "impeach the honesty, integrity, virtue, or reputation or expose the natural defects of one who is alive." The judge ordered police to return Mink's computer and barred his prosecution for libel. However, he refused to rule on the constitutionality of the law, because once the charge against Mink had been dropped he no longer had standing to challenge it. He also concluded that Mink's claim against the prosecutor for unauthorized search and seizure was barred by the doctrine of prosecutorial immunity.[74] The U.S. Court of Appeals for the Tenth Circuit reversed the decision in July 2010. Prosecutors are immune from libel suits during trial, but not during the investigative phase of a case. The court concluded that Mink had plausibly alleged that the prosecutor had violated his clearly constitutional rights.[75] On remand at the district court, Mink was granted summary judgment. The court found that no reasonable reader would have concluded that the statements in the Howling Pig were fact as opposed to hyperbole or parody" and "no reasonable prosecutor could therefore believe that it was probable that publishing such statements constituted a crime warranting the search and seizure of Mr. Mink's property."[76]

Nontraditional Media and Non-Media Defendants

The Supreme Court ignored the question of whether there should be a different standard of review for a non-media defendant versus a media defendant in *Dun & Bradstreet*,

---

[73]*In re* I. M. L. v. State of Utah, 2002 UT 110 (2002).

[74]Editor of Satirical *Web Site Won't Face Libel Charge*, Associated Press, Jan. 20, 2004 available at http://www.usatoday.com/tech/news/2004-01-20-howling-legal_x.htm.

[75]Mink v. Suthers, 613 F.3d 995 (10th Cir. 2010).

[76]Mink v. Knox, No. 84-cv-08023-LTB-CBS, 2011 U.S. Dist. LEXIS 59380 (D. Colo. June 3, 2011).

Inc. v. Greenmoss Builders, Inc. It has since pointed out in two other cases that the issue remains unresolved.[77]

It is unlikely that the Court will make such a distinction. Setting up two different standards of constitutional review would force courts to decide what constitutes a legitimate medium. Courts are loath to make this determination because it puts the government in the position of defining what constitutes real journalism – and by extension who should qualify for freedom of the press. In *Branzburg v. Hayes* (1972), the Court indicated that liberty of the press belongs as much to the "lonely pamphleteer" as it does to the largest publisher. It described freedom of the press as a "fundamental personal right . . . not confined to newspapers and periodicals."[78]

Recent cases suggest that bloggers and podcasters are entitled to the same level of First Amendment protection in libel cases. For example, a trial court in New York refused to enjoin a co-host of "DivorcingDaze," a humorous podcast about life after divorce, from making statements about her ex-husband because the First Amendment protected her comments.[79] Likewise, in *New School Communications, Inc. v. Brodkorb* (2007), a Minnesota District Court granted summary judgment to a Republican blogger sued for defamation by a Democratic political advisor because the blogger had followed sound journalistic practices in covering the allegedly defamatory story, including the use of multiple sources.[80]

Courts have differed, however, over whether bloggers and podcasters should bear the same type of liability for defamatory statements as traditional media. Blogs with a "newsy" format but a clearly biased agenda have not fared well. The first blogger to lose a libel case, David Milum, ran a website about politics in Forsyth County, Ga. According to court records, he accused a local attorney of delivering bribes to a judge from drug dealers. The attorney had represented Milam in an earlier case and, after a falling out, had refused to provide Milam with a refund. Because one of Milam's posts said "Rafe, don't you wish you had given back my three thousand dollar retainer, when I asked you too . . . ?" the posts implied a personal vendetta. A jury awarded the attorney $50,000 in compensatory damages, later affirmed by a Georgia appellate court.[81]

A college student who created UNDnews.com, a website that criticized University of North Dakota and its professors, posted an allegation that one of her professors had sexually harassed her. The professor sued her for libel and won a $3 million judgment. The former student had been suspended following a campus disciplinary hearing for stalking the plaintiff. She argued that her posts were based on the same privileged statements she had made in her disciplinary hearing. In upholding the award, the North

---

[77] Milkovich v. Lorain Journal Co., 497 U.S. 1, 20, n. 6 (1990); Philadelphia Newspapers v. Hepps, 475 U.S. 767, 779, n. 4 (1986).

[78] 408 U.S. 665, 704 (1972).

[79] *See* Leslie Kaufman, *When the Ex Writes a Blog, The Dirtiest Laundry Is Aired*, N.Y. Times, April 18, 2008, at A1.

[80] New School Communications, Inc. v. Brodkorb, CX-06-006432, slip op., at 3–4 (Minn. Dist. Ct., 1st Dist., Mar. 6, 2007).

[81] Milum v. Banks, 642 S.E.2d 892 (Ga. App. 2007).

Dakota Supreme Court clarified that while her statements during the disciplinary hearing – a quasi judicial proceeding – were privileged, she was not free to repeat them on her website.[82]

Blogs that function as gripe sites for a specific topic have been treated inconsistently. Some courts have treated statements that were clearly libelous on their own as rhetorical hyperbole in the context of the site. A federal district court in California dismissed a defamation claim against a blog critical of Art of Living, an international religious cult, finding that readers are less likely to view statements made on blogs with "heated discussion and criticism," as assertions of fact.[83]

The context of the communications precipitated a libel judgment in *Orix Capital v. Super Future Equities* (2009). Orix, a real estate, finance, and asset management business, foreclosed on a Louisiana apartment building owned by a Houston family. The Rafizadehs, who had defaulted on their loan, set up a gripe site named Predatorix.com that accused Orix of tax fraud and undergoing a federal investigation for violating racketeering laws. The defendants supplemented their accusations with court documents, deposition videos, and news articles, that later undermined their attempts to use opinion and satire as a defense when Orix sued for libel. The court concluded that the statements were meant to be taken as fact. After a two-week trial, a jury awarded Orix $2.5 million in compensatory damages and $10 million in punitive damages.[84]

Until that case, the largest libel award involving private individuals and the Internet had been $11.3 million. A Florida woman who ran an online referral service for parents of troubled teenagers sued a Louisiana woman for libelous statements she made on Internet bulletin boards accusing the plaintiff of being a "crook," a "con artist," and a "fraud." The defendant sought the plaintiff's help in extricating her sons from a boarding school where their father had placed them. The plaintiff helped in that respect but denied the defendant additional information she requested regarding a student who claimed to have been sexually abused by the same boarding school. The defendant, a Hurricane Katrina victim, did not show up at trial to defend herself. In her absence, the jury awarded the plaintiff $6.3 million in compensatory and $5 million in punitive

[82] Wagner v. Miskin, 660 N.W.2d 593 (N.D. May 6, 2003). *See also* Kono v. Meeker, 743 N.W.2d 872, 2007 Iowa App. LEXIS 2018 (Iowa App. Dec. 12, 2007) (upholding a libel judgment against two California antique dealers who described an Ohio client as a "flat-out liar, thief and cheat" after a business disagreement); Laughman v. Selmeier, No. A02-08401 (Ohio C.P. jury verdict Feb. 23, 2003) (in which a nurse accused on a patient's website of sexually assaulting him was awarded a $1,125,000 libel judgment); and Omega World Travel v. Mummagraphics, Inc., No. 05-122 (E.D. Va. jury verdict April 27, 2007) (in which the website www.cruises.com won a libel judgment against the operator of www.sueaspammer.com for listing the company as a spammer on the site).

[83] Art of Living Found. v. Does 1-10, No. 10-CV-05022-LHK, 2011 WL 2441898, at *7 (N.D. Cal. June 15, 2011).

[84] Orix Capital v. Super Future Equities, Civ. 3-06-CV-0271-B (N.D. Tex. 2009).

damages.[85] The defendant, who had no hope of paying the award, appealed it, but the award was upheld in 2007.[86]

The rise in social networking has also precipitated libel suits related to posts on Twitter, Facebook and Craigslist. Somehow it's not surprising that the first libel suit from a Twitter post would be directed at Courtney Love. The musician was sued for posting a Twitter and MySpace diatribe about a $4,000 bill from her fashion designer, Dawn Simorangkir. Love's remarks accusing the designer of theft, as well as references to prostitution and drug use, seemed to show a reckless disregard of the truth. Love's attorneys argued that the tweets were simply opinion and hyperbole that had no effect on Simorangkir's reputation.[87] Simorangkir's attorneys countered that a celebrity like Love was influential and that Twitter magnified her reach. No verdict came from the case. Love settled the suit for $430,000. Shortly afterward, she was sued again, this time by a former lawyer, over the tweet: "I was f**king devastated when Rhonda J. Holmes Esq of San Diego was bought off. . . ."[88] The attorney had represented Love in a case regarding the estate of Love's former husband, Kurt Cobain, until Love fired her and got another attorney. When Love tried to return to the firm and Holmes rejected her, Love turned to Twitter.

With only 140 characters available, a tweet has to be pretty specific to be libelous. A Cook Country, Ill., circuit judge dismissed a

Figure 9.1 The first libel suit from a Twitter post was directed at Courtney Love. Illustration: Kalan Lyra

COURTNEY ♥'S TWITTER

---

[85] Scheff v. Bock, No. CACE03022837 (Fla. Cir. Ct. default verdict Sept. 19, 2006).

[86] Bock v. Scheff, 991 So.2d 1043 (Fla. 4th Dist. 2008).

[87] Tweets can be costly, just ask Courtney Love, Associated Press, First Amendment Center, March 5, 2011, http://www.firstamendmentcenter.org/tweets-can-be-costly-%C2%97-just-ask-courtney-love.

[88] Gordon & Holmes v. Love, No. BC462438, complaint filed in Superior Court of California, May 26, 2011.

libel suit filed by a Chicago property management company against a tenant who tweeted about mold in her apartment. The defendant wrote "Who said sleeping in a moldy apartment was bad for you? Horizon realty thinks it's okay."[89] The judge concluded the tweet was too vague to meet libel standards.

The first judgment for Twitter libel occurred in the United Kingdom when a British politician tweeted that police had had to forcibly remove his opponent from a polling center during their election. It turned out to be a case of misidentification. The plaintiff was awarded £53,000 in damages and legal fees. The first libel judgment against a Facebook user was also in the UK. The defendant was sued for posting child pornography on the plaintiff's Facebook page accompanied by the suggestion that he was a pedophile. The image was tagged with the plaintiff's name, further extending its reach to the plaintiff's Facebook friends. The court awarded the plaintiff £10,000.

A Colorado man who accused his former girlfriend of prostitution and child abuse on Craigslist's "Rants and Raves" section was charged with criminal libel. Confronted by police, he said he was "just venting."[90] The charge was dropped, however, when he pled guilty to two counts of harassment instead.

Immunity for Interactive Computer Services

The ease with which Internet subscribers can post messages, both on their own websites and through other interactive websites, prompted Congress to carve out a safe harbor provision to protect online service providers from liability for their users' posts.

Section 230 of the Communication Decency Act shields operators of "interactive computer services" from liability for their users' defamatory comments. Congress enacted the provision to overrule *Stratton Oakmont, Inc. v. Prodigy Services Co.* (1995), in which a New York court held that Prodigy, an online service provider, could be considered a publisher vicariously liable for its users' posts.[91] In the United States, a publisher may be held liable for defamatory statements in a publication, but a distributor may not unless the distributor has actual knowledge of the libel. Courts assume that publishers have the opportunity to review the material in their publications before they disseminate it while distributors do not. From the court's perspective, Prodigy appeared

---

[89] *Twitter apartment mold libel suit dismissed*, WGN News/Chicago Tribune, Jan. 21, 2010, http://articles.chicagotribune.com/2010-01-22/news/1001210830_1_libel-suit-tweet-class-action.

[90] State of Colorado v. Weichel, Citizen Media Law Project, Dec. 2008, http://www.citmedialaw.org/threats/state-colorado-v-weichel.

[91] 1995 N.Y. Misc. LEXIS 229; 1995 WL 323710 (N.Y. Sup. Ct. May 24, 1995).

to be exercising editorial control over its service by using software to screen out offensive language and a moderator to enforce content guidelines on its bulletin boards and therefore qualified as a publisher.

Congress realized that if interactive services were held liable for their users' posts based on their good-faith attempts to control indecency, none would exercise editorial control. The likely consequence would be an increase in indecency and other offensive content. So it included a safe harbor provision for ISPs in the Communications Decency Act. Section 230 says: "No provider or user of an interactive computer service shall be treated as the publisher or speaker of any information provided by another information content provider."[92] The provision has also been interpreted to apply to interactive websites, forums, listservs, and blogs that allow users to post comments.

A federal court applied Section 230 for the first time in *Zeran v. America Online, Inc.* (1995). Kenneth Zeran, the plaintiff, sued AOL because it did not do enough to stop one of its subscribers from anonymously posting hoax advertisements in his name. The ads, which included Zeran's name and number, promoted t-shirts and other paraphernalia supporting the bombing of the Oklahoma federal building in which 168 victims died. The plaintiff was threatened repeatedly following the anonymous posts. When AOL failed to stop them, Zeran sued it for libel. The court concluded that AOL was immune from the suit under the CDA, even though it had been notified of the libel. The Fourth Circuit upheld the decision.[93]

Critics of the law argue that it has been abused. Sites like Campus Gossip, Don'tDateHimGirl, and the defunct Juicy Campus, have been shielded by the exemption while allowing users to post gossip unchecked. Subjects of these posts are almost powerless to retaliate. Section 230 exempts the website from liability, while its operators shield posters through coding that allows them to post anonymously. An individual who wanted to pursue a libel claim against a message board poster would have to persuade a court to issue a subpoena for the user's IP address.

Although it is most frequently used to shield ISPs from defamation claims, courts have used Section 230 to bar claims for invasion of privacy, misappropriation of trade secrets, cyberstalking, and negligence. In 2008, the U.S. Court of Appeals for the Fifth Circuit upheld a Texas court's decision to dismiss negligence claims against MySpace for failing to protect a thirteen-year-old from sexual predators by using age verification software to screen her profile for truthfulness.[94] By lying about her age the girl had circumvented a safety feature that would have prevented the public display of her profile. The court concluded that MySpace was not responsible because it was merely the distributor of third-party content, not a content provider. However, Section 230 does not shield interactive service providers against liability for users' posts if they ignore criminal acts or intellectual property claims.

---

[92] 47 U.S.C. § 230(c)(1) (2011).
[93] Zeran v. American Online, Inc., 129 F.3d 327, 330 (4th Cir. 1997).
[94] Doe v. MySpace, 528 F.3d 413 (5th Cir. 2008).

Photo Illustrations/Digitally Altering Images

Misleading and harmful information can be conveyed through imagery just as easily as through words. Digital imaging software makes it relatively easy to alter an image so that seeing is no longer believing.

The Final Call, a Nation of Islam paper, Photoshopped prison attire on a woman whose photo was randomly selected from its archives to illustrate an article titled "Mothers in Prison, Children in Crisis." The woman, Tatia Morsette, was a successful entertainment promoter who had never been incarcerated. No one tried to identify Morsette before digitally altering a photo of her holding her child while standing beside two other women.

When Morsette complained, the paper published a clarification indicating that the photo illustration was not meant to imply that the women were in prison, but it never apologized. Morsette sued for libel. The jury awarded her $1.3 million, a sum later reduced when punitive damages were taken away because the paper had not intended to harm her.[95]

Crystal Kiesau, a deputy sheriff in Buchanan County, Iowa, sued a fellow deputy for libel and invasion of privacy when he digitally altered her picture to make it appear that she was exposing her breasts. The defendant, Tracey Bantz, downloaded a picture of Kiesau standing with her K-9 dog in front of her sheriff's vehicle from a departmental website, then e-mailed the altered image to others. The jury concluded that the defamation was libel per se, which in Iowa comes with a presumption of damage, falsity, and malice in private figure cases. The Iowa Supreme Court upheld the verdict.[96] It rejected Bantz's argument that Kiesau was a public figure because she was a police officer or a limited public figure because she appeared on the website.

Libel in Fiction

Fiction is often inspired by real life. But changing the names of the "characters" in a real-life story and calling it fiction may lead to a libel claim if the characters are identifiable as real people. A story published in *Seventeen* magazine that was labeled as fiction was found to be defamatory in 1991. The central character, Bryson, who was labeled a "slut," shared characteristics with a girl named Kimberly Bryson who went to school with the author. The Illinois Supreme Court said "The fact that the author used the plaintiff's actual name [made] it reasonable that third persons would interpret the story as referring to the plaintiff despite the fictional label."[97]

A Georgia jury awarded an Atlanta woman, who was libeled in the best-selling novel *The Red Hat Club*, $100,000 in 2009. Vickie Stewart, the plaintiff and former friend of the book's author, Haywood Smith, pointed to more than 30 characteristics in "SuSu,"

---

[95] Morsette v. Final Call, 90 N.Y.2d 777 (1997).
[96] Kiesau v. Bantz, 686 N.W.2d 164 (Iowa 2004).
[97] Bryson v. News America Publications, Inc., 174 Ill.2d 77, 97, 672 N.E.2d 1207 (Ill. 1996).

one of the book's characters, that were "identifiable" as her own. Similarities between Stewart and SuSu included their hometowns, occupations, the fact that both had been engaged to men who were engaged to other women, and the circumstances of their first husbands' deaths. Several witnesses testified that they recognized SuSu to be Stewart.[98] Stewart sued for libel because she was offended by Smith's portrayal of the character as a sexually promiscuous alcoholic. Stewart believed that people who recognized her in the book would attribute these traits to her as well. *The Red Hat Club* contained a disclaimer indicating that it was a fictional work, but it was obviously not a shield. Disclaimers will not work when characters are clearly recognizable.

In an unsuccessful libel suit against the publisher of the book *Primary Colors*, a New York court wrote: "For a fictional character to constitute actionable defamation, the description of the fictional character must be so closely akin to the real person claiming to be defamed that a reader of the book, knowing the real person, would have no difficulty linking the two. Superficial similarities are insufficient."[99]

Satire and Parody

By its nature *satire* is not only critical of its subjects, who it often names, but also knowingly false. It may also include outrageous fictionalized quotations attributed to the subject, making it a prime target for libel suits. Meanwhile *parody* ridicules sacred cows through imitation. Both are protected precisely because they are outrageous and therefore unlikely to be taken seriously. The Supreme Court considers satire and parody to be a valuable part of political debate. It has said, "Nothing is more thoroughly democratic than to have the high-and-mighty lampooned and spoofed. An observant electorate may also gain by watching the reactions of objects of satiric comment, noting those who take themselves seriously and those whose self-perspective is somewhat more relaxed."[100]

In *New Times, Inc. v. Isaacks* (2004), a Dallas judge and district attorney sued a newspaper that ran a satirical article about them in its print and online editions.[101] Denton County District Attorney Bruce Isaacks and Juvenile Court Judge Darlene Whitten filed a libel suit against the *Dallas Observer* after it published an article that mocked them for arresting and jailing a 6-year-old girl for writing a book report on Maurice Sendak's classic *Where The Wild Things Are*, that included references to "cannibalism, fanaticism and disorderly conduct." The article was laced with false quotes, including one from Whitten that said: "Any implication of violence in a school situation, even if it was just contained in a first grader's book report, is reason enough for panic and overreaction . . . it's time for us to stop treating kids like children." A quote attributed to Isaacks said: "We've considered having her certified to stand trial as an adult, but even in Texas there are some limits." The article also described authorities reviewing the

---

[98] Jane Kleiner, *When art imitates life: Suing for defamation in fiction*, Nov. 4, 2010, Citizen Media Law Project, http://www.citmedialaw.org/blog/2010/when-art-imitates-life-suing-defamation-fiction.

[99] Carter-Clark v. Random House, Inc., 196 Misc.2d 1011, 768 N.Y.S.2d 290 (2003).

[100] Falwell v. Flynt, 805 F.2d 484, 487 (1986).

[101] 146 S.W.3d 144; 2004 Tex. LEXIS 787 (Tex. 2004).

child's disciplinary record "which included reprimands for spraying a boy with pineapple juice and sitting on her feet."

The article was intended as a form of commentary on another case involving a 13-year-old boy who was sent to juvenile detention for five days by Whitten for a Halloween story he wrote that depicted the shooting of a teacher and two students. The seventh grader penned the tale for a class assignment to write a scary story and, in fact, earned a 100 on it. But the principal read it and called the juvenile authorities, who sent sheriff's deputies to pull the boy out of school. Isaacks declined to prosecute the student but commented that he was a discipline problem and school authorities were "legitimately concerned."

Whitten demanded an apology from the paper but got a snarky clarification instead stating:

> Unfortunately, some people – commonly known as "clueless" or "Judge Darlene Whitten" – did not get, or did not appreciate, the joke behind the news story "Stop the madness," which appeared in last week's *Dallas Observer*.
>
> Here's a clue for our cerebrally challenged readers who thought the story was real: It wasn't. It was a joke. We made it up. Not even Judge Whitten, we hope, would throw a 6-year-old girl in the slammer for writing a book report. Not yet, anyway.[102]

New Times defended the article as rhetorical hyperbole. Lower courts denied summary judgment to the defendants, because they thought it failed "to provide any notice to a reasonable reader that it was a satire or parody."[103] But the Texas Supreme Court dismissed the case. It clarified that "the test is whether the publication could be reasonably understood as describing actual facts."[104] This must be taken from the perspective of a person of ordinary intelligence, not the weakest link. "Thus, the question is not whether some actual readers were mislead, as they inevitably will be, but whether the hypothetical reasonable reader could be."[105] Even though the article bore no disclaimer and was indexed in the news section, the court found plenty of clues that the piece was satiric.

The court rejected the plaintiffs' argument that the article was published with actual malice because defendants knew the statements in it were false. Acceptance of that argument would strip satire of all protection. It also considered the paper's attempt to clarify that the article was satire evidence of a lack of malice.

Intentional Infliction of Emotional Distress

To get around the requirement to show actual malice on the part of the defendant in a libel case, some plaintiffs have opted to sue on other theories, like intentional infliction of emotional distress and false light (an invasion of privacy tort described in the next chapter).

---

[102] *Id.* at 149 (citing Patrick Williams, Buzz, Dallas Observer, Nov. 18–24, 1999, at 9).
[103] *Id.* at 150 (citing lower court decision at 91 S.W.3d 844, 857, 859 (2002)).
[104] *Id.* at 157 (citing Pring v. Penthouse Int'l, Ltd., 695 F.2d 438, 442 (10th Cir. 1982)).
[105] *Id.*

Televangelist Jerry Falwell sued *Hustler* magazine for mocking him in a parody of a Campari Liqueur campaign.[106] Campari ran a series of ads dubbed "My First Time" in which celebrity subjects of the ads recalled their first time to try Campari. *Hustler*'s parody, titled "Jerry Falwell talks about his first time," included Falwell's picture and an "interview" in which he recounted his first sexual experience, a drunken liaison in an outhouse with his mother. The ad included the disclaimer "ad parody – not to be taken seriously" at the bottom of the page.[107] Falwell sued. Although the jury found that the ad could not "reasonably be understood as describing actual facts about [Falwell] or actual events in which [he] participated," and was therefore not defamatory, it awarded Falwell damages for intentional infliction of emotional distress.[108] The Fourth Circuit affirmed the verdict, but the Supreme Court reversed.

The Court was concerned that public figures could use the tort of intentional infliction of emotional distress to sidestep actual malice requirements in libel suits, so it extended the actual malice standard to it.

In most states, the elements required to show intentional infliction of emotional distress are:

- that the defendant's conduct was extreme and outrageous;
- that the defendant either intended or was aware of a high probability that the action would cause emotional distress;
- that the plaintiff suffered severe or extreme emotional distress; and
- that the cause of the suffering is the defendant's conduct.

In *Hustler v. Falwell*, the Supreme Court said those factors were not sufficient in cases involving public figures. It said a standard based on outrageousness, which is inherently subjective, "runs afoul of our longstanding refusal to allow damages to be awarded because the speech in question may have an adverse emotional impact on the audience."[109]

It also said that intent to harm is not sufficient because it had already held that the First Amendment protects expression motivated by hatred or ill will.[110] "Debate on public issues will not be uninhibited if the speaker must run the risk that it will be proved in court that he spoke out of hatred; even if he did speak out of hatred, utterances honestly believed contribute to the free interchange of ideas and the ascertainment of truth."[111] A contrary holding would subject political cartoonists and satirists to liability because their criticism is deliberate.

The Court held that "public figures and public officials may not recover for the tort of intentional infliction of emotional distress . . . without showing . . . that the

---

[106] Hustler Magazine, Inc. v. Falwell, 485 U.S. 46 (1988). A transcript of the oral argument is at http://www.oyez.org/cases/1980-1989/1987/1987_86_1278/argument/.

[107] *Id.* at 49.

[108] *Id.* at 57 (quoting appendix to petition for certiorari).

[109] *Id.* at 55.

[110] Garrison v. Louisiana, 379 U.S. 64 (1964).

[111] *Id.* at 73.

publication contains a false statement of fact which was made with 'actual malice.' "[112] By *false statement of fact*, the Court meant a false statement that would be taken literally – not a false statement such as the outhouse story. Through its choice to protect *Hustler*'s parody, the Court implicitly rejected the notion that knowledge of falsity in parody or satire constitutes actual malice.

In matters of public interest, private figures may be denied relief for intentional infliction of emotional distress as well. Albert Snyder, the father of a marine killed in Iraq, sued Fred Phelps, the leader of Westboro Baptist Church, for intentional infliction of emotional distress and invasion of privacy after church members picketed at his son's funeral with signs that said "Thank God for dead soldiers" and "You're going to Hell." The Kansas-based congregation believes God kills soldiers and allowed the Sept. 11 attacks on the U.S. in retribution for American tolerance of homosexuality. Snyder's son, Mathew, was targeted not because he was gay, however, but because he was a soldier and a Catholic.

Although a federal jury had awarded Snyder almost $11 million, the judgment was reversed on appeal. In an 8-1 decision, the Supreme Court sided with Phelps and his church.[113] It concluded that the First Amendment protected peaceful demonstrations when they were focused on matters of public concern. Determining whether speech is of public or private concern requires an examination of its "content, form and context." Although tasteless, Phelps' speech – delivered through signs like "America Is Doomed" and "Fag Troops" and "Priests Rape Boys" –addressed public issues regarding "the political and moral conduct of the United States and its citizens, the fate of our Nation, homosexuality in the military, and scandals involving the Catholic clergy."[114] The signs were also displayed on a public sidewalk, 1,000 feet from the funeral. Thanks to Westboro, most states have now enacted statutes dictating the minimum distance that funeral protesters must stand from a service.

Questions for Discussion

1. How does the American concept of libel law differ from other common law and civil law countries?
2. What is the difference between a public and private figure plaintiff in a libel case?
3. How does knowledge of falsity differ from reckless disregard of the truth?
4. Why have ISPs been given immunity from their subscribers' libelous posts?

[112] *Id.* at 56.
[113] Snyder v. Phelps, 131 S. Ct. 1207 (2011).
[114] *Id.* at 1217.

10 Invasion of Privacy

Privacy is the right to control access to information about ourselves. States have described it as a natural right essential to the pursuit of life, liberty, and happiness. But privacy is also a right balanced against society's need for information, which has never been greater.

Privacy law has evolved in a piecemeal fashion rather than as a response to a unified policy.[1] The Georgia Supreme Court first recognized a right of privacy based on natural law in 1905.[2] By the mid-1930s, the American Law Institute included invasion of privacy as an actionable tort in its distillation of tort law, the *Restatement of Torts*, and more courts began to acknowledge it. Today, most jurisdictions recognize a right to privacy through common or statutory law. A few states also reference it in their constitutions. But privacy protections vary considerably by jurisdiction and are generally waived if the information revealed is in the public's interest.

This chapter will discuss protections for privacy under common law and through federal and state statutes. It will also consider the extent of our right to privacy with regard to digital media at home, at work, and online.

Natural law philosophers believe individuals are endowed with certain fundamental rights, apart from "positive" rights, which are man-made.

Whose Privacy is Protected?

Privacy laws protect people from the emotional distress caused by an unexpected intrusion into their private affairs or loss of control over their personal information. Because its emphasis is on protection of feelings, rather than reputation as in defamation law,

[1] Samuel D. Warren & Louis D. Brandeis, *The Right to Privacy*, 4 HARV. L. REV. 193 (1890).
[2] *See* Pavesich v. New England Life Ins. Co., 122 Ga. 190, 50 S.E. 68 (Ga. 1905).

Digital Media Law, Second Edition. Ashley Packard.
© 2013 John Wiley & Sons, Inc. Published 2013 by John Wiley & Sons, Inc.

privacy law applies only to people.[3] Corporations and other organizations that wish to guard their information must do so through intellectual property or contract law.

As a general rule, privacy rights apply only to the living, but there are exceptions. For example, the right of publicity, which protects an individual's exclusive right to exploit the market value of his or her identity, may be inherited after death. The Supreme Court has also concluded that the Freedom of Information Act's privacy exemption may extend to a deceased individual's family members, if the potential harm inflicted on them by disclosure of the individual's records would outweigh the public's interest in the information.[4] In *National Archives and Records v. Favish* (2004), the Court considered whether a government agency could deny an FOIA requestor access to photos taken at the scene of a suicide, based on the privacy interests of the victim's family. The respondent argued that the victim's survivors had no privacy interest in the photographic records because their personal data was not included. The Court held that survivors do have privacy rights, particularly in death-scene photos. It added that the public interest in access to the photos would outweigh the family's privacy interest if the respondent were able to present evidence of government impropriety, but he had failed to do so.

Constitutional Protections for Privacy

While the U.S. Constitution protects speech and press through the First Amendment, there is no equivalent protection for personal privacy. The word privacy never appears in the Constitution. Consequently, when rights to privacy and expression compete, expression usually emerges as the victor in American jurisprudence.

In *NASA v. Nelson* (2010), the Supreme Court assumed, but did not confirm, a constitutional right to informational privacy. Plaintiffs in the case were government contractors who challenged the constitutionality of an intrusive background check ordered by the Commerce Department. After 9/11, the president issued an executive order requiring government agencies to put contractors with long-term access to federal facilities through the same background checks imposed on federal employees. The checks require contractors to divulge illegal substance use and related counseling, and to authorize the government to obtain their personal information from schools, employers and other sources during its investigation. Scientists who had been working as contractors in a NASA robotics laboratory in California for decades and never been subjected to the checks before, argued that the process violated their constitutional

---

[3] *See*, e.g., L. Cohen & Co. v. Dun & Bradstreet, Inc., 629 F. Supp. 1425, 1430 (D. Conn. 1986) (finding that privacy law concerns "the reputational interests of individuals rather than the less substantial reputational interests of corporations."); Ion Equip. Corp. v. Nelson, 110 Cal. App. 3d 868 (1980) ("A corporation is a fictitious person and has no 'feelings' which may be injured in the sense of the tort."); Felsher v. University of Evansville, 755 N.E.2d 589 (Ind. Sup. Ct. 2001) (finding a university could not rely on a privacy tort to sue a former faculty member who faked websites and e-mails in his colleagues' names, but they could).

[4] National Archives and Records v. Favish, 541 U.S. 157 (2004).

privacy "interest in avoiding disclosure of personal matters." The Supreme Court recognized this interest in two cases, *Whalen v. Roe* (1977) and *Nixon v. Administrator of General Services* (1977), but had not touched on the constitutional privacy issue for more than 30 years.[5] Writing for the Court, Justice Samuel Alito noted that in both cases the privacy interest that the Court acknowledged gave way to other considerations. He wrote that the Court was assuming, without deciding, that the U.S. Constitution guarantees a right to informational privacy. But even so, the federal law requiring background checks of private contract employees does not violate that right. In concurring opinions, Justices Antonin Scalia and Clarence Thomas agreed with the result in the case but harshly disagreed with the logic behind it. They said a constitutional right to "informational privacy" does not exist.

Nevertheless, the Supreme Court has found *penumbral* protections for privacy cast by Constitutional amendments in earlier decisions. It has observed, for example, that the First Amendment's implied right of association, the Fourth Amendment's prohibition against unreasonable searches and seizures, and the Fifth Amendment's right against self-incrimination all imply a right to privacy. Moreover, the Ninth Amendment states that the enumeration of rights in the Constitution "shall not be construed to deny or disparage others retained by the people." The Court has used this penumbral privacy theory to strike down statutes that interfere with reproductive rights and consensual sexual relations, but it has not extended it to other spheres of privacy protection.[6]

Ten states have included privacy provisions in their constitutions. Some of them protect privacy as an individual right. These include Alaska (Art. I, § 22); California (Art. I, § 1); Florida (Art. I, § 23); Hawaii (Art. I, § 6); and Montana (Art. II, § 10). Others mention a right to privacy within provisions that guard against unreasonable searches and seizures. These are Arizona (Art. II, § 8); Hawaii (Art. I, § 7); Illinois (Art. I, § 6); Louisiana (Art. I, § 5); South Carolina (Art. 1, § 10); and Washington (Art. I, § 7).

Penumbral protections are implied rights, emanating from others that are fully guaranteed. A penumbra is an area of partial illumination between full light and shadow.

Privacy Protection Under Common Law

Common law protects people against four invasion of privacy torts: (1) unreasonable intrusions into private affairs, (2) publicity given to private facts, (3) appropriation of a person's name or likeness, and (4) publication of information that unreasonably places a person in false light.

Most states protect privacy interests under common law. Nebraska, New York, North Dakota, and Wyoming are the exceptions. Nebraska and New York recognize statutory protections for privacy, but do not recognize a common law right to privacy.[7] North Dakota and Wyoming do not recognize invasion of privacy as an actionable tort.

[5] Whalen v. Roe, 429 U.S. 589, 599–600 (1977); Nixon v. Administrator of General Services, 433 U.S. 425, 457 (1977).
[6] *See* Griswold v. Connecticut, 381 U.S. 479 (1965) (striking down a Connecticut law that prevented the use of contraceptives), Roe v. Wade, 410 U.S. 113 (1973) (striking down a Texas law that criminalized abortion) and Lawrence v. Texas, 539 U.S. 558 (2003)(striking down a Texas sodomy law).
[7] *See* Roberson v. Rochester Folding Box Co., 64 N.E. 442, 447 (N.Y. 1902); Brunson v. Ranks Army Store, 73 N.W.2d 803, 806 (Neb. 1955).

States that recognize common law privacy protections do so in varying degrees. Some states recognize only two or three of the four privacy torts. Consequently, it is important to keep in mind that a decision rendered in one jurisdiction may not be applicable in another. The descriptions that follow provide general guidelines. You may need to do additional research on the particular laws of your state.

Intrusion upon seclusion

For *intrusion upon seclusion*, the plaintiff must prove that:
- there was a reasonable expectation of privacy; and
- the intrusion would have been "highly offensive to a reasonable person."

Intrusion upon seclusion is what we classically think of as invasion of privacy – the violation of a person's private space. The tort requires an intentional intrusion "upon the solitude or seclusion of another or his private affairs or concerns" that is highly offensive to a reasonable person.[8] The intrusion may be physical, such as trespassing on someone's property to peep in the windows or open the mail. Or it may be electronic, such as the use of a recording or wiretap device or illegal access to phone mail or e-mail. In assessing whether the intrusion could be construed as highly offensive, a court will consider: the degree of intrusion, the intruder's conduct, the circumstances surrounding the intrusion, the intruder's motives, the location or setting of the intrusion, and the plaintiff's reasonable expectation of privacy.[9]

Unlike other privacy torts, intrusion upon seclusion does not depend on the kind of information collected or its publication. It is based solely on the process used to gather information and whether it is highly offensive. Normal reporting practices do not constitute an invasion of privacy. It is fine to ask the subject of a story for an interview; to gather information about the person from neighbors, friends, and enemies; and to search for information through public records.

No expectation of privacy in public

The level of privacy protection accorded under common law depends on the person's reasonable expectation of privacy under the circumstances. There is no expectation of privacy in a public place. It is perfectly legal to photograph any activity conducted in plain view, or any person in public – even a child – without permission. In all states but Illinois, it is also legal to video in public without permission.

The *standing-in doctrine* allows a person to take a picture or video of anything that occurs out in the open, under the theory that the photographer is standing in for others who would have seen the same thing had they been there. An intrusion cannot be something that the general public is free to view. Based on this principle, a Washington appellate court upheld summary judgment in favor of a news station photographer who videoed his subject through a drugstore window.[10] The court pointed out that the cameraman recorded something that any passerby also could have seen.

---

[8] RESTATEMENT (SECOND) OF TORTS § 652B (1977).
[9] *See* Miller v. NBC, 232 Cal. Rptr. 668, 679 (Ct. App. 1986).
[10] Marks v. King Broadcasting, 27 Wash. App. 344, 356, 618 P.2d 512 (1980) (finding in favor of a TV news photographer, who videoed a pharmacist accused of Medicare fraud through a pharmacy window when he refused to come out for an interview).

The exception to this general rule involves photos that anyone would consider humiliating. In 1964, an Alabama court found that a newspaper's photo of a woman whose dress had blown up above her waist as she descended from a county fair ride was an invasion of privacy.[11] It noted that although she had given up an expectation of privacy in a public setting, her release did not give the newspaper a right to publish a photo that would cause embarrassment to a person of reasonable sensitivity.

The proliferation of cell phones with cameras has contributed to a more contemporary version of this problem. Worldwide, men are snapping photos under women's skirts, a phenomenon called *upskirting*, or down their shirts, a companion practice called *downblousing*. Thousands of these images wind up on photo sharing sites. More than 25 states now consider it illegal to photograph a person's private parts in a public place.[12] Federal law also prohibits the use of camera equipment to capture an image of an individual's private area without consent when the person has a reasonable expectation of privacy. Within its definition of reasonable expectation of privacy, the law includes "circumstances in which a reasonable person would believe that a private area of the individual would not be visible to the public, regardless of whether that person is in a public or private place."[13]

Full expectation of privacy at home

There is a complete expectation of privacy in one's home. This principle was established in *Dietemann v. Time, Inc.* (1971), which involved an invasion of privacy suit against the publisher of *Life* magazine.[14] Two *Life* reporters, working in conjunction with the Los Angeles District Attorney's office, visited the home of a plumber masquerading as a doctor under the pretense of requiring his medical services. While one was "examined" the other secretly filmed and recorded the plumber's diagnosis. The resulting article, published after his arrest, incorporated quotes and pictures surreptitiously gathered during the visit. The Ninth Circuit held that even though Dietemann had invited the journalists in, he was still entitled to an expectation of privacy within his home. The court determined that "One who invites another to his home or office takes a risk that the visitor may not be what he seems, and that the visitor may repeat all he hears and observes when he leaves. But he does not and should not be required to take the risk that what is heard and seen will be transmitted by photograph or recording . . ."[15]

Limited expectation of privacy at work

There is a limited right to privacy in one's workplace, depending on the setting. In *Sanders v. ABC* (1999), the Supreme Court of California held that a plaintiff's expectation of privacy in the workplace does not have to be complete to sue for intrusion. The

---

[11] Daily Times Democrat v. Graham, 276 Ala. 380 (1964).
[12] Video Voyeurism Laws, National Center for Victims of Crime, http://www.ncvc.org/ncvc/Main.aspx.
[13] 18 U.S.C. § 1801(b)(5)(B) (2011).
[14] Dietemann v. Time, Inc., 449 F.2d 245 (9th Cir. 1971).
[15] *Id.* at 249.

case involved a *Primetime Live* investigation of a psychic hotline. A reporter for the show obtained a job as a telepsychic and covertly taped conversations with other employees. Two of them sued for intrusion upon seclusion. The court held that "[i]n an office or other workplace to which the general public does not have unfettered access, employees may enjoy a limited, but legitimate, expectation that their conversations and other interactions will not be secretly videotaped by undercover television reporters."[16] This is true regardless of whether other employees are privy to the conversation. But the court cautioned "we do not hold or imply that investigative journalists necessarily commit a tort by secretly recording events and conversations in offices, stores or other workplaces. Whether a reasonable expectation of privacy is violated by such recording depends on the exact nature of the conduct and all the surrounding circumstances."[17] Some workplaces are too open to the public to suggest a reasonable expectation of privacy.

Company e-mail and phone mail is generally not considered private. If an employer runs the system, it has a right to review content on it – a subject discussed in greater depth later in this chapter.

Expectation of privacy in other areas

There is no comprehensive list of places in which privacy is protected. But in other intrusion cases, courts assumed that individuals had an expectation of privacy in a prison exercise room,[18] hospital room,[19] dressing room,[20] private dining room at a restaurant,[21] and private party.[22]

Courts have also held that people have a reasonable expectation that their Social Security numbers will be kept private. The New Hampshire Supreme Court observed that a "person's interest in maintaining the privacy of his or her SSN has been recognized by numerous federal and state statutes."[23] Consequently, "the entities to which this information is disclosed and their employees are bound by legal, and, perhaps, contractual constraints to hold SSNs in confidence to ensure that they remain private."[24] The court considered whether the unauthorized release of someone's Social Security number could be an intrusion upon seclusion in *Remsburg v. Docusearch, Inc.* (2003). The case concerned an information broker's liability for the sale of a woman's Social Security number to a stalker who murdered her. Liam Youens contacted Docusearch through its website to request Amy Lynn Boyer's Social Security number and place of employment.

---

[16] Sanders v. ABC, 20 Cal. 4th 907, 911, 1100 (1999).

[17] *Id.*

[18] *See* Huskey v. National Broadcasting Co., Inc. 632 F. Supp. 1282 (N.D. Ill. 1986).

[19] *See* Berthiaume v. Pratt, 365 A.2d 792, 795 (Maine 1976) (a surgeon who had treated a cancer patient committed actionable intrusion by photographing him in hospital bed against his will as he lay dying).

[20] *See* Doe by Doe v. B.P.S. Guard Services, Inc., 945 F.2d 1422 (8th Cir. 1991).

[21] *See* Stessman v. Am. Black Hawk Broadcasting, 416 N.W.2d 685, 687 (Iowa 1987).

[22] *See* Rafferty v. Hartford Courant Co., 416 A.2d 1215, 1216, 1220 (Conn. Super. Ct. 1980).

[23] Helen Remsburg, Administratrix of the Estate of Amy Lynn Boyer v. Docusearch, Inc., 149 N.H. 148, 156 (N.H. 2003).

[24] *Id.*

Docusearch provided the Social Security number, gleaned from Boyer's credit report, and place of employment, obtained by a subcontractor who telephoned Boyer and tricked her into providing the information. After acquiring the information, Youens drove to Boyer's workplace, fatally shot her, and then killed himself. Police later learned that Youens, who had become obsessed with Boyer in high school, maintained an online diary about stalking and killing her.

The court said that "a person whose SSN is obtained by an investigator from a credit reporting agency without the person's knowledge or permission may have a cause of action for intrusion upon seclusion for damages caused by the sale of the SSN," if he or she could prove the intrusion would have been offensive to a reasonable person.[25] Although a work address is generally not considered private information, the court held the information broker could be liable under the state's Consumer Protection Act for damages caused by its pretext call to get information it used for commercial purposes.

Publicity given to private life

Publicizing information about the private life of another person may be considered an invasion of privacy if the information is not a matter of legitimate public concern and its publication would be highly offensive to a reasonable person. In determining whether the information is of legitimate public concern, the *Second Restatement of Torts* says "the line is to be drawn when the publicity ceases to be the giving of information to which the public is entitled, and becomes a morbid and sensational prying into private lives for its own sake."[26] The private information shared, such as a medical condition, financial difficulty, sexual preference, or a humiliating experience, must be of a highly personal nature.

For *publicity given to private life*, the plaintiff must prove that:
- the private facts exposed were not of legitimate public concern; and
- publicizing them would be highly offensive to a reasonable person.

Newsworthy information is protected

The context in which the information is revealed is as important as the information itself. The publication of newsworthy information is protected from liability. Whether the information is newsworthy is a matter for a jury (or judge in a bench trial) to decide. Factors affecting that consideration include the public value of the information, the extent of the intrusion into the person's private affairs, and the extent to which the person may have voluntarily assumed a position of public notoriety.

Information must be communicated widely

A private fact communicated to one person or a small group of people does not constitute an invasion of privacy.[27] The word *publicity* differs from the word *publication*.

[25] *Id.* at 157.
[26] RESTATEMENT (SECOND) OF TORTS § 652D cmt. h (1977).
[27] *Id.* § 652D, cmt. a.

Publication refers to communication of information to a third person. Publicity refers to communication of information to the public at large, or at least to a very large group of people so that the information becomes public knowledge.[28] The means of communication is not important. It may be oral, written, or broadcast. It is the reach of the communication that matters.

The Supreme Court has refused to answer categorically whether the publication of true information may ever be punished consistently with the First Amendment. So courts are reluctant to impose liability on the publication of true facts. Some jurisdictions have refused to recognize the tort. These states include Alaska, Nebraska, New York, North Carolina, North Dakota, Oregon, Virginia, and Wyoming.

Information in public records is not protected

Once information has appeared in a public record it is no longer considered a private fact and is permissible to publish. This is particularly true of information from judicial proceedings. In *Cox Broadcasting v. Cohn* (1975), the Supreme Court considered the constitutionality of a Georgia statute that made it a crime to broadcast a rape victim's name. The Court held that "the First and Fourteenth Amendments command nothing less than that the States may not impose sanctions on the publication of truthful information contained in official court records open to public inspection."[29] It concluded that coverage of judicial proceedings fell within the press's public obligations. Records from criminal proceedings may include information about the defendant as well as the defendant's victims. Civil suits may include medical histories, mental health data, financial information, and intimate details about a person's life required to establish damages. States may not punish individuals for reproducing this information.

In fact, absent a need to further a state interest of the highest order, a medium cannot be punished for publishing truthful information obtained lawfully about a matter of public interest.[30] In *Florida Star v. B.J.F.* (1989), the Supreme Court considered whether a newspaper could be punished, under a rape victim privacy statute, for revealing a victim's name that was mistakenly included in a police report. The Court held that "[o]nce the government has placed [confidential] information in the public domain, 'reliance must rest upon those who decide what to publish or broadcast,' . . . and hopes for restitution must rest upon the willingness of the government to compensate victims for their loss of privacy . . ."[31] States that wish to protect the identity of rape victims and juvenile offenders must do so by withholding that information from public records, not by barring the media from using it. However, most media voluntarily withhold that information because they consider it the right thing to do.

---

[28] *Id.*

[29] Cox Broadcasting Co. v. Cohn, 420 U.S. 469, 495 (1975).

[30] Florida Star v. B.J.F., 491 U.S. 524 (1989).

[31] *Id.* at 538.

The passage of time

Occasionally, the media are sued for doing anniversary or "where are they now" stories that rehash information from the lives of individuals who were once publicly known but have since been forgotten. The passage of time will not make information that was once public private again. However, it does not create a license to disclose new information of a private nature about a subject who has attempted to resume a private life.

Appropriation of name or likeness and right of publicity

Appropriation, the oldest invasion of privacy tort, is committed when someone "appropriates to his own use or benefit the name or likeness of another."[32] Most states limit appropriation claims to unauthorized uses for commercial purposes.

As a privacy right, appropriation protects individuals from the emotional distress or embarrassment that might result from having their name or likeness used in an advertisement without their permission. For example, in *Cohen v. Herbal Concepts, Inc.* (1984), a court denied summary judgment to a company that used a picture of the plaintiffs (a mother and her four-year-old daughter) bathing nude in an advertisement for the defendant's cellulite removal product.[33] As private individuals, the plaintiffs were able to assert emotional harm derived from the humiliation of being pictured in the ad.

But appropriation also operates like a property right by protecting an individual's exclusive use of his or her name and likeness for economic benefit. Russell Christoff, a model who did a photoshoot for Taster's Choice in 1986, was never called back, so he assumed the company was not interested in using his photo. He was shocked to learn in 2002 that the company had been using his image on its label worldwide for seven years without compensating him. Christoff sued Nestlé, which owns Taster's Choice, for commercial appropriation of his image. A jury awarded him $330,000 in actual damages and $15 million in punitive damages, representing the company's profits from Taster's Choice while Christoff's face was on the jars. A California Court of Appeals reversed because Christoff failed to show that Nestle's $15 million profit was due to his likeness.[34] The court also held that Christoff's suit was time-barred. It applied the single publication rule, normally used for defamation, to appropriation, which requires that suits be filed within two years of first publication.[35] In August of 2009, the California Supreme Court agreed that the single publication rule applies to appropriation claims. But it did not agree that Nestlé's use of Christoff's likeness necessarily constituted a single publication. It remanded the case to a lower court to consider whether the varied uses of Christoff's likeness – on coffee jars, coupons and advertisements – amounted to a single integrated publication.[36] At that point, the parties agreed on a settlement.

For *appropriation of name or likeness,* the plaintiff must prove that:
- his or her name or likeness was used without permission; and
- the use was for commercial rather than informational purposes.

[32] RESTATEMENT (SECOND) OF TORTS § 652B (1977).
[33] 472 N.E.2d 307 (N.Y. 1984).
[34] Christoff v. Nestlé USA, Inc., 152 Cal. App. 4th 1439 (2007).
[35] Christoff v. Nestlé USA, Inc., 169 P.3d 888 (Cal. 2007).
[36] Christoff v. Nestlé USA, Inc., No. S155242 (Cal. Aug. 17, 2009).

Average individuals will find it easier to use appropriation to protect their emotional interests. It is difficult for private plaintiffs to prove that a defendant's use of their name or likeness appropriated its economic value unless they could claim value in their identities before the use. On the other hand, celebrities find greater success in appropriation's emphasis on property rights. After choosing to live in the public eye, it is hard for them to argue that appropriation of their identities has caused them emotional pain.

Right of publicity

While some states continue to categorize the property interest in identity under privacy law, approximately half recognize a separate tort called "right of publicity." Right of publicity, a tort that emerged in 1953, protects those who suffer economic rather than emotional harm from the appropriation of their identities.[37] To pursue a right of publicity claim a person must be able to show that his or her identity has economic value. The Supreme Court has observed a similarity between right of publicity and copyright law. Not only does right of publicity protect the performer's right to be compensated for his or her work, but it also provides an economic incentive for the performer to invest in the production of new acts.[38] Like other property rights, right of publicity is transferable. The right can be licensed to third parties and, in some states, bequeathed to others at death.[39]

Right of publicity is distinct from appropriation in that it protects more than name and likeness. It protects all recognizable aspects of a person's personality. Bette Midler, for example, used it to sue a company that hired someone to impersonate her voice for an ad to sell cars.[40] Jacqueline Kennedy Onassis used it to prevent a clothing manufacturer from using a look-alike model to evoke her image in an advertisement.[41] Vanna White used it to sue Samsung Electronics for a commercial with a female robot wearing a blond wig and turning letters.[42] The Vanna White case left companies questioning the limits of right of publicity. In 2001, the California Supreme Court attempted to clarify the boundary by formulating a balancing test between the First Amendment and right of publicity. It concluded that a use is fair when it adds "significant creative elements so as to be transformed into something more than a 'mere celebrity likeness or imitation.'"[43] But it is still difficult to know how courts will interpret "transformative." Electronic Arts and Activision asserted a First Amendment right to use computer-generated likenesses of musicians and athletes as avatars in video games without success. Although

---

[37] *See* Haelan Laboratories, Inc. v. Topps Chewing Gum, Inc., 202 F.2d 866, 868 (1953).

[38] *See* Zacchini v. Scripps-Howard Broadcasting Co, 433 U.S. 562, 573, 576 (1977).

[39] California, Florida, Illinois, Indiana, Kentucky, Nebraska, Nevada, Ohio, Oklahoma, Tennessee, Texas, Virginia, and Washington.

[40] Midler v. Ford Motor Co., 849 F.2d 460 (9th Cir. 1988).

[41] Onassis v. Christian Dior, Inc., 472 N.Y.S.2d 254 (Spec. Term. 1984)

[42] White v. Samsung Elecs. Am., 971 F.2d 1395 (9th Cir. 1992).

[43] Comedy III Productions, Inc. v. Saderup, 25 Cal. 4th 387, 391 (Cal. 2001).

the companies had certainly added creative elements, neither court found the avatars sufficiently transformative to justify First Amendment protection.[44]

Actress Lindsay Lohan, who has a history of substance abuse, filed a $100 million lawsuit against the financial company eTrade for violating her publicity rights with its 2010 Super Bowl commercial showing a love triangle between the eTrade baby, his girlfriend, and a rival baby named Lindsay who the girlfriend dubbed a "milkoholic." Rather than fight the case, eTrade settled out of court for an undisclosed sum.[45]

Figure 10.1   Etrade's "milkoholic" baby

News and information exemption

Courts show broad deference to the First Amendment in appropriation and right of publicity claims involving editorial content. The names and likenesses of individuals may be used for news and information purposes without their permission. If the contrary were true, individuals could use appropriation or right of publicity to stifle public criticism.[46]

Furthermore, the fact that a publication, broadcast, or film is made for profit makes no difference to the "newsworthiness" defense. Although the appropriation tort is meant to punish unauthorized commercial use of a name or image, the term *commercial use* does not refer to use in a commercial medium. A commercial use is an invitation to conduct a transaction.

The news and information exemption is not, however, a license to steal an artist's work. The Supreme Court has held that the First Amendment and right of publicity must be balanced. In *Zacchini v. Scripps-Howard Broadcasting Co.* (1977), for example, the Court rejected a news organization's argument that the First Amendment protected its right to broadcast a performer's entire act without permission.[47]

In right of publicity cases, a public figure can only recover damages for noncommercial speech by proving actual malice by clear and convincing evidence. Clint Eastwood did this in a suit against the *National Enquirer*. The tabloid ran an article that it touted as an exclusive with Eastwood. Because Eastwood never gave the *Enquirer* an interview, he sued under California's right of publicity statute. The article included quotes, scene-setting phrases (such as "he said with a chuckle") that implied the writer and star had conversed, and a byline by an *Enquirer* assistant editor. The court agreed that taken together, the magazine's actions showed an intent to convey a false impression that satisfied actual malice.[48]

In contrast, the Ninth Circuit held that the First Amendment protected *Los Angeles Magazine's* inclusion of a digitally altered photo of Dustin Hoffman in a fashion spread.

---

[44] No Doubt v. Activision Publishing, 192 Cal. App. 4th 1018 (Cal. App. 2d Dist. 2011); Keller v. Electronic Arts, 2010 U.S. Dist. LEXIS 10719 (N.D. Cal. 2010).

[45] Lindsay Lohan Gets Paid in "Milkaholic" Lawsuit, TMZ, Sept. 20, 2010, http://www.tmz.com/2010/09/17/lindsay-lohan-etrade-milkaholic-lawsuit-settlement-money-drugs-alcohol-rehab/#.Ty7mxF1127I.

[46] *See, e.g.,* Taylor v. NBC, No. BC 110922 (Cal. Super. Ct. Sept. 29, 1994).

[47] 433 U.S. 562 (1977).

[48] Eastwood v. National Enquirer, 123 F.3d 1249 (9th Cir. 1997).

Using digital imaging software, the magazine clothed Hollywood icons Grace Kelly, Marilyn Monroe, and Cary Grant in the latest fall fashions. Hoffman's photo from the film *Tootsie* was updated with a new designer gown. Hoffman won a right of publicity claim against the magazine at the district level, but the Court of Appeals reversed. It found the article's commercial aspects to be "inextricably entwined" with expressive elements that could not be separated "from the fully protected whole."[49] Also, because the magazine referred to its use of digital technology to alter the famous photos, there was no evidence that the defendant intended to mislead the public to believe that Hoffman posed for the picture.

Booth rule

A medium that uses a person's name or likeness for informational purposes is allowed to use the same piece later to advertise itself. This exception to appropriation, known as the Booth Rule, was created by the New York Supreme Court in *Booth v. Curtis Publishing Co.* (1962).[50] Actress Shirley Booth sued the publishers of *Holiday* magazine for appropriating her image to advertise the magazine. Booth had given the magazine permission to use her image in a travel feature, but had not authorized its use for advertising purposes. The court said media must be able to promote themselves through images that are representative of their content. However, the exception does not allow publications to use such images to advertise other products.

Images as art

In general, courts consider the artistic use of an image to be a protected form of expression. However, sorting out what is and is not art may be a challenge. Some states limit the art exemption to transformative rather than duplicative likenesses.[51] Others have limited the exemption to original works, but not reproductions.[52] A New York appellate court rejected a privacy claim by a Hasidic Jew who protested the unauthorized use of his image in a photography exhibit, depicting candid shots of people walking through Times Square.[53] The plaintiff, who never consented to be photographed, objected to the use of his photo based on his religious conviction that it violated the second commandment prohibition against graven images. The court concluded that the images, which were reviewed and exhibited to the artistic community, were art. The fact that the photos were exhibited and sold through a for-profit art gallery did not convert the art into something used for trade purposes.

---

[49] Hoffman v. Capital Cities/ABC, Inc., 255 F.3d 1180, 1186 (9th Cir. 2001).
[50] 11 N.Y.S.2d 907 (1962).
[51] *See, e.g.,* Comedy III Productions, Inc. v. Gary Saderup, Inc., 25 Cal. 4th 387 (2001).
[52] *See* Martin Luther King, Jr. Center for Social Change, Inc. v. American Heritage Products, Inc., 250 GA 135 (1982).
[53] Nussenzweig v. DiCorcia, 2006 NY slip op. 50171U; 6 N.Y. Misc. LEXIS 230 (Feb. 8, 2006).

Portrayal in false light

Publishing information that creates a false impression about someone, thereby casting the person in a false light, constitutes an invasion of privacy in many states. False light bears a resemblance to defamation because both torts involve deliberate misrepresentations. However, false light claims are based on the emotional harm caused by misrepresentation, rather than harm to reputation.

The misrepresentation in a *false light* claim must be highly offensive to a reasonable person to be actionable. The publisher of the information also must be at fault. In cases involving public figure plaintiffs or matters of pubic concern the appropriate standard of fault is actual malice, which is knowledge of falsity or reckless disregard of the truth.

The Supreme Court's first privacy case, *Time, Inc. v. Hill* (1967), addressed the tort of false light. Three escaped convicts held James Hill and his family hostage in their Pennsylvania home for nineteen hours. Fortunately, the family came out of the ordeal unharmed. Two of the culprits were killed in an ensuing battle with police, and the third was apprehended. Afterward, the Hills shied away from media attention, but a novel based on their experience was published the following year. The author spiced up the tale with scenes of violence. The novel was subsequently turned into a play. *LIFE Magazine*, owned by Time, published an article about the play, representing it as an accurate reenactment of the Hills' experience. Hill sued Time for deliberately misrepresenting his family's experience.

The case came on the heels of the Court's *Rosenbloom v. Metromedia* (1971) decision, extending the standard of fault in libel cases concerning matters of public interest to actual malice, even in cases brought by private plaintiffs.[54] Although *Time v. Hill* concerned false light, not libel, it too involved a matter of public interest. The Court chose to apply actual malice to it as well.[55] The following year, the Supreme Court overturned *Rosenbloom* when it announced in *Gertz v. Welch* (1974) that private figures should not be required to prove actual malice in libel cases; however it made no mention of false light.[56] A few months after *Gertz*, the Court considered another false light case involving a private figure plaintiff and a matter of public interest. The jury in the case had found actual malice on the part of the defendant. The Court did not use the opportunity to clarify whether, in light of *Gertz*, a more relaxed standard would have been sufficient. It left states to draw their own conclusions about the appropriate standard to set.[57]

For *false light*, the plaintiff must prove that:
- the published information would be highly offensive to a reasonable person; and
- the publisher of the material is at fault with respect to its falsity.

Actual malice for public figures

Public figures must show actual malice in false light cases. In *Solano v. Playgirl*, Baywatch star Jose Solano Jr. sued *Playgirl* for false light after his photo appeared on the magazine's cover between the headlines "Primetime's Sexy Young Stars Exposed" and "12 Sizzling

[54] 385 U.S. 374 (1967).
[55] 403 U.S. 29 (1971).
[56] 418 U.S. 323 (1974).
[57] *See* Cantrell v. Forest City Publishing Co., 419 U.S. 245 (1974).

Centerfolds Ready to Score With You."[58] He argued that the cover cast him in a false light by implying both that he agreed to do an interview with the magazine and that he would appear nude inside it. Finding that Solano had established a genuine issue for trial, the Ninth Circuit reversed the district court's order of summary judgment in favor of *Playgirl*. It observed that Solano might be able to prove actual malice by clear and convincing evidence because members of the editorial staff had expressed concern before publication that the cover suggested Solano would appear nude. The case was settled in 2004.

Must be believable

Like defamation, false light must be believable. A court will not find false light in a parody or spoof that no reasonable person would consider factual. A Utah court of appeals granted summary judgment to defendants in a privacy suit filed against Marriott Ownership Resorts by an employee and his spouse over an embarrassing video shown at the company Christmas party.[59] Employees were asked to give a detailed description of a household chore they hate. Later the video was edited to make it appear that they were answering the question "What's sex like with your partner?" The plaintiff was quoted as saying:

> [Y]ou have to do it and you have to enjoy doing it. And you cannot—you can't—get into the idea that this is something that you don't want to do. . . . But I've found that the goggles work very well because eye protection is a very important item.[60]

Another explained that "[i]t's one of those greasy grimy things that you just have to do at least once a year whether you want to or not."[61] Taken together in context, the court concluded that a reasonable person would recognize that the video was a spoof.

"Based on a true story"

False light cases occasionally arise from docudramas that claim to be based on a true story but are partially fictionalized. However, courts are reluctant to find false light in cases in which the overall gist of the story is true.[62] The *Second Restatement of Torts* says of false light claims that:

> The plaintiff's privacy is not invaded when unimportant false statements are made, even when they are made deliberately. It is only when there is such a major misrepresentation

---

[58] Solano v. Playgirl, Inc., 292 F.3d 1078 (9th Cir. 2002).

[59] Stein v. Marriott Ownership Resorts, Inc., 944 P.2d 374 (Utah App. 1997).

[60] *Id.* at 376.

[61] *Id.*

[62] *See, e.g.,* Seale v. Gramercy Pictures, 964 F. Supp. 918, 925–31 (E.D. Pa. 1997) (holding that the plaintiff could not support false light claims and that his right to publicity was not violated because his likeness was not used for a commercial purpose).

of his character, history, activities or beliefs that serious offense may reasonably be expected to be taken by a reasonable man in his position, that there is a cause of action for invasion of privacy.[63]

The family members of the fishing crew depicted in the movie *The Perfect Storm* sued Time Warner for false light and misappropriation. The film included a fictional scene of the captain berating his crew for wanting to go back to shore when threatened by the storm. It also included scenes that briefly portrayed the plaintiffs engaged in invented conversations. The film opened with the statement: "THIS FILM IS BASED ON A TRUE STORY." But a disclaimer at the end added "Dialogue and certain events and characters in the film were created for the purpose of fictionalization." Although most states reject false light claims concerning representations of the deceased, the plaintiffs argued that they had a relational right to sue for false light on behalf of their father, who was vilified in the movie as an obsessed boat captain, causing them pain. The Eleventh Circuit did not find the portrayal "sufficiently egregious" to warrant a relational right.[64] The Florida Supreme Court also looked at the case and held that the state misappropriation statute did not apply to the plaintiffs who were depicted in the film because their names and images, while used in a commercial film, were not used to promote a product.[65]

Random photos

False light cases can occur when publishers use unrelated photos and video to illustrate stories. Washington, D.C., pedestrian Linda Duncan sued a television news station for false light after it used her image to illustrate a story on genital herpes. Duncan was walking down a street among a crowd of people when the camera zoomed in on her and an announcer read "For the twenty million Americans who have herpes, it's not a cure."[66]

Distinguishing between false light and defamation

False light claims are not necessarily based on negative misrepresentations. *LIFE Magazine*, for example, described the play about the Hills' ordeal as "a heart-stopping account of how a family rose to heroism in a crisis." In another case, baseball Hall-of-Famer Warren Spahn sued a biographer who misrepresented him as a war hero.[67] But people are more likely to sue when misrepresentations are offensive, so most false light cases do involve negative portrayals. For this reason, they are often coupled with defamation claims. Some states accept this because the torts, although similar, respond to two different types of harm. Distinguishing between them, the Minnesota Supreme Court

---

[63] RESTATEMENT (SECOND) OF TORTS § 652E, cmt. c. (1977).
[64] Tyne v. Time Warner Entm't Co., 336 F.3d 1286 (11th Cir. 2003).
[65] Tyne v. Time Warner Entm't Co., L.P., 901 So.2d 802, 2005 Fla. LEXIS 728 (Fla. 2005).
[66] Duncan v. WJLA-TV, 10 M.L.R. (BNA) 1385 (D.D.C. 1984).
[67] Spahn v. Julian Messner, Inc., 250 N.Y.S.2d 529, 531 (1964), *aff'd,* 260 N.Y.S.2d 451 (1965).

explained: "The primary difference between defamation and false light is that defamation addresses harm to reputation in the external world, while false light protects harm to one's inner self."[68] Minnesota is one of several states that have rejected false light because the tort is too similar to defamation. Others that do not recognize false light include Colorado, Florida, Massachusetts, Missouri[69], New York, North Carolina, Texas, Virginia, Wisconsin.[70] States that do not acknowledge false light have concluded that the tort sits in tension with the First Amendment because it offers protection that overlaps defamation without providing defamation's safeguards for speech.

Defenses to Invasion of Privacy

Newsworthiness

Newsworthiness is a defense for disclosure of private facts, false light, and misappropriation. It is not a defense to intrusion claims, but it is one of the factors considered in intrusion cases when courts try to determine whether an intrusion would be offensive to a reasonable person. The term *newsworthy* is defined as "any information disseminated 'for purposes of education, amusement or enlightenment, when the public may reasonably be expected to have a legitimate interest in what is published.'"[71]

Public figures are usually considered newsworthy and receive less privacy protection than private individuals because they have voluntarily subjected themselves to public scrutiny.

Arrests are always newsworthy, even if the person arrested is later proved innocent. So are victims of crime, accidents, and disasters. William Prosser explained:

> Caught up and entangled in this web of news and public interest are a great many people who have not sought publicity, but indeed, as in the case of any accused criminal, have tried assiduously to avoid it. They have nevertheless lost some part of their right of privacy. The misfortunes of the frantic victim of sexual assault, the woman whose husband is murdered before her eyes, or the innocent bystander who is caught in a raid on a cigar store and mistaken by the police for the proprietor, can be broadcast to the world, and they have no remedy. Such individuals become public figures for a season; and "until they have

---

[68] Lake v. Wal-Mart Stores, Inc., 582 N.W.2d 231, 235 (Minn. 1998) (recognizing causes of action for intrusion upon seclusion, appropriation, and publication of private facts, but not false light).

[69] *See* Sullivan v. Pulitzer Broadcasting Co., 709 S.W.2d 475, 478–80 (Mo. 1986)(in which Missouri's Supreme Court prohibited the application of false light in defamation-type cases); *But see* Meyerkord v. Zipatoni, 276 S.W.3d 319 (Mo. App. 2008) (in which the Missouri Court of Appeals recognized false light's potential application in other types of cases).

[70] Denver Publishing Co. v. Bueno, 54 P.3d 893 (Colo. 2002); Jews for Jesus v. Rapp, 36 Media L. Rep. 2540, 2008 Fla. LEXIS 2010 (Fla. Oct. 23, 2008); Renwick v. News and Observer Pub. Co., 312 S.E.2d 405, 411 (N.C. 1984); Cain v. The Hearst Corporation, 878 S.W.2d 577 (Tex. 1994); WJLA-TV v. Levin, 564 S.E.2d 383, 395 n. 5 (Va. 2002). *See also* Jacqueline Hanson Dee, *Comment, The Absence of False Light from the Wisconsin Privacy Statute*, 66 MARQ. L. REV. 99, 99–112 (1982).

[71] See RESTATEMENT (SECOND) OF TORTS § 652D, Comment j (1977).

reverted to the lawful and unexciting life led by the great bulk of the community, they are subject to the privileges which publishers have to satisfy the curiosity of the public as to their leaders, heroes, villains and victims."[72]

However, intimate coverage of victims may cross the line. Although a television station's on-the-scene coverage of a car accident was not considered an invasion of privacy, the Supreme Court of California ruled that its coverage of victims inside a rescue helicopter, where they could claim a reasonable expectation of privacy, could constitute an intrusion upon seclusion and public disclosure of private facts.[73] Courts have found in favor of plaintiffs who sued the media for filming a dying heart attack victim and amplifying a phone conversation in which police notified parents of their son's death.[74]

Public documents

Publishing or broadcasting information that is available in a public record is not an invasion of privacy because the information is already accessible to anyone willing to comb through public files to get it. Computerization has facilitated the search process.

A surplus of "private" information exists in public documents, such as birth and death certificates, marriage licenses, divorce records, military records, professional licenses, property tax records, and wills.

Consent

A person who willingly provides information for publication or consents to photography or videotaping cannot sue for invasion of privacy later. In fact, some jurisdictions will reject a plaintiff's invasion of privacy claim based on consent, even if the consent was procured by fraud, as long as the activity disclosed is of a commercial rather than a personal or private nature. For example, the Seventh Circuit would not entertain a trespass claim from an eye clinic that gave *Primetime Live* permission to film cataract operations, even though the show's producers violated their promise not to use hidden cameras or do ambush interviews.[75] Likewise, the U.S. Court for the Eastern District of Michigan granted summary judgment to People for the Ethical Treatment of Animals in a privacy case in which the animal rights organization obtained consent to film animals being euthanized on a chinchilla farm from the owners under false pretenses.[76] It did not consider the defendant's action of placing the video with an article about the farm on its website to be an appropriation because the organization was reporting on a matter of public concern. The fact that the website also collected donations did not transform the use into a commercial endeavor.

---

[72]W. Prosser, The Law of Torts 824–26 (4th ed. 1971).

[73]Shulman v. Group W. Productions, 955 P.2d 469 (Cal. 1998).

[74]*See* Marich v. MGM/UA Telecommunications, 113 Cal. App. 4th 415 (2003).

[75]Desnick v. Am. Broadcasting Companies, 44 F.3d 1345, 1351 (7th Cir. 1995).

[76]Ouderkirk v. People for the Ethical Treatment of Animals, No. 05–10111, 2007 U.S. Dist. LEXIS 29451 (E.D. Mich. 2007).

However, this is not always the case. The Fifth Circuit held that fraudulently induced consent is the "legal equivalent of no consent" in a Texas case in which a woman sued a pornographic magazine for publishing her photo under false pretenses.[77] Jeannie Braun worked for an amusement park in San Marcos, Texas, where she performed a novelty act with "Ralph, the Diving Pig." Ralph's job in the act was to dive into a pool, swim over to Braun, and drink from a bottle of milk that she held for him. Braun had signed a consent form allowing her employer to disseminate pictures of the act for publicity purposes, as long as they were used in good taste. When a representative from *Chic Magazine* contacted Braun's employer, requesting to use a photo of the act, he was asked to describe the publication. He said it was a magazine that contained articles about men's fashion, travel and humor but neglected to mention its predominant theme. Braun later discovered her photo was sandwiched among others of a sexual nature in a section of the publication called "Chic Thrills." She sued the magazine for invasion of privacy and defamation.

Consent to publish intimate or private information may be qualified or conditioned and may even be revoked if done sufficiently in advance of publication.[78] Someone who gives consent for an interview needs to give consent for the publication of the information as well. Consent to publish a private fact may not be assumed from a person's choice to disclose the information to an individual, even an individual in the media. In *Hawkins v. Multimedia, Inc.* (1986), the South Carolina Supreme Court did not infer consent because the plaintiff, who was never informed he would be identified in an article, talked briefly with a reporter.[79]

Also, while consent is a valid defense, there are some circumstances in which it will not apply. People who are minors or mentally handicapped may not give consent on their own behalf. Consent must come from a parent or guardian. Consent may not apply if it was given a long time ago. Consent may be invalidated if the material is changed. For example, consent to use a person's image is not reliable if the image is digitally altered before publication.

Privacy Protection From Federal Statutes

Federal statutes offer specific protections for various pieces of our private lives. The first privacy statutes were passed to curb government excesses that included illegal information gathering and surveillance. These were followed by restrictions on government access to electronic communications. Later statutes imposed privacy responsibilities on private entities with regard to electronic communications, financial records, and medical records. Here are some of the most notable:

[77] Braun v. Flynt, 726 F.2d 245, 255 (5th Cir. 1984).
[78] *See* Virgil v. Time, Inc., 527 F.2d 1122, 1127 (9th Cir. 1975).
[79] 288 S.C. 569, 571 (S.C. 1986).

The Privacy Act – 5 U.S.C. §§ 552a, et seq.

The Privacy Act of 1974 provides limited protection against government collection and disclosure of personal records. The term *record* includes, but is not limited to, information an agency may have about a person's education, financial transactions, medical or employment history, or criminal background. The Privacy Act has several functions. It prevents government agencies from disclosing an individual's personal records without the subject's written permission, unless the information is part of a public record or falls within one of the Act's exceptions.[80] It entitles individuals to review government records kept about them and to request corrections if necessary.[81] The Act also prohibits government agencies from maintaining records regarding people's exercise of their First Amendment rights.[82] Government agencies may not record individuals' participation in demonstrations or Internet petitions, for example.[83]

Electronic Communications Privacy Act – 18 U.S.C. §§ 2510(1), et seq.

The Electronic Communications Privacy Act, passed in 1986, regulates access to electronically transmitted and stored information. In general, the Act did three things. It amended the Federal Wiretap Act, originally passed in 1968, to apply restrictions on wiretaps of telephones to other electronic messages, such as e-mails and electronic files, in transit. It established rules government entities must follow to collect data related to those communications, such as dialing, routing, and addressing information, through the "Pen Register and Trap and Trace Statute." It also provided protections for e-mails, texts and files stored on third party databases through the "Stored Communications Act." These provisions are explained in greater detail below.

Federal Wiretap Act – 18 U.S.C. §§ 2510–22

The Federal Wiretap Act prohibits the unauthorized interception, use, disclosure or procurement of "wire, oral, or electronic communications." An electronic communication is defined as "any transfer of signs, signals, writing, images, sounds, data, or intelligence of any nature transmitted in whole or in part by a wire, radio, electromagnetic, photoelectronic or photooptical system."[84]

The Act provides exceptions for government officials authorized by law to intercept communications. Officials who show probable cause that the interception will reveal evidence that an individual is committing, has committed, or is about to commit a "particular offense" may obtain a warrant for 30 days of surveillance. Illegally intercepted information may not be used as evidence for a crime.

---

[80] 5 U.S.C § 552a(b) (2011).
[81] *Id.* § 552(d)(1) (2007).
[82] *Id.* § 552(e)(7).
[83] *See* J. Roderick MacArthur Found. v. FBI, 102 F.3d 600 (D.C. Cir. 1996).
[84] 5 U.S.C. § 2510(12).

The Act also permits the interception of a communication with the consent of any participant in the communication. This exception has allowed reporters to secretly record their own conversations with people while investigating a story. However, some states prohibit the interception of a conversation without the permission of all participants in a communication.

Pen Register Statute – 18 U.S.C. § 3123(a)(1)

The Pen Register Statute specifies procedures that government entities must follow to collect the dialing and routing information that is ancillary to the communications collected through wiretapping. *Pen registers* capture outgoing telephone numbers. *Trap and trace devices*, like caller ID boxes, capture incoming numbers. These devices also capture e-mail addresses and URLs from web searches. The standard for getting a pen/trap order is lower than that required for wiretaps because the content of the communications is not reviewed. Authorities need only certify to a court that the information collected through the devices would be useful in an investigation. The orders also last longer than warrants issued for wiretaps – 60 days rather than 30 – and subjects of the surveillance need not be notified once it has ended.

Stored Communications Act – 18 U.S.C. §§ 2701–11

The Stored Communications Act established privacy rights related to electronic information stored by providers of electronic communications services. Congress passed the statute to plug a hole in the Wiretap Act, which applies exclusively to the interception or acquisition of a message in transit. In general, the Stored Communications Act does two things:

1. It proscribes unauthorized access to electronic mail, files and text messages stored by service providers, or to the subscriber's personal information, such as name, billing records, or IP address.
2. It also prevents service providers from knowingly disclosing the contents of subscribers' stored communications, or their personal records, to any person or entity not entitled to receive that information.

The U.S. Court of Appeals for the Ninth Circuit determined that an airline executive violated the Stored Communications Act in *Konop v. Hawaiian Airlines* (2002) by accessing an employee's password protected website without authorization.[85] The pilot who created the site used it to criticize the airline's labor practices. The executive who accessed it borrowed a password from another employee who had been granted access to it but had not used the site. The SCA indicates that a "user" of a service may authorize a third party's access to it.[86] However, because the statute defines a user as one who "(1)

---

[85] 302 F.3d 868 (9th Cir. 2002).
[86] See 18 U.S.C. § 2701(c)(2).

uses the service and (2) is duly authorized to do so," the court concluded that the employee's consent for the executive to access the site was invalid.[87]

Accessing the website without permission would have been legal if Hawaiian Airlines had housed the site on its server. The SCA prevents service providers from sharing user data stored on their systems, but not from accessing the data themselves. Effectively, this means that an employer who provides Internet service for an employee is not restricted from accessing the employee's e-mails or electronic files stored on its servers.

The law also permits access to stored communications with permission of the user. Consequently, an employer may monitor employee e-mails and files stored on a third-party service, if the employer has gained the employee's written consent to do so. Depending on the jurisdiction, implied consent also may apply if the employer has provided advance notice to employees that it monitors employee communications.[88]

Courts have interpreted the Stored Communications Act to apply to stored phone messages.[89] In 1998, *Cincinnati Enquirer* reporter Mike Gallagher was convicted of illegally accessing the voice-mail system for Chiquita Brands International while working on an exposé of the banana company's business practices. Gallagher obtained the access codes from one of Chiquita's attorneys. *The Enquirer* learned about the breech after it published an 18-page series on the company, alleging that Chiquita had engaged in illegal activities in Central America. The content of the story, compiled after a year of investigation, was overshadowed by Gallagher's unethical reporting methods. The paper paid $10 million to Chiquita in a legal settlement and printed a front-page apology for three consecutive days.[90]

In the United Kingdom, the 168-year-old paper *News of the World*, owned by Rupurt Murdoch's News Corporation, closed in 2011 after a phone hacking scandal. The paper's activities came to light in 2005, when it published information obtained from Prince William's staff. By 2011, authorities were investigating 4,000 possible cases and the paper had settled cases with movie stars, musicians and athletes. Several of its editors were also arrested.[91]

In the U.S., government entities with an appropriate court order may compel ISPs and phone companies to turn over subscribers' stored communications. The protection available to citizens against this type of government intrusion varies depending on the

[87] 302 F.3d at 880 (citing 18 U.S.C. § 2510(13)).

[88] Blumofe v. Pharmatrak, Inc., 329 F.3d 9 (1st Cir. 2003); Griggs-Ryan v. Smith, 904 F.2d 112, 116-17 (1st Cir. 1990).

[89] Bohach v. City of Reno, 932 F. Supp. 1232, 1235–56 (D. Nev. 1996)(concluding that an interception of a voicemail is covered by the Wiretap Act of the ECPA, while accessing information in voicemail storage is covered by the Stored Communications Act); See also United States v. Moriarty, 962 F. Supp. 217, 221 (D. Mass. 1997)

[90] Chiquita Brands Int'l v. Gallagher, No. C-1-98-467 (S.D. Ohio, dismissed by agreement of parties, July 19, 1999). Reporter sentenced over Chaquita voice mail theft, Reporter's Committee for Freedom of the Press, July 26, 1999, http://www.rcfp.org/node/91143.

[91] *News of the World Phone Hacking Scandal*, BBC News, Aug. 17, 2011, http://www.bbc.co.uk/news/uk-11195407; Ravi Somaiya, New outrage over hacking in another murder case; *Mother of slain girl, 8, is on list of tabloid's 4,000 probable targets*, NY TIMES, July 28, 2011, at 3.

data's age. When Congress passed the statute in 1986, it assumed that electronic communications services would provide temporary storage for subscriber messages incidental to their transmission. Government authorities who wanted access to messages in the company's possession during that brief period would need a warrant to get them. Congress assumed that after 180 days any subscriber information still on the service provider's server was abandoned and that authorities should be able to access it with a subpoena. Unlike a warrant, which requires officials to demonstrate to a court that there is probable cause to believe the subject has committed a crime, a subpoena may be issued if there is a possibility that the information sought will be relevant to the investigation.

Unfortunately, Congress did not anticipate our increasing reliance on cloud computing, which encompasses such services as Gmail, Hotmail, Google Docs and Apple's iCloud. In jurisdictions that take the statute at face value, electronic files and messages stored remotely receive less protection than files stored at home, mail sent through the postal service, or telephone calls – all of which require a warrant to review.

The U.S. Court of Appeals for the Sixth Circuit has found this part of the Stored Communications Act to be unconstitutional. In *United States v. Warshak* (2010), the court concluded "that a subscriber enjoys a reasonable expectation of privacy in the contents of e-mails 'that are stored with, or sent or received through, a commercial ISP'" and that "government may not compel a commercial ISP to turn over the contents of a subscriber's e-mails without first obtaining a warrant based on probable cause."[92]

The defendant behind the case was Steven Warshak, the owner of a company that sold Encyte, a herbal supplement purported to increase the size of a man's erection. The campaign for the supplement featured "Smilin' Bob," who was the envy of his social circle. Like Bob, the scientific claims about the drug were fabricated. Without their knowledge, customers were automatically enrolled in an auto-ship program that continued to send the pills and bill their credit cards until they demanded that it stop. When the Justice Department investigated the company for fraud, it subpoenaed Warshak's e-mails from his Internet service provider. In assessing the legality of the subpoena, the Court of Appeals considered two questions: (1) whether Warshak had a subjective expectation of privacy in his stored e-mails and (2) whether society is willing to recognize that expectation as reasonable. After concluding that the answer to both questions was yes, the court determined that the government had violated Warshak's Fourth Amendment rights by going after his e-mails without a warrant. However, because investigators were acting on what the law said at the time, the court concluded that the violation was not willful and allowed the government to use the evidence. Warshak was sentenced to 25 years in prison.

The warrant requirement for stored communications also varies by jurisdiction, according to whether the file has been accessed by the user. Some jurisdictions have concluded that because the statute defines storage as incidental to transmission, a message is no longer "stored" once the recipient has opened the file. Under this theory,

[92] 631 F.3d 266, 288 (6th Cir. 2010).

warrant protection for user messages on a third party server is limited to unread messages. The Ninth Circuit disagrees with this interpretation of the law.[93] This means that ISPs located within that circuit (Alaska, Arizona, California, Idaho, Montana, Nevada, Oregon, and Washington) are able to offer their users stronger protection.

The Stored Communications Act is more protective of private files and messages sought for civil litigation. The Act does not allow individuals or companies embroiled in lawsuits to subpoena private messages and e-mail communications from Internet service providers or social networking sites to gather evidence for their cases. Depending on the user's privacy settings, this protection may adhere to posts and wall comments on social networking sites as well.[94] Civil litigants who want access to this kind of information must subpoena it from the users themselves, which gives users the opportunity to challenge the subpoena.

Telephone Records and Privacy Protection Act – 18 U.S.C. § 1039(a)

The Telephone Records and Privacy Protection Act of 2006 makes it a criminal offense to obtain confidential phone records under false pretenses, a practice known as *pretexting*. The statute prohibits the knowing and intentional use of false or fraudulent statements or documentation to obtain confidential records from a telecommunications carrier or unauthorized access to those records via the Internet. It also prohibits the unauthorized purchase, transfer, or sale of phone company customer records. The statute applies to cell phone, landline, and voice over Internet protocol or VoIP records. Violators may be fined or imprisoned up to 10 years.

The legislation was inspired by the Hewlett Packard pretexting scandal in which the company's chairwoman hired a team of security experts to investigate HP's board of directors and members of the press to determine the source of information leaked to the media. The investigators used pretexting to obtain the phone records of board members and nine journalists who had written about the company. HP agreed to pay $14.5 million to settle a California civil suit of corporate spying for the fraudulently acquired phone records.[95]

Video Privacy Protection Act – 18 U.S.C. § 2710

Congress passed the Video Privacy Protection Act of 1988 after a newspaper published Robert Bork's video rental records during his nomination for Supreme Court justice. The statute imposes civil liability on any video provider who "knowingly discloses, to any person, personally identifiable information concerning any consumer." In addition to prohibiting the release of rental information, it requires video providers to destroy customer records within one year of an account's termination. Records may be released to police or individuals engaged in civil litigation with a valid court order. Consumers

[93] Theofel v. Farey-Jones, 341 F.3d 978 (9th Cir. 2003).
[94] Crispin v. Audigier, Inc., 717 F. Supp. 2d 965 (C.D. Cal. 2010).
[95] Damon Darlin, *H.P. Will Pay $14.5 Million to Settle Suit*, N.Y. Times, Dec. 8, 2006, at C5.

whose information has been released in violation of the statute may bring a civil action against the video provider for actual damages of up to $2,500.

Facebook's decision to reveal its users' video rentals from Blockbuster through its Beacon marketing program triggered a class action lawsuit.[96] The suit alleged that Facebook and its affiliates had violated the Electronic Communications Privacy Act and the Video Privacy Protection Act by sharing data about Facebook users with each other. Beacon tracked users' online activities off-site and reported their purchases back to their Facebook friends as a newsfeed. It was originally introduced as an opt-out feature until Facebook users rose up en masse to complain that their privacy was being violated. The suit, combined with a second concerning Beacon, led to a $9.5 million settlement, in which Facebook agreed to end Beacon and set up a privacy foundation to promote online privacy.[97]

Children's Online Privacy Protection Act – 15 U.S.C. §§ 6501, et seq.

The Children's Online Privacy Protection Act of 1998 authorizes the Federal Trade Commission to regulate Internet sites that collect personal information from children under the age of 13. Personal information is considered to be: children's first and last names, home addresses, e-mail addresses, telephone numbers, Social Security numbers, or any other personal identifiers of the child or his or her parents. COPPA authorizes the FTC to expand the definitions of personal information. In 2012 the agency was considering revising the definition of "personal information" to include geolocation information and certain types of identifiers, such as tracking cookies used for behavioral advertising.[98]

Under FTC rules, website operators must post privacy policies and get verifiable consent from a parent or guardian before collecting personal information about a child under 13. The FTC also requires operators to disclose to parents any information collected about their children and give parents the opportunity to delete the child's personal information and opt-out of future collection or use of the information. The Act also imposes a requirement that the site operator protect the confidentiality of the information it does collect.

Playdom, an operator of 20 virtual world websites, was fined $3 million for collecting information from hundreds of thousands of children.[99] It was the largest civil penalty ever imposed for a violation of COPPA. The FTC accused the company of collecting

---

[96] Harris v. Blockbuster Inc., Case No. 08-CV-155 (E.D. Texas), filed April 9, 2008; Lane v. Facebook (Case No. 09–3845 RS; March 17, 2010).

[97] Jaikumar Vijayan, *Privacy advocates hail Facebook's plan to shutter Beacon*, ComputerWorld, Sept. 22, 2009, http://www.computerworld.com/s/article/9138373/Privacy_advocates_hail_Facebook_s_plan_to_shutter_Beacon.

[98] 76 Fed. Reg. 187 (Sept. 27, 2011). The FTC was still evaluating data it had collected when this book went to publication in 2012.

[99] Operators of Online "Virtual Worlds" to Pay $3 Million to Settle FTC Charges That They Illegally Collected and Disclosed Children's Personal Information, Federal Trade Commission Release, May 12, 2011, http://www.ftc.gov/opa/2011/05/playdom.shtm.

children's ages and e-mail addresses during registration and then enabling them to post their full names, e-mail addresses, instant messenger IDs, and location, among other information, on personal profile pages and in online community forums.

In the first settlement concerning a mobile application, the FTC fined W3 Innovations $50,000 for "illegally collecting and disclosing personal information from tens of thousands of children under age 13 without their parents prior consent."[100] The company develops games for the iPhone and iTouch, including *Emily's Girl World* and *Emily's Dress Up*. The Emily apps encouraged children to e-mail "Emily" and submit blogs to "Emily's Blog" via e-mail, including "shout-outs" to friends and requests for advice.

Driver's Privacy Protection Act – 18 U.S.C. §§ 2721, et seq.

The Driver's Privacy Protection Act of 1994 is a federal regulation that bars state departments of motor vehicles from disclosing personal information about drivers without their consent. The statute was modeled on one first implemented by California after a stalker used Department of Motor Vehicle records to track down and kill actress Rebecca Schaefer.

Protection for personal information applies to photos, names, addresses, telephone numbers, Social Security numbers, driver's license numbers, medical or disability information, and accident reports, but is undermined by 14 exceptions. In 2000, Congress amended the Act to create a class of "highly restricted personal information" that includes photographs, Social Security numbers, and medical or disability information. This information is also subject to exceptions, but only four. These include use by government agencies; use in connection with any civil, criminal, administrative, or arbitral proceeding; use by any insurer or insurance support organization; and use by an employer or its agent or insurer to obtain or verify information relating to a holder of a commercial driver's license. Under any other circumstances, release of the information would require an individual's consent conveyed in writing or digitally with an electronic signature.

Fair Credit Reporting Act – 15 U.S.C. §§ 1681, et seq.

The Fair Credit Reporting Act of 1970 governs the collection and disclosure of information by consumer reporting agencies. The Act requires credit agencies to take steps to maintain the accuracy of credit reports and provide consumers with an opportunity to dispute negative information. It also gives them free access to their credit reports once a year through a government-authorized website.

In addition to credit worthiness, the Act covers information about a person's "character, general reputation, personal characteristics, and mode of living." This may include reports on criminal histories, civil judgments, bankruptcies, tax liens or practically anything else compiled from public databases by reporting agencies that sell records to third parties.

You can get a free copy of your credit report through annualcreditreport.com.

[100] Mobile Apps Developer Settles FTC Charges It Violated Children's Privacy Rule, Federal Trade Commission, Release, Aug. 15, 2011, http://www.ftc.gov/opa/2011/08/w3mobileapps.shtm.

Companies or organizations that use consumer reporting agencies for employment background checks are required to notify and obtain the applicant's consent before accessing his or her report. If a negative action is taken based on the report, the company is required to inform the applicant of that fact and provide the source of the report so the individual can investigate it. The law's purpose is to ensure that information provided by consumer reporting agencies is kept accurate and up to date. Employers that conduct their own searches of publicly accessible databases are not required to get permission from applicants first.

Right to Financial Privacy Act – 12 U.S.C. §§ 3401, et seq.

Congress passed the Right to Financial Privacy Act of 1978 in reaction to a Supreme Court decision that found consumers had no right to privacy regarding their records held by financial institutions.[101] The Act requires government agencies to provide consumers with notice and an opportunity to object before financial institutions can release copies of private financial records to the government. Usually the information is requested through an administrative summons or subpoena in conjunction with a law enforcement investigation.

Health Insurance Portability and Accountability Act

The Health Insurance Portability and Accountability Act of 1996 – or HIPPA – protects "Individually identifiable health information," that relates to:

- an individual's past, present, or future physical or mental health or condition;
- the provision of health care to an individual; or
- the past, present, or future payment for the provision of health care to an individual.[102]

The privacy provision of the Act applies to health plans, health care clearinghouses, and most health care providers who transmit health information in electronic form.

Family Educational Rights and Privacy Act, 20 U.S.C. § 1232g

Parents have a right of access to their children's educational records until the child reaches 18. After that, educational institutions may only share records with the student.

The Family Educational Rights and Privacy Act – or FERPA – protects student records. Schools that receive funding from the U.S. Department of Education are obligated to comply with the Act. The law gives parents and eligible students (those over 17) the right to inspect the student's educational records and request corrections if they believe the records are inaccurate. If the school declines, the parent or eligible student has a right to a formal hearing, after which, if no change is made, the parent or student may add a statement to the record, contesting the information on file. With some exceptions,

[101] United States v. Miller, 425 U.S. 435 (1976).
[102] Public Law 104–191 (1996), codified in various sections of the United States Code.

schools are prevented from releasing this information without the written permission of the parent or eligible student. These exceptions include disclosures to:

- other school officials, including teachers, with a legitimate educational interest;
- another school to which a student is transferring;
- specified officials for audit or evaluation purposes;
- officials in connection with a student's financial aid;
- organizations conducting studies for schools, related to student aid, testing and instruction;
- accrediting organizations;
- appropriate officials in cases of health and safety emergencies;
- school officials involved in disciplinary hearings;
- state and local officials in the juvenile justice system, pursuant to state statutes; and
- agencies or individuals with a judicial order or lawfully issued subpoena.[103]

Schools are also entitled to include certain information in student directories, as long as parents and students are given the opportunity to opt out of inclusion.

Privacy Protection Act – 42 U.S.C. §§ 2000aa, et seq.

The Privacy Protection Act of 1980 (not to be confused with the Privacy Act of 1974, discussed earlier) protects newsrooms from illegal searches and seizures of media materials for use as evidence.

State Privacy Statutes

States protect various areas of privacy through statute. Some codify the common law torts of intrusion upon seclusion and appropriation. Others duplicate federal laws that prohibit the interception of electronic communications or the release of medical information. State law also determines whether it is legal to surreptitiously record audio and video.

Audio recording

State laws prohibiting surreptitious audio recording are commonly called *wiretapping statutes*, even though they generally apply both to recordings made via wire or in person. In most states, it is legal to record a conversation without informing all parties, as long as one party involved in the conversation has consented to the recording. That party may be the person doing the recording. These are known as *one-party consent* states. States in which is it illegal to record without the consent of all parties are called *two-party* or *all-party consent* states. These include California, Connecticut, Florida, Illinois, Maryland, Massachusetts, Michigan, Montana, New Hampshire, Nevada, Pennsylvania, and Washington.

---

[103] 34 CFR § 99.31.

Federal law also permits the recording of telephone conversations with the consent of one party.[104] Traditionally, it has been thought that if the recorded conversation occurs between parties in different states, the law that applies would be either federal law or the law of the state in which the call was initiated.[105] However, California and Florida, both two-party states, have applied their own law in cases in which their residents were telephoned from one-party states and recorded without their knowledge and found liability on the part of the defendants who initiated the recordings.[106] Under the circumstances, it would be safest to ask for permission to record when calling two-party states.

Regardless of where a call may be initiated, it is not OK to record a conversation designated for broadcast without giving the other party advanced warning. The Communications Act requires an entity licensed by the FCC to provide notice to any party whom it intends to record for broadcast before the recording is captured.[107] Notice is not required, however, if the recorded party is aware that the conversation will be broadcasted.

Video recording

The use of hidden recording devices to capture video is particularly controversial. It has led to some of the most egregious privacy violations imaginable. At the same time, it has also been vital in breaking important news stories.

Use of video in private places

Video voyeurism, which is the use of hidden cameras in a location in which a person would have a reasonable expectation of privacy, such as in a bedroom, bathroom or changing room, violates federal law and is also illegal in 47 states. In fact, regulating access to private areas is generally the exclusive reason for state laws prohibiting hidden video, which largely emphasize the illegality of secretly recording someone in a state of undress with prurient interest.

Over the past few years, there have been outrageous examples of video voyeurism. A Rutgers student committed suicide after learning that his roommate was not only secretly taping his sexual relationship with another male, but also streaming the video on the Web and promoting the webcast on Twitter. The roommate was found guilty of criminal invasion of privacy.[108]

---

[104] 18 U.S.C. § 2511(2)(d) (2011).

[105] MacNeill Engineering Co. v. Trisport, Ltd. 59 F.Supp.2d 199, 202 (D. Mass. 1999); Pendell v. AMS/Oil, Inc. 1986 U.S. Dist. Lexis 26089 (D. Mass. 1986); Becker v. Computer Sciences Corp. 541 F.Supp.694, 703–05 (S.D. Tex. 1982).

[106] Kearney v. Salomon Smith Barney Inc., 39 Cal. 4th 95 (2006); Koch v. Kimball, 710 So.2d 5 (Fla. App. 1998).

[107] Broadcast of Telephone Conversations, 47 C.F.R. § 73.1206.

[108] *Richard Perez-Pena and Nate Schweber,* Roommate Is Arraigned in Rutgers Suicide Case, *N.Y. Times, May 23, 2011, at A22.* Ex-Rutgers Student Found Guilty in Webcam Suicide Case, *ABC.News, March 17, 2012.*

A Pennsylvania school district gave free MacBook laptops to students and then used the webcams inside them to spy on the students at home. The remotely activated security software loaded on the computers triggered the iSight camera above the screen to take photos every 15 minutes, capturing students in their bedrooms, sometimes in a state of partial undress. The software also captured screen shots of their activities on the Web. More than 57,000 images were recorded. When students signed the paperwork to receive the laptops, they were not told that the computer contained software that could be remotely activated. The surveillance came to light when a 15-year-old boy was called into his vice principal's office and accused of taking drugs at home in his bedroom. The student said the photo showed him eating Mike & Ike candy. His parents sued for invasion of privacy. A second student photographed also filed suit. The school district activated the software 42 times in 14 months to find lost or stolen computers, but could not explain why it continued to capture images of students once it was clear that the cameras were in their homes. The Federal Bureau of Investigation reviewed the case, but decided not to charge anyone in the district because it did not have enough evidence to prove criminal intent beyond a reasonable doubt. The school district settled the suits for $610,000.[109]

All states allow people to use hidden video cameras, commonly called nanny cams, in their homes. However, in states in which it is illegal to audio record someone without permission, the video must be captured without audio.

The freedom to record in one's own home does not extend to landlords who want to spy on their tenants. In *Hamberger v. Eastman* (1964), the New Hampshire Supreme Court found that a landlord who had installed a hidden audio transmitting and recording device in his tenants' bedroom had violated their privacy through intrusion upon seclusion.[110]

Use of video in public places

Controversies related to the use of video cameras in public places are almost always tied to state wiretapping laws rather than hidden video laws – specifically the ability of video cameras to capture audio without permission.

Businesses commonly use hidden security cameras – without audio – to guard against theft. These cameras are perfectly legal, as long as they are placed in public areas and not areas in which employees or customers have a legitimate expectation of privacy, such as restrooms, locker rooms, or changing rooms.

Government agencies are increasingly using the same type of close-circuit monitoring that companies have traditionally used to conduct surveillance of public places. This type of public surveillance is common in Europe, particularly in the United Kingdom, but is newer in the United States. Because we have no expectation of privacy in public places, the cameras are legal, as long as their audio capabilities are turned off to avoid wiretapping concerns.

---

[109]John P. Martin, *Lower Merion District's Laptop Saga Ends with $610,000 Settlement*, PHIL. INQUIRER, Oct. 12, 2010, at A01.
[110]106 N.H. 107 (1964).

Presumably, the same right should apply to citizens who want to video government officials in public places. However, there have been several disturbing cases in which police have arrested citizens who recorded them in public for violating wiretapping laws. This has occurred in Florida, Maryland, Massachusetts, New Hampshire and Illinois – all states that require all parties to consent to audio recording. Some of the videos suggested police misconduct. For example, in 2010 a bystander's video showed a New York police officer purposely knocking a man off his bicycle in a bike parade. The police officer had claimed in his report that the cyclist had tried to collide with him. After a video of the incident appeared on YouTube, the officer was fired for filing a false report.[111] Another case concerned a woman who secretly taped two Chicago police officers without their permission because she believed they were trying to persuade her to drop a sexual harassment suit against another officer. The law included an exception for secret recording when citizens had a reasonable suspicion that an illegal act was being committed. A jury acquitted her after listening to the tape and finding that she was being intimidated.[112]

The U.S. Court of Appeals for the First Circuit held in 2011 that the First Amendment protects the right to publicly record the activities of police officers in *Glik v. Cunniffe*. In 2007, Simon Glik, a criminal offense attorney in Massachusetts, was walking through Boston Common when he observed three police officers arresting a teenager and overheard a bystander say, "You're hurting him." Glik used his mobile phone to capture video of the arrest. Afterward, he was arrested and charged with violating Massachusetts' wiretap law by recording audio without permission, disturbing the peace, and aiding in the escape of a prisoner (who was already in handcuffs). Glik filed a civil complaint against the officers for violations of his First and Fourth Amendment rights.

The Court of Appeals concluded that the First Amendment not only prohibits government from abridging speech, but also "encompasses a range of conduct related to the gathering and dissemination of information."[113] The court added that this right applies equally to the press and public because "the public's right of access to information is coextensive with that of the press."[114] The court further observed that because so many of us are carrying mobile phones with cameras, bystanders are supplying pictures of current events and bloggers are breaking news stories. "Such developments make clear why the news-gathering protections of the First Amendment cannot turn on professional credentials or status."[115] Finally, the court concluded that since Glik was recording in the open, he was not violating the wiretapping law by recording secretly.

The U.S. Department of Justice took a stand on the issue in 2012, when it filed a brief in a federal case in Maryland arguing that citizens should be allowed to video police in

---

[111] Joseph Cucco, *The Expanding Trend of Criminalizing the Recording of Police Abuse*, ALBANY GOV'T L. REV., Nov.13,2010,availableathttp://aglr.wordpress.com/2010/11/13/the-expanding-trend-of-criminalizing-the-recording-of-police-abuse/.

[112] Natasha Korecki, *Influential Judge: Expanding Eavesdropping is Bad Idea*, CHI. SUN-TIMES, Sept. 14, 2011, at 18.

[113] Glik v. Cunniffee, 655 F.3d. 78, 82 (1st Cir. 2011).

[114] *Id.* at 83.

[115] *Id.* at 84.

public. In that case, the plaintiff had recorded police arresting his friend at Pimlico Racetrack. Police ordered him to surrender the phone he used to record the arrest and then deleted the video. The DOJ wrote in the brief:

> The right to record police officers while performing duties in a public place, as well as the right to be protected from the warrantless seizure and destruction of those recordings, are not only required by the Constitution. They are consistent with our fundamental notions of liberty, promote the accountability of our governmental officers, and instill public confidence in the police officers who serve us daily.[116]

The determination of whether recording the police in public violates the Constitution is not up to the Justice Department but, as the nation's leading law enforcement agency, its opinion matters.

Other courts are still considering the issue. The Seventh Circuit will review *ACLU v. Alvarez* (2011), a case in which the ACLU requested a declaratory judgment that the Illinois Eavesdropping Act, is unconstitutional because it makes recording officers in public without their permission a felony. In this case, the district court held that protecting the right to record police would be "an unprecedented expansion of the First Amendment."[117]

Many excellent investigative journalism pieces that resulted in social reform could not have been as successful without hidden cameras. But that doesn't mean courts assume that journalists are entitled to use them.

ABC lost a suit involving a *Primetime Live* hidden-camera report showing Food Lion selling spoiled meat and rat-gnawed cheese. Although there were inaccuracies in the story, Food Lion chose not to sue for libel because the taped evidence was damning. Instead it focused on the newsgathering practices used. *Primetime Live*'s producers used phony resumés to get jobs in Food Lion stores in North and South Carolina and then wore hidden cameras under wigs to document food preparation. Filming was done in the public and nonpublic areas of the stores. As a company, Food Lion could not sue for invasion of privacy, nor could it sue for violation of the wiretapping law because the secret recording occurred in one-party consent states. Instead Food Lion sued for fraud and trespass based on the fact that access to the stores was achieved through deception. The jury, which never saw the *Primetime* episode, awarded Food Lion $5.5 million in compensatory and punitive damages. The Fourth Circuit, which considered Food Lion's suit to be "an end-run" around the First Amendment, reduced the fine to $2: $1 for trespassing and $1 for breaching their legal duty of loyalty to Food Lion as employer.[118]

[116] Brief for U.S. Department of Justice Supporting Plaintiff, Sharp v. Baltimore City Police Department, Civil No. 1:11-cv-02888-BEL (D. Md. Filed Jan. 10, 2012).

[117] American Civil Liberties Union v. Alvarez, Civil Action No.: 10 C 5235 (N.D. Ill. January 10, 2011), 2011 U.S. Dist. LEXIS 2088 at *13.

[118] Food Lion, Inc. v. Capital Cities/ABC, Inc., 194 F.3d 505, 512 (4th Cir. 1999).

Workplace Privacy

Most companies monitor their employees' communications in some form to guarantee productivity, make sure that trade secrets are not being shared, prevent their resources from being used for illegal activities, and avoid liability incurred or embarrassment related to employee communications.

Companies have been held liable for the e-mail actions of their employees.[119] Chevron Corporation, for example, paid a $2.2 million settlement to employees who demonstrated evidence of sexual e-mail harassment.[120] They have also suffered public relations disasters, such as the crisis Dominos incurred when two of its employees posted a video on YouTube of themselves contaminating customer food.

According to a 2007 American Management Association survey, 66 percent of companies monitor employees' Internet use.[121] Companies monitor computer use in various ways: 45 percent track keystrokes and web content, 43 percent store and review computer files, and 43 percent retain and review e-mail messages. The survey also showed that 45 percent of employers track the telephone numbers called by employees, 16 percent record phone conversations, and 9 percent review employee phone mail.

Under the Electronic Communications Privacy Act, employers that operate as Internet service providers may tap into their own networks to access employee communications and files without liability. The service provider exception states:

> It shall not be unlawful . . . for . . . a provider of wire or electronic communication service, whose facilities are used in the transmission of a wire communication, to intercept, disclose, or use that communication in the normal course of his employment while engaged in any activity which is a necessary incident to the rendition of his service or to the protection of the rights or property of the provider of that service . . . [122]

This provision does not, however, entitle companies that provide Internet service to the public to monitor users' messages beyond what may be necessary for "mechanical or service quality control checks."[123]

Companies that do not provide their own network for communications still may avoid liability for accessing employee communications if they acquire their employees' express or implied consent to access computer files stored on another server. Continued use of a computer after being informed of an employer's monitoring policy may be interpreted as implied consent.

---

[119] *See* Burlington Industries, Inc. v. Ellerth, 524 U.S. 742 (1998); Faragher v. City of Boca Raton, 524 U.S. 775 (1998).

[120] John Yaukey, *Firms Crack Down on E-Mail*, USA TODAY, June 28, 2000, at 2B.

[121] American Marketing Association and ePolicy Institute, 2007 Electronic Monitoring & Surveillance Survey, http://press.amanet.org/press-releases/177/2007-electronic-monitoring-surveillance-survey/. (A total of 304 U.S. companies participated: 27% represent companies employing 100 or fewer workers, 101–500 employees (27%), 501–1,000 (12%), 1,001–2,500 (12%), 2,501–5,000 (10%), and 5,001 or more (12%)).

[122] 18 U.S.C. § 2511 (2)(a)(i) (2011).

[123] *Id.*

Some employees have tried to sue their employers for monitoring their computer activity under the common law tort of intrusion to seclusion. These cases usually fail because employees have no reasonable expectation of privacy on work computers. A lawsuit brought against an employer who searched an employee's personal computer files was dismissed by a Texas appellate court, which found that the employee had no expectation of privacy on a company-owned computer or to e-mails sent over a company network.[124]

Warrantless searches by government employers have also been protected when they are based on reasonable, work-related grounds. For example, the Supreme Court held in *City of Ontario v. Quon* (2010) that the search of a police officer's personal messages on a government-owned pager did not violate his Fourth Amendment rights because it was motivated by legitimate work-related purposes. The city was trying to determine if the additional fees its wireless provider was imposing for text messages were caused by employees using the pagers for personal use.[125] Likewise, the U.S. Court of Appeals for the Fourth Circuit found that a government agency's warrantless review of an employee's click stream data was not a violation of his Fourth Amendment rights because the agency's notice that it would "audit, inspect, and/or monitor" employees' use of the Internet warned employees that they had no reasonable expectation of privacy regarding computer downloads.[126]

Outside of the office, many employers also track their employees' social media use.[127] If the posts are public, employers have a right to read them. California, Colorado, North Dakota and New York have laws that prohibit employers from disciplining employees based on off-duty activity (which should include social networking sites), unless it can be shown to damage the company in some way.[128] A Connecticut statute protects off-duty speech that addresses a matter of public concern.[129] The National Labor Relations Board has also stepped in to protect workers in private companies from retaliation for social networking posts when their comments focused on work conditions. The Wagner Act (a.k.a. National Labor Relations Act) guarantees that employees can hold discussions outside of work about their labor conditions and doesn't specify where they can be held. NLRB administrative law judges have ordered employees who were fired for online exchanges with coworkers about their employment conditions reinstated.[130]

In 2012, Maryland became the first state to prohibit an employer from asking applicants or employees to disclose their passwords, or any other means of access, to personal online accounts, including social networking sites.

---

[124] McLaren v. Microsoft Corp., No. 05-97-00824-CV (Tex. Ct. App. 5th Dist. 1999), 1999 Tex. App. LEXIS 4103 at *4.

[125] 130 S. Ct. 2619 (2010).

[126] United States v. Simons, 206 F.3d 392, 396 (4th Cir. 2000).

[127] Social Networks in the Workplace Around the World, Nov. 2011, http://www.proskauer.com/ (A survey of 120 companies found that 44% of companies tracked their employees' social networking at work and away from work.)

[128] 9 Cal. Labor Code § 96(k) (West 2008); Colo. Rev. Stat. § 24-34-402.5; N.D. Cent. Code § 14-02.4-03; N.Y. Labor Code § 201-d; N.D. Cent. Code § 14-02.4-01.

[129] Conn. Gen. Stat. Ann.§ 31–51 Q (West 2003).

[130] Seth Borden, *ALJ Rules Buffalo Non-Profit Unlawfully Fired Employees for Facebook Postings*, LABOR RELATIONS TODAY, Sept. 6, 2011, available at http://www.laborrelationstoday.com/2011/09/articles/nlrb-decisions/alj-rules-buffalo-nonprofit-unlawfully-fired-employees-for-facebook-postings/.

Marketplace Privacy

One of the fastest growing enterprises online is the tracking of Internet users, using sophisticated software for the purpose of gathering data, developing profiles about them, and selling it to advertisers. Most online retailers and heavily trafficked sites on the Internet use *cookies* to gather information. These are small data files implanted on your hard drive when you visit a site. When you return, the cookie "reminds" the site about what you looked at before so it can tailor information and advertising to your interests. Standard cookies can be deleted from your browser, but advertisers are now employing a more persistent model, known as *supercookies*, or Flash cookies, that are not deleted when you clear your browser. These tracking devices, found on sites like Hulu and Pandora, are capable of storing more information, such as keystrokes made on a site, videos accessed, and other sites visited. Tracking companies also use unique

Figure 10.2   Illustration: Kalan Lyra

identifiers to follow users' activities, such as the Internet protocol address associated with a computer or the collection of attributes associated with particular mobile devices, like phones and tablets.

Internet users are generally unaware of the type and extent of information collected about them when they are online or how that information is used after it is collected. Efforts to curb tracking have been largely unsuccessful, except when trackers have made promises about their data collection practices that they failed to keep. These commitments are usually available on their websites. Of course, to find the policies, you would need to know who is tracking you.

The use of cookies to gather information from Internet users is not a privacy violation because their use falls within the Electronic Communications Privacy Act's consent exemption. DoubleClick, Google's Internet marketing company, uses cookies to gather information from computers that visit any of the thousands of websites affiliated with its network. Because cookies include a unique identifier for each computer that visits a site, DoubleClick has the power to track users across websites to build well-rounded profiles of users that it then uses to target them with ads for its clients. Plaintiffs who were targeted for profiling filed a class action suit against the company, alleging that its activities violated the Wiretap Act, the Stored Communications Act, and the Computer Fraud and Abuse Act. A federal court dismissed the claims, finding that DoubleClick's actions fell within the exemptions for the Wiretap Act and Stored Communications Act because DoubleClick's *clients* consented to its activities, and that any damages that might have occurred from the cookies did not meet the Computer Fraud and Abuse Act's threshold for minimum damages.

The Wiretap Act prohibits the intentional interception of a wire communication. But the statute includes an exception for interceptions conducted with permission by one of the parties to the communication. The communications in question occurred between the plaintiffs and DoubleClick's clients. Because DoubleClick's clients had authorized its interception of their communications, DoubleClick's actions fell squarely within the statute's exception.

The Stored Communications Act prohibits unauthorized access to a facility through which electronic information service is provided. But the statue includes an exemption that shields conduct authorized "by a user of communication service with respect to a communication of or intended for that user." The court concluded that the service through which the communications took place was not the plaintiffs' computers but their Internet service. The court reasoned that DoubleClick's clients' websites were authorized users of the Internet service because plaintiffs had voluntarily sought access to their websites through it. As such, DoubleClick's clients could authorize DoubleClick to access information intended for them.[131]

However, the use of cookies may be illegal if the tracking company exceeds its authorization. A lower court dismissed a suit against Pharmatrak, a company that used cookies to track user movements on pharmaceutical websites, based on the reasoning

The process of logging unique identifiers, information such as IP addresses, or unique combinations of attributes, such as the operating system, browser OS and version, etc., on devices is called digital fingerprinting.

---

[131] *In re* DoubleClick, Inc. Privacy Litigation, 154 F. Supp. 2d 497 (S.D. N.Y. 2001).

in *DoubleClick*. But the First Circuit reinstated the suit. The appellate court held that when website owners gave Pharmatrak permission to measure traffic on their websites, their permission did not constitute authorization to intercept communications with site users. In this case, the site owners expressly instructed defendant Pharmatrak not to gather personal information about site users and later found out that, in some cases, it had. Under the circumstances, Pharmatrak did not qualify for the immunity Double-Click had enjoyed.

False claims made about data collection practices may violate laws prohibiting deceptive marketing practices. ScanScout claimed that users could avoid data collection by setting their browsers to block its cookies. But it used Flash cookies, which could only be deleted through Adobe's website. The Federal Trade Commission found the company's claims to be deceptive. ScanScout was required to post a prominent notice on its website informing users that it collects information about their activities and to provide users with a mechanism to opt-out of that information collection.[132]

A great deal of information amassed by Internet marketers is collected from Internet users who provide it voluntarily by filling out online forms. Privacy law does not protect information that has been given away. This is so "even if the information is revealed on the assumption that it will be used only for a limited purpose and the confidence placed in the third party will not be betrayed."[133] Unless a marketer has specifically promised not to share the information it collects from users, it is within its rights to share or even sell your information to data brokers who aggregate personal information from multiple sources.

None of the common law invasion of privacy torts applies to the collection and sale of information for marketing purposes. It is not an intrusion upon seclusion because people willingly visit sites where information is collected and often provide information to them voluntarily. The information that marketers sell is not a disclosure of private facts because it is either volunteered, or in the case of information gathered surreptitiously through cookies, not considered extremely personal. Nor is the information publicly disclosed, although it is sold to other companies. False light does not apply because the user is not intentionally misrepresented. Nor does misappropriation, which would seem to be the most applicable tort because the information is used for commercial purposes. The New Hampshire Supreme Court explained that "An investigator who sells personal information sells the information for the value of the information itself, not to take advantage of the person's reputation or prestige . . ." Consequently, "a person whose personal information is sold does not have a cause of action for appropriation against the investigator who sold the information."[134]

In contrast, to the relatively loose privacy policies employed by the United States, the European Union gives individuals control over their personal data through its Data

Delete your own supercookies by following this link: http://phtshp.us/2fZi and clicking on "website storage settings panel." A pop-up window will indicate the supercookies stored on your computer. You can delete them all or individually.

---

[132] In the matter of ScanScout, FTC Decision and Order, DOCKET NO. C-4344, Dec. 14, 2011; FTC No. 102 3185, ScanScout, Inc.; Analysis of Proposed Consent Order To Aid Public Comment, 76 Fed. Reg. 223, Nov. 18, 2011.

[133] United States v. Miller, 425 U.S. 435, 443 (1976).

[134] Remsburg v. Docusearch, Inc., 149 N.H. 148, 158 (N.H. 2003).

Protection Directive.[135] Marketers cannot collect personal data from EU citizens without informing them first and explaining how the data will be used. However, even the EU is having trouble controlling cookies. In 2009, the EU passed a rule prohibiting marketers from tracking Internet users and selling their data without consumers' permission. EU marketers were supposed to offer consumers an "opt-in" option to receive cookies rather than an "opt-out" option. But the complexity of allowing users to opt-in to every cyber cookie a site wants or even needs to place on a user's hard drive has become unwieldy. An average site contains 10–20 cookies. Large sites may contain hundreds. By 2011, most countries weren't enforcing the law and the EU was considering reverting to an opt-out option.

Non-European Union nations that offer inadequate safeguards for data privacy may be blocked from doing business with EU citizens. The U.S. Department of Commerce has established a Safe Harbor Program to facilitate continued trade with EU nations. American companies that comply with EU privacy standards may join the program.

Privacy and Social Networking

Privacy concerns related to social networking range from information shared without the user's permission to data security lapses to simple errors in user judgment.

All privacy on social networking sites begins with the user agreement. Most people who click "OK" when they register for these sites don't read the terms of service, but they should because it is a binding agreement that specifies what the site can and cannot do with their information. Liability related to privacy on social networking sites is almost always connected to whether the site has violated that policy. Between 2010 and 2011, the FTC finalized privacy settlements with Google, Twitter and Facebook over privacy violations.

The Federal Trade Commission charged Google with violating its privacy policy in 2011. Google launched its Buzz social network in 2010 and attempted to capitalize on its successful Gmail service by pushing its e-mail users into the social network. Some who declined were enrolled anyway. Those who clicked on the option to "Check out the Buzz" were enrolled without being informed that their e-mail contacts would be made public.

Google's privacy policy at the time stated "When you sign up for a particular service that requires registration, we ask you to provide personal information. If we use this information in a manner different than the purpose for which it was collected, then we will ask for your consent prior to such use." The FTC asserted that Google violated its privacy policy by using data collected for e-mail for the new social network, and that the company deceived its subscribers by suggesting that they had a choice regarding participation in the Buzz. The FTC's 2011 settlement bars Google from future privacy misrepresentations, requires the company to implement a comprehensive privacy program, and mandates regular, independent privacy audits for the next 20

---

[135] European Union Directive 95/46/EC of the European Parliament and of the Council art. 4, EU O.J. L, 1995.

years.[136] Google responded by issuing one privacy policy meant to cover all of its services, which indicated that it would share data across services when consumers were logged into their Google accounts.

The FTC's settlement with Facebook was triggered by retroactive changes the company made to its privacy policy. The FTC determined that Facebook made promises to users that it didn't keep. According to the FTC's complaint,

- In December 2009, Facebook changed its website so certain information that users may have designated as private – such as their Friends List – was made public. They didn't warn users that this change was coming, or get their approval in advance.
- Facebook represented that third-party apps that users installed would have access only to user information that they needed to operate. In fact, the apps could access nearly all of users' personal data – data the apps didn't need.
- Facebook told users they could restrict sharing of data to limited audiences – for example with "Friends Only." In fact, selecting "Friends Only" did not prevent their information from being shared with third-party applications their friends used.
- Facebook had a "Verified Apps" program & claimed it certified the security of participating apps. It didn't.
- Facebook promised users that it would not share their personal information with advertisers. It did.
- Facebook claimed that when users deactivated or deleted their accounts, their photos and videos would be inaccessible. But Facebook allowed access to the content, even after users had deactivated or deleted their accounts.
- Facebook claimed that it complied with the U.S.- EU Safe Harbor Framework that governs data transfer between the U.S. and the European Union. It didn't.[137]

The settlement required Facebook to seek permission from users in the future before changing its terms of service. Like the settlement with Google, it also required 20 years of independent privacy audits.

Facebook has a pretty spotty record where privacy is concerned. In 2011, five class action suits were filed against the company when it came to light that those "Like" button widgets on pages all over the Web actually send home tracking information to the mother ship. If users log in to Facebook and then forget to click "logout" before leaving, Facebook continues to track their movements across the Web.[138] A study done by the *Wall Street Journal* found that Twitter tracks members through its widgets as well.

[136] In the matter of Google, Inc., FTC Decision and Order, DOCKET NO. C-4336, Oct. 13, 2011, FTC No. 102 3136; Google, Inc.; Analysis of Proposed Consent Order To Aid Public Comment, 76 Fed. Reg. 65, April 5, 2011.

[137] Facebook Settles FTC Charges That It Deceived Consumers By Failing To Keep Privacy Promises, FTC release, Nov. 29, 2011, http://ftc.gov/opa/2011/11/privacysettlement.shtm Facebook, Inc.; Analysis of Proposed, Consent Order To Aid Public Comment. 76 Fed. Reg. 233, Dec. 5, 2011.

[138] Amir Efrati, *Like Button Follows Web Users*, WALL STREET J., May 18, 2011, http://online.wsj.com/article/SB10001424052748704281504576329441432995616.html#ixzz1dkSj7o20. ("For this to work, a person only needs to have logged into Facebook or Twitter once in the past month. The sites will continue to collect browsing data, even if the person closes their browser or turns off their computers, until that person explicitly logs out of their Facebook or Twitter accounts, the study found.")

Other social networking problems stem from data security lapses. The FTC reached a settlement with Twitter in 2010, contending that it deceived consumers by failing to safeguard their personal information.[139] The FTC charged that holes in Twitter's security allowed hackers to obtain control over Twitter by guessing its administrative password. The hackers not only gained access to private user information, they sent out fake tweets from accounts that belonged to then-President-elect Barack Obama and Fox News, among others. David Vladeck, Director of the FTC's Bureau of Consumer Protection said "Consumers who use social networking sites may choose to share some information with others, but they still have a right to expect that their personal information will be kept private and secure."[140] As part of its settlement with the FTC, Twitter was barred from misleading consumers about the extent to which it protects the security and confidentiality of nonpublic consumer information for 20 years. It was also required to establish a comprehensive information security program, assessed for a 10-year period by an independent auditor.

In other examples of security breaches, a hacker using a security hole in MySpace accessed half a million images from private profiles and released them for anyone to download.[141] Third-party games providers on Facebook also lured subscribers into revealing their Social Security numbers.[142]

The increasing use of social networking sites and online games by minors has created more opportunities for predators to approach them. When a 14-year-old girl from Austin, Texas, was raped by a man she met through MySpace, the girl's parents sued News Corp, MySpace's owner, for negligence in failing to take reasonable steps to ensure minors' safety. The Fifth Circuit affirmed a lower court's judgment that their claims were barred by Section 230 of the Communications Decency Act, which spares online services from liability for their users' posts. But negative publicity prompted the social networking site to tighten its policies involving minors.

Users of services like Foursquare and Gowalla incur a security risk by posting their locations and linking them to Facebook and Twitter. Pictures taken with smart phones often include GPS coordinates in Exchangeable Image File Format (EXIF) data encoded in the photograph. Facebook automatically removes EXIF data from uploaded photos, but most photo-sharing sites do not.

Realistically, though, the larger danger teens face online is that they will post personal information without understanding the long-term implications of what they reveal. Schools and employers now use these sites to search for evidence of poor behavior before admitting or hiring new candidates. Raunchy language on a Twitter feed or revealing party pics on a Facebook page with inadequate privacy settings could easily undermine a young person's goals.

---

[139] In the Matter of Twitter, Inc., Federal Trade Commission Decision and Order, DOCKET NO: C-4316, March 2, 2011, FTC No. 092 3093.

[140] Twitter Settles Charges that it Failed to Protect Consumers' Personal Information; Company Will Establish Independently Audited Information Security Program, Federal Trade Commission Release, June 24, 2010, http://www.ftc.gov/opa/2010/06/twitter.shtm.

[141] Kevin Poulsen, *Pillaged MySpace Photos Show Up in Massive BitTorrent Download*, WIRED, Jan. 23, 2008, available at http://www.wired.com/politics/security/news/2008/01/myspace_torrent.

[142] Facebook Games Could Lead To Identity Theft, WBAL-TV, July 6, 2008.

Ironically, parents are helping their children join social networking sites before they even understand what privacy really means. Most social networking sites don't want to deal with the Children's Online Privacy Protection Act's strict privacy protections, so they block access to preteens. It's not hard to get around the age limit, though. Applicants just have to lie about their birth date. In its 2011 State of the Net Survey, Consumer Reports found that 7.5 million Facebook users are younger than 13 and more than 5 million are younger than 10.[143] A study conducted by Harris Interactive, in conjunction with academics from Harvard, UC Berkeley and Northwestern, surveyed more than 1,000 parents of children between 10 and 14. Nearly 20 percent of parents with 10-year-olds acknowledged their child was on Facebook. One third of parents with 11-year-olds knew their children were subscribers. And more than half of parents with 12-year-olds knew their kids had Facebook accounts. Further, 68 percent of the parents of kids with accounts helped their children create them.[144]

Anonymity Online

A lot of Internet users value anonymity – a right the Supreme Court has found worthy of protection. It has said an author's decision to remain anonymous, like other decisions concerning omissions or additions to the content of a publication, is an aspect of freedom of speech protected by the First Amendment.[145]

Without a guarantee of anonymity, distribution of information would be reduced from those who fear official, economic, and social retaliation. In the realm of political speech, the Court imposes a test of exacting scrutiny on government actions affecting anonymous speech. Restrictions must be "narrowly tailored to serve an overriding state interest."[146]

A U.S. district court struck down a Georgia statute that barred the use of pseudonyms online because it was a content-based restriction that was both vague and overbroad. Not only did it "sweep[] protected activity within its proscription," said the court, but it also failed to "define the criminal offense with sufficient definiteness" so that ordinary people could understand what conduct was prohibited.[147]

States do have a compelling interest in preventing anonymous speech that causes harm. In fraud or libel cases, for example, they must decide when it is appropriate to

---

[143] CR Survey: 7.5 Million Facebook Users are Under the Age of 13, Violating the Site's Terms, CONSUMER REPORTS, May 10, 2011, http://pressroom.consumerreports.org/pressroom/2011/05/cr-survey-75-million-facebook-users-are-under-the-age-of-13-violating-the-sites-terms-.html.

[144] Danah Doy, Eszter Hargittai, Jason Schultz, and John Palfrey, Why Parents Help Their Children Lie to Facebook About Age: Unintended Consequences of the "Children's Online Privacy Protection Act", FIRST MONDAY, Vol. 16, No. 11, Nov. 7, 2011, http://www.uic.edu/htbin/cgiwrap/bin/ojs/index.php/fm/article/view/3850/3075

[145] See MacIntyre v. Ohio Elections Commission, 514 U.S. 334 (1995) (striking down an election law against anonymous campaign literature).

[146] Id. at 347.

[147] ACLU v. Miller, 977 F. Supp. 1228 (N.D. Ga. 1997) (citing M.S. News Co. v. Casado, 721 F.2d 1281, 1287 (10th Cir. 1983) and Kolender v. Lawson, 461 U.S. 352, 357 (1983)).

require disclosure of a speaker's name. The two leading cases on the subject are *Dendrite International v. John Doe* (2001) and *Doe v. Cahill* (2005). In *Dendrite* a New Jersey appellate court developed a four-part test to determine when it is appropriate to unmask an Internet speaker.[148] The test, used by states like Connecticut, New Jersey, New York and Maryland, requires plaintiffs to:

1. make a reasonable effort to notify the anonymous poster that an identification proceeding is pending;
2. identify the exact statements the poster made;
3. present sufficient evidence to support a cause of action against the defendant; and
4. show the court that, on balance, the defendant's First Amendment right of anonymous free speech does not outweigh the plaintiff's right to identify the speaker.

In *Doe v. Cahill*, the Delaware Supreme Court relied on a simplified alternative.[149] A plaintiff must (1) make a reasonable effort to notify the anonymous poster that he or she is subject to a subpoena for identity disclosure and (2) submit evidence of a claim sufficient to survive a motion for summary judgment before the court will compel disclosure. The trial court would then balance the defendant's rights against the strength of the plaintiff's case. Courts in Delaware, Massachusetts, Pennsylvania, Texas, and Wisconsin have adopted this standard.[150]

Other states have used modified versions of these tests. Some are satisfied if plaintiffs provide some evidence to support their claim in order to learn a speaker's identity. A lower burden is also imposed on plaintiffs in copyright cases, because most courts assume that copyright law does not implicate the First Amendment.[151]

Government Surveillance

No discussion of privacy law would be complete without reference to government surveillance.

Only 45 days after terrorist attacks on Sept. 11, 2001, Congress passed the USA PATRIOT Act, an acronym for the Uniting and Strengthening America by Providing Appropriate Tools Required to Intercept and Obstruct Terrorism Act. While the PATRIOT Act gives law enforcement agencies the tools they need to fight criminal activity in the digital age, it has been criticized for its potential to violate Americans' civil liberties.

The Act amended laws discussed in this or other chapters to make it easier for law enforcement officials to conduct electronic surveillance and gain access to private

---

[148] Dendrite Int'l v. Doe No. 3, 775 A.2d 756 (N.J. Super. A.D. 2001).

[149] 884 A.2d 451 (Del. 2005).

[150] *See* McMann v. Doe, 460 F. Supp. 2d 259 (D. Mass. 2006); Reunion Industries v. Doe, 2007 WL 1453491 (Pa. Com. Pl. 2007); *In re* Does 1–10, 2007 WL 4328204 (Tex. App. 2007).

[151] Speech: Anonymity, Electronic Frontier Foundation, http://ilt.eff.org/index.php/Speech:_Anonymity (last visited Feb. 6, 2011).

records. Some of the most significant changes were made to the Foreign Intelligence Surveillance Act. FISA prescribes procedures required to conduct electronic surveillance and physical searches of people engaged in espionage or international terrorism on behalf of a foreign power.[152]

Government investigators formerly obtained orders for surveillance from the Foreign Intelligence Surveillance Court when foreign intelligence gathering was the "primary purpose" of the investigation. Now, foreign intelligence need only be a "significant" purpose of the investigation.[153] Consequently, electronic surveillance of Americans – formerly prohibited under FISA – is now allowed if Americans are conversing with foreigners under investigation. This is significant because the standard of proof a court demands for permission to conduct electronic surveillance of Americans under the federal wiretap statute is significantly higher than the standard of proof required for a FISA wiretap. Also, FISA judges refuse very few applications for surveillance and search orders. In 2010, 1579 applications were submitted and 1579 were approved.[154] In the year prior to that only one was rejected.

One of the PATRIOT Act's more controversial provisions expanded roving wiretaps in FISA investigations.[155] Authorities use roving wiretaps to intercept communications made by and to the target of an investigation, rather than to a particular phone or computer. The technique makes sense considering that a subject is likely to use more than one device for communication purposes. However, this form of surveillance inevitably intercepts the messages of all others using devices tapped for the investigation.

Another section of the Act, dubbed the "sneak and peek" provision by its critics, eliminated a requirement that authorities notify the subject of a search about the warrant at the time of the search if the court granting the warrant finds reasonable cause to believe that providing immediate notice would have an adverse affect on the investigation.[156] The legislation originally allowed officials to search a person's home or e-mail and inform the subject of the search "within a reasonable period," without specifying what *reasonable* meant. A 2006 amendment now requires authorities to notify individuals of secret searches within seven days, unless a judge approves an extension.

The PATRIOT Act also allows authorities to request a FISA court order to compel third parties that hold a subject's private communications or financial, medical or educational records to release them to investigators.[157] Federal authorities may use a *national security letter*, without court approval, to demand communication routing information from third parties, such as the phone numbers, e-mail addresses or websites accessed by the subject.[158] Orders such as these are accompanied by injunctions that forbid recipients from telling anyone other than their attorneys about them. Consequently, a

The Foreign Intelligence Surveillance Court, established by FISA, includes 11 judges from different federal circuits that are appointed by the Chief Justice to serve for staggered terms of no more than seven years. Their hearings are closed.

A national security letter is an administrative order sent by the Federal Bureau of Investigation to compel the recipient to release information.

---

[152] 50 U.S.C. § 1801 et seq. (2011).

[153] Pub. L. No. 107–56, § 218, 115 Stat. 272, 291 (2001).

[154] Foreign Intelligence Surveillance Act Court Orders 1979–2010, Electronic Privacy Information Center, http://epic.org/privacy/wiretap/stats/fisa_stats.html (last visited June 2, 2012).

[155] 50 U.S.C. § 1805(c)(1) (2011).

[156] 18 U.S.C. § 3103(a) (2011).

[157] 50 U.S.C. § 1861 (2011).

[158] *Id.* § 1861(a).

recipient of such an order would have no way to inform the subject of a search that his or her information had been demanded without going to court on the person's behalf.

The PATRIOT Act also altered the Pen Register and Trap and Trace Statute to extend its application to all electronic communications.[159] Authorities do not need a court order to install these devices. The Attorney General may authorize their use if the information likely to be obtained is relevant to an ongoing investigation to protect against terrorism or clandestine intelligence activities. The law prohibits authorities from using these devices for investigations of American citizens based solely on their First Amendment activities.

The PATRIOT Act was originally passed on a temporary basis. In 2006, Congress voted to make 14 of its 16 provisions permanent and decided to reexamine the roving wiretap and business record provisions in four years. In 2011, Congress extended them another four years.

Domestic wiretapping and the Foreign Intelligence Surveillance Act

In 2005, *The New York Times* reported that the National Security Agency was conducting a domestic surveillance program that involved the warrantless interception of e-mails and phone calls made from the United States to foreign parties.[160] President Bush authorized the secret program, which exceeded powers provided by the PATRIOT Act, in 2002. He argued that the program was legal under a 2001 congressional resolution authorizing him to use military force against terrorism. Administration sources credited the program with helping to uncover two suspected terrorist attacks.

The article, which the administration asked *The New York Times* not to run and it held for one year, suggested that AT&T and other telecommunication companies funneled international communications through the NSA, which stored them for data mining. At the time, the law required that wiretaps for communications sent abroad from the United States be obtained through a FISA court order with a particular target in mind. FISA was established in 1978 to curb domestic surveillance abuses by the NSA, the Central Intelligence Agency, and the Federal Bureau of Investigation.

AT&T faced as many as 40 private lawsuits for its complicity with the program. It is not clear how many records were drawn into the program, but estimates reach into the millions. Under the Stored Communications Act, telephone companies can be fined $1,000 for each consumer whose records are disclosed without a warrant. In arguing for telecommunication company amnesty, the administration said that the lawsuits could potentially bankrupt the companies.

In 2008, Congress voted to legalize the program through the FISA Amendment Act and granted amnesty to telephone companies that cooperated with the government.[161] The FISA Amendment Act made two important changes to the law. Under the pre-existing law, the government had to submit an application to the Foreign Intelligence

---

[159] 18 U.S.C. § 3121(c) (2007).

[160] James Risen and Eric Lichtblau, *Bush Lets U.S. Spy on Callers Without Courts*, N.Y. TIMES, Dec. 16, 2005, at A1.

[161] FISA Amendment Act of 2008, Public L. No. 110–261.

Surveillance Court identifying the particular target for surveillance, facility to be monitored, type of information sought, and procedures to be used. Under the amended Act, the Attorney General or Director of National Intelligence can apply for a mass surveillance authorization without identifying a particular target or facility to be monitored. Also, under the pre-existing law, the Foreign Intelligence Surveillance Court had to find "probable cause to believe both that the surveillance target is a 'foreign power' or agent" and that "the facilities to be monitored were being used or about to be used by a foreign power or its agent."[162] Under the amended Act, the court no longer needs to make a probable-cause determination. It is sufficient that the government assert that "a significant purpose of the acquisition is to obtain foreign intelligence information" and that the information will be obtained "from or with the assistance of an electronic communication service provider."[163]

In 2011, the Second Circuit allowed Amnesty International, the American Civil Liberties Union, media representatives, and others to challenge the constitutionality of the FISA Amendment Act.[164] A district court had ruled that the appellants lacked standing to sue the government because they had no proof that they had been subjects of government surveillance. The appellants argued that they should have standing because the government's "virtually unregulated authority to monitor international communications" engendered fear that "their communications will be monitored, and force them to undertake costly and burdensome measures to protect the confidentiality of international communications."[165] The Second Circuit held that plaintiffs did have standing to sue because "standing may be based on reasonable fear of future injury and costs incurred to avoid that injury." The government is expected to appeal the case. The blanket authorization for the law expires in 2014.

Geolocation surveillance

The Supreme Court considered whether the installation of a Global Positioning System device on a person's car for surveillance purposes constitutes a "search" that requires a warrant in *United States v. Jones* (2012).[166] The case involved a suspected drug dealer who was monitored, using a GPS device, without a warrant for 28 days. Data from the device, which was attached to the undercarriage of his automobile, provided a link to an alleged drug "stash house" that was critical to his conviction. The U.S. Court of Appeals for the District of Columbia Circuit Court overturned the conviction, holding that the admission of evidence obtained through the warrantless use of GPS tracking violated the defendant's Fourth Amendment right against an unreasonable search. Defending its actions, the government took the position that attaching a GPS tracking device to Jones' car did not constitute a "search" because he had no reasonable expecta-

---

[162] Amnesty International USA v. Clapper, Jr., 638 F.3d 118, 125–26 (2nd Cir. 2011).
[163] *Id.*
[164] *Id.*
[165] *Id.* at 127.
[166] United States v. Jones, No. 10-1259, 2012 U.S. LEXIS 1063 (Jan. 23, 2012).

tion of privacy in the area of the automobile where the device was mounted or on public roads that the car traveled. In an earlier case, the Court had concluded "A person traveling in an automobile on public thoroughfares has no reasonable expectation of privacy in his movements from one place to another."[167] That case, however, involved a defendant who had transported a container that had previously been fitted with a beeper for surveillance purposes. Because the beeper was put into the container with permission of its original owner before the defendant gained possession of it, the Court did not consider its use for surveillance to be an unreasonable search. In contrast, the Court considered the attachment of a GPS device to Jones' car without a warrant to be a property violation akin to trespass.

Although the Court was unanimous in its decision, concurring opinions demonstrated that five of the justices would have preferred to consider the broader ramifications of using such a powerful technology for surveillance. These justices clearly viewed the real issue to be less a trespass than the reasonableness of tracking citizen's movements over an extended period of time. During oral arguments for the case, several of the justices expressed concern that if warrantless GPS tracking were allowed, the U.S. might become an analog of the totalitarian state described in George Orwell's *1984*. What if, for example, police used the GPS capabilities of a service like OnStar or our mobile phones for tracking instead? Because the Court chose to construe the surveillance issue presented in *Jones* so narrowly, these types of questions remain unresolved.

The Fourth Amendment protects the "right of the people to be secure in their persons, houses, papers, and effects, against unreasonable searches and seizures."

Questions for Discussion

1. Who is and is not entitled to privacy protection? How do the rules differ from libel law? Why?
2. Why is it not safe to assume that a privacy rule that applies in another state also applies in yours?
3. Where do we have an "expectation of privacy"?
4. If you find a photograph of a cute child on Flickr.com with a Creative Commons license by the photographer to use the photo for any purpose, is it safe to use the photo commercially?

---

[167] United States v. Knotts, 460 U.S. 276, 281 (1983); *see also* United States v. Karo, 468 U.S. 705 (1984).

11 Sex and Violence

Digital media have made it easier than ever to gain access to pornography and violence. Pay-per-view, dial-a-porn, and the Internet spare individuals the embarrassment of having to go in search of the adult materials they want. Video games and simulations go one step further by enabling users to engage in virtual sex and violence.

Unrivaled access to this kind of speech has precipitated calls for censorship that reflect two schools of thought. Some want graphic representations of sex and violence controlled because they are offensive and disturbing. Others believe obscene and violent media should be controlled because they contribute to anti-social behavior. A few media scholars have argued that pornography is associated with abuse of women and children.[1] At the other end of the spectrum are researchers who doubt that violent media have any impact on behavior.

Social scientists have tried to determine the effect of media on human behavior for nearly a century with inconclusive results. Although they have observed *correlations* between the use of violent media and aggression, they are still at odds over whether cause and effect can be demonstrated outside a laboratory setting.[2] Nevertheless, the popular assumption is that media do have an impact on our behavior. Legislators have responded to this concern by prohibiting the dissemination of obscenity and restricting children's access to indecency. Some states have also imposed restrictions on children's access to violent media. Meanwhile a number of individuals have sued companies that produce violent entertainment thought to have inspired violent acts.

> Two attributes are said to be correlated when they vary together.

---

[1] *See, e.g.,* CATHARINE A. MACKINNON, ONLY WORDS 17 (1993).

[2] Paul Boxer, L. Rowell Huseman, et al., *The Role of Media Preference in Cumulative Developmental Risk for Violence and General Aggression*, 38 J. YOUTH ADOLESCENCE 417 (2009); CRAIG ANDERSON, DOUGLAS GENTILE & KATHERINE BUCKLEY, VIOLENT VIDEO GAME EFFECTS ON CHILDREN AND ADOLESCENTS (2007); Office of the Surgeon General, *Youth violence: A report of the Surgeon General* (2001) http://www.surgeongeneral.gov/library/youthviolence/; Office of the Surgeon General, *Television and growing up: The impact of televised violence* (1972), http://www.surgeongeneral.gov/library/reports/index.html.

Digital Media Law, Second Edition. Ashley Packard.
© 2013 John Wiley & Sons, Inc. Published 2013 by John Wiley & Sons, Inc.

This chapter will discuss the legal restraints that can and cannot be imposed on sex and violence in media products. It will also discuss the extent to which speech used to intimidate others and precipitate violence can be controlled.

Obscenity and Indecency

A central tenet of First Amendment law is that speech cannot be censored because it expresses unpopular ideas or opinions. In fact, Justice Oliver Wendell Holmes wrote "[I]f there is any principle of the Constitution that more imperatively calls for attachment than any other it is the principle of free thought – not free thought for those who agree with us but freedom for the thought that we hate."[3] Obscenity is the exception to that rule. In the United States, obscenity is regulated because it is offensive to others. Indecency, however, is still protected under the First Amendment.

What's the difference?

The primary difference between indecency and obscenity is that one is legal and the other is not. Indecency is constitutionally protected. All media are entitled to use it, although some limitations have been placed on it.[4] No medium is entitled to show obscenity. The Supreme Court has categorically denied its First Amendment protection.

However, because indecency and obscenity represent a continuum of adult behavior, it is not always easy to tell where one ends and the other begins. In general *indecency* encompasses profanity, references to excretory organs, nudity, and implied sexual behavior. *Obscenity* refers to explicit depictions of actual sexual conduct, masturbation, violent sexual abuse, and child pornography.

For years the Supreme Court struggled to come up with a test for obscenity that would allow communities to restrict what was most offensive without impinging on the rights of adults to produce and have access to material with sexual themes. In *Miller v. California* (1973), the Court produced the three-part test for obscenity now in use:

Miller v. California (1973) established the three-part test currently used to evaluate material challenged as obscene.

The word *prurient* refers to a deviant and unhealthy interest in sex.

- an average person, applying contemporary community standards, must find that the material, as a whole, appeals to the prurient interest;
- the material must depict or describe, in a patently offensive way, sexual conduct specifically defined by applicable law; and
- the material, taken as a whole, must lack serious literary, artistic, political, or scientific value.[5]

All three prongs of the test must be met before the material can be declared obscene.

[3] United States v. Schwimmer, 279 U.S. 644, 654–55 (1929) (Holmes, J., dissenting).
[4] *See* Federal Communications Comm'n v. Pacifica, 438 U.S. 726 (1978).
[5] 413 U.S. 15 (1973).

The first two elements of the test are judged by community standards. These can be tricky to establish because people don't like to discuss their sexual interests and stores that sell adult merchandise, which could comment on local demand, are reluctant to become involved with obscenity prosecutions. A Florida attorney defending a man charged with disseminating obscenity through the Internet used Google Trends to establish community standards.[6] Google Trends enables users to compare trends in areas based on the volume of searches for particular terms.[7] Lawrence Walters hoped the data would persuade jurors that residents of Santa Rosa County, where the case was to be tried, searched for sexual material on the Internet more frequently than they might have imagined. The data did, in fact, show that people in the area searched for terms like "group sex" and "orgy" more frequently than generic terms like "boating" or "apple pie." After the data became public, the prosecutor offered Walters's client a reduced sentence in exchange for a plea bargain; there was no trial.

Applying community standards to material on the Internet is problematic because the network has no geographic boundaries. In *Reno v. ACLU* (1997), the Supreme Court struck down a statute that applied community standards to indecency on the Internet. It observed that "the 'community standards' criterion as applied to the Internet means that any communication available to a nation-wide audience will be judged by the standards of the community most likely to be offended by the message."[8] Five years later, though, when confronted with the opportunity to strike down a law that applied community standards to commercial Internet speech considered harmful to minors, the Court fractured on the issue, leaving them in place.[9]

Since then, at least two U.S. Courts of Appeals have split on the issue. The Ninth Circuit held that, because there is no geographical control on the Internet, a national standard should be used to determine whether content on the Internet is obscene.[10] The Eleventh Circuit held that application of the *Miller* standard to Internet obscenity is still appropriate. It concluded that the local community in the region in which the material is downloaded could decide whether it is obscene.[11]

Significantly two U.S. Courts of Appeals have undermined the "taken as a whole" provision of the *Miller* test by upholding convictions from juries who had not seen the work as a whole. In *United States v. Adams* (2009), the Fourth Circuit upheld a conviction based on "representative samples" shown to the jury by a federal agent who testified that he had seen the movie in its entirety, described the film and stated that the rest of the movie's content was similar to the excerpts.[12] The Eleventh Circuit also upheld a lower court's decision to let the prosecution show the jury excerpts of films.[13]

[6] Matt Richtel, *What's Obscene? Defendant Says Google Data Offers a Gauge*, N.Y. TIMES, June 24, 2008 at A1.

[7] www.google.com/trends.

[8] Reno v. ACLU, 521 U.S. 844, 877–78 (1997).

[9] *See* Ashcroft v. ACLU, 535 U.S. 564, 584–85 (2002).

[10] United States v. Kilbride, 584 F.3d 1240 (9th Cir. 2009).

[11] United States v. Little, 365 F. App'x 159 (11th Cir. 2010).

[12] United States v. Adams, No. 08-5261, 2009 U.S. App. LEXIS 16363 (4th Cir. July 24, 2009) (unpublished opinion).

[13] United States v. Little, 365 F. App'x 159 (11th Cir. 2010).

The second leg of the *Miller* test requires the material to be "patently offensive." The Supreme Court considered the meaning of patently offensive in *Jenkins v. Georgia* (1974), a case in which a Georgia theater owner was prosecuted for distributing obscene material because he showed the film *Carnal Knowledge*. It concluded that the term encompassed representations or descriptions of "ultimate sexual acts, normal or perverted, actual or simulated" as well as "masturbation, excretory functions and lewd exhibition of the genitals."[14]

Normally obscenity involves explicit or disturbing imagery. However, in *U.S. v. Alpers* (1950), the Supreme Court held that there was no reason the obscenity statute should be limited to visual material.[15] *Alpers* concerned an obscene record album. A more recent case involved a text-only website called Red Rose, which contained fictional stories involving sex with children. The woman who ran the subscription-based site was convicted of transmitting obscenity through interstate commerce in 2008. Hers was the first conviction for obscenity without visual imagery since the *Miller* case. But the Red Rose stories were never exposed to the *Miller* test at trial. An agoraphobic, the defendant pled guilty to avoid trial in exchange for home detention.[16]

The third prong of the *Miller* test considers the literary, artistic, political, or scientific value of the work taken as a whole.[17] A national, reasonable person standard is used to judge the value of a work, rather than a community standard, under the assumption that a conservative community might judge the value of a controversial work more conservatively.

Production, distribution, and possession of obscenity

In the United States, it is a felony to knowingly produce obscene material intended for distribution through interstate or foreign commerce, or to knowingly transport obscene materials (including via a computer service) for the purpose of sale or distribution.[18] A first offense is punishable by a fine of up to $250,000 or up to five years in prison, or both. If the material is transmitted to a minor under the age of 16, the punishment can increase to 10 years.[19]

By restricting the statute's application to activities that take place through "interstate or foreign commerce," Congress brings obscenity within its jurisdiction to regulate under the Constitution's commerce clause. Congress has also imposed a requirement for *scienter* on obscenity prosecutions, meaning that individuals must know or have reason to know they are committing an illegal act before they can be held liable for it. A law that imposes liability without scienter is known as a strict liability statute. In *Smith v. California* (1959), the Supreme Court struck down a state law that applied strict liabil-

---

[14] Jenkins v. Georgia, 418 U.S. 153, 160 (1974).

[15] 338 U.S. 680 (1950).

[16] U.S. v. Fletcher, No. CR 06-329 (W.D. Pa. Aug. 7, 2008).

[17] Pope v. Illinois, 481 U.S. 497, 500–01 (1987).

[18] 18 U.S.C. §§ 1461, 1462, 1465 (2011).

[19] *Id.* § 1470.

ity to the distribution of obscenity.[20] The petitioner in the case was a bookstore owner convicted of possessing an obscene book. The Supreme Court reasoned that imposing liability on media distributors who do not have actual knowledge of the character of the material they are distributing would likely burden the First Amendment. Distributors facing strict liability would sell only what they were able to review. The natural result would be a reduction in their inventories, which would deny the public access to constitutionally protected media. This does not mean, however, that a prosecutor must prove that a distributor has actual knowledge that a particular work is obscene. A general knowledge of the material's sexual orientation is sufficient to meet the scienter requirement.

The obscenity statute is somewhat confusing as worded because it also prohibits the transport of "lewd, lascivious . . . filthy . . . [and] indecent" materials, which are protected. Despite the additional language, the Supreme Court construes the statute to refer solely to obscenity.[21] The statute also criminalizes the transmission of materials related to abortion, including any information about how, where, or from whom one can be obtained. The Justice Department does not enforce these provisions because doing so would violate the First Amendment.[22]

Possession of obscenity with the intent to sell it is illegal.[23] But possession for personal use is not. The Supreme Court held that a Georgia statute that criminalized the possession of obscenity violated the First and Fourteenth Amendments in *Stanley v. Georgia* (1969). The Court could see no reason for the statute other than to enforce morality, an inappropriate justification for state action.[24] Writing for the majority, Justice Marshall stated that "[i]f the First Amendment means anything, it means that a State has no business telling a man, sitting alone in his own house, what books he may read or what films he may watch. Our whole constitutional heritage rebels at the thought of giving government the power to control men's minds."[25] The right to possess obscenity acknowledged in *Stanley v. Georgia* does not create a "correlative right to receive it, transport it, or distribute it."[26] Although the Court has acknowledged a privacy interest in the home, no "zone of constitutionally protected privacy follows such material when it is moved outside the home."[27]

In practice, however, the degree to which the Department of Justice is willing to enforce any laws related to the production, distribution or possession of obscenity involving adults depends on the policy objectives of the current presidential administration. There were four obscenity prosecutions during the eight-year Clinton

[20] 361 U.S. 147 (1959).

[21] *See* Hamling v. United States 418 U.S. 87, 114 (1974): United States v. Orito, 413 U.S. 139, 145 (1973).

[22] *See* Janet Reno, Statement on Justice Department Policy Concerning Abortion Speech, Feb. 9, 1996, at http://www.ciec.org/trial/abort_speech.html.

[23] 18 U.S.C § 1460 (2011).

[24] 394 U.S. 557 (1969).

[25] *Id.* at 565.

[26] *See* 18 U.S.C § 1462, interpreted in United States v. Orito, 413 U.S. 139, 141–43 (1973). *See also* United States v. 12 200-Ft. Reels of Super 8mm Film, 413 U.S. 123 (1973).

[27] United States v. Orito, 413 U.S. at 141–42.

administration. The Bush administration aggressively prosecuted obscenity with more than 40 prosecutions.[28] By 2012, the Obama administration had initiated none, electing instead to focus Justice Department resources on child pornography.

Child pornography

The obscenity statute criminalizes the act of distributing, receiving, or possessing obscene depictions of a child engaged in sexual activity transported through interstate or foreign commerce, by any means, including a computer.[29] In 1977, Congress passed the Protection of Children Against Sexual Exploitation Act, which included an anti-pandering provision that makes it a crime to advertise, promote, or solicit child pornography.[30] A first offense in either case is punishable by a fine of $250,000 and imprisonment of 5–20 years.

Pointing out that "The prevention of sexual exploitation and abuse of children constitutes a government objective of surpassing importance," the Supreme Court upheld a New York law criminalizing the distribution of a sexual performance by a child under 16, even if the film would not have been found legally obscene under the *Miller* test.[31] In *New York v. Ferber* (1982), the Court gave states the leeway to adapt the *Miller* test with respect to pornographic depictions of children. A work need not appeal to the prurient interest of the average person, be "patently offensive," or be considered, as a whole, for its literary, artistic, political, or scientific value.[32] The Court held that the First Amendment does not protect photographic images of real children engaged in sexual conduct.

In *Osborn v. Ohio* (1990), the Court held that possession of child pornography in the privacy of one's home is a crime.[33] It distinguished the case from *Stanley v. Georgia*, which concerned a law prohibiting possession of obscenity on the grounds that it could lead to antisocial conduct. Statutes that ban the possession of child pornography are not concerned with the morality of the person who possesses the material, but with the child victimized through its production.

Virtual child pornography

While the transmission of child pornography online is a known problem, no one knows the extent to which virtual child pornography is. Congress attempted to address new challenges posed by digital imaging software when it passed the Child Pornography Prevention Act of 1996. The Act outlawed the possession of virtual

---

[28]Larry Abramson, *Federal Government Renews Effort to Curb Porn*, National Public Radio, Sept. 27, 2005, *available at* http://www.npr.org/templates/story/story.php?storyId=4865348.
[29]18 U.S.C. § 1466A (2011).
[30]*Id.* § 2252A(a)(3)(B).
[31]458 U.S. 747, 757 (1982).
[32]*Id.* at 763–65.
[33]495 U.S. 103 (1990).

child pornography and material that conveyed the impression of children engaged in sexual acts. The Free Speech Coalition challenged both provisions as facially overbroad, not because they actually limited protected speech, but because they had the potential to. In *Ashcroft. v. Free Speech Coalition* (2002), a narrow majority of the Supreme Court agreed that the ban on virtual child pornography was unconstitutional.[34] Referring to its decision in *New York v. Ferber*, the Court reiterated that child pornography is illegal because it is the product of sexual abuse, not because of the ideas it represents. It reasoned that if virtual child pornography is produced without children, the underlying theory to protect children from harm doesn't hold. The dissenting justices argued that virtual pornography should be banned because it could be indistinguishable from the real thing and government should not be put in the position of having to prove that an image is real to get a conviction. In some child pornography cases, the real child is never found, particularly when the images are produced overseas. However, the majority rejected this argument, saying that it "turns the First Amendment upside down . . . Protected speech does not become unprotected merely because it resembles the latter. The Constitution requires the reverse."[35]

Most of the justices agreed that the second provision, which banned material that conveyed the *impression* of minors engaged in sex, was unconstitutional because it would cover protected literary works that included themes of teenage sex and sexual abuse of children. Works like *Romeo and Juliet*, *Traffic*, and *American Beauty* might be considered illegal.

Congress responded with new legislation to allay the Court's concerns. In 2003, it passed the Prosecutorial Remedies and Other Tools to End the Exploitation of Children Today Act. The PROTECT Act amended the obscenity statute to prohibit the production or distribution of *obscene* representations of sexual abuse of children. The reworded statute capitalizes on the government's power to regulate *any* image that is obscene, regardless of whether it is real or virtual. It was used in 2009 to convict a collector of Japanese manga for possession of obscene visual representations of the sexual abuse of children.[36]

The Virginia Supreme Court upheld a graphic designer's conviction for virtual child pornography in *Christopher H. Allen v Commonwealth of Virginia* (2007). The defendant copied the faces of his stepdaughter, niece and several of their friends, all of whom were under age 10, from ordinary photos, then morphed them with images of adults engaged in sexual acts. He tried to defend his actions by saying they were protected under *Ashcroft v Free Speech Coalition*. The Court rejected that argument because Allen used images of real children. The decision stated "There is no constitutional right to possess sexually explicit morphed images of actual identifiable minors."[37]

---

[34] 535 U.S. 234 (2002).

[35] *Id.* at 254–55.

[36] United States v. Christopher Handley, 1:07-cr-00030-001, (S.D. Iowa 2010).

[37] Christopher H. Allen v Commonwealth of Virginia FE-2006-663 (2007); CBLDF Case Files – U.S. v. Handley, Comic Book Legal Defense Fund, http://cbldf.org/about-us/case-files/handley/ (last visited Feb. 9, 2012).

The PROTECT Act also adapted the pandering provision of the child pornography statute to make it illegal to advertise, promote, distribute, or solicit "any material or purported material in a manner that reflects *the belief, or that is intended to cause another to believe*, that the material or purported material is, or contains child pornography."[38] The Supreme Court upheld the provision against facial overbreadth and vagueness challenges in *United States v. Williams* (2008) by narrowing the Act's construction.[39] The Court interpreted the Act to require proof that the defendant believed he was purveying or soliciting child pornography. If the materials did not include real children, the statute's application would be limited to images that conveyed "sexually explicit conduct." It would not apply to materials in which "sexual intercourse . . . is merely suggested," such as R-rated movies. The "portrayal must cause a reasonable viewer to believe that the actors actually engaged in that conduct on camera."[40]

Age-related record keeping

To make it easier to track the ages of individuals depicted in pornography, Congress requires producers of pornographic material to document the names and dates of birth of anyone shown engaging in "actually sexually explicit conduct" and to affix a notice to the material stating the location of the records. The term *producer* applies to anyone who creates an image, digitizes or reproduces an image for commercial distribution, or inserts a digital image on a computer site or service.[41]

This provision of the Child Protection and Obscenity Enforcement Act of 1988 is known in the pornography industry as the "2257 rule," based on its section number in the United States Code. The child pornography prosecution of two filmmakers who hired Traci Lords to appear in their movies inspired the law. Lords was 15 when she started acting in hard-core films. When Congress passed the PROTECT Act, it extended the age-documentation requirement to sexually explicit material uploaded to the Web. Violators may be punished with a fine or up to five years in prison.

Sexting

Transmitting sexually explicit photos through mobile text messaging is called *sexting*. Teenagers occasionally use this tool to flirt with one another and explore their sexuality. A study by the Crimes Against Children Research Center at the University of New Hampshire found that 1.3 percent of 10- to 17-year-olds had sent or created an image of themselves that showed breasts, genitals or "someone's bottom."[42] About 7 percent had received such an image. So the problem is not particularly widespread, but it is one

---

[38] 18 U.S.C. §2252(a)(3)(B) (2011).

[39] 553 U.S. 285 (2008).

[40] *Id.* at 1840–41.

[41] 18 U.S.C. § 2257(h)(2) (2011).

[42] Kimberly Mitchell et al., *Prevalence and Characteristics of Youth Sexting: A National Study*, 129 PEDIATRICS 13 (Dec. 5, 2011).

that states have to deal with. About 4,000 instances of sexting were reported to police in 2008 and 2009. Approximately one-third of those cases ended in an arrest. Traditional child pornography laws carry felony penalties and require those convicted to register as sex offenders, stigmatizing them for life. There is a growing legislative movement to create alternative statutes that would treat consensual sexting as a misdemeanor. Other penalties may include community service, educational classes, counseling and, depending on the severity of the situation, juvenile detention. Felony charges would still apply to adults engaging in this behavior or to minors who forward images of another minor without the subject's consent.

At least twenty-one states have introduced bills on sexting. Several have already passed new laws; others have modified old ones. States in which sexting is a misdemeanor offense include Connecticut, Illinois and Texas. Other states that have decriminalized sexting or reduced the penalties for it include Arizona, Colorado, Florida, Louisiana, Missouri, Nebraska, North Dakota, Rhode Island, Utah and Vermont.[43]

Regulation of Indecency and Material Harmful to Minors

Many of the regulations Congress and the Federal Communications Commission have passed to control obscenity have included restrictions on indecency, which is constitutionally protected. In each case, courts must determine whether the government's interest in protecting children from indecent speech justifies the burden imposed on adults entitled to receive it, and whether the restriction limits no more speech than necessary.

Although the FCC has attempted to protect children from indecency over broadcast media, it has not attempted to regulate indecency transmitted through cable or satellite. This is because individuals who subscribe to these services are presumed to have selected the content with an understanding of its character. FCC oversight of these media is discussed thoroughly in Chapter 3, so it is not necessary to repeat it here. But one point is better covered in this chapter. Although indecency is permitted on cable and satellite channels, obscenity is not. Criminal sanctions may be applied to anyone who "utters any obscene language or distributes any obscene matter by means of cable television or subscription services on television."[44] Nevertheless, a lot of programming on adult channels includes real, not simulated sex, which far exceeds the FCC's definition of indecency. This occurs because the Commission's policy is not to proscribe adult programming unless it is found to be "unlawful pursuant to statute or regulation."[45] If the FCC suspects a programmer of transmitting obscenity, it will refer the matter to

---

[43] National Conference on State Legislation, 2011 Legislation Related to Sexting (Jan. 23, 2012), http://www.ncsl.org/default.aspx?tabid=22127; New Sexting Laws in 2011, Ask the Judge.info (Feb. 2, 2011), http://www.askthejudge.info/new-sexting-laws-in-2011/8570/.

[44] 18 U.S.C. § 1468 (2011).

[45] *In re* Litigation Recovery Trust, Memorandum Opinion and Order, 17 F.C.C.R. 21852, ¶ 9 (2002).

the Justice Department for criminal prosecution, but it will not act until the material has been adjudicated and found to be obscene under the *Miller* test.

Dial-a-porn

As a telecommunications service, dial-a-porn also falls under the FCC's jurisdiction. In 1998, Congress amended the Communications Act to ban obscene and indecent interstate commercial telephone transmissions. Reiterating the distinction between obscene and indecent content, the Supreme Court upheld the ban on obscene phone messages, but struck down the provision barring indecency in *Sable Communication of California v. FCC* (1989).[46] The Court pointed out that dial-a-porn does not enter the home uninvited. A user must take affirmative action to gain access to the service. It concluded that narrower restrictions on these services could protect minors from indecent speech without imposing a complete ban. Following the decision, the FCC adopted regulations that permitted dial-a-porn to offer indecent content as long as its distributors restricted access to it through the use of credit card authorization, access codes, or scrambling of transmissions.[47]

Indecency on the Internet

The government has been trying to figure out how to protect children from indecency on the Internet since 1996. Two of the laws it has passed, the Communications Decency Act and the Children's Online Protection Act – both targeted at websites – have been struck down. Another, the Children's Internet Protection Act – targeted at libraries – has been upheld.

Communications Decency Act

Congress passed the Communications Decency Act as part of the Telecommunications Act of 1996. The law made it illegal to transmit material over the Internet that was obscene or indecent by community standards if it was accessible to minors. The American Civil Liberties Union challenged the Act the day it was signed into law on behalf of websites that provided information about venereal disease and prison rape. The ACLU argued that the Act was unconstitutionally overbroad because it banned protected speech and burdened websites that had no mechanism for restricting access to minors. The government defended the Act by analogizing websites that provided indecent content to dial-a-porn services. It suggested they could defend themselves by restricting access to Internet users with credits cards or some other mechanism available to adults. The Supreme Court observed that the rule would burden nonprofit information providers who could not afford to implement such restrictions. In *Reno v. ACLU* (1997) it held that the indecency provision was both unconstitutionally vague and overbroad. The

[46] 492 U.S. 115 (1989).
[47] Restrictions on Obscene or Indecent Telephone Message Services, 47 C.F.R. § 64.201(c)(1987).

decision is especially significant because it unanimously held that the Internet is entitled to full First Amendment protection.

Children's Online Protection Act

Congress went back to the drawing board when the Communications Decency Act was struck down and emerged with a revised statute that it hoped would pass constitutional muster: the Children's Online Protection Act.[48] Congress narrowed the Act's scope by limiting its application to commercial websites that knowingly transmitted material "harmful to minors." It also attempted to eliminate vagueness by applying the *Miller* test, adding the words "with respect to minors," to define "harmful to minors" as material that:

(A)   the average person, applying contemporary community standards, would find, taking the material as a whole and with respect to minors, is designed to appeal to, or is designed to pander to, the prurient interest;

(B)   depicts, describes, or represents, in a manner patently offensive with respect to minors, an actual or simulated sexual act or sexual contact, an actual or simulated normal or perverted sexual act, or a lewd exhibition of the genitals or post-pubescent female breast; and

(C)   taken as a whole, lacks serious literary, artistic, political, or scientific value for minors.[49]

A commercial website could avoid prosecution by restricting access to adults through the use of credit cards or adult access codes.

The ACLU and the Electronic Privacy Information Center challenged COPA's constitutionality and won. The law spent the next 10 years in limbo as the government appealed the case. A federal district court in Philadelphia issued an injunction barring enforcement of the statute because it would deny adults access to speech they were entitled to receive and impose financial burdens on speakers (by requiring credit card or access codes) that might lead them to self-censor to avoid the additional cost. The Third Circuit upheld the injunction, but on a different basis. It concluded that "[b]ecause of the peculiar geography-free nature of cyberspace, [COPA's] community standards test would essentially require every web communication to abide by the most restrictive community's standards."[50] The Supreme Court concluded that COPA could not be struck down for its use of community standards. The Court's plurality opinion suggests that the justices could not come to an agreement on the issue. But the Court suggested COPA might be unconstitutional for other reasons. It upheld the injunction and sent the case back down to the district level for a broader review of

Reno v. ACLU (1997) is the landmark decision in which the Supreme Court decided that the Internet was entitled to full First Amendment protection.

[48] 47 U.S.C. § 231 (2006).
[49] *Id.* § 231(e)(2)(B).
[50] ACLU v. Reno, 217 F.3d 162, 175 (3rd Cir. 2000).

First Amendment considerations.[51] The lower court held that COPA was unconstitutional because it did not use the least restrictive means to curb speech that might harm minors and Third Circuit upheld the ruling.[52] The Supreme Court reviewed the case a second time, upholding the injunction on its enforcement based on the law's "potential for extraordinary harm and a serious chill upon protected speech."[53] It remanded the case again, asking the district court to consider whether there were less restrictive alternatives to the law. The lower court determined that filters installed by parents represented a less restrictive alternative and struck the law down again. In 2008, the Third Circuit upheld its decision for the third time, finding the Act "impermissibly overbroad and vague."[54] The Supreme Court struck the final blow in 2009 when it refused to review the decision.[55]

Children's Internet Protection Act

In 2000, Congress passed the Children's Internet Protection Act, which ties federal funding for Internet access in public libraries and schools to the installation of filtering software to block material that is obscene, child pornography, or "harmful to minors" on all computers connected to the Internet.[56] Most libraries already used filters on computers in the children's section. The American Library Association challenged the law's application to public libraries as a violation of the First Amendment. It argued that filters are inexact and block material adults are constitutionally entitled to receive – some of it unrelated to sexual content. The law specifies that adult patrons can ask librarians to remove a filter from a computer they are using for "bona fide research or other lawful purposes."[57] The ALA argued that this puts adults in the position of justifying what they want to read to a librarian.

By a 6–3 margin, the Supreme Court upheld the law in *United States v. American Library Association* (2003). It determined that the government's interest in protecting children outweighed the burden the law imposed on adult patrons.

Truth in Domain Names Act

Congress passed the Truth in Domain Names Act in 2003 to thwart the use of misleading domain names to pull Internet users into pornographic websites.[58] Knowingly using a deceptive domain name to lure a person into viewing obscene material is punishable

---

[51] Ashcroft v. ACLU, 535 U.S. 564 (2002).

[52] ACLU v. Ashcroft, 322 F.3d 240 (3rd Cir. Pa. 2003).

[53] Ashcroft v. ACLU, 542 U.S. 656, 671 (2004).

[54] ACLU v. Mukasey, 534 F.3d 181 (3rd Cir. July 22, 2008), *aff'g* ACLU v. Gonzales, 478 F. Supp. 2d 775 (E.D. Pa., 2007).

[55] Mukasey v. ACLU, 555 U.S. 1137 (2009).

[56] 47 U.S.C. § 254(h)(6) (2011).

[57] *Id.*

[58] 18 U.S.C. § 2252B (2011).

by a fine or two years in prison. If the domain name is used to deceive a child into viewing material "harmful to minors," the punishment increases to four years.

Domain names that include the words sex or porn obviously aren't meant to mislead, but websites like Teltubbies.com and Bobthebiulder.com, which contain misspellings that children are likely to make, would certainly qualify. John Zuccarini, the first person convicted of violating the law, registered sites with typos that redirected users' browsers to pay-per-click advertising sites, some with ads for free access to pornography.[59]

State Internet regulation

States are entitled to prohibit the distribution of indecent material to minors. In *Ginsberg v. New York* (1968), the Supreme Court held that a state may classify some forms of sexual expression that would not be obscene for adults as harmful to minors in order to protect their psychological and ethical development. It upheld a statute that made it a crime to knowingly sell to minors any depiction of nudity that

1. predominantly appeals to the prurient, shameful or morbid interest of minors;
2. is patently offensive to prevailing standards in the adult community as a whole with respect to what is suitable material for minors; and
3. is utterly without redeeming social importance for minors.[60]

> The *Ginsberg* test for material "harmful to minors" is a modification of the *Miller* test for obscenity.

However, regulating indecency on the Internet at the state level presents a problem. In *ACLU v. Johnson* (1999), the Tenth Circuit upheld an injunction barring New Mexico from enforcing a state statute that criminalized the dissemination of material "harmful to a minor" via computer.[61] The appellate court relied heavily on the Supreme Court's analysis of the Communications Decency Act in *Reno v. ACLU* to conclude that New Mexico's statute unconstitutionally burdened adult speech. The appellate court also agreed with the district court that the state violated the constitution's commerce clause by: (1) regulating conduct that occurred outside of the state, (2) unreasonably burdening interstate and foreign commerce, and (3) subjecting interstate uses of the Internet to state regulation. The Tenth Circuit pointed out that "the nature of the Internet forecloses the argument that a statute such [as this] applies only to intrastate communications. Even if it is limited to one-on-one e-mail communications . . . there is no guarantee that a message from one New Mexican to another New Mexican will not travel through other states en route."

[59] U.S. Department of Justice Release, "Cyberscammer" Sentenced to 30 Months for Using Deceptive Internet Names to Mislead Minors to X-Rated Sites, Feb. 26, 2004, available at http://www.usdoj.gov/criminal/cybercrime/zuccariniSent.htm.

[60] Ginsburg v. New York, 390 U.S. 629, 633 (1968).

[61] 194 F.3d 1149 (10th Cir. 1999); *See also* PSINET v. Chapman, 167 F. Supp. 2d 878 (W.D. Va. 2001) (holding that a Virginia law barring Internet material "harmful to juveniles" violated the First Amendment and the Constitution's Commerce Clause).

Violence

Sex and violence are usually grouped together among media sins, but legally they are treated very differently. Courts are much more reluctant to uphold content-based regulations targeted at violent speech or to impose liability on content producers for the harm that supposedly results from it.

Controlling access to violent speech

Fear engendered by high school shootings in Littleton, Colo., and Paducah, Ky., prompted states and communities to take a closer look at the types of video games, websites, music, and movies the shooters were consuming. Multiple states reacted by passing laws that

Figure 11.1   Illustration: Kalan Lyra

prohibited the sale or rental of violent video games to minors.[62] States assumed they could act to protect minors from violence under the same theory that allows them to protect minors from exposure to indecency.

California's statute used a derivative of the *Miller* and *Ginsburg* tests to determine whether violent video games were "harmful to minors." A game would be restricted if the range of options available to a player included killing, maiming, dismembering, or sexually assaulting an image of a human being and the acts were depicted in a manner that:

1. a reasonable person, considering the game as a whole, would find appeals to a deviant or morbid interest of minors;
2. is patently offensive to prevailing standards in the community as to what is suitable for minors; and
3. causes the game, as a whole, to lack serious literary, artistic, political, or scientific value.[63]

In *Brown v. Entertainment Merchants Association* (2011), the Supreme Court concluded that video games qualify for First Amendment protection and that California's statute imposing restrictions on their sale to minors was unconstitutional. Writing for the majority, Justice Scalia explained that. "Like the protected books, plays, and movies that preceded them, video games communicate ideas – and even social messages – through many familiar literary devices (such as characters, dialogue, plot, and music) and through features distinctive to the medium (such as the player's interaction with the virtual world)."[64]

He added that the most basic of First Amendment principles is that "government has no power to restrict expression because of its message, its ideas, its subject matter, or its content."[65] Of course, that is exactly what government does when it limits expression that incites violence or that is fraudulent, libelous or obscene. But when it limits speech based on a particular message, the regulation must stand up to strict scrutiny. The *strict scrutiny* test requires the government to show that a regulation is narrowly tailored to serve a compelling interest. In this case, California could not meet that standard because it could not "show a direct causal link between violent video games and harm to minors."

In *Brown v. Entertainment Merchants Association* (2011), the Supreme Court determined that video games are entitled to First Amendment protection.

[62] *See* Video Software Dealers Assn. v. Schwarzenegger, 556 F. 3d 950, 963–64 (CA9 2009); Interactive Digital Software Assn. v. St. Louis County, 329 F. 3d 954 (CA8 2003); American Amusement Machine Assn. v. Kendrick, 244 F. 3d 572, 578–79 (CA7 2001); Entertainment Software Assn. v. Foti, 451 F. Supp. 2d 823, 832–33 (MD La. 2006); Entertainment Software Assn. v. Hatch, 443 F. Supp. 2d 1065, 1070 (Minn. 2006), *aff'd*, 519 F. 3d 768 (CA8 2008); Entertainment Software Assn. v. Granholm, 426 F. Supp. 2d 646, 653 (ED Mich. 2006); Entertainment Software Assn. v. Blagojevich, 404 F. Supp. 2d 1051, 1063 (ND Ill. 2005), *aff'd*, 469 F. 3d 641 (CA7 2006).

[63] Cal. Civ. Code Ann. §§1746–1746.5 (2010) (overturned in Brown v. Entertainment Merchants Association, 131 S. Ct. 2729 (2011))

[64] Brown v. Entertainment Merchants Association, 131 S. Ct. 2729, 2733 (2011).

[65] *Id.* at 2733 (quoting Ashcroft v. American Civil Liberties Union, 535 U.S. 564, 573 (2002)).

Nearly all research on the effect of media violence on children shows a correlation between violent depictions and aggressive behavior, rather than demonstrating cause and effect. Those studies that have appeared to show cause and effect were done in laboratory settings away from the subjects' natural environment, so their external validity is questionable.

The Court also noted that because various media (cartoons, film and video) were used in studies demonstrating correlations between violent media and aggression, California's regulation of only video games was underinclusive. In First Amendment jurisprudence underinclusive regulations are problematic because they suggest that the government is disfavoring a particular speaker or viewpoint. California argued that violence in video games is unique because it is interactive. In refuting that notion, Justice Scalia relied on the argument that "all literature is interactive" because it draws the reader into the story.

Justice Alito, who concurred with the Court's judgment but not this reasoning, warned that the Court was too quick to dismiss the concerns of federal and state legislators, educators, social scientists, and parents regarding the social effect of a new technology. He pointed to the qualitatively different experience of assuming the role of a shooter for hours at a time as opposed to reading about a murder in a book. He also noted the availability of games that allowed players to simulate school shootings, the rape of a mother and her daughters, or ethnic cleansing.[66]

It is likely that states assumed their attempts to limit minors' access to video game violence, based on research showing a correlation between violent depictions and aggression, would be acceptable to the Supreme Court. After all, the Court had allowed them to regulate minors' access to indecency as harmful based on no research at all. But the Court didn't see it that way. In past decisions, it has clarified that obscenity and violence are different.[67] In *Brown v. EMA,* Justice Scalia explained that New York was allowed to modify the *Miller* test for obscenity to deal with sexual speech that may be harmful to minors in *New York v. Ginsberg* because it was only adjusting the boundaries of a category of speech that was already unprotected. California, on the other hand, had attempted to create a new category of content-based regulation exclusively for children. The Court found this "unprecedented and mistaken," pointing out that "minors are entitled to a significant measure of First Amendment protection, and only in relatively narrow and well-defined circumstances may government bar public dissemination of protected materials to them."

A controlling precedent in the *Brown v. EMA* case was *United States v. Stevens* (2010), a case that concerned a federal statute that criminalized the creation, sale, or possession of depictions of animal cruelty.[68] The law was meant to stop the creation and distribution of "crush videos." These are videos in which someone (often a woman in high heels) crushes a living animal for entertainment. In *Stevens,* the Court held that "new categories of unprotected speech may not be added to the list by a legislature that concludes certain

---

[66] *Id.* at 2749 (Alito J., concurring in judgment).
[67] Winters v. New York, 333 U. S. 507, 514 (1948).
[68] 130 S. Ct. 1577 (2010).

speech is too harmful to be tolerated." The Court concluded that the law was an impermissible content-based restriction because "there was no American tradition of forbidding the *depiction of* animal cruelty – though States have long had laws against *committing* it." The Court left open the possibility, however, that the crush-video statute might pass Constitutional muster "if it were limited to videos of acts of animal cruelty that violated the law where the acts were performed." Congress refined the law to focus exclusively on illegal animal cruelty. It was signed into law in December of 2010.[69]

Imposing liability on producers' violent media

While researchers continue to search for answers regarding the impact of media on human behavior, it is indisputable that people model behaviors they observe in media. Occasionally, they do so with violent results. For example, three teenage fans of the band Slayer murdered a 15-year-old girl as part of a satanic ritual, following instructions in the band's songs *Altar of Sacrifice*, *Kill Again*, and *Necrophiliac*.[70] In another case, two boys killed their mother and disposed of her body using a technique they learned from a mobster on the HBO series *The Sopranos*.[71] Some individuals have committed suicide after taking the lyrics of songs too seriously.[72] Families of victims in copycat cases occasionally sue media producers on theories of negligence or incitement to violence.

Negligence representations of violence

The families of three children murdered in a Kentucky high school shooting attempted to prove that violent media producers were partly to blame because they negligently disseminated their products to impressionable youths who were led to commit violent acts. In 1997, Michael Carneal, a 14-year-old at Heath High School in Paducah, Kentucky, shot eight of his fellow students, killing three. He was arrested and convicted of murder. A subsequent investigation revealed that Carneal visited pornographic websites; watched *The Basketball Diaries*, a movie that depicted a student shooting his classmates; and played first-person shooter video games, such as *Doom*, *Quake*, *Castle Wolfenstein*, *MechWarrior*, *Resident Evil*, *Redneck Rampage*, and *Final Fantasy*.

In *James v. Meow Media, Inc.* (2002), families of the murdered children sued the producers of these media for negligence, product liability, and racketeering.[73] The plaintiffs claimed the defendants were negligent because they knew or should have known that distribution of such material to Carneal and other young people posed an unreasonable risk to others. They argued that the defendants' violent media desensitized Carneal and caused him to commit violent acts.

---

[69] Animal Crush Video Protection Act, Pub. L. No. 111–294.

[70] Pahler v. Slayer, 29 Media L. Rep. 2627 (Cal. Super. Ct. 2001).

[71] People v. Bautista, 2006 Cal. App. Unpub. LEXIS 11714 (Dec. 28, 2006).

[72] McCollum v. CBS, 202 Cal.App.3d 989 (1988)(involving parents' unsuccessful suit of CBS records and Ozzy Osborne, following their son's suicide while listening to Ozborne's "Suicide Solution").

[73] 300 F.3d 683 (6th Cir. 2002).

A plaintiff who wants to prove that a media producer has been negligent must show: (1) that the defendant owed a duty of care to the plaintiff, (2) that the defendant breached that duty of care, and (3) that the defendant's breach was the *proximate cause* of the plaintiff's damages. To prove that the defendant owed a duty of care, the plaintiff must show that harm caused by the media product was foreseeable.

Proximate cause is the cause that directly produces an event. In other words, the event would not have occurred but for the cause.

The district court concluded that Carneal's actions were not sufficiently foreseeable to trigger a duty on the defendants' part to protect third parties from consumers of their media. It added that even if the defendants had owed a duty of care, Carneal's actions were the superseding cause of the victims' deaths. A superseding cause exists when an event occurs after the defendant's initial action that substantially causes the harm.

The plaintiffs also made the novel argument that violent elements in the film, video games, and websites were defects in the media products distributed by the producers who were subject to product liability laws. The court concluded that "thoughts, ideas and images" portrayed in these media were not products, and therefore the defendants could not be held liable for their defects. Product liability would only apply if the cassettes or DVDs malfunctioned. Finally, it rejected the plaintiffs' argument that the websites were engaged in a pattern of racketeering by distributing obscene material to minors. It did not see the connection between Carneal's violent actions and the material on the pornography sites and would not apply obscenity law to the violent sites because obscenity jurisprudence is generally applied to material of a sexual nature.[74]

A civil suit filed against media producers following the 1999 Columbine High School shootings was almost identical in scope to *James v. Meow Media*. Before killing twelve students and one teacher at their Littleton, Colorado high school, Dylan Klebold and Eric Harris immersed themselves in the same video games, pornography sites, and film that Carneal had enjoyed. In fact, Klebold and Harris wore the same clothing on the day of the shooting that the central character in *The Basketball Diaries* had worn when he shot his victims. In *Sanders v. Acclaim Entertainment, Inc.* (2002), the family of the teacher who Klebold and Harris murdered filed negligence, product liability, and racketeering claims against the same media producers sued in the Kentucky case as well as others.[75]

A federal district judge in Colorado dismissed the negligence claim, concluding that the defendants owed no duty of care to the Columbine victims. While acknowledging that the defendants "might have speculated that their motion picture or video games had the potential to stimulate an idiosyncratic reaction in the mind of some disturbed individuals," he noted that "speculative possibility . . . is not enough to create a legal duty.[76] He also agreed that product liability claims were inapplicable to intangible thoughts, ideas, images, and messages.

Other courts have reached similar conclusions with respect to music. In *Davidson v. Time Warner* (1997), a federal district court in Texas dismissed a negligence claim filed

[74] *See also* United States v. Thoma, 726 F.2d 1191, 1200 (7th Cir. 1984) (holding that obscenity jurisprudence does not apply to depictions of violence).
[75] 188 F. Supp. 2d 1264, 1272 (2002).
[76] *Id.* at 1272.

by the widow of a state trooper who was fatally shot when he stopped the driver of a stolen car.[77] The killer was listening to rap songs by Tupac Shakur, one of which described violence against police. California and Georgia courts dismissed negligence claims against Ozzy Osbourne filed by the parents of teenage boys who killed themselves while listening to Osbourne's song "Suicide Solution."[78]

Incitement to Violence

Incitement refers to the use of speech to arouse others to criminal activity. Because it is a criminal offense for pure speech – often speech directed at the government – incitement prosecutions could (and have) been used as a tool for censorship. The Supreme Court spent the first half of the twentieth century considering where its outer boundaries should lie. It now grants a great deal of latitude to speech alleged to be incitement.

The Supreme Court established the modern test for incitement to violence in *Brandenburg v. Ohio* (1969).[79] The case involved the prosecution of a Ku Klux Klan leader who was convicted for violating Ohio's criminal syndicalism statute, which prohibited "advocat[ing] . . . crime, sabotage, violence, or unlawful methods of terrorism as a means of . . . reform." At a Klan rally, Brandenburg was televised saying "We're not a revengent [sic] organization, but if our President, our Congress, our Supreme Court, continues to suppress the white, Caucasian race, it's possible that there might have to be some revengeance [sic] taken . . . We are marching on Congress July the Fourth, four hundred thousand strong."[80]

The Supreme Court reversed the decision, holding that abstract advocacy of violence must be distinguished from advocacy of imminent lawless action. It concluded that only speech "directed toward inciting or producing imminent lawless action and likely to incite or produce such action" could be denied First Amendment protection.[81] The words "directed toward" refer to intent. In other words, speech does not qualify as unlawful incitement unless harm is intended, imminent, and likely to occur.

Although *Brandenburg* was meant to apply in criminal cases involving political speech rather than entertainment, courts have applied its "intent" requirement in civil tort cases. The Louisiana Court of Appeals applied the *Brandenburg* test in *Byers v. Edmondson* (1999), a lawsuit against Oliver Stone, Warner Brothers, and other producers of the film *Natural Born Killers* filed by the victim of a couple on a murderous romp inspired by the movie.[82] Sarah Edmondson and her boyfriend, Benjamin Darrus, set out from Oklahoma on a crime spree after taking LSD and watching the movie over and over. Darrus murdered a man in Mississippi. Edmondson shot Patsy Byers during an

Brandenburg v. Ohio (1969) established the modern test for incitement to violence. Courts look for three factors: intent to cause violence, likelihood that it would occur, and that the violence would occur imminently.

---

[77] 25 Media L. Rep. 1705 (1997).

[78] *See* McCollum v. CBS, 202 Cal. App. 3d 989 (1988); Waller v. Osbourne, 763 F. Supp. 1144 (1991).

[79] 395 U.S. 444 (1969).

[80] *Id.* at 447.

[81] *Id.*

[82] Byers v. Edmondson, 712 So.2d 681 (La. Ct. App. 1998), *cert. denied*, 526 U.S. 1005 (1999).

armed robbery of the convenience store in which Byers worked as a clerk. After they were arrested, Edmondson told police that Darrus called her "his Mallory," alluding to the female character in the movie.

Byers claimed that the defendants knew or should have known that the movie "would cause and inspire people such as the defendants to commit crimes."[83] As evidence, she depended on a comment made by Oliver Stone following the movie's premiere that "The most pacifist people in the world said they came out of the movie and wanted to kill somebody."[84]

A Louisiana Court of Appeals surprised media watchers by refusing to dismiss the suit. It held that Byers had stated a valid cause of action and could proceed with the suit if she could prove intent on the part of the defendants. The court concluded that the film would lose its First Amendment protection if the plaintiffs could prove that the film incited imminent lawless activity. On remand, however, the trial court granted summary judgment to the defendants because the plaintiffs' evidence was not sufficient to establish intent. The Louisiana Court of Appeals, now having apparently watched the movie, upheld the district court's summary judgment on appeal, but for a different reason.[85] It held that intent was immaterial in the case because *Natural Born Killers* was not inciteful speech. It explained that "Edmondson and Darrus may very well have been inspired to imitate the actions of Mickey and Mallory Knox, but the film does not direct or encourage them to take such actions. Accordingly, as a matter of law . . . *Natural Born Killers* cannot be considered inciteful speech" unentitled to First Amendment protection.[86]

The judge in *Sanders v. Acclaim Entertainment* also briefly considered whether *Brandenburg* applied to the Colorado case and concluded that it did not.[87] The plaintiffs did not allege that the media producers intended Klebold and Harris to react violently to their work, the reaction was not likely, and it was not imminent.

Had it gone to trial, *Rice v. Paladin Enterprises* (1997), better known as the "*Hit Man* case," might have been an exception.[88] The plaintiffs in the case claimed that the publishers of the book *Hit Man: A Technical Manual for Independent Contractors* aided and abetted murder by printing instructions that a contract killer used to kill their family members.

Lawrence Horn hired James Perry to murder his ex-wife, his eight-year-old quadriplegic son, and his son's nurse, so he could collect a $2 million settlement paid to his son for injuries that had left him paralyzed. Perry followed the instructions in the manual to the letter. Both were convicted of murder.

The lower court granted summary judgment in favor of the publisher because it considered the plaintiffs' claim to be barred by the First Amendment, but the U.S. Court

---

[83] *Id.* at 684.

[84] ROBERT O'NEIL, THE FIRST AMENDMENT AND CIVIL LIABILITY 157 (2001).

[85] Byers v. Edmondson, 826 So.2d 551 (La. App. 2002).

[86] *Id.* at 557.

[87] 188 F. Supp. 2d 1264, 1279 (D. Colo. 2002).

[88] 128 F.3d 233 (4th Cir. 1997), *cert. denied*, 523 U.S. 1074 (1998).

of Appeals for the Fourth Circuit reversed, explaining that "speech – even speech by the press – that constitutes criminal aiding and abetting does not enjoy the protection of the First Amendment."[89] The court observed that by Paladin's own admission, it intended through its marketing campaign, "to attract and assist criminals and would-be criminals who desire information and instructions on how to commit crimes," and also that *Hit Man* actually "would be used, upon receipt, by criminals and would-be criminals to plan and execute the crime of murder for hire."[90]

The court described Paladin's manual as "the antithesis of speech protected under *Brandenburg*" because it constituted "advocacy and teaching of concrete action," the "preparation . . . for violent action and [the] steeling . . . to such action." Paladin settled the case after the court's opinion, rather than taking the case before a jury, and stopped printing the book. However, copies of it are easily found on the Internet.

New Jersey radio personality Harold ("Hal") Turner was acquitted of violating Connecticut's incitement statute based on a post he made on his Turner Radio Network or "TRN" blog. Turner was outraged over a Connecticut bill that would have removed priests and bishops from financial oversight of Roman Catholic parishes and replaced them with "boards of lay people." He believed it violated the Constitutional separation of church and state. In a blog referencing co-sponsors of the bill, State Senator Andrew McDonald and State Representative Michael Lawlor, and Thomas K. Jones, the ethics enforcement officer of the Office of State Ethics, Turner published the following:

> While filing a lawsuit is quaint and the "decent" way to handle things, we at TRN believe that being decent to a group of tyrannical scumbags is the wrong approach. It's too soft.
>
> Thankfully, the Founding Fathers gave us the tools necessary to resolve the tyranny: The Second Amendment.
>
> TRN advocates Catholics in Connecticut take up arms and put down this tyranny by force. To that end, THIS WEDNESDAY NIGHT ON THE "HAL TURNER SHOW" we will be releasing the home addresses of the Senator and Assemblyman who introduced bill 1098 as well as the home address of Thomas K. Jones of OSE.
>
> * * *
>
> It is our intent to foment direct action against these individuals personally. These beastly government officials should be made an example of as a warning to others in government: Obey the Constitution or die.
>
> If any state attorney, police department or court thinks they're going to get uppity with us about this, I suspect we have enough bullets to put them down too . . . [91]

Turner was arrested before he could publish the home addresses. He motioned to dismiss the case based on First Amendment protection for his speech. The Connecticut judge refused, observing that Turner's post explicitly advocated violence and that his promise to release the home addresses of the intended victims on the next evening suggested imminence. He concluded that it would be up to a jury to decide whether the

The irony of "The Hitman" case is that the book's author – a supposed contract killer – was in fact a single mother of two, who gathered research from movies, TV shows, and crime stories in the newspaper. She didn't even own a gun.

[89] *Id.* at 242.
[90] *Id.* at 241 (quoting parties' Joint Statement of Facts, at 58–62).
[91] Connecticut v. Turner, 2011 WL 4424754 (Conn. Super. Sept. 6, 2011) (unpublished).

violent action was likely. A jury concluded that it was not. After Turner won his case, he was escorted back to prison where he was serving the remainder of a 33-month sentence for threatening three federal judges in another post published around the same time.

Threats

Speech meant to harass or *threaten* is not protected and is easier to prosecute than incitement. A general threats statute prohibits the transmission, through interstate or foreign commerce, of any threat to kidnap or injure another person.[92] Other laws make is a crime to threaten the president, judges or clinic workers. Hal Turner was convicted of threatening three judges on his blog in an angry response to a Seventh Circuit judicial ruling upholding a ban on handguns in Chicago. According to the criminal complaint, Turner stated, "These Judges deserve to be killed." He also posted pictures of the judges, their work addresses, and a picture of the federal building where they worked with notations indicating "Anti-truck bomb barriers."[93] Turner was convicted after three trials; the first two ended with deadlocked juries.

Threats are open to interpretation, of course. Some are overt; others are implied. Most threats are expressions of momentary anger and would never be realized, as in "I'm going to kill my boss if he asks me to work on the weekend again." According to the Supreme Court, "true threats" are "those statements where the speaker means to communicate a serious expression of an intent to commit an act of unlawful violence to a particular individual or group of individuals."[94] Assessing what a speaker means to communicate can be difficult. Most courts rely on the objective standard of whether the threat, regardless of its character, is a statement that a *reasonable person* would foresee as likely to be interpreted by its recipient as a serious expression of intent to harm.

The Supreme Court concluded that threats fall outside the realm of protected speech in *Watts v. United States* (1969).[95] But it also warned that law enforcement officers have to be careful because threats are frequently characterized by hyperbole. In *Watts*, an 18-year-old Vietnam War protester said to fellow demonstrators, "If they ever make me carry a rifle, the first man I want to get in my sights is L.B.J. [President Lyndon Baines Johnson]." He was arrested for violating a federal statute that makes it a felony to "knowingly and willfully . . . make any threat to take the life of, to kidnap, or to inflict bodily harm upon the President of the United States."[96] Only six years had passed since President John F. Kennedy's assassination, so the Court took death threats against the president seriously, but it also realized that threats must be examined in context. It said "a statute such as this one, which makes criminal a form of pure speech, must be inter-

Courts consider the use of the hypothetical "reasonable person" to be an *objective* standard to measure a defendant's actions because it does not take the defendant's particular characteristics (e.g. hotheadedness) into account in assessing the appropriateness of behavior.

The Supreme Court denied First Amendment protection to "true threats" in *Watts v. United States* (1969).

[92] 18 U.S.C. § 875 (2011).
[93] United States v. Harold Turner, Crim. No. 09-542 (N.D. Ill. Sept. 8, 2009).
[94] Virginia v. Black, 538 U.S. 343, 360 (2003).
[95] 394 U.S. 705 (1969).
[96] 18 U.S.C. § 871(a) (2011).

preted with the commands of the First Amendment clearly in mind. What is a threat must be distinguished from what is constitutionally protected speech."[97]

The context of the speech determined the outcome of *Planned Parenthood of the Columbia/Willamette v. American Coalition of Life Activists* (2002), better known as the Nuremberg Files case.[98] A Portland, Oregon, jury ordered the defendants, a coalition of abortion protesters, to pay $109 million in damages for threatening four abortion providers by circulating their names and addresses on "wanted"-style posters and a website the doctors described as a hit list. Neither the posters nor the website explicitly threatened violence against the doctors, but the plaintiffs successfully argued that they constituted true threats when viewed within the context of a wave of violence against abortion providers.

During the 10 years preceding the case, there were 39 bombings, 99 acid attacks, 7 murders, and 16 attempted murders of doctors and clinic workers, according to the National Abortion Federation.[99] Four of those murdered were doctors. Three of them had been identified on similar wanted-style posters. The last to die was Barnett Slepian, whose name appeared on the Nuremberg Files website, along with 200 other abortion providers. The names of murdered doctors appeared on the list with a line through them. The names of injured doctors appeared shaded in gray. Slepian's name was crossed off the site only hours after his murder.

Plaintiffs brought the suit under the Freedom of Access to Clinic Entrances Act, which creates a right of action against anyone who by "threat of force . . . intentionally . . . intimidates . . . any person because that person is or has been . . . providing reproductive health services." In March of 2001, a three-judge panel on the Ninth Circuit reversed the lower court's decision in favor of the plaintiffs. In its view, the district court allowed the jury to find ACLA liable for putting the doctors in harm's way by focusing too much on the context of the speech, which involved violent acts by third parties, and too little on the content, which never directly authorized or threatened harm. The court focused more on the issue of incitement. But that decision was short-lived.

The plaintiffs requested the whole court to reevaluate the case in an en banc hearing. The full court affirmed the lower court's verdict. The majority opinion, written by Judge Pamela Rymer, explained, "by replicating the poster pattern that preceded the elimination of [other] doctors . . . ACLA was not staking out a position of debate but of threatened demise."[100] In 2009, George Tiller, another doctor depicted on a wanted poster and named on the Nuremberg Files website, was murdered in his church.[101]

As the Hal Turner and *Planned Parenthood* cases have shown, a threat does not have to be conveyed directly to the subject of the statement. But its mode of communication

---

[97] Watts v. United States, 394 U.S. 705, 707 (1969).

[98] 244. F.3d 1007 (9th Cir. 2001), reh'g en banc granted, 290 F.3d 1058 (9th Cir. 2002).

[99] National Abortion Federation, NAF Violence and Disruption Statistics, www.prochoice.org/pubs_research/publications/downloads/about_abortion/violence_statistics.pdf.

[100] Planned Parenthood of the Columbia/Willamette v. American Coalition of Life Activists, 290 F.3d 1058, 1086 (2002).

[101] Joe Stumpe and Monica Davey, *Abortion Doctor Slain in Kansas Church*, N.Y. Times, June 1, 2009, at A1.

must be such that the subject is likely to see it. In *United States v. Alkhabaz* (1997), the Sixth Circuit held that the defendant's private e-mail exchange with a friend regarding his fantasies of harming a woman who bore the same name as his classmate was not a true threat.[102] In contrast, in *United States v. Jeffries* (2011), the defendant's act of posting a video on YouTube, promising to kill the judge overseeing his child custody dispute if the judge made the wrong decision, and then publishing links to the video on Facebook was considered a true threat. In this case, the defendant's threat, which never identified the judge by name, was distributed among a sea of 100 million other videos, where it might never have been noticed. But the act of posting links to it on Facebook, so those familiar with the case would see it, ensured that the threat would be received.[103]

Cyberstalking, cyber harassment, and cyberbullying

Engaging in a course of conduct that involves the electronic transmission of threats directed at a specific person also may be classified as cyberstalking or cyber harassment. *Cyberstalking* is the use of the Internet to stalk a victim. It is generally characterized by a pattern of behaviors that includes credible threats of death or injury, or malicious behavior, such as encouraging third parties to harm or harass the victim. *Cyber harassment* involves attempts to torment an individual through repeated contacts, but unlike cyberstalking, usually does not involve a credible threat of bodily harm. Both cyberstalking and cyber harassment are prohibited by federal law.

The federal stalking statute applies to anyone who, with the intent

> to kill, injure, harass, or place under surveillance with intent to kill, injure, harass, or intimidate, or cause substantial emotional distress to a person in another State or tribal jurisdiction . . .
>
>   uses . . . any interactive computer service, or any facility of interstate or foreign commerce to engage in a course of conduct that causes substantial emotional distress to that person or places that person in reasonable fear of the death of, or serious bodily injury . . . [104]

A Montana man was convicted of violating the statute after sending his ex-girlfriend 22 threatening e-mails and 50 threatening text messages. One text message with the subject heading "I'm going to slit your throat" stated "It would make be fill [sic] so good to see you bleed as you gasp for air. I hope your are [sic] ready for retribution, because it is coming. You are going down bitch."[105] In addition to the threatening correspondence, he sent her pictures of dismembered women.

Most cyberstalking crimes are committed by people who know the victim. Those committed by strangers are usually directed toward someone in the public eye. For

[102] United States v. Alkhabaz, 104 F.3d 1492 (6th Cir. 1997).
[103] US v. Jeffries, 10-CR-100 (E.D. Tenn. Oct. 22, 2010)(refusing to dismiss the case); Jim Balloch, *Army soldier gets prison time for threatening Knox judge in YouTube song*, KnoxvilleNews.com, June, 2, 2001, http://www.knoxnews.com/news/2011/jun/02/army-soldier-gets-prison-time-threatening-knox-jud/?print=1.
[104] 18 U.S.C. § 2261A (2011).
[105] United States v. Jeffrey Grob, 625 F.3d 1209 (9th Cir. 2010).

example, Tina Knight, a general assignment reporter for a television station in Ohio, was stalked for 14 months by an obsessed fan. She took a job in West Virginia in an effort to escape him, but his e-mails followed her and even included pictures of him taken in various locations in her new town. None of the messages contained explicit threats, but their volume, inclusion of sexual references, and suggestions that he was watching her were sufficient to connote a threat. One said

> "You don't know where I'm at. I might be in your house in Dunbar [, West Virginia]; you don't know that. . . . I know all of your neighbors. . . . And I have access to all that information, just like anybody else does who knows where to find it. I have an enormous amount of things about you that I'm not going to disclose unless I have to. I'm not going to tell anybody about it except if you lie to me. I might not say anything to you at the time, but that might come back, you know. . . . I know the names of all your relatives and where they live. . . . I know your brothers' wives['] names, their ages, their Social Security numbers and their birth dates . . . and their property values. . . . Maybe I live on 20th street in Dunbar. . . . Maybe I watch you with binoculars all the time and maybe I don't.

He was convicted under the federal statute of stalking, cyberstalking and telephone harassment.

In both of these examples, the defendants intimidated their victims through direct messages. A federal court in Maryland dismissed cyberstalking charges against a man alleged to have posted thousands of intimidating messages on Twitter, under various usernames, about the leader of a Buddhist sect that had kicked him out for nonBuddhist-like behavior.[106] The judge noted that, unlike e-mails and phone calls, Twitter messages could be blocked and therefore did not constitute stalking.

Cyber harassment criminalizes the use, in interstate or foreign communications, of a telecommunications device, whether or not conversation or communication ensues, to annoy, abuse, threaten, or harass someone anonymously.[107] The first person convicted for violating the law was a South Carolina man who sent harassing e-mails to a Seattle resident for six years. He also disseminated false information about the victim to her co-workers and posted sexual invitations in her name in chat rooms.[108] The perpetrator turned out to be a boyfriend from a relationship that had ended eight years earlier. Authorities in Washington relied on the federal law because the state had no cyberstalking or cyber harassment law at the time. Now most states do.

The first cyberstalker convicted in the U.S. was prosecuted under a California statute in 1999. Gary Dellapenta, a former security guard, was angered when a female acquaintance rebuffed his attention. He posted Internet personal ads in her name, indicating that she fantasized about being raped. The ads included her home address, phone number, physical description, and directions to disable her alarm system. Six men visited

---

[106] United States v. William Lawrence Cassidy, No. TWT 11-091 (MD Filed 12-15-2011).

[107] 47 U.S.C. § 223(a)(1)(C) (2011).

[108] Vanessa Ho, *Cyberstalker enters guilty plea*, SEATTLE POST INTELLIGENCER, July 29, 2004, at B1.

her home before police learned the identity of the poster and arrested him. Fortunately, she was never harmed.[109]

National attention drawn to the cyber harassment of 13-year-old Megan Meier precipitated a wide-scale adoption of cyberstalking and cyber harassment statutes across the country. Megan, an insecure teen who had previously suffered from depression, developed a MySpace friendship with 16-year-old Josh Evans, who seemed wonderful at first but after 16 weeks turned on her cruelly. After weeks of attention that made her feel good about herself, Josh sent her a message that he didn't want to be friends with her anymore because he had heard that she wasn't very nice to friends. Afterward she saw messages posted by others, saying she was fat and a slut. Her father said the last message Megan received told her everyone hated her and that the world would be a better place without her. That day Megan hung herself in her closet.[110]

Six weeks later, Megan's parents learned that Josh Evans never existed. Megan had recently ended an on-and-off-again friendship with a girl who lived down her street. The girl's mother, Lori Drew, got an employee to create the fake profile so she could learn what Megan was saying about her daughter. The mother, daughter, and employee sent Josh's messages. Another girl in the neighborhood was also drawn into the ruse. Her mother told the Meiers the truth after learning about it from her daughter.

Missouri, which had no cyberstalking or cyber harassment law at the time, was powerless to charge Drew with anything because she had not broken the law there. However, a federal prosecutor in California, where MySpace's servers are located, indicted Drew under the Computer Fraud and Abuse Act – a law normally reserved for computer hackers – for accessing protected computers without authorization to get information used to inflict emotional distress on the girl.[111] The government based its case on the notion that violating MySpace's terms of service, requiring that subscribers provide "truthful and accurate registration information" and "refrain from promoting information that is false or misleading," amounted to an "unauthorized access" of MySpace in violation of the law. A jury cleared Drew of felony computer-hacking charges, but convicted her of three counts of misdemeanor computer fraud.[112] The judge later acquitted Drew of the charges, reasoning that the case was really one of breach of contract and that convicting someone for violating a website's terms of service would empower a website's owner to determine what constitutes a crime.[113]

Unfortunately, there have been several cases of children who have committed suicide after being bullied both in school and online.[114] Many states have responded by enacting

---

[109] Greg Miller and Davan Maharaj, *N. Hollywood Man Charged in 1st Cyber-Stalking Case*, L.A. Times, an. 22, 1999, http://articles.latimes.com/1999/jan/22/news/mn-523.

[110] Megan Meier Foundation, *Megan Meier's Story*, http://www.meganmeierfoundation.org/megansStory.php (last visited Feb. 8, 2012).

[111] U.S. v. Drew, Crim. No. 08-00582 (C.D. Cal. indictment filed May 15, 2008).

[112] Jeremy Kohler and David Hunn, *Drew juror says most saw case as a felony*, St. Louis Post-Dispatch, Dec. 2, 2008, A1.

[113] Correy Stephenson, *Cyberbullying Conviction Reversed in U.S. District Court*, Lawyer's Weekly, Sept. 1, 2009.

[114] Susan Donaldson James, Immigrant Teen Taunted by Cyberbullies Hangs Herself, CBS News, Jan. 26, 2010 (describing the deaths of teens in Vermont and Massachusetts).

cyberbullying statutes. *Cyberbullying* refers to electronic harassment targeted at minors by minors. Most cyberbullying laws direct schools to adopt regulations to protect minors from this type of activity as well as more traditional bullying. These laws are a boon to victims who need protection from online harassment, but they have to be used carefully. Schools administrators are finding that navigating their responsibilities with respect to student speech posted off campus is complicated.

Occasionally administrators try to use cyberbullying or harassment laws to punish speech that is merely rebellious. In Indiana, the state supreme court overturned a delinquency charge against a 14-year-old girl accused of harassing her principal. The student posted expletive-laced comments about him on a fake MySpace profile a friend created in his name.[115] A lower court held that the girl's actions, if carried out by an adult, would have violated Indiana's law against cyber harassment. In Indiana, as in other states, it is an offense to use electronic communication to transmit an obscene, indecent or profane message to a person "with intent to harass, annoy, or alarm" the person. . . ."[116]

It was clear from the student's posts that she was angry because her principal had criticized her piercings:

hey you piece of greencastle s**t. what the f**k do you think of me know [sic] that you cant [sic] control me? Huh? ha ha ha guess what ill [sic] wear my f**king piercings all day long and to school and you cant [sic] do s**t about it! ha ha f**king ha! stupid bastard.[117]

Unfortunately, in true teen drama queen fashion, she added to the rant: "die . . . gobert . . . die" and "F**K MR. GOBERT AND GC SCHOOLS!"

The site's creator had granted only 26 MySpace "friends" access to it. The Indiana Supreme Court pointed out that in order to violate the statute's intent requirement the accused must have had some expectation that the speech dubbed harassment would reach its target.[118] But in this case, there was no evidence to show that the petitioner had reason to expect that the principal would learn about the site or read it. In fact, he only became aware of the girl's posts because one of the students with access to the site showed him a printout from it. The girl had also created a site of her own that was publicly accessible. But her comments on it – aside from its title, which associated the principal's name with another expletive – were a reaction to her friend's punishment for the private profile. The Indiana Supreme Court found the girl's page to be a "legitimate communication of her anger and criticism" of the principal and school regarding the disciplinary actions it took against her friend for her private profile.[119]

Most recently, courts have begun to consider alleged stalking cases involving Twitter. In one, a man taunted a woman by posting 8,000 tweets about her. Some of the posts predicted her death. When she blocked the messages, more appeared from different accounts. Federal authorities arrested the poster and charged him with stalking. But a

---

[115] A.B. v. State of Indiana, 885 N.E.2d 1223 (Ind. 2008).

[116] Indiana Code § 35-45-2-2(a)(4) (2004).

[117] A.B. v. State of Indiana, 885 N.E.2d at 1225.

[118] *Id.* at 1226.

[119] *Id.* at 1227.

federal judge dismissed the case.[120] The legal question was whether in posting a public message on Twitter the accused was engaging in direct personal communication to harass the victim, or simply ranting from a public platform. The defendant had not been indicted for threatening the victim. The court believed Twitter was a public platform and that the poster's diatribes, although they may have inflicted emotional distress, were protected.

Hate Speech

Hate speech is a form of communication that disparages individuals or groups on the basis of characteristics such as ethnicity, race, religion or sexual orientation. The United States is unique among democratic nations in its protection for hate speech. Hate speech is a crime in Australia, Brazil, Canada, Denmark, France, Germany, India, the Netherlands, South Africa and the United Kingdom. In fact, at least 175 countries are party to the Convention on the Elimination of All Forms of Racial Discrimination, which, among its many provisions, obligates signatories to make "all dissemination of ideas based on racial superiority or hatred" a punishable offense.[121] The United States is a party to the convention as well but has refused to enact legislation contrary to First Amendment principles.

Justice Louis Brandeis expressed a common view held in the United States about unpopular speech – that when the malady is falsehood or bias "the remedy to be applied is more speech, not enforced silence."[122] One exception to the rule is *fighting words*, which may be regulated to avoid a disturbance of the peace. These are "words that people of common intelligence would know would be likely to cause a fight."[123] Because the doctrine only applies to face-to-face confrontations likely to ensue in violence, it has no bearing on digital media.[124] Hate speech filtered through a website, text message, e-mail, or television program does not constitute fighting words and is protected by the First Amendment.

Action motivated by hate is not protected, however. Almost all states and the federal government have enacted some form of legislation meant to counter hate crimes motivated by personal characteristics, such as race, color, religion, national origin, ethnicity, gender, disability, or sexual orientation. The federal statute, for example, allows juries to triple the punishment for a crime if they find that it was motivated by the victim's personal characteristics.[125]

[120] U.S. v. William Lawrence Cassidy, 2011 U.S. Dist. LEXIS 145056; 40 Media L. Rep. 1001 (D. Md. 2011). Somini Sengupta, *Judge Dismisses Twitter Case*, N.Y. TIMES, Dec. 16, 2011, at B9.

[121] International Convention on the Elimination of All Forms of Racial Discrimination, Mar. 7, 1966, 660 U.N.T.S. 195.

[122] Whitney v. California, 274 U.S. 357, 377 (1927) (Brandeis, J., concurring).

[123] Chaplinsky v. New Hampshire, 315 U.S. 568 (1942) (finding fighting words to be of "such slight social value" as to be unworthy of First Amendment protection).

[124] *See* Gooding v. Wilson, 405 U.S. 518 (1972) (finding that fighting words must be limited to face-to-face conflicts, involving words "that have a direct tendency to cause acts of violence by the person to whom, individually, the remark is addressed").

[125] 18 U.S.C.S. Appx § 3A1.1 (Lexis-Nexis 2008).

Questions for Discussion

1. What is the difference between indecency and obscenity?
2. Why is it legal to possess obscenity in the home, but not to download it at home over the Internet?
3. What is the difference in the approach that American courts take regarding indecency and violent speech and their potential impact on children?
4. Are the makers of violent films, games, and music lyrics liable to the families of victims harmed by people inspired to act violently after using such media? Why or why not?

12 Commercial Speech and Antitrust Law

At one point, purely commercial speech was considered to be unworthy of First Amendment protection.[1] Although this is no longer true, commercial speech is still afforded "lesser protection" than other forms of speech.[2] The government can control advertising that is deceptive or misleading or that promotes transactions that are themselves illegal. It may impose reasonable time, place, and manner restrictions on commercial speech. It also may subject commercial speech disseminated through broadcast media to certain requirements or restrictions based on its scarcity and pervasiveness rationale.

The Supreme Court initially justified this difference in protection on the view that commercial speech held a "subordinate position in the scale of First Amendment values" and that requiring parity of protection for it would eventually dilute the First Amendment's power to protect noncommercial speech.[3] As its view on commercial speech developed further, the Court suggested that the First Amendment protects advertising's "informational function." When advertising is false or misleading, it is not serving an informational function and is therefore not protected.

> Commercial speech is protected for its *informational function*. Because false advertising does not serve an informational function, it is not protected.

The regulatory agency with the largest impact on commercial speech is the Federal Trade Commission, which protects consumers against unfair or deceptive trade practices. However other government agencies also regulate commercial speech related to their specialty areas. The Federal Communications Commission, for example, imposes some restrictions on advertisements intended for broadcast media. The Food and Drug Administration regulates advertisements related to food, drugs, cosmetics and tobacco products. The Securities and Exchange Commission regulates advertising for financial products. The Department of Transportation regulates advertising for air travel.

---

[1] *See* Valentine v. Chrestensen, 316 U.S. 52 (1942).
[2] *See* Central Hudson Gas & Electric Company v. Public Service Commission, 447 U.S. 557, 563 (1980).
[3] *Id.* at 562 (quoting Ohralik v. Ohio State Bar Ass'n, 436 U.S. 447, 455–6, (1978)).

Digital Media Law, Second Edition. Ashley Packard.
© 2013 John Wiley & Sons, Inc. Published 2013 by John Wiley & Sons, Inc.

The Federal Trade Commission, in collaboration with the Justice Department, also makes decisions about mergers that could lead to anticompetitive practices. When proposed mergers involve communication companies that not only threaten competition but diversity of expression, the FCC becomes involved as well.

This chapter will examine the meaning of commercial speech, the evolution of its protection under the First Amendment, the principal legal test that applies to it, policies and restrictions related to advertising, and antitrust action intended to preserve speech.

What is Commercial Speech?

At its most basic, *commercial speech* is "speech that proposes a commercial transaction."[4] But the Supreme Court has also defined commercial speech more broadly as "expression related solely to the economic interests of the speaker and its audience."[5] Classically, we think of commercial speech as advertising, but the term has also been applied to in-person solicitations,[6] parties at which products were sold,[7] direct mail offers, and even pamphlets about diseases that mention a specific product.[8] We are now at a point at which commercial activity has expanded to encompass e-mail promotions, texts, social media marketing and other areas that cross the line between advertising and public relations. The Court will soon have to decide whether these new forms of marketing constitute commercial speech and, if so, whether its current perspective on the level of constitutional protection accorded to commercial speech should remain.

Advertising and First Amendment Protection

Protection for commercial speech is in the process of evolution. In the 1940s, the Supreme Court determined that advertising was not protected. It had established a two-tier approach to speech protection. Within that paradigm, the First Amendment protected core expression – particularly political, cultural or artistic speech – while offering essentially no protection to categories of speech deemed to be of "such slight social value as a step to truth" that government could prevent people from using them without offending the constitution. The Court placed advertising in the latter category, where *false* advertising remains today. *Truthful* advertising has since secured a kind of second-class protection subject to greater government regulation than core expression. Recent decisions by the Court suggest, however, that protection for commercial speech will continue to expand.

[4] Board of Trustees v. Fox, 492 U.S. 469, 482 (1989).
[5] Central Hudson Gas & Electric Corp. v. Public Service Commission of New York, 447 U.S. 557, 561 (1980).
[6] Breard v. Alexandria, 341 U.S. 622 (1951).
[7] Board of Trustees v. Fox, 492 U.S. 469 (1989).
[8] Bolger v. Youngs Drug Product Corp., 463 U.S. 60, 66 n.13 (1983).

Advertising first earned constitutional protection through its association with political speech. The Supreme Court held that an ad alleged to have been defamatory in *New York Times v. Sullivan* (1964) was protected political speech.[9] The ad in question was what we would now call an "advertorial." It described police resistance to civil rights demonstrations in Alabama. The Court was motivated by political concerns again in *Bigelow v. Virginia* (1974), when it struck down a law that barred media from publishing advertisements for legal abortion services.[10] It held that speech is not devoid of First Amendment protection simply because it appears in the form of advertising.

It was not until 1976 that the Supreme Court protected advertising for its own sake. In *Virginia State Bd. of Pharmacy v. Virginia Citizens Consumer Council, Inc.*, the Court struck down a law that prevented pharmacists from advertising drug prices. The government argued that the ban was necessary to discourage people from selecting cut-rate pharmacies likely to provide them with reduced services. The Court concluded that government couldn't protect people from supposed harm by keeping them in ignorance. It held that there is not only a right to advertise but also a reciprocal right to receive advertisements.[11] Writing for the majority, Justice Blackmun explained that in a free-enterprise economy, "the allocation of our resources at large will be made through numerous private economic decisions. It is a matter of public interest that those decisions, in the aggregate, be intelligent and well informed. To this end, the free flow of commercial information is indispensable."[12]

The Supreme Court crystallized its policy on commercial speech in the landmark case of *Central Hudson Gas & Electric Company v. Public Service Commission* (1980). The case concerned the constitutionality of a New York Public Service Commission rule, passed during an energy shortage, which prohibited advertising that promoted energy consumption. Here the Court recognized the state's interest in limiting energy use and that the regulation under consideration seemed to advance that interest. However, it concluded that the regulation limited more speech than necessary to accomplish its goal.

Even truthful commercial speech may be regulated if the regulation passes the *Central Hudson* four-part test.

The Court held that protection for commercial speech "turns on the nature both of the expression and of the governmental interests served by its regulation."[13] It established a four-part test to evaluate the constitutionality of regulations applied to commercial speech. A court must determine that:

1. the expression concerns a lawful activity and is not misleading;
2. the governmental interest in the regulation is substantial;
3. the regulation directly advances that interest; and
4. the regulation is no more extensive than necessary to serve that interest.[14]

---

[9] 376 U.S. 254 (1964).
[10] 421 U.S. 809 (1975).
[11] 425 U.S. 748 (1976).
[12] *Id.* at 765.
[13] Central Hudson, 447 U.S. at 563 (1980).
[14] *Id.* at 566.

The first prong is an entry-level consideration. The First Amendment does not protect speech that is false or misleading or that promotes illegal activity. Because unprotected speech may be regulated constitutionally, there would be no need to employ the rest of the test.

After reviewing the case based on these criteria, the Court concluded that while New York's interest in energy conservation was substantial and advanced by the regulation, a complete ban on advertising burdened too much protected speech. For example, it prevented the petitioner from advertising energy-efficient appliances. In that respect, the regulation violated the First and Fourteenth Amendments.

The Court applied the *Central Hudson* test in the mid-1990s to strike down state laws meant to discourage liquor consumption by banning the inclusion of alcohol content on beer labels or retail liquor prices in advertising.[15] It used the test again in 2002 to strike down a restriction that prevented pharmacies from advertising the sale of compound drugs, in an effort to discourage their wide-scale production.[16] Each time, the Court found that the regulations either failed to directly advance government interests or were more extensive then necessary to accomplish the government's goal.

Most recently, in *Sorrell v. IMS* (2011), the Supreme Court appeared to move toward even greater protection for commercial speech by suggesting that regulations that target it are a form of *viewpoint discrimination*. The case concerned a Vermont restriction that prohibited pharmacies from selling their records of doctors' prescriptions to data miners and marketers who could use the information to market brand-name drugs to physicians more effectively. The state defended the law by arguing that "pharmaceutical marketing has a strong influence on doctors' prescribing practices." It clearly wanted to encourage doctors to prescribe generic drugs; it also wanted to protect medical privacy. The Court did not dispute the state's interests in these goals. However, it did not feel that the regulations advanced them in a permissible way. Subjecting the regulation to heightened scrutiny, the Court found the law to be both a content- and speaker-based restriction because it disfavored a particular type of speech – marketing – and a particular type of speaker – pharmaceutical companies. It stated again that "the 'fear that people would make bad decisions if given truthful information' cannot justify content-based burdens on speech." It also noted that privacy was not protected by the regulation because pharmacies were allowed to share the data for other purposes.

> Viewpoint discrimination, which is antithetical to First Amendment principles, refers to government regulation of speech based on its preference for or dislike of the particular message it contains.

The right to reject advertising

Just as the First Amendment protects the right to advertise, it protects the right to reject advertising. The Supreme Court has said that the term free speech comprises "the decision of both what to say and what not to say."[17] Requiring a medium to accept advertising it does not want to run would be a form of compelled speech.

---

[15] Rubin v. Coors Brewing Co., 514 U.S. 476 (1995); 44 Liquormart, Inc. v. Rhode Island, 517 U.S. 484 (1996).
[16] Thompson v. Western States Medical Center, 535 U.S. 357 (2002).
[17] Riley v. National Fed'n of the Blind of North Carolina, 487 U.S. 781, 796–97 (1987).

The Supreme Court held that there is no right of access to broadcast media in *CBS v. Democratic National Committee* (1973).[18] The DNC requested a declaratory ruling from the Federal Communications Commission stating that broadcasters had no right to refuse to sell time to responsible entities who wanted to solicit funds or comment on public issues. The FCC rejected its request. The Supreme Court upheld the FCC's decision. It pointed out that forcing a private medium to accept advertising would interfere with producers' rights to exercise editorial control over the content of the medium and require them to sacrifice other content they would have preferred to run in the space or time occupied by the compelled ad.

This case, along with another in which the Supreme Court held that there is no right of access to newspapers, has come to stand for the proposition that there is no right of access to private media.[19] This principle also applies to the Internet. A Delaware district court dismissed a suit against Google, Yahoo! Inc., and Microsoft Corp. for refusing to run ads for particular websites in *Langdon v. Google, Inc.* (2007).[20] Christopher Langdon sued the search engines when they declined to run ads for his websites criticizing North Carolina's attorney general and the Chinese government. Filing on his own behalf, Langdon alleged that the defendants' refusal to run his ads violated his First Amendment rights and constituted fraud because Google refused his ads for reasons that were not stated in its content policy. The court pointed out that, as private entities, the search engines could not violate the plaintiff's First Amendment rights. However, a court order compelling the defendants to run Langdon's ads would violate their First Amendment rights. The defendants were also entitled under Section 230 of the Communications Decency Act to refuse objectionable content.

However, the media may not reject advertising for discriminatory reasons.[21] Nor can it refuse advertising in violation of antitrust laws, discussed later in this chapter.[22] Broadcast media are also required to accept advertisements from federal candidates before an election and to provide equal access to state and local candidates should they choose to accept ads for state or local elections.

Regulation of Unfair and Deceptive Advertising

The primary agency responsible for controlling unfair and deceptive ads is the Federal Trade Commission. The FTC was created in 1914 to regulate unfair competition, but in

---

[18] 412 U.S. 94 (1973); *see also* Clark County Sch. Dist. v. Planned Parenthood, 941 F.2d 817, 824 (9th Cir. 1991) (holding that advertising space in school newspapers and yearbooks is not a public forum and schools may reject advertising).

[19] *See* Miami Herald Publg. Co. v. Tornillo, 418 U.S. 241 (1974) (upholding a publisher's right to refuse to run editorial replies).

[20] 474 F. Supp. 2d 622 (D. Del. 2007).

[21] *See* Pittsburgh Press Co. v. Pitt. Commn. of Human Rel., 413 U.S. 376, 391 (1973) (prohibiting a publication from carrying advertisements for jobs in sex-designated columns).

[22] *See* Lorain J. Co. v. U.S., 342 U.S. 143, 155–56 (1951); Home Placement Serv. v. Providence J. Co., 682 F.2d 274, 281 (1st Cir. 1982).

1938 its role was expanded to include consumer protection. The agency draws its power to prohibit deceptive advertising from Section 5 of the Federal Trade Commission Act, which states that "unfair or deceptive acts or practices in or affecting commerce" are unlawful.[23]

Unfair acts or practices

Normally consumers survey product or service options, compare costs and benefits, and make their own choices. An act or practice that impedes consumers' ability to make those choices effectively may be considered unfair if it *causes substantial injury that consumers cannot reasonably avoid on their own and is not outweighed by countervailing benefits to consumers or competition.*[24] It may also consider established public policy in determining whether an act is unfair, but only as a supplementary criterion. This usually amounts to determining whether its own actions would be in accord with legislative and judicial determinations in the area.

The injury must be substantial

Substantial injury generally involves monetary harm. But the injury may also involve unwarranted health or safety risks. Even if the harm is relatively slight, it may be deemed substantial if it affects a broad population. For example, an unnecessary transaction fee of $2 imposed on a phone bill may be small in isolation, but quite large when spread over a phone company's many consumers.

The FTC does not consider emotional impact in its calculation of injury. It is, therefore, not concerned with whether consumers find particular forms of advertising tasteless or offensive.

The injury must not be one that consumers could have avoided on their own

The Commission's role is to protect consumer choices, not to second guess the choices they make. Consider the practice of selling sugary sodas – a product with no redeeming value beyond taste. Clearly they are bad for us, but we know that, and we don't have to buy them. The FTC concerns itself with practices that make it hard to sort out the information we need. For example, a consumer agreement designed to confuse consumers and then later take advantage of them would be considered unfair. So would a company's practice of failing to disclose a potential danger associated with its product that a reasonable consumer would not anticipate.

The injury is not outweighed by countervailing benefits

The commission employs a cost/benefit analysis when it is considering whether a practice is truly unfair. Take, for example, the authentication procedure that most companies

---

[23] 15 U.S.C. § 45(a) (2011).
[24] *Id.* at § 45(n).

use when you shop online. It takes very little effort to register for an account on iTunes or Amazon, and once the company has your credit card information, you need only sign in with your password to shop. Passwords are convenient, but also easily stolen. How many extra steps would you be willing to take to secure your account information? The FTC balances proposed remedies against their potential inconvenience to consumers or the extra costs that companies will have to incur.

Deceptive advertising

The FTC considers three factors when determining whether an advertisement is deceptive: *whether the ad contains a representation, omission, or practice that is likely to mislead; how a consumer acting reasonably in the circumstances would be likely to interpret the ad; and whether the ad's deception is material.*[25]

There must be a representation, omission, or practice likely to mislead

Deceptive ads may include false oral or written misrepresentations about a product or service, omissions meant to lead consumers to false conclusions, misleading price claims, and false warranties. Advertisers that make particular claims, whether explicitly stated or simply implied, must have a "reasonable basis" for them. The level of evidence required depends on the claim made. The FTC is most concerned about health and safety claims. It requires advertisers to support health and safety claims with "competent and reliable scientific evidence" gathered through studies and tests conducted using appropriate methodologies and evaluated by qualified reviewers.[26]

The act or practice must be considered from a reasonable consumer's perspective

When assessing an ad, the FTC looks at it from the perspective of a "reasonable person" – not someone who is overly sensitive or gullible. If a reasonable person could interpret the ad in more than one way, one of which is false, the seller will be held liable for the false interpretation.

The agency also considers the ad from the perspective of its intended audience. If the ad is targeted toward children, the FTC will consider the ad from the perspective of a reasonable child, who due to lack of age or experience would be less qualified than an adult to filter exaggerated claims. If the ad is targeted toward people who are sick, overweight, or elderly, the FTC will consider the ad from the perspective of audiences who may be more vulnerable to magic cures or scams.

---

[25] FTC Policy Statement on Deception, Appended to Cliffdale Associates, Inc., 103 F.T.C. 110, 174 (1984).
[26] Federal Trade Commission, In the matter of Nestlé Healthcare Nutrition, Inc., File No. 092 3087, consent order, May 18, 2010; Nestlé HealthCare Nutrition, Inc.; Analysis of Proposed Consent Order to Aid Public Comment, 75 Fed. Reg. 140 (July 22, 2010).

When assessing an advertisement, the FTC considers the ad in its entirety, rather than divorcing particular words or phrases from the whole. Disclaimers in mouse print or spoken at lightning speed at the end of an ad will not be accorded any weight if the rest of the ad implies something else. Disclosures that qualify a claim must be displayed "clearly and conspicuously." If a disclosure is made through a hyperlink, the link should be prominently displayed near the claim. The FTC also considers the fact that people skim ads and websites, so accurate information in the text of an ad may not make up for a deceptive headline.

The representation, omission, or practice must be material

Deceptive statements or omissions are considered material if they are likely to affect a consumer's purchasing decision. Certain categories are presumptively material. These include implied claims, if there is evidence to show that the seller intended to make an implied claim, and express claims about a product's performance, features, safety, price, or effectiveness. In contrast, subjective statements, regarding taste, smell, or appearance, are considered subject to consumer interpretation and are much less likely to attract the FTC's attention.

According to the agency's Statement on Deception, "A finding of materiality is also a finding that injury is likely to exist because of the representation, omission, sales practice, or marketing technique . . . Injury exists if consumers would have chosen differently but for the deception."[27]

FTC Actions Against False Advertising

Consumers who spot deceptive marketing practices can file a complaint with the FTC, which will investigate them and respond with the action it considers appropriate. The Commission's preferred course of action in false advertising cases is to seek voluntary compliance with the law though a consent order. A *consent order* is a negotiated settlement in which the advertiser agrees to refrain from further deception without having to admit any wrongdoing. For example, in a consent agreement with the FTC, WebTV agreed to stop advertising that it could offer people the same level of Internet access and content through their TVs that they could achieve through a computer.[28] Consent orders carry the force of law. Violation of the order can result in a fine of $11,000 per ad per day.

Consent agreements often involve not only the promise to discontinue deceptive advertising, but a settlement of some kind. Reebok, for example, reached a $25 million

---

[27] FCC Policy Statement on Deception, appended to Cliffdale Associates, Inc., 103 F.T.C. 110, 174 (1984) ¶ 33, http://www.ftc.gov/bcp/policystmt/ad-decept.htm.
[28] *See In re* WEBTV Networks, Inc., FTC Docket No. C-3988 (Dec. 8, 2000) (consent order).

agreement with the FTC after the agency determined that it had used unsupported claims in print, television, and Internet advertisements for its EasyTone and RunTone shoes. The company advertised that the shoes had "been proven to lead to 28 percent more strength and tone in the buttock muscles, 11 percent more strength and tone in the hamstring muscles, and 11 percent more strength and tone in the calf muscles than regular walking shoes."[29]

If the advertiser does not agree to stop the offending ad, the FTC will issue an administrative complaint against it and the case will go before an administrative law judge. In an administrative proceeding, parties present evidence and witnesses as they would in a trial, and the administrative law judge acts as fact finder. At the end of the proceeding, the administrative judge issues an initial decision, stating the facts and relevant law. The Commission then makes its final determination to dismiss the case or issue a cease and desist order. *Cease and desist orders*, which remain in force for 20 years, require an advertiser to discontinue a particular practice and avoid further deception. An advertiser has 60 days to comply with the order or launch an appeal in the federal court system. The advertiser may petition a U.S. Court of Appeals to review the Commission's decision, either in the circuit in which the company is based or where the alleged deception was carried out.

If a fraudulent act is particularly egregious and ongoing, the FTC may go straight to federal court to file a complaint against the advertiser. For example, in *FTC v. Accusearch, Inc.* (2008), the Commission asked for an injunction to stop an information broker from selling consumer telephone records to third parties without the consumers' knowledge.[30] The company advertised on its website that it could deliver anyone's phone records for a fee, and it did after obtaining them through illegal methods. A Wyoming district court permanently enjoined the company from selling or advertising the sale of telephone records and made it return $200,000 in ill-gotten profits.

Courts may also demand corrective advertising in false advertising cases, require defendants to pay restitution to duped consumers, and force them to disgorge ill gotten gains.

In 2010, the U.S. Court of Appeals for the First Circuit upheld a judgment for the FTC, forcing the company Direct Marketing Concepts to disgorge $48 million for deceptive marketing. The company used infomercials to advertise its Coral Calcium and Supreme Greens products. In the infomercials, the marketers claimed that all diseases are caused by a condition called acidosis and that their products cured diseases by making the body more alkaline. The supposed expert on the infomercial said

---

[29] Federal Trade Commission v. Reebok International, Ltd. Case: 1:11-cv-02046 (N.D. Ohio Sept. 29, 2011); Reebok to Pay $25 Million in Customer Refunds To Settle FTC Charges of Deceptive Advertising of EasyTone and RunTone Shoes, Federal Trade Commission Release, Sept. 28, 2011, http://www.ftc.gov/opa/2011/09/reebok.shtm. Reebok also settled a class action suit for this claim for $28.5 million, *In re* Reebok Easytone Litig., No. 4:10-cv-11977-FDS (D. Mass. Oct. 6, 2011).

[30] Civil Action No. 06-CV-0105 (D. Wyo. 2008); FTC File No. 052 3126.

> You can have heart disease, cancer, lupus, fibromyalgia, multiple sclerosis. Name the disease, they're all caused by acidosis. . . . We've been studying the coral calcium and I can tell you there are tens of millions of people, millions of testimonials. I've had 1,000 people tell me how they've cured their cancer. I've witnessed people get out of wheelchairs with multiple sclerosis just by getting on the coral.[31]

Courts have determined that penalties properly begin with consumers' losses, so fines often represent the company's gross revenue rather than its profits after expenses.

Many of the cases the FTC pursues through the courts involve health or credit scams. A federal district court in Texas awarded the FTC a $105.7 million judgment in 2004 against a telemarketing company named Assail. Among other things, the company targeted consumers with poor credit histories by promising advance-fee credit card packages for credit cards that never came. The scam defrauded hundreds of thousands of people. The court imposed lifetime telemarketing bans on the defendants.[32] The company's owner, Kyle Kimoto, was later sentenced to 29 years in prison.[33]

FTC Advertising Guidelines

FTC advertising guidelines may be found at www.ftc.gov/bcp/guides/guides.shtm.

The FTC offers guidelines to advertisers to help them avoid marketing practices that would be considered unfair or deceptive under the Federal Trade Commission Act. The guidelines are administrative interpretations, not binding law.

Endorsements and testimonials

Endorsements and testimonials are common in advertisements and the FTC has enacted rules for their use. Expert endorsements may only come from someone truly qualified to give an opinion on the subject.[34] Dr. Packard, the professor, would not be allowed to give an opinion on the effectiveness of a particular drug, for example.

The FTC claims the right to hold both advertisers and endorsers liable for false or unsubstantiated claims made in an endorsement and for failure to disclose material connections between the advertiser and endorser that might influence the endorsement. Consumers expect experts and celebrities to be paid for endorsing a product in an advertisement, so it is not necessary to disclose that information. However, celebrities must disclose their relationships with advertisers when making endorsements in contexts other than traditional ads, such as talk shows or social media. Regardless of the venue, they also have a duty to reveal unexpected material connections such as sharing profits from the sale of the product.[35]

[31] Federal Trade Commission v. Direct Marketing Concepts, Inc. 624 F.3d 1, 5 (1st Cir. 2010).
[32] Federal Trade Commission v. Assail, Civ. No. W-03-CA-007 (W.D. Tex. Sept. 24, 2004).
[33] U.S. v. Kimoto, 560 F. Supp. 2d 680 (S.D. Ill. 2008); Update on Kimoto Case, Re: United States v. Kyle Reid Kimoto, Case Number 2007R00169, http://www.justice.gov/usao/ils/Programs/VWA/kimoto.htm.
[34] Expert endorsements, 16 C.F.R. § 255.3.
[35] Disclosure of material connections, 16 C.F.R. § 255.5.

Endorsement rules also apply to bloggers. The FTC considers the post of a blogger, who receives cash or in-kind payment to review a product, to be an endorsement. Its rules require bloggers who make an endorsement to "disclose the material connections they share with the seller of the product or service."[36]

A person who is paid to endorse a product may not claim that the endorsement is freely given. If the endorser claims to use the product, he or she must in fact use it. Likewise, advertisements that claim to be using endorsements by actual consumers must be using the statements of actual consumers.

In 2011, the FTC won a $29.8 million judgment against a company that misled consumers through a variety of marketing ploys for its product and services, including false testimonials.[37] In promotional materials for one product called Grant Connect, the company promised millions of dollars in free government grants. According to the FTC, the company began using testimonials before the service had its first consumer. In testimonials for a work-at-home business offer, only one of the testimonials seemed to have come from someone who had been a customer.

Testimonials must reflect customers' typical experience with a product.[38] If they do not, the company will be required to disclose the results that consumers could generally expect. It is no longer enough to say that results may vary. Claims made about the effectiveness of a drug or device must be substantiated. If the company has sponsored an organization that has supplied research for the product, it must disclose that connection.[39]

Comparative advertising

The FTC encourages the use of brand comparisons in advertising because it can be helpful to consumers making purchasing decisions, encourage product improvement, and lead to lower prices. However, the advertiser must identify the basis for the comparison and the comparison must be accurate. An advertiser cannot engage in disparagement of competing products through the use of false or misleading pictures, depictions, or demonstrations.

Subliminal advertising

Subliminal advertising is supposed to act on consumers subconsciously by transmitting messages to them below the threshold of their awareness. Although it has never been proved to be effective, the FTC does not allow subliminal advertising because the practice is deceptive. The Federal Communications Commission also has a policy against subliminal advertising because the agency considers it "contrary to the public interest."[40]

---

[36] Guides Concerning the Use of Endorsements and Testimonials in Advertising, 16 C.F.R. § 255.

[37] Federal Trade Commission v. Grant Connect, No. 2:09-CV-01349-PMP-RJJ (D. Nev. Oct. 25, 2011), 2011 U.S. Dist. LEXIS 123792.

[38] Consumer endorsements, 16 C.F.R. § 255.2.

[39] General considerations, 16 C.F.R. § 255.1.

[40] See Public Notice Concerning the Broadcast of Information By Means of "Subliminal Perception" Techniques, 44 F.C.C. 2d 1016, 1017 (1974).

Nevertheless, advertisers occasionally use it. Messages have been hidden in films, on television, in print, and flash advertisements on the Internet.

Subliminal advertising was an issue in the 2000 presidential election when Senators Ron Wyden and John Breaux asked the FCC to investigate commercials that attacked Al Gore's prescription drug proposal while displaying the word RATS for one-thirtieth of a second longer than the rest of word BUREAUCRATS. The agency questioned 179 stations that aired the ad, finding that they either did not know the word was there or knew that it was there but assumed that because it was visible it did not constitute subliminal advertising. The Commission determined that no further action was warranted on its part because it could only punish the stations, not the Bush campaign for placing the ad.

Vance v. Judas Priest (1990) presents the most in-depth discussion of subliminal messaging.[41] The plaintiffs were parents of two boys who made a suicide pact while listening to the Judas Priest album *Stained Glass*. One succeeded in killing himself; the other was gravely injured. A song on the album called "Better by you, better than me" contained the hidden words "do it." A federal district court in Nevada ruled that subliminal messages are not protected by the First Amendment and constitute an invasion of privacy if they are intended to manipulate the recipient's behavior. However, because the plaintiffs did not prove that the defendants intended to put subliminal messages in the album and scientific evidence did not support the effectiveness of subliminal messages, the court ruled in favor of the defendants.

Advertising and Foreseeable Harm

Normally the company advertising a particular product or service is responsible for false or deceptive advertising, but third parties such as advertising agencies and web designers may be held liable for false advertising as well if they contribute to the ad's preparation or are aware that its content is deceptive or unfair. The FTC considers it the duty of advertising agencies and web designers to verify the information used to substantiate claims in ads. It will hold them responsible if they know or *should have known* that the claims were false. Accepting a client's assurance that the ads are substantiated is not enough.

Publishers and broadcasters are rarely held liable for advertising unless they take part in the production of the ad or it is obvious from the ad's content that it is likely to cause harm. Courts assume that publishers do not have a duty to investigate the claims of advertisers because requiring them to bear that burden would draw time and attention away from their own speech.

Ohio's First District Court of Appeals reiterated this point in *Amann v. Clear Channel Communications, Inc.* (2006).[42] The appellate court upheld a lower court's grant of

---

[41]Vance v. Judas Priest, No. 86-5844/86-3939, 1990 WL 130920 (D. Nev. Aug. 24, 1990).
[42]165 Ohio App. 3d 291(2006).

summary judgment in favor of Clear Channel on claims that the company negligently failed to verify the content of its advertisements and committed negligent misrepresentation by airing a false ad on a Cincinnati radio station. The advertisements at issue promoted a "guaranteed 10% income plus plan" that turned out to be a fraudulent investment scheme. The appellate court held that Clear Channel had no duty to investigate claims made in the ad. It also held that running the ad was not a negligent misrepresentation on Clear Channel's part because the tort of negligent misrepresentation, which involves supplying false information for the guidance of others in their business transactions, requires a defendant to intentionally direct information to a specific or limited group of people rather than a general audience.

Although a medium has no duty to investigate claims in an ad, it can be held liable for publishing an advertisement that "on its face, and without the need for investigation, makes it apparent that there is a substantial danger of harm to the public."[43]

In *Braun v. Soldier of Fortune* (1992), the Eleventh Circuit upheld a $4.3 million award against the magazine for negligently publishing an ad for a contract killer. The ad read: "GUN FOR HIRE: 37-year-old professional mercenary desires jobs. Vietnam veteran. Discrete and very private. Body guard, courier, and other special skills. All jobs considered." Two men who read the ad hired the mercenary to kill their business associate, Richard Braun. The victim's son, Michael Braun, was also wounded in the attack. The Court of Appeals held that the First Amendment permits liability for the negligent publication of an ad that poses a clearly identifiable and unreasonable risk.

Braun was one of three cases filed against *Soldier of Fortune*. One was settled out of court.[44] Another, *Eimann v. Soldier of Fortune*, was decided in the Fifth Circuit.[45] The Court of Appeals for the Fifth Circuit reversed a $9.4 million jury verdict against the magazine in a wrongful death action brought by the son and mother of a murder victim. In that case the ad placed by the hired gun was less explicit: "EX-MARINES – 67–69 'Nam Vets, Ex-DI, weapons specialist – jungle warfare, pilot, M.E., high risk assignments, U.S. or overseas." The family argued that the magazine was negligent in publishing the ad, particularly since its advertising had been associated with crimes before. Applying Texas law, the court noted that negligence liability requires: the existence of a duty, a breach of that duty, and an injury proximately caused by that breach. The court concluded that *Soldier of Fortune* owed no duty to refrain from publishing the ad in this case because it was facially innocuous and "the ad's context–at most–made its message ambiguous."[46]

False Advertising and the Lanham Act

While the FTC enforces rules intended to protect the public at large, private citizens and companies harmed by unfair competition may sue for false advertising under Section

---

[43] Braun v. Soldier of Fortune, 968 F.2d 1110, 1119 (11th Cir. 1992).
[44] Norwood v. Soldier of Fortune Magazine, Inc., 651 F. Supp. 1397 (W.D. Ark. 1987).
[45] 680 F. Supp. 863 (S.D. Tex. 1988), rev'd 880 F.2d 830 (5th Cir. 1989).
[46] *Id.* at 834.

43(a)(1) of the Lanham Act – the same provision that prohibits false designation of origin in trademark cases. The statute provides a civil claim against anyone who "uses in commerce . . . any false of misleading representation of fact, which . . . in commercial advertising or promotion, misrepresents the nature, characteristics, qualities, or geographic origin of his or her or another person's goods, services or commercial activities."[47] The false claims may pertain to the advertiser's product or the competitor's product and may be comparative or noncomparative.

To successfully prove a claim under the Lanham Act, a plaintiff must establish that the defendant made:

1. a false or misleading statement of fact about a product;
2. such statement either deceived, or had the capacity to deceive a substantial segment of potential consumers;
3. the deception is material, in that it is likely to influence the consumer's purchasing decision;
4. the product is in interstate commerce; and
5. the plaintiff has been or is likely to be injured as a result of the statement at issue.[48]

The Lanham Act empowers courts to issue injunctions to stop false advertising. A plaintiff also may recover monetary damages if he or she can show that consumers relied on the false advertising to the detriment of the plaintiff's business or, alternatively, that the defendant deliberately published false comparative claims.[49] A plaintiff who can show willfulness or bad faith on the part of the defendant, may be awarded the defendant's profits from the false advertising.[50] A court may also demand that the defendant do corrective advertising to counteract false claims.

Because the focus of the Lanham Act is unfair competition, it is not meant to provide a private cause of action for consumers hurt by false advertising. Consumers who want to pursue independent claims normally do so through state consumer protection acts.

Categories of falsity

Courts categorize misleading advertisements as literal falsity, implied falsity, and puffery. *Literal falsity* involves false statements of fact. *Implied falsity* refers to statements that are literally true, but which are phrased in a misleading way. *Puffery* describes exaggeration and subjective claims that no consumer would be likely to take as fact. The first two categories are illegal, but the third is not.

Literally false statements are classified as either *establishment claims*, in which the defendant has based the advertised claim on some evidence (e.g., "Tests prove" or

---

[47] 15 U.S.C. § 1125(a)(1) (2011).

[48] *See* Pizza Hut, Inc. v. Papa John's Int'l, Inc., 227 F.3d 489, 495 (5th Cir. 2000).

[49] *See* U-Haul Int'l, Inc. v. Jartran, Inc., 793 F.2d 1034 (9th Cir. 1986).

[50] *See* ALPO Petfoods, Inc. v. Ralstan Purina Co., 997 F.2d 949 (D.C. Cir. 1993).

[51] *See* BASF Corp. v. Old World Trading Co., 41 F.3d 1081 (7th Cir. 1994); Johnson & Johnson-Merck Consumer Pharms. Co. v. Rhone-Poulenc Rorer Pharm., Inc., 19 F.3d 125, 129–30 (3rd Cir. 1994).

"studies show" . . .) or *bald claims* in which the defendant has made an unsupported assertion.[51] To establish the falsity of an ad with an establishment claim, a plaintiff must show that the defendant's studies do not sufficiently support the claim.[52] To establish the falsity of an ad with a bald claim, the plaintiff must disprove the claim.[53] A plaintiff who can prove that an advertisement is literally false will not be required to show that consumers were actually deceived by it.

If the falsity in an ad is only implied, however, the plaintiff will have to provide evidence that the advertisement is capable of misleading the public. Plaintiffs usually do this by submitting surveys that show consumers received the implied false message from the ad. Some circuits require the plaintiff to show that the ad actually deceived consumers. Others are satisfied with a showing that the ad had a tendency to deceive.

Sometimes it is difficult to tell whether an advertisement should be classified as literal or implied falsity. *Time Warner Cable, Inc. v. DIRECTV, Inc.* (2007) addressed this problem.[54] Time Warner sued DIRECTV for false advertising, contending that the satellite provider's advertising campaign promoting its high-definition programming made the literally false claim that cable HD service is inferior to satellite HD service. A district court, which agreed, awarded summary judgment to Time Warner on its claim and enjoined DIRECTV from further use of the campaign. DIRECTV appealed, arguing that its television commercials were not literally false because they did not explicitly state that DIRECTV's HD programming was superior to any other cable provider's service.

The U.S. Court of Appeals for the Second Circuit reviewed two of DIRECTV's television advertisements. The first, starring Jessica Simpson as Daisy Duke from the movie *Dukes of Hazzard*, went like this:

Simpson: Y'all ready to order?
          Hey, 253 straight days at the gym to get this body and you're not gonna watch me on DIRECTV HD?
          You're just not gonna get the best picture out of some fancy big screen TV without DIRECTV.
          It's broadcast in 1080i. I totally don't know what that means, but I want it.

Figure 12.1

The commercial originally ran with an accompanying tagline that read "for picture quality that beats cable, you've got to get DIRECTV." When Time Warner complained, the tagline was changed to: "For an HD picture that can't be beat, get DIRECTV." The Second Circuit found the ad likely to be proven literally false. Writing for the court, Judge Straub said "These statements make the explicit assertion that it is impossible to

[52] *See* Southland Sod Farms v. Stover Seed Co., 108 F.3d 1134, 1144 (9th Cir. 1997); EFCO Corp. v. Symons Corp., 219 F.3d 734, 740 (8th Cir. 2000).
[53] *See* United Industries Corp. v. Clorox Co., 140 F.3d 1175, 1182 (8th Cir. 1998).
[54] 497 F.3d 144 (2007).

obtain 'the best picture' – i.e., a '1080i'-resolution picture – from any source other than DIRECTV. This claim is flatly untrue."[55]

DIRECTV's second television ad, which follows, was a take-off on the science fiction series *Star Trek*, with William Shatner reprising his role as Captain Kirk:

> Mr. Chekov: Should we raise our shields, Captain?
> Captain Kirk: At ease, Mr. Chekov.
>   Again with the shields, I wish he'd just relax and enjoy the amazing picture clarity of the DIRECTV HD we just hooked up.
>   With what Starfleet just ponied up for this big screen TV, settling for cable would be illogical.

The ad was followed by the same revised tagline: "For an HD picture that can't be beat, get DIRECTV."

The Second Circuit, acknowledged that the Shatner ad was more ambiguous because it did not make an explicitly false assertion. In determining whether the ad could be interpreted as literally false, it chose to adopt the "false by necessary implication" doctrine. The First, Third, Fourth, and Ninth Circuits have already accepted the doctrine, which requires courts to analyze advertising messages in context. The Second Circuit held that "an advertisement can be literally false even though it does not explicitly make a false assertion, if the words or images, considered in context, necessarily and unambiguously imply a false message.[56] However, it warned "if the language or graphic is susceptible to more than one reasonable interpretation, the advertisement cannot be literally false."[57] Applying the "false by necessary implication" doctrine, the Court of Appeals affirmed the district court's conclusion that the statement "settling for cable would be illogical," in context with the rest of the ad, amounted to a false claim that cable's HD service is inferior to DIRECTV's HD service.

Although DIRECTV's television ads did not name Time Warner explicitly, the Second Circuit upheld the lower court's injunction against it. In a market in which Time Warner was the only cable alternative, it would be obvious to viewers that the comparative ads were directed toward it. However, the Court of Appeals reversed the injunction as it applied to DIRECTV's Internet advertisements, because it considered them to be "nonactionable puffery."

Puffery

Puffery involves the use of subjective statements that are not capable of measurement, such as "Downy makes your clothes smell April fresh," the meaning of which is open to

---

[55] *Id.* at 154.
[56] *Id.* at 148.
[57] *Id.* at 158.

anyone's interpretation. It also includes hyperbole that consumers are unlikely to believe, such as one gamemaker's boast that it made "The Most Advanced Home Gaming System in the Universe."[58] Papa John's protected puffery – "Better Ingredients. Better Pizza" – was both opinion and exaggeration.[59] The FTC's stance on puffery is to ignore it as long as it does not imply a statement of fact and consumers are unlikely to take it seriously.[60] Courts also consider puffery acceptable as long as it doesn't cross the line into believability.

Puffery is almost always described in verbal terms. The Second Circuit's opinion on puffery in *Time Warner v. DIRECTV* was significant because it addressed the use of visual puffery. The Court of Appeals held that puffery includes "visual depictions that, while factually inaccurate, are so grossly exaggerated that no reasonable consumer would rely on them in navigating the marketplace."[61]

DIRECTV's banner advertisements for high-definition satellite service began with an image that was impossible to discern because it was so highly pixilated accompanied by the slogan "SOURCE MATTERS." After a moment, the pixilated image split. One side of the screen, labeled DIRECTV, was crystal clear. The opposite side, labeled "OTHER TV," remained pixilated and distorted. Viewers were prompted to "Find out why DIRECTV's picture beats cable." The Court of Appeals found that it would be "difficult to imagine that any consumer, whatever the level of sophistication, would actually be fooled" by the exaggerated imagery.[62]

False Advertising and State Law

All states have consumer protection laws to protect against unfair and deceptive trade practices. Consumers may use these laws to recover damages when false advertising harms them. Businesses and individuals may use them in lieu of the Lanham Act to seek redress for deceptive competitive practices that do not involve interstate commerce. State laws also empower attorneys general to investigate claims on behalf of the public. Attorneys general from 32 states sued the manufacturers of the nutritional supplement Airborne for making unsubstantiated claims that the product could ward off colds. They reached a multi-state settlement for $7 million in December of 2008.[63] Without admitting guilt, the company also agreed to a $23.3 million settlement in a separate class

[58] *See* Atari Corp. v. 3DO Co., No. C 94-20298 RMW (EAI), 1994 WL 723601, at 1 (N.D. Cal. May 16, 1994).

[59] Pizza Hut, Inc. v. Papa John's Int'l, 227 F.3d 489 (5th Cir. 2000).

[60] FTC Policy Statement on Deception, U.S.S.G. § 2B1.1(b)(7) (Nov. 1, 2001).

[61] Time Warner Cable v. DIRECTV, 497 F.3d at 148.

[62] *Id.* at 160.

[63] *Airborne Can't Say Product Treats Flu and Colds; $7 Million Payout to 32 State Attorneys General*, THE SEATTLE TIMES, Dec. 17, 2008, at B2.

action suit for false advertising in California.[64] Both suits occurred after ABC reported that the lone study demonstrating Airborne's effectiveness was conducted without doctors or scientists.[65]

Advertising "Sin" Products and Services

Essentially, if a service or product is legal, advertising it must be legal as well, but it took the Supreme Court a while to come to that conclusion. For many years, the government has tried to control what might be called "sin" products and services – that are immoral or unhealthy, like gambling, alcohol, and tobacco products – by controlling advertisements for them.

In *Posadas de Puerto Rico Associates v. Tourism Company of Puerto Rico* (1986), the Court considered whether Puerto Rico could prevent its casinos from promoting themselves in Puerto Rico or using the word "casino" on paraphernalia, such as matchbooks and napkins.[66] The local government legalized gambling to attract the tourist trade but didn't want to tempt its own residents, so it banned casinos from promoting their services to Puerto Ricans. A local casino sued, claiming the law violated the First Amendment by suppressing commercial speech. The Supreme Court took the position that if Puerto Rico had the power to restrict casino gambling, it must have the power to ban advertisements for casino gambling.

The Court overruled *Posadas* in 1996, finding that it "clearly erred in concluding that it was 'up to the legislature' to choose suppression over a less speech-restrictive policy."[67] In *44 Liquormart, Inc. v. Rhode Island*, the Court said "The *Posadas* majority's conclusion on that point cannot be reconciled with the unbroken line of prior cases striking down similarly broad regulations on truthful, nonmisleading advertising when non-speech-related alternatives were available."[68]

Advertisements for alcohol

Most states limit regulation of alcohol marketing to efforts intended to reduce youth exposure to alcohol ads. Alabama, for example, prohibits alcohol advertising that targets minors.[69] Connecticut prohibits alcohol ads that include images of minors or that associate alcohol with athletic achievement.[70] Ohio prohibits billboard advertising of

---

[64] $23.3M Settlement in Airborne False Ad Suit, FindLaw, March 4, 2008, http://commonlaw.findlaw.com/2008/03/233m-settlement.html.

[65] Does Airborne really stave off colds? Good Morning America, ABC, Feb. 27, 2006.

[66] 478 U.S. 328 (1986).

[67] 517 U.S. 484, 509 (1996).

[68] *Id.* at 509–10.

[69] Ala. Admin. Code § 20-X-7-.01 (e).

[70] CT Reg. § 30-6-A31(a)(6).

alcoholic beverages within 500 feet of any church, school or public playground.[71] New Hampshire, Pennsylvania and Utah prohibit alcohol advertising on college campuses.[72]

Alcohol is advertised on television. The liquor industry imposed a voluntary ban on radio advertising in 1936 and on television advertising in 1948, but the industry's trade group, the Distilled Spirits Council of the United States, voted to lift the ban in 1996. NBC became the first network to broadcast ads for distilled spirits in 2001.

Advertisements for cigarettes

Advertisements for cigarettes, small cigars, and smokeless tobacco products are prohibited on any medium that falls within the FCC's jurisdiction.[73] The ban, imposed by the Federal Cigarette Labeling and Advertising Act, applies to broadcast, cable, and satellite media. It also requires that ads placed in other U.S. media for cigarettes and smokeless tobacco products include the same kinds of health warnings that appear on the products' packaging. Billboard ads for smokeless tobacco products are exempted from this rule.

Congress gave the Food and Drug Administration authority to regulate tobacco in 2009.[74] Following a model practiced in Canada, Congress required the introduction of color graphics depicting the negative health consequences of smoking on cigarette packaging and directed the FDA to implement those regulations. The FDA selected nine images for use as graphics. They included photos of cancerous lungs, oral cancer, a baby in an incubator and a corpse on an autopsy table. The new warnings with graphics were to appear on the top 50 percent of the front and back of cigarette packages and on the top 20 percent of cigarette ads. It also limited tobacco manufacturers' use of color for labeling and advertising to black text on a white background. Five tobacco companies filed suit against the FDA, claiming that the advertising and labeling restrictions violated their First Amendment rights by confiscating the top half of their packages and compelling them to engage in speech that harmed their interests. A federal district court in the District of Columbia agreed that the graphic images violated the cigarette companies' speech rights. Applying strict scrutiny, the court stated, "The government has failed to carry both its burden of demonstrating a compelling interest and its burden of demonstrating that the rule is narrowly tailored to achieve a constitutionally permissible form of compelled commercial speech."[75] The presiding judge questioned the size of the labels and the FDA's evidence that they would be

---

[71] Ohio Admin. Code § 4301:1-1-44(D)(1).

[72] Center on Alcohol Marketing and Youth, State Alcohol Advertising Report: Current Status and Model Policies, April 2003, www.camy.org/action/Legal_Resources/state_laws.pdf.

[73] 15 U.S.C. §§ 1331–41, 4402 (2011).

[74] Family Smoking Prevention and Tobacco Control Act, Pub. L. No. 111–31, 123 Stat. 1776 (2009).

[75] R.J. Reynolds Tobacco Co. v. FDA, No. 11-1482 (D.D.C. Feb. 29, 2012); See also Commonwealth Brands, Inc. v. FDA, No. 1:09-CV-117-M (W.D. Ky. Jan. 4, 2010)(enjoining enforcement of the no-color rule because it violated the Central Hudson Test).

effective, concluding that their purpose went beyond warning the public about the dangers of smoking to advocating against the sale of a legal product. The appeals process to follow is expected to be lengthy.

Tobacco advertising was significantly curtailed in 1998 by a court settlement between major tobacco companies and 46 states' attorneys general who sued the industry to recover public health costs related to smoking illnesses. Tobacco companies are prevented from marketing their products to children through the use of cartoon characters, apparel with brand-name logos, and brand-name sponsorships of concerts and games with a significant youth audience. The settlement also prohibits payments to promote tobacco products in movies, TV shows, and video games and limits use of ads on billboards and public transit.

Advertisements for gambling

By 2003, advertisements for Internet gambling were ubiquitous on television and the Internet. At that point, the Justice Department voiced its view that providing online gambling services is illegal and that accepting advertisements from them constituted aiding and abetting an illegal activity.[76] In 2004, U.S. marshals seized more than $2 million from the Discovery Network in advertising revenue prepaid by Paradise Poker because the money was generated from illegal online gaming and intended for its further promotion.[77] In 2006, the *Sporting News* settled with the Justice Department for $7.2 million to avoid criminal charges for advertising online gambling. There have been, however, several proposals in Congress, to repeal laws that are interpreted to prohibit online gambling. Many states are attracted to the potential revenue that could be generated from taxing the activity.

States already make a great deal of money through state-sponsored lotteries, which are legal to advertise on television as long as the advertisements appear on a station in that state or another that conducts such a lottery. It is also legal to broadcast advertisements for lotteries conducted by a nonprofit or government organization, with state permission, as an occasional promotional activity or for lotteries sponsored by an Indian tribe pursuant the Indian Gaming Regulatory Act.[78]

Casino advertising, which was formerly banned on broadcast television, is now legal, regardless of where the station or cable system is located.[79]

---

[76] *See* Correspondence from John G. Malcolm, Deputy Asst. Attorney General, Criminal Division, U.S. Dept. of Justice (June 11, 2003). A copy of the letter can be viewed at http://www.igamingnews.com/articles/files/NAB_letter-030611.pdf.

[77] *See* Matt Richtel, *U.S. Steps Up Push Against Online Casinos by Seizing Cash*, N.Y. Times, May 31, 2004, C1.

[78] *See* 18 U.S.C. § 1343 (2011). *See also* FCC Consumer Facts, Broadcasting, Contests, Lotteries and Solicitation of Funds, http://www.fcc.gov/cgb/consumerfacts/contests.html (last visited Feb. 8, 2012).

[79] *See* Greater New Orleans Broadcasting Ass'n v. United States, 527 U.S. 173 (1999).

Advertising to Children

Because children can influence their parents' purchasing decisions and have some discretionary income of their own, they are a target audience for advertising. But their inexperience makes them more vulnerable to advertising and therefore worthy of greater protection. The Children's Television Act of 1990 limits advertising in television programs produced for children aged 12 and younger to 10.5 minutes of commercials per hour on weekends and 12 minutes of commercials per hour on weekdays.[80] The FCC applies this rule to broadcast, cable and satellite television. If a program includes an advertisement for a product associated with the program – for example, an ad for Jimmy Neutron toys during *The Adventures of Jimmy Neutron* – the FCC will regard the show as a "program-length" advertisement.

Because the FCC is concerned that young children may not be able to distinguish between some programming and commercial content, it requires the insertion of "bumpers" between programs and ads.[81] Statements like "We'll be right back after these messages," cue children that a commercial is coming. This requirement also suggests, although it has not yet been tested, that product placement and embedded advertising is prohibited in children's programming.

The display of website addresses in programming for children aged 12 and under is permitted only if the website meets the following criteria:

- it offers a substantial amount of bona fide program-related or other noncommercial content;
- it is not primarily intended for commercial purposes, including either e-commerce or advertising;
- the home page and other menu pages are clearly labeled to distinguish the noncommercial from the commercial sections; and
- the page of the website to which viewers are directed is not used for e-commerce, advertising, or other commercial purposes . . . [82]

If a program character is being used to sell a product on the website, referred to as *host-selling*, the character must appear in a commercial section of the website that is clearly separated from the noncommercial section.

The Children's Online Privacy Protection Act also requires that websites obtain verifiable parental consent before collecting personal information from children under 13.

---

[80] 47 U.S.C. § 303a (2011).

[81] Policies and Rules Concerning Children's Television Programming, 6 FCC Rcd. 2111, 2117–18 (1991).

[82] Children's Educational Television: Guide, http://www.fcc.gov/cgb/consumerfacts/childtv.html (last visited Feb. 8, 2012).

The rule applies to commercial websites and online services for children and to general websites that know they are collecting information from a child.

Marketing Intrusions

Limitations on commercial speech have been put in place in an effort to safeguard personal privacy and productivity and to curtail fraudulent marketing practices. Congress has imposed restrictions on telemarketing, junk faxes, and spam in particular.

Telemarketing

The Federal Trade Commission prescribes rules against deceptive telemarketing under the Telemarketing and Consumer Fraud and Abuse Prevention Act.[83] The rules require telemarketers to promptly disclose the purpose of the call as well as the nature and price of any goods and services. It prohibits telemarketers from calling people before 8 a.m. or after 9 p.m. or calling people who have stated previously that they do not wish to receive calls from the seller or charitable organization.[84] The FTC implemented the National Do-Not-Call registry to make it easier for people to refuse telemarketing calls. Telemarketers are required to "scrub" their call lists every 31 days to ensure they do not contain numbers placed on the registry.[85] The FTC will fine telemarketers $16,000 per violation.

Register for the National Do-Not-Call list at www.donotcall.gov.

The law does not apply to political organizations and charities. It also does not apply to companies with which you have established a business relationship. A company may call for up to 18 months after the date of your last purchase or payment on a product. However, if you ask not to be called again, the company must honor that request. Subsequent calls could also result in a fine of up to $16,000.

The FTC also prescribes rules to prohibit deceptive ads for those 900 numbers that charge by the minute.[86] Ads for pay-for-call services must clearly and conspicuously disclose the cost of using the number. They may not target children under 12, unless they offer educational services, and are prohibited from targeting individuals under 18 without stating that consent to use the service is required by a parent or guardian.

Junk faxes

The Telephone Consumer Protection Act prohibits the use of "any telephone facsimile machine, computer, or other device to send an unsolicited advertisement to a tele-

---

[83] 15 U.S.C. § 6101 et seq. (2011).

[84] Abusive telemarketing acts or practices, 16 C.F.R. Part 310.4(c).

[85] 16 C.F.R. Part 310.4(b)(3)(iv).

[86] 15 U.S.C. § 5711 (a)(1) (2011).

phone facsimile machine."[87] The law applies to unsolicited advertisements sent to personal and business home numbers. The Junk Fax Prevention Act of 2005 amended the law to allow unsolicited faxes to people with whom the sender has an established business relationship.[88] However, the Act also establishes a process receivers may use to opt out of future transmissions. Senders must include contact information on the fax that receivers can use to stop the communications and honor such requests within 30 days.

Spam

Junk e-mail, or *spam*, outpaced legitimate e-mail for the first time in 2003. To get the problem under control, Congress passed the Controlling the Assault of Non-Solicited Pornography and Marketing Act, better known as the CAN-SPAM Act.[89] The statute isn't limited to bulk messaging though. It applies to "any electronic mail message the primary purpose of which is the commercial advertisement or promotion of a commercial product or service."[90] It also applies to e-mail that promotes content on commercial websites.

The CAN-SPAM Act prohibits marketers from using materially false or misleading header information (the "From," "To," and "Reply-To" lines) or routing information (the domain name and e-mail address) in commercial e-mails. Messages must include subject lines that reflect the content of the message and be labeled as advertisements. They also must include a functioning return e-mail address or Internet link that recipients can use to opt out of additional messages. Senders have 10 business days to honor a recipient's request and are barred from selling or transferring the person's e-mail address to others. Commercial e-mails must also include the physical location of the sender.

The FTC treats spam violations as an unfair or deceptive practice and may subject the spammer to penalties of up to $16,000 per violation (in other words, per e-mail sent).[91] State attorneys general may bring civil charges against violators of the CAN-SPAM Act and seek statutory damages of up to $250 per e-mail, not to exceed $2 million.

Sexually oriented commercial e-mail may not be transmitted to recipients who have not given their prior consent for it. The FTC requires sexually oriented spam to include the warning "SEXUALLY-EXPLICIT" in the subject heading. When opened the initially viewable content must include only the following:

[87] 47 U.S.C. § 227 (2011).
[88] Restrictions on telephone solicitation, 47 C.F.R. § 64.1200.
[89] Public Law 108-187, 117 Statute 2699, codified at 15 U.S.C. §§ 7701–13, 18 U.S.C. 1037 and 28 U.S.C 994.
[90] 15 U.S.C. § 7702(2)(a).
[91] CAN-SPAM Act: A Compliance Guide for Business, http://business.ftc.gov/documents/bus61-can-spam-act-compliance-guide-business (last visited Feb. 8, 2012).

- the phrase "SEXUALLY-EXPLICIT";
- clear and conspicuous identification that the message is an advertisement;
- notice of the opportunity to decline further messages from the sender;
- a functioning return e-mail address or link to decline the messages.[92]

Violations are punishable by fines or imprisonment of up to five years.

The statute also directed the FCC to develop rules to prohibit wireless spam, which is not only annoying but costly to receive.[93] The FCC has since banned the transmission of commercial text messages that include an Internet domain name to mobile devices. The ban does not apply to messages from commercial senders who already have an established business relationship with the consumer through prior transactions; however, even these retailers must provide an opportunity to opt out of their messages. The FCC does not prohibit commercial text messages transmitted solely to mobile numbers without the inclusion of an Internet address. However, short-message-service spam can be punished if the receiver has included the number on the national Do-Not-Call list.

The Department of Justice can pursue criminal penalties against spammers who commit fraud by knowingly:

- accessing a computer without authorization, and intentionally initiating the transmission of multiple commercial electronic mail messages through it;
- using a protected computer to transmit multiple commercial e-mails, with the intent to deceive or mislead recipients;
- falsifying header information in multiple commercial e-mails;
- registering or using information that materially falsifies the identity of the actual registrant, for five or more e-mail accounts or two or more domain names, and using them to transmit multiple commercial e-mails; or
- falsely representing oneself as the registrant or the legitimate successor to the registrant of five or more Internet Protocol addresses, and using them to transmit multiple commercial e-mails.[94]

The term "multiple" refers to more than 100 messages sent in a 24-hour period, 1,000 messages in a 30-day period, or 10,000 messages in a 1-year period.

By the time Congress enacted the CAN-SPAM Act, many states had already developed their own anti-spam laws. The federal statute supersedes state laws, except for provisions that prohibit falsity or deception in any part of a message.[95]

To report wireless spam, forward the message to your mobile provider at 7726 (which spells spam). Your provider will text you back to ask for the spammer's number.

[92] Requirement to place warning labels on commercial electronic mail that contains sexually oriented material, 16 C.F.R. § 316.4.
[93] Restrictions on mobile service commercial messages, 47 C.F.R. § 64.3100.
[94] 18 U.S.C. § 1037 (2011).
[95] 15 U.S.C. § 7707(b) (2011).

Public Relations

Public relations and advertising are both branches of the marketing function. Advertising has been thought of as speech that transmits a message to consumers through space or time purchased in a medium, such as a magazine, billboard or television show. In contrast, PR does not rely on purchased space to communicate a message. PR professionals use news releases to transmit information to the media, hoping that the media will then convey that information to the public, bearing the imprimatur of media credibility. They also use their own channels of communication, such as newsletters, brochures and annual reports, to reach their audiences. The use of digital media as a communication tool has blurred the traditional distinction between advertising and public relations. Both professions use e-mail, social media and websites to reach their target audiences. From a marketing perspective, that blurring is a good thing; advertising and PR messaging should be seamless. But from a legal perspective, that blurring creates confusion regarding the level of First Amendment protection that should be accorded to both. Commercial speech is entitled to First Amendment protection, but only to the extent that it is serving an information function. False commercial speech is not protected. If public relations is classified as commercial speech, it would be subject to the same constraint.

Is public relations commercial speech?

The question of whether government can regulate the truth of statements made through public relations as it can other forms of commercial speech was addressed in *Nike v. Kasky* (2003).[96] For years, Nike was dogged by accusations that its athletic products were produced in sweatshops in underprivileged countries. The company defended its labor practices in press releases and letters to the media. Activist Mark Kasky, who argued that Nike's claims were untrue, sued the company under California laws prohibiting false advertising and unfair competition.

A California district court accepted Nike's argument that its statements were part of an ongoing political controversy and therefore deserving of full First Amendment protection. It dismissed the case and a California appellate court upheld the dismissal. But in 2002 the California Supreme Court reversed. A majority of the court accepted Kasky's argument that company speech carried out through public relations is conducted for the purpose of promoting a company's image so that the public will want to buy its products or services. In that respect, PR appears to be commercial speech. The court held that speech should be considered commercial if it is (1) conducted by a commercial speaker, (2) to an intended audience of potential customers, and (3) the content of the message is commercial in character.[97] The state supreme court's test was a modified version of one applied by the U.S. Supreme Court in *Bolger v. Youngs Drug*

---

[96] 27 Cal. 4th 939 (2002).
[97] *Id.* at 961.

Products Corp. (1983) to analyze expression that contains both political and commercial elements.[98]

Nike's attorney argued that treating press releases and letters as the equivalent of advertising would limit companies' First Amendment rights to engage in political speech. Taking the opposite perspective, the California Supreme Court pointed out that if companies' press releases and letters were fully protected speech, companies could misrepresent their actions in them with impunity. This was not a novel idea on the part of the California court. The U.S. Supreme Court has stated that "[a]dvertisers should not be permitted to immunize false or misleading product information from government regulation simply by including references to public issues."[99]

The U.S. Supreme Court initially granted certiorari to review the case and then changed its mind, indicating that a decision on its part would be premature because California courts had not yet decided whether Nike's speech was false. The case was remanded back for that determination but never went to trial. Kasky settled with Nike in exchange for the company's donation of $1.5 million to the Washington, D.C.-based Fair Labor Association. Meanwhile, the California Supreme Court's decision regarding PR as commercial speech stands and could be applied again.

Social media promotion

The management of social media is largely considered to be a public relations function. However, when used for messaging that is consistent with other advertising, it has been considered commercial speech. The Department of Transportation fined Spirit Airlines $50,000 in 2011 for posts on Twitter that violated its regulations on unfair and deceptive trade practices.[100] On its Twitter feed, Spirit Airlines posted *"Check out our [fares] ~ from just $9* each way!"* It failed to include that the one-way rate required a round-trip purchase and that extra fees and taxes applied. A link included in the tweet took consumers to an Internet site that disclosed the fact that extra fees applied, but consumers had to click on a second link to find out what the costs were. The Twitter posts were made in conjunction with a billboard and poster campaign that also neglected to include the specific costs.

Antitrust Law

Antitrust laws prevent anticompetitive behavior that has a negative impact on the marketplace. In a properly functioning economy, market competition provides incentives to offer consumers better goods at lower prices. Within the communication sector, antitrust laws serve another function. They ensure that media consumers receive access

---

[98] 463 U.S. 60, 66–67 (1983).

[99] *Id.* at 67–68.

[100] Consent order (Spirit Airlines) issued by the Department of Transportation, Nov. 21, 2011, Docket OST 2011-0003, Violations of 49 U.S.C. § 41712 and 14 CFR 399.84.

to a diversity of "media voices." There are three federal antitrust laws: the Sherman Act, the Clayton Act, and the Federal Trade Commission Act.

The Sherman Act

Congress passed the Sherman Act in 1890 to break up monopolies and trusts when it became apparent that single companies were controlling entire markets. The Sherman Act prevents "every contract, combination in the form of trust or otherwise, or conspiracy, in restraint of trade or commerce."[101] The statute empowered the government to break up monopolies like Standard Oil (Exxon's forerunner) and the American Tobacco Company. The Justice Department used the Sherman Act to break up AT&T's monopoly on the telephone system in 1982, leading to the largest divestiture in history.[102] In the 1990s, the Justice Department used it to go after Microsoft.

The Sherman Act does not ban monopolies per se. It bans attempts and conspiracies to monopolize an industry. A company may reach a superior market position by offering a better product, through particularly effective management, or simply through historic accident. It is only when a company reaches power through improper conduct or attempts to wield its power in an exclusionary or predatory way that it violates the Sherman Act.

Likewise, the Sherman Act does not require the government to take the term monopoly literally. It does not have to wait until a single firm dominates an industry to act. It is sufficient that the firm have "significant or durable market power" – in other words, "the long term ability to raise price or exclude competitors."[103] Courts normally require that a company hold a 50 percent market share of an industry in a particular geographic area before considering its monopolistic potential.

> Companies become monopolies when they have the power to control prices or suppress competition within their product market.
>
> Trusts are combinations of firms colluding to reduce competition.
>
> A divestiture is the disposition or sale of a company's subsidiaries or assets.

The Clayton Act

In 1914, Congress passed the Clayton Act to close loopholes in the Sherman Act that allowed companies to continue to engage in monopolistic practices. The Clayton Act prohibits a variety of monopolistic behaviors including:

- *exclusive sales contracts*, which require buyers to purchase certain commodities from one seller;
- *price discrimination*, which occurs when sellers charge buyers different prices for the same commodity;
- *predatory pricing*, in which sellers cut their prices below costs temporarily to undercut their competitors and drive them from the market;

---

[101] 15 U.S.C. §§ 1–7 (2007).

[102] United States v. American Telephone & Telegraph Co., 552 F. Supp. 131 (D.D.C. 1982), *aff'd in* Maryland v. United States, 460 U.S. 1001 (1983).

[103] FTC Guide to Antitrust Laws, Single Firm Conduct: Monopolization Defined, FTC website, http://www.ftc.gov/bc/antitrust/monopolization_defined.shtm (last visited Feb. 9, 2012).

- *tying agreements*, which involves conditioning the sale of a particular commodity on the buyer's agreement to purchase a second product or service; and
- *interlocking directorates*, which occurs when competing corporations have at least one director in common on their boards of directors.[104]

The Clayton Act also empowered the government to review and evaluate mergers and acquisitions that were likely to have a detrimental impact on competition.

The Federal Trade Commission Act

The Federal Trade Commission Act, also passed in 1914, was established to prevent "persons, partnerships or corporations" from engaging in unfair competition.[105] The law applies to corporations and other for-profit entities. However, the FTC will exercise its jurisdiction over non-profits as well if their activities are substantially dedicated to providing economic benefits to their for-profit members.[106]

The FTC's Bureau of Competition has the power to challenge mergers and acquisitions that are likely to violate antitrust laws. It is particularly interested in industries likely to affect a substantial portion of the population, such as health care, pharmaceuticals, professional services, food, energy, and certain high-tech industries like computer technology and Internet services.

The FTC prefers to obtain voluntary compliance from individuals or corporations accused of violating antitrust law. As in false advertising cases, it will begin by drawing up a consent order that the company can sign, agreeing to discontinue the behavior without having to admit any wrongdoing. If the company violates the consent order, the FTC may pursue civil penalties or injunctive relief in a federal court.

If the FTC cannot reach a consent agreement, it will file an administrative complaint to initiate a formal proceeding before an administrative law judge. The administrative judge will issue a preliminary decision based on the facts presented and the applicable law. The Commission will then issue the final order, which may be contested before a U.S. Court of Appeals.

The FTC takes some cases directly to federal court, particularly if an injunction is needed quickly to prevent a particular action. It might, for example, request an injunction to block a proposed merger until it has the opportunity to fully investigate the merger's implications.

Shared antitrust jurisdiction

The Federal Trade Commission shares responsibility for the enforcement of antitrust laws with the Justice Department's Antitrust Division. Companies are required to notify both agencies before entering into mergers valued at an annually adjusted threshold

---

[104] 15 U.S.C. §§ 12–27 (2011).

[105] *Id.* § 45(a)(2).

[106] California Dental Ass'n v. Federal Trade Commission, 526 U.S. 756 (1999).

figure – in 2012 it was $66 million – so the proposed deals may be reviewed for anti-competitive potential. The agencies do independent reviews to consider whether a proposed merger will be likely to lead to a more concentrated market that impedes the entry of competing firms.

The FTC may impose civil actions on antitrust violations, and the Justice Department may impose criminal sanctions if necessary. The Federal Communications Commission also shares the responsibility of evaluating proposed mergers among telecommunications companies with the FTC and Justice Department. Its responsibility is to ensure that such firms continue to operate in the public convenience, interest, and necessity.

In 2011, the Justice Department filed an antitrust lawsuit to block AT&T's attempt to purchase T-Mobile because the merger would reduce the field of mobile carriers with national reach from four to three. AT&T, which had 27 percent of the mobile phone marketshare would have had 44 percent after a merger with T Mobile. This type of action is rare. In an average year, the agencies review around 1,000 merger proposals and 95 percent present no problems.[107] In cases in which there are competitive issues, the FTC is generally able to work out a consent agreement to resolve them, usually by requiring one or both companies to sell part of their assets.

State antitrust law

States also have antitrust laws that can be used to control intrastate anticompetitive behavior. These are enforced by the attorney general's office. State attorneys general also may bring federal antitrust suits on behalf of their state's residents. Nineteen states attorneys general joined the Justice Department in challenging a 2010 merger between Ticketmaster, the nation's largest ticket seller, and Live Nation, the largest concert promoter. The merger would have removed Live Nation's fledgling ticketing business as a competitor. Ticketmaster eventually agreed to a settlement in which it would license its ticketing software to other competitors, sell a division that sold tickets to college sporting events, and agree not to retaliate against venues that worked with other ticket sellers by blocking the artists it represents from playing in them. The merger didn't expand the market share of either company significantly, but it did create a powerhouse able to manage artists, book them at venues it owns, and sell tickets for the concerts.

Class action and individual civil claims

Businesses may use the Sherman and Clayton Acts to sue rival companies that have harmed them through anticompetitive practices. This legal remedy offers consumers indirect protection from anticompetitive practices that otherwise would lead to higher prices for fewer product choices. However, antitrust laws were never intended as vehicles to allow consumers to directly challenge anticompetitive behavior that causes *them* harm.

---

[107] FTC Guide to Antitrust Laws: Mergers, http://www.ftc.gov/bc/antitrust/mergers.shtm (last visited Feb. 3, 2012).

Nevertheless, the Ninth Circuit considered a legal challenge by consumers of cable and satellite television programmers, like NBC Universal and Disney, and distributors, like Time Warner and DIRECTV, based on the Sherman Act. In a class action suit, the plaintiffs argued that the practice of bundling high-demand channels with low-demand channels in cable and satellite packages is anticompetitive. The court initially dismissed the suit, finding that the plaintiffs' allegations of widespread harm to consumers, through increased prices and reduced choices, were insufficient to justify application of the Sherman Act without evidence that rival distributors were harmed.[108] On rehearing, the court considered plaintiff's alternative argument that bundling channels forces independent distributors, who might offer consumers smaller packages or a la carte channel choices, out of the market. But when plaintiffs could not prove that, the court dismissed the case again.

Microsoft

No company has been a greater target for antitrust investigations than Microsoft, which has been found guilty of violations in the United States and the European Union. In 1998, the U.S. Department of Justice, 20 states, and the District of Columbia sued Microsoft for antitrust violations based on its monopoly of the market through its Windows operating systems and Internet Explorer browser. The software giant was accused of abusing its dominant position to drive out competing browsers by tying licensing agreements for its operating system to the use of Explorer. Microsoft also intertwined Explorer's code with the Windows operating system so it worked better with Windows than competing browsers users might install later. The district court judge assigned to the case concluded that Microsoft was a monopoly and ordered it be divided into two companies: one to produce the operating system and another to produce software.[109] The break-up order was more than the Justice Department anticipated and it took the unusual step of appealing the decision with Microsoft. The U.S. Court of Appeals for the District of Columbia vacated the order but upheld the decision that Microsoft had engaged in illegal conduct.[110]

Microsoft reached a settlement with the Department of Justice and some of the states, which was affirmed by a federal court in 2002. The company agreed to license its protocols so third parties could create middleware products, such as browsers, e-mail clients, media players and instant messaging applications, which would work with its operating system. It also agreed to license its operating system to PC manufactures on an equal basis and not to retaliate against them if they preinstalled software on their computers that competed with Microsoft's applications. But the settlement did not require Microsoft to remove code that made its software work better with the Windows' operating system. Nine states refused to sign the agreement because they considered it insufficient. The consent degree expired in 2011.

[108] Brantley et al. v. NBC Universal, Inc. et al., No. 09-56785 (9th Cir. March 30, 2012), Brantley et al. v. NBC Universal 2011 WL 2163961 (9th Cir. June 3, 2011).
[109] United States v. Microsoft, 97 F. Supp. 2d 59, 2000 U.S. Dist. LEXIS 7583 (D.D.C. 2000).
[110] United States v. Microsoft, 253 F.3d 34 (D.C. Cir. 2001).

In the European Union, Microsoft was penalized for tying the use of its Windows Media Player to its operating system. Microsoft was ordered to make a version of Windows without the media player and to share information with rival companies that wanted to produce competing software intended to work with Windows. The EU's investigations of Microsoft for antitrust violations have cost the company approximately $2.5 billion in fines and penalties.[111]

Antitrust law and the media

Although it is not always apparent from increasing levels of media consolidation, antitrust laws do apply to the media. In *Associated Press v. United States* (1945), the Supreme Court rejected the argument that the First Amendment immunized media from antitrust laws.[112] The Associated Press' bylaws, requiring members to transmit local news to AP and no one else, presented a serious obstacle for newspapers that were excluded from AP membership. The problem was compounded by a system that allowed AP members to deny membership to new competitors. When the Justice Department accused AP of violating the Sherman Act, AP argued that its actions were protected by freedom of the press. The Supreme Court observed that the irony of that argument was that it would prevent the government from protecting that freedom. It concluded that the First Amendment provides "powerful reasons" for the application of antitrust laws to the media. Writing for the majority, Justice Black said, "Freedom to publish is guaranteed by the Constitution, but freedom to combine to keep others from publishing is not."[113]

The Court had already shown its willingness to step in to prevent media monopolies in *National Broadcasting Company v. United States* (1943).[114] In the late 1930s, the FCC determined that NBC, which owned two national networks, was in a position to dominate broadcasting. It ordered the company to divest itself of one of its networks and the Supreme Court upheld the order. The network sold became the American Broadcasting Company.

In 1951, the Supreme Court held that a medium's right to refuse advertising did not extend to practices intended to drive out its competition.[115] The petitioner in *Lorain Journal Company v. United States* was an Ohio newspaper that refused to carry ads from businesses that also advertised on a local radio station. The Court held that a publisher's decision to reject advertising from businesses that also purchased ads from a competing media operation was an antitrust violation.

The FCC and the Court continued to express a commitment to media diversity through the 1960s and 1970s. In *Red Lion v. FCC* (1969), Justice Byron White said "It is the purpose of the First Amendment to preserve an uninhibited marketplace of ideas

---

[111] Microsoft Corp. v. European Commission, Case T-201/04, O.J. C 269 (2007), available at http://curia.europa.eu/jurisp/cgi-bin/form.pl?lang=EN&Submit=rechercher&numaff=T-201/04.

[112] 326 U.S. 1 (1945).

[113] *Id.* at 20.

[114] 319 U.S. 190 (1943).

[115] *See* Lorain Journal Company v. United States, 342 U.S. 143 (1951).

To learn what media companies actually own, visit the site "Who Owns What," sponsored by Columbia Journalism Review, at http://www.cjr.org/resources/.

in which truth will ultimately prevail, rather than to countenance monopolization of that market, whether it be by the government itself or a private licensee . . ."[116] However, government moved in a more conservative direction in the 1980s and 1990s. Deregulatory policies led to the elimination of a number of ownership restrictions, which resulted in more media consolidation.

Public perception is now that government agencies handle media consolidation too lightly. In the twenty-first century, that trend toward consolidation now encompasses new media technologies. For example, the FTC and Justice Department approved News Corporation's $580 million acquisition of the social networking site MySpace.com in 2005, Google's $1.65 billion purchase of the video site YouTube in 2006, and Microsoft's $8.5 billion acquisition of Skype in 2011. In a particularly controversial 2008 decision, the FTC, FCC, and Justice Department approved a merger between Sirius and XM Radio that reduced the number of satellite radio providers from two to one. A key factor in the decision was that both companies were struggling to build a sufficient audience base to stay afloat. Because demand for the service was low, the agencies thought it unlikely that the merger would enable Sirius-XM to increase prices significantly.

In 2011, the FCC and Justice Department also approved a merger between Comcast, the nation's largest cable company and residential Internet service provider, and broadcasting company, NBC universal. The combined company now owns or is invested in more than 140 media properties, including 40 television channels and 3 film companies.[117] Comcast made several concessions to get permission for the merger. It agreed to give up management of Hulu, an Internet video site, partially owned by NBC Universal, which offers competitive choices in programming. It also agreed to expand local news coverage, programs for Spanish-speaking viewers, and Internet access for schools.

Contracts and Electronic Signatures

A *contract* is an agreement between two or more people that involves a promise by one party in exchange for a counter promise by the other. Online contracts are now just as enforceable as contracts created on paper. This means that when you enter a website and click on a button that says "I accept," your acceptance to the site's terms is binding.

For example, if you are a Facebook user, you have agreed to assign Facebook a

"non-exclusive, transferable, sub-licensable, royalty-free, worldwide license to use any IP content that you post on or in connection with Facebook."

The terms "transferable, sub-licensable" mean that Facebook can grant others the right to use your intellectual property, including your photos and videos. Likewise, if you subscribe to Twitter, you have agreed to grant Twitter

[116] 395 U.S. 367, 390 (1969).
[117] Who Owns What, Comcast, Columbia Journalism Review, http://www.cjr.org/resources/index.php?c=comcast (last visited Jan. 17, 2012).

Figure 12.2   Illustration: Kalan Lyra

"a worldwide, non-exclusive, royalty-free license (with the right to sublicense) to use, copy, reproduce, process, adapt, modify, publish, transmit, display and distribute such Content in any and all media or distribution methods (now known or later developed)."

The terms of use associated with both services, as well as YouTube and LinkedIn, also require users to accept California's jurisdiction over any legal dispute that might arise through the use of these services, as well as the application of California's law.

Your click on these contracts, known as *clickwrap agreements*, is binding because it is the equivalent of a digital signature. To facilitate electronic commerce, Congress passed the Electronic Signatures in Global and National Commerce ("E-SIGN") Act.[118] The federal statute, in effect since 2000, vests electronic signatures and documents with the same legal force of traditional signatures and printed documents. It defines *signature* broadly as "an electronic sound, symbol, or process, attached to or logically associated with a contract or other record and executed or adopted by a person with the intent to sign the record."[119] The term *process* can be understood to mean a click on an "OK" or an "I accept" button.

In order to be enforceable, a contract must include at least two things: a *consideration* (a benefit exchanged for something) and some level of equality between the parties. Clickwrap agreements don't leave room for negotiation. A user either accepts the terms or is denied the service or access to a particular site sought through the agreement.

Nevertheless they have been upheld by courts, which see them as vital to the function of electronic commerce. In *Feldman v. Google* (2007), a lawyer whose firm purchased pay-per-click advertising from Google sued the search engine for negligence because the company failed to protect him from click fraud.[120] *Click fraud* occurs when individuals maliciously click on a competitor's ad repeatedly to drain the competitor's advertising budget. Adometry, an ad measurement firm, estimated in 2011 that 15 to 25 percent of advertising clicks on search engines were fraudulent.[121] In fact, in 2006, Google agreed to a $90 million settlement to end a class action lawsuit against it emanating from its failure to prevent click fraud.[122]

Lawrence Feldman had assented to Google's terms of agreement, specifying that the forum for any legal action between them would be California and that California law would apply. Feldman, who filed suit in Pennsylvania, argued that Google's contract should not be enforced because he was not given notice of its terms and the contract was *unconscionable*, meaning it was characterized by unequal bargaining positions or hidden terms.

The court determined that Feldman was given reasonable notice of the terms through Google's scroll-down window, and

(Continued)

---

[118] 15 U.S.C. §§ 7001 et. seq. (2011).

[119] *Id.* § 7006.

[120] Feldman v. Google, 513 F. Supp. 2d 229 (E.D. Pa. 2007).

[121] Online Ad Fraud: A Business Model at Risk, Adometry, May 24, 2011, http://www.youtube.com/watch?v=zwtEl-NUI2s&feature=youtu.be.

[122] Lane's Gifts and Collectibles v. Google, Inc., No. CV-2005-052-1 (Miller Co., Ark. Cir. Ct. 2006).

that by clicking on a button that said "Yes, I agree to the terms above" he had assented to them. Internet users do not always read the terms in these agreements because they are impatient to move forward. One study conducted in 2002 estimated that 90 percent of Internet users did not complete them and 64 percent agreed to them without reading anything at all.[123] But that doesn't make them any less binding. While recognizing that the contract was one-sided, the court did not consider Google's terms to be unconscionable because Feldman still had the choice to advertise elsewhere.

Moreover, a website's terms may be binding on others who access the site using someone else's account. In *Motise v. America Online* (2004), Michael Motise filed suit against AOL in New York for releasing his private information to a third party who used it illegally. AOL motioned to dismiss the case because its terms of service specified that legal actions must be filed in Virginia. The plaintiff argued that he never agreed to those terms because he was using his stepfather's account. The court considered the plaintiff to be the account holder's sub-licensee. It said "Any other conclusion would permit individuals to avoid the Defendant's Terms of Service simply by having third parties create accounts and then using them as the Plaintiff did."[124]

Certain agreements still require paper. These include wills, adoption papers, divorces, evictions, notices canceling insurance or utilities, court orders, and product recalls.[125]

Questions for Discussion

1. What justification has the Supreme Court given for granting lesser First Amendment protection to commercial speech?
2. How does the Federal Trade Commission deal with false advertising?
3. How do literal falsity, implied falsity, and puffery differ? Which are illegal?
4. Should public relations be fully protected by the First Amendment, even if it is false, or should it be treated like advertising?

---

[123] Adam Gatt, *The Enforceability of Click-Wrap Agreements*, 18 COMPUTER L. & SECURITY REP., 404–10 (2002).

[124] Motise v. America Online, 346 F. Supp. 2d 563, 566 (S.D. N.Y. 2004).

[125] 15 U.S.C. § 7003 (2011).

Appendix: How to Find the Law

To be confident of your knowledge of the law, you need to know how to find it. Fortunately, most legal resources are now available through computerized databases and the Internet. Below are the primary sources of law and directions to read citations used with them.

Constitutions

Constitutions are the ultimate source of law for a political body. The U.S. Constitution can be found online through the Government Printing Office website at http://www.fdsys.gov. State constitutions can be found online at http://www.constitution.org/cons/usstcons.htm. Citations indicate the applicable jurisdiction in abbreviated form, article, section (indicated by §) and clause, for example, *U.S. Const. art. III, §2, cl.2*, expanded for clarity below:

Jurisdiction	Article	Section	Clause
U.S. Const.	art. III	§ 2	cl. 2
N.Y. Const.	art. I	§ 9	cl. 2

Federal and state codes

Federal, state, and municipal laws are arranged topically in codes. Federal statutes are amassed in the United States Code (U.S.C.), which is divided into 50 titles, categorized by subject. Title 17, for example, contains copyright law. Citations indicate the title of the U.S. Code, the section number, and the date of the compilation, e.g. *17 U.S.C. § 106 (2000)*, expanded for clarity below:

Digital Media Law, Second Edition. Ashley Packard.
© 2013 John Wiley & Sons, Inc. Published 2013 by John Wiley & Sons, Inc.

Title	Code	Section	Date
17	U.S.C.	§ 106	(2000)

The U.S. Code is published every six years. In between editions, the government releases annual supplements. The official version is available through the Government Printing Office website at http://www.gpo.gov/fdsys/. Annotated versions of the U.S. Code, such as the U.S. Code Annotated (U.S.C.A.) and the U.S. Code Service (U.S.C.S.), are available through commercial databases like Westlaw and Lexis-Nexis. The citations are similar, but the publisher is often included with the compilation date, for example, *17 U.S.C.A. § 106 (Thomas/West 2000)*, expanded for clarity below:

Title	Code	Section	Publisher and Date
17	U.S.C.A.	§ 106	(Thomson/West 2000)
17	U.S.C.S.	§ 106	(LexisNexis 2000)

State codes also come in official and commercial annotated versions, for example, the Iowa Code and the Iowa Code Annotated. Citations to state codes include the name of the code, the section number and the date of the compilation:

Iowa Code § 321 (2005)
Iowa Code Ann. § 321 (Thomson/West 2005)

State statutes can be found easily through commercial databases like Lexis or Westlaw, but are also available on the Internet though Cornell's Legal Information Institute at http://www.law.cornell.edu/statutes.html.

Administrative regulations and executive orders

Federal agency rules, proposed rules, and notices, as well as executive orders and other presidential documents, are published daily in the Federal Register (abbreviated as either FR or Fed. Reg.), which can be found at http://www.gpo.gov/fdsys. Citations to agency notices include the volume number, abbreviation for Federal Register, page number, and publication date, for example, *73 Fed. Reg. 143* (June 30, 2008), expanded for clarity below:

Vol.	Publication	Page	Date
73	Fed. Reg.	143	(June 30, 2008)

Citations to executive orders include the same information preceded by the executive order number:

Exec. Order No. 13,462, 73 FR 11805 (March 4, 2008)

Federal department and agency rules published in the Federal Register are eventually codified in the Code of Federal Regulations (C.F.R.), located at http://www.gpoaccess.gov/

CFR/. The C.F.R. is divided into 50 titles related to specific subject areas. Citations include the title, abbreviation for Code of Federal Regulations, section number, and date, for example, *16 C.F.R. § 255.1 (2008)*, expanded for clarity below:

Title	Code	Section	Date
16	C.F.R.	§ 255.1	(2008)

Court opinions

Court decisions are initially released as slip opinions, published on court websites, arranged by date or docket number. Eventually, these decisions are collected in bound volumes called case reporters that are paginated, annotated, and accompanied by topical digests. The commercial services that produce case reporters sell access to the same information through Westlaw and Lexis-Nexis. These searchable, full-text databases are expensive, but often available to college students free through their university libraries. Findlaw.com offers searchable versions of slip opinions for free.

Supreme Court decisions are published in United States Reports (U.S.), the official case reporter for Supreme Court decisions, and the commercial reporters Supreme Court Reporter (S.Ct.), U.S. Law Week (USLW), and United States Supreme Court Reports, Lawyers' Edition (L.Ed. or L.Ed.2d). Oral arguments can be heard online through the Oyez Project at http://www.oyez.org.

Citations to Supreme Court cases provide the case name, volume, abbreviated name of the reporter, beginning page of the case, and date the case was decided, for example, *Reno v. ACLU, 521 U.S. 844 (1997)*. It is sufficient to reference a case by its official citation, but some authors and courts supply parallel citations to make a case easier to find:

Case name	Vol.	Reporter	Page	Year
Reno v. ACLU,	521	U.S.	844	(1997)
Reno v. ACLU,	117	S.Ct.	2329	(1997)

U.S. Court of Appeals opinions are reported in the Federal Reporter (F., F.2d, F.3d). Volumes for 1950–93 are online at http://bulk.resource.org/courts.gov/c/F2/. Citations include the case name, volume, abbreviated name of the reporter, beginning page of the case and, in parentheses, the circuit in which the case was decided and date, for example, *Taubman Co. v. Webfeats, 244 F.3d 572 (7th Cir. 2001)*, expanded for clarity below:

Case name	Vol.	Reporter	Page	Circuit Year
Taubman Co. v. Webfeats,	244	F.3d	572	(7th Cir. 2001)

Selected U.S. District Court opinions appear in the Federal Supplement (F. Supp.). Citations include the case name, volume, abbreviated name of the reporter, beginning page of the case and, in parentheses, the district in which the case was decided and date, for example, *Doe v. MySpace, 474 F. Supp. 2d 843 (W.D. Tex. 2007)*, expanded for clarity below:

Case name	Vol.	Reporter	Page	Federal District Year
Doe v. MySpace,	474	F. Supp. 2d	843	(W.D. Tex. 2007)

State court opinions appear in regional reporters that collect opinions from several states. These include: West's Atlantic Reporter, North Eastern Reporter, North Western Reporter, Pacific Reporter, South Eastern Reporter, South Western Reporter, and Southern Reporter. The citation 807 A.2d 847 (Pa. 2002), for example, indicates that the opinion appears in volume 807 of the Atlantic Reporter, second series, on page 847, and that the case was decided by the Pennsylvania Supreme Court in 2002. Some states also have their own reporters.

Secondary sources

Secondary sources of information, such as law review and journal articles, can provide helpful background and analysis to understand a legal issue. Digital versions of law reviews are available by subscription through Westlaw, Lexis-Nexis and Hein Online. Findlaw.com compiles some full text versions of law reviews at http://stu.findlaw.com/journals/general.html.

A law review citation includes the author's name, article title, journal volume, abbreviated journal name, page on which the article begins, and date of publication. A second page number refers to a specific citation in the text:

> Dan Hunter, Cyberspace as Place and the Tragedy of the Digital Anticommons, 91 Cal. L. Rev. 439, 491 (2003)

This citation indicates that the article "Cyberspace as Place and the Tragedy of the Digital Anticommons" written by Dan Hunter, appears in volume 91 of the California Law Review, printed in 2003, beginning on page 439, with a particular reference on 491.

Helpful sites with government information include:

Library of Congress, for copyright information, http://www.loc.gov.

Library of Congress Thomas, for pending bills and legislative history, http://thomas.loc.gov/home/thomas.php.

U.S. Patent and Trademark Office, for trademarks and software patents, http://www.uspto.gov.

U.S. Federal Communications Commission, for telecommunications regulations, http://www.fcc.gov.

U.S. Federal Trade Commission, for advertising and antitrust rules, http://www.ftc.gov/.

U.S. Department of Justice and the *Federal Bureau of Investigation* for information on computer and other federal crimes at http://www.justice.gov/ and at www.fbi.gov.

Glossary

actual damages   An award given to the plaintiff in compensation for a loss or injury, also known as compensatory damages.

actual malice   A standard of fault in defamation cases. Plaintiffs are required to prove that the defendant published the defamation with knowledge of its falsity or reckless disregard of its truth.

administrative rule   Agency regulations that carry the force of law, promulgated by independent administrative agencies and federal departments in the course of supervising the implementation of statutes or executive orders.

agency   Any executive department, military department, government controlled corporation, or other establishment in the executive branch (including the Executive Office of the President), or any independent regulatory agency to which the Freedom of Information Act is applicable.

amicus curiae   A Latin term for "friend of the court." The name for a brief submitted on a matter of law by someone who is not a party to the case but who wishes to influence its outcome.

antitrust law   Law intended to inhibit anticompetitive behavior that harms rivals and has a negative effect on the marketplace.

appellant   The party who files an appeal in a civil or criminal case after losing a case at the trial level.

appellee   The party who must respond to an appeal in a civil or criminal case.

applied challenge   A challenge to a law based on its effect on a particular party.

arraignment   A legal proceeding in which a defendant is formerly charged and issues a plea of innocence, guilt or no contest.

binding precedent   A precedent that a court must follow because the opinion was issued in the same jurisdiction by a higher court.

categorical speech restriction   The doctrine that certain categories of speech contribute so little to the life of social dialogue that they are unworthy of First Amendment protection.

cease and desist order   A final order, issued after a trial or administrative hearing, to prevent a party from continuing to engage in activity deemed harmful or illegal.

choice of law   An area of procedural law specifying rules for selecting the law applicable in a case involving parties from different states.

Digital Media Law, Second Edition. Ashley Packard.
© 2013 John Wiley & Sons, Inc. Published 2013 by John Wiley & Sons, Inc.

civil law A body of law addressing the rights of private individuals with respect to one another.

class action lawsuit A lawsuit filed on behalf of particular population that might have been harmed by the defendant company.

Code of Federal Regulations A compilation of rules issued by federal departments and independent administrative agencies in the United States.

collective mark A distinctive name or mark used to identify a membership organization that may be registered for protection under trademark law.

commercial speech Speech that proposes a commercial transaction.

common carrier A nondiscriminatory conduit for others' speech.

common law A body of law based on court decisions. Also known as caselaw.

compensatory damages A penalty meant to compensate a victim for actual damages incurred.

concurring opinion An opinion by an appellate court judge that agrees with the majority regarding the holding, but arrives at its conclusion through different reasoning.

conflict of laws The body of procedural law that establishes the rules for determining jurisdiction, the choice of law and enforcement of judgments in transborder conflicts, either at the state or national level.

consent agreement A legal document, often issued by administrative agencies, in which parties voluntarily agree to the terms of a settlement to avoid litigation.

contract An agreement between two or more people that involves a promise by one to do something in exchange for a counter promise by the other.

contempt of court Failure to obey a court order or to exercise proper decorum in the courtroom.

content-based restriction A restriction intended to prevent a particular type of speech or message.

content-neutral restriction A restriction intended to prevent speech (usually based on its time, place or manner) regardless of the particular type of speech or message that is conveyed.

criminal law A body of law that specifies behavior prohibited by the state, based on its potential harm to society, and its punishment.

cyber harassment The use of the Internet to torment an individual through repeated contacts.

cyberbullying Electronic harassment targeted at minors by minors.

cybersquatting Registering a domain name that is identical or confusingly similar to someone's protected trademark with "bad faith" intent to profit from the mark.

cyberstalking The use of the Internet to stalk a victim, generally characterized by a pattern of behaviors that includes credible threats.

declaratory judgment A court order in a civil case explaining the rights and responsibilities of the parties in the case, without awarding them damages or requiring them to take a particular action.

defamation A false communication that exposes a person to hatred, contempt, or ridicule, or that lowers a person's stature in the community.

defendant The party against whom a civil suit is filed or a crime is prosecuted.

deposition A pre-trial legal proceeding in which witnesses are asked questions under oath before a court reporter.

derivative An adaptation of an earlier work. Copyright law protects a creator's right to control the use of an original work as well as any derivative versions that might be created from it.

dissenting opinion An opinion by an appellate court judge that disagrees with the opinion supported by the majority of the court.

discovery   The process that opposing parties undertake before a trial begins to acquire relevant information and documents from each other in an attempt to learn all pertinent facts that might affect the litigation and avoid surprises at trial.

DSL   An acronym for direct subscriber line, a two-way data connection that provides broadband access through telephone lines.

electromagnetic spectrum   The range of radiation through which signals of all types are transmitted. The spectrum is divided into frequencies ranging from cosmic-ray photons, gamma rays, x-rays, ultra-violet radiation, visible light, infrared radiation, microwaves and radio waves.

en banc   A court of appeals sits en banc when all (or most) of the justices hear a case together. Appellate cases are normally assigned to a three-judge panel.

enforcement of judgments   An area of procedural law specifying rules for enforcement of judgments.

equity   A system of law that furnishes remedies for wrongs that would not be recognized under common law or for which there is no adequate remedy under common law.

errors and omissions policy   Professional insurance coverage to compensate for the cost of negligent actions made in service to others.

ex rel.   An abbreviation for the Latin term ex relatione. It is used in the title of a legal proceeding brought in the name or on behalf of the government, but based on the complaint of an individual who has a personal interest in the matter.

executive orders   A policy directive that implements or interprets a statute, a constitutional provision or a treaty.

facial challenge   A challenge to a law, as it is written, either because the law is overbroad or vague or both, based on its potential capacity to limit protected behavior.

fair use   A doctrine that allows the use of a copyrighted work, without the copyright holder's permission, in some circumstances. Favored uses include criticism, comment, news reporting, teaching, scholarship, or research. However, these are not without limitations. The law does not specify how much one may use.

false statement of fact   A false statement that is likely to be taken literally.

Federal Register   The daily digest of proposed and final administrative regulations issued by federal executive departments and independent administrative agencies in the United States.

fighting words   Words exchanged in a face-to-face conflict that a reasonable person would understand would be likely to elicit violence.

first sale doctrine   The legal principle that the lawful owner of a copyrighted work may sell, transfer or dispose of the physical work without infringing on the copyright owner's distribution right. The doctrine assumes that possession of the work is transferred without the creation of any additional copies.

foreseeable harm   Harm that a reasonable person would be able to predict as the likely outcome of a particular action.

forum non conveniens   A doctrine in common law legal systems that allows a court that legitimately could exercise jurisdiction over a case to reject the case if it determines that litigating the case in that jurisdiction would pose a particular hardship to some of the parties in the case and a competent alternative forum exists.

grand jury   A group of citizens impaneled for a period of time, usually one year, to determine whether the evidence presented by a prosecutor warrants an indictment. Grand jury hearings are closed to the public.

hate speech   A form of communication that disparages individuals or groups on the basis of characteristics such as ethnicity, race, religion or sexual orientation. Hate speech is legal in the United States, although hate crimes (which are characterized by action) are not.

holding   The court's decision in a case about a legal question.

hyperbole   A statement so characterized by exaggeration that no one would believe it.

implied falsity   Assertions that are literally true, but which are phrased in a misleading way.

In rem proceeding   A lawsuit or legal action directed toward property that is in dispute, rather than a particular person. The court determines the status of property in relation to the legal rights of all persons involved.

incitement   The use of speech to arouse others to criminal activity.

incorporation doctrine   A legal doctrine that applies parts of the Bill of Rights, originally meant to serve as a constraint on federal power, to the states through the Due Process clause of the Fourteenth Amendment. Prior to the Fourteenth Amendment's ratification, the Supreme Court interpreted the First Amendment as applicable only to the federal government.

indecency   Material that encompasses profanity, references to excretory organs, nudity, and implied sexual behavior.

indemnity agreement   A contract in which one party agrees to accept financial responsibility for any loss or damage that might result from a particular action taken by another.

indictment   A formal accusation charging someone with a crime.

injunction   A court order rendered through equity law that requires a defendant to take a particular action or to refrain from a particular action.

inline link   The placement of an HTML link for an image on one website into the code of another website, creating the illusion that the image is part of the second site. These are also called embedded links.

intermediate scrutiny   A middle level of judicial review (also called heightened scrutiny) that courts employ when a government regulation burdens a constitutional right in pursuit of some other goal. In a First Amendment context, it applies to content-neutral regulations that burden speech. To withstand review, the regulation must further an important government interest through means that are substantially related to the goal and burden no more speech than necessary.

interrogatives   Written questions that parties in a civil suit answer under oath prior to trial.

journalist's privilege   A qualified privilege to protect a source of information.

jurisdiction   A court's authority to hear a particular case, based on its subject matter and the geographic region in which the case is initiated.

jurisprudence constante   A doctrine in civil law legal systems that suggests that, while courts are not bound by earlier decisions, they should defer to them in situations in which there is a consistent pattern of decisions employing the same reasoning on a topic.

legal person   An entity subject to legal rights and duties, which may be a natural person or a corporation.

legislative history   All documents, such as committee reports, floor debates and transcripts of hearings, that accrue during the enactment of a law. Courts turn to a statute's legislative history, also known as its statutory construction, when they are trying to interpret ambiguous wording.

libel   Defamation in printed or broadcast form.

libel per quod   A statement that is not facially defamatory. Its implication must be judged in context.

libel per se   A statement that is obviously damaging to reputation. An example would be accusing someone of cheating or stealing.

libel tourism   The practice of forum shopping in order to file a libel suit in the most plaintiff-friendly jurisdiction that will accept it.

limited-purpose public figure   A person who voluntarily thrusts him or herself into the spotlight in regard to a particular public issue or controversy but remains a private figure in all other aspects of life.

literal falsity Assertions that include false statements of fact.

long-arm statutes A statute specifying the conditions under which a court may exercise personal jurisdiction over an out-of-state defendant.

majority opinion The dominant opinion expressed by an appellate court, which provides the holding.

mechanical license The type of license required to reproduce a sound recording, on another CD for example.

misappropriation The acquisition or disclosure of a trade secret by someone who knows or has reason to know that it was acquired improperly and that its use is unauthorized.

mitigation An effort to lessen damage.

multi-channel video programming distributors Distributors of paid programming options like cable or satellite.

musical work A composition of music and lyrics generally owned by the songwriter or a music publisher.

obiter dictum The part of a court's opinion that provides explanation and analogy, as opposed to the holding, which provides the court's decision. It is known as dicta in its plural form.

obscenity Material that encompasses explicit depictions of actual sexual conduct, masturbation, violent sexual abuse and child pornography, identified through the *Miller v. California* test.

opinion A statement that cannot be proved, not because there is too little evidence but because it is subjective.

overbreadth doctrine A doctrine stipulating that a law may be struck down as unconstitutional if it has the potential to proscribe a substantial amount of protected speech along with its proscription on unprotected speech.

P2P The acronym for the peer-to-peer communication model that describes an informal network formed among Internet users who exchange files directly from each other's hard drives.

parody A derivative work that imitates the characteristic style of the original work to poke fun at it.

payola The practice of paying someone to promote a product on air.

penumbral rights Implied rights, emanating from others that are fully guaranteed.

performance license The type of license required to perform a copyrighted musical work.

personal jurisdiction The court's right to exercise its control over parties involved in a case, based on their residence in or contacts with a particular area.

persuasive precedent A precedent that a court may elect to follow, because the court considers it well reasoned, but is not obligated to follow. Courts look for persuasive precedents in other jurisdictions when there is no legal precedent on a particular legal question in their own jurisdiction.

petitioner The party who petitions an appellate court for the opportunity to challenge a lower court's decision when the court has the prerogative to accept or deny the appeal.

pharming A fraudulent practice that redirects users from legitimate commercial websites to malicious ones that look identical in an attempt to steal the user's personal information.

phishing An identity theft scheme that tricks people into revealing their personal identifying information or financial data, through the use of fraudulent e-mails that mimic documents from their financial institutions.

phonorecords A term used in the Copyright Act to apply to any sound recording, regardless of the medium on which it is stored.

plaintiff A party who files a civil suit against a defendant.

plurality opinion The controlling opinion in an appellate court case when there is no clear majority. The opinion that garners the most support.

police power The legal authority reserved for the states under the Tenth Amendment to preserve and protect the health, safety, and welfare of their citizens. The power of the federal government to prosecute crimes is limited by the Constitution to certain areas, such as commerce.

precedent (binding and persuasive) A legal principle drawn from a court decision that provides authority for judges deciding similar cases later. A binding precedent is one that a court must follow. A persuasive precedent is one that is issued in another jurisdiction which the court may be persuaded to follow, but may also reject.

pretexting The act of misrepresenting one's identity or purpose to acquire personal data about someone else.

prima facie A Latin legal term meaning "on first face" or "on first look." In a prima facie case, the evidence is sufficient to establish a presumption of fact.

prior restraint A form of censorship that takes place before material is published. Prior restraint is considered a more egregious form of censorship than punishment after publication.

private figure A person who has not voluntarily exposed him or herself to the increased risk of defamation or privacy violation by seeking media attention and who has no special access to the media.

private international law The body of law that applies to transborder conflicts. In the United States it is more commonly called "conflict of laws."

procedural law A body of rules regulating access to and operation of the legal system.

proximate cause The cause without which an event would not have occurred.

prurient Characterized by a deviant and unhealthy interest in sex.

public domain A term applied to a range of works that are not protected under intellectual property law and are therefore free to be used in any way.

public figure A person who willingly assumes a position in the public arena and has ready access to the media.

puffery Statements characterized by exaggeration and subjectivity that no consumer would be likely to take as fact.

punitive damages An award given to the plaintiff in addition to actual damages, which serves as additional punishment for the defendant's actions.

rational basis test The lowest level of judicial scrutiny applied in cases in which no fundamental right appears to be threatened. To withstand review, the government must show that the restriction is a reasonable means of achieving a legitimate government goal.

reasonable person In legal parlance, a hypothetical person who exercises orginary care and judgment.

redaction The process of blacking-out parts of a document requested under the Freedom of Information Act, to protect sensitive information within, so that the remaining information may be made available to the requester.

remand When an appellate court returns a case to a lower court for further action.

respondent The party who is required to answer a petition for appeal.

respondeat superior A Latin term that means "let the master answer" for the deeds of the servant. The common law doctrine holds that employers are liable for injuries caused by employees acting on their behalf. The theory allows plaintiffs to probe deeper pockets.

satire A literary work that uses wit, irony or sarcasm to attack a person's foolishness or vice.

scienter Knowledge of wrongdoing.

service marks A distinctive name or mark used to identify a business in the service industry that may be registered for protection under trademark law.

service of process   Providing notice that legal action is forthcoming by providing the opposing party with a copy of the complaint.

slander   Defamation through spoken words of limited reach.

SLAPP suits   Defamation suits filed to intimidate or punish legitimate critics. SLAPP is an acronym for Strategic Lawsuit Against Public Participation.

sound recording   A final musical product produced in a studio by musicians, producers and sound engineers, distinct from the musical work, made up of words and musical notes.

sound recording license   The type of license needed to play a copyrighted rendition of an artist's work.

sovereign   A legally independent body, such as a state or a nation.

spam   Indiscriminate and excessive e-mail sent for marketing purposes.

specific jurisdiction   A type of personal jurisdiction that a court may exercise over nonresidents outside its borders, if their conduct precipitates harmful or damaging effects within its territory and asserting jurisdiction over them does not violate their rights of due process.

stare decisis   The common law doctrine that precedents are to be followed. In Latin it means "to stand by that which is decided."

statute of limitations   A statute setting the time limit to initiate a legal action.

strict liability   Liability incurred regardless of scienter.

strict scrutiny   The highest level of judicial review applied by courts when the government imposes restrictions impinging on a constitutional right. It is applied, for example, when the government restricts speech based on the ideas it conveys. To withstand review, the restriction must be justified by a compelling government interest, be narrowly tailored to achieve that interest, and use the least restrictive means to achieve that interest.

subject matter jurisdiction   The particular issues that a court is empowered to decide.

summary judgment   A decision rendered by a court in favor of either the plaintiff or the defendant in a civil suit when all factual issues have been discovered and the evidence presented suggests that the party would win at trial.

synchronization license   The type of license needed to incorporate a musical work into another work, such as a video. A sound recording license is also needed if the artist's rendition of the musical work is used.

testimonial   A statement made in support of a particular product or claim.

threat   A serious expression of an intent to commit an act of unlawful violence to a particular individual or group of individuals.

tort   A negligent or intentional civil wrong that harms a person or infringes on a right, not involving breach of contract, which is litigated under civil law.

trade dress   Distinctive aspects of a brand's image, other than its mark, such as its packaging, color, size and shape, which may be protected under trademark law.

trade libel   False allegations that harm the market for a particular product.

trademark   A distinctive name or mark used to identify a manufactured good that may be registered for protection under trademark law.

trademark dilution   The lessening of the capacity of a famous mark to identify and distinguish goods or services.

trademark infringement   The use of a mark, without permission of its owner, on a product or in an advertisement for a product or service in a manner that is likely to confuse consumers about the source of the product or service.

vagueness doctrine   A doctrine stipulating that a law may be voided for vagueness if it is not drafted clearly enough to give a reasonable person of average intelligence notice of what constitutes a crime.

viewpoint discrimination Government regulation of speech based on its preference for or dislike of the particular message the speech contains.

voir dire The process used for jury selection in which attorneys question prospective jurors to assess their suitability.

work for hire A work prepared in the scope of employment, in which intellectual property rights vest in the employer rather than the employee who directly produced it.

writ of certiorari A formal petition to a court to hear an appeal.

Table of Cases

Index

Digital Media Law, Second Edition. Ashley Packard.
© 2013 John Wiley & Sons, Inc. Published 2013 by John Wiley & Sons, Inc.

Political Science

Marcus A. Stadelmann, PhD

Professor of Political Science at the University of Texas at Tyler

for
dummies®

A Wiley Brand

Political Science For Dummies®

Published by: **John Wiley & Sons, Inc.**, 111 River Street, Hoboken, NJ 07030-5774, www.wiley.com

Copyright © 2020 by John Wiley & Sons, Inc., Hoboken, New Jersey

Published simultaneously in Canada

For general information on our other products and services, please contact our Customer Care Department within the U.S. at 877-762-2974, outside the U.S. at 317-572-3993, or fax 317-572-4002. For technical support, please visit https://hub.wiley.com/community/support/dummies.

Wiley publishes in a variety of print and electronic formats and by print-on-demand. Some material included with standard print versions of this book may not be included in e-books or in print-on-demand. If this book refers to media such as a CD or DVD that is not included in the version you purchased, you may download this material at http://booksupport.wiley.com. For more information about Wiley products, visit www.wiley.com.

Library of Congress Control Number: 2020940324

ISBN: 978-1-119-67484-9 (pbk); ISBN: 978-1-119-67483-2 (ebk); ISBN 978-1-119-67477-1 (ebk)

Manufactured in the United States of America

V10019873_071720

Contents at a Glance

Table of Contents

Introduction

A s a professor of political science, some of the most frequently asked questions I receive from students include the following: Why study political science? Why should different forms of government and world politics matter to me? Why study political theory and learn about foreign cultures? Most students assume that political events occurring either at home or in faraway countries don't impact their daily lives and are therefore not too concerned about them. Why would someone in Texas care about a new senator being elected in Oregon? Why would a college student living comfortably in the U.S. care about what's happening in Central Asia? What is globalization, how does it impact us, and why care about it? Why read a book written by an old Greek guy who has been dead for thousands of years? Because learning these concepts helps define how people come together and the importance of being a citizen of the world.

By reading this book and becoming a student of political science, you'll acquire the necessary tools to become familiar with, study, and hopefully become interested in both domestic and international political affairs. I hope that this political interest will then get you involved and encourage you to participate in politics.

Studying politics isn't easy. Many factors shape it — individuals, such as leaders of political parties and countries; international organizations, such as the United Nations; domestic factors, such as political cultures and public opinion; and even disasters, such as the COVID-19 outbreak. Albert Einstein put it best almost a century ago when asked why men could discover the structure of the atom but were unable to keep it from destroying the world, stating: "This is simple, my friend; it is because politics is more difficult than physics."

About This Book

This book is intended as an introduction to the study of politics and political science. I assume no prior knowledge of the political process or the discipline of political science. While writing this book, I've strived to be nonpartisan, meaning that I didn't write with any type of political ideology in mind. I also didn't attempt to push certain political ideas and concepts while ignoring others.

One of the purposes of this book is for readers to come to their own conclusions and become more informed citizens and participate in not just debates on politics but in the political process. With politics being the process of making decisions for the public, it affects us all. Therefore, citizens need to be educated on the issues of the day and must be willing to participate in politics.

Whenever the text discusses certain concepts, such as federalism, I provide not only a definition of the term but also real-life examples of the concept. I show how it's being applied in countries and how it works. I draw many examples from democracies, mostly located in Europe, but I also focus on the rest of the world, especially in the section on international organizations, globalization, and warfare.

I designed this book to provide a solid foundation on the discipline of political science. It will prove to be helpful whether you're studying political science, writing a paper, or reading to expand your knowledge. I tried to make the book entertaining by including little-known tidbits on many topics. So whether you're a political science student or just someone interested in the discipline, this book is for you. My hope is that this book will prove one point: Politics matters, and everyone needs to get involved in it.

Conventions Used in This Book

The information in some chapters is relevant to more than just that chapter. When this is the case, I include cross-references to these chapters by chapter number. For example, I discuss the U.S. Constitution in Chapter 5. However, I also analyze specific constitutional powers of the American legislature and executive in Chapter 6.

Icons Used in This Book

As you read and enjoy this book, you'll see two different icons that alert you to specific aspects related to political science, its subfields, and major writers and their works.

REMEMBER

This icon points out important information you should be aware of as you read the section, the chapter, or the book. This icon covers only the most important events, people, and issues.

TECHNICAL STUFF

Historical information often case-specific, including treaties, important battles, strategic doctrines, and other relevant material or events have this icon beside them. This information isn't necessary for grasping certain concepts but is required for a political scientist in the making.

Beyond the Book

In addition to what you're reading right now, this book comes with a free access-anywhere Cheat Sheet that includes a list of political scientists and their major works as well as a handy bank of major political science concepts. To get this Cheat Sheet, simply go to www.dummies.com and type "Political Science For Dummies Cheat Sheet" in the Search box.

Where to Go from Here

Feel free to start with any chapter in the book that interests you. Keep in mind that all the chapters are nonlinear, so you can start with any topic in any chapter. Happy reading!

1

Understanding Political Science

Chapter 1

Discovering the Discipline of Political Science

olitical science is the study of politics and more precisely power. *Politics* is the process by how government decisions are made. It involves some members of society making decisions for all of society because they hold political power over others. Politics, in turn, determines who gets what, where, when, and how. For this reason, politics is an ongoing competition between individuals, groups, or even nation-states. In the United States, politics can involve two interest groups competing for benefits from the government. At the international level, politics could be a competition for natural resources, such as oil, or new powerful allies.

A political scientist is interested in who holds political power in a society, what type of political institutions (forms of government) are best suited to bring about the least amount of conflict, and what form of government is best for its citizens. To be more precise, political scientists are interested in who gets elected to office, how elections are won, how policy is made, how leaders maintain themselves in power, and the all-important question, why does war occur and could it be prevented?

This chapter looks at the study of politics and political science, including the beginnings of political science.

Looking at Politics and Political Science

Many believe that political science is a way of training for future politicians. Although taking a political science class can be helpful if you want to venture into politics, this isn't what political science is all about. Political science is a method or a way to study politics.

REMEMBER

Political science is an academic discipline that studies the relationship between people and political institutions. A discipline is a field of study usually represented by an academic department at a college or university. Political science is a discipline, and so are history, sociology, and biology.

Politics impacts people daily, and most of the time they're not aware of it. Politics determines tax rates, the way businesses are run, the textbooks a child uses in high school, and even how much a person pays for a gallon of milk in the grocery store.

Going back to the history of political science

The founder of the discipline of political science is the famous Greek philosopher Aristotle (see Figure 1-1). He referred to political science as a master science, because everything in life can be political in nature. Aristotle was the first political scientist to collect data and then base his research on it.

TECHNICAL STUFF

Aristotle and his teacher Plato were concerned with the decline of his home city-state Athens. He wanted to know what caused the decline of his beloved Athens and more important how to save Athens. So he sent his students to the other Greek city-states to gather data. He wanted to know why some city-states were doing well and why others weren't. Based on the data his students collected, Aristotle wrote his famous book *Politics*. In it, he describes the various forms of governments and institutions his students discovered in the Greek city-states. Then he discusses his own preferences. Political science and normative theory (see Chapter 2) were born.

REMEMBER

The term *politics* comes from the ancient Greek *polis,* which means city-state. The first person to use the term was Aristotle, who lived during the time of the Greek city-states dominating Greek politics. So politics for Aristotle referred to the interaction between the Greek city-states.

FIGURE 1-1:
Greek
philosopher
Aristotle is
credited with
founding political
science.

TECHNICAL STUFF

A *city-state,* or polis, was the dominant political structure of ancient Greece. Each city-state had an urban center, walls for protection, and controlled a piece of the surrounding countryside. There were over 1,000 city-states, and the largest ones were Athens, Sparta, Corinth, Thebes, Syracuse, and Rhodes. Each city-state ruled itself and had a different form of government. For example, Athens was a democracy while Sparta was ruled by two kings and a council of elders.

Being a part of the social sciences

Political science is a part of the social sciences. Social sciences study how people interact with each other, how they behave toward others, and how power is distributed and used within societies. Social sciences include anthropology, economics, criminology, political science, sociology, and psychology. The social sciences that political science heavily draws on contribute to political science in the following manner:

>> **Sociology:** The discipline of sociology studies human beings and how they interact. Sociology focuses on how small and large groups form and become large organizations, even nation-states. Political scientists use sociology to

explain the behavior of small groups, such as members of a parliament, and the creation of large groups, such as nation-states. In addition, studies are conducted on how people acquire and maintain power within groups.

» **Economics:** The discipline of economics is important for the political scientist. Economics and politics often intersect. The political scientist uses economics to examine government programs such as social security or to discuss international trade agreements or even punitive sanctions.

» **Anthropology:** Anthropology is the study of ancient and modern-day cultures. The discipline is useful for political scientists when conducting culture studies (see Chapter 3). Anthropology allows the political scientist to compare processes, norms, and institutions in different societies. For example, political scientists for decades have studied cultural aspects that maintain or destroy democracy in a nation-state. Also, as Chapter 12 shows, certain cultural traits can make societies more aggressive and warlike in the international arena. Anthropology helps find these cultures and hopefully change them to prevent global conflict.

» **Psychology:** Psychology studies the way human beings think and behave within the national or international system. The political scientist can use psychology to analyze people, studying voting behavior in countries or examining the leading politicians in different countries to see how and why they make certain decisions.

All social sciences have impacted and still impact the discipline of political science. It's impossible to be a political scientist without having knowledge of the other social sciences.

Being fragmented

The discipline of political science itself isn't a cohesive discipline but actually is made up of various subfields, which in turn are broken down into more subfields. They are

» **American politics:** The study of American politics involves studying American political institutions such as Congress or the presidency, as well as local or state governments. For example, the study of Texas politics falls into this category. Further, it includes the role of political parties and interest groups as well as the American electorate. Today, subfields within American politics have developed. They include public administration, which studies bureaucracies; public policy making; and the role of courts, which looks on the evolution of the constitution.

>> **Comparative politics:** Comparative politics studies other nations and cultures. It creates theories and frameworks that explain why and what happens and then identifies similar patterns and differences between political systems. Comparative Politics compares, for example, American culture to Swedish culture or looks at the voting behavior of Australians and compares it to U.S. voters. In addition, comparative politics studies various forms of governments (authoritarian, totalitarian, or democratic) and creates theories or concepts on the foundations for democracy (see Chapter 3).

>> **International relations:** International relations studies relationships between nation-states. It looks at international conflict, diplomacy, and international organizations and discusses issues such as human rights and terrorism. It also has two subfields: international political economy, which analyzes how economics and politics impact each other, and foreign policy studies, which looks at the interaction of countries with foreign nations.

>> **Political theory:** Political theory studies the great thinkers of the past and present. Most political scientists believe that the great Greek philosophers Aristotle and Plato set the foundation for political science. Political theory studies how and why people behave in a certain way politically and develops theories about the nature of people, the nature of liberty and freedom, ethics, and the role of the individual within a political system. It further includes studies on political ideologies, such as fascism, communism, and the various types of democracies.

Studying Political Power

Political science is the study of power. The discipline is enamored with the concept of power, namely how A gets B to do what A wants. Therefore, political science studies who holds power and how it's being used.

REMEMBER

Political power is the ability to get others to do what you want. It can take force or peaceful means, such as persuasion, to achieve this. Political power is exercised over people in many ways. In the U.S., for example, the federal government exercises political power over its population by forcing its citizens to pay taxes. Who would volunteer to pay taxes once a year unless the federal government had the power to force someone to pay up! Most important, this use of power of the U.S. government is considered rightful by its population. Therefore, the federal government possesses the legitimate use of power over its population.

REMEMBER

The term government describes the people and institutions that are responsible for making laws and policies in a country.

Exercising political power

In the U.S. and other federal societies, such as Germany, states or regions also exercise political power over their population. In the U.S., the states set speed limits on their roads, and in Germany, states have the power to set tax rates.

Finally, specific people, such as teachers, can also exercise political power. Whenever teachers assign homework, they're exercising political power over students. Student consider teachers to have authority and their use of power legitimate and therefore will do something, such as homework, they wouldn't normally do for fun. Authority refers to a general agreement that a person has the right to make certain decisions and that these decisions should be complied with.

Different thoughts on political power

TECHNICAL STUFF

Both ancient and modern political scientists were concerned with how power is used in societies. The famous Greek philosophers Socrates, Plato, and Aristotle believed that political power should be held by the best educated in society and should be used for the good of society (for more on the ancient Greek philosophers, see Chapter 14).

Niccolo Machiavelli (see Chapter 15) disagreed in his seminal work *The Prince.* He argues that power is needed to maintain the security of the state both at home and internationally. His work focuses on how to acquire power and then use it for the good of the state. Fellow political philosopher Thomas Hobbes not only agrees but also claims that political power shouldn't be used for ethical governance but to prevent conflict both domestically and internationally.

The more modern theorists such as John Locke and Jean-Jacques Rousseau (see Chapter 15) argue differently. They believe that the people should exercise political power in a nation-state and need to be able to hold their leader accountable. For Locke, whose work became the foundation for the American political system, a contract exists between leaders and citizens on how to exercise political power. If leaders violate the contract, the people can remove them from their positions.

More recent thinkers such as John Rawls (see Chapter 19) have added the components of social justice and economic equality to their theories.

Views on who holds the power

One of the ongoing questions in political science is how can the researcher determine who holds power in a society. Over time, six different explanations were developed.

>> **Bureaucratic theory:** Bureaucratic theory assumes that bureaucracies in countries hold power and make the most important decisions for society. It's therefore not politicians nor other leaders but top-level bureaucrats who run a country. They work for the good of the country, not to amass wealth, and their policies are based on what's best for a country. When studying France or Japan, two countries with powerful bureaucracies, bureaucratic theory can be used to study political power.

>> **Pluralism:** Pluralism, as developed by James Madison (see Figure 1-2) in Federalist Paper Number 10, believes interest groups will be created as societies become more economically and socially complex. People will join together to push for their own interests and for government benefits. These interests can be economic, professional, ideological, environmental, or even religious. All these diverse groups will now compete for public benefits, ensuring that public policy will benefit not only a few people but a majority in the country. Political power is therefore held by interest groups, representing the people.

As soon as one group of citizens feel disadvantaged, they'll begin to organize and compete for benefits. Suddenly, many interest groups are competing for political benefits and hopefully balancing each other out overall. Pluralism assumes that everybody will get a little bit from policymakers, but nobody will get everything he asks for. This balance makes every interest group accept lawmakers' policy decisions without complaining or, more importantly, without taking action against policymakers.

FIGURE 1-2: James Madison is the developer of pluralism.

Source: James Madison/Alamystock Photo

>> **Corporatism:** Corporatism also deals with interest groups. However, there are not tens of thousands as in the U.S., but a lot less. There may be only three. These groups are large and powerful and directly deal with the government when it comes to policy making. Therefore, a few but very powerful interest groups hold power in a society. The political scientist needs to study these to find out who holds power in a society. Examples of corporatist countries include Germany, Austria, and most of Scandinavia.

>> **Elite theory:** Elite theory, as created by the great Italian social scientists Vilfredo Pareto and Gaetano Mosca, states that every society has an elite that holds political power. That elite differs from society to society. In some societies, it's blood based, meaning you have to be born into it. A monarch with a ruling aristocracy comes to mind. In other places, wealth puts you into the elite. The more money you have, the more influential you'll be. This is often the case in capitalist countries like the U.S. or Great Britain. Another determinant of power is religion; Iran is governed by a religious elite. Membership in organizations such as an elite political party, for example, the Communist Party of the Soviet Union, or the military can put someone in the elite. A military dictatorship such as found in Chile from 1973 until 1990 under General Pinochet is an example. In a nutshell, elite theory states that in every society an elite holds political power.

>> **Marxism:** A Marxist believes that whoever holds economic power also holds political power. In other words, control of the economy equals control of government. In a capitalist society, the economy is controlled by the upper and middle classes, and therefore they control government. In a feudal society, the king and his aristocracy control the economy and therefore government (for a detailed discussion of Marxism, see Chapter 17).

Checking on sources of political power

Two models explain where political power comes from. First is the percolation-up model. It assumes that power rests with the citizens of a country. The citizens in turn elect leaders and give them political power to run the country on their behalf. If the citizens are satisfied with their leaders, they can reelect them. On the other hand, if they're dissatisfied, they can replace them. An example is a representative democracy.

The second model assumes the exact opposite. It's called a drip-down model. Here, ultimate power doesn't rest with the citizens but with the leadership of a country. For example, in authoritarian and totalitarian systems, the leader has ultimate power and makes policy for the country. The citizens have no input and can't hold the leadership accountable. Historically, this type of power model was the most widespread of the two. Examples include the monarchies of the past, totalitarian systems such as the Soviet Union, and more modern dictatorships such as Belarus or Iran.

Searching for Sources of Legitimacy

A successful government has to have its population recognize its legitimacy. If the population recognizes its government as legitimate, it will follow its leaders' decisions, and no force needs to be used when implementing policies. For example, if a police officer pulls you over for speeding, you recognize his powers of doing so. In other words, you see his use of power as legitimate and will abide by it. Governments can acquire legitimacy in various ways, as I discuss in the following sections.

REMEMBER

Legitimacy is the belief that the government's power over its population is rightful. This results in the exercise of power by a government without having to resort to force. A government that has a high level of legitimacy also has a high level of authority. Its citizens obey laws without having to be forced to.

Political structures

Certain political structures such as democracy can be helpful when it comes to legitimacy. If a government is chosen through democratic elections, it acquires legitimacy. The voters perceive this government to be based on popular will, and they're more likely to follow its lead.

Results

A second source of legitimacy are results. If a government is successfully providing its population with what it needs and desires, its legitimacy increases. For example, if a government is successful with its economic policies, providing its people with economic security, its legitimacy increases. The same will happen if a successful war is fought or the country is able to maintain security for its population. However, if a government fails to provide what people need or want, the population will turn against it. It will then lose legitimacy.

History

History matters when it comes to legitimacy. For example, if a regime has lasted for centuries, as the U.S. or the British governments have, the population is used to it, has a lot of pride in the system, and is more likely to find it legitimate.

Habit

Habit can make a difference when it comes to legitimacy. In any society, people will become socialized to find a government legitimate. The acquisition of political beliefs and values is referred to as political socialization and is usually accomplished by the family and parts of government, such as the educational structures (political socialization is discussed in more detail in Chapter 3). If children have been successfully socialized, they will abide by government rules because they believe that their government is legitimate. Later in life, they pass this habit on to their children. Governments that have been around for a long time have citizens who habitually consider it legitimate.

International recognition

International recognition makes a difference. If a government is recognized by the rest of the world, especially great powers such as the United States and China, as legitimate, its population is less likely to turn against it. Furthermore, legitimate governments can expect international aid in times of an economic or political crisis, which in turn will help maintain legitimacy among its people. For example, a loan by the International Monetary Fund (see Chapter 13) can help governments continue providing basic economic need to their populations. Only countries considered legitimate by the United Nations or other international organizations qualify for this kind of aid. In a nutshell, international legitimacy provides domestic legitimacy.

Religion

Religion can be a powerful source of legitimacy. If a government can tie its rule to a predominate religion, it automatically receives legitimacy. During the middle ages, most kings were absolute rulers, holding all political power in their countries. They tied their rule to religion, claiming that they had received the divine right to rule from God. God had installed them onto their throne, and any kind of insubordination or worse move against their authoritarian rule would be a move against God. Today, these types of regimes are rare. Iran is a good example where religion provides the government with legitimacy.

Nationalism

Finally, nationalism, defined as pride in one's country, can be a source of legitimacy. Often newly created states can receive legitimacy from a person or an event that unified the nation and instilled national pride into a population. A good example is the U.S. after the War of Independence against Great Britain. The country had been split on whether to wage a war of independence against British rule, and many colonists didn't believe in independence. The new country needed to become legitimate. The first president was war hero George Washington, and his name provided legitimacy to the newly established republic. While colonists may not have liked the new constitution or the leaders of Congress, they wanted to support General Washington. Many other prominent leaders, such as Thomas Jefferson and James Madison, followed, providing the country and its newly created institutions with legitimacy.

Chapter **2**

Shaping Research in Political Science: Looking at Major Approaches

Since its academic beginnings in the late 19th century, three major methodological schools of thought have dominated the discipline of political science; they are traditionalism, behavioralism, and post-behavioralism. This chapter looks at these three schools of thought in detail.

REMEMBER

A *methodology* is a general research strategy used by a political scientist. It dictates how research is undertaken and how results can be interpreted. For example, a methodology determines how data is collected and analyzed.

In addition, political science uses theories to explain behaviors and events. The field of political science deals with three types of theories: grand, medium-range, and narrow-range theory. All of these are also covered in this chapter.

Starting with Traditionalism

Not surprisingly, political scientists in the late 19th century to the 1940s were more like the historians of the day. They picked similar problems to study and used similar techniques to study them. This methodological period is called traditionalism. When using the traditionalist approach, while researching a problem, political scientists would engage in the following activities:

>> **Description:** Traditionalist political scientists were descriptive in nature. They described structures and their features in detail instead of trying to explain.

For example, when looking at a legislature, such as the U.S. Congress, political scientists described its structures and functions. They discussed in detail the powers given to Congress by the constitution, the way Congress passed bills, and how many committees both Houses of Congress had. In addition, they described electoral laws for countries and how people could run for office. When looking at the U.S. Constitution, political scientists would detail the powers given to all three branches of governments and the relationship between the federal government and states. There was no analysis of how Congress actually worked and how and why members of Congress voted on certain bills.

>> **Formal legalism:** Formal legalism refers to traditionalists studying formal structures such as political institutions, examples being legislatures and executives, and focusing on written documents such as constitutions. Traditionalists excluded studying human beings working in these institutions on purpose. In other words, they needed to discuss the structures but ignored the people working in these structures.

>> **Normative theory:** Normative theory is an explanation of events and people's behavior, which includes a researcher's personal preferences. Instead of being neutral, under this theory, it's perfectly acceptable to include values, personal preferences, and personal beliefs into research. After creating a normative theory, it isn't necessary to test it.

TECHNICAL STUFF

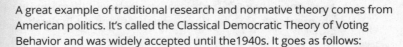

A great example of traditional research and normative theory comes from American politics. It's called the Classical Democratic Theory of Voting Behavior and was widely accepted until the1940s. It goes as follows:

In a democracy, voters are rational voters.

Voters know about issues and candidates' stances on issues and are able to base their votes on issues and candidate preferences.

Voters cast a vote based on knowledge.

This is considered a rational vote.

Because democracies create these rational voters and the U.S. is a democracy, rational voters exist in the U.S.

>> **Conservativism and the status quo:** Political scientists who identified as traditionalists wrote in support of their governments or political regimes. For traditionalists, it was unacceptable to criticize their current government. They did research to support the current regime. Do keep in mind that many political scientists of the time conducted their work in authoritarian regimes (see Chapter 4) and couldn't, even if they wanted to, publicly criticize their government. Imperial Germany (1871–1918) is a good example of this.

>> **Eurocentrism:** Most traditionalists were Eurocentric. All that means is that they focused their work on Europe. And for research purposes, this included the U.S., which was considered European because it was populated by Europeans. The rest of world was colonized and didn't matter much to political scientists. This didn't change until the end of World War II, which resulted in the decolonization of most of the world, especially Africa and Asia.

>> **Begin parochial:** Most traditionalists believed that the European races were superior to other races found especially in Africa. Political scientists and historians in France, for example, focused on the moral obligation to spread the superior French culture to its African colonies to educate and improve local culture. The inequality of races was one of the most controversial aspects of traditionalism and disappeared from political science research after World War II.

Traditionalism dominated political science for almost a century but started to decline in the 1940s. More and more political scientists felt uncomfortable with its Eurocentric and conservative orientations. Most important, political scientists conducted new empirical studies, which undermined traditionalist theories.

Switching to Behavioralism

Behavioralism is the study of human beings and their behavior. Behavioralism was a direct response to the failures of traditionalism and was an attempt to turn political science and the social sciences overall into real scientific disciplines. For decades, people looked down on the social sciences because they weren't considered real or hard sciences like biology, chemistry, and physics. The reason was that political scientists didn't test theories, brought their own values into their research, and couldn't create universal theories.

REMEMBER

A *universal theory* is a general explanation of behavior and events that has to be able to explain over time (ahistorical) and its explanations have to hold true everywhere. Universal theories are the backbone of the natural sciences and consist of *universal laws*. A universal law is a relationship that holds true everywhere and also over time. For example, x has to cause y everywhere and over time.

The concept of a paradigm was developed in 1962 by Thomas Kuhn in his book *The Structure of Scientific Revolutions* (University of Chicago Press). A *paradigm* is a scientific worldview (ideology) that shapes and guides a researcher in political science. The paradigm tells the political scientist what to research, how to research the specific problem, and what type of conclusions the researcher can draw. In other words, it sets the parameters for research. Paradigms can help with research but are also very restrictive. For example, traditionalism is a paradigm. It tells the political scientist what to study, in this case, institutions and constitutions, how to study the two, by describing them, and what type of conclusions to draw. To study actual human behavior would be outside of the paradigm and wouldn't be acceptable to the rest of academia. The researcher would be shunned by his colleagues and his research wouldn't be published. The researcher's career would be over.

To gain respect from the other real sciences, political science started to attempt to turn itself into a hard science beginning in the 1950s. Suddenly, political scientists tested theories and attempted to create grand theories, necessary to qualify as a natural science.

Being a behavioralist

By 1954, behavioralism successfully replaced traditionalism as the dominant paradigm (see nearby sidebar) in political science. It brought about the following changes to political science research.

Trying to explain

Traditionalism made a point to describe only institutions and constitutions. It didn't analyze the people running these institutions or try to explain their behavior. Behavioralism changed this. Now, political scientists begin to study human behavior and actually explain and analyze the inner working of institutions and constitutions. For example, instead of just describing Congress, the researcher now focuses on members of Congress and why and how they vote a certain way. Instead of describing the great battles of World War II, the political scientist now tries to explain why war broke out and how decisions were made during the war. In a nutshell, explanation replaced description in political science research. Today only a few traditionalist political scientists remain, mostly in Europe.

Emphasizing human behavior

Instead of focusing on institutions and constitutions as traditionalism did, behavioralism focuses on actual human beings and how they act. Instead of just describing human behavior, researchers now want to explain human behavior. Why do people engage in certain acts? How do they act when they suddenly find themselves in positions of power? Why do members of Congress vote in a certain way? Why do people go to war? All of these are questions political scientists now ask. Behavioralists therefore try to explain human behavior.

Employing empirical theory

Empirical theory explains human behavior and events and tests them to see whether they're true. The political scientist stops assuming when trying to explain, and testing of theories becomes the norm for the discipline.

Traditionalism uses normative theory (see earlier section on traditionalism) when engaging in research. It was acceptable for traditionalists to bring their own personal preferences and values into their research. There was no need to test theories. Behavioralists reject this type of research. For them, bringing personal values into research makes findings not just unscientific but also unacceptable and biased. Political science for them needs to be a real science, using theories that have been tested and are value-neutral. For this reason, instead of creating explanations of behavior and events based on personal preferences, behavioralists want to test their theories. This is possible only if you employ empirical theory.

Using mathematics

Mathematics is one of the most objective disciplines in academia. It's a natural or hard science, and people believe that it's impossible to bring values (personal influences) into mathematical research. It makes no difference whether a person is a liberal, conservative, or even communist; when political scientists undertake research using mathematics, they all come to the same conclusions. Adding, subtracting, and using advanced mathematical formulas are all objective and value-free activities.

Not surprisingly, using mathematics to test theories appeals to behavioralists, who believe in objectively testing theories. The best way to tell the academic world that you're being truly scientific and objective is to test a theory using mathematics, especially statistics. How can people bring their personal norms and values into statistics? Beginning with behavioralism, the use of mathematics in political science is encouraged, and today quantitative analysis has become the norm.

REMEMBER

Quantitative analysis is research using numbers derived from survey research, such as public opinion polls or other data sets previously created by other social scientists. Its opposite is *qualitative research,* which is research using nonnumerical data. In other words, the political scientist deals with some research to which mathematics can't be applied. Examples are field studies by anthropologists or detailed case studies.

Being truly objective

Like natural scientists, behavioralists believe that researchers can be truly objective when they're conducting their research. Personal beliefs and preferences don't matter and can be set aside during research. For example, a behavioralist believes that both an American researcher and a Russian researcher can look upon a certain event the same way and draw the same conclusions from the event, regardless of time and location.

For example, when studying the outbreak of war, the American political scientist could have researched an event 200 years ago and the Russian researcher could have studied it today. Both would come to the same conclusion. It is therefore possible to perceive events the same way, regardless of time, location, cultural upbringing, and personal preferences. This school of thought is called *positivism* or the French school of thought.

TECHNICAL STUFF

Positivism or the French school of thought was developed in the 19th century by French philosopher Auguste Comte. Positivism applies natural science techniques to study societies. It further stresses science and knowledge and advocates testing of all theories. Positivism believes that true objectivity exists and that all scientific experiences are based on sensory experiences — that is, social scientists can collect data using scientific observation, without bringing their own values into the research. This means that what you observe in the 18th century you'll observe in the 21st century and then draw similar conclusions. Perception makes you aware, and researchers perceive it the same way regardless of time and place. True objectivity and grand theory is thus possible.

Being liberal

Unlike traditionalism, behavioralism is based on the classical liberal school. It begins to question government decisions but at the same time also works with governments to find solutions to present-day problems.

For example, the Kennedy administration worked closely with political scientists to tackle issues such as spreading democracy or maintaining political stability in the newly created nation-states in Africa and Asia. While traditionalism supports government policies, thereby creating legitimacy for many governments, behavioralism isn't afraid to critique governments and regimes and often gets involved with government in the policy-making process.

Going global

Unlike traditionalism, behavioralism studies the whole world. The Eurocentric view of the past disappears and more studies focus on the newly created Third World. After World War II ended, the large colonial empires of the British and French collapsed, and suddenly new countries were created mostly in Africa and Asia. This allowed for the political scientist to move away from purely studying Europe. Decolonization has created more and more exciting options to study, and behavioralism takes advantage of this.

Turning the social sciences into a real science

For centuries, the social sciences, of which political science is a part of, felt inferior to the natural sciences because they weren't considered real or hard sciences, in the same boat as physics or chemistry, because they didn't have any grand theories. Grand theories, which are universal in nature, are the backbone of the natural sciences. Unless you have grand theories, you're not a real science. Physical laws, for example, transcend time and hold true everywhere. Now that is a real science.

Political science especially didn't have any of these grand theories. So during the behavioralist period, it set out to get a few. Systems theory, an example being the Theory of Hegemonic Stability, which I discuss in Chapter 8, and culture theories, such as the Civic Culture Theory, which I cover in Chapter 3, come close to grand theory in political science. Using grand theories and being truly objective in research can qualify the discipline as a natural or real science.

Moving Leftward with Post-Behavioralism

Unlike both traditionalism and behavioralism, the school of post-behavioralism has a specific birth date. It was created by David Easton, one of the great political scientists of our time (see Chapter 19). He coined the term in his address to the American Political Science Association in 1969.

He argued that the school of behavioralism was necessary in the 1950s and had done a lot of good for the discipline. However, by trying to become a natural science, political science had forgotten what it was all about. Political scientists are supposed to deal with current problems the world is facing and help people in the process. Instead, according to Easton, behavioralists ignored the current world and its problems, instead focusing only on trying to make political science become a real science. In the process, they created grand theories that were so abstract and complex that they couldn't be applied to the real world. Easton urged a compromise. He argued that political science should keep a part of behavioralism but ignore other parts of it. Thus the term *post-behavioralism*. I explain the parts of behavioralism that were kept and what were discarded in the following sections.

Agreeing with behavioralism

Post-behavioralism did not initiate a complete break from behavioralism. Instead, it kept quite a few of behavioralism's core ideas. These include:

>> **Explaining and studying human behavior:** Post-bevioralists believe that political scientists should study human behavior and not just institutions and constitutions as traditionalists did. In addition, the emphasis on examination instead of description needed to be kept, because you could solve only current problems and help people by trying to analyze, explain, and find solutions.

>> **Using empirical theory:** The use of empirical theory needed to be maintained. Obviously, it wasn't good enough to just assume and bring your own biases into your research if you wanted to solve current problems. The researcher had to use mathematics, especially statistics, to conduct testable research. Only empirical theory could guarantee explanations to deal with modern-day problems.

>> **Having a global perspective:** Political scientists needed to maintain their emphasis on the newly developing countries in Asia and Africa. Eurocentrism had to be rejected because, by the late 1960s, most nations weren't in Europe or the Americas but were located in Africa and Asia. Therefore, the study of nation-states had to be moved into the developing world.

Differing from behavioralism

While accepting many of behavioralism's ideas and concepts, post-behavioralism had some big differences. First, there was major disagreement over whether political science and the rest of the social sciences should try to become a real science like the natural sciences. The question was why political science should be like chemistry if it meant giving up doing real-world research that could actually help people. Also, many political scientists flat out rejected the idea that a social scientist could actually conduct objective or value-neutral research. Most post-behavioralists rejected the notion of positivism (see the section "Being truly objective," earlier in this chapter), instead adhering to a school of thought referred to as historicism.

TECHNICAL STUFF

Historicism is also called the German school of thought. Major German philosophers, such as Georg Friedrich Hegel and Karl Mannheim, supported it in the 19th and 20th century. The idea is that all human thought is socially determined and relative to time. In other words, everybody, including the political scientist, receives values from the environment she grew up in, and these values will determine how (1) research is conducted, and (2) what conclusions can be drawn from that research. A political scientist growing up in the U.S. won't interpret the results of research in a similar fashion to someone who grew up in Russia.

Post-behavioralists also believe that all thought is bound by the time period you grow up in. Someone growing up in the 1850s perceives research differently from someone conducting research in the 21st century. Therefore, true objective knowledge is impossible. People are subjective, formed by the environment they grew up in, even if they claim to be objective in nature.

Post-behavioralists also argue that objectivity doesn't exist and that not just all social scientists are subjective but everybody is. Society needs to accept this.

Post-behavioralists don't believe that grand theory can be discovered in the social sciences, including political science, and don't support even attempting to create it. For them, grand theory is so abstract that it can't be used to explain current problems and therefore there's no use for it. They argue that the political scientist should forget about turning political science into a real science and should also forget calling for pure objectivity in research because it doesn't exist.

Finally, post-behavioralists advised for more third-world studies and fewer studies of the advanced world. They were especially concerned with the emphasis behavioralism placed on democracies. Many behavioralist theories worked best in established democracies and weren't adaptable to other forms of government.

Post-behavioralists became fully third-world oriented and will often travel to third-world countries to immerse themselves in local cultures to better understand the local cultures and their politics.

REMEMBER

By the 1980s, many more political scientists studied third-world countries than advanced industrialized countries, and there was even a shortage of European and Soviet scholars in the U.S.

Comparing Political Science Theories

In this book, the term *theory* is used on many occasions. What is a theory? Are theories important to the field of political science? The answer is a clear yes. Without theories, the discipline of political science is quite useless. Theories are an integral part of the study of political science, especially some of its subfields such as international relations and comparative politics.

A *theory* is defined as a general explanation of behavior or events. It can be applied across many cases and is not specific to one. A theory therefore tries to explain why a certain event has occurred or why people behave in a certain way. For example, we have theories of why World War II occurred or why Adolf Hitler acted the way he did. Chapter 12 outlines theories explaining why war and other international conflict occur.

Theories are designed to not only explain but also predict behavior and events. If a political scientist can predict what causes a certain event, such as warfare, it may be preventable. For example, one of the theories in Chapter 12 claims that democracies are less likely to go to war than other forms of governments. If this is true, then democracy needs to be spread throughout the world, and slowly war will disappear. This has been the cornerstone of American foreign policy since the end of World War II.

Read on to find out more on the three types of political science theories: grand, medium range, and narrow range.

Creating theories

The first step on the way to create a theory is to come up with a hypothesis. All a hypothesis is, is a testable proposition. An example: Women are more liberal than men. This is a basic proposition or proposal. Next, researchers set out to test the proposition. They collect information or data empirically — that is, based on observable evidence. In this case, they could create a public opinion survey and administer several polls in different countries. They then quantify the results, measure them with numbers, and test them. If the hypothesis proves true, they've created a theory. The aforementioned hypothesis, women are more liberal than men, is actually wrong. It holds true in the U.S. but is wrong in other countries, where men are more liberal.

Grand theory

Grand theories are the most prestigious and sought after. They claim to provide explanations or predictions over time and space. In other words, they claim to be universal in nature. The concept of grand theory comes from the natural sciences such as physics and chemistry. A good example is the mixing of two chemicals. After you mix the two, a certain result occurs. The result will be the same whether you mix the chemicals in Africa or Europe (space) or whether you mix the two today or in two years (time).

It's tougher to create such theories in the social sciences such as political science or sociology. However, a few grand theories have been created in political science, and one of the most famous ones, the theory of the civic culture, states that only one specific culture can sustain democracy in the long run, and unless you create it, democracy will collapse in a country. As soon as the culture is created, democracy is here to stay in a country. It doesn't matter where you create it (space) or when you create it (time). Therefore, it's universal in nature and can be used to predict whether democracy can succeed in a country. See Chapter 3 for more details.

Medium-range theory

Medium-range theories claim to provide answers to questions asked a majority of the time but not all the time. Therefore, they're not universal in nature. Medium-range theories are most often used in political behavior studies. A good example is the theory that women are more liberal than men. Although that holds true in the U.S., Great Britain, and Germany, it's not true in France or Spain. So the theory is valid most of the time but not all the time. That makes it a medium-range theory and not grand theory, which has to be valid all the time.

Narrow-range theory

Narrow-range theories are useless in the field of political science. They're discouraged by the field, and political scientists who use them are looked down upon. Narrow-range theories claim to occasionally provide an explanation for behavior or events. In other words, a narrow-range theory can explain an event once in a while. So if the questions are what causes war, a narrow-range theory could explain only why war can occur once in a while and not provide an explanation of why war occurs a majority of the time or all the time.

Looking at Historical Sociology

Historical sociology is one of the newer schools in political science. It traces its origins back to the 19th century but didn't become popular until the 1960s. In the 19th century, some of the most famous social scientists, including Emile Durkheim, Karl Marx, and Max Weber, were active, and all were historical sociologists. They based their works on historicism, believing that all academic work in the social sciences is subjective and biased, because researchers bring their own values into their research. For this reason, they were attacked by positivists who believed that the social sciences could be a true science and value-neutral.

Historical sociology understands that the present is a product of the past and can be understood only by using a historical approach. People make history under circumstances encountered from the past. A society is constructed historically by individuals who are constructed historically by society. Individuals are shaped by society, which in turn influences their thinking. Therefore, the political scientist has to focus on the historical and social period of a person to detect the true meaning behind a scholar's work.

So what is historical sociology and how does it work? First, the social scientist looks at one or more societies and analyzes the way groups within society interact with each other. These groups can be classes, like in modern society, or castes like in more traditional societies. The way these groups interact in turn shapes form of government and policy outcomes.

For example, the way social classes interact with each other can determine what form of government a society has. Barrington Moore, Jr. demonstrates this in his classic work *Social Origins of Dictatorship and Democracy* (Beacon Press). His research shows that social class alliances shape governments. Whenever an aristocracy aligns itself with the peasantry, a fascist government develops. If, however, the working class aligns itself with the peasantry, socialism is the result. Finally, if an aristocracy aligns itself with the middle classes, capitalism develops.

Seeking Benefits: Rational Choice Theory

With the advent of political economy (see Chapter 13) in the 1970s, political science sees a fusing of the disciplines of political science and economics. Suddenly, research techniques from both disciplines are available to the researcher, one of them being rational choice theory. Political scientists use rational choice theory to explain human behavior and also state behavior. The theory is fairly simple: People and countries will, based on the information they have at the time, engage in actions from which they benefit the most. At the same time, they'll also engage in actions from which they'll lose the least. Quite simply, people, such as politicians and even countries, will do what is best for them and what will cause the least damage to them.

Chapter **3**

Dealing with Political Culture

Every nation-state in the world contains one or more different cultures. A culture determines the language people speak, the religion they practice, and their behavior toward others. It's based on the traditions found in a society and the history people have shared. At the same time, people also have a distinct political culture. A political culture is defined as a set of attitudes and practices held by citizens that in turn shapes their political behavior in society. In other words, a political culture determines how people feel about their political system and whether they support it. Not surprisingly, governments take a keen interest in attempting to shape political culture.

This chapter discusses the importance of political culture and how it shapes society. The concepts of civic culture and political socialization are important points to political culture as well as moving from materialism to postmaterialsm. Read on to find out more on these topics.

Analyzing Political Culture

In his work *The Republic* (see Chapter 14), Plato discusses the importance of political culture and political socialization for a political regime. The political culture of a society shapes political values and political behavior and has to be in line with the political system. If it isn't, the long-term survival of the regime is in question. For this reason, according to Plato, the young in a society have to be politically socialized, which is a fancy term for being politically indoctrinated, with the values of the regime. Only political socialization can guarantee survival of the regime in the long run. (See the later section "Working on Political Socialization" for more on political socialization.)

The importance of political culture

Every society instills certain political values into its people. Political values are defined as deeply held views about how government is supposed to work and what a person's role in a political system is. These beliefs and values are what shapes the political culture of a nation. The political culture of a country is thus determined by the history of a people and its religious, economic, and social values. If a government is able to manipulate a political culture, it can enhance support by the people. Therefore, interfering in the shaping of a political culture has become commonplace in the world.

Both democracies and authoritarian governments attempt to influence the political culture in a country. In totalitarian societies, such as the Soviet Union, classes designed to indoctrinate the population are mandatory at all school levels. In the U.S., civic education classes, designed to accomplish similar objectives, are also required in most states.

Touching on political socialization

REMEMBER

Political socialization refers to the process of how people acquire their political values (see the section "Sustaining Democracy: The Civic Culture," later in this chapter, for more information).

Many governments of all types use the process of political socialization to intervene in the creation of a good citizen. Governments can do so through the educational process, control of the media, a state religion, public events such as military parades, and commemoration of past events.

Noting citizenship

The concept of citizenship is a part of political culture. In every society, people are told what makes a good citizen and what type of characteristics citizens should possess.

Every sovereign nation-state in the world has different citizenship requirements and expects citizens to behave in a certain manner. Three examples of different citizenship requirements are

>> **Jus soli (Latin for "right by territory"):** In a country following the law of jus soli, everybody born in its territory automatically becomes a citizen. France and the United States use this law.

>> **Jus sanguinis (Latin for "right by blood"):** Countries following jus sanguinis bestow citizenship rights based on blood. For example, a person is automatically a German citizen if one of his parents was a German citizen, regardless of whether he ever visited or lived in Germany. (As a side note, Germany will allow individuals to become citizens if they have legally lived in Germany for eight years and apply for citizenship.)

>> **Israel's law of return:** It makes every Jewish person a citizen as soon as he moves permanently to Israel. This can be called citizenship by religion.

Looking at the variances of political cultures

Some nation-states have more than one culture. These states, such as Afghanistan and Iraq, are made up of different groups, with different religious traditions, and they don't even share a common language. Instead, they share loyalty with their tribe and consider it, and not the national government, the ultimate source of power. They don't share a culture or history with the majority group. This usually results in political struggle for power and often civil war and the possible breakup of a nation-state.

Political cultures vary from society to society. In the U.S., a spirit of rugged individualism survives, where people believe in small government and put the emphasis on individual achievement. In other societies, such as France or Japan, people look to a strong and powerful state for guidance, while individualism is subjugated to the concept of communalism. The community matters in Japan, not the individual.

Changing political cultures

Political cultures do change over time. However, changes come slowly because people are set in their ways and refuse to change their attitudes and behavior.

A good example of a political culture slowly changing involves racial intermarriage in the U.S. Until the 1960s, a majority of all Americans, including African Americans, opposed racial intermarriage. This attitude began to slowly change in the 1960s, and it took another half a century for most Americans to consider racial intermarriage acceptable.

Political cultures aren't static and can change over time. The easiest way for a political culture to change is to face a major crisis. Economic crises have changed cultural attitudes toward governments. For example, the Great Depression beginning in 1929 led to a support of government intervention in the economy in the form of a welfare state. At the same time, the economic crisis of 2007/2008 resulted in many Americans losing trust in their government and becoming more cynical in nature.

In other societies, the same can happen. In Japan, for example, decades of no or low economic growth have changed a culture that was very supportive and proud of its form of government. The average Japanese today is more cynical and less likely to be proud of government. Political scandals and wars can have similar effects. Watergate, for example, made American culture more negative toward government, and the invasion of Iraq in 2003 had a similar effect.

Sustaining Democracy: The Civic Culture

The seminal work on political culture was published in 1963 by Gabriel Almond and Sidney Verba. Titled *The Civic Culture: Political Attitudes and Democracy in Five Nations* (SAGE Publications, Inc.), the work was in response to the collapse of democracy in Europe in the 1920s and 1930s and in Africa in the 1950s. In both instances, democracies were established in former authoritarian countries (colonies in Africa) but survived for only a few years. (See Chapter 16 for more information on failures of democracy.)

REMEMBER

The civic culture is the only culture that can sustain democracy over time in a country.

Almond and Verba believed that political cultures could be used to explain the failure of democracy. For them, democracy needed a certain, specific culture, which they titled the civic culture, to survive in the long run. So they set out to discover the characteristics of a civic culture. They believed that if they discovered a political culture that could sustain democracy, they could change other cultures to create this civic culture and then make sure democracy survived. In their research, they discovered the following five components of a civic culture, necessary to sustain a democracy:

>> **A large middle class:** A large middle class has to exist in a democracy, because it's the class most likely to possess democratic values. If the middle class is small and other nondemocratic classes such as an aristocracy or a radicalized working class dominate society, there's a good chance that an authoritarian regime can come to power.

>> **A secular society:** A society has to be secular with no state religion in place. Religion has to be kept out of government, because many religions hold nondemocratic values. If religion dominates society like in Iran today, democracy isn't possible.

>> **Pluralism:** A democratic society has to allow for the creation of political parties and interest groups to represent the will of the people. In other words, people have to be able to organize and express their wishes to government.

>> **A culture of consensus:** A society has to agree on the major political issues shaping it. These include form of government and economic structure. Almost all Americans agree that democracy is the best form of government and that a form of capitalism is the best economic structure for a society. In Russia, on the other hand, such a consensus doesn't exist. About one-third of all Russians believe in democracy and capitalism, while the other two-thirds support either strong man rule or a return to communism. This makes it tough for democracy to set foot in Russia.

>> **Permission of moderate change:** Government and its people have to be willing to change over time. With societies and the world constantly changing, there has to be a willingness to accept change and adapt to it. Societies that don't change, for either political or religious reasons, will fall behind globally and become pariah nations. In addition, they'll face constant battles at home between citizens ready for change and those who want to stick with the status quo. Iran and Afghanistan are two good examples of such societies.

Being behavioral in nature

The civic culture is a classical behavioral study (see Chapter 2). Almond and Verba researched human behavior through empirical testing. For this reason, they set out and interviewed 5,000 people — 1,000 in each one of the five countries they had selected for their research. The five countries were two successful democracies, the U.S. and Great Britain; two classical failures of democracy, West Germany and Italy; and one lesser developed country, Mexico. The attempt was to find a culture in these five countries that could sustain democracy in the long run. If that was possible, a blueprint for democracy could be created to bring this civic culture to other countries. This in turn would allow for democracy not only to be spread globally but to actually maintain it over time.

Asking questions

In their study, Almond and Verba decided to personally interview 5,000 people in five countries. The most relevant questions concerning political culture were centered on these topics:

» **Cognition:** They asked people whether they were familiar with their national government, knew about officeholders, and most important, knew how they could participate in the political process. The results were that knowledge of government and participation were high in Great Britain, West Germany, and the U.S. At the same time, cognition was high in northern Italy and low in southern Italy. In Mexico, cognition was low at the national level; however, at the local level, Mexicans were keenly aware of their political structures.

» **Feelings toward the system:** Feelings of pride and support of the current form of government were very high in Great Britain and the U.S. In West Germany, people weren't very proud of the structure of the system but supported it because it was efficient and delivered the goods. In Mexico, people were proud and supported their local system, but not their national political structure.

» **Partisanship:** In both the U.S. and Great Britain, partisanship was low. Political science usually measures partisanship in a society by asking the following question: "Would you allow your child to marry someone with a different partisan identification?" Although this wasn't a problem in Great Britain and the U.S., parents not having much of a problem being a Democrat and their child marrying a Republican, it matters in the other three countries. In both West Germany and Italy, people expressed great partisanship by refusing to consider such a marriage. In Mexico, the question wasn't relevant because Mexico at this time was a one-party state ruled by the PRI (Institutional Revolutionary Party).

» **Civic obligation:** The questions of civic obligation involved feeling an obligation to participate in politics by voting or participating in other ways. In both the U.S. and Great Britain, civic obligation was high, while in West Germany, people expressed an obligation to vote, but that was about it. In Italy and Mexico, feelings of civic obligation were low.

» **Civic competence:** Civic competence refers to the public believing that it has an obligation to join and participate in civic organizations such as charities and religious organizations or just volunteering and helping members of the community. The U.S. scored highest in this category, with Great Britain coming in second. In West Germany and Italy, civic competence was low, most people believing that it was the government's obligation to help the needy. In Mexico, civic competence was high at the local level but almost nonexistent at the national level.

>> **Trust:** This category refers to whether people trust the government to do what is right. While Americans and the British had a high level of trust in their government, West Germans and Italians did not. Mexicans, on the other hand, showed trust in the local government but not the national government.

Based on results from these questions, Almond and Verba categorized cultures in the five countries they studied and came up with not just one civic culture but three political cultures they found in each country. Furthermore, each country had a mix of the three cultures. See more on this in the next section.

Finding three political cultures

The three cultures Almond and Verba found in each of the five countries are parochial political culture, subject political culture, and participant political culture.

Parochial political culture

In a parochial political culture, people don't care very much about their national government. They don't have a lot of information on it, have no attachment to it, and make no demands on it. In other words, people expect nothing from their national government and want it to leave them alone. They don't like or dislike it and don't participate in national politics.

At the same time, the parochial population is very close to their local form of government. In Mexico, for example, the people were familiar with their small city government structures, knew their mayors, and participated in local elections. They felt close to the locality and supported it.

Parochial cultures can still be found in remote parts of the U.S., such as rural West Virginia, and in tribal societies, such as Afghanistan and some African countries.

Subject political culture

In a subject political culture, citizens tend to have a high level of political information. They're familiar with many important issues of the day and know how to participate in the political process. However, they feel powerless and believe that their opinions don't matter. In other words, they lack political efficacy. Further, they don't have an attachment to the political system and don't express any positive emotions toward it. They just expect benefits from government. As long as the government delivers the goods, subjects tend be passive and accept the political system in place. However, as soon as government is unable to deliver the goods anymore, they can easily turn against it and demand a change of government or the political system itself.

Good examples of countries where the majority of the population are/were subjects are the Soviet Union or present-day China. Citizens in both countries are/were well informed and expected the political structure to deliver benefits to them.

Participant political culture

In a participant political culture, political scientists find the true democratic citizens. They understand how the political process works and they're interested in the issues of the day. When they vote, they base their vote on knowledge of issues and candidate stances on issues. For this reason, they can hold their government accountable, and if they dislike what they see, they can replace it. Participants are further proud and supportive of their political system. They believe that they hold political power and can influence policy making. In other words, they believe that they have political efficacy. Finally, participants are active at all levels of politics; they don't just vote but also volunteer for civic organizations. They're not afraid to discuss politics at the dinner table and with friends. Participants are truly the backbone of a democracy.

REMEMBER

Political efficacy refers to people feeling that they have some input in decision-making. In other words, they don't feel powerless.

Needing three political cultures to sustain democracy

Instead of picking one of three political cultures discussed in the previous section, Almond and Verba claim that a country needs a mix of all three cultures to sustain democracy. A pure parochial society wouldn't exist very long. Keep in mind that parochials feel no love or loyalty to a national government, instead focusing purely on the local level. If a whole nation consisted of people who don't like the nation or the government in charge, it would collapse.

At the same time, a nation full of subjects would result in the collapse of democracy, too. If every citizen was just a follower who would obediently abide by government rules, government could soon turn authoritarian. The Soviet Union and Nazi Germany, for example, consisted of pure subject cultures, with citizens blindly obeying government decisions.

Now what about a pure participant society? Could you imagine if every American citizen was a pure political animal? What would happen to the system if more than 150 million people were active in politics and demanded benefits from government? According to Almond and Verba, this would result in a system overload. Government couldn't deal with that many demands, and people in turn would take action against government if they didn't get what they asked for.

For this reason, Almond and Verba advocate for a mix of the three cultures. Every democracy has to have all three cultures to survive in the long run. A democracy needs people who just don't care about politics, have no knowledge of what's going on, and don't participate (parochials). At the same time, government often has to make controversial decisions for the good of the country, such as increasing taxes to pay off government debt or fund new programs. In this scenario, a democracy needs subjects who will complain bitterly about these decisions but won't take any action against government.

Finally, participants are needed to hold the government accountable. Whenever government makes a decision, it needs to know that its citizens will hold it accountable for these decisions. Almond and Verba refer to this as *anticipated reaction.* Government and its leaders make decisions based on how they believe people will react to their decisions. Often no reaction will come, but a rational leader believes that it will, and so policy is made, which is acceptable to most people.

TECHNICAL STUFF

In the last few decades, fewer and fewer people have been voting in democracies. This has concerned many, but the concept of anticipated reaction comes to the rescue. Anticipated reaction refers to political leaders assuming that the people will react to their policies and, if objecting, will organize into political parties or join interest groups and, most important, will participate in voting. Therefore, every rational politician will do his best to represent the people. It's out of fear of people becoming upset and holding political elites accountable that politicians attempt to do their best to represent people. Recent examples of people organizing because they were upset with government decisions include the Tea Party movement as a reaction to Obamacare in the U.S. and the creation of new populist parties in Europe, such as the Alternative for Germany as a reaction to mass migration from the Middle East and Africa.

Working on Political Socialization

Political Socialization is the process of how people acquire their political values. The political values people possess in turn will shape their political behavior within the state. Political socialization teaches children political values and norms that will later impact their political behavior. The objective of political socialization is the same for every government: to create a populace that is well socialized and supports the current form of government. For this reason, many governments directly intervene in the socialization process. This can be done through educational structures and even religion.

Goals of political socialization

Studies have shown that successful political socialization has to create loyalty to the political system in the following areas:

» **Loyalty to the state:** This is the most important because, without it, states will collapse at some point. If a majority of the people opposes the existence of the state they live in, there's no future for the state.

Recent examples include Yugoslavia and Czechoslovakia, both states that collapsed because a majority of the people opposed the state itself. Loyalty toward the state is created through nationalism and patriotism. The goal is to instill pride into a people through patriotic activities, such as singing the national anthem before sports events and pledging allegiance to the flag of a country.

» **Loyalty to the political structure:** Loyalty toward the state is important but not sufficient for the survival of a government. Besides supporting the country, the populace also has to support the current government structures and the ideas they're based on.

In the U.S., the government is based on democracy and capitalism. For this reason, the government has to artificially create loyalty toward these two. In civic education classes, mandatory in most states, children are taught about the virtues of democracy and how great capitalism works for the well-being of most Americans. At the same time, the evils of authoritarianism and communism are imprinted into children's minds. Polls show that a vast majority of all Americans support and are very proud of their form of democracy, while a smaller majority also supports various forms of capitalism.

» **Loyalty toward the current government:** Loyalty toward the current government in power is a necessity. A populace has to be socialized to accept their favorite candidate losing and still supporting the new government elected. Even though a favorite candidate may have lost, people still have to consider the new government legitimate. If they don't, they could turn against government and political violence can result.

When Hillary Clinton lost the presidency to Donald Trump in 2016, many American were shocked and dismayed. However, nobody took up arms and initiated political violence to overthrow the newly elected Trump administration. This signals that Americans are well socialized into accepting losing elections and living with a president they didn't support. In other countries, such as Kenya, this wouldn't have happened. The losing side would have initiated political violence, and civil war would have broken out.

Agents of political socialization

How do citizens of a nation become socialized? In other words, what and who are the institutions that transmit political values to people? *Agents of political socialization* refer to the various institutions and people that will have an impact on a person's learning of values and norms of political behavior. The following sections explore these questions.

Trusting family

The family is still the most important agent of political socialization today. Parents are who children see the most in early life, and this allows for parents to imprint children politically. Even if governments attempt to indoctrinate children through school or youth organizations, as the Soviet Union did, they fail. While schools preached socialist messages in the Soviet Union, the Russian grandmas back home would tell children stories about the czars and teach them about religion. Lenin considered Russian grandmas among the most dangerous group of people during the Russian Revolution.

Therefore, families do matter, and parents influence political behavior. A majority of all people perceive politics as their parents did and also base their voting behavior on their parents' voting behavior. Even a like or dislike for government can be transferred as can trust and distrust. It's important to point out that most parents act as an unconscious agent of political socialization. All this means is that parents don't consciously attempt to indoctrinate their children, but children overhear parents discussing political issues and model their political behavior on their parents' political behavior.

TECHNICAL STUFF

Studies have shown that young men who grow up in single-parent households tend to be more authoritarian than other males. The reason is that they must often assume the role of the man in the household early on in life, which changes their behavior. On the other hand, if children are allowed to have a say in family decision-making, they tend to be more democratic later in life.

Going to school

During school years is when the government can attempt to influence political socialization. Often, governments will make a conscious attempt to indoctrinate children and create citizens loyal to their country and government. This is accomplished through a curriculum that emphasizes history and civic education classes in such a way as to instill nationalism, pride in the country, and patriotism in children.

Creating a political culture curriculum has an added benefit. In many countries, subcultures exist, such as ethnic minorities, and many immigrants may have arrived recently. They still practice their native cultures. Through government-guided education, they can learn a unifying language and a common history. In other words, the educational structure can make sure they'll become good citizens.

Studies have shown that government attempts to socialize children can have the most impact in middle school. Before middle school, children are too young to understand complex political concepts such as separation of power in the U.S. or scientific communism in the Soviet Union. One of the few things young children understand is the concept of authority and loyalty to one person. So early on, loyalty to a political leader can be taught. This in turn enhances legitimate authority in a nation. Many American schools teach the idea that the police have legitimate authority over people, and for this reason, young children are more likely than teenagers to support police.

At the high-school level, conscious political socialization is too late. By the time students enter high school, their political values have been fully formed. Even if the government attempts to indoctrinate at this time, it's too late. Political opinions can rarely change at this age. Therefore, political socialization needs to happen at the middle-school level.

Finding friends

Friends can be very influential in socializing a person politically. Especially in cases where a young person is apolitical, a friend who is very much interested in politics can make a difference. The friend may drag the youngster along to political rallies and constantly talk politics. This will make a difference. Another example involves peer groups. If a person moves to a new neighborhood, say, a country club suburban area, he may change his political beliefs to fit into a new peer group.

Going to church

Religion can become an important agent of socialization. If a person is deeply religious and her religion takes many political stances, the person will adopt these issue stances as a part of her political values. For example, the Catholic Church opposes abortion, and many devout Catholics follow the church's teaching and oppose abortion as well.

Listening to the media

Today, the media is becoming more important in political socialization. More and more American children grow up in one-parent households, and after school, they're alone at home watching television or engaging in social media. The absence of family has given the media an opening to socialize children. It's not just news programs, rarely watched by children, that can impact a child's belief systems, but just about any show on television that portrays certain behavior, a certain lifestyle, or analyzes events in a certain way.

REMEMBER

In most societies, the government regulates parts of the media and thereby controls the flow of information to the public. In authoritarian and totalitarian societies, the government assumes direct control over the media and allows only certain information to be dispersed to the public. This allows the government to politically socialize people and manipulate their political values.

Belonging to a minority group

Most societies contain minority ethnic groups. In the U.S., for example, African Americans constitute a minority and have developed certain political traits. For example, African Americans tend to be more liberal than American whites and are more likely to vote for the Democratic Party. They're also more likely to perceive police as racially biased. These ideas are socialized into young black children and will stick with them for the rest of their lives. Today, more than 90 percent of all African Americans vote consistently for the Democratic Party in the United States.

Living through major political and economic crises

A certain catastrophic event can change people's political values and their political behavior. For example, the Great Depression changed American values and, in turn, voting behavior. Before the Great Depression, most American believed in small government and voted Republican. The Great Depression changed all of this. Suddenly, people favored government intervention in the economy through a welfare state and began to vote Democratic. This lasted until the late 1960s, when the war in Vietnam and race relations changed Americans again.

Changing later on in life

Although most people won't change their political attitudes and behavior during their lifetime, a few do. There are two ways that can happen. First, there is adult socialization. This can be brought about by economic changes in a person's life. A person can grow up poor and a staunch Democrat. However, later in life, he grows wealthy, moves to a nice neighborhood, and is now surrounded by conservative peers. This can change his political attitudes. He becomes conservative, especially on economic issues.

The second way a person can change his political attitudes is through a process called elite socialization. This can happen if a person makes it into an elite group, such as a business group or a political group. A good example are new members of the U.S. Senate. They start out rebellious, wanting to change things around in the Senate. They may want to change the rules of conduct or propose radical policies. Over time, they figure out that unless they change their political attitudes and behavior, they'll be very unsuccessful Senators never passing any bills. This can cost them reelection. To be a successful Senator, they'll have to work through the system and adapt. As soon as they do, elite socialization has happened, and it has changed their political attitudes and behavior.

Moving from Materialist to Postmaterialist

The concepts of materialism and postmaterialism have been used by the discipline of economics for decades. Recently the two concepts have been adapted by political science to show how the shift from a materialist society to a postmaterialist society can change the political culture of a country and subsequently the politics in a country.

In a materialist society, people are trying to fulfill their basic needs. Basic needs include food, shelter, and ways to get to work and take care of the family. People in materialist societies are mostly concerned with economic security, they tend to be deeply religious, and issues such as law and order matter to them.

After several decades of economic growth, a materialist society evolves into a postmaterialist society. Suddenly, basic economic needs of citizens have been met, and society now is less concerned with economic survival and has money left over to spend on more than just basic needs. The issues society is concerned about also change. Instead of economic security, people now focus on individual freedoms, social equality, and overall quality-of-life issues.

This shift from a materialist society to a postmaterialist society redefines politics in a country. The following changes can be detected:

>> **Religion loses importance in society.** Fewer and fewer people attend church services and are willing to base their vote on religious issues.

>> **Union membership declines.** With society doing well economically, there's less of a need for unions and fewer and fewer people are willing to join. In turn, unions are getting weaker in the political realm.

» **Social class becomes less important in politics.** Most of the citizens in a postmaterialist country consider themselves middle class, and class distinctions cease to be of importance.

» **New issues become important to the public.** With people having less to worry about economic security, they can now focus on other issues of importance. These issue include a worry about the environment and social equality. Green movements are born, and issues such as gender equality and gay rights come to the forefront.

» **People demand more direct democracy.** With a society becoming not only more prosperous but also more educated, people want change. They now call for the use of referenda and initiatives to allow for the people to be more involved in policy making.

» **A more educated electorate is less willing to base its vote on straight political party line.** Instead, ticket-splitting becomes commonplace. The whole political process now becomes personal. With people voting less for the party than for the candidate, politics becomes personalized and image driven. People vote for candidates and not a political party anymore. Suddenly, a candidate's image becomes paramount, and party issue stances matter less.

2
Comparing Governments

Examine what political scientists do.

Look at comparative politics by comparing the foundations for democracy and the rule of law — constitutions. Examine two constitutions: the U.S. and the New Russian Constitution.

Check out the institutional structures of democracies. Dig in to the legislative, executive, and judicial structures and both parliamentary and presidential systems.

Uncover political processes in democracies, explore political parties and interest groups and their role in democracies, and then evaluate the cornerstone of democracy: voters and voting.

Chapter **4**

Discussing Different Forms of Government

When doing research in political science, a variety of forms of government are found. While many are familiar with the types of democracy, who knows about the differences between authoritarianism and totalitarianism? While there were only a few totalitarian regimes in human history, there are many examples of authoritarian countries today and in the past. Another important aspect when comparing nations are systems of government, which refers to the distribution of power within states. In other words, are countries federal, consisting of states with independent powers, such as the United States, or unitary where all power is held by the central government.

Identifying Types of Governments

When studying political science, you come across a variety of governments. From democracies to totalitarian regimes, governments do vary. What type of government or regime is out there in the world today? Table 4-1 gives examples of the various forms of government.

TABLE 4-1 **Forms of Government**

Forms of Government	Power Structure-Holder of Political Power	Examples
Monarchy	One, a king or prince	Saudi Arabia, Medieval France
Aristocracy	A small ruling elite or class, usually based on hereditary qualifications	Ancient Sparta
Oligarchy	A small group based on characteristics such as wealth or religion	Iran, ancient Venice
Totalitarian	One all-powerful supreme leader	Stalinist Russia and Nazi Germany
Authoritarian	One leader with a small elite	Egypt, fascist Italy
Democracy	Many; the people	United States, Great Britain, the Roman Republic
Anarchy	Nobody; no leader or government in charge; can occur during or right after a civil war	Libya, Somalia

Diving in to democracy

TECHNICAL STUFF

The term *democracy* comes from ancient Greece. *Demos* in Greek refers to "the people" while *cracy* means "rule by." Therefore, the term *democracy* translates to "rule by the people." Today, two types of democracies exist.

Direct democracy

Arriving on the scene first, direct democracy was practiced by the ancient Greeks and Romans. In a direct democracy, the citizens make all decisions themselves. In other words, citizens make policy. They gather on occasion in a large place and discuss and then vote on policies for the state. These policies can include laws or bureaucratic appointments. No politicians are elected because the citizens themselves make all decisions. Direct democracy has become rare. It still exists at the local level in New England and in countries like Switzerland.

A direct democracy is the most democratic form of government in existence. The people themselves make policy for their country. However, it's tough, almost impossible, to have direct democracy in countries with large populations. The concept worked well in small city-states, such as Athens, or the Roman Republic. It would be unworkable in the U.S. Where would more than 150 million American citizens meet to make policy directly, and how could they ever agree on anything?

Representative democracy

The second type of democracy is referred to as a representative democracy. In a representative democracy, such as the U.S. or Great Britain, citizens don't make policy for the country directly. Instead, they vote for a representative, or office holders, who will act on and make policy on their behalf. If the representatives follow the people's wishes, implementing policies they support, they'll get reelected. If, on the other hand, they anger the population, the people can replace them with new and hopefully better representatives.

Representative democracies work well in larger countries and give the people the freedom to disengage from politics. They don't directly have to participate in decision making. They can pick someone else to do it for them. However, this can result in a major problem. Often, many citizens choose not to participate, allowing for a small minority to take over policy making. In the U.S., for example, almost 40 percent of the people don't vote for president. Every president for the last 100 years has actually been elected by a minority of the people. Is this still democracy?

Today, two types of representative democracies exist: parliamentary democracy and presidential democracy.

PARLIAMENTARY DEMOCRACY

Parliamentary democracies are very common in Europe and also found in Australia and New Zealand. Germany and Great Britain are the two major examples of parliamentary democracies. In a parliamentary democracy, the people don't vote for their executive, be it a prime minster or chancellor, directly; instead, they vote for a member of a legislature. The legislature then selects the executive. It's usually the majority political party that gets to select the executive. The following diagram shows how parliamentary democracy works in Great Britain:

Citizens ⟶ Parliament (legislature) ⟶ Prime minister (executive)

Parliamentary systems tend to be dominated by the executive. The British prime minister has to have a majority in parliament and controls his political party with an iron fist (see Chapter 6). Instead of having separation of power and checks and balances between the legislature and the executive, there exists a fusion of power, where the two branches of governments are intermixed. All power is in the hands of the executive.

For this reason, it's easy to pass legislation, and parliamentary systems tend to respond quickly to the public's wishes for new policies.

PRESIDENTIAL DEMOCRACY

Presidential democracies are common on the American continents and are also found in a few European countries such as France. In a presidential democracy, the concept of separation of powers exists. The two institutions, the legislature and the executive, are elected separately and constantly check each other. So citizens vote twice, once for the president (executive) and once for the legislature. In the U.S., the voters select the president and members of Congress separately. The following diagram shows the presidential system in the U.S.

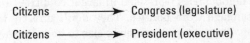

As the diagram shows, the two structures are independently elected by the people and share powers when it comes to policy making. This in turn results in a system of checks and balances between the two. Presidential systems take longer to bring about political change, because two institutions have to implement them. Overall, this brings about moderate change.

Testing totalitarianism

As the term implies, in a totalitarian state, the government exercises total control over its citizens. The government controls the social, political, and economic aspect of a person's life, and the person enjoys no freedoms whatsoever. Totalitarian regimes are rare in history. The two most prominent governments that qualify being called totalitarian are Nazi Germany (1933–1945) and Stalinist Russia (1929–1953). See Figure 4-1.

At the same time, there were many dictatorships and monarchies that restricted people's freedoms, but none of them was able to become totalitarian in nature. What makes a government totalitarian? To qualify as totalitarian, a government has to control all aspects of a person's life and meet the following six characteristics:

» **One-party state:** There has to be one major political party that controls all aspects of not only the government but also a person's life. It's the only legal party, and people have to join it to advance politically or economically in a totalitarian society. No opposition parties are tolerated.

FIGURE 4-1:
Adolf Hitler of Germany (a) and Joseph Stalin of Russia (b) were leaders of former totalitarian governments.

(a)

(b)

Source: (a) Wikimedia Commons; (b) Library of Congress

In Germany, the National Socialist Workers Party (NSDAP) fulfilled this role, while in the Soviet Union, the Communist Party of the Soviet Union (CPSU) had a similar role. Citizens joined the party at a young age and were being consistently indoctrinated throughout their lives. The party was there at every stage of their lives. The Hitler Youth in Germany and the Young Octobrists in the Soviet Union are examples of such youth political party organizations. Children were not just politically indoctrinated but were also taught how to fight and show extreme devotion to the totalitarian leader. These party organizations became like second families to many children. They spent weekends with the party, not their families, made friends in the organizations, and often would find their future spouse at party events. Later, when becoming adults, children would join the regular party.

» **One dominant ideology:** One ideology explains political and economic life to the average citizen. This ideology justifies why government is in power and why certain leaders are all-powerful. The ideology further lays out the economic structure of the country and even explains its foreign policy. Chapters 16 and 17 look at both fascism and communism and how the two were used to justify Stalin's and Hitler's rule. The average citizen is indoctrinated with this ideology throughout life. Political party organizations at all levels of life will familiarize citizens with the ideology. In addition, educational structures, including universities, will teach the ideology, and it permeates all aspects of the media.

» Total control over the media: Government has to fully control all aspects of the media. This includes television, the radio, and newspapers. No news from nonapproved government sources can enter the country, and the population can have access to only government-approved news. The average citizen is allowed to know only what the government wants him to know. The government controls not only the news but also education, the arts, and even movies. Everything a citizen sees is government-approved. In both the Soviet Union under Stalin and Hitler's Germany, the government did exercise total control of the media. It was virtually impossible for the average German or Russian to get information that wasn't biased or government-controlled.

Today, it has become a lot tougher to control the media, which now includes the Internet and social media. With globalization (see Chapter 13), it has become virtually impossible to totally isolate a population and control its access to other news sources.

» Control over the police: Government has to not only control the regular police to maintain law and order but also establish a secret police to control its population. This secret police has to instill a culture of fear into the average person so that he won't question or turn against the regime. Everybody in the country needs to know the kind of punishment he'll face if he questions or turns against the regime. Both the NKVD in the Soviet Union and the Gestapo in Germany performed this function. Mass killings and torture of dissidents was common, and every Russian and German knew the punishment for opposing the regime. In turn, opposition to both totalitarian regimes was minimal.

» Control over the military: History has shown that most dictators are toppled by their own militaries. Control over the military is difficult to accomplish in most authoritarian regimes, even monarchies. In a totalitarian society, it's different because the military is brought under the total control of the regime.

In the Soviet Union, Stalin executed almost all his officer corps during the Great Purges in the 1930s to bring the military under his control. This assured him total loyalty of the military.

In Germany, Hitler struck a deal with the military, eliminating the socialist wing of his national socialist party, which in turn led the German military leadership to acquiesce to his rule. Later, a force separate from the military was created to assure that in the event the military turned against Hitler, there would be another military branch to protect him. This was the infamous SS.

In both countries, within a few years of totalitarian rule, the military lost its independence and became a tool of the ruling regime.

» **Control over the economy:** To qualify as a totalitarian regime, a government has to control its economy. In the Soviet Union, all property was nationalized and owned by the government, and the government planned for the economy, abolishing the free market. Government control of the economy was a given.

Germany was different. In Germany, private property and ownership of business existed, but the government often intervened, telling businesses what to produce and how much to charge for it. Often, the government itself became the largest purchaser of privately produced goods.

Only if a government controls all six areas can it be labeled totalitarian. If it meets only five or fewer of the criteria, it's considered authoritarian instead of totalitarian. With technological advances today, it's very unlikely that any government could ever qualify as totalitarian again. It has become impossible to control all aspects of the media, to prevent a country's citizenry to be kept in the dark for long periods of time.

Answering to authoritarianism

An authoritarian government has less power over its citizens than a totalitarian government. Although it still controls many aspects of its citizens lives, it doesn't exercise complete control. Authoritarian leaders usually don't possess an official ideology that penetrates a society. More important, there's no powerful political party that runs the state for the leadership and permeates all aspects of society.

Totalitarian leaders possess a high level of charisma that results in a very high level of public support. Thy tend to be good speakers and are able to solicit dedication from the masses. Authoritarian leaders are the opposite. Many of them aren't charismatic, and the level of public support they enjoy is low, usually based on specific issues or fear of a secret police.

The level of control over a person's public life may be the same as that found in a totalitarian society, but control of the private lives of citizens is missing.

Total control of the media and the military is also missing. In many instances, authoritarian leaders are replaced by their own militaries. In addition, with the advent of globalization, it has become tougher to control a country's economy. The state-controlled economies of the Soviet era have disappeared, and today even authoritarian regimes like China see their economies easily impacted by other economies.

Finally, the level of legitimacy is very high in totalitarian regimes. People have been indoctrinated to support the leader and often are swayed by his charismatic style. Plus, a high level of nationalism is found in a totalitarian society. Often totalitarian countries have been wronged in the past and now are ready to right the wrong. In authoritarian regimes, neither is found. Further, the level of corruption is low in totalitarian regimes while it can be very high in authoritarian regimes.

Dividing Powers

One of the fundamental aspects of a political structure such as a state is the distribution of power among its parts and various levels. They're called systems of government. The amount of power held by the central government determines the system of government a state has. The three major systems of government distributing power are a unitary system, a federal system, and a confederation.

Centering on a unitary system

In a unitary system, most power is located with the central government. Although lower levels of governments, such as counties or departments, can exist, these don't have independent powers. All power is derived from the central government. These lower levels of governments implement policy made at the central level. They can't change or even question these policies.

France is a great example of a unitary system. It has lower levels of governments called departments. There are 95 departments in mainland France and 5 overseas departments in places like Martinique in the Caribbean. Each department is run by a department council, elected by the people and headed by a department president. The departments have limited powers. Their major function is to implement policies made by the central government in Paris. So while France looks like a federal system on paper having subnational levels of governments, in reality, it's unitary because these levels have no independent powers.

A good example involves education. In France, the Department of Education sets the high-school curriculum for the whole country. So everybody in France knows that at 11:00 a.m. all students in 10th grade study Algebra in every region of France. The same goes for laws and regulations. There are no variances between Northern France and Southern France when it comes to things such as building codes. Everybody knows what to expect from laws and regulations, and nobody can be surprised. Other examples of unitary systems include the Netherlands and Japan.

Focusing on federalism

In a federalist state, subnational levels of governments not only exist but have independent powers. These powers are reserved by a constitution for these subnational levels of governments and can't be taken away by the central government. Examples are states in the U.S. and the Laender (federal states) in Germany. Both of these subnational levels of governments have independent powers guaranteed by federal constitutions. Additionally, these lower levels of governments are represented at the national level in upper houses of governments such as the U.S. Senate or the German Bundesrat.

The central government usually maintains full power over the military and monetary and foreign policy, but the lower levels of governments do exercise important powers. In the U.S., for example, the states have power over school curricula and can decide on matters such as whether to have the death penalty, what the speed limit should be, and most recently whether to legalize recreational drugs. In Germany, the Laender can also set school curricula and have important powers of taxation.

The next question is why have a federal political structure? Are there advantages and disadvantages over a unitary system?

Dissecting federalism versus a unitary system

A federal form of government works best in large diverse countries like the U.S. An argument can be made that government should be close to the people, and therefore local government is the best form of government. Local government and even state government allows for the people to closely monitor their elected representatives and make sure that the policies implemented represent them. It's not too difficult to go to a city council meeting, sit in, and make sure you're being represented by the city council member you elected.

In a unitary system, observation and supervision is much more difficult. How can a citizen travel to Washington, D.C., to observe Congress at work and make sure it's being representative of the local population? The further away a government is located from most of its population, the more difficult it becomes to check on it.

Advantages and disadvantages of federalism and unitary systems

Federalism works better in a large diverse nation. How can a central government represent the many different groups making up the United States? In the U.S., there are many local and regional differences. Local and state governments are much more likely to represent these differences compared to a central government thousands of miles away. Federalism therefore allows for diversity in the U.S. to be better reflected than a strong all-powerful central government. The state government of Louisiana, for example, is much more likely to be aware of and reflect Cajun culture than the central government in Washington, D.C., thousands of miles away.

Unitary governments, on the other hand, totally ignore any form of diversity in a country. All decisions are made at the central level, ignoring local differences. This often results in citizens being opposed to policies because they don't reflect their values. Not surprisingly, unitary forms of governments are better suited for less diverse and more homogenous nations. This explains why it works so well in France or the Netherlands.

Are there any advantages to unitary systems? Yes, there are. The major advantage of a unitary system is its uniformity. The same types of policies apply to every part of a nation, which makes it easier for both people and businesses to know what to expect. A person in France knows exactly which laws and regulations are in effect regardless of the part of France he's in. A good example are building regulations for private homes. In the U.S., regulations vary from state to state. This can be tough on prospective home owners and also builders who construct homes across states. In France, the regulations are the same everywhere in the country. This makes it easier for both buyers and builders.

A second very topical example involves taxation. In a unitary system, taxes (personal income, sales, and property) are the same throughout the country. There's no reason to move to another part of France to avoid paying higher taxes. In the U.S., taxation is high in some states and low in others. With the states being able to set their own rate for income, sales, and property taxes, some states are more expensive to live in than others. This has led to a mass exodus from high-tax states to low-tax states. Today, California, one of the states with the highest tax rates, is losing population, while Texas, a low-tax state, is gaining people rapidly and will at some point overtake California as the most populous state in the union.

Finally, unitary systems do better with public education. With the central government setting similar high standards for the whole nation, nobody is allowed to deviate from it, while the central government provides the funding for education. Today, both France and Japan have some of the highest educational standards in the world.

Going federal

There a few reasons to create or join a federation. First, some smaller states facing a common foreign threat can join to become more powerful and protect each other. You can make a good argument that one of the major reasons the 13 original American colonies came together to create the United States of America was because they faced a common threat from several European powers, especially Great Britain, France, and Spain. By combining and joining resources, the 13 colonies were suddenly able to establish a viable economy, implement a system of taxation, and especially create a common military force to face any future threats.

Second, federalism can be a prerequisite to create a new nation-state. It's implausible that the 13 original states would have joined a unitary system. A federation allowed each to maintain its own way of doing things. In other words, not just local culture but also the power of local leaders was protected by federalism. Local autonomy makes it easier for previously independent states to join a new federation. Other examples include Brazil and Argentina in Latin America.

Checking on confederations

Today, confederations have become a rarity. A confederation is a very loose organization of localities or states. In a confederation, these localities and states hold all the political power. The central government itself has none or only a few powers.

A great example is the first government created by the U.S. after the Revolutionary War was won. During the Articles of Confederation, all powers were held by the original 13 states, while the central government around the Continental Congress held few powers. Soon, many in the U.S. noticed that for political and economic reasons, the confederation had to be changed into a federation. Without the power to tax or regulate commerce, the new Continental Congress didn't have the monies to create a military to defend the country, and trade between the states was chaotic. For this reason, a new constitution with a federal form of government was written and ratified. A good example of a confederation today is Switzerland where the central government has few powers but real power is exercised at the *canton* (German for state) level.

Failing — The Articles of Confederation

In 1774, 12 of 13 colonies (Georgia refused to attend) agreed to set up a united legislature, the Continental Congress. The Continental Congress turned into a national legislature during the Revolutionary War and became the new central government after the War of Independence against Great Britain had been won.

In 1781, the Continental Congress passed the Articles of Confederation, creating a confederation between the 13 former colonies. After the states ratified the Articles of Confederation, the Continental Congress renamed itself the Congress of the Confederation and became a weak national legislature. It had no real powers, including the power to tax or the power to create a national army. The real power remained within the 13 states.

The confederate form of government caused immediate problems for the new country:

>> **No power to tax:** Without the power to tax, the Continental Congress couldn't establish a large military, needed with the British, Russian, and Spanish empires still in North America.

>> **Unable to redeem war bonds:** With the war over and the national government unable to tax, nobody redeemed the bonds. Many patriotic people who bought war bonds to support the war for independence lost their life savings when they couldn't redeem the bonds. Not surprisingly, people complained.

>> **Trade issues:** Trade became a problem, with the states treating each other like they were foreign countries. How can a united country be established when its members impose trade restrictions against each other?

Introducing federalism

By 1785, many prominent politicians in the U.S. were worried. They felt that the new country was in serious trouble and that the new government, created by the Articles of Confederation, wasn't working. For this purpose, a national meeting in Philadelphia was called to change or revise the Articles of Confederation. This meeting, also referred to as the Constitutional Convention, began in May of 1787. Its original purpose was just to change the Articles of Confederation, not to write a new Constitution. The convention lasted until September 1787, and the delegates actually overstepped their authority and voted to approve a new constitution for the country, which changed the country from a confederation to a federation.

Classifying the three systems of governments

After studying the various systems of governments, it's now possible to classify them. Table 4-2 presents the three systems of governments, the level of centralization for each one, and examples for each system.

TABLE 4-2   **Three Systems of Governments**

System	Level of Centralization	Examples
Unitary	All power is centralized with a central government.	France, Japan
Federal	Some power is reserved for subnational levels of governments such as states.	United States, Germany
Confederation	Subnational levels of government have most power. The central government is weak.	Switzerland, the United States under the Articles of Confederation (1781-1789)

Chapter 5

Setting the Rules: Constitutions

J ust about every country in the world has a constitution. Constitutions are written documents that outline the whole structure of a political system. The constitution of a country determines what type of executive and legislature a country has and what form of government a country possesses. It could be a democracy, an authoritarian form of government such as a dictatorship, or even an old-style monarchy. In other words, constitutions set the rules for governments.

In addition, constitutions don't just formalize government structures; they also justify the governments' right to govern and can even include national ideals.

Besides providing for the structure of government, constitutions also provide for the rights and obligations of citizens. While the U.S. Constitution did so early on, with the passage of the Bill of Rights, other constitutions didn't provide for these rights until the 20th century or later.

This chapter highlights two constitutions. The first one is the U.S. Constitution, considered by many to be the oldest constitution in the world. The second constitution is the Russian Constitution of 1993. It's one of the newer, more comprehensive constitutions and contains some similarities to the U.S. Constitution.

Looking at Constitution Basics

REMEMBER

A constitution is defined as the basic principles and laws according to which any country, state, or organization is governed.

REMEMBER

Just because a country has a constitution doesn't mean that its leaders are willing to follow it. In Stalinist Russia, there was a fairly democratic constitution in place that limited the powers of government. Stalin and the communist party chose not to follow it, and in reality, Stalin ran the country with an iron fist often ignoring his own constitution. Therefore, it's necessary to study a constitution in two ways:

» Research what a constitution provides. Study its provisions on government structures and citizens' rights.

» Make sure that a country's leadership is actually following the provisions within a constitution.

TECHNICAL STUFF

Constitutions come in all sizes. Some constitutions are very short and vague. For example, the U.S. Constitution consists of only seven articles that outline the structure of government and discuss powers that the government should possess. Even though 27 amendments have been added since, the U.S. Constitution is still very short and often vague, leaving it open to interpretations by politicians and federal judges. (For more information on articles and amendments, see the section "Checking out constitution components," later in this chapter.) Other constitutions are lengthy and specific. They provide for every possible political and even economic situation and discuss rights and obligations of citizens in much detail. For example, some constitutions list minimum wages and retirements plans and even provide for environmental protection.

REMEMBER

Most countries, including the U.S., have written constitutions. A few such as Great Britain do not. Government in Great Britain is based on tradition, custom, and acts of parliament instead.

WHO'S COUNTING?

India has the longest constitution in the world with 146,385 words, while the Kingdom of Monaco has the shortest constitution with only 3,814 words. The original U.S. Constitution contained only 4,543 words, which put it among the shortest constitutions in the world. Even with 27 amendments added, the U.S. Constitution is still quite short, containing only 7,500 words today.

Discovering the purpose of constitutions

A constitution sets out a general vision for society, creates political structures, and establishes how these structures will function. A constitution places limits on the power a government can exercise and establishes rights for those who are governed; this is called *constitutionalism.* The first great example of constitutionalism was in 1215 when the English King John agreed to having his powers limited by a constitution that protected the political rights and liberties of the English nobles from the potential capriciousness of rulers in the Magna Carta.

REMEMBER

Constitutionalism is a doctrine that a government's authority comes from and is limited by a constitution. Governments are, therefore, both empowered and limited by constitutions; this is the basis of constitutionalism. The primary political structure of any government is its constitution. It is a society's most basic law.

In constitutionally governed nations, like all democracies, the constitution limits government and protects citizens' rights. Totalitarian and authoritarian governments, however, aren't limited by their constitutions. In such societies, constitutions are often violated and exist only for show. The Soviet Union is a good example of this.

The basic purpose of a constitution is to be the highest law of the land. Leaders are supposed to follow their constitutions and abide by the rules a constitution establishes. Constitutions are documents that are supposed to be in place for as long as the state exists that they helped create. For this reason, the amendment process is time-consuming and cumbersome. In many democracies, such as Germany, it takes a two-thirds vote in both houses (the lower and upper house, or the Bundestag and the Bundesrat in Germany; see Chapter 6) to amend the constitution. Other democracies, such as France, hold a constitutional referendum letting the people themselves decide if and how to change the constitution. The founding fathers of the United States made sure that it would be tough, almost impossible to change the constitution. Therefore, they put one of the most cumbersome processes in place to change the U.S. Constitution.

Checking out constitution components

Constitutions usually consist of several components. First, constitutions can contain *preambles,* which are basically symbolic statements, very general in nature, indicating the values of a nation. Preambles are not required or vital for a constitution and have no legal meaning. However, they express the writers' intent and motives and show the basic principles contained in the document. For example, the U.S. Constitution contains the following preamble.

> We the people of the United States, in order to form a more perfect union, establish justice, insure domestic tranquility, provide for the common defense, promote the general welfare, and secure the blessing of liberty to ourselves and our posterity, do ordain and establish this constitution for the United States of America.

Also found in constitutions are the articles, or clauses. They contain the foundation for a political structure as well as specific rights and obligations of both government and citizens. In the U.S. Constitution, there are seven articles that outline the new form of government and its relation with the states as well as an amendment process.

Every constitution finally contains an amendment process. Amending a constitution refers to the process of changing or altering a constitution. In the U.S. Constitution it is Article V that outlines the amendment process (see the section "Making changes," later in this chapter).

Creating a New Country: The U.S. Constitution of 1789

The U.S. has the oldest democratic constitution in the world today. How is it possible that a constitution that is more than 225 years old, drafted in 1787, is still functioning today with minimal changes? How can such an old document still be applicable to a changing society and new issues the founding fathers had never foreseen, such as terrorism and climate change? The answer is to be found in the nature of the Constitution itself.

The U.S. Constitution is a brief procedural constitution. The Constitution doesn't go into much detail when it comes to societal matters but provides a structure for government. Parts of it are vague and open to interpretation. The U.S. Supreme Court has the power to interpret vague parts of the Constitution through the power of judicial review.

TECHNICAL STUFF

The power of judicial review was established in the court case Marbury v. Madison in 1803. It refers to the powers courts have to declare laws of Congress and acts of the president unconstitutional. This in turn nullifies the laws or acts of the executive. Only a few other democracies, such as Germany, have given the court system the power of judicial review. In most democracies, the power of judicial review doesn't exist.

The lack of specificity and detail in the U.S. Constitution is a historical reflection of the necessity of compromise when the founding fathers drew up the Constitution in 1787. Only a vague document with as few details as possible could have received majority support at the Constitutional Convention held in 1787 in Philadelphia. It also proved helpful later during the process of ratification. The states would have never approved a document that would have contained many specific policies restricting their powers.

Finally, the framers of the Constitution knew that a vague document could easily be adapted to changing times with only minor changes in the form of amendments if necessary. Therefore, the U.S. Constitution is a flexible document adaptable to changing times. This is why the U.S. Constitution is referred to as a living document.

Framing the U.S. Constitution

The 13 colonies making up the original United States had been a part of British America since 1607. In 1774, 12 colonies (Georgia refused to attend) set up a united legislature, called the Continental Congress, to unite against British oppression. When the Revolutionary War broke out in 1775, the Continental Congress turned into a national legislature. After the war had ended in 1783, independence was declared, and the Congress assumed the role of a new national government.

In 1781, the Congress passed the Articles of Confederation, creating a confederation between the 13 former colonies. For this reason, the Congress renamed itself the Congress of the Confederation and became a weak federal legislature. It was without real powers, especially the power to tax and the power to create a national army. The real power remained within the 13 states.

The Congress survived until the Constitution created a new form of government in 1789 and was then replaced by the Congress of the United States.

Facing problems

From 1781 when the Articles of Confederation were passed until 1789 when they were replaced with the Constitution of the United States, the new country faced severe problems created by a weak national government. The problems included:

>> The new country couldn't support a large military, because the national government didn't possess the power to tax. This was dangerous with the British, Russian, and Spanish empires still in North America.

>> With the Revolutionary War over and the national government not having the power to tax, the national government couldn't redeem the war bonds used to finance the war against Britain. Many Americans who bought war bonds to support the war for independence lost their life savings when they couldn't redeem the bonds.

>> Trade between the 13 states making up the new United States of America became problematic. Each state treated the other states like foreign countries, imposing tariffs and other trade restrictions against their goods. Some states even possessed their own currencies.

Writing a constitution

By 1785, many prominent politicians in the U. S. were worried. They felt that the newly established government, created by the Articles of Confederation, wasn't working. They were worried about an economic collapse of the 13 colonies and feared a foreign invasion. Therefore, they decided that the Articles of Confederation had to be amended, or changed. For this reason, a national meeting in Philadelphia was called to change or revise the Articles of Confederation. The Constitutional Convention began in May of 1787. Its original purpose was just to change the Articles of Confederation. The convention lasted until September 1787. Instead of amending the Articles of Confederation, the delegates voted to approve a new constitution for the country.

The delegates decided to write a brand new document, the Constitution of the United States, because they believed that revising the Articles of Confederation wouldn't create a strong enough, unified country. The new Constitution of the United States replaced the Articles of Confederation and set up a new form of government. The Constitution created the following form of government:

>> A new federal government, where the states and the federal government shared powers (federalism)

>> A legislature with two chambers (bicameral) with a House of Representatives (selected by the people) and a Senate (equally representative of the states, with each state sending two Senators)

>> An executive, or presidency, elected by an electoral college every four years

>> A Supreme Court, with justices nominated by the president and ratified by the Senate

TECHNICAL STUFF

The delegates at the Constitutional Convention faced a big dilemma: Should they create a parliamentary or a presidential republic? In a parliamentary republic, the legislature, not the citizens, selects the executive. In a presidential republic, voters choose the president. This can result in a divided government, with one party controlling the legislature and the other the presidency. The founding fathers opted for a presidential republic, because they believed in the concept of separation of powers, where the executive and the legislature share powers and constantly check on each other. They didn't want to put too much power in the hands of an executive who also controls the legislature, as is the case in Great Britain.

REMEMBER

A presidential system, such as the one found in the U.S., creates moderate policies. It involves lots of compromise, because the executive and Congress have to bargain with each other to be successful. In a parliamentary system, such as found in Great Britain, the executive always gets what it wants, because it controls the legislature.

Using checks and balances

The system of checks and balances in the Constitution is a feature unique to the U.S. The delegates at the convention, afraid of a strong executive, such as the monarchy of George III they had just experienced, wanted to make sure that the president wouldn't be able dominate the new government. So they decided to implement checks on the president's power. The delegates looked at policy areas they considered the most important and then put checks on presidential powers in these areas. For example, in the area of war making, the president is the commander in chief of the U.S. Armed Forces, but Congress has the power to fund and declare war. Therefore, it takes both institutions, the presidency and Congress, to agree, before the U.S. can go to war.

In other foreign policy areas, the same happens. The executive can negotiate treaties with foreign powers, but the Senate has to ratify them. The president appoints ambassadors to foreign countries, but again the Senate has to consent to her choices. Congress further received the power to override a president's veto with a two-thirds vote in both houses of Congress, and the House of Representatives can even impeach a president and then the Senate can vote to remove her. Finally, the U.S. Supreme Court can declare any act of the president and any laws passed by Congress unconstitutional, thereby nullifying them.

Forming an electoral college

Another unique feature of the U.S. Constitution is the electoral college. In most democracies, either parliament elects the executive, Germany being an example, or the people get to directly vote for their president, as is the case in France. It's different in the U.S. The electoral college, established by the Constitution, consists of electors who have the power to choose the president and vice president.

The U.S. founding fathers were afraid that citizens weren't educated enough to cast a rational ballot and could be easily duped by a demagogue running for office. Therefore, they believed that people should be able to only indirectly pick the executive. The people can vote for electors who then choose the president. However, these electors aren't bound by the people's choices. So if the people make a mistake, selecting someone unfit for office, the electors can rectify this mistake when voting for president. They can basically select someone else they like better.

The first electoral college, which met in 1789, consisted of representatives from all the states that ratified the Constitution. Depending on the state, either the people or the state legislatures chose the respective delegates for the electoral college. In the electoral college, each delegate cast two ballots. Whoever won the most votes became the president of the United States; the runner-up was named the vice president.

This system led to confusion. In 1800, Thomas Jefferson and Aaron Burr received the same number of votes, even though most electors favored Jefferson for president and Burr for vice president. The electors had to cast two ballots without being able to differentiate between president and vice president. The 12th Amendment fixed the system in 1804 by mandating separate ballots for the president and vice president.

In 1961, the 23rd Amendment allowed the District of Columbia to cast three votes in the electoral college, even though it doesn't have statehood. Today, the electors in the electoral college represent all 50 states and the District of Columbia. The electors, in turn, are chosen by their respective state legislatures. Each party, Democrats and Republicans, draws up a list of electors. Whichever party wins the state in the presidential election gets to use its list in the electoral college. The only exceptions to this rule are found in Maine and Nebraska, where one electoral vote goes to the winner of each Congressional district in the state and two votes go to the winner of the state itself. The number of electors representing each state equals the number of members of Congress (members of the House of Representatives plus the two senators) for each state. Today, there are 538 total votes in the electoral college, and a candidate has to win 270 to become president. If nobody has a majority in the electoral college, the vote goes to the House of Representatives.

Getting stronger

Over the last 200 years, the U.S. federal government has been getting stronger. The Constitution addresses the issue of federal versus state relations in the 10th Amendment. The 10th Amendment states that "the powers not delegated by the

Constitution, nor prohibited by it to the States, are reserved to the States respectively, or to the people." The Constitution allocates a few powers to the federal government in Article 1, Section 8. They are called enumerated powers. These include

>> The power to declare war

>> The power to coin money

>> The power to regulate foreign commerce

>> The power to raise and support armies

>> The power to establish a federal court system

Powers directly prohibited to the states are few. They include signing treaties with foreign powers or taxing imports from foreign countries.

In the beginning, the states assumed that everything else not mentioned in the Constitution were powers they possessed. However, over time, things began to change. The states began to lose more and more power to the federal government.

The court system, namely the Supreme Court, over time enhanced the powers of the federal government. In *McCulloch v. Maryland,* the court ruled in 1819 that the federal government possessed so-called implied powers. These powers aren't expressly listed in the Constitution but can be implied from the necessary and proper clause found in Article 1, Section 8, of the Constitution. The clause, also called the elastic clause, states that the federal government has all powers that are necessary and proper to carry out its enumerated powers. So the court argued that the federal government has the power to create a national banking system, because this could be implied from the constitutional power to coin money.

The Supremacy Clause found in Article 6 of the U.S. Constitution also has been frequently used to enhance the powers of the federal government at the expense of the states. The Supremacy Clause states that national laws and treaties are supreme over state laws when in compliance with the U.S. Constitution.

Using three principles

The U.S. Constitution is based on three principles. First, there is separation of powers. All that means is that the government itself is divided between a legislative branch (Congress), an executive (president), and a judiciary (federal court system). This assures that not one branch can become dominant and run the country by itself.

Second, there is the concept of checks and balances. Checks and balances refers to the three branches of government not just sharing powers but constantly checking on each other. This prevents one of the three from taking over the political system. For example, the executive negotiates treaties with foreign countries. Then, the Senate comes in and must ratify the treaty before it goes into force. Finally, the Supreme Court could determine a treaty unconstitutional, thereby nullifying it. By the time the treaty is valid, all three branches of government have been involved, being able to check each other in the process.

The final principle of the constitution is federalism. Federalism refers to a political structure that divides power between national and subnational levels of government, such as states. These subnational levels of government, or states in the United States, have reserved powers that can't be infringed upon by the federal government.

REMEMBER

One of the reasons the founding fathers opted for a federal system is to placate the states. Under the Articles of Confederation, the states had all the powers. Many of the delegates at the Constitutional Convention believed in states' rights. The sharing of power between federal and state governments proved to be the ideal compromise. Without it, the states would have never ratified the constitution.

As of 2018, out of 193 countries, 27 are federal and 166 are unitary. Interestingly, the federal countries tend to have larger, more diverse populations and cover more of the world's land area. The federal nations make up 40 percent of the world's population and about 50 percent of the world's land mass. The largest federal societies are the United States, Canada, Brazil, Argentina, Germany, Australia, India, and Russia.

Protecting citizens' rights

Constitutions include the distribution of power among institutions and also basic individual rights. They establish the role of citizens and the role of government in a society and prevent government abuse. Most recent constitutions, such as the Russian Constitution discussed later, have extensive sections on citizens' rights. The U.S. Constitution doesn't. Even with the addition of the Bill of Rights, the U.S. Constitution isn't very specific when it comes to civil rights and civil liberties. Other constitutions are and also include social and economic rights. The Bill of Rights, or the first ten amendments to the U.S. Constitution, guarantee the following rights:

Amendment 1: Freedom of Religion, Speech, Assembly, and the Press

Congress shall make no law respecting an establishment of religion, or prohibiting the free exercise thereof; or abridging the freedom of speech, or of the press; or the right of the people peaceably to assemble, and to petition the government for a redress of grievances.

Amendment 2: The Right to Bear Arms

A well-regulated Militia, being necessary to the security of a free State, the right of the people to keep and bear Arms, shall not be infringed.

Amendment 3: The Housing of Soldiers

No soldier shall, in time of peace be quartered in any house without the consent of the owner, nor in time of war, but in a manner to be prescribed by law.

Amendment 4: Protection from Unreasonable Searches and Seizures

The right of the people to be secure in their persons, houses, papers, and effects, against unreasonable searches and seizures, shall not be violated, and no Warrants shall issue, but upon probable cause, supported by Oath or affirmation, and particularly describing the place to be searched, and the persons or things to be seized.

Amendment 5: Protection of Rights to Life, Liberty, and Property

No person shall be held to answer for a capital, or otherwise infamous crime, unless on a presentment or indictment of a Grand Jury, except in cases arising in the land or naval forces, or in the Militia, when in actual service in time of War or public danger; nor shall any person be subject for the same offense to be twice put in jeopardy of life or limb; nor shall be compelled in any criminal case to be a witness against himself, nor be deprived of life, liberty, or property without due process of law; nor shall private property be taken for public use, without just compensation.

Amendment 6: Rights of the Accused in Criminal Cases

In all criminal prosecutions, the accused shall enjoy the right to a speedy and public trial, by an impartial jury of the State and district wherein the crime shall have been committed, which district shall have been previously ascertained by law, and to be informed of the nature and cause of the accusation; to be confronted with the witnesses against him; to have compulsory process for obtaining witnesses in his favor; and to have the Assistance of Counsel for his defense.

Amendment 7: Right of Trial by Jury

In Suits at common law, where the value in controversy shall exceed twenty dollars, the right of trial by jury shall be preserved, and no fact tried by a jury, shall be otherwise reexamined in any court of the United States than according to the rules of the common law.

Amendment 8: No Excessive Bail, Excessive Fines, and Cruel and Unusual Punishment

Excessive bail shall not be required, nor excessive fines imposed, nor cruel and unusual punishments inflicted.

Amendment 9: Other Rights Kept by the People

The enumeration in the Constitution of certain rights, shall not be construed to deny or disparage others retained by the people.

Amendment 10: Powers Kept by the States

The powers not delegated to the United States by the Constitution, nor prohibited by it to the States, are reserved to the States respectively, or to the people.

Making changes

The longest surviving constitution in the world today is the U.S. Constitution. One of the reasons it survived for more than 200 years is the fact that it's a living constitution. All that means is that it can be changed periodically to adapt to an ever-changing social and political environment.

There are two ways to propose changing or amending the U.S. Constitution. First, an amendment can be formally proposed by a two-thirds vote of both Houses of Congress. Second, it can be requested by two-thirds of the state legislatures at a national convention. The second method has never been used.

Next, the resolution proposing the amendment is shipped to the states, where it has to be ratified (formal consent) by three-fourths of the state legislatures (38 states) or by special conventions held in three-fourths of the states. The second method has been used only once in 1933 when the 21st Amendment was passed, which repealed the prohibition on alcohol (18th Amendment).

REMEMBER

It's difficult to the change the U.S. Constitution. Since ratification by the states in 1788, close to 11,000 amendments have been proposed. Only 27 have passed. This is a success rate of less than one-tenth of a percent.

Of the 27 amendments that were successfully added to the U.S. Constitution, 10 were added in 1791. They are called the Bill of Rights, guaranteeing Americans, according to James Madison, rights of citizens and rights of property.

Two amendments, the 18th and the 21st, cancel each other out. The 18th Amendment, passed in 1919, implemented Prohibition, and the 21st Amendment repealed Prohibition in 1933.

This really leaves only 15 formal amendments since 1791, a very low number given the dramatic societal changes in the last 231 years.

It's important to point out that most of the 15 amendments have effectively made our form of government more democratic by increasing the number of Americans eligible to vote and giving more power to the people. For example, the 13th

Amendment prohibits slavery, the 14th Amendment extends legal protection to everyone, and the 15th Amendment gives former slaves the right to vote. The 17th Amendment allows for direct popular election of senators, and the 19th extends voting rights to women. The 24th Amendment bars poll taxes, and the 26th Amendment lowers the voting age to 18.

Checking on a New Document: The Russian Constitution

While the U.S. Constitution is the oldest living federal constitution in the world today, the Russian Constitution is one of the newest. It came into effect only in 1993 after the Russia people voted to approve it in December of 1993 with 54.5 percent of the vote.

Similar to the U.S. Constitution, which in many ways was a response to British oppression and authoritarian rule, the Russian Constitution is a response to 75 years of communist rule, including the brutal dictatorship of Joseph Stalin from 1929 to 1953.

While there are some similarities between the two constitutions, there are also many differences. The current Russian Constitution is quite lengthy and detailed, guaranteeing many economic and social rights for its citizens. This is quite common with current constitutions, while older constitutions are shorter, mainly outlining the political structures of a country.

Looking at similarities

The Russian Constitution creates a democratic federal republic similar to the U.S. and Germany. The Constitution gives ultimate political power to the Russian people with the right to free elections, allowing them to replace any government in power if they choose to do so. In addition, the Constitution provides some direct democracy to the people, by allowing for referenda to change the Constitution.

Similar to the U.S., the Russian Constitution creates a federal government with lower levels of government that have independent powers. However, like in the U.S., there is a provision in the Constitution that declares federal law superior to lower levels of law.

Noting the differences

Being a newer constitution, the Russian Constitution deals with many social and economic rights. For example, it guarantees a minimum wage and social security for the elderly as well as benefits for the disabled. The Constitution further guarantees a right to private property but also allows for public, or state-owned property. Today about 40 percent of the Russian economy is state owned.

As a direct response to years of communism where only publicly owned property existed, specific business rights are listed in the Russian Constitution. They include the right to own and sell property, the right to inherit property, and the right to establish a business. There also is a protection against expropriation of property. In other words, property is protected from nationalization by the state.

The Constitution also expressly allows for Russians to choose their own job, guarantees the right to unionize and the right to strike, and guarantees unemployment benefits and a right to a safe work environment. Rights to healthcare and free education are also guaranteed.

TECHNICAL STUFF

As a direct result of the communist era, the Russian Constitution prohibits a state ideology, like communism or fascism; and ideological diversity within the Russian state is guaranteed. The Constitution further declares Russia a secular state with no state religion. Any type of government-sponsored religion is expressly prohibited.

REMEMBER

Political diversity and a multiparty system are guaranteed. However, the government can prohibit organizations that are opposed to the Constitution or are threatening the integrity of the Russian state. This includes separatist movements in Russia today. Further, any political party or interest group that can bring about social, racial, national, or religious strife can be banned. This clause in the Constitution can be used to outlaw any political party or interest group that the Russian government determines to be a threat to the Russian state.

Structuring government

The Russian Constitution provides for a political structure similar to the one created by the U.S. Constitution. It calls for an executive (president), a bicameral legislature, the State Duma and Federation Council, and a judiciary. The State Duma is the lower house of parliament elected by the Russian people to five-year terms. It contains 450 members who enjoy full immunity from the law. The Duma is currently controlled by President Putin's party, United Russia. United Russia has controlled the Duma since 2007 and received about 74 percent of the seats in the 2018 elections.

The upper house in Russia is called the Federation Council. Each of the 85 regional levels of government sends 2 members to the Council for a total of 170 members. Members of the upper house are nonpartisan, and a region's delegation is appointed by the governor of the region (one delegate) and by the regional legislature (one delegate). An additional 10 percent of all members of the Federation Council are appointed by the president.

Each institution is supposed to be independent of each other and is supposed to check on the others, preventing one from becoming dominant. This, however, has not happened. President Putin's party, United Russia, controls both legislative houses, giving him full control of government.

Similar to the U.S., the president of Russia is the dominant political figure in the country. However, in Russia, the president has the power to unilaterally run the country without the input of other political institutions. In other words, it'd be like an American president being able to run the country by himself because he dominates both Congress and the judiciary.

TECHNICAL STUFF

The Russian president is independently elected for a six-year term by the Russian people. He has the right to run for a second term but is then term-limited. The Constitution gives him many powers that he can use to dominate the political system. For example, the Russian president is the head of state and only he can make foreign policy. He is in charge of the Russian military and can declare martial law, assuming military control over the country. He can further make domestic policy by issuing decrees and edicts and has the power to pardon and give foreigners asylum in Russia.

Guaranteeing civil rights and liberties

A major part of the Russian Constitution deals with inalienable rights every citizen possesses. Again, this part of the Constitution is a direct response to 75 years of communism. The Constitution guarantees equality before the law and equality of gender. It further states that government can't discriminate against any Russian citizen on the basis of sex, race, nationality, origin, place of residence, religion, or membership in public organizations.

The Constitution also guarantees a right to privacy, which includes a right to private phone conversations and any form of correspondence. Police can't enter a home in Russia unless a federal law or court order is in place.

REMEMBER

A part of the Russian Constitution even guarantees the right to travel freely domestically and abroad, and choose a place to live.

REMEMBER

While capital punishment is legal, the Russian Constitution prohibits torture and medical and scientific experiments on people.

The Russian Constitution also contains sections similar to the Bill of Rights found in the U.S. Constitution (see the section "Creating a New Country: The U.S. Constitution of 1789"). Rights similar to the U.S. 1st Amendment, such as freedom of the press, assembly, religion, and especially freedom of speech, are guaranteed. In addition, the Russian Constitution guarantees the right to counsel, prohibits double jeopardy, provides for a right to appeal, and outlaws self-incrimination.

The Russian Constitution also list obligations citizens have toward the Russian State. Example are the obligation to pay taxes and the obligation to serve in the military.

Changing the Russian Constitution

In January 2020, the president of Russia, Vladimir Putin, proposed changes to the Russian Constitution to the Russian people. Next, both houses of parliament approved a referendum in March of 2020. A referendum was then called for in April of 2020, but subsequently postponed due to the COVID-19 pandemic. A new date had not been set at the time of this writing.

Instead of voting on each amendment (there are 14) separately, the Russian people voted on the entire revised constitution as a whole.

Some of the proposed changes are very controversial because they clearly help President Putin and his political party stay in power for the foreseeable future. The proposed changes include

>> Previous presidential terms will be discounted, and the two-term limit will begin anew after approval of the newly revised constitution by the Russian people. This will allow President Putin, who was term-limited as of 2024, to serve two more terms until 2036 when he would be 81 years old.

>> Parliament receives the power to approve the prime minister. Right now, parliament can only consent to the president's choice.

>> A presidential candidate has to live in Russia for 25 years before the person can run for office.

>> The upper house, the Federation Council, can now propose to the president the removal of federal judges. This includes both the Constitutional and Supreme Courts. This gives President Putin, who currently controls the upper house, the power to remove justices at will, guaranteeing him control over the judiciary in Russia.

>> All heads of law enforcement have to be appointed by the president with consultation of the Federation Council. This will allow for President Putin, who controls the Federation Council, to control the police in Russia.

>> The minimum wage can't be lower than a subsistence wage, and pensions will be indexed to inflation.

Chapter **6**

Comparing Political Institutions: Systems of Government

When dealing with *political institutions*, defined as the governmental structures that make, enforce, and apply policies in countries, two possible political systems in democracies come into play. They are presidential systems and parliamentary systems.

In presidential systems, such as the United States, the people elect the executive (president), and the executive usually isn't responsible to the legislature (in the United States, the Senate and House of Representatives, also known as Congress) and often has no ties with legislators. Presidents pick their own cabinet (which includes persons such as the vice president and the secretary of defense), usually not selecting many current members of the legislature. The legislature, in turn, is separately elected by the people, and a system of separation of powers exits. Both branches have to share powers, which results in a system of checks and balances where each branch constantly checks the other. On the negative side, that battle between the two branches often results in a bitter partisan warfare between the president and the leaders of Congress, which results in deadlock and policy making is ignored.

In a parliamentary system, the legislature (parliament) picks the executive, usually a prime minister or chancellor, and no separation of power exists. Instead, there's a fusion of power. The executive has to be a member of the legislature and is usually the leader of the biggest party in parliament. This allows for the executive to have majority backing in parliament at any time, allowing the executive to make policy efficiently and without much opposition.

This chapter looks at the three branches of government: legislative, executive, and judicial, with a closer look at the U.S. and British political structures. I also examine bureaucracy because civil servants are an important component to shaping government policies. The chapter concludes with a look at the judiciary, using a comparison of the U.S. Supreme Court to the German Federal Constitutional Court.

Comparing Democratic Political Systems

When studying political systems, namely the institutions that make up a government, two major types of government possible in democracies are found. They are parliamentary and presidential systems. Further, each system can be structured in two different ways: a federal or a unitary way. What are the differences between the two? The following section explores this question.

Parliamentary democracies versus presidential democracies

One of the great advantages of a parliamentary democracy is the lack of gridlock when it comes to policy making. Keep in mind that the executive has to have a majority in parliament and is therefore likely to get her policies approved without much opposition. In addition, strong, powerful political parties exist in most parliamentary democracies. In both Great Britain and Germany, the executive dominates her political party, and party deviation isn't allowed. Political parties follow the lead of the executive, often without questioning it.

For this reason, prime ministers or chancellors can act like powerful presidents. If they have solid majorities in parliament, they'll know in advance that their policies will get passed. This will allow them to act like independently elected executives, and instead of judging a political party, voters judge the executives.

One of the few ways to check an all-powerful executive in a parliamentary system is through a vote of no confidence.

A *vote of no confidence* in parliament is a vote to support the ouster of the government. Votes of no confidence are rare and almost never succeed. For it to work, the majority party or coalition actually has to vote against its own executive. In other words, it votes itself out of power. However, if it works, a new leader has to emerge and create a new majority to govern; if this isn't possible, new elections will have to be held.

A good example is Germany. The German parliament, called the Bundestag, which is the lower house of parliament in Germany, picks the chancellor. The chancellor can be removed only in regularly scheduled elections, held every four years, or in a vote of no confidence, which is unlikely to happen because the chancellor's party is the majority party in parliament. Only once in the history of the Federal Republic of Germany has a chancellor been removed through a vote of no confidence, and that was back in 1982.

Some political scientists argue that a major advantage of a parliamentary system is that it creates multiparty systems. In a two-party system, it's argued that parties are all-encompassing, including so many different political beliefs and values that they can't fully represent any. Therefore, third parties are needed in two-party systems to truly represent all beliefs. However, third parties are rare because they know they can't win in two-party systems. In multiparty systems, combined with proportional representation, third parties can win seats even if they receive a small amount of votes. This allows for many parties in parliament representing every group and individual in a country (for a discussion of electoral law and party systems, see Chapter 7).

Another difference is that presidents are usually term-limited. The U.S. president is limited to two terms and so is the Brazilian president. The Mexican president is actually limited to only one term. In parliamentary systems, executives are usually not term-limited. In Germany, Chancellor Merkel has been in power for 15 years (since 2005), and former Chancellor Kohl served 16 years from 1982 to 1998. In Great Britain, Margaret Thatcher served 11 years as prime minister from 1979 to 1990.

In many parliamentary democracies, minority governments are common — that is, a government lacking a majority in parliament. This type of government is at the mercy of smaller parties that tolerate it. However, if they withdraw their support, the government falls. This happens quite frequently in Italy and Israel.

Unicameralism versus bicameralism

While most (two-thirds) democracies are bicameral in nature, with an upper and lower house and the lower house being the dominant structure, there are exceptions. Some democracies are unicameral in nature and have only one house. Most unicameral democracies are found in fairly small countries, which are very homogeneous, such as Ukraine, Bulgaria, Croatia, and Finland. There isn't a lot of diversity to be found in these nations. Most bicameral democracies are larger, containing millions of more people, and have a fairly large minority population. Examples are the U.S., Germany, Russia, and India.

Being unicameral has certain advantages:

>> **Unicameral structures are more cost-effective.** Instead of having two houses with hundreds or even thousands of parliamentarians to pay for, you have only one house with fewer parliamentarians to take care of. Costs not only include salaries for parliamentarians but also maintaining the bureaucratic upkeep for two houses. A unicameral structure could cut cost in half. Congress with two houses costs the U.S. taxpayers almost $13 million a day. This equals close to $6 billion a year. Cutting one of the two houses could result in savings of at least $1 billion or more.

>> **Unicameral legislatures by definition are more efficient.** This is common sense. Instead of having to have legislation debated and passed by two houses, it needs to be dealt with by only one house. This speeds up the process of debating and then passing legislation. Studies have shown that unicameral legislatures pass bills quicker than bicameral legislatures.

Is one type of legislative structure better than the other? The answer seems to depend on the distribution of powers in a democracy. Most countries that use federalism (see Chapter 4), where you have levels of government with independent powers below the national level, are bicameral in nature. This isn't surprising. If subnational levels of government with independent powers exist, they also expect to be represented at the national level, usually in an upper house or Senate.

If a country, however, is unitary in nature with all powers being centralized at the national level, it makes sense to have only legislative structure. Today, most countries in the world have opted to be both unitary and unicameral in nature.

Studying the U.S. Congress

The U.S. Congress is one of the most studied political systems in the world — not just because it's one of the most powerful legislatures but because it's one of the oldest legislatures still in existence today. It's often referred to as the first branch of U.S. government simply because it was the first branch of government created by the founding fathers in Article 1 of the Constitution.

For the founding fathers, the legislature mattered most, and it received more coverage in the Constitution than the executive or judiciary. Being admirers of the British legislative structure, the founding fathers modeled the U.S. legislative structure partially on it. They set up a bicameral structure with two houses, the House of Representatives and the Senate. Each had its own purpose. The House of Representatives was elected by the people and served as a representative of the people. Its purpose was greatly influenced by John Locke's social contract theory (see Chapter 15). It was a body voted upon by rational voters every two years so that the public could frequently hold it accountable and replace representative who didn't serve the public well.

On the other hand, the Senate wasn't directly elected by the public but selected by state legislatures and was supposed to put a brake on some of the people's demands. Similar to the ancient Greeks, the U.S. founding fathers didn't fully trust the people. Therefore, one house represented the people, and the second house was there to prevent popular demands that were deemed as too excessive.

All of this changed 126 years later, in 1913, when the 17th Amendment to the Constitution was passed. It provided for the direct election of U.S. senators by the people.

REMEMBER

The U.S. Constitution contains specific *enumerated powers* in regard to Congress. Enumerated powers are powers specifically given to a branch of government. The legislative powers include the powers to collect taxes, coin money, declare war, raise armies and navies, establish federal courts below the Supreme Court, regulate citizenship, and regulate interstate commerce.

Prior to 1913, when the Senate was selected by the states, the senators were the representatives of the states in charge of protecting states' rights. Many consider the Senate to be slightly more powerful than the House of Representatives because it has additional powers the House does not possess. These are called *advise and consent powers.* These powers refer to the Senate having the power to consent to treaties a president has negotiated with foreign powers and the right to ratify a president's choices for the executive branch, like his cabinet, ambassadors, and federal justices, including Supreme Court justices.

TECHNICAL STUFF

The founding fathers even included what is today referred to as the elastic clause in the Constitution. The clause is so vague that virtually any power can be implied from it. The elastic clause, also called the necessary and proper clause, states that Congress has the power to "make all laws which shall be necessary and proper for carrying into execution the foregoing powers, and all other Powers vested by this Constitution." This clause can be interpreted to give Congress any kind of power necessary and proper to fulfill its duties and obligations.

HOW DOES IMPEACHMENT WORK?

Both houses of Congress participate in impeaching and removing members of the executive, including the president. The House of Representatives starts the impeachment process by investigating wrongdoings of any member of the executive branch, including the president. If the House of Representatives finds any wrongdoing, it can impeach the president, which means he now has been charged of wrongdoing. Only a simple majority vote is needed in the House of Representatives to impeach. After impeachment, the House hands the matter over to the Senate. The Senate then becomes the judge and jury while a few select members of the House act as prosecutors. It then takes a two-thirds vote in the Senate to convict and remove any federal official, including the president.

Other powers given to Congress are the power to impeach and remove members of the executive branch from office. This includes members of the cabinet, the federal judiciary, and even the president.

REMEMBER

Three presidents in U.S. history have been impeached by the House of Representatives. They were Andrew Johnson in 1868, who had succeeded Abraham Lincoln after his assassination; Bill Clinton in 1998; and Donald Trump in 2019. In all three cases, the Senate refused to convict the president and didn't remove him from office. All three presidents were able to complete their terms.

STRUCTURING CONGRESS

When the first Congress of the United States met in 1789, it consisted of 65 members in the House of Representatives and 26 senators from 13 states, with each state sending two senators. Today, Congress has 535 members with 100 Senators, two from each of the 50 states, and 435 members of the House of Representatives.

The size of a state's delegation in the House of Representatives is based on the population of a state. Originally, one representative represented 30,000 residents living in the district. The more a population grew in a state, the more members it would get in the house. In 1929, Congress passed the Permanent Apportionment Act, which capped the number of seats in the U.S. House of Representatives at 435 members. Today, a member of the House of Representatives represents about 700,000 people in a district. While the number of seats is fixed at 435 today, seats are reapportioned every 10 years. Some states will gain and some states will lose seats depending on population growth or population decline.

Looking at Great Britain

Great Britain has a bicameral structure, including the House of Commons elected by the people and representing the common person in Great Britain. It also has an upper chamber called the House of Lords, representing the British upper classes, namely its aristocracy and clergy. Both houses were designed to check the British monarch and her powers, to make sure Great Britain didn't go back to a period of absolute monarchy.

Until 1911, the House of Lords could be considered the more powerful of the two institutions, but that changed with the Parliament Act of 1911. Before this point, the House of Lords had an absolute veto power over all legislation passed by the House of Commons. Today, the House of Lords has the power only to reflect on and delay bills, but the House of Commons can override them. For this reason, today, the House of Commons is the dominant structure in Great Britain while the House of Lords has become a more deliberative body. The house that represents the will of people has been given more power than the house that represents a small minority of the public. The lower house of parliament selects the prime minister in Great Britain, who in turn dominates policy making in the country.

REMEMBER

In most democracies today, the lower house of the legislative structure holds most of the power, because it's considered to represent the will of the people. The lower house gets to pick the executive and make policy for the country. However, because lower houses are selected in districts representing localities, they're more likely to represent local issues instead of national issues. The upper house, on the other hand, is a more deliberative body dealing with national and not just local issues. Often, upper houses can only consult and delay legislation but not actually make it. France is a good example of this. Germany and the U.S. are exceptions to this rule because in both countries the upper houses do have equitable powers to the lower house.

Great Britain is also the origin of electoral law for most democracies (see Chapter 7). It uses a single-member district electoral law where the country is divided into districts and the person who wins the most votes in a district is elected to office. Most democracies today use proportional representation where political parties get seats based on the proportion of the votes they receive in an election. Single-member district electoral law in turn encourages a two-party system, where only two parties have a real chance of winning office, while proportional representation results in multiparty systems, where more than two parties have a chance of winning office (see Chapter 7).

The British system of government has become a model for most democracies because of the legacy of the British Empire. When most British colonies became independent after World War II, many adopted the British system of democracy. Today, major countries using the British model include the U.S., Canada, Australia, New Zealand, and Ireland.

Analyzing Executives

Executives have been around a lot longer than legislators. The kings and emperors of the past were executives running countries without legislatures. Legislatures didn't matter much in politics until the 17th century when they began to exert their powers first in Great Britain. For this reason, when people use the term *government*, they're usually referring to the executive and not a legislature.

The U.S. presidency

The U.S. president today is the most powerful executive in the world. He is the center of attention for the world media, and just about every person in the world knows him. This wouldn't have been the case in the 18th century when the office of the president had just been created and was weak in comparison to what it has become today. The founding fathers had perceived the presidency as a fairly weak institution, still being afraid of the monarchy in Great Britain. In Article 2 of the Constitution, the founding fathers outline the powers of the president, called the *expressed powers of the executive*. There aren't many of them and some are vague by definition.

The Constitution formally mentions the following powers in Sections 2 and 3 of Article 2 of the Constitution. The powers are listed in the order found in the Constitution:

>> **Commander in chief of the armed forces:** This power has caused much controversy in recent years. Many presidents have interpreted it to mean that they have the power to make war, even though Congress has the constitutional power to declare war.

>> **Granting reprieves and pardons:** The president has the power to pardon anyone for federal, but not state, offenses. The only exception is impeachment. The president can't pardon someone who has been impeached.

>> **Making treaties:** The president has the power to negotiate treaties with foreign countries, but the Senate later has to ratify the treaties.

>> **Appointing Supreme Court justices and ambassadors:** The president has the power to appoint justices of the U.S. Supreme Court and ambassadors. In both instances, the Senate has to approve his choices.

>> **Convening Congress to special sessions:** In emergency situations, the president has the power to call Congress into a special session.

>> **Receiving ambassadors:** The president has the right to receive foreign ambassadors and other foreign dignitaries to discuss policy with them.

>> **Ensuring that the laws are faithfully executed:** That's all the Constitution says about this power. Today, presidents interpret it as the power to make policy, as outlined in the annual budget the president submits to Congress.

The Constitution further provides the president with delegated powers, where Congress can give power to the executive in times of emergencies. In addition, there are inherent powers, which are not expressly stated in the Constitution but can be inferred from it.

A final power of the president can be found in Article 1, Section 7, of the Constitution — the president's veto power. It mentions that the president possesses the power to veto legislation passed by Congress. The president has ten days to veto a bill and has to explain to Congress why he cast the veto. Congress then has the option to override the president's veto. This requires a two-thirds majority in both houses of Congress.

If Congress passes a bill within ten days of adjourning, the president can cast a *pocket veto.* All he has to do is let the bill sit on his desk until Congress adjourns and the bill has been vetoed. Pocket vetoes can't be overridden, because Congress has no chance to vote on the veto. Therefore, Congress is careful not to pass legislation too close to adjournment unless the president guarantees that he won't veto the legislation. Most vetoes stand, or are not overridden by Congress. Less than 4 percent of all vetoes in U.S. history have been overridden.

Evolution of the U.S. presidency

In the beginning, most U.S. presidents were weak and let Congress take care of running the country. They were figureheads legitimizing the newly created country. Occasionally, a strong president did emerge, such as Andrew Jackson in 1828, but after his two terms had ended, Congress took back over running the country. It wasn't until Franklin D. Roosevelt (FDR) came to power in 1933, in the wake of the Great Depression, that a strong presidency was created and was here to stay. FDR is widely considered the first modern president, transforming the U.S. executive into the powerful institution it is today. Instead of Congress, the presidency now deals with economic and foreign policy making.

Today, the U.S. executive performs many functions in U.S. politics. He has become the preeminent politician in the U.S. Some of the president's roles include

>> **Head of state:** The president symbolizes the United States. Other countries judge the U.S. by what kind of president the U.S. public elects.

- » **Commander in chief:** The president heads the U.S. military. The public looks to him to commit troops into combat. The public also holds him accountable for the successes or failures of military operations.

- » **Chief foreign policy maker:** The president is expected to make foreign policy, meet foreign leaders, and negotiate treaties. The public holds him responsible for successes and failures in foreign policy.

- » **Chief executive:** The president is in charge of the federal bureaucracy, which includes the cabinet departments, the Office of Management and Budget, and the military.

- » **Chief legislator:** Today, the president is responsible for most major legislation. He proposes the budget and uses his veto power to shape policy. The president acts, and Congress usually reacts to his policies.

- » **Crisis manager:** Whenever crisis strikes the country, the U.S. public looks to the president to act. After the outbreak of the new coronavirus COVID-19 in early 2020 in the U.S., the public expected President Donald Trump, not Speaker of the House of Representatives Nancy Pelosi, to tackle the problem.

- » **Leader of his party:** The public, as well as party supporters, look at the president as the leader of his party. If the president does well, the public will usually reward his party in the elections. If he performs poorly, the public will usually punish his party.

Today, the president is the chief politician in the U.S. However, he still has to share his powers with Congress on many occasions, and Congress can keep his power in check, if necessary.

Great Britain's prime ministry

Many claim that Great Britain had the first democratic form of government in the world. While this isn't necessarily true, it did have the first form of parliamentary democracy. Great Britain uses a parliamentary system where voters cast a vote for parliament, which then in turn selects the executive. A parliamentary democracy is based on a fusion of power, where one structure, the legislature, also selects the executive.

The majority party or majority coalition in parliament actually selects the British prime minister. The prime minister then picks his cabinet, where he becomes primus inter pares, or "first among equals." In reality, though, the prime minister dominates the cabinet and thus makes policy. He can fire members of the cabinet at will if they disapprove of his policies. In a parliamentary system, cabinet members have to be picked from parliament and are therefore members of the legislature and executive at the same time. They're usually seasoned political veterans who excel at policy making and negotiation and bargaining with other members of the legislature.

TECHNICAL STUFF

A cabinet is composed of appointed officials selected by the executive. Each official leads a specific department or ministry, such as the Ministry of Defense in Great Britain. (*Note:* In the U.S., the term *department* is used, while in most of the world, departments are referred to as *ministries*. So in Great Britain, it's called the Ministry of Defense, and in the U.S., it's the Department of Defense.) In Europe, an executive can enlarge a cabinet at will and then cut it back if necessary.

However, in presidential systems such as in the U.S., members of the executive cabinet are rarely members from the legislature. Most of the time they come from the private business sector, or the military and even academia. In the case that members of Congress are appointed to the cabinet, they have to resign their seat in Congress.

Which cabinet system is better? In the European case, you have cabinet members who are career politicians. They know the rules of institutions and politics, have background on the issues they represent, and have great ties to the legislature. This makes them more likely to get policies passed in an efficient manner. However, they lack any fresh perspective or new ideas and are more likely to support the status quo than advocate for reform.

Most members of U.S. cabinets do not have a power base in the legislative as cabinet members in Europe have. They do not know the rules of a legislature, are not familiar with the process of bargaining and compromising to get legislation passed, and are not policy experts in the position they are in. Therefore they are less effective in policy making and it is easier for an executive to get rid of them. They're usually not well known and instead of actually making policy they have become bureaucrats only implementing policies made by the President and his closest advisors.

Going Bureaucratic

Whenever people hear the term *bureaucracy* or *bureaucrat*, they usually cringe. They think of rules and regulations and a lot of red tape. So what is bureaucracy? Bureaucracies are large organizations that are supposed to implement policies made by government, both legislative and executive. Bureaucrat refers to career civil service that staff government agencies at all levels, so for example, the U.S. has federal, state, and local bureaucrats.

Many call the bureaucracy a permanent government because legislators and executives come and go over time, but the bureaucracy stays in place. Therefore, it's imperative to have a professional bureaucracy that works for the nation and not for its own benefits. The first professional bureaucracy was developed in France in the 1790s. In the U.S., on the other hand, a professional bureaucracy didn't develop until the late 19th century. Instead, a system based on patronage was in place, which was called the spoils system. The idea behind the spoils system was that all federal jobs could be freely handed out to party supporters or family.

The French bureaucracy

France has one of the most professional bureaucracies in the world. The French bureaucracy became professionalized after Napoleon took over France after the French Revolution had failed by 1794. Napoleon decided that France needed a more effective bureaucracy. He centralized the system, overcoming regional differences in France, and divided the country into 96 prefects to carry out government policy. Great universities were created where national level bureaucrats were trained for their profession. Only the best and brightest in France were allowed to enter these universities. It didn't matter whether students had money or a title; all that mattered was whether students were bright and willing to sacrifice for France. In these universities, students were trained to work for the good of the country and not to enrich themselves.

The U.S. bureaucracy

In the U.S., on the other hand, becoming a bureaucrat wasn't based on merit until the 20th century. A spoils system had been created and was based on the concept of patronage, which refers to handing out government jobs based on political party and/or family ties.

Andrew Jackson was the first U.S. president to widely use the spoils system extensively. Following Jackson, almost all federal appointments were based on party or family ties. The first president to tackle the spoils system was Chester Arthur. In 1883, President Arthur pushed for Congress to pass the Pendleton Act, the first major civil service reform bill in U.S. history. The Pendleton Act established the following provisions:

>> Political tests for federal officeholders were banned.

>> Alcoholics, even if they were loyal party alcoholics, could not be hired.

>> Competitive tests for some (14,000 out of 131,000) civil service positions became mandatory.

>> Future presidents were allowed to make more civil service positions closed to the spoils/patronage system.

The spoils system survived until the Wilson administration (1913–1921), when the Civil Service Reform Act was passed and outlawed the practice. From now on, hiring for the bureaucracy at all government levels had to be based on merit.

REMEMBER

Most civil servants (bureaucrats) in the U.S. work at the state or local level. Only 15 percent of all civil servants work for the federal government. Local bureaucrats can include police, firefighters, and teachers.

Settling Disputes

The third branch of government is the judiciary, or the judicial system. The judicial system interprets laws, making sure that they're in compliance with a constitution or other legal traditions, such as acts of parliament. The power of judiciaries differs from country to country. In some countries, such as the U.S., judiciaries have the power to nullify laws of the legislative and acts of the executive, in turn making law themselves. This is called the power of judicial review. In other countries, such as Great Britain, where no written constitution exists, laws passed by parliament are the supreme law of the land and can be changed only by parliament itself. Judicial power is, therefore, considerably weaker in Great Britain.

The judiciary is the least democratic branch of the three branches of government. While citizens can replace legislators and executives in elections if they disagree with their decisions, judges are isolated from popular will. They're usually appointed for life, like in the U.S., or have lengthy terms, like in Germany, and are therefore not faced by the public will.

Classifying law

When studying the law, you'll notice that there isn't just one type of law but many. In addition, different countries use different types of laws. Following is a discussion of the most common types of laws in the world.

>> **Higher law:** Law made by God.

>> **Natural law:** Rights that come from nature and not rules of society. These rights are common to all people.

LAWYERS BY THE NUMBERS

When analyzing the number of lawyers in a country, the U.S. comes out way ahead. Today, the U.S. has 281 lawyers for every 100,000 people. Great Britain, in comparison, has only 94 lawyers per 100,000 people, and Japan has a measly 7 lawyers per 100,000 people.

>> **Positive law:** Law written by people.

>> **Common law (also called case law or judge-made law):** Body of law derived from previous decisions made by courts or tribunals. Common law is based on precedent and relies on the concept of stare decisis, which is Latin for "let the decision stand." Judges can modify but not change previous judicial decisions. The U.S. and Great Britain use common law.

>> **Roman Catholic law (also called canon law or code law):** This comprehensive and written collection of laws are arranged in books and based on the laws of the Catholic Church. In 1804, the Napoleonic code codified law in France, and later the code spread throughout Europe and Latin America. When using code law, judges don't have the power to make or modify law; they can only apply it. France, Germany, and most other democracies use Roman Catholic law.

>> **International law:** International law is defined as a body of rules and principles that are binding upon civilized states. It consists of the works of great writers, treaties, and customs and can't be enforced (see Chapter 9). International law is designed to impact the behavior of states and maintain peace within the global arena.

>> **Constitutional law:** Body of laws, defined as rules, doctrines, and practices, that govern the operation of a political community such as a state. Constitutional law isn't static but can change over time.

>> **Administrative law:** Body of laws created by bureaucracies when they interpret and implement rules. Administrative laws cover the structure, power, and duties of bureaucracies.

Being supreme: The U.S. Supreme Court

The U.S. Supreme Court is the highest of all the federal courts in the United States. It has the power to strike down laws of Congress and acts of the president. It also can overturn and change any judicial decision made at a lower level. In recent years, it has had an impact on every American with decisions such as legalizing gay marriage and banning any restrictions on campaign donations to candidates running for office.

TECHNICAL STUFF

The U.S. Supreme Court can overturn any State Supreme Court ruling because of the Supremacy Clause. The Supremacy Clause is contained within the Constitution in Article 6 and states that the laws of the United States (federal law) are the supreme law of the land.

When making decisions, U.S. Supreme Court justices can employ two schools of thought:

>> **Judicial restraint:** Judicial restraint refers to justices believing that their rulings should be based purely on what's written in the Constitution. If an issue isn't mentioned in the Constitution, the legal system shouldn't be able to deal with the issue.

>> **Judicial activism:** Judicial activism believes that courts can go beyond what's mentioned in the Constitution. They argue that times have changed since 1789 when the Constitution went into effect and that even though an issue may not be mentioned in the Constitution, such as abortion or restrictions on social media, decisions can be inferred from it.

REMEMBER

In the U.S., courts have the power of judicial review. Judicial review refers to the ability of courts to overturn laws of the legislative and acts of the executive that violate the U.S. Constitution. This allows for the court system to make policy. The federal judiciary has the power to strike down the will of the majority. Justices are appointed for life and can act freely, ignoring the popular will.

Comparing two higher courts

A good comparison of two similar judicial systems are the U.S. Supreme Court and the Federal Constitutional Court in Germany. The two courts are similar, because they both possess the power of judicial review, enabling them to overturn legislation.

Established in 1949, the Federal Constitutional Court has become the most popular institution in Germany today. Unlike the U.S. Supreme Court, it consists of two chambers with eight justices each. Each chamber deals with different issues. One deals with conflicts between the federal government and the German states. The second chamber deals with civil rights and civil liberties issues. The judges are picked by both the upper and lower houses of the German parliament, with each picking half with a two-thirds vote. Each judge gets to serve a 12-year nonrenewable term and has to retire at the age of 68.

The U.S. Supreme Court has one chamber with nine justices. They deal with any kind of issue and are appointed for life. Supreme Court justices can be replaced only if one of them voluntarily retires or resigns or dies. In addition, Congress can impeach them and remove them from office. Similar to presidential impeachments, the House of Representatives has to convict and then impeach a justice, and the Senate has to try to remove the justice. In the history of the Supreme Court, only one Supreme Court Justice was ever impeached. It was Samuel Chase, who was impeached in 1804 for publicly criticizing President Jefferson. The Senate, however, refused to remove him from office.

Chapter 7

Elections, Political Parties, and Interest Groups

emocracies are based on the concept of popular will. In other words, it is the people who make policies either directly or indirectly (see Chapter 4 for a discussion of the types of democracies). In a representative democracy, most democracies today are representative democracies; the public is represented by elected officials who make policies on behalf of the people. Thus, elections provide the major link between government and people. Elections allow for the public to not only impact policy making but to also hold our officeholders accountable. Political parties and interest groups are additional links between the government and the people. They facilitate political participation and aggregate interests, which allows the public to participate in policy making and hold office holders accountable. In conclusion, without popular elections, political parties and interest groups democracy would not be possible.

Studying Elections

Elections provide the major link between people and government in a democratic society. Through elections, people can hold their government accountable and also change its policies. Elections, therefore, have two purposes. First, they're the means for people in democracies to not only hold their government accountable but also change it. Second, they're the means to initiate policy change if so desired. However, for that link to work, people have to, first of all, vote and, second, know who to vote for.

REMEMBER

When studying elections, two major electoral systems can be analyzed. They are the single-member district electoral system and proportional representation. The *single-member district electoral system* is an electoral system in which the person who wins the most votes in a district is elected to office. *Proportional representation*, on the other hand, is an electoral system in which seats are allocated based on the proportion of the vote a party receives.

Authoritarian regimes also hold elections. They're designed to bring about international legitimacy and increase support back home. China regularly holds elections, even though only communist party-approved candidates are allowed on the ballot.

Explaining voting behavior

For decades, political scientists have tried to explain voting behavior in democracies. Many theories were created but most don't seem to fully explain voters. Following are some of the more popular models. All have some merit, and to truly explain voting, all of them should be used to explore the outcome of an election.

The Columbia model

Beginning in the 1940s, sociologists developed the Columbia model of voting. This model focused on group behavior. It stated that group membership determined how people voted. In other words, a person was born into a certain group, and this group membership determined how that person voted. For example, if a person was born into a union household, union membership determined the vote. Or if a person was born a Catholic, religious membership determined how she voted. Today, race or gender, major determinants of the vote, constitute group membership.

The Michigan model

Social scientists from the University of Michigan conducted a major study on voting behavior in the 1950s. The model they created is labeled the Michigan model and is based on the 1952 and 1956 U.S. presidential elections. It stated that people base their vote on a psychological attachment to a political party. A *psychological attachment* is when people develop a form of group identity, affiliating with a political group, namely a political party. This attachment is called *partisan identification*, and it determines how people vote.

The echo chamber effect theory

American political scientist V. O. Key, Jr. set out to create his own theory on voting behavior. He called it the echo chamber effect theory. He stated that voting echoes, or reflects, the political environment. When parties are similar, supporting the same issues, people have to base their vote on party identification. However, when parties begin to differ, providing the electorate with different issues, people are prone to base their vote on issues.

Economic theories of voting behavior

Many economic theories on voting behavior claim that voters are rational. Economists such as Anthony Downs claim that voting behavior can be explained by looking at the state of the economy. Downs claims that rational voters base their vote on their pocketbook and on which candidate they expect to provide them with more benefits (expected utility). If they receive what they expected, they'll reelect the candidate. If not, they'll vote against the candidate. In other words, if the economy is doing well, incumbents benefit, and if not, challengers have a good shot at winning office, because voters will blame incumbents for the poor state of the economy.

Retrospective versus prospective voting

Retrospective voting occurs when incumbents decide to run for reelection. Voters can look at an incumbent's record and then decide whether they like this record. If so, they'll reelect the incumbent. *Prospective voting* is the opposite. It's rare and happens only when there's no incumbent. In this case, voters have to make an educated guess on who would be the better candidate and then make their choice.

Determining the vote

When studying voting behavior in democracies, several characteristics determining the way citizens' vote can be discovered. Among the factors influencing voting, the following stand out:

>> **Age:** One of the major determinants of the vote today is age. Turnout has a tendency to increase with age. Voters in most democracies are middle aged or older, while the young are least likely to vote.

>> **Gender:** One of the hottest topics in political science is the gender gap. Who is more likely to vote, women or men? Interestingly, the gender gap is country

specific. In France, for example, men are more likely to vote than women. In the U.S., on the other hand, women are more likely to vote than men. So, yes, there is a gender gap when it comes to voting, but it's country specific.

>> **Education:** The level of education a person achieves is another major factor in determining voter turnout. People are more likely to vote if they're well educated. A good education results in people being more aware and informed about issues. They also know about candidates and their stances on issues. They not only know how to participate but want to participate. The level of education a person has is the most important determinant of the vote today.

>> **Income:** Directly related to education, studies have shown that high-income people are more likely to vote. This shouldn't be surprising. High-income people are more concerned about issues such as taxes, and a change in government policies is more likely to impact them. Very simple, high-income people have more at stake in elections and so they turn out and vote.

>> **Partisan identification:** Partisan identification is an attachment a person has with a political party. Strong partisans habitually vote for their party regardless of candidates running for office. Partisan identification is usually imprinted on young adults by their parents through political socialization (see Chapter 3). If both parents possess the same partisan identification, the child has an 80 percent chance of having his parents' partisan identification. Strong partisans turn out to vote in high numbers. So the higher the number of strong partisans in a country, the higher the turnout will be.

TECHNICAL STUFF

Recent trends don't bode well for partisan identification. Even in Europe where partisan identification has always been strong, it's on the decline. In countries such as Germany and Great Britain, where partisan identification was high, this decline resulted in more ticket splitting and the creation of new parties, such as the Green Party in Germany, which now attracts a large number of former Social Democratic voters. In turn, voter turnout has seen a small decline in Europe in the last decades.

Partisan identification was never very high in the U.S. For this reason, the U.S. sees more crossover voting and ticket splitting than other democracies.

>> **Religion and class:** Both religion and class used to be major determinants of the vote. However, they have declined in importance in recent years. In the U.S., for example, it used to be the case that Catholics formed a solid voting bloc for the Democratic Party. This has changed, and today the Catholic vote is evenly split between the parties. With fewer Europeans and Americans professing to be deeply religious, religion is less of a predictor of the vote today compared to the past.

Class is in the same boat as religion. In most democracies, fewer people identify with a specific social class, and, therefore, union membership is down. So today, class voting is down in every industrialized democracy.

Political Parties — Necessary for Democracy

For nearly a century, a debate has raged within the field of political science on whether political parties are necessary for a democracy to function properly. In 1942, E. E. Schattschneider claimed in his classical study *Party Government* (Routledge) that political parties created democracy, and modern democracy is unthinkable save in terms of parties. Political scientist Samuel Huntington agrees with Schattschneider, claiming that parties are found in every working democracy and that they're necessary to organize participation, aggregate interest, and serve as the link between society and the government.

Political parties are therefore necessary, because they act as a link between the government and the people. By supporting and voting for political parties, people can have some input on political decisions, thus feeling represented. This feeling will make them more likely to support government.

This chapter assumes that Schattschneider's and Huntington's viewpoints are correct and that every democracy in the world needs a fully developed and functioning party system.

Defining a political party

What is a political party? Former U.S. President James Madison gives a widely used definition of a political party in Federalist Paper No. 10. According to Madison, a party or, as he calls it, faction can be defined as "a number of citizens, whether amounting to a majority or a minority of the whole, who are united and actuated by some common impulse or passion, or of interest, adverse to the rights of other citizens or to the permanent aggregate interest of the community."

Modern definitions of political parties vary. First, some political scientists define a political party as a group that seeks to elect candidates to public office by supplying them with a label by which they're known to the electorate. Anthony Downs provides another and more detailed definition of political parties, stating that political parties are "a team of men (and women) seeking to control the governing apparatus by gaining office in a duly constituted election."

REMEMBER

Both definitions agree on two major characteristics that political parties have to meet. First, political parties want to elect people to public office. Second, political parties provide a label or cue to their supporters facilitating the contesting of elections.

When examining political parties in a democracy, political scientists analyze a political party in three different ways. V. O. Key, Jr. first suggested this in his seminal work *Politics, Parties, and Pressure Groups* (Crowell). Key urged political scientists to differentiate between political parties and other groups, such as interest groups, by recognizing that political parties are tripartite structures composed of the following three different components.

>> **The party in the electorate:** The party in the electorate includes all the individuals who identify with a political party and support the party on Election Day.

>> **The party as an organization:** It analyzes the party's structure at the national, state, or local level. For example, political scientists can study a political party's structure by focusing on the number of national offices, their staff, budgets, and rules of behavior for party officials. In addition, the party's organizational view includes an analysis of the party's involvement in the selection of candidates.

>> **The party in government:** This third and final component of political parties consists of elected party officeholders. This includes executives, members of parliaments or congresses, as well as state legislators and local officeholders if they exist. Studies involving this component include, for example, the voting behavior of members of the House of Commons in Great Britain (see Chapter 6).

HOW POLITICAL PARTIES DIFFER IN THE U.S.

The U.S. differs when it comes to regulating political parties. Unlike other democratic constitutions, such as the German or French constitution, political parties aren't mentioned or regulated by the U.S. Constitution. The founding fathers believed that political parties were a source of corruption and division. Not only did they divide the newly founded country on partisan lines, but they also prevented the common person from judging issues on her own.

George Washington believed that political parties were so dangerous that he warned against them in his Farewell Address in 1796. This negative attitude toward political parties has persisted in the U.S., and many Americans still perceive political parties as a necessary evil and a source of corruption.

With political parties not mentioned or regulated at the national level, the states had to step in. So today, state constitutions, not the U.S. Constitution, regulate political parties in the U.S.

REMEMBER

Political parties are usually regulated by constitutions found in democracies. In other words, the constitution of a democracy provides political parties with a blueprint of how to organize, how to recruit members, and how to select candidates for office. For example, in Germany, the constitution allows for only dues-paying party members to select candidates for parliament within each parliamentary district. If someone doesn't belong to a political party or doesn't pay his membership dues, he can't be involved in the candidate selection process.

Dealing with party systems

When studying political parties globally, political scientists distinguish between several types of political party systems.

Party systems differ by how many parties are active in the system and whether these parties have a legitimate shot at winning office. They are classified in the following way:

>> **One-party system:** One-party systems are usually found in authoritarian and totalitarian societies. For example, the Soviet Union had a one-party system in which only one party, the Communist Party of the Soviet Union, was legal and was allowed to run candidates for office. The party further controlled every aspect of government and the economy. China is an example of this today.

>> **Two-party system:** Two-party systems are found in many democracies, including the U.S. and Great Britain. In a two-party system, only two parties have a legitimate chance of winning office. There are other or third parties, but they can't win office. They act as a valve for discontentment, and if they advocate popular policies, these policies are taken over by the two major parties, in turn destroying the third party. A good example is the Socialist Party of the U.S. (see Chapter 17), which saw most of its platform adopted by the Democratic Party in the 1930s, thus destroying it.

>> **Multiparty system:** Multiparty systems are the most widely found form of party system today. They have several parties competing, and all of them are strong enough to win seats. This results in coalition governments, at times unstable, and usually produces moderate policies by the government. Italy and Denmark are examples of multiparty systems.

TECHNICAL STUFF

Party systems can change over time. Germany had a two-party system for quite some time. Only the Christian Democratic Party (CDU) or the Social Democratic Party (SPD) had a chance of winning a majority of the vote. This has changed today. New parties such as the Green Party, the Party of the Left, or the Alternative for Germany (see Chapter 16) have emerged and have become strong enough to matter. Often, smaller third parties can become kingmakers in these countries. In other words, without their support a coalition or minority government cannot be formed. This is called a two-plus party system.

Causing different party systems

Electoral law within a country can impact the party system a country possesses. For example, the U.S. has had a two-party system for most of its history because of American electoral law. The U.S. uses single-member district electoral law. This type of electoral law is simple: The candidate who wins a majority of the vote wins office. For example, the U.S. is divided into 435 congressional districts. Whoever wins the most votes in a district in a general election is elected to office.

At the same time, this type of electoral law discriminates against third or minor parties. Even if a third party manages to get 20 percent of the vote, it won't be able to gain any seats in Congress. Only the two major parties have a legitimate chance of winning a majority of the vote in each district. Single-member district electoral law is the major reason countries have a two-party system.

Most of the rest of the democratic world, especially Europe, uses proportional representation (see the "Studying Elections" section, earlier in this chapter). In a proportional electoral system, political parties receive seats in legislatures based on the proportion of the vote they receive nationwide in an election. For example, if a political party receives 20 percent of the vote, it will receive 20 percent of the seats in the legislature. This type of electoral law creates many smaller or third parties, because they know that they'll receive seats in a parliament even if they don't win a majority of the vote or even come in second or third. In turn, a multi-party system, where more than two parties are represented in a legislature, results.

TECHNICAL STUFF

A great example of the impact of electoral law on party systems is the National Front in France. When President Mitterrand of France changed the electoral law in 1986 from single-member district representation to proportional representation to placate his communist allies, the extreme right National Front suddenly found itself with 35 seats in the National Assembly, receiving close to 10 percent of the vote. By 1988, France had switched back to its traditional single-member district electoral law, and the National Front was decimated, receiving only one seat in parliament, despite receiving the same amount of votes as in 1986.

A second determinant of a party system is the structure of parties themselves. In a two-party system, political parties are all-encompassing. All-encompassing parties aren't very ideological or extreme and represent a plethora of political viewpoints. For example, in the U.S., the Republican Party is open to both liberal and conservative Republicans. Being open to all viewpoints on major political issues forces political parties to constantly bargain, mediate, and then compromise within the party itself. This results in moderate policies, acceptable to all factions within the party. This in turn reflects the moderate nonideological nature of the American electorate.

In addition, all-encompassing parties are very flexible and can easily absorb popular issues of the day, especially if they were brought forward by minor or third parties. Not only are issues being absorbed but also supporters of third parties. For example, the Democratic Party absorbed progressive issues such as the creation of a welfare state and union rights from the Socialist Party in the 1930s. This resulted in socialist voters supporting the Democratic Party and the subsequent decline of the Socialist Party in the U.S.

In comparison, in Europe, each faction within the Republican Party — conservative, moderate, and liberal — would have its own political party. This would allow each faction to pursue more extreme policies, not having to bargain and compromise with a more moderate faction within the party.

Classifying political parties

When studying political parties, political scientists classify them into cadre and mass parties. *Cadre parties* are decentralized, with real power vested at the local level, and led only at the national level by informal committees. Cadre parties have no dues-paying mass membership, and their functions are purely electoral. In other words, they're in it to win elections at all cost. A cadre or electoral party has only one goal in mind — win office. Its policies tend to be moderate, because it has to appeal to a large segment of society, and therefore rarely supports radical change. Both the Democratic and Republican parties in the U.S. are cadre parties.

Mass parties, found mostly in Europe, are very centralized. Power is vested in a small leadership group, which runs the party with an iron fist. Mass parties have a large dues-paying membership, which can run in the millions. Their main purpose is not to win elections but to stay true to their beliefs (ideology). Mass parties would rather lose elections instead of compromising on issues. After winning an election, mass parties tend to be very radical and uncompromising in nature. The British Labor Party is a good example of a mass party today. Instead of changing its stances on issues, it was willing to lose the last election in Great Britain.

TECHNICAL STUFF

A third type of party is usually found in authoritarian or totalitarian societies. It's called a *devotee party*. A devotee party is organized around one person, usually a dictator or strongman. The National Socialist German Workers' Party (NSDAP), which was built around Adolf Hitler, is an example.

Functioning in a democracy

Political parties are considered by many to be essential for a democracy to function well. The following sections explore the functions political parties perform in a democracy.

Providing partisan identification

Political parties are a major determinant of the vote in democracies through partisan identification. The concept of partisan identification is psychological in nature. Studies have shown that most voters in a democracy have a psychological attachment to a political party and that this attachment determines how people vote. Therefore, partisan identification — whether identifying as a Republican or Democrat in the U.S. or as a Conservative or Socialist in Great Britain — determines how people vote. Voters vote conservative not because they necessarily know about conservative stances on issues but because they identify with a conservative party.

Independents are voters who don't identify with a political party. Partisans are voters who identify with a political party.

REMEMBER

Socializing the public

A second function of political parties is called political socialization (see Chapter 3). Political socialization refers to the process of how people acquire their political beliefs and values. The type of political beliefs and values people hold shapes how they act within their political system. People acquire their political beliefs through what is called agents of political socialization (see Chapter 3). By socializing voters, political parties are an agent of political socialization in many countries.

Political parties have an interest in instilling political values into the public. They can create lifelong supporters who will support the party during good and bad times. However, to become an agent of political socialization, political parties have to have close contact with the voters in a society, and the public has to perceive parties as being important. Political parties, therefore, organize meetings, provide entertainment, such as party picnics, and even organize travel for members. In other words, parties have to have contact with the average person.

Recruiting candidates and running their campaigns

Another function of political parties is to first recruit and then nominate candidates for political office. Parties attempt to recruit the strongest possible candidate to run for office to enhance their chances of winning office. Next, the party nominates the candidate and then runs his campaigns for office, by providing campaign funds and a campaign staff.

This in turn gives the party control over the candidate. The party is now able to punish the candidate for deviating from the party line by denying him renomination. This ultimately ends the candidate's political career.

While American political parties performed this function a century and a half ago, times have changed. With the introduction of the direct primary, candidates today don't need the party anymore in the U.S. to win nomination for public office. They can recruit and nominate themselves and even run their own campaign if they have the necessary resources. This has resulted in non-party backed candidates upsetting party establishment favorites in primaries and less party discipline in institutions such as Congress.

The direct primary is an election that allows the public, and not political parties, to pick a party's nominee for office.

Mobilizing voters

Another function parties perform is the mobilization of voters, especially on Election Day. Political parties try to get people to vote. Political parties initiate contact with voters by contacting them. They can call voters, stop by their homes, or text or email them. This is done on Election Day and weeks before an election, to make sure that voters will go out and vote.

Providing information

One of the most important functions of a political party is to provide the voters with information they can use to make decisions on Election Day. For this reason, political parties formulate ideas and propose policies and programs to the voters in their *party platforms* — a document that outlines a party's policies and principles. In other words, the party platform presents proposed policies to the voters. Voters then are supposed to study the party platform and base their vote on the party's proposals. While political parties create platforms outlining their policy proposals in every democracy, most voters don't bother to read the party platforms.

A second way to provide voters with information is for political parties to publish newspapers and even own news channels. In many European countries, major parties publish daily or weekly newspapers, which their supporters read. This allows for the party to control the information their supporters receive and can shape public opinion.

Political parties are major sources of political information in most democracies with the exception of the U.S. In the early years of the republic, it was quite different. The two major parties, the Federalists and the Democratic–Republicans, published their own newspapers, providing their supporters with information, albeit skewed in nature. Today, neither party publishes newspapers or runs a news channel. At the same time, American parties do provide voters with a limited amount of information, usually during election time. Through television or radio commercials, pamphlets, or even debates, the parties make the public aware of how they stand on the most important issues of the day.

Organizing government

One of the major functions of a political party is to organize the policy-making machinery at all government levels. Could you imagine the German parliament with more than 700 members without any kind of machinery in place to organize and run its affairs? You'd have to get more than 700 individuals together to legislate. This involves procedures on how to write and pass bills and how to get legislation passed. This result would be anarchy, and nothing would get accomplished. Here is where political parties come in. They organize the policy-making process by establishing rules and procedures and then make sure its members support the party's policies and vote for its bills.

Aggregating interests

A last function of political parties, shared with interest groups (see the section "Interest Groups: Influencing the Government," later in this chapter), is called *interest aggregation.* Interest aggregation is the act of joining with like-minded citizens to acquire political power.

Most citizens in democracies don't possess a lot of political power by themselves. For example, if an individual travels to Paris to meet with a French senator to discuss policy, the senator likely wouldn't agree to meet with him. However, if the individual presents a petition, signed by thousands of potential voters, the situation changes. Instead of presenting only one interest, the individual now represents the interest of thousands, and a representative will meet with and take his interests into account. Interest aggregation is usually accomplished by joining a political party or specific interest groups.

Realigning with another party

One of the most widely used concepts in the study of voters and elections is the concept of critical realignment, developed by V. O. Key, Jr. in an article in 1955. This concept was designed to explain the shifting of party dominance in American elections but can be easily applied to other democracies.

The idea involves the changing of groups that make up political parties. For example, both major parties in the U.S., the Republican and the Democratic Party, aren't cohesive but are made up of many groups supporting the parties for different reasons. Some of the core groups making up the Democratic Party are unionized workers, African Americans, Mexican Americans, and the Jewish population. When one of these core groups leaves a party and moves to the other major party, a realignment occurs. For example, white Southerners used to be a core group of the Democratic Party. Beginning in the 1960s, they began to leave the Democratic Party, and by the 1980s, they had joined the Republican Party. In other words, a realignment occurred. In a few, very rare instances, this shift of a core group from one to the other party can bring about the creation of a new majority party. In this instance, a critical realignment occurs.

In other circumstances, a dealignment can occur. In a dealignment, groups leave their respective political parties, but they refuse to realign themselves with a new party. Instead, they remain largely independent, supporting different parties depending on the election. For example, in the U.S., Southern Democrats dealigned as early as 1964 and then supported George Wallace and the American Independent Party in 1968, Nixon and the Republican Party in 1972, and the Democratic Party headed by Jimmy Carter in 1976. White Southerners finally realigned themselves with the Republican Party beginning in the 1980s.

Interest Groups: Influencing the Government

Interest groups today have become a major player in democratic politics. An *interest group* is an organization that seeks to influence public policy. Interest groups attempt to influence all branches of government — the legislative, the executive, and the judiciary — to pass policies that are favorable to their cause and their members and also block policies that would cause harm to their cause. In addition, interest groups actively seek new members and supporters to increase their political clout, in turn increasing political participation.

TECHNICAL STUFF

The U.S. leads the world in the number of interest groups, and in no other democracy have interest groups become as influential. Americans join interest groups to influence policy making at the local, state, or national level. When touring the U.S. and studying American politics, the famous French philosopher Alexis de Tocqueville noticed the prevalence of interest group politics in the country. He subsequently labeled the U.S. as "a nation of joiners."

When analyzing the impact of interest groups on politics in a country, two major theories were created to explain interest group involvement. They are pluralism and elite theory.

Going pluralist

Pluralist theory can be first seen in Federalist Paper No. 10, written by James Madison. Pluralism believes that as societies become more economically and socially complex, interest groups will arise. People will join together and create interest groups. They'll then push for their own interests and government benefits. These interests can be economic, professional, ideological, environmental, or even religious in nature.

Suddenly, a society has a plethora of interest groups, and they now compete for public benefits. This competition among interest groups assures that public policy will be a result of bargaining and compromising by interest groups. Public policy won't benefit just a few, but the many.

As soon as one group feels disadvantaged, it will begin to organize to be able to compete with other interest groups. Suddenly, many interest groups are competing for political benefits and hopefully balancing each other out in the long run.

The idea behind pluralism is that everybody will get something he asks for but nobody will get everything he asks for. This will make every interest group accept policy decisions by lawmakers.

TECHNICAL STUFF

Corporatism, like pluralism, involves interest groups. However, instead of competing for government benefits as interest groups do in a pluralist society, in a corporatist society, interest groups directly participate in policy making. There are usually fewer interest groups in a corporatist society and they work directly with government when it comes to policy making. Germany is an example of a corporatist society.

Being elitist

Elite theory takes a different point of view. It believes that not all interest groups are created equal but that some are more powerful than others. Over time, they acquire a monopoly on power in the political system. At this time, they'll be able to dominate other interests, now being able to push for public policies benefiting only them and their members and not the public overall. Not being able to be counterbalanced by weaker interest groups, they further their very narrow self-interest at the expense of the many. Elite theorists believe that interest groups aren't responsible to the public and they overrepresent business and the wealthy.

Differing from political parties

What is the difference between a political party and an interest group? Political parties are much broader, all-compassing organizations, as discussed earlier, and represent large segments of the population. Interest groups are narrower in scope, represent a small segment of the population, and push for policies that directly benefit their members and supporters. While political parties nominate and run candidates for elected office, interest groups do not. However, they attempt to influence elections by publicly supporting candidates who agree with them on issues.

REMEMBER

In the U.S., political parties and interest groups are complementary in nature. While they both compete for supporters and donations, they support each other on passing legislation that will benefit both. Often activists from interest groups closely aligned with political parties will join political parties and continue their activities in these.

Classifying types of interest groups

Are all interest groups the same, or do different types of interest groups coexist? Interest groups can be classified in the following way:

>> **Economic:** Most interest groups in the world are economic interest groups, including unions, either independent or government controlled, and business organizations.

>> **Professional:** These organizations represent a small but powerful segment within society, and they're actively pushing for legislation benefiting a small group of members. Examples include medical associations or groups representing a small segment of the economy, such as lawyers.

>> **Public:** Some countries, usually advanced industrialized economies, have public interest groups. Public interest groups push for policies benefitting the majority of the people and not just a small minority of members.

>> **Government:** Government structures themselves can act as interest groups. In federal societies, local governments often act as interest groups competing for a slice of the federal budget. In societies such as France or Japan, the federal bureaucracy itself lobbies government for more funding for their agencies.

>> **Ideological:** These are usually very ideological in nature and push for certain very narrow policies. A good example are extreme right- or left-wing groups or environmental organizations.

Joining interest groups

Why do people join interest groups? First, most people join an interest group to receive material benefits. For example, workers join unions to receive higher wages and the ability to work in a safe environment.

Second, people join for ideological reasons. Especially in countries that have a weak party system, for example, the U.S., people join interest groups instead of political parties. While an environmentalist can join the Green Party in Germany, he would join the Sierra Club, an environmentalist interest group, in the U.S., because a green party has no chance of winning seats in state legislatures or the U.S. Congress.

Finally, solidary incentives have increasingly come to the forefront. In today's societies, many people don't possess a large social support structure. They're separated from their family structure, single or divorced, and often feel lonely. Interest groups have tapped into this market. Interest groups provide a person with the opportunity to join a large group of like-minded people to socialize with. Many interest groups are socially active, having dinners or game nights. Here, supporters can meet and socialize with each other.

Being powerful

What determines the influence interest groups have in a democratic society? Keep in mind that interest groups don't run candidates for office but are active in politics by taking a part in political campaigning and by lobbying. *Lobbying* is defined as contacting members of the legislative, executive, or the judiciary in an attempt to influence public policy or administrative decisions. Interest groups provide public support, mobilize their members to vote, and spend money on behalf of candidates. There are six sources of interest group power:

>> **Size of membership:** The larger the membership of an interest group, the more powerful it will be in politics. Even though an interest group might not have a lot of financial resources, it can make up for this by having millions of members who will vote on Election Day.

>> **Monetary resources:** The more money interest groups can spend on candidates running for office, the more powerful they'll be.

>> **Intensity of members' conviction:** Certain interest groups, such as the National Rifle Association (NRA) in the U.S., have a large pool of very dedicated members. These members feel strongly about an issue, in this case the right to bear arms, and are likely to not only give money to the organization but also base their vote on a specific issue.

>> **Prestige of membership:** The prestige of an interest group also matters. Some interest groups consist of members who enjoy a lot of prestige in a society. This will make the interest group more powerful when dealing with policy makers. A good example is the American Medical Association.

>> **Leadership skills:** Often an exceptional leader can overcome a lack of membership in an interest group or even a lack of monetary resources.

>> **Organizational structure:** The organizational structure of an interest group can make a big difference. For example, interest groups that are headquartered in not just one location, such as the capital of a country, but have offices in every region of a country will be more influential. Organizational structure, in other words, determines the political power an interest group possesses.

Checking out interest group functions

Interest groups fulfill several functions in a democracy. They include

>> **Interest aggregation:** Individuals by themselves usually lack political power and can't influence public policy making. However, when they join with other individuals who hold similar interests, they can acquire political power.

REMEMBER

In countries with strong political parties, such as Germany or Great Britain, people join political parties to aggregate their interests. In societies with weak political parties, such as the U.S., they join interest groups instead.

>> **Electioneering:** Electioneering refers to interest groups becoming active in campaigns for political office. By electing candidates friendly to their policy demands, interest groups will be more likely to get what they want from policy makers. Campaign activities by interest groups can include monetary donations, urging their members to vote for certain candidates, providing campaign volunteers, and mobilizing their members on Election Day.

>> **Providing Information:** Interest groups have become a major source of information for policy makers. Most politicians are not specialists in policy areas and so they have to rely upon information from other sources to be able to make a rational policy choice. It is here where interest groups step in. They will provide policy makers with credible information on issues dear to them. Policy makers will then use this information in the policy-making process. The information provided by interest groups is usually credible and nonbiased because if interest groups lie to policy makers they will never be trusted again and lose their political influence. In some democracies, it is even a crime to lie to policy makers when providing information to them.

>> **Shaping public opinion:** Interest groups are well aware that policy makers care about public opinion and attempt to follow the public's wishes. They do want to be reelected. By shaping public opinion, interest groups indirectly influence policy making. Therefore, interest groups will use the media, for example TV commercials, or even social media to provide the public with information favorable to their demands. By convincing the public that their demands are just and also beneficial for the average person, the public will fall in line and now support interest group demands.

3

Going Global: International Relations

IN THIS PART . . .

Find out more about the ever-expanding field of international relations, ranging from the causes of international conflict to international economic relations.

Discover concepts trying to explain and understand world politics.

Find theories that explain and predict world politics.

Look at international organizations, such as the United Nations, and international law. Both were designed to maintain peace and regulate conflict if it should occur.

Read about political violence, from the causes of warfare to modern-day terrorism. Get a detailed analysis of Cold War events.

Focus on international economic relations, with a close look at various economic theories and the current process of globalization.

IN THIS CHAPTER

» Checking out the origins and theories of international relations

» Getting a sense of realism

» Taking a look at idealism

» Discovering how global humanism works

» Looking at constructivism

Chapter **8**

Thinking Globally: The Study of International Relations

Why study international relations? The answer is simple: Events in foreign places do matter. The isolationism of the 19th century isn't an option for the United States anymore. Whenever an event takes place across the globe, it has an impact, major or minor. By studying global problems and analyzing their roots, not only can international relations be understood, but possible solutions to international conflicts come to light. Society can further acquire knowledge about issues, other cultures, their politics, and how international politics affect us.

Understanding the Origins of International Relations

The study of international relations is almost as old as humankind itself. As soon as people organized into groups, first as small as tribes and later as large as nation-states, they began to interact with each other. Suddenly, international relations was born.

REMEMBER

International relations is the study of organized groups of people interacting with each other across political boundaries. These groups can be small, like tribes, or large, like the great empires of the past. Today, a discussion of international relations (world politics) refers to states interacting with each other.

Creating states

REMEMBER

The current international system made up of states was created in the 17th century. After the Treaty of Westphalia of 1648, states were slowly created, and today they are the most common form of organized groups at the international level.

TECHNICAL STUFF

Although the state is the most common unit in international relations today, that has not always been the case. Throughout history, many different units have interacted and created the foundation for an international system. In ancient times, large empires, such as the Roman or Persian empires, interacted. An international system was even created by the small city-states of ancient Greece and the middle-age Italian city-states when they were interacting with each other. However, the creation of the modern state system didn't occur until 1648.

In 1648, the Treaty of Westphalia ended the Thirty Years' War (1618–1648) in Europe. The Thirty Years' War was one of the most devastating wars Europe had ever experienced, killing close to one-third of all the people in Germany alone. The Treaty of Westphalia set the foundation for a new international structure in Europe, replacing the old empires. Newly created entities called states were created. They have known boundaries, a population that identifies with them resulting in a growing nationalism, and they were recognized by international law (see Chapter 9). The concept of the state quickly spread throughout Europe and then in the 19th century to the Americas. By the 20th century, the state was the prevalent government structure around the globe. It still is today.

REMEMBER

The term *nationalism* is usually defined as loyalty and devotion by a people to a nation. The French Revolution of 1789 and the subsequent Napoleonic conquest of most of Europe instilled nationalism into many conquered European countries. People began to strongly identify with the state they lived in and with its common culture, history, and language.

Getting familiar with international relations terms

To better understand the concepts of international relations, get to know these common terms:

>> **Bipolarity:** An international system dominated by two great powers. It usually forms two large hostile blocs such as the Soviet Union and United States during the Cold War.

>> **Hard power:** Using military force or economic measures, such as economic sanctions, to force another nation to do something it wouldn't have done based on its own free will.

>> **Hegemon:** The leading power in the international system that has dominant influence on other states.

>> **International relations:** The study of relationships between countries.

>> **Multipolarity:** More than two great powers dominating the international system.

>> **Power:** The ability to make other nations do something they wouldn't do based on their own free will.

>> **Soft power:** Using measures other than military or economic force to get another country to do your bidding.

>> **State:** Also referred to country. States are entities with defined territorial boundaries and have ultimate control within their boundaries. This is referred to as sovereignty (see Chapter 9). States are the primary actors in international relations today.

>> **Unipolarity:** One great power or hegemon dominating the international system.

Getting into the Theories of International Relations

One of the major tasks of political scientists is to explain why certain events occur or have occurred in the international system. For example, what has led to a decline in warfare between countries since the end of the Korean War, and why did World War II occur? These are important questions to ask, and to answer them, political scientists use three different approaches, or levels of analysis.

REMEMBER

A level of analysis is a technique used in explaining global events. The three different techniques that political scientists use to research world politics are the individual, the state, and the systemic level of analysis.

TECHNICAL STUFF

Political scientist Kenneth Waltz first proposed these three levels of analyses in his book *Man, the State, and War* (Columbia University Press) in 1959. In his work, he uses the term *images,* but today it's more commonly referred to as levels of analysis. For Waltz, these three levels allow different ways to study, explain, and predict events in the international environment.

Individual: The first level of analysis

The first level is called the individual level — it's the study of the impact of people on world politics. Political scientists focus on the actions of certain individuals, their intentions, plans, and actual policies. Some researchers even go as far as to study certain common characteristics of human nature. Similar to many philosophers and even religions, many political scientists believe that people are flawed (see the discussion of realism later in this chapter), some even evil, and that this causes aggression and warfare throughout the world.

The first level of analysis focuses on certain select individuals and tries to determine how they've impacted world politics. The study is on their background, their beliefs, and, most important, their actions.

Looking at individuals and their backgrounds often can be used to explain the outbreak of conflict within the international system. Many books have been written trying to explain the outbreak of World War II. To provide an explanation, some political scientists have used the first level of analysis. They've focused on major political leaders, such as Adolf Hitler, Joseph Stalin, and even Franklin Delano Roosevelt, to determine how these individuals contributed to the outbreak of World War II. More recent works have focused on Saddam Hussein, the former leader of Iraq, to see how his personality and his decisions contributed to the invasion of Kuwait in 1990 and the subsequent U.S. invasion of the country in 2003.

State: The second level of analysis

The second level of analysis studies states and not people. The focus is on one or more states and the study of its political and economic structures, including type of government (democratic or authoritarian), political parties (single or multiparty system), media (free or government controlled), political ideologies (democratic, fascist, or communist), and even the political culture of a people.

A controversial approach falling into the second level of analysis category are culture studies. These studies claim that we have and have had certain cultures that are more war prone than others. For example, both Germany and Japan and more recently Serbia have been accused of having had warlike cultures. This in turn made them more aggressive within the international system resulting in World War I and World War II and more recently the conflict in the former Yugoslavia.

Systemic: The third level of analysis

The third level of analysis is the systemic or global level. Political scientists study the interaction of states and nonstate actors such as international organizations and nongovernment organizations, for example, multinational corporations, in the global arena. These interactions often shape state behavior. Examples are plenty and include actions the United Nations has undertaken, such as leveling sanctions against Serbia in the late 1990s to prevent further Serb atrocities against their own population and neighboring countries, or demands by the International Monetary Fund (IMF) insisting that a member state implement certain economic policies before it would lend more money to a state.

Other third-level theories, such as balance of power theory (see "Balancing power: The balance of power theory" section, later in this chapter), look directly at the impact of the international systemic structure, assuming that it's responsible for nation-state actions in the global arena. In these theories, the system shapes nation-state policies and behavior in the international arena and not the personalities of leaders or factors within the nation-state (first and second level of analysis explanations).

Getting Real: The Power of Realism

The school of realism is the oldest school in international relations. It can be traced back to the ancient Greeks. It's most famous adherents are Niccolo Machiavelli and Thomas Hobbes (discussed in Chapter 15). The idea behind realism is that world politics is all about struggle for power between nations. The following points discuss realism:

>> It is the dominant school of thought in international relations before World War I and after World War II.

>> The idea behind realism is that world politics is all about struggle and a quest for power in the international system.

>> States are the key actors in the present international system. International organizations, such as the United Nations, are secondary actors.

>> Every state tries to become more powerful because only power can guarantee survival of a state.

>> This struggle for power results in conflicts between states.

>> Anarchy, or lawlessness, dominates the international arena. There is no world government that can enforce laws or punish aggression.

>> Because there's no authority, such as a world government, to prevent conflict, every state is on its own. In other words, every state lives in a self-help system where the strong will survive and the weak will perish.

>> Security necessitates a strong powerful military and a good economic foundation.

>> Military force is a necessity. You not only have to possess it, but you also have to be willing to use it. The use of military force to acquire power and assure the survival of the country is justified at any point.

>> International morality is not relevant. The highest moral goal of a country is to assure its own survival.

>> High politics dominates. With the security of a state being the ultimate objective, only foreign policy matters, because only it can guarantee security.

>> Idealism, discussed later in this chapter, is utopian: A realist believes that idealists are utopian. Their ideas are based on wishful thinking about the nature of people. Realists advocate looking at the real world and not at how things should be.

Balancing power: The balance of power theory

The balance of power theory is one of the oldest realist theories used to study international relations. The balance of power theory was used by statesmen in ancient Greece and Rome and advocated by great writers such as the Italian political philosopher Niccolo Machiavelli (see Chapter 15). The theory is based on the idea that states interact with each other and that this interaction causes our present-day international state system. Beginning with the signing of the Treaty of Westphalia in 1648, it became the dominant foreign policy concept of the day.

From King Louis XIV of France to the great Prussian ruler Frederick the Great to even Napoleon, balance of power became the foundation for foreign policy. It can be used to explain foreign policy events from the Concert of Vienna (see Chapter 10), which ended the Napoleonic Wars, to World War I (1914–1918).

Seeing how the theory works

The balance of power theory is fairly simple in nature. It stipulates that all great powers — at least two are needed for the theory to work — are similar in size and power. The power of a country is measured in both military and economic terms. If this is the case, the world will be in balance and peace will result. If, however, one country grows too powerful, it will upset the balance. This in turn will result in conflict, even war, because the system is out of balance. To rebalance the international system, other nations will have to combine and rebalance the system. This is done using warfare. For example, Germany grew rapidly economically and militarily in the late 19th century. By 1914, it had upset the balance of power in Europe and other countries such as France, Great Britain, and even Russia combined against it. The resulting conflict, World War I, rebalanced the system by weakening Germany.

Noting whether it's still applicable today

For balance of power theory to work, certain preconditions have to be in place. First, as previously mentioned, all the great powers have to be similar in size and power, both economically and militarily. This isn't always the case. After World War II, the U.S. enjoyed a period of unipolarity, or sole power, because it was the only great power left. It took the Soviet Union years to catch up and rebalance the system. The same happened after the Soviet Union collapsed in 1991. The U.S. had again become the hegemon, or sole superpower in the world. It took a decade for other powers such as China, Russia, and the European Union to become relevant again.

Second, a willingness to use force has to be in place for balance of power to work. Countries have to be willing to use force to rebalance the international system. Examples are the Napoleonic Wars and World War I.

Third, a system of flexible alliances has to be in place. This refers to countries switching allies quickly to rebalance the system. To be able to do so, you need to forsake a former ally and align with a former enemy if needed. Great Britain, for example, fought France for hundreds of years and was on good terms with Germany. However, when Germany became too powerful in the late 19th century, it switched sides quickly and aligned itself with its former enemy France against former ally Germany.

Fourth, an agreement on rules of conduct during warfare has to exist. If you go to war against a country, you have to keep in mind that that country could be a future ally. Therefore, a war can't be too devastating because any enemy is a future friend.

Finally, to be able to conduct a foreign policy based on balance of power, you have to have skilled foreign policy leaders. The need to constantly monitor the international arena for any possible upset of the balance of power and the willingness to bargain and compromise with not just allies but also enemies takes time and especially diplomatic skills.

Avoiding conflict: The power transition model

The power transition model is a realist model developed by political scientist A. F. K. Organski in 1958. It is a theory developed to explain peace and conflict in international relations.

The power transition model arrives at the exact opposite conclusion that balance of power theory does. The transition theory states that any balance — two or more powers being equal — results in conflict. Therefore, any kind of balance, or states being similar in power, needs to be avoided. Instead, one all-powerful country (the technical term is *hegemon*) is needed to maintain peace and stability within the international system. This all-powerful country dominates the system, polices it, and maintains the peace. However, whenever another great power rises and suddenly equals the hegemon, it challenges the hegemon, and conflict occurs. Therefore, a balance within the system leads to conflict, while an imbalance — one power dominating the system — results in peace.

REMEMBER

Conflict will occur only if a rising secondary power is dissatisfied with the way the hegemon runs the international system. As long as it benefits from the system, it won't challenge the hegemon but will continue to become more powerful over time.

For example, many believe that the U.S. became the hegemon for a second time after the Soviet Union collapsed in 1991. The U.S. dominated the international arena and maintained peace within it. Whenever aggression by minor countries occurred, such as in 1990 when Saddam Hussein invaded Kuwait, the U.S. would take care of business, in this case with Operation Desert Storm, and resolve the conflict. However, today the U.S. is clearly not the hegemon anymore, being challenged by China and a rapidly rising Russia. But both China and Russia do benefit economically from the international system and so far have decided not to challenge the U.S. but rather sit back and have the U.S. police the world while they continue to get more powerful militarily and economically. At some point, however, a challenge to the U.S. may occur, especially from China.

Noting neorealism

Neorealism isn't a new school in international relations but an update to classical realism. Neorealism accepts all the foundations of realism, such as the fact that the state is the key unit of analysis, that anarchy is at the root of the international system, that states pursue power for security, and that states are rational actors, which engage in policies that will benefit them and guarantee their security in the long run.

Neorealists also agree that a strong military with a willingness to use military force as a foreign policy tool is necessary to survive in the international arena. However, neorealists find realism lacking in many areas. They believe that classical realism is inadequate because it ignores the role international law and international organizations can play in international relations. Further, realism doesn't account for global economic integration and the impact domestic politics can play on a country's foreign policy. Can you really ignore public opinion or the role of interest groups when studying the foreign policy of a nation?

Neorealists thus argue that political scientists today have to not only study *high politics* (foreign and security policy) but also focus on international organizations and international law as well as *low politics* (domestic politics, such as economic and social policy).

For this reason, a more comprehensive approach to the study of international relations is needed. The integration of international organizations, international law, and low politics completes realism, giving a comprehensive approach to the study of world politics.

An example of neorealist theory is called the theory of hegemonic stability and was developed by Robert Gilpin in his seminal work *War & Change in World Politics* (published in 1981 by Cambridge University Press). The work details how countries become all powerful and then create international systems from which they benefit. However, over time, these hegemons decline and are replaced. The work further discusses in detail the reasons these hegemons decline and mentions ways to prevent decline.

In other words, check out the rise and decline of nations. Figure 8-1 presents the theory in a nutshell.

Following are three possible results of hegemonic or world wars:

>> The hegemon wins the war, and no major changes occur to the international system. The challenger is beaten back, and the world returns to the status quo.

» The challenger wins the hegemonic war, and a new international system from which the challenger benefits the most is established.

» Both hegemon and challenger destroy each other, and a third power by default becomes the new hegemon and establishes a system from which it benefits the most.

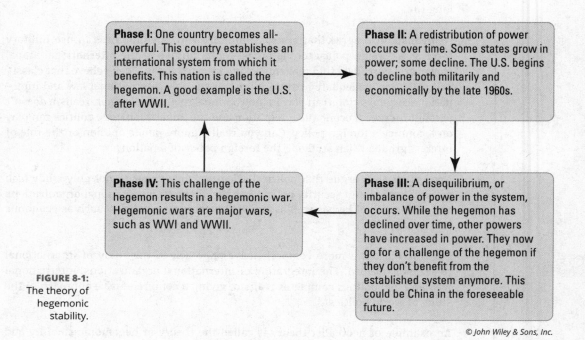

Phase I: One country becomes all-powerful. This country establishes an international system from which it benefits. This nation is called the hegemon. A good example is the U.S. after WWII.

Phase II: A redistribution of power occurs over time. Some states grow in power; some decline. The U.S. begins to decline both militarily and economically by the late 1960s.

Phase IV: This challenge of the hegemon results in a hegemonic war. Hegemonic wars are major wars, such as WWI and WWII.

Phase III: A disequilibrium, or imbalance of power in the system, occurs. While the hegemon has declined over time, other powers have increased in power. They now go for a challenge of the hegemon if they don't benefit from the established system anymore. This could be China in the foreseeable future.

© John Wiley & Sons, Inc.

FIGURE 8-1: The theory of hegemonic stability.

History provides examples of all three possible outcomes. By 1800, France under Napoleon had become the hegemon on the European continent. So the rest of Europe combined and challenged the new hegemon, and by 1814, France had been defeated and the previous international system was restored. The Concert of Europe (see Chapter 10) was established and maintained peace in Europe for about 100 years.

Second, by 1900, Germany had grown both economically and militarily in Europe and presented a challenge to the then–hegemon Great Britain. By 1914, a hegemonic war broke out, World War I. However, the hegemon prevailed, the challenger was defeated, and no changes occurred to the international system.

The third example revolves around World War II. The hegemon was still Great Britain with the U.S. going back to isolationism after World War I. The new challengers were once again Germany and this time also Italy and Japan. During the ensuing hegemonic war, the hegemon and all challengers were either destroyed or weakened, and there was a power vacuum. The U.S. by default slid into it and became the new hegemon. Next, it established our current international system.

Moving into hegemonic decline

Why do great powers decline over time? This question is all important for the U.S. With the U.S. being the hegemon for most of the time since the end of World War II, it's imperative to discover the causes of decline. If we can determine these causes, it may be possible to slow down or even reverse them. The next sections list some causes of decline and some possible solutions to them.

Overextension

With a hegemon having to control and police the international system it created, overextension, or imperial overstretch, sets in over time. Today, the U.S. has to have military bases all over the world to respond to any form of aggression quickly. In addition, military alliances, such as NATO in Europe, have to be formed to be able to exercise control globally. Although NATO has proven to be very beneficial containing first the Soviet Union during the Cold War and now Russia, this has come at an enormous cost to the U.S.

Currently, the U.S. spends the most of any country in the world on its military, more than 3 percent of its GDP, while most allies don't spend even the 2 percent minimum requested by NATO in 2014. Possible challengers such as China do spend quite a bit but don't come even close to the U.S.'s military spending (see Chapter 13). Over time, massive military expenditures can cripple an economy because the monies spent can't be used on other necessities such as keeping up a country's infrastructure or being put into research and development.

The law of increasing cost of war

The hegemon has to have the most powerful military in the world and constantly develop newer and better military technology. This is expensive, and often after the development of new weapons systems, allies and possible challengers will receive the technology for free or just steal it.

The law of stagnation

The law of stagnation is an old economic concept trying to explain why some economies grow and some don't. It stipulates the following: For an economy and a country to grow, it has to have low consumption of goods by its population, high investment in research and development in the economy, and low protection costs. For a hegemon, however, protection costs are very high, and its population consumes more than it should, which leads to not very much monies available for investment. Because investment in new technology and new infrastructure makes an economy strong and a country powerful in the long run, and the hegemon is now lacking in investment, the hegemonic country begins to decline.

Changes in economic structures

History has shown that growth in the manufacturing sector makes a country powerful. Industries such as steel, chemicals, and the military industrial complex turned the U.S. into the hegemon after World War II.

By becoming the most powerful country in the world and creating an international system from which it benefited the most, especially economically, the U.S. became very prosperous within decades. This resulted in a shift in the economy. The manufacturing sector began to decline, and the service sector increased. Although the service sector is necessary and often more profitable than the manufacturing sector, it doesn't contribute much to a country's economic power. The steel industry is one of the backbones of any powerful economy, not Starbucks selling fancy coffee.

Population growth

Although population growth is necessary for a powerful country, too much of it can be detrimental. With the U.S. growing in wealth, it became the envy of the world. Citizens from other countries wanted to share in the U.S. wealth, and more and more began to emigrate to the U.S. While legal immigration can be very beneficial, the best and the brightest wanting to move to the U.S., illegal immigration can have mixed results. Many illegal immigrants tend to be less educated and have lower skill levels than legal immigrants. For this reason, they take manual labor jobs many American citizens won't take because they believe they are too qualified. These include jobs in construction, meatpacking, and agriculture. At the same time they also rely on the hegemon's extended welfare benefits, especially free education and subsidized housing. When an economy begins to decline or economic crisis suddenly strikes, this can become an economic and political problem for the hegemon.

Solutions to decline

What can be done about these factors contributing to the decline of the hegemon? Following are some answers.

>> **Cut protection costs.** One attempt to reverse decline involves cutting the costs of protection. The U.S. has worked on this for decades. American military bases all over the world have been closed, and allies have been asked to contribute more. For example, NATO has been asked to spend more on its military and has actively contributed in the war against terrorism in Afghanistan, lowering American costs.

>> **Bring in an ally.** A new powerful ally can be brought in on the hegemon's side. Its power makes up for the hegemon's decline of power. In the early 1970s, the U.S. actively courted China as an ally against the Soviet Union. Today, relations with China have become more problematic and the emphasis has shifted to India.

>> **Reduce consumption.** To lower consumption within the hegemon's economy, hard and often politically impossible choices are needed. Keep in mind that people love to buy products (consume). Who doesn't want to have the newest iPhone? However, by consuming too much, especially by going into debt to consume, money is taken away from investment. Investment is what made the hegemon's economy powerful. The only way to reduce consumption in a society is to take purchasing power from citizens. This involves higher taxes and higher interest rates. It would be political suicide for any politician to advocate for this. For this reason, most hegemons historically have not been able to stop decline and have been replaced by another country at the top.

Doing Good: Idealism

Idealism, which is a school within liberalism (for a discussion of liberalism see Chapter 15), is the second major school of thought in international relations. It also goes back centuries. Great philosophers such as John Locke and Immanuel Kant, as well as great economists like Adam Smith and David Ricardo, can be counted among idealists. Idealism at its core has the assumption that people are good by nature, have the ability to reason, can be educated, and can change if required. Idealism becomes the dominant school of thought between the two world wars. World War II discredits it, and realism comes back to the forefront. Idealists believe in the following points:

» **Peace:** According to idealism, human nature is peaceful and good. Government in turn can be corrupted and become dangerous. Especially authoritarian regimes are dangerous for the world community. So democracies — where good people are in charge — need to be established to prevent warfare. For this reason, democracy needs to be spread throughout the world.

» **Human rights:** With people being naturally good and having an inherent dignity, governments have no right to deprive people of these rights. For this reason, human rights have to be respected by governments. If governments commit violations of their citizens' human rights, the international community has the right to intervene. Human rights are therefore at the forefront of idealism and not national self-interest as a realist would advocate.

» **International morality:** When pursuing a foreign policy, the concept of morality does matter. Certain immoral, reprehensible acts — even if they may be beneficial for the country — can't be allowed. This includes using certain types of weapons, such as poison gas, or the assassination of foreign leaders.

» **Moral values:** They do matter and people have an inherent dignity, which needs to be respected and protected.

» **Military force:** The use of military force is rejected, and peace is the ultimate objective.

» **Anarchy and aggression:** Idealists believe that anarchy and international aggression can be overcome by the creation of international institutions, such as the League of Nations or the United Nations, and the strict enforcement of international law.

» **International organizations:** War has become so horrific that it can't occur again. To outlaw it, an international organization, such as the League of Nations and later its successor the United Nations, had to be created to punish all offenders to peace. The concept of collective security, where an attack on one member equals an attack on all members, is behind the creation of the League of Nations and the United Nations. It basically outlaws war.

» **Conflict:** Instead of going to war, countries in conflict need to use international law or international organizations, such as the United Nations, to settle disputes.

>> **Harmony of interests:** Every nation struggles to improve its economic and political situation. By collaborating — helping each other out — everybody benefits and will be better off in the long run.

>> **Economic equality:** People have a right to be well off and not to suffer. For this reason, economic success and progress needs to be brought to all countries. This in turn will make the world a more peaceful place.

Being Equal through Global Humanism

Global humanism is a more left-leaning challenge to older, more traditional theories, such as idealism and realism. A global humanist believes that cooperation among all states is the ultimate goal of world politics. Increased cooperation, especially economic interdependence, will benefit every state. By being tied closer together, every state can experience the benefits of cooperation and trust, and a willingness to share will result.

Global humanism believes in the concept of equality, as expressed in the General Assembly of the United Nations, with all nations being equal regardless of military and economic power. Here are some more points that identify with global humanism:

>> **Share and share alike.** The more advanced economies have an obligation to share with the lesser developed economies. This involves a free transfer of technology as well as the forgiveness of international debt carried by the Third World.

>> **Make peace, not war.** The foreign policy of all states should be based on the principle of nonviolence; all military actions and even threats are rejected, and the primary objective of any foreign policy should be the establishment of world peace and the guarantee and protection of human rights.

>> **Everyone is equal.** All the world's problems need to be solved in cooperation and not unilaterally by any country. International organizations need to solve problems in a democratic fashion. The United Nations should be turned into a true world government, making policy for all states, and the International Court of Justice should be a world court with the power to enforce its decisions.

The spirit of cooperation should dominate the international arena, and all states need to pursue a foreign policy based on ethical principles and the highest morality as established by the world community.

Striving for Change with Constructivism

One of the newest approaches to international relations is constructivism. Developed in the 1980s and 1990s, it focuses on the values and norms that guide the behavior of states. This school of thought believes that all aspects of international relations are based on the social environment of the time they were created. Therefore, the realist assumption that the international system lacks order and states have to pursue a policy that is power based is historically and socially determined. Therefore, it can be changed.

TECHNICAL STUFF

For constructivists, all international arrangements and outcomes aren't predetermined but are human constructs and can be changed at any time. World politics is shaped by the constant interaction between states, and if changes occur within these states, international goals and objectives also change. For example, if states realize that cooperation can benefit them more than constant conflict, they'll begin to cooperate and are less likely to engage in conflict. The idea that states have to compete for power, which leads to conflict, is actually a human construction and not determined by the international system itself. It was created hundreds of years ago, but the times have changed.

Today, most states have recognized that cooperation and using international organizations, such as the United Nations, and respecting international law is more beneficial in the long run than pursuing a policy of power. In other words, if people's perceptions can change within countries, this will bring about change in the global social environment, which can change international politics. Like domestic politics, international politics is fluid and not set in stone.

Chapter 9

Creating Some Order: International Law and Diplomacy

Both realists and neorealists (see Chapter 8) believe that anarchy is at the core of the international system. There is no world government, no rules of behavior by states that can be enforced, and no world police to maintain law and order in the international system. Therefore, every country is on its own and is responsible to maintain its own security. This necessitates power, both economic and military. The whole international system is, therefore, based on nations constantly struggling to become more powerful. This results in conflict.

International law, which creates rules of behavior for nations, and international institutions, such as the United Nations (see Chapter 10), was created to overcome some of this anarchy, or lawlessness, within the international system. This chapter covers international law and diplomacy, and Chapter 10 discusses international organizations.

Defining International Law

Three structures — international organizations, international law, and diplomats — together provide the international system with some order and interaction with each other as the following diagram shows. None could work without the other, and all three are dependent on each other. For example, international organizations can make international law while they're being created by international treaties (law). At the same time, diplomats staff international organizations and are protected by international law. Finally, diplomats are responsible for the most current international law.

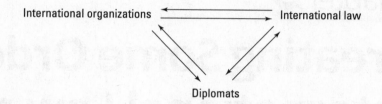

International organizations ⟶ International law

Diplomats

TECHNICAL STUFF

International law is defined as a body of rules and principles that are binding upon states. It's designed to overcome some of the anarchy within our international system, reduce conflict, and make the foreign policy of nations more predictable. Therefore, international law is designed to impact the behavior of states and maintain peace within the global arena.

International law is both similar and at the same time different from domestic law by establishing rules of behavior for nations. International law prescribes and prohibits certain behavior by states. In other words, it tells the world what actions are allowed by states and which ones are prohibited. There is, however, one major difference: Domestic law is enforceable by sovereign countries, while international law is not. If a person commits a crime in the United States, he will be punished by the U.S. government. For example, if a person breaks into a department store and steal goods, he'll be punished by the government and go to jail. Punishment for crimes acts as a deterrent and hopefully discourages people from engaging in such actions.

On the other hand, if a country violates international law, no such enforcer exists. No world government, no world police, and no international court system have the power to punish and then enforce the punishment. Following international law is voluntary and determined by a country's own national interest. If the national interest demands that you violate international law and you're powerful enough to so, a country can freely do so without having to expect any type of punishment.

International law, however, does create some law and order and predictability within the international system. Most nations do follow it most of the time, which does reduce conflict and allows for some predictability within the international system.

Studying Sources of International Law

There are four major sources of international law. The first are the great writers of the past, who have set the foundation for current international law. The second are international treaties signed on by a vast majority of all nations. Third are international organizations, such as the United Nations (see Chapter 10), which can on occasion make international law. Finally, there is customary international law. It consists of general practices accepted as law. It can be written and unwritten. In other words, states respect and follow certain rules consistently and these rules become a part of international law. An example is the prohibition of torture.

I discuss the first two sources of international law in detail in the following sections.

Reviewing the great writers of international law

When analyzing international law, two great individuals, both academics and philosophers, are studied. They are Hugo Grotius and Jean Bodin.

Hugo Grotius (see Figure 9-1) is usually referred to as the father of international law. He was born in the Netherlands in 1583. Early on, his parents determined that he was a child genius. He wrote poetry at the age of 9 and received a university degree at 14. In 1609, he published his first major work, *Mare Liberum (The Freedom of the Seas),* in which he argued that the oceans couldn't be claimed by any person or country but were the property of humankind. Thus, the oceans are free from the control of any state with the exception of a small territorial zone adjacent to a country. Today, this territorial zone is 12 miles.

REMEMBER

Grotius's ideas on the freedom of the oceans still stand today. Not one country can claim the open sea, commonly referred to as international waters, and the resources below the oceans are considered common property of humankind under the control of the United Nations.

FIGURE 9-1:
Hugo Grotius,
father of
international law.

Source: Wikimedia Commons

When the Thirty Years' War (1618–1648) broke out, Grotius was shocked by the barbarism of the war and decided that certain ground rules for warfare had to be established. He argued that war can be legal in only a few instances and that the use of force is justified only in these cases. In addition, a country had to abide by certain rules when exercising its right to use force.

Grotius argued that the legitimate use of force is limited to only a few situations. These include the right for a country to defend itself and the right to engage in reprisals, which refers to recovering lost property or territory. In other words, if another country wrongs you, you have the right to punish it.

Here are some of the current ground rules which are based on the concepts Grotius established:

>> Only a legitimate authority has the right to declare war — for example, the United Nations or a state that has been wronged by another state.

>> A country is permitted to go to war only if it has just cause. Just cause involves self-defense or the protection of the human rights of the citizens of another state. A nation can go to war only to correct a wrong and not for revenge.

>> War is only a last option, after all other alternatives, such as negotiations or arbitration by the United Nations, have been exhausted.

For Grotius, who was shocked by the atrocities committed during the Thirty Years' War, it was important that only legal and moral means can be employed to conduct a war. Civilian mass casualties were unacceptable, and today the use of biological or chemical weapons are considered unacceptable, too.

>> If a country has a legitimate reason to go to war, a formal statement, such as a declaration of war, is required. The final goal of any war is to reestablish peace, and it can't involve conquest of an enemy or parts of its territory.

Jean Bodin (see Figure 9-2) is the second major writer. In his work, *Les Six Livres de la République (The Six Books of the Republic)*, published in 1576, he developed the concept of sovereignty. Sovereignty is also called the essence of statehood. It's what makes a country legitimate in the eyes of the world.

FIGURE 9-2:
Jean Bodin created the concept of sovereignty.

Source: Wikimedia Commons

BEING A SOVEREIGN COUNTRY

Sovereignty has several aspects to it. Only if a country meets all aspects can it be considered a sovereign country. The concept of sovereignty is absolute for any nation and disappears only if the country is dissolved or annexed by another power. For example, when the sovereign state of Czechoslovakia decided to dissolve itself peacefully in 1993, it lost its sovereignty. Instead, two new countries, the Czech Republic and Slovakia, were created. Both are now considered sovereign nations.

A sovereign country enjoys complete power over its domestic and foreign policy. It can decide what form of government to have, what economic structures it wants, and how to treat its citizens as long as their human rights aren't violated. The sovereign country further has the right to engage in any actions to preserve its sovereign independence. In other words, no authority at the international level, such as the United Nations, is above the sovereign state, unless the state voluntarily confers authority on the international organization it joins.

Today, to be recognized by the world as a sovereign country, the following characteristics have to be in place:

>> A country has to have the ability to conduct its own foreign policy. Only states that make their own foreign policy are considered sovereign. For example, Greenland isn't considered a sovereign country because Denmark makes its foreign policy.

>> A country has to have the ability to make and enforce laws for its citizens. A sovereign country has full jurisdiction over its citizens and anyone else in the country, such as legal or illegal people and even foreign citizens visiting the country. For example, if Americans travel to Turkey for a vacation, they're bound by Turkish law and not American law and will face consequences if they decide to break Turkish law, even if American law differs.

>> Sovereign countries have the power to admit to and expel foreign citizens from their territory. Nobody has the right to enter a sovereign country unless he was legally admitted.

>> A sovereign country also has the right and obligation of noninterference. In other words, a sovereign state can't interfere in the affairs of another sovereign state and can expect other states not to intervene in its own domestic affairs.

EXCEPTIONS TO SOVEREIGNTY

The United Nations has created and approved exceptions to the right of noninterference.

First, the international community can interfere in a sovereign state's domestic affairs, if the United Nations approves. A good example occurred in 1999 when the United Nations approved military actions against Serbia. Serbia at the time was involved in a long conflict with Bosnia and Kosovo and was accused of human rights violations.

Second, since 2001, the international community has the right to intervene in a country's domestic affairs if that country violates the human rights of its own citizens, such as genocide on its own population.

Third, if another country commits crimes against your own citizens within its own borders, a country has the legal right to interfere in that country's affairs to protect its citizens. A good example is the invasion of Grenada by the United States in 1983. The Reagan administration accused Grenada of threatening American students studying at a local medical school and subsequently invaded the island to protect American citizens.

Finally, if a sovereign country prepares an attack against you, you have the right to interference in that country's affairs to prevent the attack. These so-called pre-emptive strikes against other countries are legal if these countries threaten your sovereignty now or in the future. The American attack on Afghanistan in 2001, to topple the Taliban regime implicated in the September 11, 2001, attacks, are a recent example.

Examining international treaties

International treaties are another source of international law. Treaties are legally binding agreements between two or more sovereign countries. If a majority of all nations sign on to a treaty, it can become a part of international law. However, treaties are binding only on countries that have actually signed and ratified them. The United States has refused to sign many multilateral international agreements recently (see Chapter 10).

REMEMBER

Treaties are also known as agreements, protocols, covenants, or conventions. Today, all international treaties have to be registered with the United Nations, which acts as a depository for all treaties. More than 500 treaties are registered with the United Nations today.

A country can voluntarily sign treaties, or it can be forced to sign them. After the end of World War I, for example, Germany was forced to sign the Treaty of Versailles, which became one of the contributing factors to the outbreak of World War II.

Can a country get out of a treaty after it has signed on to it? Most of the time, treaties are here to stay and countries are bound by them, but here are some areas that may break a treaty:

» **Expiration date:** Some treaties have expiration dates, and after a treaty expires, countries aren't bound by them anymore. For example, the treaty between the Chinese Empire and Great Britain handing Hong Kong over to the British empire had a 100-year expiration date attached to it. It expired in 1997, and Hong Kong was returned to now communist China.

» **Mutual consent:** Some treaties can be ended by mutual consent. In other words, all nations decide that a treaty has lost its value or an obligation has been performed, and they therefore decide to end the treaty. In 1967, the United States and West Germany decided to end a treaty that had given the U.S. the right to intervene in domestic affairs if democracy was threatened in West Germany. West Germany had become a model democracy, and the U.S. decided there was no need for the treaty. So both countries ended it.

» **Action performed:** Some treaties contain a clause demanding a certain action. If that action is performed, the treaty is null and void. Often, treaties force countries to make monetary compensation to other countries, and after this obligation has been fulfilled, the treaty ceases to exist.

» **Destruction of a state:** The destruction of a sovereign state can result in treaties becoming null and void. How can a treaty still be in force if the country that signed it disappears from the international arena?

The three treaties discussed in the following sections are all great examples of how treaties become a part of international law. They're still adhered to today by the world.

ASSIGNING A TREATY TO A LAND MASS

Recently, a new type of treaty has become popular. It's called a dispositive treaty. Previously, two or more countries signed a treaty, and if one of the signees ceased to exist as a country, the treaty and possible obligations attached to it would also disappear. This new type of treaty called a dispositive treaty fixed this. A dispositive treaty isn't attached to a sovereign country but a land mass. If the country disappears from the international arena, the land mass is still there, and the treaty stands. So, for example, if Italy would dissolve itself into several states, all the treaties signed by Italy would be null and void. However, a dispositive treaty would still stand and be applicable to a successor state because it's attached not to a country but to a piece of land.

The Outer Space Treaty

By the 1960s, both the United States and the Soviet Union were working on space programs. The U.S. had successfully put a man on the moon, and the Soviet Union was able to put a man into orbit for the first time. Suddenly, fears arose that the two powers would use outer space and the moon and the stars for their own political and military purposes. For this reason, the international community got together with the help of the United Nations to make sure that outer space and the moon and stars could be used only for peaceful purposes. After long negotiations, a treaty was signed in 1967 to accomplish this. Today, 150 nations have signed on to the treaty, and it has become one of the most successful treaties since the end of World War II. The treaty stipulates the following:

>> No country has the right to contaminate outer space. For example, no nuclear waste can be stored in outer space.

>> No country can militarize outer space. For example, no nuclear weapons can be put in outer space or on the moon.

>> The moon and the stars can be used only for peaceful purposes.

>> Any nation has the legal obligation to tell the rest of the world when it engages in activities in outer space or on the moon. For example, every time a country puts a satellite into space, it has to inform the rest of the global community what it's doing.

>> Any country whose activities in outer space cause damage to another country is legally liable. For example, if a satellite comes crashing down and destroys property in another country (which actually did happen when a Soviet satellite crashed into a Canadian home), the country has the legal obligation to compensate the other country for the damages it caused.

>> If a country's astronaut, due to an accident or mistake, comes back to earth and lands in a foreign country, he has to be treated like a diplomat. He has immediate full diplomatic immunity and has to be returned to his home country without being detained or questioned.

The Antarctica Treaty

The Antarctica Treaty, better known as the Antarctic Treaty System (ATS), is another great example of a treaty becoming international law. It was signed in 1961, and the Outer Space Treaty was in part based on it. The treaty turns Antarctica, the only continent without a native human population, into the possession of humankind and prohibits any kind of military activity, especially the testing of nuclear weapons, on the continent.

According to the treaty, Antarctica can be used only for peaceful purposes. Therefore, scientific research and exploration can be conducted, even by military personnel. Interestingly, any research findings have to be shared with the rest of the world, and every time new research teams are deployed by a country, the whole world has to be informed. Other countries also retain the right of surprise inspections to make sure no military activity occurs. For example, the U.S. has the legal right to inspect a Russian research facility in Antarctica to make sure the Russians don't engage in secret military activities.

The treaty also stipulates that Antarctica can't be turned into a waste dump, and any storing of waste, especially nuclear waste, is prohibited. By 2019, 54 countries had signed the treaty, including major powers such as the U.S., Great Britain, France, and Russia. The major exception is China, which hasn't yet formally signed the treaty.

The Law of the Sea

A third example of a treaty becoming international law is the Law of the Sea Treaty. It's based on the writings of Hugo Grotius, discussed previously. The Treaty has been updated many times, the last major update occurring in 1982, and stipulates the following:

>> **Internal waters are controlled by its nation.** Any internal waters, such as rivers and lakes, are controlled by the nation the body of water is contained in. For example the U.S. exercises full control over Lake Michigan.

>> **There is a territorial sea.** It's the part of an ocean that is adjacent to a country. For example, the Gulf of Mexico borders the U.S., mostly Florida. Therefore, the U.S. controls it. Territorial waters can extend 12 miles from a country into the open sea. Until 1982, territorial waters could extend only 3 miles in to the open sea.

>> **No one country can claim the high or open sea.** This includes the great oceans of the world, such as the Atlantic Ocean or the Indian Ocean. No power can claim these oceans; they are the property of humankind.

REMEMBER

Today, many countries claim fishery, or economic zones, which can extend up to 200 miles from a country into the high sea. These economic zones have become important today because they can contain important natural resources such as oil or natural gas.

TECHNICAL STUFF

The resources contained under the oceans and outside of the 12-mile territorial waters and the 200-mile economic zones are considered the property of humankind. They are controlled by the United Nations. In 1994, the United Nations established the International Seabed Authority (ISA), which can authorize the right to mine for natural resources under the oceans. However, countries or private corporations have to pay a fee or royalties to be able to do so.

Connecting with Diplomacy

When countries began having relations with each other, it became necessary to create permanent structures in countries to facilitate having constant contact between nations. These facilities are called embassies, consulates, or even trade missions and are staffed by professionals diplomats.

A *diplomat* is a professional with special training, usually provided by a country's foreign service. According to the Vienna Convention on Diplomatic Relations, which has become a part of international law, the functions of diplomats are

>> **Representation:** Diplomats must represent their country in a foreign nation and must support their country's political positions. Other countries will judge a country by the quality of its diplomats, which in turn can enhance a country's prestige abroad. The more professional a country's diplomats are, the more respected a country will be globally. Historically, the British and French foreign services are the most professional foreign services in the world.

>> **Observation:** Most diplomats are in foreign countries to observe. They read newspapers, watch television, listen to the radio, and have contact with the local population. They then write reports summarizing their observations. Diplomats are, therefore, more like teachers, observing and reporting activities, and not like James Bond–type spies.

>> **Negotiation:** Diplomats are trained in the art of negotiation. They're involved in negotiating treaties and trade agreements. Diplomats always have to keep their own country's interest in mind and have to be patient, friendly, and aware of other cultures or customs.

>> **Support:** Most low-level diplomats are involved in activities providing support to citizens traveling abroad. These activities include dealing with lost passports, stolen wallets, or helping citizens accused of criminal activity in foreign countries.

To be able to fulfill these activities at the highest level, diplomats need to be trained well. In the U.S., future diplomats attend special foreign service training where they're taught foreign languages and are made aware of other nations' cultures and customs.

REMEMBER

The U.S. didn't have a professional foreign service until 1924 when Congress passed the Rogers Act, also referred to as the Foreign Service Act of 1924. It created the U.S. foreign service, which is headed by the secretary of state and is in charge of all diplomats and their assignments.

Being a successful diplomat

While undergoing training, diplomats must also have the following characteristic to be successful in presenting their country well:

» **Truthfulness:** Diplomats always have to be truthful and can't lie. If they do, they'll lose all credibility and nobody will ever trust them again. In addition, it will hurt the prestige of the sending country, and other nations will be less likely to deal with it.

» **Precision:** Diplomats have to be accurate and precise in their reporting. They can't leave out vital information or, even worse, exaggerate facts. They must keep in mind that their reports are the foundation for their country's foreign policy.

» **Calmness:** Diplomats need to keep their temper in check. Foreign diplomats may prod them or possibly insult them, but they need to keep their calm. Diplomats with a bad temper have caused wars in the past.

» **Modesty:** Good diplomats are modest in nature and don't brag about their country's personal wealth. This can be very offensive to other diplomats coming from poorer, mostly third-world countries.

Regulating diplomacy: The Vienna Convention on Diplomatic Relations

The Vienna Convention on Diplomatic Relations is one of the oldest treaties on file and has become a part of international law. When the modern nation-states were created after 1648, it became necessary to regulate diplomatic relations between countries. Permanent missions, today called embassies, were established and staffed with diplomats. A system of rules was established to regulate diplomatic activities and to protect diplomats serving abroad. To be able to do so, the Reglement de Vienne (Vienna Regulations) was agreed upon in 1814/1815 and has been updated several times since. The latest update was the Vienna Convention on Diplomatic Relations of 1961. The following discusses the most important rules and regulations in regard to diplomacy in force today.

» Diplomatic relations between countries are by mutual consent. In other words, both states have to agree to have diplomatic relations, and a state can't be forced to have relations with another country. Currently, the U.S. has no diplomatic relations with North Korea or Iran and can't be forced to start having diplomatic relations with the two.

BECOMING A DIPLOMAT IN THE U.S.

Becoming a diplomat in the U.S. isn't easy. First, a person needs to study a topic related to international diplomacy, such as political science, international relations, history, sociology, or anthropology. A bachelor's degree in one of these disciplines is a must, and a master's degree is encouraged to make an applicant more attractive to the foreign service.

A foreign language is another requirement. Some foreign languages, such as German, French, or Spanish, aren't much in demand. A more exotic language, such as Russian, Chinese or any Middle Eastern language, will make the applicant more attractive to the foreign service.

The final step is to take a very competitive national exam, the Foreign Service Exam. The exam consists of an interview, a written test, and a simulated negotiation exercise. Finally, the applicant has to pass a background check and a medical exam. Then, after passing all the steps, the successful candidate may have to wait for up to a year until a vacancy opens up in the foreign service. At this point, the applicant will be finally admitted to the foreign service.

» After agreeing to diplomatic relations, the two countries will have to find a piece of land to build the respective embassies on. These embassies are exempt from local laws and have to be protected by the receiving country. In 1979, Iran failed to protect the American embassy in Teheran. The embassy was attacked by Iranian militants and American diplomats were taken hostage. This was a clear violation of international law, and President Carter authorized a rescue attempt that failed. The American diplomats were finally released in January 1980.

» The country that receives a foreign diplomat has to agree to the specific diplomat. For example, when the Russian government sends a new ambassador to the U.S., the U.S. government has to agree to receive him, and vice versa.

» At any time, a country can declare a diplomat persona-non-grata (nonacceptable), and that diplomat will have to return to his home country. Just recently, the U.S. declared two Chinese diplomats unacceptable for having spied on American military installations, and they were sent home to China.

>> Diplomats enjoy full diplomatic immunity while serving abroad. They can't be detained or arrested for any type of crime they may commit or be accused of. Their residencies and even their families enjoy the same type of immunity. The worst that can happen to a diplomat is that he will be asked to leave the country he's stationed in. For example, in 1997, a diplomat from the former Soviet Republic of Georgia drove while being intoxicated in Washington, D.C., and killed an American citizen. The U.S. government couldn't arrest him and charge him with murder.

Note: Diplomatic immunity can be waived by the country the diplomat is from. In this case, the government of Georgia waived the diplomat's immunity after intense pressure from the American government, and he was returned to the U.S. and subsequently tried and sentenced to prison.

Chapter **10**

Creating Order through International Organizations

The modern state system created in 1648 brings about a need for continuous contact between states, especially the great powers of Europe. Both international law and diplomacy (see Chapter 9) and the creation of international organizations fill this need.

This chapter covers the first true international organization regulating relations between states, the Concert of Europe. It provided the foundation for future international organizations, such as the League of Nations and the United Nations.

Next the chapter looks at the League of Nations, the predecessor to the United Nations, and discusses its failures and final dissolution in 1946. Most of the chapter then deals with the United Nations, established in 1945, covering its origins, its purpose, and its structure. The final section of the chapter deals with the protection of human rights in the current international arena.

Getting Together in Europe — The Concert of Europe

After Europe had been at war for more than 20 years, the great European powers — Great Britain, France, Russia, Prussia, and Austria — decided that it was time to restore peace in Europe and come up with a set of rules to prevent future conflicts. They held a Congress (meeting) in Vienna from 1814 until 1815, and here they established what is today called the Concert of Europe. The Concert of Europe lasted until the outbreak of World War I and provided Europe for almost a century with peace (despite some minor conflicts).

The Concert of Europe was based on following international law to solve conflict peacefully and on maintaining the balance of power in Europe (see Chapter 8). Some of the greatest diplomats of the time, such as Prince Metternich of Austria, oversaw the system. The idea behind the Congress System was simple: As long as all great powers in Europe were similar in size and power and followed established rules, no conflict would occur. Whenever a problem or conflict arose, the five great powers would call for a Congress and get together to discuss the issue and resolve it peacefully.

Between 1815 and 1884, there were 17 Congresses held by the great powers to help resolve disputes and maintain peace in Europe. Among the most famous and influential Congresses held was the 1878 Congress of Berlin, which prevented war in the Balkans and resulted in the creation of many Eastern European states such as Bulgaria and Romania. The second Congress of Berlin, held in 1884, still impacts the world today. It divided up Africa among the major European powers to avoid conflict over colonies and established most current African countries and their borders.

Calling for a League of Nations

The outbreak of World War I in 1914 changed everything. By 1914, the five great powers had formed a rival two-alliance system in Europe consisting of the Triple Entente (Great Britain, France, and Russia) and the Triple Alliance (Germany, Austria-Hungary, and Italy). These two alliances slowly undermined and then destroyed the Concert of Europe, which was based on the balance of power in Europe and on resolving conflicts peacefully. By 1914, the two-alliance system had replaced the Concert of Europe and the concert system collapsed. World War I was the result.

By 1918, when World War I ended, the world was in shock. World War I was supposed to last for only a few months, and most Europeans believed it would be a traditional war fought by professional militaries. Nobody foresaw the use of poison gas or new weapons like the tank and airplanes. Many politicians, including U.S. President Woodrow Wilson, decided that war had become so horrible that it could not occur again. Woodrow Wilson, therefore, proposed the creation of an international organization, called the League of Nations, to prevent future wars.

In January of 1918, President Woodrow Wilson outlined his famous Fourteen Points as a condition for peace in Europe. After Germany surrendered in November of 1918, he was ready to put his points into place. Right away, he ran into problems.

Coming up with 14 points

President Wilson proposed 14 points as a condition for peace in Europe and believed, if implemented, these policies would outlaw war in the future. The most famous of his 14 points were:

» **Abolition of secret diplomacy:** Many politicians and academics had blamed secret diplomacy for the outbreak of World War I. Wilson proposed that all diplomatic activity be made public so that everybody had a chance to scrutinize it.

» **Reduction of armaments:** The reduction was through arms control, where countries limited the amount of weapons they possessed, and disarmament, where countries destroyed existing weapons.

» **Removal of international trade barriers:** Wilson was an idealist (see Chapter 8), who believed that closer economic cooperation between states resulted in less conflict among nations.

» **The restoration of the Belgium state (occupied by Germany) and the creation of a new Polish state:** Poland had ceased to exist as a state since the Seven Years' War (1756–1763), where it had been divided between Germany, Russia, and Austria.

» **Creation of a League of Nations:** The League was to be an international organization open to all sovereign countries in the world. This new organization was based on the concept of collective security, where an attack on one member equaled an attack on all members, thereby outlawing war.

Although President Wilson was successful in implementing some of his points, he failed with others. He did succeed in restoring Poland and Belgium and creating the League of Nations.

The U.S. Senate refused to ratify the treaty allowing for the United States to join the League of Nations, because it feared the commitment of American troops to fight international aggression. Ironically, President Wilson created the League of Nations, and received a Nobel Peace Prize for doing so, but his own country refused to join the organization.

Starting weak as an international organization

The League of Nations was up and running by January 1920. It was headquartered in Geneva, Switzerland, and 41 countries joined it. From the beginning, the League was handicapped because some of the most powerful countries in the world had either refused to join or weren't allowed to join. These included the U.S., Germany, and Russia. For this reason, the two most powerful countries left, Great Britain and France, took over the League and used it as a foreign policy tool to further their own interests. This undermined the credibility of the organization from the beginning.

Structuring the League of Nations

The structure of the League of Nations was very similar to the current United Nations. The League Assembly was the legislative part of the League of Nations. Every member country had one vote, and the assembly met once a year. If there was an act of aggression or any other problem, the League could be called into session at any time. The assembly's major functions included allowing new states to join the League and control of the budget for the organization. The major problem with the League Assembly was that all voting had to be unanimous, giving each member country an absolute veto. Not much was accomplished because of this.

Using a League Council

The League Council was very similar to today's Security Council (see the next section). The Council's main task was to maintain peace globally and punish any type of international aggression. In the beginning, only four countries sat on the Council: Great Britain, France, Japan, and Italy. In 1926, Germany was allowed to join. The Council met five times a year to oversee the state of the world. It also could be called into session during times of crisis.

Failing in times of crisis

Very quickly, problems with the League of Nations became visible. First, unanimous voting allowed for any member to block actions demanded by the rest of the

League, which resulted in inaction. Second, the great powers used the League freely to pursue their own political interests, and whenever they committed an act of aggression, it went unpunished.

TECHNICAL STUFF

Italy, a member of the League Council, freely committed acts of aggression that went unpunished. For example, it invaded Ethiopia in 1935. The League verbally condemned the Italian aggression but took no effort to stop it. Japan was the other Council member that violated the League's rules against aggression. It attacked Manchuria in 1931, and again the League failed to respond. By the 1930s, it had become clear that the League of Nations was a paper tiger without the willingness to punish international aggression.

Third, the League didn't believe that it had the power to intervene within a country's internal affairs, even if a country violated its citizens' human rights. Therefore, the League ignored the genocide committed by Soviet leader Stalin on the Ukraine. The League just stood by as millions died without lifting a finger.

Finally, major powers decided to start to leave the League after noticing its ineffectiveness or for being condemned for an act of aggression that they had committed. This left the League even weaker and more helpless. Germany and Japan left in 1933 and Italy four years later. The Soviet Union was expelled in 1939 after it attacked Finland. Suddenly, the league was left with only two great powers, Great Britain and France.

By the time World War II started in 1939, the League had become a weak organization without any credibility and was powerless to prevent the war.

Needing a United Nations

As early as 1941, before the U.S. even entered World War II, President Franklin D. Roosevelt and British Prime Minister Winston Churchill decided that a new organization was needed to maintain peace in the world. They believed that the League of Nations was fundamentally flawed and needed to be replaced. For this reason, they signed the Atlantic Charter in 1941, which called for disarmament, economic cooperation after the war, and the creation of a new international organization to keep peace globally. The 26 nations that signed on to the charter further renounced the use of force to make territorial gains.

In January of 1942, these 26 nations signed the Declaration of the United Nations, which became the foundation for the future United Nations. Every country that signed on to the declaration pledged to fight the Axis powers — countries opposing the allies, mainly Germany, Italy and Japan — and to create a new international organization to maintain peace in the world after the war had been won.

After agreeing on the structure of the new United Nations in 1944, 50 countries met in San Francisco to approve the U.N. Charter, establishing the United Nations. The United Nations came into existence on October 24, 1945, and was moved to New York City, where John D. Rockefeller had donated the land to house the newly established organization (see Figure 10-1).

FIGURE 10-1:
United Nations headquarters in New York City.

Source: Library of Congress

A few month later, April 26, 1946, the League of Nations was disbanded, and all its assets were transferred to the United Nations.

REMEMBER

President Franklin D. Roosevelt coined the term *United Nations* for the future international organization replacing the League of Nations.

Sharing similarities with the League of Nations

The United Nations and the League of Nations share many similarities. Basically, the objective of maintaining peace in the world and avoiding conflict remain the same. The concept of collective security where an attack on one country equals an attack on all member countries also remains intact. Structurally, there are many similarities, too. The League Council was renamed Security Council and was asked to maintain peace in the world. It also had permanent members that received an absolute veto power.

The League Assembly was turned into the General Assembly, where each member state received one vote. The major difference between the League Assembly and the General Assembly of the United Nations was in voting procedures. While the League Assembly had to pass resolutions unanimously, the new General Assembly of the United Nations can pass most policies by a simple majority vote (a few select have to be passed with a two-thirds vote).

Setting up a Charter for the United Nations

The Charter of the United Nations is basically a constitution for the U.N. It consist of 19 chapters and discusses the purpose, structure, and functions of the organization. It's binding on all member states. All signatories have to agree to

- » Equality of all states, regardless of size, military, or economic might
- » Respect for international law and renunciation of force to gain territory
- » Maintenance of international peace and security
- » Development of friendly relations among states
- » Respect of equal rights and self-determination of people
- » Promotion of human rights and fundamental freedoms
- » A belief in equal and fundamental rights of all individuals

At the same time, signatories also have to fulfill obligations. These include

- » An obligation to enforce the charter by refusing aid to any state that is violating it
- » An obligation to settle all international disputes peacefully and not to use force
- » The renunciation of the use of force to gain territory from another sovereign state
- » Noninterference in a state's domestic affairs except if allowed by the United Nations

To see the full Charter of the United Nations, check out `www.un.org/en/charter-united-nations`.

Looking at the six structures of the United Nations

The Charter of the United Nations (see previous section) outlines the structure of the United Nations. According to it, the United Nations consists of six different structures or organs. The following sections outline those structures.

The Security Council

The Security Council is the most powerful of the six structures making up the United Nations.. It was specifically established to maintain peace throughout the world and only it is able to punish aggression and mediate conflict.

The Security Council deals with any threat to peace. This can be open warfare between states or conflict within a state. Today, the Security Council also acts in cases of domestic oppression, human rights violations, and genocide.

REMEMBER

Only the Security Council can recommend the use of force to punish aggression or vote to send peacekeepers to hostile parts of the world (for more on peacekeepers, see the section "Keeping the peace," later in this chapter). The use of force is usually a last resort, and the Security Council has rarely given the go-ahead to initiate military force.

CREATING A SECURITY COUNCIL

The Security Council consists of 15 member states. Five are the permanent members of the Security Council — the U.S., Russia, China, France, and Great Britain. They are the only members that have the power of absolute veto, meaning that they can veto any resolution before the Council and thus prevent any kind of action by the Council.

The other ten members rotate on a two-year basis and are picked by the General Assembly. They don't have the power of veto. The United Nations has placed some geographical limitations on the ten nonpermanent members. Two have to come from Western Europe and one from Eastern Europe. Two member states have to be from Asia and three from Africa. And, finally, two need to come from Latin America.

All resolutions in the Security Council, if no veto has been cast, are passed by a 60 percent majority vote. In other words, 9 out of 15 votes are required to pass any kind of resolution.

The International Court of Justice

The International Court of Justice (ICJ) is the third structure making up the United Nations. Many people call it the "World Court," and it's located in The Hague in the Netherlands. The Court consists of 15 judges, jointly selected by the Security Council and the General Assembly. The judges serve nine-year terms and can stand for reappointment. Established in 1945, the Court doesn't deal with many cases, having heard only about 177 of them since its inception. That equals to about two and a half cases a year. The Court's main functions are to settle legal disputes between U.N. member states and to give advisory opinions on legal questions submitted to it by the United Nations.

REMEMBER

Keep in mind that the ICJ is very different from any domestic court. While domestic courts can render legally binding decisions and enforce them, the ICJ can't. The ICJ differs from domestic courts in the following ways:

» **No compulsory jurisdiction exists.** The ICJ can't pick any cases as domestic courts can. For it to be able to rule on a case, both states involved in a dispute have to agree to have the case heard by the Court. In other words, a country can commit an act of aggression and then refuse to have the case heard by the Court.

» **It isn't bound by its previous decisions,** whereas U.S. domestic courts are (stare decisis). The ICJ can use the doctrine of "ex aequo et bono," which means that it can render a judgment on the basis of what is just and fair at the time and doesn't have to base its decision on precedent.

» **The Court's decisions can't be enforced and are therefore more advisory in nature.** While the Security Council has the legal power to enforce the Court's decision, one of the permanent members of the Council can veto it.

   In other words, the two parties to a case have to voluntarily agree to not only have the case heard but also abide by the decision. On occasion in the past, more powerful countries have refused to abide by the Court's ruling after it went against their national interests.

The Economic and Social Council

The Economic and Social Council (ECOSOC) is the fourth structure making up the United Nations. It consists of 54 member countries selected by the General Assembly. Each nation serves a three-year term and then gets replaced with a different country. ECOSOC is in charge of 14 specialized agencies and five regional commissions (one each in Africa, Asia, Latin America, Europe, and Western Asia/Middle East), which are the major U.N. forums to discuss international economic, social, and cultural issues. Recent issues ECOSOC has dealt with include elimination of poverty, starvation, women's rights, human rights, illegal drugs, and education. ECOSOC further initiates studies and organizes international conferences to discuss these issues globally.

Today, ECOSOC has become a major part of the United Nations discussing important issues of the day and passing policy proposals (resolutions) on them. Each resolution passed goes to the General Assembly for discussion. In other words, ECOSOC can only recommend policies to the General Assembly and not make policy itself.

The Secretariat and the Secretary General

The Secretariat is the fifth structure and is the United Nations bureaucracy. It administers all U.N. programs and monitors the various agencies attached to the United Nations. It provides basic services such as translating speeches and documents and organizing international conferences. It further serves as the body's research organization, compiling social and economic data and preparing reports for the United Nations to use. Finally, the Secretariat is also the United Nations media and information center. It publishes reports and books and maintains the organization's website.

The Secretary General heads the Secretariat and is the agency's top administrator. The Secretary General is in charge of the United Nations budget and is required to present an annual report to all members on the state of the United Nations. The Secretary General is also considered the world's top diplomat, traveling the globe and providing assistance in settling disputes peacefully. The United Nations has had nine Secretary Generals. The current (2020) Secretary General is Antonio Guterres from Portugal, who is serving his first term.

The Trusteeship Council

The Trusteeship Council is the final structure of the United Nations. It was created to administer former colonial holdings and transition them to independence. The last trust territory was Palau, which received independence in 1994. Since then, the operations of the Trusteeship Council have been suspended; however, the General Assembly or Security Council can call the Trusteeship Council back into session at any time.

Budgeting for an international organization

The budget of the United Nations for the fiscal year 2018–2019 was $5.4 billion with an additional $6.5 billion for peacekeeping missions (the budget excludes funding for other organizations attached to the United Nations such as the World

Health Organization, the United Nations Development Program, and the World Food Program). The United Nations is funded by its 193 members, using a formula based on a country's gross national product (GNP), external debt, and per capita income. The formula creates percentage shares per country, ranging from 22 percent to 0.001 percent, and is reviewed every three years. Currently, based on the formula, the United States has to pay 22 percent of the United Nations' budget. China ranks second with 12 percent. The top 20 economies in the world pay about 84 percent of the United Nations' budget. The other 173 countries pay only 16 percent of the budget.

Keeping the peace

Peacekeeping has become the most visible and the most expensive function of the United Nations today. In 2019, 97,509 peacekeepers served in 13 countries at a cost of $6.69 billion. Since the first peacekeeping operation in 1948, which was put into place to supervise the cease-fire between the newly created state of Israel and the surrounding Arab states, there have been 71 peacekeeping missions with 13 still ongoing. More than 130 nations have contributed troops to United Nations peacekeeping missions, and more than 1 million men and women have served as peacekeepers. Sadly, 3,892 of them were killed while serving.

Peacekeeping

The United Nations defines peacekeeping as "a unique and dynamic instrument developed by the Organization as a way to help countries torn by conflict create the conditions for lasting peace." Functions of peacekeeping include not just negotiating cease-fires to end conflicts but also making sure that no new conflicts arise.

Peacekeepers monitor and observe the peace established between countries, assist in implementing peace agreements, and often serve as a buffer zone between two hostile countries.

Peacekeeping forces are divided into two categories. First, there are observers. These peacekeepers don't carry any weapons and monitor only cease-fires or peace agreements between nations. Second, there are the peacekeepers. They are lightly armed, and they have the right to defend themselves if attacked.

REMEMBER

Peacekeepers can be deployed in a conflict between two countries only if both countries agree to the deployment. In other words, consent has to be given by both countries. If one country changes its mind, peacekeepers have to be withdrawn right away.

Peacemaking

In the 1990s, a new function for peacekeepers was created. With interstate warfare becoming less common, more and more conflict arose within countries. This change in international violence resulted in a new task for peacekeepers, referred to as peacemaking. Today, peacemaking has overtaken peacekeeping as the major function of the United Nations.

How does peacemaking differ from peacekeeping? While traditional peacekeeping involves maintaining the peace between two countries, peacemaking involves creating and maintaining peace within a country. Peacemaking often involves state building or even state rebuilding. After a state has fallen apart due to civil strife, peacemakers come in to rebuild it. Peacemakers aren't always trained soldiers, and their functions involve police functions (restoring law and order), monitoring elections, rebuilding an infrastructure, creating an educational structure, and establishing medical services. Peacemakers often are police officers, engineers, medical doctors, teachers, and academics.

Approving peacekeeping and peacemaking operations

According to the Charter of the United Nations, the Security Council has to authorize the use of peacekeepers and peacemakers. To use peacekeepers and/or peacemakers, the following steps have to be taken. First, the Security Council approves the use of peacekeepers and peacemakers. Next, the Department of Peacekeeping Operations plans for the deployment of U.N. forces. It asks for contributions of troops from member states (the U.N. doesn't possess an independent military force) and then puts the force together. Usually, the country that supplies the most troops gets to name the commander of the force.

TECHNICAL
STUFF

Today, peacekeeping has become big business for many third-world countries. The United Nations pays $1,410 daily for every soldier who is used as a peacekeeper. Many third-world countries have taken advantage of this and are contributing thousands of ill-equipped and untrained soldiers to make millions in profit.

REMEMBER

On rare occasions, the United Nations will contract with an outside force to function as a peacekeeper/peacemaker. The U.N. has used NATO in the former Yugoslavia and Afghanistan for this purpose.

Guaranteeing human rights

Human rights are commonly defined as rights essential to human beings. Without human rights, human beings can't fully develop and reach human potential. Human rights are rights possessed by all individuals by virtue of being human, regardless of their status as citizens of particular states or members of a group or organization.

Human rights can be classified into three categories. These are usually labeled first-, second-, and third-generation human rights.

Since 1948, the United Nations has been working on the three categories of human rights. It started with first-generation human rights and then slowly moved to second- and third-generation rights. The most important covenants or treaties in regard to human rights are in the next sections.

First-generation human rights

First-generation human rights refer to civil and political rights. The Constitution of the United States guarantees many of these rights. Examples are first amendment rights, such as freedom of speech, assembly, press, and religion. Also included are equality before the law, a right to impartial trials, and prohibition from arbitrary arrests.

Political rights include the right to contribute to policy making through free electoral participation and rights associated with the rule of law.

Finally, general rights of every human being are included — such as, prohibition on slavery, torture, and other forms of cruel and unusual punishment.

Second-generation human rights

Second-generation human rights are usually economic rights. Examples are the right to food and shelter as well as the right to an adequate standard of living and protection against unemployment.

Further economic rights include the right to join unions and a guarantee of welfare benefits such as social security.

Third-generation human rights

The third category of human rights refers to social and cultural rights, such as the right to an education, the right to peaceful development, the right to self-determination, cultural diversity, the protection of minority cultures, and the right to live in a healthy environment. For example, the right not to live in a heavily polluted area is a third-generation human right.

Setting up the International Bill of Human Rights

The International Bill of Human Rights consists of the three most important pieces of international legislation in regard to human rights. They are the Universal Declaration of Human Rights (1948), the International Covenant on Civil and Political Rights (1966), and the International Covenant on Economic, Social, and Cultural Rights (1966).

The Universal Declaration of Human Rights (1948)

The most comprehensive definition of what human rights actually entail was given to us on December 10, 1948, when the General Assembly of the United Nations adopted and proclaimed the Universal Declaration of Human Rights.

After World War II had ended, the international community was shocked by the atrocities committed during the war. The United Nations decided that human life had to be protected and human rights mattered. For this reason, the United Nations created the Human Rights Commission in 1947. It was chaired by former First Lady Eleanor Roosevelt (see Figure 10-2).

FIGURE 10-2: Mrs. Eleanor Roosevelt reporting to Pres. Harry Truman on her trip to Geneva as a representative of the U.N. Human Rights Commission.

Source: Eleanor Roosevelt with Harry Truman/Getty images

Under Eleanor Roosevelt's able leadership, the commission created the Universal Declaration of Human Rights, or UDHR. International experts on human rights from all over the world and belonging to many different religions came together to work on the declaration. The committee decided that human rights were indivisible and that all the rights listed in the UDHR were linked to each other.

The UDHR lists basic principles, such as dignity, liberty, and equality in the first two articles, while the latter articles address issues such as political, economic, cultural, and social rights.

All signatories agreed that human rights were guaranteed in their respective countries.

REMEMBER

Like all other United Nations General Assembly resolutions, the UDHR wasn't binding on any nation in the world but just a recommendation on how to treat human beings. For this reason, the United Nations decided to turn it into international law through a series of treaties, binding on all signatories. These treaties created the International Bill of Human Rights.

The International Covenant on Civil and Political Rights (ICCPR)

The International Covenant on Civil and Political Rights (ICCPR) is a multilateral treaty passed by the United Nations General Assembly in 1966. It went into force in 1976. The treaty mandates that all signatories guarantee civil and political rights of individuals. Examples include freedom of speech, freedom of assembly, and freedom of religion. In addition, the right to due process and fair trial are included. The final right is the right to be able to participate in policy making through free electoral processes. As of 2019, 173 nations have signed and ratified the treaty. Twenty nations, including, Cuba, China, and Saudi Arabia, have not yet ratified the treaty.

The International Covenant on Economic, Social, and Cultural Rights (ICESCR)

The same year, 1966, the United Nations also passed the International Covenant on Economic, Social, and Cultural Rights (ICESCR). It also came into force in 1976.

All signatories to the treaty have to provide their citizens with economic, social, and cultural rights. Examples include the right to unionize, the right to receive an adequate education, and the right to an adequate standard of living. Therefore, the treaty deals with second- and third-generation human rights.

As of 2018, 169 countries have signed and ratified the treaty. The U.S. hasn't ratified the ICESCR because it believes that second- and third-generation human rights aren't inherent rights of people but rather desirable social goals, which have to be implemented by respective states, with America's help if so desired.

Today, most countries agree on first-generation human rights; however, there's a split in the international community on whether second- and third-generation human rights are actual rights or desirable social goals.

Chapter 11

Not Going to War: The Cold War 1946–1991

From the creation of the modern state system in 1648 until the end of World War II, Europe had controlled most of the world. Both military and economic power had been concentrated in the hands of the great European powers, which in turn had subjugated most of the world. World War II changed all of this. When the war ended, Europe laid in ruins and the great powers of the past, Great Britain, France, Italy, and Germany, had lost their great power status, both militarily and economically. This changed the international system from a multi-polar one, with more than two great powers playing a role in international politics, to a bipolar system with only two powers, the United States and the Soviet Union, dominating the international system. In other words, World War II changed international affairs forever by creating a bipolar structure resulting in conflict between the two great powers left. The conflict between the United States and the Soviet Union is referred to as the Cold War, an era dominated by competition between the two new superpowers, smaller conflicts fought by allies and proxies of the two superpowers as well as the nuclear arms race.

This chapter deals with the causes of the Cold War and highlights Cold War events. The second part of the chapter then looks at the nuclear arms race.

Explaining the Cold War

When World War II ended in 1945, the United States and the Soviet Union were the last two great powers standing. They had been collaborating for the last four years to defeat Germany, but conflict between the two began. With the defeat of Germany, Italy, and Japan as well as the collapse of the British and French empires, a power vacuum had been created in Europe and Asia. The Soviet Union, under the leadership of Joseph Stalin, was eager to fill this vacuum and assume control of the European continent. It began to expand aggressively by 1946, beginning what is known as the Cold War. The Cold War lasted for 45 years until the Soviet Union collapsed in 1991.

Why did the Cold War break out? Was it inevitable, or are there people or countries to blame? There are many explanations for the outbreak of the Cold War, and the next sections discuss some of the most common and popular ones.

Using systemic explanations

Systemic explanations, as discussed in Chapter 8, believe that the international system itself is the major cause of conflict within the international system. For systems theorists, the leaders of countries don't matter much and neither do conditions within states themselves. What matters is only the system.

They argue that with the collapse of the multipolar international structure after World War II, a new structure, namely a bipolar one, was created. In a bipolar structure, the two major powers always clash. It makes no difference who they are — they could have been South Africa and Argentina, and the two would have still clashed.

Applying history

A second explanation uses history. Many historians look at the Cold War as a continuation of hostilities that began in 1917, when tsarist Russia collapsed and the United States began to meddle in Russian affairs.

In 1918, the U.S. was very upset after tsarist rule in Russia had collapsed and Vladimir Lenin, who had taken over the country in the fall of 1917, nationalized all property, including foreign-held property. This included American-held investments. The U.S. decided to intervene in the Russian Civil War (1918–1921) to defeat Lenin. For several years, the U.S. supplied weapons to the anti-Communist forces and even deployed Marines on Russian soil. According to many historians, this resulted in distrust between the U.S. and Russia, which became the Soviet Union in 1922. The Cold War, therefore, is just a continuation of conflict that started way back in 1918.

Misinterpreting actions

A third explanation focuses on individual perceptions of events during World War II. The theory claims that the two sides misunderstood the actions undertaken. For example, Joseph Stalin never forgave the Allies for not opening up a second front against Germany until 1944. He wanted it a lot earlier than 1944 to provide relief to his troops.

Stalin believed that the Western leaders purposely delayed a second front so that he and Adolf Hitler would destroy each other. The Allies, on the other hand, believed that Stalin had agreed to free democratic elections in Eastern Europe after it had been liberated from the Germans. Stalin had done so, but for him, Soviet-style elections were democratic.

Basically, there were many misunderstandings and misperceptions of actions, which pushed the Soviet Union and the U.S. into the Cold War after World War II.

Trying to protect itself

A fourth explanation uses *geopolitics.* Geopolitics is an academic approach that looks at both the geography and political history of a country. It then tries to predict a country's behavior based on these two variables.

For example, the Russian people for centuries had been afraid of the West, not just because of the West's industrial superiority but mainly because of historical invasions by Western powers. From Napoleon, the Crimean War, to World War I and World War II, Western powers, be they German or French, had repeatedly invaded Russia.

Therefore, a buffer zone protecting Russia from the West was needed. This security or buffer zone was Eastern Europe. By virtually colonizing Eastern Europe, turning all of Eastern Europe into client states and forcing it to join the Warsaw Pact, the Soviet Union was finally able to get its security zone.

Therefore, Soviet expansionism was based on geography and history. Stalin accomplished what other Russian leaders had tried to do for centuries.

Being aggressive

The final and most common explanation for the outbreak of the Cold War looks at Communism. Many consider Communism an aggressive, expansionist ideology whose ultimate goal is world domination. In a speech to the Communist Party Congress in 1946, Stalin supported this explanation. He proclaimed that he would lull the West into a sense of security and then crush it after it had become weak and complacent.

By the late 1940s, most American and European leaders looked at the Soviet Union as an aggressive, expansionist power, striving for world domination. It had to be stopped at all costs.

Highlighting the Cold War

By 1946, the Soviet Union had violated both the Yalta and the Potsdam agreements, which called for democracy in Eastern Europe. Instead, the Soviet Union imposed Communist dictatorships. Joseph Stalin didn't stop there. He helped initiate Communist uprisings in Greece and Turkey, and by 1947, Communist victories in the two countries seemed possible. The U.S. had had enough, and President Harry Truman decided to act.

Containing the Soviet Union

In 1946, George F. Kennan (see Figure 11-1) created the policy of containment. He had been the deputy chief of the U.S. mission in Moscow since 1944 and had become worried of Soviet promises and policies. By 1945, Kennan started to believe that the Soviet Union wouldn't abide by any of the agreements it had signed with the U.S. and Great Britain during World War II. The Soviet Union, therefore, posed a great threat to the Western world.

In April 1946, Kennan sent his "Long Telegram" from Moscow in which he tried to explain his concerns to the State Department. In the telegram, Kennan outlined a policy of containment of the Soviet Union, arguing that the Soviet Union was an inherently expansionist power that had to be contained by the West, namely the U.S. By 1947, the policy of containment became the official policy of the U.S.

George Kennan's telegram was published as an article titled "The Sources of Soviet Conduct" in the magazine *Foreign Affairs* in 1947.

FIGURE 11-1:
George F. Kennan, American diplomat and creator of the policy of containment.

Source: Library of Congress

TECHNICAL STUFF

The concept of containment advocates for the U.S. to not only provide countries threatened by Communism with military and economic aid but also surround the Soviet Union with pro-American alliances to prevent it from expanding. The North Atlantic Treaty Organization (NATO), established in 1949, was a part of the policy of containment.

Coming together

The concept of collective security, stating that an attack on one member equals an attack on all members, became the foundation for NATO. The Soviet Union knew that if it tried to expand by subverting or attacking a NATO member, such as Denmark, it would face the might of all the other members of NATO, including the U.S.

To back up the idea of collective security, President Truman stationed four U.S. Army divisions in European NATO countries. Collective security worked well; no NATO member was ever attacked by the Soviet Union.

The Soviet Union responded in 1955 by setting up the Warsaw Pact, which included all its Eastern European client states. The purpose of the Warsaw Pact was similar to that of NATO.

The goal of U.S. foreign policy was to contain the Soviet Union globally. It established security organizations similar to NATO all over the world. Examples include SEATO in Asia, the ANZUS Pact with Australia and New Zealand, and the Baghdad Pact in the Middle East. Finally, with military alliances with Japan and South Korea, the U.S. was able to complete global containment of the Soviet Union.

Saving Greece and Turkey: The Truman Doctrine

Stalin was emboldened by his successes in Eastern Europe. He then turned to Southern Europe. The Soviet Union began to actively support communist uprisings in Turkey and Greece. President Truman decided that he had to act.

For this reason, President Truman addressed Congress on March 22, 1947, and outlined what was to become the Truman Doctrine. The Truman Doctrine called for $400 million in military and economic aid for Greece and Turkey to save the countries from Communism. In addition, President Truman sent U.S. military advisors to both countries to help train government forces fighting Communist rebels. By 1950, the U.S. government had provided $600 million in aid to Greece and Turkey, saving both countries from Communism.

TECHNICAL STUFF

The Truman Doctrine became an official part of U.S. foreign policy and marked a permanent commitment by the U.S. helping foreign countries threatened by Communism. From now on, the U.S. provided non-Communist governments with U.S. aid if threatened by Communism.

Restoring Europe: The Marshall Plan

When World War II ended, Europe laid in ruins. The economies of most countries had been destroyed by the war, and widespread poverty existed. This dire economic situation helped create popular support for Communist parties, which promised to provide for the basic needs of all.

In both France and Italy, the Communist Party became the largest party by 1947, and it looked like they could come to power democratically. President Truman knew he had to act. Together with his Secretary of State George C. Marshall, President Truman announced the European Recovery Program, later known as the Marshall Plan, in June of 1947.

The Marshall Plan was both economic and political in nature. The U.S. offered billions of dollars in loans to any European country that applied for it. After receiving U.S. aid, a country had to buy U.S. goods with the money, therefore stimulating the U.S. economy. Later, of course, the loans had to be repaid.

Politically speaking, President Truman knew that U.S. loans would help restore economic prosperity to Europe, which in turn undermined the possibility of Communist electoral successes on the continent. History proved him right. Neither the Italian nor the French Communist Party grew strong enough to come to power in their respective countries.

Between 1947 and 1951, the U.S. provided more than $13 billion in Marshall Plan aid to Europe, undermining Communist parties everywhere on the continent.

Feeding millions: The Berlin Airlift

The four victorious allies of World War II — the U.S., the Soviet Union, Great Britain, and France — divided Germany and its capital of Berlin into four zones of occupation. In 1947, the British economy was on the verge of collapse, and Britain found itself unable to care for its zone of occupation. It asked the U.S. for help. The British zone was then fused with the American zone of occupation, creating the Bi-zone.

Later, France, in similar bad economic shape, asked the U.S. to fuse its zone with both the British and the American zones, creating what was called Trizonia, which became West Germany in 1949.

Alarmed, the Soviet Union decided to punish the Western allies by shutting off all access to West Berlin, which was geographically located within the Soviet zone of occupation. The idea was simple: Prevent food from getting into West Berlin and starve the Germans into submission. President Truman implemented the Berlin Airlift in June 1948 to feed the starving population of Berlin. For the next 11 months, the U.S. flew food to the city, feeding close to 2 million people. During the height of the crisis, an American plane landed in Berlin every minute of the day.

In May of 1949, the Soviet Union caved and ended the blockade, and a new country, West Germany, came into existence. The Soviet Union followed suit quickly and created Communist East Germany.

Going to war in Korea

In June 1950, the Cold War turned into a hot war, when North Korea invaded South Korea. Korea had been divided by American administrators along the 38th parallel, with U.S. troops occupying the Southern part and Soviet troops occupying the Northern part of the Korean Peninsula.

By 1950, South Korea was controlled by a pro-Western dictator while North Korea was under Communist control. Open warfare broke out when North Korean forces invaded South Korea on June 25, 1950. The Communist forces advanced quickly, and President Truman decided to act. He sent U.S. troops, later supported by United Nations forces from 15 member countries, to defend South Korea. The U.S. fought back the Communist forces and started to push them back into North Korea.

The U.S. ignored warnings from the Chinese, who asked the U.S. not to invade North Korea. The U.S. crossed into North Korea. China entered the war on the North Korean side. This stopped the U.S. advance. By 1951, prewar borders were restored, and for the next two years, the two sides fought each other to a standstill. President Dwight Eisenhower ended the war in 1953, by threatening North Korea and China with the use of any weapon at his disposal, including nuclear weapons. Within months, the war was over and the prewar borders were restored.

Just talking: The Doctrine of Rollback

Dwight Eisenhower became president in 1953 and made changes to U.S. foreign policy. Instead of only containing Communism, Eisenhower wanted to roll back Communism by liberating Communist countries. This new doctrine of rolling back Communism turned out to be mostly rhetorical in nature. The U.S. refused to help the Hungarians, who rose up against Soviet control in 1956, as well as France and Britain during the Suez Canal Crisis (I explore these further in the following sections). In both instances, President Eisenhower wasn't willing to risk military confrontation with the Soviet Union.

Rising up against Communism: The Hungarian uprising of 1956

Hungary was one of the Eastern European countries dominated by the Soviet Union. A pro-Soviet regime ran the country with an iron fist. In 1956, the Hungarians, led by reformist leader Imre Nagy, attempted to leave the Soviet bloc. Believing that President Eisenhower would back them, they seceded from the Warsaw Pact. Soon, the Soviet tanks rolled in, killing an estimated 50,000 Hungarians in two weeks, while the U.S. did nothing. Hungary remained Communist until 1989.

Taking back a canal: The Suez Canal crisis

The Suez Canal crisis of 1956 brought the world close to nuclear war. Both Great Britain and France jointly owned the Suez Canal, located in Egypt, since 1875. In 1956, a new revolutionary government in Egypt took over the canal. Great Britain and France invaded and took the canal back.

Egypt at the time was closely aligned with the Soviet Union, which threatened Britain and France. Both of these close NATO allies turned to President Eisenhower for help. He, however, refused, fearing that Great Britain and France would attempt to recolonize the Middle East.

Without U.S. backing, Great Britain and France had to stand down and were forced to withdraw from Egypt. France decided that it needed its own nuclear forces, and General De Gaulle, after becoming President of France in 1958, developed nuclear weapons for France and pulled the country out of NATO. France didn't fully rejoin NATO until 2009.

Building the Berlin Wall

Since the creation of an East German state in 1949, millions of East Germans had fled the communist country by crossing into West Germany. With no real border fortifications in place in Berlin, thousands left there every day because it was the easiest place to leave the country.

By the early 1960s, the number of people fleeing presented a major problem for East Germany. The country's best educated and most skilled citizens were leaving. East Germany faced a brain drain and a shortage of skilled laborers.

In August 1961, the Soviet Union and the Communist East German government built a wall to close off East Berlin to prevent people from fleeing the country (see Figure 11-2). Border guards received the order to shoot to kill anyone attempting to leave East Germany.

FIGURE 11-2:
Building the Berlin Wall in 1961.

Source: Library of Congress

Over the next decades, more than 100 people were shot and killed attempting to flee East Germany. The Wall became a symbol of the Cold War, and its fall in 1989 signaled the collapse of Communism in Eastern Europe.

The Cuban missile crisis

In October of 1962, the U.S. discovered that the Soviet Union was building missile sites for nuclear missiles in Cuba. Cuba, which had gone Communist in 1959, was the ideal site for the Soviets to counter American missiles targeting the Soviet Union in Europe. Instead of invading Cuba, as the military had urged, President John F. Kennedy decided to blockade the country. The U.S. stated that it would intercept any Soviet ship heading for Cuba to make sure that no missiles or missile parts could reach the island. In addition, President Kennedy demanded that all Soviet weapons and bases be removed from Cuba. At the last minute, the Soviet Union decided to back down and recalled its ships heading for Cuba. The U.S., in turn, promised not to invade Cuba or topple the Communist Castro regime. A world war was narrowly avoided.

Note: Soviet leader Nikita Khrushchev was removed after backing down during the Cuban Missile Crisis.

Staying Communist: The Brezhnev Doctrine

In 1968, a reformist government came to power in Czechoslovakia. Its leader was a social democrat who attempted to slowly move Czechoslovakia toward the political center. He was interested in improving the standard of living for his people and wanted closer ties with the West.

The Soviet Union saw this as a direct threat to its dominance over Eastern Europe and invaded the country in 1968. The new leader, Alexander Dubček, was removed, a hardline government restored, and Soviet Premier Leonid Brezhnev stated that from now on the Soviet Union would make sure that any country that had gone Communist would remain Communist. This became known as the Brezhnev Doctrine.

Getting stuck in Vietnam

In 1945, France regained control over its colony Indochina, consisting of what today is Laos, Cambodia, and Vietnam. Indochina had been conquered and occupied by the Japanese during World War II, and a native force organized by Communist leader Ho Chi Minh fought the Japanese while France was focused on the war in Europe. After World War II ended, Indochina was returned to France, which refused to implement reforms, such as local autonomy, demanded by Ho Chi Minh and the Communists. A bitter eight-year war of independence began.

Aiding France in Vietnam

The U.S. at first decided to stay out of the conflict. However, after China went Communist in 1949, U.S. policy changed. President Truman didn't want to see another country go Communist in Asia, so he sent military and economic aid to France to help it fight Communism.

Despite increasing levels of American aid, the French forces started to lose ground, and by 1954, the war was lost. In a last-ditch effort, France asked the U.S. for more direct help, including air strikes against the Communist forces.

Instead, the Eisenhower administration pushed for peace talks. At the 1954 Geneva conference, the French agreed to withdraw from Indochina, and Vietnam was divided into a Communist North and anti-Communist, pro-Western South. Elections to unify the country were scheduled for 1956.

Starting military involvement by the U.S.

By 1956, it looked like the Communists might win the elections, so the U.S.-backed South Vietnamese government refused to hold elections. In response, the North started a Communist uprising in the South, and President Eisenhower decided to intervene. He sent military and economic aid and committed military advisors to train the South Vietnamese military.

Later, Presidents Kennedy and Lyndon B. Johnson escalated U.S. involvement by sending troops to aid South Vietnam. When the war began to turn in the North's favor in 1964, President Johnson issued the Gulf of Tonkin report to Congress in August 1964. The report claimed that North Vietnamese forces in the Gulf of Tonkin had attacked U.S. warships. To punish this obvious act of war by North Vietnam, President Johnson asked for Congress to pass the Gulf of Tonkin Resolution, which allowed him to escalate the war in Vietnam. Congress passed the resolution, and the U.S. increased its troop presence to 200,000 and started to bomb North Vietnam. In addition, the U.S. asked some of its Asian allies to contribute troops to help out. By the end of 1965, South Korea, Australia, New Zealand, Thailand, and the Philippines had committed troops.

By 1967, the war was taking a horrible toll on the U.S. About 15,000 soldiers had died so far, and the war had cost the U.S. $25 billion. The American public and the president were ready to end the war. However, North Vietnam rejected initial peace proposals. Instead of negotiating, North Vietnam launched a major offensive against the U.S. and its allies in January of 1968. The campaign began during the Vietnamese New Year's celebrations, or the Tet holidays. Every large city and provincial capital in South Vietnam was attacked by the North Vietnamese forces and its South Vietnamese allies, the Vietcong.

Fighting back: The Tet Offensive and Vietnamization

American forces fought back the attack, and the Tet Offensive turned out to be a major U.S. victory. Eighty-five thousand Communist troops were killed, which eliminated the Vietcong as a viable fighting force. From then on, the U.S. fought regular North Vietnamese soldiers.

By 1968, American troop strength in South Vietnam suddenly reached 500,000. Casualties increased, and after being elected in 1969, President Richard Nixon decided it was time to act. He recalled 90,000 troops by the end of 1969. When he was up for reelection in 1972, only 30,000 American troops remained in South Vietnam. When secret peace talks collapsed, President Nixon decided to bomb North Vietnam back to the bargaining table. The air strikes proved to be the most severe in history to this point, but they did bring North Vietnam back to the bargaining table.

REMEMBER

President Nixon's strategy was called Vietnamization. It called upon South Vietnam to do more of the fighting so that the U.S. could withdraw its troops. In addition, President Nixon proclaimed what became known as the Nixon Doctrine, which stated that Asian countries fighting Communism could only expect military and economic aid from the U.S. in their fight against Communism — the U.S. wouldn't send any more troops and would begin to recall troops from Vietnam. The objective was to make sure that countries would fight Communism without the help of American troops.

Coming to a close

President Nixon finally settled the conflict in 1973 with the Treaty of Paris, which returned Vietnam to its divided prewar status.

The two Vietnams broke the agreement shortly thereafter, and the war dragged on for two more years. Without U.S. support, the South Vietnamese army collapsed, and on April 30, 1975, the South Vietnamese capital of Saigon fell. The war was over, and the country unified under Communist control. At its height, more than half a million American soldiers fought in Vietnam, and more than 50,000 of them wouldn't return.

President Bill Clinton finally reestablished diplomatic relations with Vietnam in 1996, and today the two countries enjoy a cordial relationship.

Invading Afghanistan

In 1979, the Soviet Union for the first time during the Cold War used its own troops to invade a country that was not a part of the Warsaw Pact. This shocked the world and resulted in both Europe and the U.S. to begin a process of rearmament to fight off Soviet aggression.

After the fall of the Afghan monarchy in 1973, Afghanistan was taken over by the Communist Party, which established a pro-Soviet government. By 1979, the ruling Communists in Afghanistan were fighting an anti-Communist insurrection and decided to leave the Soviet sphere of influence. Using the Brezhnev Doctrine, the Soviet Union invaded in late 1979. President Jimmy Carter felt that he had to act. He boycotted the 1980 Olympic Games in Moscow and imposed a grain embargo against the Soviet Union.

In addition, the U.S. began to support freedom fighters in Afghanistan, called the Mujahedin, who were fighting against the Soviet Union. The U.S. soon supplied advanced weaponry to the Mujahedin. The deliverance of Stinger missiles especially hurt the Soviet Union, because the Afghanis could shoot down Soviet aircraft. This took air superiority away from the Soviets.

For the next decade, the Soviet Union fought a battle against Western-supported Afghan freedom fighters. After losing close to 15,000 men and wasting billions of dollars, the Soviet Union finally withdrew from Afghanistan in 1989. The Soviet military was demoralized and Afghanistan was in shambles, with more than 1 million dead and 5 million displaced.

Destroying an empire

In 1985, Mikhail Gorbachev became the new leader of the Soviet Union. Young and energetic, he was ready for change. So he altered Soviet foreign policy. Gorbachev realized that his country was in decline and that only peaceful relations with the West could assure Soviet survival. Therefore, he not only renounced the idea of world Communism but also started to pursue arms control and disarmament negotiations with the U.S.

To save much-needed resources, Gorbachev decided to end Soviet involvement in Afghanistan. He ordered the pullout of all Soviet troops from Afghanistan by 1989. After the Soviet Union had fully withdrawn, a bitter civil war broke out in Afghanistan between a Communist puppet government and various Mujahedin factions, including the Taliban who consolidated power by 1996.

Gorbachev further cut support to Soviet-dominated regimes and militant groups all over the globe. Within months, many pro-Soviet regimes either collapsed or changed their policies, suddenly becoming friendly to the U.S. and the West. Examples include Mozambique, Ethiopia, Nicaragua, Angola, and Cambodia. Only Cuba, North Korea, Vietnam, Laos, and China chose to continue to pursue the Communist path.

By 1988, Gorbachev was ready to let Eastern Europe go free. Starting with Hungary and Poland, most of Eastern Europe went democratic by 1989. After the fall of the Berlin Wall in 1989, Germany even unified by 1990. Soviet dominance over Eastern Europe was now over.

At home, Gorbachev ended the monopoly of power of the Communist Party of the Soviet Union (CPSU), allowing for multiparty elections by 1990, and was ready to implement a new mix of socialism and capitalism. He even allowed for Glasnost, or intellectual and cultural openness, which included freedom of the press, and allowed for freedom of dissent.

This new freedom of expression stimulated nationalism within the Soviet republics. By 1990, the three Baltic States — Lithuania, Estonia and Latvia — proclaimed their independence; after a failed coup by hardliners against Gorbachev in the summer of 1990, the President of Russia, Boris Yeltsin, began to dismantle the rest of the Soviet Union, resulting in the collapse of the Soviet Union in late 1991. The Soviet Union was replaced with 15 independent countries, the largest and most powerful being the Russian Republic. The Cold War was finally over.

Analyzing Strategic Doctrines and the Arms Race

A study of the Cold War also involves an analysis of the nuclear arms race and strategic doctrines associated with it.

In 1945, the U.S found itself with a monopoly on nuclear weapons. Even though the Soviet Union had been working on nuclear weapons since the 1930s, it had been unsuccessful in developing them. This changed in 1949 when the Soviet Union successfully tested an atomic bomb.

Even though it was in possession of an atomic bomb, the Soviet Union still presented no threat to the U.S. It didn't have the capability of delivering the bomb, because it had no long-range bombers and therefore couldn't strike the U.S. mainland.

HOW TO CARRY A NUCLEAR WEAPON

There are four types of ballistic missiles capable of carrying one or more nuclear warheads.

- The intercontinental ballistic missile (ICBM), with a range of greater than 3,500 miles, designed to target another continent.

- The intermediate-range ballistic missile (IRBM), with a range of 1,500 to 3,420 miles. This missile can target other continents or can be used on the same continent.

- The medium-range ballistic missile (MRBM), designed to be used on the same continent. It has a range of 600 to 1,500 miles.

- Short-range ballistic missiles (SRBM), with a range of less than 600 miles. These are able to carry nuclear warheads and are used for regional conflicts. They are usually low cost, easily transportable, and easy to conceal.

This allowed for the Eisenhower administration (1953–1961) to implement a strategic doctrine referred to as "Massive Retaliation." This doctrine threatened a massive nuclear attack on the Soviet Union or Communist China if they attacked a U.S. ally or any other friendly country. Relying purely on nuclear weapons allowed for Eisenhower to cut back the size of the military and save money needed to balance the budget, which he did.

The Doctrine of Massive Retaliation lost its credibility in 1957, when the Soviet Union perfected its missile technology. Suddenly, the Soviet Union could target the U.S. mainland. A doctrine threatening a nuclear attack for any minor infraction wasn't credible anymore.

REMEMBER

A new doctrine, named "Flexible Response," was developed. It stated that the U.S. would reserve its options when responding to Soviet aggression. The U.S. could use either nuclear or conventional weapons. This allowed the U.S. government flexibility when responding to aggression and also left the enemy guessing.

Becoming superior one more time

The American public began to panic after it found out that the Soviet Union possessed nuclear missiles. It seemed that Soviet missile technology, coupled with Sputnik, the first Soviet satellite in orbit, made the U.S. vulnerable. The U.S. poured billions into missile technology, and by 1959, it had developed two intercontinental ballistic missiles (ICBMs), both liquid-fueled, the Atlas and Titan missiles. The first American missiles were housed in silos and, similar to cars, had to be fueled before being launched. This could take up to half an hour. By the mid-1960s, this flaw was overcome with the development of the Minuteman missile, which contained solid fuel and could be launched in about a minute.

The U.S. didn't stop there. In the early 1960s, the U.S. government commissioned the development of submarine-launched missiles. The government knew that the Soviet Union didn't have the capability to track American submarines. So what better deterrent than to put nuclear missiles onto a submarine? The Polaris missile, the first American submarine-launched ballistic missile (SLBM), developed in the early 1960s, would prove to be the most feared weapon the U.S. possessed.

The "TRIAD" Doctrine soon supplemented the concept of flexible response. The U.S. government wanted to make sure that it could retaliate against the Soviet Union even after the Soviet Union had launched a nuclear first strike.

This meant that some of the U.S. nuclear arsenal had to survive a Soviet first strike. TRIAD assured this. It stipulated that the U.S. would have three different types of strategic nuclear forces. First, the U.S. had land-based missiles stored in underground silos. Second, strategic bombers were used to carry some nuclear weapons. The third part of TRIAD was submarine-launched missiles. This assured the U.S. a second-strike capability. Even if the Soviet Union destroyed all land-based missiles and shot down all strategic bombers, the U.S. could still retaliate with submarine-based nuclear weapons.

With both countries having second-strike capabilities, by the 1960s, a new strategic doctrine was born. It was simply called MAD, or "Mutually Assured Destruction," because any attack by one superpower would end up destroying both.

Getting creative in the 1970s

The 1970s was a banner decade for the production of new and more destructive weapons. These weapons, such as the cruise missiles, are commonly used today, and constantly improved upon.

Multiple Independently Targetable Reentry Vehicle (MIRV)

This technology, developed by the United States, allows for more than one nuclear warhead to be put onto missiles. In the past, each missile could carry only one warhead and could reach only one target. MIRV allowed for the deployment of many warheads onto one missile, and each warhead was able to reach different targets. For example, the American MX missile, deployed in the 1980s, could hold up to ten warheads, and each warhead could strike a different Soviet target. In other words, one MX missile could destroy the ten largest Soviet cities.

The Soviet Union countered with the development of the SS18 (surface-to-surface) missile, which could hold up to 18 warheads, targeting 18 different locations in the U.S. By the 1980s, more than 90 percent of all American and Soviet ICBMs had been MIRVed. Today only five countries, the United States, Russia, China, France, and Great Britain, have MIRV missiles systems, while India and Israel are believed to be working on them.

Inventing flying bombs: Cruise missiles

The other major technological breakthrough of the 1970s was the development of the cruise missile. Cruise missiles are similar to little airplanes, using a jet engine and flying at subsonic or supersonic speed. They're essentially flying bombs. They can be short, medium, or long range, similar to ballistic missiles. Being less expensive, small, and mobile, cruise missiles soon became a mainstay of the U.S. military arsenal.

Cruise missiles have many advantages over conventional missiles. They can be fitted with either a conventional or nuclear warhead and can be launched from just about any location, be it above or underground, in the air, or even in submarines. Even more important, they can be recalled at any time, unlike ICBMs, which as soon as they're launched are on their way and not recallable. Finally, cruise missiles can fly under radar and are virtually undetectable until it's too late to destroy them. By the 1980s, cruise missiles became the fourth leg of the American TRIAD.

REMEMBER

For two decades, the U.S. had a monopoly on cruise missiles, but today many other nations possess them, including not only the great powers such as Russia, Great Britain, China, and France, but also countries like Germany, India, Israel, Sweden, Norway, Taiwan, and Pakistan. Currently, both Russia and the U.S. are working on hypersonic cruise missiles that can fly at five times the speed of sound.

Going into space

In 1980, Ronald Reagan won the U.S. presidency. It was a time of American decline. The war in Vietnam had been lost, South Vietnam was now Communist, the Watergate scandal had forced President Nixon to resign, and the Soviet Union had extended its influence into Africa and Central America. To make the U.S. stronger, President Reagan embarked on a massive rearmament program. The Soviet Union tried to match it, further contributing to its economic decline.

In 1983, President Reagan announced the Strategic Defense Initiative (SDI), commonly called Star Wars. It involved the construction of a laser-based missile shield that could destroy any incoming Soviet missile in outer space. SDI was supposed to make the U.S. and its allies immune to any Soviet nuclear threat and restore the West's superiority. However, the technology to build SDI was not yet available and the project was scrapped by the Clinton administration in 1993 after the Cold War had ended.

The Soviet economy was in such bad shape that the country couldn't match U.S. military spending. Therefore, the new Soviet leader Gorbachev decided to stop the arms race and get back to the negotiating table. Gorbachev's efforts, however, were too late for the Soviet Union, and the country collapsed in 1991.

Chapter 12

Dealing with Political Violence: War and Terrorism

Since the beginning of time, war has been one of the most popular ways of resolving disputes between peoples. Despite the enormous costs of war, whether measured in human lives or destruction of property and military hardware, nations have been prone to use war as the mechanism to resolve conflicts.

War is one of the most examined topics in the field of political science. A general explanation of warfare, which would allow political scientists to predict the outbreak of war, is the ultimate goal. Predicting and explaining warfare then allows early intervention to prevent or at least limit warfare. However, so far, political scientists haven't been able to create such a general explanation, and international conflict seems to be a part of life. The abolition of war and other forms of political violence seems to be a dream.

This chapter focuses on warfare, including causes and financial implications. It also takes a look at terrorism and how it plays a part in warfare and the consequences it wreaks.

Examining Warfare

Warfare became regulated after the creation of the modern state system (see Chapter 8), and between 1648 and 1914, war was an accepted means of foreign policy. It was fought by either mercenary or civilian draft armies but didn't harm the civilian population or the infrastructure of countries. Rules were in place on how to treat prisoners of war and defeated nations.

With the end of the Cold War in 1991 (see Chapter 11), many hoped that political violence within the international system would decline. While conflict between countries, or interstate warfare, did decline, conflict within nations increased.

Discovering the types of war

One of the most comprehensive studies on warfare is the Correlates of War Project. It was started in 1963, last updated in 2010, and looks at political violence from 1816 to 2007 — almost 192 years. The study qualifies war as any armed conflict that results in at least 1,000 battle-related deaths or fatalities per calendar year. Based on this definition, four types of war exist:

>> **Interstate wars:** These are armed conflicts between sovereign states within the international system. Ninety-five interstate wars occurred, from major wars, such as World War I and World War II, to smaller wars, such as the Polish-Lithuanian War of 1920.

Overall, more interstate wars occurred in the 20th century than in the 19th century, proving that the Concert of Europe (see Chapter 10) was successful in maintaining peace in Europe for almost 100 years. More recent examples of interstate wars include the Iraqi invasion of Kuwait in 1990 and the war between the Republic of Georgia and Russia in 2008.

>> **Intrastate wars:** These are armed conflicts that take place within nations, fought between a government and a nongovernment entity, such as a group trying to topple a government or attempting to secede from a nation. Civil war usually results.

Intrastate wars have been on the rise since the 19th century and today have become the fastest-growing category of conflict, almost tripling in number in the last 40 years. There have been 335 conflicts. Recent examples include the civil wars in Syria and Libya.

>> **Extra-state conflicts:** These are armed conflicts fought between a state and a nonstate entity, such as a colony or an international organization. Any colonial war qualifies, as does the conflict in the former Yugoslavia, which resulted in warfare between NATO (international organization) and the state of Serbia.

There were 163 of these wars, and they were more common in the 19th century. Most extra-state wars were between colonial powers and their colonies. They have become rare today.

» **Nonstate wars:** This type of armed conflict refers to conflict between two nonstate entities. To qualify as a nonstate war, groups not affiliated with a government have to commit acts of political violence.

These wars are a recent phenomenon. Examples include terrorist groups in a country fighting each other, such as the current conflict between two terrorist groups, ISIL and the Taliban, in Afghanistan.

Changing warfare

An interesting phenomenon occurred in the last half decade. Conflicts between countries have declined quite a bit. At the same time, conflicts within countries, such as civil war, and conflicts with nonstate actors, such as terrorist groups, have increased. The wars of the past, fought between states and their armies and involving large battles with mass casualties, seem to be a thing of the past. Today's wars are fought between smaller groups, involving fewer people and fewer casualties.

The two major reasons for this change in warfare are the advent of nuclear weapons and the end of the Cold War (see Chapter 11). Nuclear weapons make it irrational to go to war. Why attack a country that can annihilate you in return?

With the end of the Cold War in 1991, political violence declined globally. Most of the world turned away for Communism and embraced the U.S.-created international system.

CHANCES OF WINNING

Historically, nations that initiated war against other nations had a good chance of winning; why else would they initiate a war? Data show that nations that initiated a war before World War I were victorious about 75 percent of the time. The end of World War II changed this. Since 1945, the percentage has declined to 33 percent, meaning that nations that start a war today are more likely to lose than to win a war. For this reason, interstate war, or war between two or more countries, has declined while intrastate war, or war within a country, has increased.

Looking at the Causes of War

Most political scientists are hoping that the study of war will allow the researcher to discover the underlying causes of warfare. This would allow a political scientist to predict and hopefully prevent the outbreak of war. The following sections cover the five most common explanations of warfare studied by political scientists today.

Economic

Economic explanations of warfare are very popular within academia. They claim that the major cause of warfare is rooted in a country's economic structure. The less developed an economy, the more aggressive a country will be. It's not political evolution, such as a change of government, that determines whether a country goes to war, but economic evolution resulting in prosperity.

A good example is the work of political scientist John Mueller who argues in his work *Retreat from Doomsday: The Obsolescence of Major War* (Zip Publishing) that since 1945, none of the top 44 richest countries have gone to war against each other. Mueller claims that the more prosperous countries get, the less likely they are to go to war. The reason is economic interdependence (see Chapter 13). Having your economies closely intertwined means that going to war would only undermine economic prosperity in each country. Why battle a country that is beneficial to your economy?

On the other hand, many of the richest 44 countries have attacked other, less developed and less prosperous societies. According to Mueller, the conclusion is that economic and not political development of countries seems to be the key in eliminating war in the long run.

Sociological

Joseph Schumpeter, an Austrian economist and sociologist, covered in his book *The Sociology of Imperialism,* published in 1918, sociological reasons of warfare. Schumpeter focuses on group studies in his explanations of warfare. He argues that every society is made up of groups that interact with each other to create a nation. The way these groups (some social scientists call them classes) interact can determine how aggressive a society is in the international arena and how likely it is to initiate international conflict.

Schumpeter argues that in many societies, groups exist that have only one purpose: fighting wars or initiating conflict. For example, in imperial Germany, the ruling aristocracy, or Junkers, were born and bred to fight. Their only purpose was to fight wars to protect the country and expand its geographic borders. Whenever international problems arose, that group was ready to go to war, not wanting to bargain or compromise. The result was an aggressive foreign policy.

Not surprisingly, when the German aristocracy ran the country during the second German Empire (1871-1918), it pursued a very aggressive imperialistic foreign policy. It initiated conflict with Great Britain, by building the second largest fleet in the world, challenging the British Empire and alienating the Russian Empire with its protectionist economic policies. In charge of Germany, the Junkers acted exactly like they were supposed to act. They were aggressive and warlike. They didn't consider warfare evil but something that was aspired to. Similar aggressive ruling classes can be found in Japan, Russia, and more recently, Serbia.

Schumpeter's conclusion is that whenever a class similar to the Junkers or the Samurai in Japan leads a country, that country is more likely to initiate international conflict or even open warfare.

Psychological

Many famous psychologists, including Sigmund Freud, Konrad Lorenz, and even philosophers like Friedrich Nietzsche, have argued that violence is a part of human nature. In other words, states don't make war; people do.

They argue that human nature is similar to animal nature, with humans being naturally competitive, territorial, and aggressive. English poet John Milton put it best in his classical statement that "war is inevitable, because men are irrevocably bad." For this reason, to explain the causes of war, political scientists need to study human nature.

It is argued that humans are inherently violent, selfish, and driven by passion and not reason. Political scientists, who study the causes of international aggression, have to accept this and focus on changing human nature.

For many social scientists, war is learned behavior. While people are inherently violent, warfare itself is learned behavior. They claim that people who grow up in violent environments where warfare is glorified will be more likely to engage in violent behavior in the international arena. As John Stoessinger states in his seminal work *Why Nations Go to War* (published by Cengage Learning): "Aggression may be inherent, war is learned behavior and as such can be unlearned and ultimately selected out entirely."

For this reason, the personalities of people, especially leaders, shaped by the environment they grow up in matters. It will determine how they act in the international arena and can be a powerful determinant in predicting a country's aggressiveness internationally.

Ideological

Many political scientists claim that countries go to war because of differing ideologies or worldviews, such as Fascism, Communism, or even liberalism.

REMEMBER

Ideologies are political beliefs that shape a person's expectations and actions. In other words, an ideology shapes how people act within their domestic and international political environment.

Communism is considered an aggressive, expansionist ideology, because world Communism, or domination of every country in the international arena, is its goal. For this reason, many blamed Communist expansion for causing the Cold War (see Chapter 11).

Liberal democracy could be the answer to ideologies causing aggression. Many politicians and social scientists claim that democracies are more peaceful and less likely to go to war than other political structures, such as authoritarian systems or traditional monarchies.

American foreign policy follows this line of thought. Since the end of World War I, the goal of U.S. foreign policy has been to try to establish democracies throughout the world. The assumption is that this will result in less conflict over time.

The big question, however, is: Are democracies more peaceful than other forms of government? The answer is an interesting yes and no. Warfare between true democracies is rare. In other words, democracies are less prone to fight each other but are as likely to go to war as other forms of governments. Therefore, democracies don't fight each other, but they target other forms of governments, such as authoritarian states or monarchies. For example, Great Britain has never fought a war with another established democracy, but it did battle with Argentina, run by a military junta, over the Falkland Islands in 1982. The U.S. also hasn't fought a war with another established democracy, but it did attack Afghanistan and Iraq, both run by authoritarian governments, in 2001 and 2003, respectively.

Why, then, are democracies less likely to battle each other? First, democracies are run by their citizens, who can put a brake on aggressive leaders or governments by voting them out of office. Second, the concepts of free speech and freedom of the press make democratic citizens more informed and less likely to be duped by their governments into going to war. Third, economic cooperation between democracies makes war less likely, because countries will be better off by trading than by going to war. Why attack a country that provides a market for your goods?

Finally, violence as a tool in conflict resolution is considered unacceptable within democracies; therefore, democratic leaders are less likely to use it internationally. The rise in democratic forms of governments is another explanation of why international conflict, especially interstate wars, is on the decline since the end of World War II.

Systemic

Many believe that the international system itself determines how states act within it. Therefore, the international system is the major cause of warfare and not specific people or countries. Political scientists employing the systemic level of analysis are less concerned about specific leaders, such as Adolf Hitler or Napoleon, or the social or economic structures of societies, but study the international structure intensely.

For them, the most important issues to study are the way states interact and how they're situated within the international system. For example, two states that are similar, both in military and economic power, but have different forms of governments will act the same in the international system. In contrast, states that are similar in domestic terms, both democracies, for example, but different in their relationship to the international system will have different policies.

For this reason, the U.S., a liberal capitalist democracy, and the Soviet Union, a Communist system, acted in a similar fashion in the international system during the age of the Cold War (1946–1991). What mattered weren't domestic structures, but the fact that both were superpowers situated in a similar position within our international system. If it had been China and France, which were the two superpowers at the time, both of them would have acted exactly as the U.S. and the Soviet Union did, because the system, and not the domestic structure or people, determines a country's security policies.

Dealing with Terrorism

After the Cold War had ended with the collapse of the Soviet Union in 1991, political violence, especially warfare between countries, declined. However, within years, a new form of political violence emerged, terrorism. *Terrorism* is the deliberate use of violence against civilians for political or religious ends. While terrorism had always been a part of the world, it had been confined to just a few countries. Suddenly in 2001, a new type of terrorism arose. In political science, we refer to it as transnational terrorism, a form of terrorism that sets its targets around the world.

REMEMBER

Terrorism is a highly subjective concept. One person's terrorist is another person's freedom fighter. For example, while most Spaniards consider the Basque Fatherland and Liberty (ETA) a terrorist group, many Basques look upon them as a group fighting for Basque freedom, namely independence from Spain.

Terrorism itself is nothing new in world politics. Acts of terrorism are actually a lot older than the term itself. For example, in the 1st century BC, Jewish holy warriors committed acts of terrorism against Roman troops and civilians stationed in Judea, whom they considered occupying forces. In India, the Thugee cult committed acts of terrorism in the name of their god by randomly strangling nonbelievers.

One of the most famous and historically impactful terrorist attacks occurred in 1914, when the Serbian-sponsored Black Hand movement assassinated Archduke Francis Ferdinand, the heir to the throne of Austria-Hungary, resulting in the outbreak of World War I.

TECHNICAL STUFF

The term *terrorism* is a result of the French Revolution when the revolutionary French Jacobins implemented a Reign of Terror, killing tens of thousands between 1793 and 1794. These acts of violence were known as *La Terreur*, which gave us the term terrorism.

Studying characteristics of terrorism

Terrorism has the following six characteristics:

>> **Premeditated acts of violence.** Acts of terrorism are well planned and not random or impulsive acts of violence. Sometimes they are years in the planning.

>> **Political and/or religious in nature.** Its objectives are the change of a political order, for example, the destruction of a country or the overthrowing of a specific government. Terrorists in Afghanistan today are attempting to overthrow the pro-American government in charge, while terrorists in Spain want to destroy the Spanish state.

>> **Targets often include civilians.** Terrorism doesn't target only the military but especially civilians.

>> **Attacks are usually not carried out by official representatives of countries,** such as the militaries or police forces of specific states. Instead, subnational groups within countries, either political or religious in nature, commit these acts of terrorism. In Spain, for example, the ETA, drawing its strength and support from the Basque region of Spain, carries out terrorist attacks.

>> **Acts are psychological in nature.** They're designed to instill fear into a population. Often compared to theater, terrorism strikes symbolic targets to undermine the will of a people. Striking at department stores, targeting women and children, like the Red Army Faction (RAF) did in West Germany in the 1970s, was designed to undermine the will of the German people in their support of democracy. Today Al Qaeda and ISIL use similar objectives when striking bazaars in Iraq or Syria.

A good example of the psychological nature of terrorism are the Red Brigades, a terrorist group operating in Italy in the 1970s and 1980s. They committed most of their terrorist attacks on Saturdays so that they could achieve maximum publicity in the Sunday newspapers read by a vast majority of all Italians. Sunday attacks, on the other hand, were rarely heard of. Not many people read the Monday paper. For this reason, it's said that the media needs terrorism to create news and that terrorism needs the media to succeed.

>> **Acts aren't just designed to deliver a political or religious message** but often are used to provoke a reaction by the people that are being targeted. A violent response to an act of terrorism can win a terrorist group's support among the global public, allow it to attract more recruits, and divide public opinion within the international community.

For example, terrorist acts committed by Hezbollah against targets in Israel usually lead to an Israeli reaction, such as an airstrike against Hezbollah targets in Lebanon, which in turn increases support for Hezbollah in neighboring Muslim countries and around the globe. The response also polarizes the public in Israel and therefore weakens the Israeli government in the long run.

Taking in types of terrorism

Terrorism has recently changed by adding religious undertones. Previously, terrorism had been mostly associated with national liberation of minority groups in countries. Examples are groups like the Irish Republican Army (IRA) in Northern Ireland and the Basque Fatherland and Liberty (ETA) in Spain, which wanted to bring about independence for a small group contained within a larger country.

Both groups engaged in terrorist acts to get the attention of the world and make the world familiar with their causes. Both groups didn't engage in terrorist acts designed to bring about mass casualties, because this would have been self-defeating, undermining support at home and abroad. Who would support the cause of a group killing women and children?

For example, in 2004, an Al Qaeda–affiliated terrorist group struck Spain, killing 191 civilians in the bombing of the Madrid commuter train system. At first, the ETA was suspected. ETA right away forcefully denied any part to this terrorist act and condemned it strongly for causing mass civilian casualties. Terrorist acts like this would only result in a loss of support for their cause, independence from Spain.

Religious terrorists like Al Qaeda and ISIL, on the other hand, aren't constrained by this, because they kill for divine purposes, rationalizing mass casualties. Overall, four different types of terrorism exist, as I explore in the next sections.

Nationalist terrorism

Nationalistic terrorism is where a small minority within a country tries to get the attention of the world in its quest for independence. These groups need both international and domestic support in their quest for independence, and therefore their acts of terrorism are quite limited. They can't engage in acts of terrorism resulting in mass casualties because that would turn world opinion against them. So they mostly target police and military installations, not civilians. This type of terrorism has been the most successful form of terrorism in gaining international sympathy and support.

Religious terrorism

This form of terrorism is the most rapidly growing today. Religious terrorists use violence for a divine purpose and therefore aren't constrained by any kind of political considerations like nationalistic terrorists are. Religious terrorists will kill at will, and the number of civilian casualties isn't a concern for them. Al Qaeda, discussed later, is one of the most prominent examples of a religious terrorist group today. Other religious terrorist groups include ISIL, Hamas, and Hezbollah.

State-sponsored terrorism

State-sponsored terrorism is the support of terrorist activity by a specific country's government against its own population or another country. The objective is to undermine domestic opposition or another country and its government.

The bombing of Pan Am Flight 103 in 1988 is an example of this. Pan Am Flight 103 was on its way from London to JFK airport in New York City when it was blown up over Lockerbie, Scotland, killing 270 people — 259 people on board the plane and 11 on the ground by debris.

After years of investigations, Scotland Yard determined that the mastermind behind the bombing was a Libyan intelligence officer. The Libyan government headed by its longtime leader Muhammad Qaddafi accepted responsibility, but not guilt, for the act in 2003 and compensated the victims' families each $8 million for their loss. Qaddafi then renounced terrorism as a political tool.

Ideological terrorism

Ideological terrorism involves extreme right- or left-wing groups using terrorism to destroy the government in their country. The Red Brigades and the RAF are examples of this.

The Red Brigades was a Marxist-Leninist terror organization. It formed in 1970 with the objective of bringing about the downfall of the Italian government and the creation of a revolutionary state. Its most famous attack occurred in 1978 when it kidnapped former Italian Prime Minister Aldo Moro, killing five of his body guards and murdering him 54 days later. The Red Brigades was finally destroyed in the mid-1980s.

The RAF, also known as the Baader-Meinhof Gang, named after two of its founders, was active in West Germany at the same time. Like the Red Brigades, it was a revolutionary organization, supported by Communist East Germany, which wanted to destroy the West German democratic state. Founded in 1970, the group finally disbanded in 1998, after killing 34 people in various terrorist attacks.

Going to War with Evil

A good example of a transnational terrorist group studied by political scientists today is Al Qaeda or "the base." Al Qaeda is considered a transnational terrorist group because it is not supported by any government and is financially independent. It has a global organizational structure, an annual budget, and it sets its targets worldwide. With a budget of over $30 million annually, Al Qaeda has a larger budget than many developing countries and it even has some governmental structures, such as a media committee and a media spokesman. Today, it has become one of the most infamous terrorist groups worldwide.

Al Qaeda was responsible for one of the most heinous terrorist activities in recent years, the September 11, 2001, terrorist attacks against the United States, and has been responsible for a string of attacks on the U.S. and its allies. These include

>> The killing of U.S. marines in Somalia in 1991/1992

>> The bombing of the World Trade Center in 1993

>> The bombing of U.S. embassies in Kenya and Tanzania in 1998

>> The bombing of the U.S. warship USS *Cole* in Yemen in 2000

>> The destruction of the World Trade Center, as well as the attack on the Pentagon and additional plane hijackings, in 2001

>> The bombings of the London public transportation system in 2005

In addition, Osama bin Laden, the founder of Al Qaeda, was also implicated in failed assassination attempts on Pope John Paul II and former President Bill Clinton.

Today, the organization trains its members in Afghanistan, Pakistan, Iraq, and Sudan and then sends them all over the world to prepare for terrorist attacks. Presently, Al Qaeda has members in more than 100 countries, including the U.S., Russia, Great Britain, France, Germany, and even remote places like Bosnia and Chechnya.

How a terrorist group begins: Al Qaeda

The origins of Al Qaeda can be traced back to the Soviet invasion of Afghanistan in 1979 when thousands of Muslims went to Afghanistan to fight the Soviets after the Soviet Union had invaded Afghanistan. One of the groups was the International Muslim Brigade, recruited in religious places throughout the world by Osama bin Laden. He and his holy warriors deserve much credit for the Soviet defeat in Afghanistan. When the Soviets finally left the country in 1989, bin Laden founded the Islamic Army, which he later turned into Al Qaeda, and returned to Saudi Arabia.

REMEMBER

The founder of Al Qaeda, Osama bin Laden, was the son of a Saudi billionaire. One of more than 50 children, bin Laden was a multimillionaire. After completing degrees in engineering and public administration, bin Laden turned into a radical when the Soviet Union invaded Afghanistan in 1979.

After Iraq invaded Kuwait in 1990, bin Laden offered the Saudi government his Islamic Army to expel Iraq from Kuwait. Instead, the Saudi government asked for American help, and half a million American soldiers were sent to Saudi Arabia to prepare for the expulsion of Iraq from Kuwait. bin Laden was enraged by this act, having non-Muslim soldiers stationed in Saudi Arabia, and was openly critical of the Saudi government. He was banished for his criticism and left for Sudan in 1992.

While in Sudan, bin Laden acted like a businessman. He ran a construction business, building roads throughout Sudan, and invested in local businesses. Many of his laborers were battle-hardened freedom fighters from Afghanistan. Sudan expelled bin Laden in 1996 due to continued American and Saudi pressure. The Sudanese government seized all his assets, but about 300 construction workers went with him into exile. They would become the core of his terrorist organization.

Evolution of a terrorist leader

bin Laden went back to Afghanistan where he became close friends with the leader of the Taliban, Mullah Omar, and fought in the ensuing civil war on the side of the Taliban, a fundamentalist Muslim sect. With his help, the Taliban took over the country, and bin Laden stayed and became an honored guest of the Taliban regime. His Al Qaeda units became a part of the Taliban military. He permanently settled in Afghanistan after Saudi Arabia renounced his citizenship for attempting to undermine the Saudi ruling family.

In 1998, bin Laden issued a fatwa (religious ruling) in which he called for a holy war against all Jews and Crusaders (Christians). This included a call for the killing of all U.S. citizens, whether military or civilian. President Clinton in turn offered a $25 million bounty for the capture of Osama bin Laden.

TECHNICAL STUFF

Osama bin Laden's hatred for the U.S. can be traced to three sources:

>> He objected to U.S. troops in Saudi Arabia. For him, these Christian troops desecrated the most holy places in the Muslim world, Mecca and Medina.

>> He objected to the U.S. backing Israel. He wanted to destroy Israel and expel all nonbelievers from the Middle East.

>> He advocated the overthrowing of all pro-U.S. regimes in the Middle East. So he called for a holy war, or Jihad, against all infidels (non-Muslims, or Muslims collaborating with non-Muslims). To eliminate these infidels, all means were acceptable.

The terrorist attack on the United Sates on September 11, 2001, led to the U.S. attacking Afghanistan, which was harboring bin Laden, to destroy Al Qaeda. When the ruling Taliban refused to hand over bin Laden, the U.S. initiated Operation Enduring Freedom on October 7, 2001, which destroyed the ruling Taliban regime. bin Laden was forced to go into hiding. He successfully hid from U.S. forces for almost a decade.

Osama bin Laden was killed May 2, 2011, by U.S. special forces (Navy Seals) while living in Pakistan.

Exploring the Costs of War

Not surprisingly, the nuclear arms race, discussed in Chapter 11, had been prohibitively expensive. Surprising is the fact that since the end of the Cold War in 1991, global military spending didn't consistently decrease but actually increased beginning in 1999 and, by 2008, reached Cold War levels one more time.

Since the 1930s, the U.S. has spent an extraordinary amount of its budget on the military. Spending remained high through World War II and the Cold War, but military budgets were cut during the Clinton administration when it became clear that the U.S. was the sole remaining superpower. However, military spending accelerated again with the terrorist attacks of September 11, 2001, and the subsequent invasions of Afghanistan and Iraq.

As Figure 12-1 shows, the U.S. spends the largest amount of money of any country in the world on the military. In fact, it spends about one-third of all military spending worldwide. However, current spending represents a big decline in spending. As recently as 2009, the U.S. spent almost half of the world's military spending on its military.

Global Military Spending in 2018

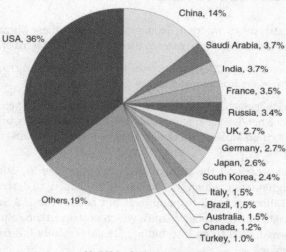

USA, 36%
China, 14%
Saudi Arabia, 3.7%
India, 3.7%
France, 3.5%
Russia, 3.4%
UK, 2.7%
Germany, 2.7%
Japan, 2.6%
South Korea, 2.4%
Italy, 1.5%
Brazil, 1.5%
Australia, 1.5%
Canada, 1.2%
Turkey, 1.0%
Others, 19%

FIGURE 12-1: Global military spending in percentages.

SOURCE: Stockholm International Peace Research Institute
ANDREA VILLARI/Stars and Stripes

Currently, the U.S. spends almost 2½ times as much money on its armed forces compared to its closest challenger, China. And it spends 13 times as much on its military as Great Britain, the closest U.S. ally.

The amount of money the top two countries, the United States and China, spend on their military budgets is unlikely to decline in the near future. While the U.S. is fighting in Iraq and Afghanistan, China is rearming at a massive pace. The country seems to be set on joining the rank of true superpowers, both economic and military, in the foreseeable future.

Chapter 13

Mixing Disciplines: International Political Economy

The discipline of international political economy (IPE) studies international political and economic relationships between countries. IPE is an interdisciplinary approach, incorporating the disciplines of political science and economics and also relying on history, sociology, and even anthropology to study the relationship between states in the international economic arena. IPE developed as a field within international relations in the 1970s with the first oil crisis and the collapse of the Bretton Woods system.

The political aspect of IPE deals with the interaction of countries and the creation of the international system through which economic interactions occur. The economic aspect of IPE deals with the exchange of goods and services between states.

This chapter covers the creation of the institutions making up the current liberal international economic order. Next, it focuses on major economic theories used over the last centuries. Finally, global economic inequality, the cause of decline of third-world economies, and globalization are covered.

Fusing Economics and Politics

In a totally free international economic system dominated by the free market, a free exchange of goods and services between countries based on what English economist David Ricardo called a harmony of interests occurs. Each nation produces what it can produce most cost-effectively and efficiently and then trades for goods and services it has a hard time producing. Ricardo referred to this as *comparative advantage.* Countries export what they're best at producing, while they import goods they have a tough time producing. In a system like this, every nation would benefit from trading with each other and also would be dependent on each other, and therefore international harmony and peace would be created.

Sadly, this concept ignores the political aspects of IPE. Economics can't be divorced from politics; therefore, a free international market system doesn't exist. National governments care first about their own citizens and try to provide them with as many benefits as possible. Often this conflicts with the free international market.

While pure economics may demand that many industries in advanced industrialized nations should be closed because they can't compete with cheaper goods produced in developing countries, politics won't allow this. What government would shut down core industries, such as steel or chemicals, putting millions of workers out of jobs, just because it would be cheaper to buy these goods from other countries? Instead, governments implement protectionist policies, where they protect their own industries from foreign competition. These policies can include trade restrictions, such as tariffs (import taxes), import quotas, or voluntary trade restrictions.

Security issues also interfere with a totally free international market system. Just taking a pure economic point of view, the U.S. should stop producing steel and import it at cheaper prices from countries like South Korea or Brazil. However, steel is the backbone of the military industrial complex, and what country would shut down such an important industry and be totally dependent on another country in the international system? The idea of a totally free market system dominating international economics is utopian and thus not feasible in international politics.

Creating a New Economic Order

The present international economic order was established by the U.S. after World War II. It was based on the concept of economic liberalism, referring to a philosophy that advocates free trade between nations to increase wealth in all nations.

Free trade, in turn, is defined as unrestricted (no state-imposed restrictions such as tariffs or other import taxes) commerce between nations. Political scientists refer to the post–World War II era as the liberal international economic order.

REMEMBER

The current international economic order is also referred to as the Bretton Woods system, because the foundation for it was laid at Bretton Woods in New Hampshire. The Bretton Woods system advocates for free international trade and also attempts to manage the international money system to prevent another Great Depression. It created three international organizations: the International Bank for Reconstruction and Development (IBRD), better known as the World Bank, which is officially attached to the United Nations; the International Monetary Fund; and the General Agreement on Tariffs and Trade (GATT). The next sections discuss all three.

Designing a World Bank

The International Bank for Reconstruction and Development (IBRD), or World Bank, was established in 1944 and is headquartered in Washington, D.C. Today, it has 189 member countries, has offices in more than 130 countries, and employs more than 10,000 people globally. Originally, the World Bank was designed with two purposes in mind: to help rebuild the war-torn economies of the world after World War II, and to help with the economic development of the Third World. Here, the objective was to reduce poverty and hunger through increasing international trade and foreign investment in developing countries. While many Third-World countries in 1945 pushed for the World Bank to be used to help them develop right away, the U.S. decided that first Europe had to be rebuilt.

After the European economies had recovered, the priorities of the World Bank began to change. By the 1960s, the industrialized world had recovered from the ravages of World War II, and the World Bank could focus on development instead of reconstruction. For this reason, the U.S. set up the International Development Association (IDA) as a part of the World Bank, which makes low interest rate loans to developing countries.

Beginning in 1968, the World Bank became a major source of low interest rate loans to developing countries. By 2020, the World Bank sponsored more than 12,000 projects with a total commitment of $45.9 billion distributed in credits, loans, grants, and guarantees. World Bank loans have been used to help with the following:

» Supplying safe drinking water

» Building schools and training teachers

- » Increasing agricultural productivity through modern technology
- » Building and maintaining infrastructure
- » Combating environmental problems
- » Expanding health care, especially for women and children

Finally, the World Bank has become one of the largest research centers in the world. It supplies data, including poverty rates, trade relations, globalization, and the status of the environment, on all developing economies.

Establishing the International Monetary Fund

The International Monetary Fund (IMF), created in 1945 at Bretton Woods and coming into force by 1947, has the same objective as the World Bank. With the end of World War II, the economies of the industrialized world had to be rebuilt. The IMF was designed to help with this rebuilding process and also with overseeing the international monetary system to make sure that a situation resulting in another Great Depression would never occur again.

TECHNICAL STUFF

During the 1930s, the industrialized world had protected its domestic economies through tariffs and other trade barriers, while devaluing its currencies to keep its goods cheap abroad. With every country doing this, disaster struck and the international trade system collapsed. The IMF was supposed to prevent this from ever occurring again.

The IMF was designed to be a global institution that would ensure currency exchange rate stability and encourage its member countries to eliminate exchange restrictions that hindered trade. Every country that joined the IMF had to agree to keep its exchange rate stable unless a fundamental disequilibrium, such as a recession, had to be corrected. This monetary stability was created by pegging each member's currency to the dollar, which in turn was pegged to gold. This system collapsed in 1971, when the U.S. suspended the convertibility of the dollar into gold.

TECHNICAL STUFF

Since the collapse of the Bretton Woods system in 1971, after the U.S. stopped the convertibility of the dollar into gold, the IMF has allowed members the freedom to choose any exchange arrangement they want. Countries can float their currency freely, peg it to another currency such as the British Pound, or even adopt the currency of another country. Other choices include forming a currency bloc, such as the European Union did when it created the Euro in 2002.

A second feature of the IMF allows for members to borrow from the fund. Originally, the idea was for members to put money into the IMF when economic times were good and then to take it back out when needed. In addition, the IMF allows a country to borrow more than the country has contributed with a small interest charge attached to the loan. However, if a country takes a loan from the IMF, it has to implement austerity policies the IMF develops specifically for the country to alleviate its economic problems. These measures usually involve hard choices, such as cutting spending, increasing interest rates to combat inflation, and exporting more at the expense of consumption back home. All these policies aren't very popular, especially with Third-World governments, which take out a majority of IMF loans today.

Developing the General Agreement on Tariffs and Trade

The General Agreement on Tariffs and Trade (GATT) came into existence in 1948. GATT was designed to increase international trade by lowering trade barriers, such as tariffs and other import taxes between countries. In the beginning, 23 countries signed on to GATT, and the international organization worked the following way: If the U.S. gave France, also a member, a break by lowering tariffs on wine, it would have to give the same break to all other members of GATT. In other words, if trade barriers are lowered between two member states, this action is automatically applied to all the other member states of GATT.

While GATT allowed exceptions to this principle, such as agricultural subsidies and voluntary trade restrictions, it did stimulate free trade among all member states, and countries were lining up to join GATT. In 1995, when membership had reached 122 countries, GATT was transformed into the World Trade Organization, or WTO.

The WTO is based on the same principles as GATT and designed to stimulate free trade. Unlike GATT, the WTO is a more powerful organization and can deal with such issues as subsidies and even intellectual property rights. It has a permanent headquarters in Geneva, Switzerland, and the power to actually enforce violations of WTO rules. For the first time, an international economic organization acquired the power to impose sanctions on member states that violate trade agreements.

Discovering Economic Theories

Economics is a social science discipline that deals with the production, distribution, and consumption of both goods and services domestically and globally. Adam Smith defined economics as the study of the causes of wealth of nations.

Throughout history, many economic theories been developed to explain how people and nations prosper. I discuss the most influential ones in the following sections.

Economic liberalism

The role of the state has been an ongoing discussion in international economics. As early as the 18th century, economists clashed on what the proper role of a government within a country's economy, and also globally, should be. In his seminal work, *The Wealth of Nations*, published in 1776, Adam Smith argued for a smaller role of government in the economy. Smith believed that the free market should dominate the economy and that government's role is a small one, only making sure that the free market can work undisturbed. For Smith, the state has three roles to perform in a domestic economy:

>> **The state has to provide for a defense of the country.** With the international system full of hostile countries, every country needs to be able to protect itself. The free market by itself won't fulfill this function; therefore, the government has to step in. The government's obligation is to create a military force sufficient to protect the country from foreign interferences.

>> **The government has to establish laws so that the free market can work undisturbed.** The government's obligation is to provide law and order in a society so that economic transactions can freely and peacefully occur. If an economic transaction occurs, with one person selling a good to another, society needs to make sure that this transaction is protected. In other words, stealing or forcefully obtaining goods from another person has to be illegal and punishable by the law. If not, who would buy goods if they could just take them?

>> **For economic transactions to properly occur, an infrastructure has to be in place.** In other words, an economy has to have roads, canals, and other means of transportation in place for economic transactions to work. Goods have to be able to reach the markets to be sold, and people have to be able to easily move to facilitate trade.

Smith didn't believe in government having no role whatsoever in a domestic economy, but he believed that it should be quite limited and not interfere with the free market. Smith himself didn't apply his ideas to international economics, but some of his followers, like economist David Ricardo, did. International liberal economists advocate the following:

>> **International trade:** Economic liberalism argues for free trade between nations, without much government interference, because the belief is that it will lead to increased efficiency and accumulation of wealth for all the nations involved. It should be the free market and not government that determines what goods are produced by countries and traded globally. So a system needs to be in place that pushes for free trade and prohibits unrestricted government intervention through policies such as tariffs or other trade barriers.

>> **International currency markets:** Governments should stay put and not interfere much with economic transactions occurring between countries. One of the few areas government should intervene is in the creation of international currency markets, mainly through adjusting and regulating exchange rates to facilitate international economic transactions. Obviously, dealing with a country that has a nonconvertible currency wouldn't make much sense for any international business.

TECHNICAL STUFF

David Ricardo made that point in his theory of comparative advantage. The theory advocates that countries need to set aside their political differences and focus on economics. Every nation struggles to improve its economic and political situation. By collaborating, everybody benefits and will be better off in the long run. Ricardo advocated that nations produce what they're best at producing. In other words, nations should produce only goods that they can efficiently and cost-effectively produce. The country then will trade these goods to other nations for goods it can't produce in an efficient manner. This will make nations dependent on each other, creating interdependence, and everybody will be better off in the long run.

Mercantilism

Mercantilism is one of the oldest economic theories around. It, unlike economic liberalism, believes that politics and economics are related and that economics is supposed to serve a nation's interest. In other words, political power and security of a nation are considered superior to economic activity, and all economic transactions are designed to enhance state power. Mercantilism was the dominant economic theory from the 15th to the 18th century, and then it slowly lost out to economic liberalism.

For a mercantilist, international economic relations are designed to increase a country's wealth and power. Spain, for example, acquired colonies in Latin America for political and not economic reasons. The Spanish crown exploited these colonies and amassed wealth. This wealth could be used to create larger, more powerful armies, which in turn were being used to acquire more wealth and power through increased colonization and acquisition of more territory. Any international economic transaction that's beneficial to the state is acceptable, while any transaction that's detrimental to state power is not. Mercantilists are, therefore, less concerned with economic relations that benefit two or more countries than with economic transactions that benefit one country.

In addition, any kind of economic dependence is unacceptable for a mercantilist. Interdependence is considered dangerous for the survival of the state. Mercantilists reject Ricardo's theory of comparative advantage because it leads to foreign dependence of a nation. Dependence then equals danger and weakness, because a country is dependent on another country for a vital product. What if that other country stops trading with you and suddenly you have no more access to a vital good like steel?

Mercantilists advocate the domestic production of vital goods even if they're produced inefficiently and in a costly manner. In addition, vital industries have to be subsidized and protected from foreign competition to assure survival. Protectionist policies, where a nation protects its markets from foreign competition with means such as tariffs and other trade restrictions, are considered necessary. Therefore, mercantilists believe in an active role of the state in economic relations, be they domestic or international.

State capitalism

A modern variant of mercantilism is state capitalism or etatism (statism in French). This economic theory believes that the government has the right and even obligation to intervene in the economy. This can be accomplished through direct ownership of enterprises or other forms of economic planning. Statism isn't socialism or Communism, because private property is legal and the majority of the economy is privately owned.

A good example of a state capitalist society is France. In France, the government has the power to directly intervene in the economy to bring about necessary changes. For example, in the 1980s, French President Mitterrand (1981–1995) decided that it was time to revamp the French economy to make it more globally competitive. The French bureaucracy was given the order to create a list of industries needed for the 21st century for France to be able to compete on the global market. A second list of industries was also created. It contained industries that were outdated and could be eliminated.

When the list was completed, it included industries such as aerospace, electronics, atomic energy, undersea exploration, and telecommunications. All of these were considered vital for the 21st century. Industries such as textile and shipbuilding were deemed dated and had to be destroyed. Through control of the banking structure and the financial markets in France, the French government was able to extend interest-free loans, subsidies, and grants to specific privately held enterprises, which proceeded to create the industries deemed necessary by the government.

The government not only provided the funds to create new industries but also became the first buyer of these newly produced goods. For a private company, this meant free or almost free money to create industries and also a guaranteed buyer for its goods. In other words, it was a win-win situation for private business in France.

As a result, France today is a leader in many sectors of the international economy, especially atomic energy and undersea exploration. Interestingly, after experimenting with economic liberalism in the 1990s under French President Chirac (1995–2007), France has recently moved back to statism. After the economic downturn in late 2008, French President Sarkozy (2007–2012) declared economic liberalism dead and proclaimed a return to statism.

A similar situation can be observed in Russia. After the fall of Communism in 1991, Russian President Boris Yeltsin (1991–1999) attempted to transition Russia quickly to a free market economy guided by the concept of economic liberalism. This attempt ended in utter failure, and by the late 1990s, the Russian economy was in shambles. Yeltsin's successor Vladimir Putin (2000–present) slowly transitioned the economy back to a statist format. Unlike France, the state in Russia directly took over privately held industries. Today, the Russian state controls more than 40 percent of the economy directly, mainly in the energy sector.

State socialism

State socialism is quite different compared to state capitalism. State socialism advocates a direct state role within a nation's economy, but private property isn't allowed. In other words, the state owns all the property in a society. A prime example is the former Soviet Union where the state owned all the property and a private market wasn't allowed to function. Instead, there was a centrally planned economy where the state was in charge of production, consumption, and even pricing of goods.

REMEMBER

In the Soviet Union, a centralized economic planning agency, by the name of Gosplan, prepared for the production of about 5 million goods in five-year cycles in its infamous five-year plans. Gosplan had to decide what kind of products the Russian public needed, how these products would be produced, how they would reach the consumer, and how much the consumer would pay for these products. Not having the gift of perfect foresight, surpluses and shortages were common in the Russian economy. For example, Gosplan had to figure out how much heating oil was needed every year for five years in advance. However, Gosplan couldn't know what the weather conditions would be every year, so it took an educated guess. If it was on target, there was enough oil for everybody. However, if a severe winter struck, there wouldn't be enough heating oil for the Russian public, and it would freeze. If there was a warm winter, on the other hand, surpluses resulted. By the 1980s, the Soviet economy was in shambles and the whole system collapsed in 1991. Centralized planning today is found only in a few surviving Communist countries, such as North Korea.

Examining Population and the Division of Wealth

In 2020, the world's population will reach about 7.8 billion people, with about 6.5 billion of those people living in poor or less-developed countries, referred to as LDCs. The following sections look at global economic inequality and terminology associated with the study of it.

Defining terms

When discussing global politics, we often use the terms *North* and *South:*

>> North usually refers to the world's richest countries, such as the United States and Western Europe, which are located in the Northern hemisphere.

>> South refers to countries located in the southern hemisphere, which are traditionally less developed.

Historically, political scientists used the terms *First, Second,* and *Third World* when classifying the international economic system:

>> The First World was the advanced industrialized world, which included the United States, Western Europe, and Japan.

>> The term *Second World* referred to the Communist countries of Eastern Europe and the Soviet Union.

>> The term *Third World* was coined by the French historian Alfred Sauvy in 1952 and referred to most of Africa, Asia, and even Latin America. Third-World countries exhibited similar characteristics, such as poverty, high birth rates, and low life expectancy.

REMEMBER

It became necessary to add the term *Fourth World* for countries that have seen no economic or social progress in the last 35 years. Many of these countries have even experienced a decline in their economy, exhibiting negative growth rates, seeing an increase in poverty, and experiencing a decline in life expectancy. Countries such as Haiti or Zambia fit the bill.

Looking at global inequality

Today, billions of people live in poverty. Global inequality is greater today than it has ever been in history. It's estimated that the richest 25 percent of the global population earns about 75 percent of the world's income, and the poorest 75 percent receive only about 25 percent of the world's income. This inequality isn't necessarily evenly divided between countries but is caused by several very poor countries with very large populations.

If you take rural China, India, and Indonesia, you have almost half of the world's population. However, this population receives only 9 percent of the world's income. On the other hand, if you take the U.S., Japan, Germany, France, and Great Britain, combined about 13 percent of the world's population, you have about 45 percent of the world's income. Regionalism is also major determinant of global income. While income has steadily increased in the Americas, Europe, the Middle East, and Oceania, it has declined rapidly in Africa.

Despite these shocking numbers, the number of people living in extreme poverty has declined over the last few decades. In 1995, almost one-third of the world's population lived in extreme poverty. Today, the number has declined to about 10 percent.

REMEMBER

Extreme poverty is defined by the World Bank as making less than $1.90 a day. Forty-one percent of all people in Sub-Saharan Africa live in extreme poverty. This is actually down from 59 percent in 1996. The decrease in poverty is mostly due to the efforts of two nations, China and India, who have almost 3 billion people combined.

Causing Economic Decline in the Third World

For decades, political scientists have attempted to determine the reason for this North-South divide and the slow development or even underdevelopment in the Third and Fourth Worlds. The next sections look at some of the more commonly advanced causes for Third-World economic and social problems. Not one of them can provide a full explanation for the problems the Third World is facing today, but a combination may be able to provide an answer for specific problems.

Colonialism

A popular perspective, especially in the Third World, is that the major reason the Third World is lagging behind the advanced industrialized world is colonialism. Most countries in the southern hemisphere were colonies at certain times in their history and exploited for their material goods and cheap labor. Usually, colonies were exploited by the colonial powers, and often the locals were treated like slaves. They were forced to work for pennies, under horrific conditions, and afterward were sold the goods they helped produce for an increased profit, putting them into the poorhouse. Under these conditions, the Third World was constantly exploited with no way to develop economically.

In addition, present day African borders were drawn by European colonial powers without taking national or ethnic determinations into account. Often, warring tribes and historical enemies were put into the same colony, which today has become a sovereign state. However, these new states now contain hostile ethnic and tribal groups that reject the state, often resulting in civil strife or even civil war.

At the same time, colonial rulers provided for a viable infrastructure, such as roads, railroads, and ports, and trained locals in bureaucratic techniques. More important, not all colonies grew up to become poor Third-World countries. Just take a look at South Korea and Singapore. Also, some countries that were never colonized are doing well, such as China or Thailand, and some are doing poorly, such as Ethiopia or Iran. Cleary, the colonial experience itself isn't a full explanation for the status of the Third World today.

Dependency theory

Very popular in the 1970s, this theory claims that the First World has underdeveloped the Third World on purpose. The theory states that the First World, labeled the *core*, forces Third-World economies, labeled the *periphery*, to produce only certain goods, such as agricultural goods or natural resources (primary goods), which are then exported to the First World at low cost. First-World countries use these resources to produce secondary goods (manufactured goods), which are sold back to the Third World for a profit. This allows First-World economies to grow and develop, while under these conditions, Third-World economies can never develop economically and will always remain underdeveloped. In the long run, they'll become dependent on the First World and its advanced industries and technology.

While certainly making a valid point, a major problem of the theory is that it can't explain why certain Third-World countries have done so well in the international economy and have elevated themselves out of the Third World into First-World status. South Korea, Taiwan, Singapore, and even Brazil and Chile are major examples of this.

Third-World elites

Another popular approach assigns blame for the current conditions within the Third World to the native ruling elites. Popularized by Robert Bates (1981), this theory claims that Third-World elites have made the strategic choice to industrialize at any cost. By doing so, they're ignoring the lessons learned from the first and second industrial revolutions in Europe. Europe and the U.S. began to industrialize from the countryside, with a solid agricultural sector in place. In the Third World, the small inefficient agricultural sector is exploited and destroyed to get resources to industrialize. Without it, the Third World will never fully industrialize. In other words, strategic choices made by Third-World elites are to blame for the current situation in the Third World. Even worse, Third-World elites are destroying any kind of possibility for future economic development.

Domestic factors

Domestic factors, such as the following, account for the dismal performance of many Third- and Fourth-World countries.

>> **A lack of a viable infrastructure exists.** To be able to industrialize, an infrastructure, including roads, canals, ports, and railroads, need to be in place. With an infrastructure lacking, it's impossible for an economy to take off.

>> **A social infrastructure needs to be in place.** To develop a country, it needs a population that's literate and has access to basic necessities, such as food and healthcare.

>> **A lack of personal and financial security characterizes many Third-World countries.** With laws protecting economic transactions and private property not being in place or not being enforced, economic development can't and won't take place. For example, a country won't see any domestic or foreign investment without these laws in place, instead experiencing massive capital flight from the few people who actually possess some wealth.

>> **A lack of viable domestic political institutions won't allow for a country to develop economically.** Without a functioning bureaucracy to enforce rules and a police force to protect the population from arbitrary decisions by autocratic leaders, development won't occur.

International organizations

Another factor attributed to underdevelopment in the Third World is the First-World domination of international organizations. Most present-day international organizations, like the United Nations, the World Bank, and the IMF, were established by the First World when it set up the international liberal economic order after 1945. Their purpose was to stimulate free trade and help the countries with the most advanced export capabilities, namely the advanced industrialized Western world. For example, voting within the IMF isn't based on the concept of equality like the General Assembly of the United Nations but on economic size of the member states. For this reason, the U.S. together with Western Europe controls almost 50 percent of the votes within the IMF, giving control over the IMF to the First World.

A good example of the use of the IMF is the international debt crisis, discussed in the next section, where the First World was able to use the IMF to not only rescue the Third World but also demand economic changes within many Third-World countries.

To remedy this bias within the international structure, the Third World decided to organize. In 1964, the Group of 77, consisting of 77 Third-World countries formed within the United Nations to push for Third-World interests. Today, 135 countries belong to the group of 77. By the 1970s, the Third World called for a New International Economic Order, which would increase Third-World power in international organizations and trade agreements with the First World. So far, this effort has proven fruitless.

The international debt crisis

In October 1973, the first oil crisis struck the world. In 1973, Egypt had invaded Israel, which not only brought the world to the brink of war but also led Arab allies of Egypt to increase the price of oil dramatically. The Arab petroleum-exporting countries wanted to punish the U.S. for resupplying Israel militarily by restricting the supply of oil through an oil embargo. This dramatically increased the price of oil for not just the advanced industrialized world but also many Third-World countries. The embargo lasted until 1974.

Suddenly, many oil-producing countries made huge profits and put much of their newly acquired currency back into major Western banks. Having an abundance of currency in their coffers, banks lowered their interest rates. Third-World countries, which didn't have the option of passing on the increased price of oil to their impoverished consumers, as the advanced industrialized world did, faced hard choices. Should they increase the price of oil and oil-related products such as gasoline for their populations, which would have caused popular unrest, or should they just go out and borrow money to make up for the increase in spending on oil?

With ample money supplies, Western banks offered low variable interest loans, which made the choice an easy one for many Third-World countries. However, instead of borrowing at fixed interest rates, which had a slightly higher interest rate associated with them, they opted for variable interest rates. A few years later, this choice came back to haunt them.

In 1979, the second oil crisis struck after the Iranian Revolution and this time caused massive inflation in the advanced industrialized world. To combat inflation, interest rates were increased in most Western countries, including the U.S., and suddenly variable interest rates saw a huge increase. By 1980, many Third-World loans had interest rates of 20 percent or more attached to them. Many Third-World countries couldn't afford debt payments anymore. If countries like Mexico and Brazil would have defaulted on their outstanding loans, many Western banks, such as Bank of America or Citibank, would have collapsed.

Remembering the beginning of the Great Depression in 1929, the U.S. decided to bail out the Third World and the Western banking structure. For this reason, the Reagan administration increased American lending to the IMF so that the IMF could be used to restructure or outright buy Third-World loans. The IMF proceeded to restructure Third-World loans by turning them into long-term loans with fixed interest rates attached to them. This allowed for many Third-World countries to avoid defaulting on their loans, because they had lower but longer payments to make. In the end, however, many Third-World countries were still stuck with high foreign debts and are still paying the price today.

Multinational corporations

A final component in the development or underdevelopment of Third-World countries are multinational corporations, or MNCs. There are both pluses and minuses when it comes to multinational involvement in Third-World countries. Here's a look at the positive side:

>> MNCs invest heavily in Third-Worlds countries, thus providing not only jobs but also facilities and even an infrastructure to get their goods to the international markets.

>> Indirectly, through the provision of jobs and salaries, MNCs stimulate the local service economy from restaurants to grocery stores.

>> MNCs provide new and needed technology and management techniques and pay taxes to the host nations.

On the negative side,

>> MNCs lower wages, and the work environment for the locals isn't always the best.

>> Much of the profit generated in Third-World countries doesn't stay in the Third World but is repatriated.

>> Often, MNCs are tempted to intervene in local political affairs, including not just bribery but even overthrowing governments. They interrupt local culture with new ideas and new customs, which often conflict with many traditional cultures.

In conclusion, MNCs are both good and bad, and an evaluation of their involvement in Third-World countries should be country-specific. In other words, you shouldn't applaud or condemn MNCs as a whole but should study their impact on specific countries to draw appropriate conclusions.

Seeking Globalization: An Integration of Countries

The concept of globalization has become one of the most widely used terms in IPE today. Globalization refers to the integration of countries through increasing trade and contact. It's defined as a widening, deepening, and speeding up of a world-wide interconnectedness in all aspects of contemporary social life, from the cultural to the criminal, from the financial to the spiritual.

Although globalization could be found in the 19th century among many European powers, only recently has globalization occurred on a global scale. With the creation of the Bretton Woods system (see "Creating a New Economic Order," earlier in this chapter), increasing contact and trade began between many countries, and today almost every nation's economy has become closely tied to the economies of the rest of the world. The term we use to describe this phenomenon is *interdependence*.

Any event — be it economic, scientific, or even cultural — within any society will have an impact on the rest of the globe. An American economic downturn, such as experienced in late 2007, won't only hurt the American people anymore but will start a major recession in the rest of the world. An outbreak of a pandemic disease, such as the new coronavirus COVID-19, won't just impact the country of origin, China, but within weeks will affect the rest of the world. Even the emergence of an American pop phenomenon, such as Lady Gaga, will have an impact on the rest of the globe.

Measuring globalization

International trade is the major way we measure globalization today. We take the sum of imports and exports and then divide it by gross domestic product (GDP) to get a correct measurement of international trade. The higher the percentage, the more connected an economy is globally. In other words, the higher the percentage, the more interdependent a country is globally.

REMEMBER

GDP measures all economic transactions within a country. GDP per capita divides the overall GDP of a country by its population to measure a country's wealth.

Foreign direct investment (FDI) is the second major example of globalization. The term refers to one country participating in the economic activities of another country. This can be done directly, through the ownership of property in foreign countries, or indirectly. The ownership of mines, oil fields, and factories are an example of direct foreign investment. A more indirect way of foreign investment includes joint ventures, transfer of management techniques and new technology, and even the purchase of foreign stocks and bonds. Today, trillions of dollars are exchanged every year in the form of foreign investments. While traditionally the most foreign investment occurs between the advanced industrialized world, this has been rapidly changing, with more and more foreign investment occurring in Third-World countries.

REMEMBER

To be able to invest in a foreign country or trade with a foreign country, a stable currency system has to be in place. This is usually referred to as a *monetary system.* This monetary system determines the value of a nation's currency in relation to another nation's currency, allowing investors, buyers, and sellers to calculate the costs of economic transactions. In other words, the monetary system determines a state's currency exchange rate in relationship to other nations' currency rates.

Comparing countries: The KOF Index of Globalization

The KOF Index of Globalisation, developed by the Swiss Federal Institute of Technology, measures three dimensions of globalization: economic, social, and political. Figure 13-1 shows the increase of globalization from 1970 to 2017. As the figure shows, international economic integration has increased from about 35 percent in 1970 to about 62 percent globally in the last 47 years.

TECHNICAL STUFF

The KOF Index measures globalization in economic, social, and political dimensions, using 42 variables and on a scale from 1 to 100. The higher the score for a country, the more globalized (integrated) a country is.

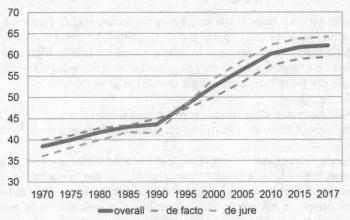

KOF Globalisation Index
World average

Source: Gygli, Savina, Florian Haelg, Niklas Potrafke, and Jan-Egbert Sturm (2019): The KOF
Globalisation Index – Revisited, Review of International Organizations, 14(3), 543-574

FIGURE 13-1:
The KOF Index of
Globalization.

The economic aspects of the KOF Index include both trade and international finances. It measures both exchange of goods and services, including tariffs, taxes, and trade restrictions. The financial aspect looks at foreign investment as well as investment restrictions and international investment agreements.

The social aspects of the KOF Index include personal contact, information flows, and cultural globalization. For example, personal contact includes tourism, migration, and international student exchanges. Information flows can include access to television and the Internet and freedom of the press. Cultural globalization can include the number of American fast-food places abroad and the protection of civil rights, including gender equality.

Finally, the political aspect looks at the numbers of embassies a country has, how many international treaties a country has signed, how many international organizations a country belongs to, how often a country participates in U.N. peace-keeping missions, and how many international nongovernment organizations (NGOs) are located within a country.

REMEMBER

NGOs are private organizations not connected to a government. They raise money and find volunteers to help the population in Third-World countries. They often work with local government to help the local population with issues such as disease, hunger, and natural disasters. Doctors Without Borders and the Children's Defense Fund are examples of NGOs.

The KOF Index demonstrates that globalization has spread throughout the world since 1970. However, regional differences exist. In Africa, for example, many areas are barely topping the 30 percent level, which shows a very weak level of economic interconnectedness. In other areas, such as in many Western European countries, the KOF Index number has actually topped the 90th percentile, showing an almost perfect level of economic interdependence. In Western Europe, this is obviously the result of European integration through the European Union, but other countries such as Australia and Canada are following suit quickly.

In the most recent index, Switzerland was the most highly globalized country in the world, followed by the Netherlands and Belgium. Switzerland was strongly globalized across all categories. The two least-integrated countries in the world are Eritrea and Somalia, both located in Africa.

REMEMBER

Smaller countries tend to be more integrated with the global economy than larger countries, which aren't as dependent on trade. For this reason, the U.S. occupies the 59th spot on the KOF Index.

At present, globalization is becoming a global phenomenon, slowly overcoming the North-South divide discussed earlier in this chapter. While only about 20 percent of all goods traded globally were exported by developing economies in 1980, this number has changed quite dramatically. By 2005, developing countries had increased their level of trade/exports to 32 percent, and by 2030 that level of trade/exports is expected to increase to 45 percent.

Seeing the light at the end of the tunnel

As many liberal economists had hoped for, free trade is slowly able to overcome the North-South divide. The creation of a global free market economy has the potential to overcome the gap between the First and Third World. Certainly, this won't happen overnight but may take another generation or two. The First World seems to have realized this and has recently opened its exclusive club called the Group of Eight (G-8), including the eight largest economies of the world, to new members. Many are from traditional Third-World countries, such as Indonesia and Brazil.

The most recent example of globalization is the creation of the G-20 in 1999. The Group of Twenty (G-20) includes 19 countries and the European Union. Combined, these 20 economies represent about two-thirds of the world's population, 80 percent of the world's trade, and 85 percent of the world's GDP. Its major focus is the maintenance of international financial stability and trade. In other words, the G-20 represents an attempt to deal with international economic crises globally.

4 Going from Classical to Modern Political Ideologies

Take a look at the first classical political science writers in ancient Greece. They truly are the founders of political science, and their writings still impact political science and politics today.

Turn to modern writers who have impacted world politics and democratic institutions globally. Not surprisingly, they impacted the American founding fathers.

Read a discussion of modern-day political ideologies, and then explore both liberalism and conservatism in their classical and modern form and two authoritarian ideologies: Fascism and Communism.

Chapter **14**

Starting in Greece: The Roots of Political Science

Political theory and political philosophy refer to thinking about how a better political world could look and how to create it. Often this involves criticism of the current political structure, which involves all practices and institutions that are a part of government. While *political philosophy* deals with more abstract topics such as justice in society, *political theory* is more concerned with theories of politics and how they were created. Political theory, therefore, deals with topics such as defining various forms of governments, while political philosophy studies concepts, such as what makes a government legitimate.

TECHNICAL STUFF

Political theory is one of the four major subfields making up political science (see Chapter 1). Political philosophy on the other hand is related to both disciplines, political science and philosophy. It deals mainly with ideal political institutions and ideal human political behavior.

This chapter travels to ancient Greece and looks at political theory and political philosophy through the eyes of three great Greek philosophers: Socrates, Plato, and Aristotle. Ancient Greece is considered the birthplace not only of Western civilization but also of political science, especially the subdiscipline of political theory. The Greeks were the first great philosophers. They created a culture that valued speech and debate and not only made it a part of their daily lives but also gave these qualities an elevated status in society. The Greek philosophers were especially concerned with knowledge and reason and, in the realm of politics, with justice. They studied which type of political regime would create the most ethical and most just political community.

Studying Ancient Greece and the Start of Political Science

About 2,500 years ago, ancient Greece was not just one nation-state but a collection of city-states making up its own little international system. Each one of these city-states was referred to as a polis — this is where the term *political science* comes from. These city-states had different political structures: Some were absolute monarchies, some dictatorships, and some even democracies. This allowed the Greek philosophers to study a variety of political regimes, compare them, and come up with an ideal form of government — the beginning of political science!

At this time, many great accomplishments occurred in the social and natural sciences, such as mathematics, biology, and chemistry. Most important for this book, political science and political philosophy were also created. For the next several hundred years, political science would be closely linked to Greek political philosophy, and later on Christian theology (see Chapter 15).

In ancient Greece, three philosophers, Socrates, Plato, and Aristotle, set the foundation for not just the discipline of political science but also all of Western political thought. We still debate their ideas today, and without them, many concepts such as democracy wouldn't be possible. These early philosophers didn't just deal with the general question of life, asking questions such as "What is the purpose of life" and "How can we be happy?" but they studied political regimes trying to discover the best form of government and rights citizens and rulers should possess.

The next sections highlight each of the great Greek philosophers.

DEFINING HAPPINESS

The term *happiness* is used quite a bit by the Greek philosophers. It's important to note that happiness for them was quite a bit different from what we understand the term to mean today. It wasn't being happy because we bought a new car, got a new mate, or started a family, but the term referred to leading a just and virtuous life and contributing to the public good.

Questioning Everything: Socrates

It's believed that Socrates was born in 470 BCE in Athens, Greece. Most of the information on his ideas is secondhand because Socrates never wrote any books or articles and didn't even write his ideas down on paper. So it was up to his students, especially Plato, to collect his ideas and put them on paper.

Socrates (see Figure 14-1) was born into an artistic family. His father was a sculptor and his mother was a midwife. Like his father, Socrates was trained as a stonemason and became a sculptor. However, his great passion was studying, especially philosophy. He read the texts of the leading philosophers at the time. Before becoming an educator, Socrates served in the military as a foot soldier. He proved to be a good and brave soldier, serving in several battles during the Peloponnesian War.

FIGURE 14-1: Greek philosopher Socrates.

Introducing inductive reasoning

When not fighting in wars, Socrates spent his time in Athens preaching his new style of philosophy, which involved questioning everything.

REMEMBER

Socrates's major contribution to Western political thought was the application of the inductive method, more commonly referred to as the scientific method, into inquiry. Using the scientific method, scientists observe a certain event, look for patterns explaining the event, and then come up with a testable proposition (hypothesis). If testing proves the hypothesis correct, a theory, or general explanation of behavior and events, has been created (see Chapter 2).

Inductive reasoning refers to arguments where the conclusion is probable from reasoning and testing. The inductive method allows students to discover facts for themselves through observation and examples that will support the conclusion.

The Socratic teaching method is still the most common form of instruction at many American universities and law schools. Inductive instruction refers to the teacher giving many examples of how a concept works. The students then notice how the concept works through the use of examples. *Deductive reasoning,* on the other hand, refers to a case where the conclusion is already a given without any testing necessary.

Taking a critical look at politics

Socrates soon became very controversial in Athens. His teaching style involved questioning, observation, and then criticism. When he applied this style to politics, his students began to question the current political structure and its leaders. Soon he and his students believed that the current leadership in Athens didn't possess wise and just values and implemented policies to benefit only themselves and not for the public good.

Socrates further believed that it was the duty of everybody to live an ethical life, and if ethics conflicted with the current political rules, it was legitimate to oppose these rules.

The city of Athens wasn't amused by Socrates critiquing the ruling elites and asked him to stop teaching his beliefs and values. Socrates refused and was arrested and subsequently sentenced to death. He was executed for corrupting the youth of Athens in 399 BCE.

Putting Political Philosophy into Play: Plato

Many consider Plato (see Figure 14-2) to be the first Western political philosopher. He was the first to put his thoughts into writing and even put Socrates's thoughts on paper.

FIGURE 14-2:
Early Western
political
philosopher,
Plato.

Source: National Archaeological Museum of Naples

REMEMBER

Plato was a playwright before he became a political philosopher. Most of his works are therefore not just straight books dealing with his ideas but fictional dialogues with his mentor Socrates, other Greek philosophers, and even his family and friends.

In his works, *The Republic* and *The Laws,* Plato basically presents his political philosophy. Often, it's difficult to know which ideas are from Socrates and which come from Plato. The reason is that while Plato himself is never a character in his own plays, he often expresses his ideas through Socrates's character in his works. Plato's works focus on an investigation of political and ethical questions. In a nutshell, throughout his career and his works, Plato always focused on his belief that politics should be used to bring about justice in society. This in turn required ethical rule.

TECHNICAL STUFF

Plato gives us one of the most famous terms in the Western world: *platonic love.* Today, platonic love refers to a relationship with another person that isn't sexual in nature. For Plato, sexual relations were a distraction from becoming a true philosopher dealing with more important issues such as justice and ethics in society.

Advocating for ethics

Plato was in many ways the exact opposite of Socrates. He was born around 428/427 BCE into a wealthy and politically active Athenian family and died at the age of 81 in 347 BCE. Plato received the best possible education at his time and was schooled in philosophy, poetry, and gymnastics. One of his philosophy teachers was actually Socrates, who would also become his mentor.

In his 20s, Plato perceived that the Athenian leadership was self-serving and didn't act in the public trust. Instead, he believed that Athenian leaders had become unethical, pursuing only their own self-interest. The execution of Socrates and the crushing loss in the Peloponnesian War were signs of this. For Plato, the Athenian government had become an unjust regime, and he advocated for a just regime to come to power headed by people who possess wisdom and have studied philosophy.

After Socrates's death, Plato left Athens and traveled through southern Italy and Egypt studying with other philosophers. When he returned to Athens around 387 BCE, Plato, then 40 years old, opened his own philosophical academy, considered the world's first Western university. Here, he taught students from all over Greece, including his favorite student Aristotle, who would become a future teacher at the academy.

TECHNICAL STUFF

Plato gave us the term academia, which refers to a group of professors and researchers working in a place of higher education. The term can be traced back to the spot Plato picked for his school which was located north of Athens in a place called Akademia.

Believing in just behavior

Plato outlined most of his political ideas in his works *The Republic* and *The Laws*, which he wrote around 360 BCE. In his book *The Republic*, Plato explores the best political orders for society and the way to truly live a good, ethical life. For him, both are connected to philosophic inquiry and the study of natural sciences, including mathematics.

Plato argues that just behavior by a person is vastly superior to unjust behavior. He even states that no harm can come to a good man, even if he gets killed, as long as the man is engaged in just behavior. Only unjust behavior, which damages the soul, can harm someone.

In addition, Plato argues that being a just person is what results in happiness. It's better to be a just person who is considered unjust than be an unjust person considered to be just. A person can be truly happy only if he leads a just life.

Dividing into classes

Similar to Socrates, Plato believed that people aren't solitary beings. People are social creatures who need to congregate with others to survive. Therefore, the creation of a polis, or state, is a natural result of humans banding together. Plato further believed that every polis had to have a class structure based on the inherent inequalities of people. This class structure also corresponded to different aspects of the human soul. For every class, there was a different part of the human soul that dominated and guided people's behavior.

According to Plato, the ideal polis should consist of three classes of people:

>> **Class I:** This class has citizens who engage in economic activity and includes farmers, artisans, and merchants. Their activity fulfills the economic desire and needs people have. This class is needed, because without having their basic needs met, humans can't move on and become active in higher activities such as philosophy. The behavior of this class is determined by desires such as economic success and wealth. Their soul, using Plato's terminology, is driven by the appetite portion of their soul, which drives them to fulfill their desires without regard for other citizens.

>> **Class II:** The citizens in this class defend the polis and maintain law and order. This group includes the military and the police. Their activity fulfills the needs for security in a polis. Again, humans can't move on to higher activity, such as philosophizing about life, unless they feel protected and secure. This class, according to Plato, needs to be taught strength, courage, and, most important, restraint. The people in this class need to be able to fight bravely but have the understanding that they're not to take over the state. They're driven by the spirit part of their soul, which results in their courage and strength but also compassion and empathy for other people.

>> **Class III:** In this class, the citizens rule the republic and have to have the knowledge and wisdom to guide the people. According to Plato, these guardians have to be trained at a young age and instilled with wisdom, courage, and restraint. They need to be schooled in the areas of philosophy, the natural sciences, and mathematics, and then they can rule a society wisely and justly. The people in this class are driven by the rational part of their soul, which is based on knowledge and wisdom. Only their rule can result in a just society, where rulers pursue the public good.

REMEMBER

Note that Plato doesn't advocate a democracy in his writings but rather says a polis should be ruled by a few well-educated and just persons. For him, democracy could result in mob rule, with the majority oppressing the minority, which he blamed for the death of his mentor, Socrates.

Creating an elite

Plato believed a city should be ruled by a small elite of philosophers who combine political power and philosophic wisdom. They're not interested in worldly things but strive for justice within their city. They're called philosopher kings or guardians. The guardians live in communal arrangements, and their children are raised communally. This results in selectively breeding a new stock of guardians. The guardians possess no wealth and own no land. They're supported by a tax on the other classes. For Plato, this is an ideal situation. Each class gets what it wants. The farmers control wealth to satisfy their appetite. The soldiers receive military honors and prestige, which satisfies their happiness. The guardians can set aside their own desires, can focus on their studies, and rule wisely and justly, because they can't benefit from their policies. *Note:* Plato doesn't exclude women from the ruling elite. Women are as capable as men when it comes to studies, and they can become guardians, too.

Plato isn't very optimistic when it comes to the future of his ideal polis. He believes that, over time, the ruling class will lose its values and turn to the values of the other classes. He fears that instead of pursuing justice and the common good, the leaders will attempt to achieve military honors and then attempt to enrich themselves. The final result will be tyranny of the few, such as a dictator, or tyranny of the many, such as democracy. Plato isn't fond of democracy because he perceives it as a system where the ignorant many (the public) oppresses the enlightened few.

Seeking a Scientific Approach: Aristotle

Aristotle (see Figure 14-3) was Plato's best student and lived from about 384 BCE to 322 BCE. Aristotle joined Plato's academy at the age of 17 and then stayed at the academy as a teacher.

After Plato's death, Aristotle decided to leave and travel for the next 12 years. He even served as a tutor for Alexander the Great of Macedonia. When he returned home to Athens, he decided to follow in his mentor Plato's footsteps and create his own philosophical academy, the Lyceum.

Unlike Plato's academy, which taught only political philosophy, Aristotle decided to focus on a full range of academic disciplines. With his father being a physician, Aristotle had developed a keen interest in the natural sciences, such as biology and physics. For this reason, Aristotle decided to take a more empirical approach to politics. Unlike Plato, who dealt mostly with the abstract, Aristotle focused on a more scientific approach. He wanted to collect data, test it, and then come up with conclusions and suggestions about politics.

FIGURE 14-3:
Greek philosopher and creator of the academy, the Lyceum, Aristotle.

Source: Library of Congress

Creating communities

Most of Aristotle's political ideas are summarized in his work *Politics*. In it he argues that people are social and political animals who assemble in communities. Creating communities is a natural development of people. People start at the most rudimentary level, creating a family community, because of their desire to procreate. The family is, however, too small to survive on its own. It can't feed or protect itself, so families band together to join into a village community.

Then, families begin to specialize in acquiring traits necessary for the village to survive. Some members of the village become farmers, some stonemasons, and some other artisans. However, the village is still too small to guarantee security against the outside world. It's vulnerable to foreign attack, and so the villages combine to create the polis (state). At this level, a large community of people has been created, and now economic and political security is guaranteed. The polis has become economically self-sufficient, and basic human needs such as food and shelter and safety have been met. It's at this point that humans can advance and focus on more abstract ideas, such as what form of government is best.

Being human: A look at humanity and politics

Aristotle believed that people were social creatures, by nature assembling in groups, and that through human interaction in groups, politics is born. Aristotle used to say man is a political animal. For him, thoughts about political life had to be the main aspect of political philosophy. Philosophy, in turn, was the true master science; therefore, political philosophers were the true kings of society.

What distinguishes people from animals? For Aristotle, it's the ability to reason that makes people unique. Like animals, people have biological and instinctive traits. However, that's where the similarities end. Only people possess the ability to think, especially in an abstract way. It's this ability to reason and pursue knowledge that differentiates people from animals.

While Plato believed that the pursuit of knowledge was enough to make people content, Aristotle argues that to be truly happy, a person has to take the pursuit of knowledge into politics. In the polis (state) is where a person is able to do so, where people have been freed of trying to fulfill basic necessities. They have the ability to take political philosophy to its highest level, and their thoughts can impact actual decision-making. Philosophy and politics have to be fused to actually matter, and knowledge and action have to become one. Therefore, an ideal leader has to have not only knowledge but also the political skills to lead a society. For Aristotle, this combination is easiest visible in the ability to debate. During a debate, knowledge can be carried into a call for action.

Political leaders need to have the wisdom to know what's right and the political skills to carry out their ideas. Aristotle's ideas on politics have influenced many European rulers and also the founding fathers of the United States.

Classifying forms of governments

Aristotle was concerned about the decline of his home state of Athens, so he sent out his students to the other city-states in Greece to collect data. He wanted to know which type or form of government worked best, which constitutions were the most just, and which type of government was able to survive in the long term.

After his students returned, he sat down to compose his work *Politics* in which he outlined various types of constitutions and forms of governments. Unlike Plato, Aristotle didn't argue for just one constitution and one form of government. He believed that all types of governments could have merit, if the ruler or rulers were wise and just. At the same time, all forms of governments could be horrible if bad rulers had been installed. So he created the first typology of forms of governments depending on the type of ruler in place:

» **Government by One:** This form of government is headed by one ruler. As long as the constitution is well-written and the ruler is just and wise, Aristotle labels it a monarchy. If the ruler however is unjust, enriching himself at the expense of the people, Aristotle labels it a tyranny.

» **Government by Few:** This form of government is dominated by a small elite. As long as the government has a well-written constitution and the elite pursues just and fair policies, Aristotle labels it an *aristocracy*. However, if the elite puts its own interests ahead of the public's, he labeled it an *oligarchy*.

» **Government by Many:** If many citizens are allowed to rule and the constitution is a well-written, just document, Aristotle labeled this form of government a *polity*. If, however, the majority pursues policies from which only it benefits, in turn hurting and discriminating against minorities, he labeled this system a *democracy*.

Aristotle took economics into account when classifying governments. For him, the good of the community mattered. He was afraid that in all three types of governments, leaders would turn against other citizens to claim economic benefits hurting society at the expense of less-fortunate citizens. It could be a tyrant enriching himself at the expense of his people or a small minority, labeled an oligarchy, that grew wealthy at the expense of the many. Interestingly, Aristotle was also afraid that in a democracy, the many could turn on the few, being jealous of their possessions and political power.

For Aristotle, the best scenario was in the middle where everybody was economically viable. In other words, Aristotle advocated for a society with a large middle class, which had its economic needs met and where just policies benefiting the majority were implemented. These ideas clearly impacted the American founding fathers when they drew up the Constitution of the United States.

Putting Ethics to Use

Ethics is a branch of philosophy defined as dealing with what's good and what's bad and the moral obligation to do what's good. Ethics prescribes what people should and shouldn't do. It studies concepts such as fairness, justice, and morality.

Serving the public first

The contributions of Socrates, Plato, and Aristotle involved the combination of ethics and politics. According to all three, politics is designed for leaders who have to put the public's interest over their own. Politics isn't for self-enrichment of a person or a group of people but for the enrichment of society. Therefore, politics isn't for everyone. Only the most enlightened leaders, or philosopher kings, to use Plato's term, can serve the people and subjugate their own self-interest to the wishes of society. The U.S. founding fathers were familiar with these ideas, and therefore the American form of government is a direct result of some of the Greek philosophers' concerns.

Designing the U.S. government

Looking at the creation of the U.S. government is a good case study on ethics and politics. The original U.S. Constitution is a response to the Greek philosophers' fear of a corrupt and unethical government. The concept of separation of powers was designed to result in a system of checks and balances. Each part of the government, using Aristotelian terminology, the one, the few, and the many, constantly checks on each other, thereby assuring a government that's just and has rules with the best possible outcome for society in mind. If one of three becomes corrupt and self-serving, the other two are still there to check and make sure this doesn't happen.

The government of the many is represented in the U.S. House of Representatives. The American people vote for all the members of the House of Representatives and are represented by them. All members of the House of Representatives can be held accountable by the people through elections. This gives the people the power to replace corrupt, unethical representatives. While members of the House of Representatives represent fairly small constituencies, the Senate was elected by the state legislatures, representing larger communities, namely whole states. It, too, can be checked; Senators could be impeached for unethical behavior.

If the many get out of hand trying to go after the few, such as the wealthy, they can be stopped by other parts of the government structures. For example, the U.S. Supreme Court represents the few. It currently has nine members appointed for life. Supreme Court justices can be impeached only for criminal behavior and therefore have the freedom to do what they believe is right and just. The Supreme Court has the power to nullify and overturn laws made by the many, if it considers these laws to be unconstitutional.

The presidency is equivalent to a government by one. The U.S. president has a considerable amount of power but is quite weak compared to other presidencies, such as the one in France. The U.S. president has to share powers with Congress, and his actions can be overturned by the court system. So if he turns out to be self-serving and corrupt, he can be held accountable by both the many (Congress), through impeachment and then removal, or the few (Supreme Court) by overturning his executive actions.

Chapter 15

Going Modern: Middle Ages to the Present

Modern political theorists deal with an empirical approach. Instead of philosophizing about how the world and people should be (as the Greek political theorists did; see Chapter 14), they wanted to study the world as it really is. Therefore, they looked at actual leaders and people and how they behaved. For them, politics wasn't about being ethical and wise but about who possesses power and how they used it for the good of the state and its people.

This chapter deals with the most influential post-Greek theorists, whose thoughts still impact the world today. They are Niccolo Machiavelli, Thomas Hobbes, John Locke, Montesquieu, Jean-Jacques Rousseau, Edmund Burke, and Adam Smith. But first, a discussion of two Catholic political theorists is in order. Then, to round out the chapter, I examine the theories of classical conservatism and classical and modern liberalism.

Taking a Lesson on Catholic Theory

In this section, I discuss two catholic political theorists. Both fused ancient Greek political thought with catholic teachings to set the way for the Renaissance and the rediscovery of ancient Greek and Roman thought. Without their contribution there might not have been a Renaissance or future philosophizing about the value of individuals or social contracts.

Saint Augustine (354–430)

One of the early Catholic theorists who fused Plato's teaching with catholic thought was Saint Augustine (see Figure 15-1). In his work *The City of God*, Augustine becomes one of the founding fathers of the political theory of Christianity. He explored the relationship between the individual and a divinely created natural order. According to Augustine, natural law regulating the world could be understood only through prayer and devotion to God. For this reason, monasteries and nunneries were built to create institutions to encourage these practices. In these institutions, specialists devoted entirely to God could study and try to understand natural law and order.

FIGURE 15-1: Saint Augustine, a founding father of the political theory of Christianity.

Source: Ann Ronan Pictures/Print Collector/Getty Images

According to Augustine, natural order could be achieved only in heaven, and the only option for people on Earth was to submit to the church and its teachings. The city of man, in Augustine's words, was sinful and therefore needs earthly authority such as religion and the state to maintain law and order. Only in the afterlife, in the city of God, can true justice be found and prevail.

Saint Thomas Aquinas (1225–1274)

Saint Thomas Aquinas (see Figure 15-2) was a Catholic theorist who tried to reconcile Aristotle's teachings with Catholic beliefs by incorporating both faith and reason in his work. His major work is *Summa Theologia*, in which he integrates reason and God's natural order. He argued that political theorists could use them to understand the meaning of God's plan for people.

FIGURE 15-2: Saint Thomas Aquinas, Catholic theorist and author of *Summa Theologia*.

Source: Library of Congress

Aquinas fusing reason and religion was a first during this time. Augustine had relied on faith and religious traditions to understand God's plans; Aquinas advocated the use of reason to do so. The idea that people could use reason to understand human nature was called *humanism* and opened the way for the Renaissance. If reason can unlock the natural order of things and everybody possesses reason within him, he should put individual judgment at the center of political life. The time to have divine plans interpreted by only clergy and kings was over, and individuals could do it themselves.

Augustinian thought supported traditional forms of authority, such as religion and the state, by advocating that only the church and state can understand natural law. If, however, citizens can understand and interpret natural law, they can begin to receive and share power in a community and become their own authority. The time for religious and traditional authority was over.

Revolting against religion

The humanist idea, that people could understand natural law and religion, resulted in the Protestant Reformation initiated by Martin Luther (1483–1546). Luther believed in a powerful God but argued that individuals themselves had to develop a relationship with God. The church could assist in doing so through its teachings and guidance, but in the end, the individual faces God alone. Suddenly, the individual was put at the forefront of religion, and not a church or a state. Not surprisingly, if the individual becomes the focus for religion, he also becomes the focus for political thought.

Understanding Power

This section focuses on five of the most famous modern theorists, who all used an empirical approach to studying politics. Their ideas still impact the social sciences today. Instead of using a normative approach and focusing on how politics ought to be, they believed that it was necessary to use an empirical approach and study how politics was actually practiced. Three of the five (Hobbes, Locke, and Rousseau) were contact theorists, who studied the relationship between individual and the state. The other two dealt with the study of power (Machiavelli) and the relationship of political institutions (Montesquieu).

Niccolo Machiavelli (1469–1527)

To this day, Niccolo Machiavelli (see Figure 15-3) is one of the most influential and controversial political philosophers in history. Just about every political scientist and also every politician, be they democratic or authoritarian, has read his works. Machiavelli wrote during the period of the Renaissance (French for "rebirth") in Europe. The Renaissance resulted in a cultural reboot of the old Greek and Roman ideas on philosophy, politics, and even architecture. In the area of politics, it resulted in feudalism and later the creation of the nation-state (see Chapter 8). For Machiavelli, the overwhelming interest of society was order. Order could be produced only in a well-led state. Therefore, any means to get to this well-led state were acceptable.

FIGURE 15-3:
Niccolo
Machiavelli,
influential
Renaissance
philosopher.

Source: Wikimedia Commons

REMEMBER

Italy had one of the first international systems in the world. It was a mini-state system consisting of five city-states. They were Florence, Naples, Venice, Milan, and the Vatican. They all competed for political power and dominance. This resulted in the birth of diplomacy and international relations in, first, Italy and later the rest of Europe (for a detailed discussion, see Chapter 8 and Chapter 9).

Looking at early life and workings

Machiavelli was born in 1469 in Florence, Italy. He came from a prominent Florentine family, and his father was an attorney. Machiavelli grew up at a time of great political upheaval and military conflict. The Pope and foreign powers, such as France and Spain as well as the Holy Roman Empire, battled for power and influence among the Italian city-states. Alliances changed constantly, battles were fought by mercenary armies, and governments fell often.

Machiavelli studied Latin, some Greek, and grammar and rhetoric. In 1494, he was put in charge of the production of official Florentine government documents, and in 1498, he was appointed Second Chancellor of Florence after the ruling Medici family was toppled by French troops and a democratic republic was created. Machiavelli was put in charge of the city's foreign affairs, becoming Florence's top diplomat. He traveled on behalf of Florence throughout Italy and even to the Spanish court. Not surprisingly, his career as a diplomat influenced his political thought and his writings.

During his tenure, Machiavelli was put in charge of the Florentine military. He decided to use a citizens' militia instead of a mercenary army to defend the city, a first at that time in Italy.

During this time, Machiavelli began to study Roman history and published some of his early essays. The theme of his essays was that a ruler had to deal with rebellious people, or enemies, the way the Romans did; they needed to be either destroyed or bought off and brought into the fold.

Despite Machiavelli's best efforts, the Republic of Florence was destroyed by Spanish troops with the help of the papacy, and the Medici family returned to power in 1512. Machiavelli was subsequently banished after being imprisoned and tortured. He left for exile in 1513, where he wrote his two major works, *The Prince* and *Discourses on Livy*.

Machiavelli retired from public service and traveled through Europe. By 1520, he had made up with the Medici family and was back in politics, becoming the official historian of Florence. He finished his book on Florentine history in 1525 and, nearing the end of his life, switched from politics to theater plays. Machiavelli died in 1527 at the age of 58, but his work lives on to this day.

Writing "The Prince"

The Prince, written in 1513, is Machiavelli's masterpiece. The work wasn't published until after his death, in 1532. In *The Prince*, Machiavelli assumes the role of a teacher to a new prince just installed to power. Many consider Machiavelli the true founder of modern political science because he studied the actual world as it was and didn't deal with utopias as the ancient Greeks had done. For Machiavelli, it wasn't about justice and ethics in government but about how to acquire and maintain political power. The necessity to acquire political power justified any actions, even ones that could be considered immoral.

In his work, Machiavelli portrayed politics for the first time as a struggle for power. He further outlined ways a ruler can successfully lead his nation. To understand Machiavelli, you need to look at the historical context of his work. Studying the conflict between the Italian city-states and the rest of Europe, Machiavelli believed that Italy had to unify to compete with the threat of great European powers such as France, Spain, and England. In addition, he decided that politics is all about power and that religion, morals, and ethics don't belong in politics unless they can be used to enhance state power. Machiavelli wrote *The Prince* to offer the ruling Medici family a blueprint on how to gain and, more important, maintain political power.

According to Machiavelli, leaders should be concerned only about power. They need to employ whatever tactics necessary to acquire more power. Only power can guarantee their and their state's survival in the long run. Machiavelli believed that power can be maintained through the use of force, the threat of the use of force, and by the buying of enemies and turning them into allies.

Following rules

Machiavelli became the first political consultant in history in his works. He believed that a successful ruler should have the following characteristics:

>> **Self-interest:** Unlike the ancient Greeks and the Catholic Church, Machiavelli believed that a ruler who uses self-interest and seeks power isn't immoral or sinful but is just following human nature.

>> **Power of a lion and cunningness of a fox:** Machiavelli believed a successful ruler needed both of these traits to survive.

>> **Use of force:** For Machiavelli, the use of force to protect a country from external and internal threats was legitimate. Violence is an instrument for the ruler to use to maintain himself in power and to enhance his power. The use of force isn't immoral, because morality is removed from politics. The end truly justifies the means.

Machiavelli also thought the use of violence could save lives by preventing more violence in the future. In other words, it's better to turn against a domestic or external enemy while it's still weak than to wait until it gets stronger. To wait only results in more bloodshed.

>> **Ready to go to war:** A ruler needs to establish a large military force to protect himself and the state.

>> **Being feared:** Machiavelli thought it was better to be feared than to be loved. As long as the fear doesn't turn into hatred, the ruler is safe.

>> **Just and fair:** A just ruler shouldn't take a person's property to enrich himself, because he will create a lifelong enemy. Also if a leader has to engage in acts of extreme violence, he has to have a reason for it. If there's a reason to punish an opponent, the ruler has to act quickly and decisively. He has to be assertive and finish off his opponents quickly. A ruler can't be seen as indecisive, for this will lower his esteem among the people.

>> **Have good, capable advisors:** However, he needs to make the most important decisions himself.

>> **Be manipulative, to a degree:** A good ruler has to use religion to manipulate the people. People will follow a divine ruler easier because he has been anointed by God.

Thomas Hobbes (1588–1679)

Thomas Hobbes (see Figure 15-4) is another founding father of modern political theory. He truly was a Renaissance man, not only excelling at political philosophy but also working in history, the law, theology, and even the natural sciences, specializing in physics. In his major work *Leviathan*, Hobbes set out to prove scientifically that Machiavelli's claim that power was the most important variable in politics was correct. He did so by analyzing human behavior and its relationship with the state. In other words, Hobbes created one of the first social contract theories.

FIGURE 15-4:
Thomas Hobbes,
a founding father
of modern
political theory.

Source: Wikimedia Commons

REMEMBER

Social contract theories usually include a study of human behavior in the *state of nature* — people living before a society or civilization has been created — and, most important, an analysis of human behavior with no government in place. Social contact theories conclude with a recommendation on the best form of government.

Similar to Machiavelli, Hobbes believed in the study of power in politics. He also opposed the old Greek philosophers and their normative approach, advocating instead for a scientific approach to politics involving rigorous testing. This was one of the reasons Hobbes was close to Galileo, who used a scientific approach (mathematics) to show that the sun and not the Earth was at the center of our galaxy.

Making a power play

Like Machiavelli, Hobbes believed that politics was about the quest for political power and that political power had to be used to maintain law and order in a society. He thought a study of human behavior was the first step because all people pursue power in their lives. This lust for power is a part of people because they pursue their own self-interest and pleasure in life. The more power they have, the more successful they'll be in their quest.

This struggle for power, in turn, results in conflict between people in a true state of nature with no government present. According to Hobbes, people will clash for three reasons:

>> **Competition for material goods:** Everybody wants certain goods, and there isn't an infinite amount of goods so people will compete for them.

>> **Fear and insecurity:** If people acquire power, they'll also acquire security. This quest for power will result in violence between men.

>> **Glory:** Glory will come from acquiring power, and men want more glory to enhance their reputations, which in turn enhances their power.

Therefore, there's a constant state of warfare in the state of nature. Everybody will fight everybody with no notions of right or wrong. The world will be dominated by civil war and constant violence. For this reason, a strong state is needed to restrain people. For Hobbes, society results because people fear each other.

Creating a state

According to Hobbes, people will voluntarily leave the state of nature and give up their freedoms for a more secure environment as provided by the state. They voluntarily surrender all their freedoms to a central authority for peace and security. In his work, *Leviathan*, Hobbes further argued that a strong centralized monarchy would be the best form of government to guarantee security for society, because in a parliamentary democracy, you'd find decentralization and more people having power. These parliamentarians would all strive for power, resulting in constant struggles in parliament. Instead of guaranteeing security for the people, parliament becomes a source of conflict itself.

Hobbes also rejected federalism and believed in one strong all-powerful unitary monarchy where all power is centralized in a monarch who himself is above the law. For Hobbes, the purpose of government isn't to provide justice and equality but security for the population.

Working toward political philosophy

Thomas Hobbes was born in 1588 in Westport, England. Not much is known about his childhood, only that he was born prematurely after his mother heard that the Spanish armada was invading England. His father was the vicar of the local church, but he was a violent man often getting into fights. Eventually, he abandoned his family. Young Thomas was raised by his uncle, a wealthy glove manufacturer. This proved to be a blessing for Thomas, who received a private education and went to Oxford University to study physics and logic. After Hobbes decided to leave Oxford for Cambridge, he graduated with a bachelor of arts degree from Cambridge in 1608.

As was common among young academics back then, Hobbes became the private tutor to an aristocrat. He was lucky to be selected to be the private tutor of William Cavendish, the Earl of Devonshire. Not only did Hobbes serve as his tutor, but he also stayed on to serve as the tutor for his son. As the tutor to a prominent and wealthy aristocrat, Hobbes was able to travel throughout Europe with his student, allowing him to meet many of the great minds of Europe. His academic interest at the time was mostly in the area of translating classic Greek texts into English.

To his great dismay, Hobbes was fired in 1628, when the Earl of Devonshire died, and Hobbes had to look for a new job. He turned to political philosophy. Continuing his work as a tutor for several aristocrats, Hobbes was able to live in Paris, travel throughout Europe, and even meet Galileo Galilei in Italy.

Hobbes returned home to England during times of political turmoil. The English Civil War began in 1642, which increased Hobbes's interest in politics. Hobbes supported the royalists in their fight against the Puritans, who favored a parliamentary system of government.

In 1647, living in Paris, Hobbes received the job as tutor for future King Charles II of England. This relationship proved to be beneficial for Hobbes because the king became his protector. After he returned to England, Hobbes published his major work *Leviathan* in 1651, in which he outlined his political philosophy. The book became a hit but was very controversial. In 1666, Hobbes was tried as a heretic but Charles II protected him. However, the English government decided that his works couldn't be published anymore and that he had to stop writing about human nature and politics. So for the rest of his life, Hobbes went back to translating ancient Greek texts such as the *Odyssey* and the *Iliad* into English. Thomas Hobbes died at the age of 91 of a stroke in 1679.

John Locke (1632–1704)

John Locke (see Figure 15-5), similar to Thomas Hobbes, was an English political philosopher. Unlike Hobbes, who was a monarchist, Locke sided with the parliamentary opposition and supported the Glorious Revolution that weakened the British monarchy and imposed parliamentary supremacy. Locke set out to disprove Hobbes in his work titled *Two Treatises of Government,* which was published in 1690. With his work, Locke founded a new way of thinking that viewed human beings as principled, bright, and capable of self-rule and self-government. Therefore, a limited government and more personal liberties in society are possible. With these ideas, Locke became the godfather of classical liberalism, which in turn influenced the American Revolution and subsequently the U.S. founding fathers when they wrote the Constitution.

FIGURE 15-5: John Locke, English political philosopher and godfather of classical liberalism.

Source: Library of Congress

Making property a priority

Similar to Hobbes, Locke was an empiricist and wanted to use a scientific approach to study politics. For Locke, the state of nature consisted of a primitive society where people were free of any state control and acted rationally to better their lives. In his *An Essay Concerning Human Understanding*, Locke argued that people were born tabula rasa, or with a blank slate. They come into the world without any preconceived ideas and are instead shaped by the environment they grow up in.

For both Locke and Hobbes, human nature is determined by both reason and self-interest. Hobbes believed that human beings are driven by desires while Locke believed that their rational side dominates. People are largely peaceful and cooperative and are driven by a desire to acquire private property. Reason and self-interest teaches them not to harm each other or take another's possessions. According to Locke, reasoning teaches people "that no one ought to harm another in his life, liberty, or possessions."

For Locke, the state of nature was a state of liberty where everybody is free and enjoys the right to property. Locke considered the right to own property a God-given right and believed that people would work their property and become prosperous. Not owning property or not being industrious was a violation of life in the state of nature. With these ideas, Locke also became a founding father of capitalism.

Forming a social contract

According to Locke, the ideal state was "a state of peace, good-will, mutual assistance, and preservation." Now the big question is, if the state of nature is so wonderful, why would people want to leave it and create a government that constrains some of their freedoms?

According to Locke, there are threats to people. These threats can be both domestic and foreign. Foreign powers can be a major threat to an unprotected people, and domestically laws have to be in place to protect people against any violations of the law and any injustices. Therefore, people have to come together to form a society and create a government. They need to enter into a social contract and establish a limited government to protect society from foreign aggression and establish laws, based on natural laws, such as the right to property in a society. Government needs to pass laws aligned with natural laws and be able to punish those who violate the laws. Locke further argued that the government should consist of a legislature to enact just laws, an executive to enforce them, and a judiciary to mediate conflict.

Locke's most controversial statement comes at this point. He argued that, if government does a poor job or violates the social contract, people have the right to revolt. This statement appealed to many and contributed to both the French and American Revolutions.

THE PRINCIPLE OF PARLIAMENTARY SUPREMACY

The Revolution of 1688, or Glorious Revolution, was a result of King James II, a devout Catholic, wanting to force England to convert to Catholicism. After Anglican bishops were prosecuted in 1688, anti-Catholic riots broke out in England. This resulted in a bloodless revolution driving King James II into exile in 1688. The throne was offered to Prince William III of Orange (the Dutch Republic). In 1689, parliament met and made William and his wife, Mary, joint monarchs. However, at the same time, a bill of rights was passed by parliament that stripped the monarchy of major powers such as the power to raise and fund armies without the consent of parliament. The principle of parliamentary supremacy had been established.

To this day, the British monarch can't be a Catholic. The reason is simple: The king or queen of the United Kingdom is also the head of the Church of England (Anglican Church).

Studying philosophy and medicine

John Locke was born into a middle-class family. His father was an attorney, was politically active, being a Puritan, and had fought in the English Civil War on the parliamentarian side. One of his father's friends, a parliamentarian, sponsored him, and young John was able to attend the prestigious Westminster School in London and later Oxford University to study medicine and philosophy.

Lock's medical degree got him his first job when he was appointed the personal physician of Lord Ashley. After saving Lord Ashley's life and Ashley becoming Lord Chancellor of England, Locke began to prosper. However, when civil strife broke out one more time, with King James II persecuting the Anglican Church and its leaders, Locke was forced to flee to the Netherlands. He lived there from 1683 to 1688 and worked on several texts at the same time. The most famous of them *The Two Treatises on Government* was published after his return in 1688 at the end of the Glorious Revolution. Locke became an intellectual hero among the anti-monarchist forces, and he died in 1704 as one of the most respected political theorists at the time.

Montesquieu (1689–1755)

Another major modern political theorist was Charles-Louis de Secondat, Baron de La Brede et de Montesquieu — whew! what a mouthful. He was more commonly known as just Montesquieu (see Figure 15-6) and was a major political theorist who had a great impact on the political structure of the United States. Because of him, the U.S. currently uses the concept of separation of powers, where government consists of various branches constantly checking on each other to make sure none of them dominates.

FIGURE 15-6:
Montesquieu, political theorist and author of *The Spirit of the Laws.*

REMEMBER

Montesquieu advocated dividing political power among an executive, a legislative, and a judiciary. All these institutions have to be independent of each other to be able to check each other.

Montesquieu was born in 1689 near Bordeaux, France. He was the son of a minor nobleman and came from a military family. After his mother passed when he was only 7, he was sent to a private school where he received a top-notch education. In 1705, he began his studies in law at the University of Bordeaux and became a lawyer by 1708. Next, he moved to Paris to gain experience in his profession.

After his father's death, Montesquieu inherited his estate and married wealthy. Leaving the day-to-day operations of his estate, which included a vineyard, to his wife, he began to focus on political philosophy and was one of the first scholars to compare Christianity and Islam.

Montesquieu became famous, moved to Paris, and, in 1728, joined the prestigious Academie Francaise. He traveled through Europe visiting Austria, Hungary, Italy, Germany, Holland, and England, where he lived for two years until 1731. Returning to France, he began to work on his political ideas. He published an essay on the English Constitution and, in 1750, his masterpiece *The Spirit of the Laws.* It was 1,086 pages long and today is considered one of the major works in the social sciences and the law. In his work, Montesquieu classified various forms of government and created the concept of separation of powers.

Not surprisingly, Montesquieu's work didn't sit well with the absolutist royal government in France, and even the Pope criticized it. By 1751, it was on the list of banned books in France, but Montesquieu had become a household name, and his ideas would influence the founding fathers of the U.S. when they wrote the Constitution a few decades later. Montesquieu died of a fever in 1755.

Jean Jacques Rousseau (1712–1778)

Jean Jacques Rousseau (see Figure 15-7) was born in Geneva, Switzerland, in 1712. His mother died at childbirth and his father, a watchmaker, had to flee the city after getting into trouble with the law. Young Rousseau, only 10 years old, was therefore forced to live with his mother's family. He despised them and fled the city at the age of 16 to find adventure all over Europe. He converted to Catholicism and lived in the Kingdom of Sardinia and France. His life changed when he met the Baroness de Warens, who took him in as both her steward and her lover. She provided him with an education and Rousseau studied philosophy and music.

FIGURE 15-7:
Jean Jacques
Rousseau, author
of *The Social
Contract.*

Source: Library of Congress

Rousseau moved to Paris at the age of 30 and joined a club of young intellectuals. He began to write music, including several operas. At the age of 37, Rousseau decided to switch to philosophy and in 1750 he published his first major work, *A Discourse on the Sciences and the Arts*.

In 1754, Rousseau decided to return to Geneva and converted back to Calvinism. Back in Geneva, Rousseau proceeded to write some of his major works, including *The Social Contract* in 1762. The work, which contained a criticism of unjust government, resulted in him having to renounce his citizenship in Geneva. In addition, his works were being banned in France. Until his death of a stroke in 1778, Rousseau lived as a fugitive moving between Switzerland, France, and England.

Rousseau was the last of the great social contract theorists. Rousseau published his major work *The Social Contract* in 1762, and it became one of the most influential books in political theory. Rousseau argued that man was free and without chains in the state of nature. There was no government and no law. Rousseau thus believed that people are born free and live in a state of nature without government.

According to Rousseau, people behave as noble savages helping others in need until the introduction of private property happens. For him, private property creates a class structure in society. Suddenly, inequalities exist and people begin to change. Their goodness is destroyed and envy and greed take over. For this reason, government and laws become necessary. However, society should be a voluntary community based on the wishes of all of society. Rousseau calls this the *general will.* The general will represents the community and not individuals who could be selfish and narrow-minded. In a good society, people can be free again and enjoy life similar to the one in the state of nature.

REMEMBER

Rousseau's contract theory calls for economic equality and equality before the law. Everybody has the right to be involved in politics, not just the propertied classes. Under his contract theory, people surrender their natural rights to a general will (society) and in turn will have a say in what the general will should be. This is called a *direct democracy.* Everybody in a society is required to abide by the general will, and those who object will be forced to comply.

By getting together voluntarily through a social contract, people retained some of their freedom and could leave society at any point, if the government decided to infringe upon their freedom. Rousseau further argued that the power to make policy should remain with the people and government should just try to implement policies made by the people. He clearly believed in a direct democracy like the ones found in ancient Greece and Rome.

Moving to Classical Conservatism

Classical conservatism, also known as European conservatism, is based on the ideas of both Machiavelli and Hobbes (see earlier in this chapter) as well as the teachings of the Catholic Church. Although classical conservatism is rare in the U.S., it's prevalent in Europe. Classical conservatism today is the dominant ideology of most of Eastern Europe, especially countries such as Hungary and Poland, and can also be found in major conservative political parties in Germany and in Southern Europe.

Saving traditional beliefs and institutions

Classical conservatism was a reaction to the liberal ideas of the French Revolution. Conservatives were dismayed by the political violence and destruction of traditional concepts and institutions during the French Revolution. Conservative political theorists like Edmund Burke (1729–1797), shown in Figure 15-8, believed that liberals give human beings too much credit and that people aren't always rational. People have irrational passions and emotions that can result in them destroying traditional beliefs and institutions without much thought, which can result in violence and chaos. The French Revolution is a great example of this.

EDMUND BURKE E:SQ.ᴿ

FIGURE 15-8:
Edmund Burke, statesman and philosopher.

Source: Granger

For Burke, traditional beliefs and institutions have achieved legitimacy in a society because people have become used to them and tend to support them. So change should occur gradually, and existing institutions need to be slowly changed and not destroyed overnight.

Defining conservative views

Classical conservatism strives to maintain traditional beliefs and institutions. To accomplish this, classical conservative theorists support the beliefs covered in the next sections.

Identifying human flaws

Classical conservatives have a morbid view of human nature. They believe that human nature is flawed and that people are driven by their emotions and passions. Instead of relying on reason, they rely on their feelings. Therefore, they possess emotions such as hatred and greed and are by nature materialistic. Conservatives further believe that human nature can't be changed and that the world is stuck with a flawed human population.

In a state of nature, as envisioned by Rousseau (see earlier in this chapter), people wouldn't be kind to each other or help out when required but would instead take what they could and harm each other. For this reason, a strong state is needed to protect people from themselves. Clearly, classical conservatism is very Hobbesian in nature.

Maintaining a strong government

Because people are flawed and irrational, a strong centralized government is needed to enforce law and order. People are violent by nature; therefore, society places greatest emphasis on law and order. Everything else, including personal freedoms and natural rights, comes second. A society can survive only if a powerful state can maintain law and order. For this reason, government needs to be strong and very centralized. A weak government wouldn't be able to effectively maintain law and order.

Building an elite

There's also a belief that a natural elite, the best and brightest in society, should be in control of government. It's important to point out that conservatives don't advocate for a blood elite, like an aristocracy, or a monied elite, found in capitalist societies. They believe that God has given people different abilities and that some are just better equipped to handle running a government. These few select people can be detected through a rigorous educational structure that separates the brightest from the average and allows for only the best students to advance to higher education. The higher educational levels should be free of charge and then create the natural elite running the country. This belief is similar to the Catholic idea of predestiny, which states that God predestines a whole life for a person.

Focusing on community

Classical conservatives believe in communalism, not to be confused with Communism (see Chapter 17). Communalism advocates the belief that the community, the many, matter more than the individual, or the one. For this reason, policies should benefit the majority and not just a select few. So, for example, if an individual acquires a disease that can be spread, he needs to be isolated from the community. The community has rights, the right to be protected from a potentially dangerous individual, which are superior to the individual's rights. Every policy government implements needs to protect or benefit the community and not the individual. Community rights always trump individual rights.

Incorporating traditionalism

Classical conservatives support traditionalism. For them, the past needs to be studied and past wisdoms need to be incorporated into today's society. Society should be guided by the collective historical wisdom of a people. Conservatives believe in change but advocate for a slow gradual change to existing institutions and beliefs.

Controlling emotions

Finally, classical conservatives advocate for the instilling of discipline into a population. With people being flawed and not being able to control their emotions, it becomes necessary to instill patience and discipline into them. The two institutions best suited to do so are the educational structures and religion.

Advocating for Classical Liberalism

Classical liberalism began in England in the 17th century, when major political theorists such as John Locke began to discuss the relationship between individual and society. These discussions involved the rights and responsibilities that not only individuals but also government had in society. In addition, the right to own property was incorporated into classical liberalism, and soon classical liberalism and capitalism became a part of each other.

Leaving the economy alone

Another founding father of classical liberalism was Adam Smith (see Figure 15-9). Smith was a Scottish economist, who published *The Wealth of Nations* in 1776, which created the concept of laissez faire capitalism. Unlike the predominant economic theory of the time, mercantilism (see Chapter 13), Smith advocated for an economy driven by the supply and demand of goods people produce and consume.

FIGURE 15-9: Adam Smith, founding father of classical liberalism.

Source: Library of Congress

For Smith, it wasn't the amount of gold a country possessed that mattered but a market based on the laws of demand and supply. Trade made a nation great, not the protection of domestic markets through tariffs and subsidies. Only domestic and international competition resulted in the cheapest and best products being produced. Smith argued that a protected market would stagnate and become uncompetitive. Therefore, it's best for government to leave the economy alone and focus on its limited role in society (see Chapter 13).

According to Smith, the laws of supply and demand allow the market to regulate an economy. Supply and demand determines what products will be produced, how much of a product will be produced, and how much it will cost. If people want more of a good, quantities of goods increase; if they want less, production goes down. If a good is too expensive, nobody will buy it, and the price will have to be lowered. If the good is, however, too cheap, it sells out quickly and its price increases. Therefore, the free market, and not the government, should regulate an economy. Smith believed that government should stay out of the economy and play a small role in a person's life (see Chapter 13 for a full discussion of the role of government in a free market society).

Believing in people

Classical liberals believe in individual rights. For them, the individual, not the community, matters; in other words, individual rights trump communal rights. Classical liberals further advocate for personal freedoms, especially freedom of religion. The Bill of Rights (see Chapter 5) added to the U.S. Constitution is a great example of classical liberal beliefs.

Liberals share the idea with conservatives that people aren't perfect. They believe that the average person is driven by their emotions and desires but is still rational; however, this is where similarities with classical conservatism ends. Classical liberals draw different conclusions from human nature. They believe that people are flawed and shouldn't be handed a lot of government powers because they can't be trusted. Instead, government should be weak and decentralized. The closer government is to the people, the easier it is for the people to check up on government.

Finally, classical liberals believe that while human beings are flawed, they can be changed and they can be improved upon and turned into productive citizens in a society.

REMEMBER

Today, classical liberalism is called American Conservatism in the U.S. People still refer to it as classical liberalism in Europe and the rest of the world.

REPRESENTATIVE DEMOCRACY

According to classical liberalists, individuals set free of government control will prosper and achieve their true potential, which in turn benefits society overall. Classical liberal theorist John Stuart Mill argued that a good government should be a government that allows its people to pursue their own self-interest and achieve their own true potential without government interference. The best form of government for Mill was a representative democracy, where people would select representatives to make policy on their behalf. This form of government allows people to be able to vote representatives out of power if they dislike what their representatives are doing. Mill argues that the more active people are in politics, the more satisfied they'll be with their government.

Putting the Government Back in Charge: Modern Liberalism

After the economic downturns of the late 19th century, it became clear that there were times when a free market economy was not self-regulating as Adam Smith had assumed. Market failures happened and monopolies were created, controlling a segment of the market. This destroyed competition and allowed for companies to fix prices of goods and produce goods of lesser quality. In addition, a class society was created with a few very wealthy, a fairly large middle class, and a substantial working class. Many of the poor were working in despicable work environments, with long hours, and still didn't make enough money to afford to feed their families. Even child labor was legal at this time.

This resulted in the creation of modern liberalism, which calls for the government to come back and regulate businesses and protect society. A larger, more powerful government was needed to take care of people in need. The average citizen had to be protected from an imperfect market system and especially market failure. Modern liberals, therefore, called for a welfare state with unemployment benefits to protect the unemployed when the market goes into a recession and a pension system to protect the elderly.

Furthermore, modern liberals called for the outlawing of child labor, a safe work environment, and wage and hour laws. They championed a 40-hour workweek and a minimum wage and the right to unionize and strike. Finally, modern liberals advocated for government healthcare and free education for all citizens. To finance all these new programs, they called for a progressive taxation system that taxed the wealthy at higher levels than the poor. This is called progressive taxation.

By the early 20th century, banking and the finance system were regulated, and monopolies were broken up to restore the free market system.

REMEMBER

Modern liberalism is the liberalism that started with Presidents Woodrow Wilson and Franklin D. Roosevelt in the U.S. and is still advocated by presidents such as Bill Clinton and Barack Obama. For them, government needs to protect people from market failures, such as a recession, and ensure social equality in the country. Modern liberals believe in capitalism but not a completely free market because government is needed to ameliorate some of its damaging aspects.

Finally, when it comes to progress and change, modern liberals are all for it. They believe that socioeconomic situations change constantly, so people and government policy need to adapt to these changes. While having traditions is nice, often these traditions deal with outdated politics and social situations and need to change quickly. Therefore, progress demands sudden and frequent change.

Chapter **16**

Moving to the Right: Fascism, Neofascism, and Right-Wing Populism

T his chapter deals with three right-wing ideologies. The first one is fascism. It is an authoritarian ideology which was widespread until the end of World War II. Afterwards, it was replaced by neofascism, which still believes in many fascist ideas but does accept democracy and is intent on using democratic means to come to power. Finally, I discuss right-wing populism, a fairly new ideology becoming prominent in the 1990s. While it accepts democracy, it does target certain groups, using them as scapegoats for current problems a society is facing.

REMEMBER

A political ideology is a belief system (Weltanschauung) that shapes how people see and analyze politics and who they support or vote for. It shapes the way people see the world and how they act within a political system (nation-state). An ideology affects people's outlook on the world and the role they play in it. It determines how people see everything and everybody.

Getting a Sense of Fascism

Unlike classical liberalism or European conservatism (see Chapter 15), Fascism is a fairly recent political ideology. Fascism is an authoritarian ideology (in Germany, totalitarian; see Chapter 4), which is highly nationalistic, militaristic, and in some instances openly racist. Similar to Communism, Fascism became a powerful ideology, challenging the democratic ideal in the interwar period (1919–1939).

TECHNICAL STUFF

Although most Fascist governments can be found in Europe, the movement was global. Examples of countries where Fascist movements existed but didn't take control of government include France, where the Cross of Fire, later renamed the French Social Party, had close to 1 million members and, by 1939, elected 3,000 mayors and 12 members of parliament; the Middle East, such as the Syrian National Socialist Party or the Green Shirts in Egypt; Latin America, where Fascist parties played an important part in several countries; Mexico, where the Gold Shirts existed; Brazil, where the Brazilian Integralist Party had 200,000 members and even attempted a coup in 1938; and even the U.S. with the Black Legion, an offshoot of the Ku Klux Klan, which had 60,000 members in the 1930s.

Fascism varied from country to country, but it had a common political and economic structure. Politically, Fascist regimes created one-party states headed by a charismatic leader, such as Benito Mussolini in Italy, Adolf Hitler in Germany, or Francisco Franco in Spain. The objective was the creation of a totalitarian state where the leader controlled every aspect of people's lives (see Chapter 4). This necessitated total control over people's surroundings. To accomplish this, the Fascist state took control over the media, including the fine arts, the police and military, the educational structure, and even religion. A small elite — not based on money as in a capitalist society, instead distinguishing itself by classless values such as honor, sacrifice, and complete loyalty to the leader — supported the political structure. The masses followed blindly, any kind of opposition not being tolerated.

In the area of the economy, the Fascist state was very interventionist. The state controlled the economy, even nationalizing industries if necessary, and established an authoritarian corporatist structure, where the state together with state-controlled unions and large business and agricultural organizations engaged in economic policy making. The interest of the state, and not profit, dominated a Fascist economy.

Starting Out: The Beginnings of Fascism

Beginning with Benito Mussolini's takeover of Italy in 1922, Fascism soon spread into Eastern, Central, and Southern Europe as well as parts of Latin America and Asia. By 1939, when World War II broke out, Fascist countries included Italy, Germany, Spain, Portugal, Hungary, Romania, Bulgaria, Slovakia, and even Argentina and Japan.

Coming first: Benito Mussolini

Benito Mussolini (1883–1945), seen in Figure 16-1, was an Italian journalist who grew up in a socialist household. Not surprisingly, he started his career in journalism as a devout socialist. By 1912, he became the editor for the socialist newspaper *Avanti*, which had a circulation of 100,000 readers. His reputation grew, and soon he became one of the best journalists in Italy.

FIGURE 16-1:
Benito Mussolini, Prime Minister of Italy.

Source: Wikimedia Commons

In 1914, on the eve of World War I, Mussolini went against many in his own party, the Socialist Party of Italy, by supporting going to war. He saw the war as a chance to advance socialism by destroying the monarchies in both Austria-Hungary and

Germany, allowing Italy to expand in Europe and become a great power. His support for Italian entrance into World War I led to his ouster from the Italian Socialist Party, so he joined the Italian Army to fight in the war. He served until 1917 and was discharged after being wounded. By the time World War I ended in 1918, Mussolini had become an ardent nationalist who advocated for the expansion of the Italian Empire in Europe, and especially in Africa, to acquire necessary space to expand economically.

After Italy was denied any spoils after the end of World War I (Italy had expected territorial gains from Austria), it experienced political and economic turmoil from 1919 to 1921. Pure anarchy broke out, and hordes of dissatisfied workers and peasants roamed through the country, taking over businesses and large estates. The Italian aristocracy and middle classes looked for protection, which the Italian state couldn't provide.

Mussolini began to organize the Blackshirts, a collection of war veterans who were heavily armed, and he hired them out to protect the Italian elite, industrialists, and large landowners. His reputation grew, and his Blackshirts grew in numbers. Many Italians looked to him as someone who could save Italy by restoring order. Mussolini promised to provide political stability by ending democracy, abolishing political parties and elections, and creating a government based on strong central rule.

On October 27 and 28, 1922, Mussolini's Blackshirts marched on Rome, the capital of Italy, and demanded the appointment of a Fascist government. The king of Italy consented to make Mussolini the prime minister at the sight of his 30,000 Blackshirts. Mussolini demanded and received dictatorial powers by 1923, and in 1924, he turned Italy into a one-party state with himself as leader. He was called Il Duce (the leader). The first Fascist state was born, and the ideology spread rapidly. Mussolini ran Italy for the next 21 years until 1945, when he was executed by Communist partisans.

Causing Fascism

What caused the rapid spread of Fascism during the interwar period? Fascism was a direct response to rapid industrialization and the political, cultural, and economic turmoil after World War I. The ideology became especially popular in countries that stood on the losing side or believed that they had been betrayed by the victorious allies, for example, Italy. This also included Germany, Austria, and most of Eastern Europe.

Many scholars consider Fascism a response to the crisis of the old liberal democratic system and capitalism after World War I. In both Italy and Germany, the democratic institutions in place after the war failed. Millions began to believe that the democratic institutions and the capitalist economic system were unable to provide political and economic solutions to dealing with the economic crisis and political turmoil of the late 1920s and thus turned to different political ideologies, namely Fascism and Communism. This dissatisfaction with democracy was coupled with a revolt against modern society. People resented the cultural and political changes brought about by industrialization, capitalism, and democracy. Fascism offered a way out by providing modernization from above, which left many traditional beliefs and structures intact.

The economic and political devastation in the interwar period resulted in a reactionary mood in many countries clamoring for the glory of the past. Industrialization had resulted in a growing prosperous middle class but also created a desolate lower middle class, disillusioned farmers, and a poor working class. While the middle classes became a core support group of democracy, the working classes turned to the left, supporting either socialist or Communist causes. The other two classes, the lower middle class and the farmers, felt like they had to bear the burden of industrialization, losing both economic and political power. So they turned to parties on the right, which promised a return to traditional times when these two groups mattered in society.

Fascists advocated a rejection of liberal democratic values, a forsaking of reason, and a return to the mythical glory of the past.

The story behind Fascism

The term *Fascism* was coined by Benito Mussolini. It's derived from the Italian *Fasces,* which refers to a bundle of elm or birch rods, a symbol of authority in ancient Rome. It's difficult to define Fascism because the ideology varied widely from country to country. Therefore, it's easiest to discuss the term by focusing on what Fascism is against.

Often, the ideology is defined as an anti-ideology because it's clearer in opposing other viewpoints than creating a coherent ideology itself. Fascism is based on irrationalism. It directly rejects the idea, created during the Enlightenment, that people are rational beings who can understand the world using science and technology. For a Fascist, life is inexplicable and people are driven by emotions and passions, not rational thought. Instead of trying to understand the world, a person should be driven by action and will. As Mussolini stated on many occasions, "Feel, don't think." Adolf Hitler echoed him stating, "Action, not talk."

Fascists believe that people have to be led by small elites. They, therefore, reject democracy because it allows for majority control over a nation, which results in inferior political and economic outcomes as demonstrated by the turmoil of the 1920s and 1930s.

Fascism further advocates a fierce nationalism, which often results in violent forms of racism. This coupled with militarism and imperialism often advocates the restoration of past empires. The result is a very aggressive, expansionist foreign policy, with the objective of creating vast empires to sustain the Fascist states. For example, Mussolini in Italy actively attempted to restore the Roman Empire, while Francisco Franco in Spain was hoping to conquer parts of Africa, and Hitler in Germany was hoping for conquest of Eastern Europe and parts of the Ukraine.

Fascist core beliefs

When analyzing fascism more closely, the following core beliefs come to light.

Opposing Marxism

One of the core beliefs of Fascists is their opposition to Marxism (see Chapter 17) of any kind. This includes Communism, all forms of socialism, and even social democracy.

Despising democracy

Fascists also oppose any form of democracy. Fascists believe in the rule of an all-powerful leader assisted by a small elite group. They consider the majority of the people incapable of making decisions that are good for the country. Only a small group, which can distinguish itself through traits such as honor, complete loyalty to the all-powerful leader, and extreme nationalism, should help run the country.

Rejecting liberalism

Fascists reject the notion of liberalism (see Chapter 15) because it emphasizes individual rights. For Fascists, the individual doesn't matter much, and only the community matters. All individual rights are subjugated to the rights of the community. Individualism only encourages dissent among the people and attracts decadent values, such as materialism, selfishness, sexual decadence, and opposition to religion. Only through Fascism can a person overcome immorality and became a productive citizen working for the good of the nation.

Standing for authoritarian corporatism

Fascists reject the notion of individual profit. Although owning property is acceptable, using it to make money at the expense of a nation isn't. Under an authoritarian corporate system, the state is dominant and can tell state-controlled unions and private business and farming organizations what to produce and what the costs of products should be.

The German steel industry, for example, was told what to produce — tanks, instead of consumer goods — and the state then purchased these goods from industries. Private business still made profit but not at the expense of the nation. Profits were much lower, as they would have been in a capitalist economy. Everybody worked for the good of the nation and not the individual.

The following quote expresses the idea behind a Fascist economy best: "Capitalism is a system by which capital uses the nation for its own purposes; Fascism is a system by which the nation uses capital for its own purposes."

Eliminating class conflict

Unlike under Communism (see Chapter 17), classes weren't destroyed in a Fascist system. The idea was that all classes — upper, middle, and lower class — were equal and should be equally respected by society. In Germany, for example, the idea wasn't to destroy the old aristocracy but to have it work hand in hand with the lower classes. To become a member of the ruling elite, class background didn't matter. A poor person could distinguish himself by having characteristics such as honor, self-sacrifice, and blind loyalty to the leadership. In other words, everybody, regardless of background, could make it into the elite. This was one of the reasons Fascism had so much appeal with the lower classes.

Coveting expansionism

Every Fascist regime showed a drive toward expansionism. It either wanted to reclaim empires of the past, such as Mussolini who wanted to restore the Roman Empire, or believed that it needed more lands to take care of an expanding population and acquire more economic resources. In Germany, the claim was that the German people needed Lebensraum, or living space, to be able to become a great power. The German Empire needed to feed a growing population and get more natural resources to economically expand. This necessitated the conquest of Ukraine, the bread basket of Europe. Other examples include Polish Fascists who wanted to restore the great Polish-Lithuanian Empire, Finnish Fascists who wanted to create a greater Finland, and Croatian Fascists who wanted to create a greater Croatia.

Valuing the military

Military values were important in Fascist societies. Fascists appreciated courage and obedience to higher authorities. In addition, just about every Fascist leader had a paramilitary organization attached to his Fascist political party. These were separate military organizations, which were completely loyal to the leader and could be used for protection of the ruling Fascist elite or for putting fear into the population. For example, Mussolini had the Blackshirts, and Adolf Hitler had his Brownshirts (SA).

War is considered a part of life for Fascists. It's natural and not necessarily bad. Fascists closely follow Charles Darwin's idea of the survival of the fittest and Herbert Spencer's ideas of natural selection. It's through war that nations advance. Only the strong will survive, and the weaker nations will disappear. The idea of survival of the fittest is closely tied to this. Only the best and most powerful have the right to survive while the weak need to be destroyed. That is how society advances.

REMEMBER

Some of Mussolini's and Hitler's most famous quotes include military values. Mussolini said: "Better to live an hour like a lion than a hundred years like a sheep" and "War is to men, what maternity is to women." Hitler followed it up with "Victory is to the strong and the weak must go to the Wall" and "The new man is slim and slender, quick like a greyhound, tough like leather, and hard like Krupp steel."

Considering racism

Not all Fascist governments or movements were openly racist, and if they were, their targets differed. In Germany, racism was directed against Jews. Hitler and his government blamed the Jewish population for everything, from the loss in World War I to the Great Depression. This form of racist hatred resulted in the Holocaust, which killed 6 million Jews by 1945. In Bulgaria, on the other hand, the Fascist government targeted the Gypsy population and protected the Jewish population from German atrocities; and in Croatia, the government targeted the Serb minority. In Fascist countries such as Spain and Portugal, racism wasn't a part of official policy. However, political opponents were targeted.

Many Fascist societies believe that they're the master race and that other races have to be subjugated or even exterminated to assure the survival of the master race. In Germany, Hitler and his followers believed that the Nordic race, including the German race, was the dominant race called the Aryan race (ironically, the term *Aryan* originated in India, and not in Europe). Similar to Fascist Germany, Argentine Fascists, or Russian Fascists, consider themselves racially superior. In a nutshell, many Fascists, regardless of where they live, consider themselves racially superior.

Defending religion

Many Fascist governments and movements, especially in deeply Catholic countries such as Spain or Argentina, portrayed themselves as defenders of the faith. Often, the Catholic Church, afraid of Communism, an atheist ideology (discussed in Chapter 17), supported Fascist regimes. The relationship between church and state in Germany was more complicated. While the Nazi regime tolerated Christianity and most Germans were Christian, it also emphasized a return to the Nordic gods and Teutonic rituals to slowly undermine Christianity in Germany.

The end of World War II and the defeat of Germany, Italy, and Japan ended the period of Fascism. A few Fascist regimes survived in countries such as Spain and Portugal until the 1970s, but defeat in World War II and Fascist atrocities during the war severely discredited Fascism and undermined its mass appeal. However, today many scholars believe that Fascism isn't dead but only dormant, and with revisions, the ideology could stage a comeback in the future.

Rising of Neofascism

By the end of World War II in Europe, Fascism had been discredited. In some countries, such as Germany, Fascist movements were declared illegal. It looked like Fascism had died out. However, by the late 1940s, Fascism, now called neo-fascism, staged a small comeback in several European countries and especially in Latin America.

Similar to classical (pre-1945) Fascism, neofascism (post-1945) stands for extreme nationalism, scapegoating of ethnic minorities, and vehemently opposing Communism. However, neofascism has major differences from classical Fascism:

>> **Shifting blame from one ethnic group to another:** Instead of being anti-Semitic, neofascists looked for and found other ethnic groups to blame for current political and economic problems. In countries such as France and Italy, non-European immigrants were blamed for just about any problem the countries were facing. In Germany, guest workers from Turkey suffered a similar fate.

>> **Accepting democracy:** Neofascists realized that authoritarian forms of government had lost appeal to the people of Europe after World War II. They also knew that using violence to come to political power wasn't possible, so they claimed that they had accepted democracy and were willing to come to power democratically. Fascist parties were renamed to sever their ties to the past and stated that they were ready to use democratic means, namely elections, to participate in politics. Violence as a means of coming to power was renounced.

>> **Abolishing paramilitary units:** Instead of wearing uniforms and greeting each other with Roman salutes (as did the Blackshirts in Italy), neofascist politicians wore suits and ties and shook hands. The idea was simple. People shouldn't be reminded of the violent past of Fascism but look at it as a new and democratic alternative to established political parties.

>> **Changing economic beliefs:** Instead of advocating for authoritarian corporatism (see the earlier section "Standing for authoritarian corporatism"), they stood for a free market economy. They became economic liberals.

LOOKING AT MODERN NEOFASCISM IN ITALY

A great example of a neofascist party is the Italian Social Movement founded in 1946. The Italian Social Movement was at first headed by Mussolini's minister of propaganda, Giorgio Almirante. Right away, the party prohibited its members to wear the black shirts (uniforms) of the past and to greet each other with the Roman salute. It further accepted democracy and participated in every election. The party's major issue in the beginning was the fight against Communism. Italy at this point had a powerful Communist party, which by the late 1940s had become the second-largest party in the country. The Italian Social Movement called for authoritarian corporatism and stood for conservative political values, such as opposition to divorce and abortion.

By the 1980s, it had become a small party in Italy, never receiving more than 10 percent of the vote. In the 1990s, then leader Gianfranco Fini changed the party's name to National Alliance. Officially rejecting dictatorship and political violence and embracing free market economics, the party soon became a mainstay of Italian politics. By 1995, it attracted almost 14 percent of the vote and joined a coalition government with conservative Prime Minister Silvio Berlusconi. Suddenly, a neofascist party was a part of the government in Italy.

In 2009, the National Alliance joined a new political coalition, the People of Freedom, and it seemed that neofascism was dead in Italy. However, a radical wing of the party, still neofascist, opposed the joining of the new coalition and left. They created a new neofascist party called Brothers of Italy. It won 4.4 percent of the vote in the 2018 elections and currently sits at almost 7 percent of the vote. Italian neofascism is, therefore, still around, and the party is ready to join a populist right alliance in future elections.

Challenging the Elite: Populism

Populism is an anti-elite political movement. It taps into the frustration of ordinary people with their government. The people are frustrated by their economic, political, or social circumstances and resent current elites running their countries. These elites are referred to as *the establishment*. Populists believe the establishment places its own interests above the interest of the people. The establishment is considered corrupt and self-serving, ignoring the wishes of the common person. Worse, populists believe that their current economic, social, and political situation is due to a lack of support by the current government and that government works only for a select few.

The term *populism* can be traced back to a Russian movement that referred to itself as *narodniki,* which means "populists" in English. Today, populism can be defined as a movement that challenges the established values and rules of the political establishment. Another definition is simpler: All populism is, is taking the people's opinions and political wishes into account.

Making a path for populism

Populism can be either right or left wing. Populism on the right usually includes an anti-immigrant (legal or illegal) feeling, and blame is shifted not only to the government but also to recent migrants. Populism on the left is more likely to blame the rich and global capitalism for current problems in societies. Right-wing populism is more common in Western and Eastern Europe today, while left-wing populism dominates Southern Europe. Examples of populist leaders include Victor Orban in Hungary and the late Hugo Chavez in Venezuela.

Even though they're democratically elected, populist leaders have a tendency to move their countries toward being borderline authoritarian. They usually attack establishment institutions, such as the media or the judiciary, and try to intimidate, change, or even control them. Examples abound in Eastern Europe. In countries such as Hungary and Poland, the political left has been decimated, and only right-wing populist parties have a chance of controlling government. Slowly, governments there have taken control over the media and the court systems as well as parts of the economy.

Populist leaders in democracies are willing to work within the established institutions to come to power. They create their own parties or take over existing parties and then try to take control of government democratically. They reject violence as a means of coming to power, preferring to win elections. While they claim to represent the people, they're willing to exclude certain groups within society. These groups become their scapegoats, and they're usually tied to current government policy. In both France and Germany, Muslim migrants and refugees fulfill that function. In both instances, governments invited or allowed these groups to enter their countries, against the wishes of the people, and as soon as social and economic problems arose, populist parties blamed government for them.

Causing populism

What causes populism to appear in countries? While there are many causes, three stand out.

>> **A major ongoing economic crisis occurs.** The recession of 2007/2008, for example, resulted in the Tea Party movement in the U.S., which fairly quickly turned right populist. In Greece and Spain, on the other hand, the economic crisis and continued European Union bailouts resulted in left-leaning populist movements putting blame on the world capitalist system and the European Union.

>> **A government decision results in social and economic problems.** In 2015 and 2016, Chancellor Merkel of Germany allowed close to 2 million refugees, mostly from Muslim countries, to enter Germany. Soon, economic problems resulted and crime increased. Within a year, a right populist party, the Alternative for Germany (AfD), saw increased support when it started to oppose open border policies. Today, the AfD, which wants to expel theses migrants and refugees, sits at about 15 percent support and will soon be the largest party in the former East Germany.

>> **A populist leader emerges and claims to represent the people against the establishment.** These populist leaders tend to be charismatic, great speakers who know exactly what the public wants. They use the language of the common person and not the intellectual elites. A good example is U.S. President Donald Trump. Although the elites make fun of him during presidential addresses or campaign appearances, he connects with the common person. He uses their language and discusses the issues they're concerned about, which aren't necessarily the issues the establishment cares about in Washington, D.C.

Swinging Right: Right-Wing Populism in Europe

One of the most fascinating phenomena in recent European history has been the rise of right-wing populism in Europe after the collapse of the Soviet Union in 1991. While many had predicted the collapse of right-wing politics with the demise of Communism, the populist right discovered new issues it could rally around. They were the influx of ethnic minorities, mostly illegal immigrants and refugees, and economic decline and hardships. Suddenly, populist right parties, which had enjoyed only marginal support after World War II, found issues they could use to appeal to a larger segment of the European population. From France to Italy and Austria to Hungary, to even Germany today, many European countries experienced a rise of right populist parties.

The next sections looks at two of the major right-wing populist parties in Europe. The first is the National Front, renamed National Rally in 2018, in France, whose leader Marine Le Pen came in second in the 2017 French presidential elections and is currently one of the two frontrunners for the 2022 presidential election in France. The second is the Alternative for Germany (AfD), a new right-wing populist party in Germany that shocked the world when it came in third in the 2017 German parliamentary elections and ranks, at the writing of this book, second in German public opinion polls.

Building of a right-wing populist party in France: The French National Front

The National Front was founded in 1972 by Jean-Marie Le Pen (see Figure 16-2). The party was created through a fusion of many right-wing nationalist movements and parties with Le Pen's own New Order movement, to combine the French right into one powerful force. Le Pen himself started his political career as a student by selling monarchist newspapers while studying political science. He later enlisted in the French Foreign Legion and served in Indochina, Egypt, and later Algeria, where he was an intelligence officer supposedly torturing natives during interrogations.

FIGURE 16-2: Jean-Marie Le Pen, founder of the National Front.

Source: Wikipedia

The newly established party right away became controversial. Its campaign slogan "France for the French" was the same slogan used by the French Fascists in the 1930s, and the party targeted immigrants, mostly Muslim. With France having high unemployment and an increased crime rate, these immigrants became scapegoats for the current state France was in. The party that housed many former Fascists became more controversial when it downplayed the Holocaust. Le Pen's bodyguards wore helmets and battle gear, reminiscent of the Blackshirts in Italy, and Le Pen openly stated his admiration of Fascist dictator Francisco Franco of Spain.

REMEMBER

In some cities controlled by the National Front, censorship was imposed when it removed leftist-leaning books from public libraries. Instead, people could check out only materials supporting the viewpoint of the National Front.

TECHNICAL STUFF

Le Pen won a seat in the French parliament in 1958 and served one term, losing in 1962. It wasn't until 1986 that he was elected to the National Assembly again. He lost his seat two years later. Concurrently, he also became a member of the European parliament in 1984, losing his seat only once in 2004, for one year, after attacking a female socialist parliamentarian.

The National Front had its first breakthrough in the 1984 European elections, when the party took about 11 percent of the popular vote. Two years later, it gained 35 seats with 10 percent of the vote in the French parliamentary elections. For the next decade, the National Front consistently polled between 12 and 15 percent of the vote, with Le Pen receiving 15 percent of the vote in the 1995 French presidential elections. In these last elections, the party was able for the first time to gather substantial support outside industrial areas. Especially in rural areas and areas inhabited by Muslim immigrants in the South of France, the National Front was suddenly winning as much as 30 percent of the vote.

TECHNICAL STUFF

The election of 2002 proved to be the highlight of Le Pen's political career. The incumbent conservative President Jacques Chirac was the clear frontrunner, but the major opposition party, the French socialists, were damaged by a combination of political and sex scandals. In the first round of the French presidential elections, Le Pen was able to beat out the socialist candidate, Jospin, coming in second with 17 percent of the vote. In the subsequent run-off elections, incumbent president Chirac easily beat Le Pen with 82 percent of the vote. Five years later, Le Pen received 11 percent of the vote for president, coming in fourth. It was then that the National Front began to decline. In the subsequent parliamentary elections of 2007, the party received less than 5 percent of the vote. Financial problems began to set in, and Le Pen had to sell off National Front–owned property, such as campaign headquarters and cars. Many proclaimed the party to be over for the French National Front. With an ancient leader and an outdated extremist party platform, it seemed to be destined to become a small fringe party with a core of old male supporters. At this time, Le Pen decided to retire. He was succeeded by his daughter Marine in 2011, who saved the party by turning the party into a populist right party.

Becoming right-wing populist

Marine Le Pen (see Figure 16-3) took over as the chair of the National Front in 2011. The National Front was on the decline, having money problems and not being able to extend its support beyond the traditional 10 to 12 percent of the vote it had received for most of the last 30 years. Marine realized that to be able to attract more support, she had to transform the National Front into a modern mainstream political party. For this reason, she renamed the party "National Rally" and transformed it into a modern right populist party, shedding a lot of the party's historical baggage.

FIGURE 16-3: Marine Le Pen, chair of the National Rally party.

Source: Wikipedia

Marine abandoned the party's anti-Semitism, chauvinism, and revisionist versions of World War II, and even expelled her own father, who had created the party. She openly appealed to young and female voters. With this change, the party has seen its support steadily increase, as seen in the 2017 presidential and the 2019 European parliamentary elections.

With France experiencing economic decline, high unemployment, and mass immigration, coupled with an increase in crime, Marine had found her issues. Like her father, the major issue she has used to appeal to voters was the fear of Islamification of France. However, she didn't attack Muslims personally, instead focusing on the threat Islam poses for women's rights and secularism in France.

For this reason, her rhetoric seemed less harsh than her father's, and she didn't come across as bigoted or racist. Instead, many looked upon her as a defender of women's rights and a protector of the secularism of the French Revolution.

In addition, Marine brought the National Rally into the 21st century technologically. She began to focus on social media, targeting tech-savvy first-time voters. Online and Facebook polling became a part of her campaign, helping her discover issues for her 2017 presidential campaign.

Finally, Marine adopted a new strategy for recruiting candidates to run for office. Instead of relying on older, often discredited rightists associated with her father, she turned to young, well-educated, and articulate candidates. This has resulted in 55 percent of all French university students proclaiming in a recent survey that they'd consider voting for the National Rally.

Advocating change

Marine's call for restricting legal immigration to 10,000 per year, down from the current 200,000 per year, resonated with French voters. She further advocated a 10 percent tax on all French companies that hire foreign workers and don't employ French citizens instead.

At the same time, Marine promised to expel all illegal migrants from the country and stop providing free healthcare and education to them. She further called for an end to multiculturalism and advocated for the de-Islamization of France. For this reason, Marine has advocated for a ban on wearing religious symbols in public, including public schools. This includes headscarves worn by Muslim women.

Marine successfully shifted economic blame away from the French people by blaming globalism and international organizations, such as the European Union, the European Central Bank, and the World Trade Organization (see Chapter 13) for the current economic crisis. As an alternative, she offered the closing of French markets to foreign competition and tariffs against foreign goods. She, therefore, presented a new mercantilist vision for the country (see Chapter 13), breaking with the party's traditional neoliberalism. Under Marine's leadership, the National Rally has embraced traditional French statism, advocating a strong government role in certain aspects of the economy.

The government, according to Marine, should be entrusted with healthcare, education, transportation, banking, and energy. To appeal to female homemakers, she proposed paying homemakers a salary, raising incentives for women to stay at home to start a family.

Major social policy changes include supporting same-sex civil unions, but not same-sex marriage, and becoming pro-choice. Furthermore, the National Front switched its position on the death penalty, now opposing it.

Under Marine's leadership, the National Rally received the most votes in the 2019 European parliamentary elections in France, about 23 percent of the vote, and she advanced to the second round in the 2017 presidential election. Even though she lost to the current French President Macron, she received close to 34 percent of the vote, the best showing in the history of the party.

Today, Marine Le Pen has positioned herself to be a strong contender for the 2022 French presidential elections.

Wanting change: The Alternative for Germany (AfD)

On September 24, 2017, Germany went to the polls, and Chancellor Angela Merkel, in power since 2005, was expected to easily win reelection, and maybe even receive the absolute majority of seats in the German parliament, which had been denied to her in her previous three elections. To the surprise of many, it was not the Chancellor who made news but a brand-new party on the populist right of the political spectrum, *Die Alternative fuer Deutschland* (Alternative for Germany), or AfD. Winning a surprising 12.6 percent of the vote and 94 seats in parliament (out of 709 seats), the AfD managed the best populist right showing since the creation of the Federal Republic of Germany in 1949.

Upcoming Alternative for Germany

AfD is the newest party on the German political scene. It was founded only seven years ago, in April of 2013, by a group of German intellectuals, economists, and business leaders. They opposed Chancellor Merkel's bailout policies of Southern Europe, especially Greece. Soon, the party received its nickname, the Professors' Party. Most of its leaders were former Christian Democrats, who in the past had supported Chancellor Merkel. However, her decision to bail out Greece repeatedly with German taxpayer money had left them disillusioned and moved them away from her Christian Democratic Party.

The group, headed by Bernd Lucke, a professor of economics at the University of Hamburg, believed that the German taxpayer was forced to pay for the mismanagement of Southern European economies and therefore not only called for an immediate end to the bailout of Southern Europe but also an end to the common European currency, the Euro. The AfD instead advocated a return to the German mark.

The party successfully tapped into the resentment of German voters. To the great surprise of the German political establishment, the AfD, only five months old and with almost no financial resources, won 4.7 percent of the vote in the German national elections in 2013, which saw Chancellor Merkel reelected. The party did, however, miss the 5 percent necessary under Germany electoral law to enter the German parliament and received no seats.

Encouraged, the party leaders turned to the upcoming elections to the European Parliament in May of 2014 while deciding to forego campaigning for state elections in Germany. The 5 percent hurdle wasn't in force for the European parliamentary elections, and the party felt hopeful that it would do well enough to clear the 3 percent hurdle to win seats. The party's strategy proved successful, and on May 25, 2014, it won 7.1 percent of the vote, a little over 2 million votes, and received seven seats in the European parliament.

Becoming stronger

In 2015 and 2016, Chancellor Merkel decided to allow for close to 2 million Muslim refugees to enter Germany. Suddenly, the AfD had found a second and more powerful issue to garner political support.

Within a year, the major issues in Germany weren't bailouts and rejection of the Euro but Muslim migration and the problems it had created. The AfD became the only major party that would openly oppose migration, becoming critical of the Merkel government, and advocated not only for an end to migration but also the expulsion of migrants and a rejection of their Islamic faith.

With migration becoming the dominant issue in Germany by 2016, support for the AfD skyrocketed. In 2016 the AfD picked its new party slogan, "Islam is not a part of Germany," and advocated for the ban of all Islamic symbols such as the burka, minarets, and the call to prayer.

The AfD advocates for a change to the German Constitution in regard to refugees. It wants to make sure that only political refugees are allowed to enter Germany and not economic refugees, who just want to better their lives.

The party officially rejects the concept of multiculturalism and believes that it will only tear a country apart. People who flee to Germany should integrate or be deported. German should become the official language, and migrants should be forced to learn it or be deported. Therefore, the AfD demands that all prayers and sermons in mosques be held in German and demands a ban on the burka and hijab. Further, no Islamic instruction should be provided in public schools.

The AfD also advocates for constitutional changes. The party believes in the concept of direct democracy and wants to implement referenda similar to France and Switzerland to have the public directly make policy. The AfD advocates for term limits, namely a two-term limit for the chancellor and a four-term limit for parliamentarians. The party also wants to eliminate special healthcare benefits for parliamentarians, forcing members of parliament to have the same health insurance as the average person.

Finally, in the realm of social politics, the AfD advocates stipends for having and raising children to overcome the impending population crisis and also opposes abortion for the same reason. In the realm of economics, the AfD advocates for a lowering of the sales tax and an increase in the minimum wage and also rejects social quotas (affirmative action) for jobs.

With this agenda, the AfD entered the 2017 German parliamentary elections, and the party surprised everybody by coming in third with 12.4 percent of the vote. In more recent state elections in the former East Germany, the AfD received almost a quarter of the vote and is now poised to become the strongest political party in the east of Germany.

Chapter **17**

Going Left: Communism, Socialism, and Social Democracy

This chapter deals with political ideologies of the left. I start out by discussing the reason for the sudden rise of socialist ideas in the 19th century. Next, I cover the core ideas of Marxism and subsequent contribution to Marxism by both Lenin and Mao in the 20th century. Finally, the move from socialism to social democracy by many socialist parties is covered and a specific example in the Social Democratic Party of Germany is provided.

Causing Socialism

Socialism was a response to the changing economies of Europe created by the First and Second Industrial Revolutions. The First Industrial Revolution started in England in the 18th century and didn't disrupt society much. While businesses were created, they were small, often run from homes, and the social structure didn't change in a society.

The Second Industrial Revolution, beginning in the 19th century, changed all of this. With the advent of modern technology, such as the steam engine, mass production of goods became possible. Suddenly, large factories were created in cities, and thousands of peasants moved to the cities to create the working class. In other words, farmers became workers. With a working class being created, there was suddenly a call for unions to combat the horrific work conditions and long work hours. The foundation for socialist ideas was created to protect the new working class.

By the 19th century, it became clear that capitalism was producing a society based on economic inequality. The gap between rich and poor became greater, and political theorists became worried that this would produce a society where a few grew very wealthy, while the many were exploited. Socialist theories were created to combat this exploitation of the workers. They advocated for an economically productive society without any class distinctions, where nobody faced exploitation, resulting in hunger and poverty.

Major political theorists such as Karl Marx, Friedrich Engels, and later on Vladimir Lenin set out to provide not only an explanation of the current political and economic conditions but also solutions for the current state of social and economic exploitation of the working classes. Their theories explained how and why the working classes were exploited and claimed that when socialism bore fruit and a society was prosperous and productive, Communism would follow.

In a Communist society, besides having no upper, middle, or lower classes, there was no need for a government, laws enforced by police, or even money. Society had advanced to a state where, economically and also technologically, people could take what they needed. A Communist utopia was created where everybody shared in the wealth of society. There was no need for private property or government; everything was commonly owned, and the community made all decisions together.

REMEMBER

Core ideas of socialism include

>> **Public ownership of property:** All property is owned by society; therefore, no private property exists in a socialist society.

>> **Central economic planning:** Instead of a free market, there's a centralized planning agency that plans for all of society.

Starting with Karl Marx

Karl Marx, the father of Communism, is one of the most famous German philosophers of the 19th century (see Figure 17-1). He created some of the most controversial political and economic theories in the last two centuries. For this reason, Marxism is taught not just in political science departments but also in history, economics, and sociology departments. Karl Marx truly had an impact on all the social sciences, and it's important to remember that many non-Marxist academics agree with some of his ideas. While Marx presents a critique of capitalism, he leaves his followers no blueprints on how to implement his economic ideas.

FIGURE 17-1:
Karl Marx, the father of Communism.

Source: Library of Congress

REMEMBER

Karl Marx wasn't the first political theorist to discuss the idea of Communism. Communism is defined as the idea of people living and working together. All property is communally owned, and everybody works for the good of the community and not for themselves. The ancient Greeks already discussed this idea, as did the early Christians. Marx was, however, the first theorist to try to explain how Communism could be achieved.

Marx objected to classical liberalism (see Chapter 15) because it supported individual rights, neglecting the community, and the pursuit of individual wealth and happiness at the expense of the community. Marx further rejected capitalism for similar reasons. He argued that in a capitalist society, different classes would develop. Some would be property owners and wealthy, while others would be poor and exploited, barely surviving. For him, this was unacceptable.

Therefore, a new way of living was needed. Marx came up with a brand-new theory explaining history and class exploitation and provided for the first time a way of how to achieve Communism.

Marx's political theories

Karl Marx's philosophical and political theories are outlined in his early works *The Germany Ideology* and *The Communist Manifesto.*

Karl Marx believed that humans distinguished themselves from animals because they could produce goods. In other words, only humans can take a certain item, such as coal, and produce a good, such as steel. They can create tools and weapons and advance society. For Marx, each person has the potential and urge to produce goods. This potential is, however, stifled in a class society as found in capitalism. A rigid class structure will keep the bright working-class kid from developing his potential and producing and creating new goods. Class structures stifle any kind of potential for the lower classes and therefore result in a lack of progress. Marx thus argued for a classless society.

LIVING IN EXILE

Karl Marx was born in 1818 in the city of Trier, located in the Kingdom of Prussia. He studied first at the University of Bonn, but his father transferred him to the University of Berlin, because Marx was constantly drunk and started fights in Bonn. In Berlin, Marx received his PhD in philosophy in 1841. After publishing the *Communist Manifesto* with his best friend Friedrich Engels, in 1848, which discusses the idea of class revolution to destroy the ruling aristocracy and middle classes in Europe, he had to flee Prussia and moved to London. He spent the rest of his life in London in exile. In 1867, Marx published the first volume of *Das Kapital,* his economic opus. By the mid-1870s, Marx had become disillusioned because none of his predictions seemed to come true. He died in 1883 still in exile in London.

In a Communist society, it's different. It is based on the concept of communalism and everything is owned by the community, and people are provided for by the community. They receive free housing and food. In turn, they spend half of the workday producing goods for the community, and the other half they take off and explore their creativeness. In other words, they can develop their potential.

REMEMBER

Communalism assumes that all human beings are social by nature. Therefore, individualism is rejected, and only the community matters. The good of the community is always superior to the good of the individual.

People are freed from the struggle for survival, constant competition, and boredom at work. This freedom allows people to come up with new ideas and create new technologies and innovations to increase production. This in turn increases the overall well-being of the community.

REMEMBER

Karl Marx's most famous statement explains the core of his ideas on Communist society: "From each according to his abilities, to each according to his need." In other words, people will have their basic needs covered by the community while they in turn work and produce for the community.

Advancing through history

Marx uses the famous German philosopher Georg Friedrich Hegel's concept of the dialectic to explain history. The dialect is a theory of motion that explains how history moves from one phase to another. According to Hegel, the dialectic moves from a state of unity (thesis) to a state of disunity (antithesis) and then results in a state of new unity (synthesis). For Marx, who believes that history is determined by economics, these states reflect economic structures. The catalyst to move from one structure to another is class struggle.

TECHNICAL STUFF

Karl Marx was an economic determinist. He believed that political power derives from economic power. In other words, whoever controls the economy also controls government. To use Marxist terminology, whoever controls the means of production, namely physical structures such as factories and tools, to make and manufacture goods, is in charge of government.

Marx's theory outlines the following stages of human history, each based on a mode of production, defined as how society is organized to produce goods and services. The stages are slavery, feudalism, capitalism, and then Communism (revolutionary socialism). His theory goes by the following:

>> **Slavery:** Slavery is the oldest mode of production (economic structure). In a slave-based society, the economy is agricultural in nature and slaves are needed to work the fields. Private property exists and the two classes are property owners and slaves.

- » **Feudalism:** In feudalism, the dominant economic class is the aristocracy, while the exploited classes are the peasants (back then, serfs) and later on the middle classes. After a few centuries, a middle class develops in the larger cities. They have no political power but do have economic power. Therefore, they became dissatisfied with their status in society and initiate class struggle against the ruling aristocracy. This results in a period of disunity (antithesis). The class struggle results in a victory for the middle classes, and a new period of unity (synthesis) results. It's called capitalism, where the middle classes have economic and therefore political power.

- » **Capitalism:** In a capitalist society, a new class is created by industrialization, the working class. It's exploited by the middle classes. After a while, it starts to initiate class struggle, rebelling against the ruling middle class. The struggle, if victorious, destroys the middle class, and socialism has been achieved.

- » **Socialism:** During the socialist period, the working classes are in charge, and all property is state owned. Instead of having a free market regulate the economy, a centralized command economy is put in place where an agency plans for the whole economy. A powerful state is created to eliminate the remnants of other classes, such as the aristocracy and the middle class.

- » **Communism (revolutionary socialism):** At this stage, class struggle ends and classes disappear, because only the working classes are left. The dialectic has reached its end, and a Communist society has been achieved, where all property is communally owned, and there's no more need for a government.

Today communism is often referred to as revolutionary socialism in academia.

Moving towards class struggle

As discussed earlier, Karl Marx believed that human beings are shaped by the production of goods. However, soon class structures are put in place, which hamper human development. In a capitalist society, for example, two classes exist: the middle classes, or bourgeoisie (French for "middle class"), and the working class, the proletariat.

The remnants of older classes, the aristocracy, and the peasants usually align themselves with one of the two. The middle classes control the means of production, such as technology, tools, and industrial facilities, while the working class produces the goods. The working class just slaves away to survive, while the middle classes enhance their wealth.

After a period of exploitation, the working classes become alienated from their political and economic system. They believe that the system will impoverish them and hamper their personal development. They acquire what Marx calls *class consciousness*, when the class they belong to, the proletariat, matters and loyalty toward the current government is shifted to their class. Politically alienated and economically miserable, the working class is ready to initiate class struggle and destroy capitalism.

According to Marx, the middle classes also control government. For him, control over the economy equals control over government. The middle class–controlled government uses not only force to oppress the working class but also indoctrination through the educational structures and religion (see Chapter 3) to maintain itself in power. For this reason, the working class has to destroy both the political and economic structures in capitalism to be able to move on to socialism.

Socialism is a necessary stage on the way to Communism. After the working class successfully initiates class struggle and destroys capitalism, socialism can be achieved. In a socialist society, classes continue to exist and have to be slowly destroyed by an all-powerful state. Only then can a classless society exist and move to Communism.

During the socialist phase of a society, all property is state owned. Private property ceases to exist at this point. Free markets also disappear, and the economy is controlled by the central government through an economic planning agency.

With the socialist economy in full swing, workers can cut back their work hours and work on their potential. Centralized planning overcomes capitalist inefficiency and wastefulness. People can enjoy economic equality, and crime slowly disappears. At this stage, there's no more need for a government, and government slowly withers away. In its place is a decentralized structure where policies are made by factory managers and community leaders. They in turn are elected by the people.

Marx's economic theories

Karl Marx outlined his economic theories in three books: *Das Kapital, Volumes I, II, and III*. However, some of his ideas were quite utopian, such as assuming that technology over time would resolve the problem of shortages of materials such as natural resources and that one agency could plan for a whole country. These assumptions led to disaster when implemented by the Soviet Union. I discuss three of Marx's major economic theories in the following sections.

The labor theory of value

The labor theory of value states that all goods produced in an economy should be valued based on the time and labor it costs to produce them. In other words, the resources used to produce goods and consumer demand shouldn't matter. For example, if it takes ten hours to produce a watch, the watch should be valued at ten hours of labor and nothing else. The materials it takes to produce the watch don't matter, and neither does consumer demand for watches. Therefore, a plastic watch and a gold watch would cost the same.

The theory of surplus value

The theory of surplus value explains how workers are exploited by the capitalist class and later end up receiving a class consciousness, initiating a violent class struggle against their oppressors, destroying capitalism, and replacing it with Communism. The theory argues the following way: A worker is paid a low wage, say, a dime an hour, to produce a good for a business owner (capitalist). The product the worker produces is, however, worth a quarter and will be sold by the capitalist to a store or even back to the worker for 50 cents. The worker, therefore, gets exploited twice. First, he doesn't get a fair wage for what he produces; and second, he is forced to buy the product he produced at an even more inflated price. If that goes on for every product in an economy, the workers very soon will be in the poorhouse. Workers and their families are now starving, and they have no choice but to initiate class struggle, or to revolt against the capitalist system. For workers, this is a matter of life and death. Rebel against the system or slowly starve to death. This rebellion will result in a class revolution, which will replace capitalism with Communism.

The law of concentration

The law of concentration explains what Marx calls monopoly capitalism. According to Marx, over time, an economy comes to be dominated by large-scale businesses or monopolies. In the early stages of capitalism, an economy is evenly divided between workers and the bourgeoisie. Over time, the small business capitalists shrink in size because large businesses take over their business.

For example, one hundred years ago, the U.S. had tens of thousands of small mom-and-pop grocery stores. Over time, many of these were bought by larger grocery chains, or they just couldn't compete with them anymore and went out of business. Today, there are very few but very large grocery store chains found in the U.S. Therefore, thousands of capitalists, business owners, disappear at the expense of a very few large businesses. This trend continues until only a few grocery store chains are left and they become monopolies. To make matters worse, many of these former property-owning capitalists have to become workers to survive — that is, former grocery store owners have to work for large supermarket chains. If that happens, the number of capitalists will decline while the number of workers increases. This make a class revolution more likely.

REMEMBER

Monopolies a very large industries that dominate a sector of an economy. This allows monopolies to manipulate prices and charge more for their goods. In turn, the average person gets more impoverished.

This has certainly happened in the U.S. in many sectors of the economy. On a few occasions, the government even had to step in and break up these monopolies, an action Marx never foresaw. A good recent example is the breakup of AT&T in the 1980s because it had a monopoly over the phone industry.

Realities of Marx's theories

When Marx died in 1883, he was a disillusioned man. His theories hadn't come to fruition, and many started to question his writings. Lenin (see the section "Updating Marxism: Lenin" in this chapter) added to Marx's theories not only to justify his own rule but also to explain why parts of Marxism hadn't yet happened. Other Communist scholars such as Antonio Gramsci followed after Lenin, each trying to update Marxism and explain why a class revolution hadn't yet happened.

TECHNICAL STUFF

Many current scholars believe that Marxism didn't occur because capitalist systems put policies into place that he never foresaw. With the introduction of the welfare state and laws protecting unions and workplace conditions, workers had less of a reason to revolt against capitalism. Suddenly, programs sprang up, such as unemployment benefits, social security, and a minimum wage, that allowed workers to live well. Ironically, workers in the U.S. lived a better life than workers in the socialist Soviet Union. Why would workers rebel against a system from which they benefitted?

Updating Marxism: Lenin

Vladimir Ilyich Ulyanov (Lenin), seen in Figure 17-2, was born in 1870 in the Russian city of Simbirsk. He came from a solid middle-class family, and his dream was to become a lawyer. His life changed when his older brother Alexander was executed in 1877 for participating in the assassination attempt on Tsar Alexander II. Suddenly, Vladimir decided to oppose the tsarist regime in Russia and went underground to plot revenge. He changed his name to Lenin and was arrested for plotting against the tsar. He was subsequently exiled to Siberia and in 1900 decided to leave Russia and went into exile in Switzerland. In 1903, Lenin became the leader of the major faction within the Russian Social Democratic Labor Party (RSDLP).

FIGURE 17-2:
Lenin, Russian revolutionary and political theorist.

Source: Library of Congress

Lenin decided to return to Russia during the 1905 uprising against Tsar Nicholas II, but after the uprising's failure, he quickly returned into exile. While in exile, Lenin published his most famous work *Imperialism the Highest Stage of Capitalism* in 1916, followed by *The State and Revolution* in 1917. When World War I began to go badly for the imperial Russian regime, Lenin decided it was time to go home and instigate what's known as the October Revolution. After the October Revolution was successful, Lenin consolidated power in Russia by 1918 and became involved in the Russian Civil War, which lasted from 1918 to 1921. After emerging victorious from the Russian Civil War, Lenin created the Soviet Union in 1922. A series of strokes killed Lenin by 1924.

Lenin's contributions to Marxism

Lenin contributed to classical Marxism in three major ways:

>> **Creating a small elite party:** Lenin believed that a socialist party shouldn't be a mass party, with a democratically elected leadership. Instead, the party should consist of a very small intellectual elite, which he called the vanguard of the proletariat, which made policy for the people. Lenin didn't trust the average person to know and do what's right and therefore believed that only a very small Communist elite should run the country.

At the same time, a small amount of freedom was permitted within the party itself. Lenin called this democratic centralism. Inside the Communist Party, free discussion was allowed, but as soon as the leadership made a decision, everybody within the party had to fall in line and support it.

>> **Updating the dialectic stages:** In his second major work, *The State and Revolution,* Lenin decided to update the stage of socialism in the dialectic (see earlier) as used by Karl Marx. This move was quite self-serving because Russia in 1917 was still mostly feudal and only recently had started to develop economically.

According to Marx's theories, Russia wasn't yet ready for Communism but had to be capitalist first. So Lenin decided to skip the phase of capitalism in Marx's dialectic. According to Lenin, a powerful state had to be created to bring about economic development and exterminate the remnants of both feudalism and capitalism and only then could Communism follow. Not only did Lenin justify the future political structure of the Soviet Union in the book, but he also called for genocide on everybody who could possibly oppose Communism in the future.

>> **Explaining the absence of a class revolution:** In his work *Imperialism, the Highest Stage of Capitalism,* Lenin tried to explain why no class revolution had occurred in capitalist societies yet (see the next section). He also provided an explanation for the outbreak of World War I.

Dissecting Lenin's pivotal work

Lenin wrote *Imperialism, the Highest Stage of Capitalism* in 1916. In it, Lenin presented an economic explanation for the outbreak of war and an update to classical Marxism. For him, imperialism (colonialism) was the highest stage of capitalism and necessary for capitalism to survive. He explained that imperialism would generate higher profits for capitalist societies, which allows for capitalists to share some of the profits with the working class, especially what he called the labor aristocracy, such as labor union leaders. Satisfied, this labor aristocracy supported the political status quo and didn't initiate a class revolution as Karl Marx had predicted.

Lenin presented an interesting theory here focusing on Marxist economics. By the time World War I broke out in 1914, Karl Marx's theories had been called into question. His prediction of a working class revolution seemed to be wrong. Lenin set out to update Marx and save some of Marx's ideas in the process.

According to Lenin, World War I was caused by the capitalist system itself — not the assassination of Archduke Ferdinand of Austria-Hungary by Serbian terrorists or the complex and confusing secret alliance system that caused the war.

Lenin believed Marx was right in his core assumptions and theories. All workers were exploited in capitalist societies, and within time, due to the effects of monopoly capitalism (see "The law of concentration" earlier in this chapter), a majority of the population would be turned into impoverished workers. These workers were unable to purchase necessary goods, because they were exploited by the capitalists. The capitalists faced the problem of overproduction and underconsumption. They produced goods nobody at home could afford to buy with the exception of a very small capitalist minority that was well off. New markets for their goods needed to be found. Therefore, the major capitalist powers in the world set out to acquire new markets for their goods, namely colonies.

Workers had become so impoverished that they were ready to initiate class struggle to survive, in turn overthrowing the capitalist system and replacing it with a socialist one. Colonialism proved to be a solution for this problem, too.

Colonialism proved to be the savior of capitalism because it solved the previously mentioned two problems. First, colonial powers made enormous profits by exploiting natives in the colonies. They did so by extracting cheap natural resources and labor from the colonies and then shipping them back to the colonial mother- or fatherland, providing jobs for the working class. These natural resources were then transformed into finished goods sold domestically and, more important, exported back to the colonies where the natives had to buy the goods at a premium.

This allowed the colonial powers to make huge profits, which they shared with their working class, in turn improving the livelihood of these workers, who lost their will and reason to initiate a revolution against their capitalist government. The population in the colonies, however, became impoverished over time.

As long as capitalist countries could be imperial powers, holding colonies, there was enough profit to share with the working class and no revolution would occur. Over time, however, the world ran out of colonies. Soon, there were a limited number of colonies in the world, and by 1914 the supply of colonies was exhausted.

To survive, the capitalist powers had to take colonies from other capitalist imperial powers, which resulted in World War I. The war would destroy capitalist powers, and the workers would then rise and initiate a class revolution replacing current capitalist governments with socialist ones.

TECHNICAL STUFF

As history would prove, Lenin was wrong in his assumption that World War I would destroy capitalism, and soon a new theory of how capitalism through imperialism causes war was developed. This more recent theory follows the aftermath of colonization of a country. Not surprisingly, the colonized peoples of countries weren't happy with their status and sooner or later would rebel against their colonial powers. This caused widespread warfare among colonial powers and their colonies, providing for another example of how capitalism through imperialism can cause warfare. Examples include the wars in Indochina (1945–1954) and the war for Algeria, where France fought its colonies for more than a decade at high human costs.

Traveling to Asia: Maoism

Maoism is the third major attempt at Communism discussed in this chapter. Mao Zedong, seen in Figure 17-3, knew right away that Marxism and Leninism weren't a perfect fit for China in the 1920s. China was preindustrial, with the vast majority of all Chinese living in the countryside. They were being exploited by a landed aristocracy. There was little industry in China, and a small working class was concentrated in a few large cities. According to Marx, a class revolution couldn't occur in China because the revolutionary class, the working class, was missing. China first had to go through industrialization and create a capitalist society with a large working class, and only then could it go Communist.

FIGURE 17-3:
Mao Zedong, founding father of the People's Republic of China.

Source: Library of Congress

TECHNICAL STUFF

Mao Zedong was born in 1893 in Shaoshan, China. He was the son of a wealthy farmer and received a good education, including a tutor familiar with Western ideas such as nationalism and socialism. In 1911, Mao became a supporter of the revolution that overthrew the Chinese monarchy, and in 1917, he completed his first academic work, "A Study of Physical Culture," in which he infused Confucianism with the Western concept of nationalism.

In 1919, Mao applied to the best university in China, Beijing University, but he was rejected. Disappointed, Mao decided to move to the capital anyway and became a librarian at Beijing University to be close to academics. Here, he was introduced to the works of Marx and Lenin, and in 1921, he became one of the 13 original founding members of the Chinese Communist Party.

In 1927, Chinese nationalist leader Chiang Kai-Shek began his quest to destroy the Communists, and Mao had to flee in 1934 to the remote mountainous parts of China. The Communists, however, were saved by the Japanese attack on China in 1937, because Chiang Kai-Shek had to focus on defending his country instead of wiping out the Communists.

After the defeat of the Japanese Empire in 1945, a civil war broke out in China between the Communists and nationalists. The Communists won the civil war with Soviet help, and in 1949, China went Communist, and Mao established the People's Republic of China. He ran the country until his death in 1976.

Mao had no intention to wait until capitalism established a large working class in China. So, he decided to make a few changes to Marxist/Leninist theory. According to Mao, it wasn't the working class in China that was being exploited and had the potential to become the class initiating a revolution; it was the peasants in rural areas. Thus, for Mao, the peasants were the class that would initiate class struggle and destroy the current form of government.

The cities, on the other hand, with a few workers and a larger middle class, were parasites that lived off the peasants' work, exploiting them; and therefore, the peasants had to destroy them. For Mao, the countryside was the site of progress and not the cities.

Mao further believed in the concept of permanent revolution. Both Marx and Lenin believed that a working class revolution would destroy capitalism and then socialism would take care of remnants of other classes and set the foundation for Communism. As soon as Communism was achieved, there'd be no need for another revolution. Mao disagreed. He believed that after a few years or decades, people become complacent and capitalist ideas resurface in society. Therefore, another revolution, a cultural one, was needed to eliminate or reeducate the people who had lost their Communist spirit. In 1965, Mao implemented the Cultural Revolution to purge Chinese society with disastrous political and economic results.

Finally, Mao agreed with Lenin that the common person wouldn't be able to make rational decisions for the country. Only a small intellectual elite in charge of a powerful political party could do so — thus, the creation of the Chinese Communist Party, which still runs China at the time of this writing.

Going Democratic: Social Democracy

The term *democratic socialism, or social democracy,* comes from Imperial Germany (1871–1918). The largest party in Germany by 1900 was the Social Democratic Party of Germany (SPD). It was allowed to freely participate in politics, organizing campaign rallies and distributing campaign information. It even elected members to the imperial parliament and dominated German unions. The party was very successful in demanding higher wages for its members, and Imperial Germany even provided for the German people the first welfare state in the advanced industrialized world. By 1900, Germans were receiving pensions and government healthcare and could receive unemployment benefits. In other words, German workers did well compared to workers in Great Britain and even the United States.

German political theorists such as Eduard Bernstein argued that there was no need for a class revolution in Germany and that the working class could receive economic and political power by working with other political parties through the political system, especially after Germany went democratic in 1918. During the Weimar Republic (1918–1933), the German socialists elected a president of Germany and were well represented in the German parliament. By the late 1920s, the German socialists had toned down their revolutionary rhetoric and even abandoned most of Marxism. They were willing to work through a democratic system to receive political representation and economic benefits for their workers.

After the party had been outlawed and its members had been persecuted during the period of national socialism (1933–1945), it staged a comeback when World War II ended. It became the second largest party of the newly created West Germany. By the time West Germany became a sovereign country one more time in 1954, the party decided to officially abandon Marxism. It did so in 1959, stating that the SPD was a fully democratic party, rejecting class revolution and all forms of political violence, and that the party would use the democratic system to come to power and get benefits for their constituency. The party further stated that it would accept the concept of private property but would continue to call for certain state-owned industries such as public utilities. In addition, the party advocated for a large welfare state protecting the working class in times of economic crisis. (*Note:* Welfare state benefits include pensions, unemployment benefits, healthcare, holidays, and even maternity benefits.) To finance this large welfare state, which is very expensive to maintain, the Social Democrats put a system of progressive taxation into place. Progressive taxation is fairly simple: The more a person makes, the higher his taxes will be.

The reformed Social Democrats would subsequently control the West German and later all German government from 1969 until 1982 and again from 1998 until 2005. They had truly become a social democratic party, rejecting Marxism.

REMEMBER

Democratic socialism or social democracy is the mildest form of socialism, advocating for the retention of private property in a society and establishing a large welfare state to protect the people.

TECHNICAL STUFF

The United States also had a socialist party in its history, The Socialist Party of America. Founded in 1901, the Socialist Party was headed by Eugene Debs and became a mainstay in American politics until the end of World War II. Running on a platform of union rights, the creation of a welfare state, and the nationalizing of certain core industries, such as public utilities, the party appealed to the American working class and many intellectuals. By 1912, the party had almost 120,000 members and received close to a million votes, or 6 percent of the vote, in its quest for the presidency. The party began to decline when the Democratic Party, under President Franklin D. Roosevelt, took over most of its agenda. After the welfare state was created and unions achieved political power with the Wagner Act, the Democrats absorbed many of the former socialist supporters and the party disappeared by the early 1970s.

Following are differences between social democracy and Communism:

>> Social Democrats don't believe that a class revolution is necessary to transform a society. Instead, they're willing to use the electoral process in a democracy to peacefully come to power and change society.

>> Social Democrats don't reject the idea of civil rights and liberties. For them, individuals do matter and their rights need to be protected. Total conformism as is found in a Soviet-type society and a police state aren't acceptable to them.

>> Social Democrats do believe in private property but support the government owning certain industries, such as public utilities.

>> Social Democrats further believe in economic equality, which can be achieved through progressive taxation.

For these reasons, social democracy does appeal to all classes in a society. In many European countries, middle- and lower-middle-class people vote for social democratic parties.

5

The Part of Tens

Check out a list of the ten most influential books in political science.

Discover ten modern political scientists everybody should be familiar with.

Chapter **18**

Ten Political Science Books Everyone Should Read

Readers who want to learn more about political science than they'd find in a regular textbook should take a look at the ten books listed in this chapter. They're not only classics in the field but also still relevant today. My hope is that you pick one or more of the books and decide to not only read it but afterward come to the conclusion that it still matters today.

For example, after reading Aristotle's *Politics*, written in the 4th century BCE, you may realize that the book written more than 2,000 years ago is still applicable to politics today. Or after reading *The Prince* written by Machiavelli in 1513, you may be surprised that Machiavelli's ideas and conclusions on power can be used to explain Russia's or China's foreign policy in the 21st century.

Therefore, in each of the books listed in this chapter, you'll find interesting, often eye-opening or shocking revelations still applicable to today's world. Do keep in mind that the ten book choices are my personal suggestions. Feel free to disagree with my choices. You may even disagree with the conclusions I draw from the books or may find new observations and draw your own conclusions. I hope that you'll discuss the books with friends or classmates or even recommend them to your book club for future reading materials.

Without further ado, here's my list of the ten political science books everyone should read.

Politics (335–323 BCE)

Most political scientists consider Aristotle's book *Politics* the first real political science book. In this seminal work, Aristotle discussed why people create communities and later, on the polis (state).

Aristotle argued that, as members of a community, people enjoy economic and political security and can focus on advancing personally, focusing on more abstract ideas such as what type of political community is best. Suddenly, politics was born.

For Aristotle, the ability to think and philosophize is what makes people happy, not personal wealth or power. People have to take the pursuit of knowledge into politics to be truly happy. This way their thoughts and beliefs can impact actual decision-making in the polis. Philosophy and politics have to be fused, and knowledge has to result in action. A good ruler needs to know what's right and then have the ability to put these policies into place.

Finally, *Politics* was the first political science work that classified different types of governments. Aristotle wanted to know which type of government was best — a monarchy, an aristocracy, or a democracy. So he created a typology of various forms of governments found in Greece at the time. His conclusions were controversial. Instead of making a case for democracy, Aristotle decided that all forms of governments have merit as long as the ruler is wise and just. So for Aristotle, the best form of government depended on the type of ruler. For a detailed discussion of Aristotle's life and work, see Chapter 14.

The Prince (1513)

The Prince was written by Niccolo Machiavelli in 1513 but wasn't published until after his death in 1532. It has become one of the most controversial books in the history of political science. *The Prince* is basically a how-to guide for a ruler on coming to power.

For Machiavelli, it's all about power, and every action that contributes to the acquisition of more power is ethical and moral. Therefore, ethics and justice aren't what matter for a ruler but the acquisition of power. Leaders should be concerned about power because only it can guarantee their survival and the survival of the state itself. The best way to maintain power is through the use of force or the threat of the use of force.

In addition, the book discusses the characteristics a successful ruler has to have and the specific policies he needs to follow to maintain himself in power. For a detailed discussion of Niccolo Machiavelli and his work, see Chapter 15.

Leviathan (1651)

Leviathan, written by Thomas Hobbes and published in 1651, is another must-read for anyone interested in political theory or philosophy. In the work, Hobbes tried to explain why people desire the creation of a strong centralized state. Hobbes agreed with Machiavelli that life is a pursuit for power. For him, people are self-centered, egotistical, and on a constant quest for power. This results in conflict, and without a strong state, only the strong will survive. Therefore, in a state of nature, with no government present, constant conflict and violence occurs. For this reason, people willingly give up their freedoms for the creation of a state that provides them with security.

Hobbes further argued that the most secure society for a people is an absolute monarchy, where the monarch herself is above the law. For Hobbes, the purpose of a government was to provide security for its citizens and not to advocate for notions such as justice or equality in a society. For a detailed discussion of Thomas Hobbes and his works, see Chapter 15.

Two Treatises of Government (1690)

In many ways, John Locke and Thomas Hobbes were the exact opposites. Hobbes believed in a strong centralized form of government, while Locke advocated for the opposite. In his work *Two Treatises of Government,* Locke argued that people are actually rational, they want to better their lives, and they want to own property. People are, therefore, peaceful and want to become prosperous. They're capable of self-rule and self-government. This allows for weak, limited government, providing people with personal freedoms.

Locke argued that people form communities or a state only because of foreign threats and the need for domestic laws and their subsequent enforcement. Only a state, weak and limited in nature, can provide for external and internal security to guarantee against any legal violations and injustices.

Locke even described the government structures that should be in place. He advocated for a legislative to make laws, an executive to enforce the laws, and a judiciary to mediate conflict. In his conclusion, Locke went as far as calling upon people to revolt against any government that's unable or unwilling to stay true to its purpose. For more on John Locke and his work, see Chapter 15.

The Wealth of Nations (1776)

The Wealth of Nations was written by Adam Smith, a Scottish economist, and published in 1776. It has become the bible for people believing in laissez faire (hands-off) capitalism.

Smith argued in his work that the free market should regulate a country's economy, and government needs to stay out of the economy. Smith believed that, in a few instances, government has a role to play in the economy, but these are very limited. Government functions include protection from foreign nations; therefore, government needs to establish a military force. In addition, government needs to provide for an infrastructure, such as roads and canals, to facilitate economic transactions. Finally, a legal system has to be put in place to make and enforce laws protecting mostly economic transactions in the free market. For more on Adam Smith, see Chapter 15.

The Communist Manifesto (1848)

The *Communist Manifesto* was written by Karl Marx and Friedrich Engels in 1848. In it, the authors outline their concept of historical materialism (see Chapter 17) in which they trace history from feudalism to capitalism and finally Communism. They discuss the concept of class struggle, showing how the working class is consistently exploited by the bourgeoisie and how it becomes impoverished. That, in turn, results in a violent class revolution where the working class will overthrow capitalism and become the ruling class and outlaw private property.

The second section of the work contains demands by the two authors, such as a progressive tax, the nationalization of all property, the abolition of private property, the abolition of child labor, and the right to a free education for all classes. The final section of the work then distinguishes Communism from other forms of socialism. For more on Karl Marx and Friedrich Engels, see Chapter 17.

The American Voter (1960)

The American Voter was written by Angus Campbell, Philip Converse, Warren Miller and Donald E. Stokes, four professors from the University of Michigan. The book was based on the first large-scale study of American voters in the 1950s. The authors wanted to know what Americans based their vote on — issues, candidate images, or something else. The results were surprising and established the Michigan model of voting.

The Michigan model found that most Americans based their vote on partisan identification and not knowledge of candidates and issues. *Partisan identification* refers to people having an emotional attachment to a political party, which they usually inherit from their parents through a process called political socialization (see Chapter 3). In other words, voters voted for the Democratic Party candidates because they were Democrats and not because they knew about issues the Democratic Party favored. The Michigan model was the first voting behavior model to discover this.

The model further discovered a group of voters called independents, or people who have no attachment to a political party. According to the study, these independents have the least knowledge of all voters but often decide elections. The study was later duplicated by Donald Stokes and David Butler in Great Britain with similar results.

Man, the State, and War (1959)

Man, the State, and War was published in 1959. In the book, Kenneth Waltz creates the three images or levels of analysis approach to explain causes of war in the international system. Using this approach, Waltz focuses on individuals, nation-states, and the international system itself, in that order. He studies each image and gives explanations of how each can tribute to the outbreak of war.

» First-image explanations involve individuals such as major leaders or top-level diplomats. Waltz examines how first-image explanations can be used to explain the outbreak of war.

» Second-image explanations involve nation-states. Here, Waltz studies a country to discover how domestic factors, such as political culture or economic structures, can contribute to conflict in the international system.

» Third-image explanations focus on the international system. The international system is dominated by anarchy and all nations' thirst for power to acquire security. This results in conflict between states. Therefore, the international system, anarchic in nature and without a world government to enforce laws and punish aggression, is the major source of conflict for Waltz.

For a more detailed discussion of Waltz and his works, see Chapters 8 and 19.

Who Governs? (1961)

Who Governs? is one of the best-known books in American political science. It was written by Robert Dahl and published in 1961. In the book, Dahl attempts to rebut elite theorists who claimed that political power in the United States was centralized in a small power elite, which is interconnected and which occupies all positions of power, while most people lacked political power.

To disprove elite theorists, Dahl studied political power distribution in New Haven, Connecticut, to see whether a small elite was running the city and holding all power. He was surprised to find that there wasn't just one elite but a number of elites or groups competing for political power. One group dominated certain aspects of city politics, such as trash collection, while another one was in charge of another part of the city. This resulted in these elite groups constantly competing for political power and having to bargain and compromise with each other. This is the definition of pluralism as envisioned by James Madison (see Chapter 7). Therefore, pluralism was at work in New Haven, Connecticut, and there wasn't one dominant power elite to be found.

Dahl later on coined the term *polyarchy*, which refers to political systems, such as the U.S. system, that are open and inclusive. Everyone can join elite groups, and their power is limited by the people through free elections.

Who's Running America? (8th Edition, 2017)

Who's Running America?, now in its 8th edition, was written by Thomas R. Dye. The book is an example of elite theory, which claims that a small power elite runs the United States. For Dye, however, the position a person holds in an institution puts that person into the elite. In other words, institutional positions are the sources of power. For example, the position of Secretary of State has power attached to it, and whoever holds the position is suddenly a member of the power elite running the U.S. Therefore, all political scientists have to do is identify the institutional power positions in the U.S., and then it's possible to know not only how many positions exist but who currently holds them.

Dye further argues that some members of the elite can hold more than one position at a time and that the power elite is interconnected through family background, schooling, and even race, religion, and gender.

In the work, Dye finds that there isn't just one coherent elite in the U.S. but two. They are the conservative Sunbelt Cowboys, for example, George W. Bush, and the more liberal Establishment Yankees, for example, Barack Obama. The two elites agree on major issues such as form of government (democracy) and economic system (capitalism). However, they differ on smaller issues such as tax rates, military spending, and the legality of the death penalty. Sunbelt Cowboys are conservative on economic, social, and foreign policy issues, while Establishment Yankees tend to be liberal on these issues. The two elites usually correlate with political party affiliation, Sunbelt Cowboys being Republicans and Establishment Yankees being Democrats, but do not have to. The two elites constantly compete for power and alternate holding positions of power in the U.S.

Chapter **19**

Ten Modern Political Scientists

I n this chapter, I undertake a truly difficult task: selecting the top ten modern political scientists. First, what is "modern"? For the purposes of this chapter, I've chosen political scientists only from the 20th and 21st centuries. Therefore, I've excluded all the great classical writers. You can read about them in Chapters 14 and 15. Political science officially became a discipline in 1903 in the United States, so I picked this date as a starting point for my list. Also, if I included all the classical writers, it'd be impossible to pick just ten.

Second, I've selected only political scientists who were either born in the U.S. or taught at American universities. Some choices are no-brainers because they had such an enormous impact on the field of political science. Others may be more controversial because they dealt with topics that aren't considered politically correct. So feel free to disagree with my choices. They're obviously very subjective in nature, and every political scientist could easily come up with different choices to put into their top-ten list.

Without any further ado, here are my picks for the top ten modern political scientists.

David Easton

David Easton was born in June 1917, in Toronto, Canada, and died at the age of 97 in 2014. He received his PhD in political science from Harvard University in 1947 and subsequently taught at the University of Chicago from 1947 to 1997.

At the University of Chicago, Easton turned a fledgling political science program into one of the best in the U.S. From 1968 to 1969, he served as president of the American Political Science Association (APSA), where he coined the term *postbehavioralism* in 1968. Postbehavioralism was an attempt to turn political science into a discipline that focused more on actual political, economic, and social problems while still being scientific in nature. (For a discussion of postbehavioralism, see Chapter 2.) In 1997, Easton was appointed a distinguished research professor in the Department of Political Science at the University of California, Irvine, where he closed out his long, distinguished career.

Easton's contributions to political science focused on systems theory, defined as a set of related units that interact constantly with each other (see Chapter 8 for the concept of the international system). He argued that the political system integrates all activities through which policy is made. His concept of a political system is commonly known as the black box theory or the input/output theory. It's used to explain how government actually works.

Gabriel Almond

Gabriel Almond was born in 1911 in Rock Island, Illinois, and died in 2002 at the age of 91 in Garden Grove, California. He studied at the University of Chicago and received his degree in political science in 1938. He subsequently taught at Brooklyn College, now the City University of New York. After volunteering for the war effort, Almond worked for the Office of War Information, analyzing enemy propaganda. He went back to academics in 1947 and received a job at Yale University. After teaching both at Yale and Princeton, he left for Stanford University in California in 1963 and taught there until his retirement in 1993.

Gabriel Almond is most famous for bringing behavioralism (see Chapter 2) to comparative politics. His most famous work is *The Civic Culture*, published in 1963 (see Chapter 3). In it, Almond and his coauthor Sidney Verba applied the concept of political culture to political stability and tried to determine which culture is most suited to sustain democracy. *The Civic Culture* was the first large-scale study in political culture exploring the relationship between citizen participation and attitudes toward the political system.

Hans Morgenthau

Hans Morgenthau was one of the major writers in international relations. He was born in 1904 in Coburg, Germany, and went to the universities of Berlin and Munich. He emigrated to the United States in 1937 and subsequently taught at the University of Chicago and the City University of New York. He died in 1980 in New York City.

Morgenthau is widely considered the godfather of classical realism in the U.S. (see Chapter 8). In his classic *Politics Among Nations* (1948), he argued that idealism (see Chapter 8) had allowed Nazi Germany and Fascist Italy to rise to power and commit international aggression, and now that World War II was over, it was time to abandon idealism for realism. For him, political scientists need to look at the world as is and not how it should be. According to Morgenthau, states are rational actors and realize that they'll need to be powerful to survive in the international system. Political scientists, therefore, need to study the relationship between states and their quest for power.

In the 1960s, Morgenthau became an advisor for President John F. Kennedy but dissented on his policies toward Vietnam. Morgenthau became one of the most vocal critics of the Vietnam War, which led to his dismissal by the Johnson administration.

Kenneth Waltz

Kenneth Waltz was another prominent scholar in the field of international relations. Many consider him to be the father of neorealism (see Chapter 8). He was born in 1924 in Ann Arbor, Michigan, and went to Oberlin College. He served in the army during World War II and attended Columbia University after the war ended. He was called up when the Korean War broke out and served from 1951 to 1952 as a first lieutenant. After the war, he returned to Columbia to continue his studies, earning his PhD in political science in 1954.

After teaching at Columbia University, Swarthmore College, and Brandeis University, Waltz took a position at the University of California, Berkeley, where he stayed until his retirement in 1997. He became a professor emeritus and later continued teaching part time at Columbia University until his death at age 89 in 2013.

Waltz's first major contribution to the field of international relations came in 1959 when he published his book *Man, the State, and War: A Theoretical Analysis,* in which he used three levels of analysis to study the causes of war (see Chapters 8 and 18). His second major work, titled *Theory of International Politics,* published in 1979, became the foundation for neorealism. In it, Waltz argued that to study the politics of states, you must look at the structure of the international system. He argued that the system is dominated by anarchy and that it's shaped by the distribution of power among the various states. For example, in a bipolar system, two great powers exist, and the way they interact shapes the structure of the system.

Vladimir Orlando Key

Vladimir Orlando Key was born in 1908 in Austin, Texas. He received his PhD from the University of Chicago in 1934, specializing in American politics. He joined the faculty of the University of California at Los Angeles for several years and then moved on to Johns Hopkins, Yale, and finally Harvard University. He stayed at Harvard University until he died at age 55 in 1963.

Key was a pioneer in the study of American politics. He was the first political scientist to study interest groups and their impact on politics in the U.S. In addition, Key created the concepts of realignment and dealignment in American voting behavior (see Chapter 7) as well as the echo chamber effect theory on voting behavior, which states that voting reflects the political environment of the time.

Samuel P. Huntington

Samuel P. Huntington was born in 1927 in New York City. After serving in the U.S. Army, he received his PhD from Harvard University in 1951. He subsequently taught most of his life at Harvard University from where he retired in 2007, shortly before his death in 2008.

He is mostly remembered for his paper "Clash of Civilizations," published in 1993, which was later (1996) turned into a book titled *The Clash of Civilizations and the Remaking of World Order.* In this highly controversial book, Huntington argued that the world had become divided into seven or eight civilizations. These civilizations differ based on religious, historical, and cultural values. For this reason, Huntington argued that future wars would be fought not between nation-states, as had been the case the previous four centuries, but instead between civilizations, an example being a conflict between Christianity and Islam. He cited Islamic extremism as an example of his theory.

John Rawls

John Rawls was an American political theorist who dealt with the issues of justice and equality in society. He was born in Baltimore, Maryland, in 1921 and died in Massachusetts at the age of 81 in 2002. After he received his bachelor's degree from Princeton University, Rawls volunteered for the army and served in the Pacific, receiving a Bronze Star. After he observed the destruction caused by the dropping of the atomic bomb on the Japanese city of Hiroshima as a part of the U.S. occupying force in Japan, he retired from the military and returned to Princeton for his PhD. Rawls taught at both Princeton and Cornell universities and then moved to Harvard, where he taught for almost 40 years. In 1999, Rawls was presented with the National Humanities Medal by President Clinton.

Rawls's major contribution to the discipline was his theory of justice as fairness, outlined in his 1971 book *A Theory of Justice*. In it, Rawls argued for a political system based on social justice, which entails equal basic rights, equality of opportunity, and promoting the interest of the least advantaged in society. To garner support for his argument, he asked readers to pick the society they'd like to live in if they wouldn't know what kind of social position they'd hold in society.

Francis Fukuyama

Yoshihiro Francis Fukuyama was born in Chicago in 1952. He received his PhD from Harvard University, where one of his professors was Samuel P. Huntington (discussed earlier). After working for the private Rand Corporation, he joined the faculties of Johns Hopkins and George Mason universities before moving on to Stanford University, where he still teaches.

In his major work *The End of History and the Last Man*, published in 1992, Fukuyama argues that the struggles between all competing political and economic ideologies have come to an end with the collapse of the Soviet Union and Communism in 1991. The world has settled on one major ideology, liberal democracy. Therefore, the end of history has been reached, and liberal democracy has been triumphant and is here to stay.

Fukuyama has been politically active in conservative circles, working for the Reagan administration. However, he opposed the war in Iraq, beginning in 2003, and has been openly critical of neoconservatism in the U.S.

Robert Gilpin

Robert Gilpin was an American political scientist who specialized in international political economy. He was born in Burlington, Vermont, in 1930 and died in 2018 at the age of 87. He received his PhD from the University of California, Berkeley, after serving for three years in the U.S. Navy. He taught at Princeton University for 36 years (1962–1998) and then became a professor emeritus. At Princeton, he was appointed the Dwight D. Eisenhower Professor of International Affairs and also was a faculty associate of the Center of International Studies.

In his work *War and Change in World Politics,* published in 1981, Gilpin created the theory of hegemonic stability (see Chapter 8), which claims that every hegemon (superpower) creates an international structure for its own benefit. However, other states will also benefit, because the hegemon has created and maintains a system from which not just it but many nations, especially allies, benefit. Gilpin further explained the causes for the rise and decline of powerful nations.

Robert O. Keohane

Robert Owen Keohane was born in 1941 in Chicago, Illinois. He received his PhD in political science from Harvard University and subsequently taught at several universities across the U.S., including Stanford University, Harvard University, and Duke University. He is currently on the faculty at Princeton University.

Keohane is one of the most prominent scholars in international relations. Many consider his books *Power and Interdependence* (1977) and *After Hegemony* (1984) to be major contributions to the creation of the field of political economy. Keohane is famous for neoliberal institutionalism, an approach to international relations that discusses the use of international institutions, such as the United Nations or the International Monetary Fund (IMF), by nation-states to advance their own interests while also benefiting other nations. Instead of believing in power politics as realists had done, Keohane advocates for interdependence and cooperation. Using this approach, states can still benefit and get more powerful, but it doesn't come at the expense of other nations. For Keohane, pursuit of self-interest by states can lead to cooperation, which benefits all involved.

Index

free market system, 196, 248–249, 250, 292

free trade, 197, 201

French Revolution, 245

French school of thought, 24

friends, as agents of political socialization, 42

Fukuyama, Francis, 301

G

G-20 (Group of 20), 213

G-8 (Group of 8), 213

GDP (gross domestic product), 211

gender, influence on voting, 97–98

General Agreement on Tariffs and Trade (GATT), 199

General Assembly, U.N., 151, 154

general will, 244

geopolitics, 165

Georgia, 144

German school of thought, 26–27

Germany

  amendment process in, 65

  balance of power theory, 121

  Berlin Airlift, 169

  Berlin Wall, 171–172

  bicameralism, 82

  chancellors, 81

  citizenship requirements, 33

  corporatism in, 108

  democratic socialism in, 285–286

  Federal Constitutional Court in, 93

  federal government, power of, 12

  federalism in, 57

  historical aggressive foreign policy, 184–185

  Nazi regime, 38, 52–55, 258

  partisan identification, 98

  party systems in, 101

  populism in, 262

  power of judicial review, 66

  right-wing populism in, 263–267

  theory of hegemonic stability, 124

  vote of no confidence in, 81

Germany (Federal Constitutional Court), 93

Gilpin, Robert, 123, 302

global economic inequality, 204–205

global humanism, 129

global level of analysis, 119

globalization, 210–213

Glorious Revolution, 241

Gorbachev, Mikhail, 175–176, 180

Gosplan, 203–204

government. See also specific forms

  defined, 11

  forms of

    defined by Aristotle, 226–227

    overview, 49–50

  legitimacy, sources of, 15–17

  loyalty to, 40

  systems of

    classifying, 61

    confederations, 59–60

    federal versus unitary system, 57–59

    federalism, 57

    overview, 56

    unitary system, 56

grand theories, 25, 27, 28–29

Great Britain

  bicameral structure in legislature, 85

  civic culture in, 35–37

  lack of constitution, 64

  Magna Carta, 65

  parliamentary democracy in, 51

  partisan identification, 98

  prime ministers, 81, 88–89

  principle of parliamentary supremacy, 241

  Suez Canal crisis, 170–171

  U.N. Security Council, 152

Great Depression, 34, 43

Greece, 168, 262

Greece (ancient), 8–9, 218

Greek philosophers

  Aristotle

    communities, creating, 225

    forms of government, 226–227

    founding of political science, 8–9

    general discussion, 224–227

    humanity and politics, 226

    Politics, 8–9, 225, 226, 290

    view of political power, 12

Italy
  civic culture in, 35–37
  Fascism in, 253–254
  in League of Nations, 149
  Marshall Plan, 168–169
  neofascism in, 260
  Niccolo Machiavelli, 232–235
  Red Brigades terrorist group, 189, 191

J

Jackson, Andrew, 87, 90
Japan, 33, 34, 56, 59
Jefferson, Thomas, 70
Johnson, Andrew, 84
Johnson, Lyndon B., 173
judge-made law, 92
judicial activism, 93
judicial restraint, 93
judicial review, power of, 66, 91, 93
judiciary branch, 91–94
Junkers, 184–185
Jus sanguinis (right by blood), 33
Jus soli (right by territory), 33
just behavior, 222
justice as fairness, theory of, 301

K

Kennan, George F., 166–167
Kennedy, John F., 172
Keohane, Robert O., 302
Key, V. O.. Jr., 97, 100, 106
Key, Vladimir Orlando, 300
KOF Index of Globalization, 211–213
Korean War, 169–170
Kuhn, Thomas, 21

L

labor theory of value, 277–278
laissez faire capitalism, 248–249, 292
law of concentration, 278
law of increasing cost of war, 125
law of stagnation, 126

Law of the Sea Treaty, 140
laws, types of, 91–92
lawyers, number of, 92
Le Pen, Jean-Marie, 263–265
Le Pen, Marine, 263, 265–267
League Council, 148
League of Nations
  general discussion, 146–149
  similarities with United Nations, 150–151
left-wing ideologies. *See also* Communism; Marxism
  Maoism, 283–285
  populism, 261
  social democracy, 285–286
  Socialism, 271–272
  Vladimir Lenin, 279–283
Legal Committee, 154
legalism, formal, 20
legislative branch, 82–85
legitimacy, 15–17, 56
Lenin, Vladimir, 164, 279–283
levels of analysis, 117–119, 293–294
Leviathan (Hobbes), 236, 237, 238, 291
liberal democracy, 301
liberal international economic order, 197
liberalism
  behavioralism and, 24
  classical, 239, 247–249
  Fascist rejection of, 256
  modern, 250
lobbying, 110
Locke, John, 12, 239–241, 291–292
low politics, 123
lower houses of legislative structure, 85
loyalty to political system, creating, 40
Luther, Martin, 232

M

Machiavelli, Niccolo
  balance of power theory, 120
  general discussion, 232–235
  The Prince, 12, 234, 290–291
  realism, 119
  view of political power, 12

multinational corporations (MNCs), 119, 209–210

multiparty systems, 81, 101

Multiple Independently Targetable Reentry Vehicle (MIRV), 178–179

multipolarity, 117

Muslim migration, 264, 268

Mussolini, Benito, 253–254, 258

mutual consent to end treaties, 138

N

Napoleonic Wars, 120

narrow-range theories, 29

National Alliance, 260

National Front (France), 102, 263–267

National Rally party (France), 265–267

National Rifle Association (NRA), 110

nationalism, 17, 40, 56, 116, 256

nationalist terrorism, 190

NATO (North Atlantic Treaty Organization), 125, 127, 158, 167, 171

natural law, 91

Nazi Germany, 38, 52–55, 258. *See also* Fascism

necessary and proper clause, 83

neofascism, 259–260

neoliberal institutionalism, 302

neorealism, 123–125, 299–300

Netherlands, 56

NGOs (nongovernment organizations), 119, 212

Nixon, Richard, 174

Nixon Doctrine, 174

nongovernment organizations (NGOs), 119, 212

noninterference, right of, 136–137

nonstate wars, 183

normative theory, 20, 23

North, defined, 204

North Atlantic Treaty Organization (NATO), 125, 127, 158, 167, 171

NRA (National Rifle Association), 110

nuclear arms race

  cruise missiles, 179

  Flexible Response Doctrine, 177

  MAD Doctrine, 178

  Massive Retaliation Doctrine, 177

  MIRV, 178–179

  SDI, 179–180

  TRIAD Doctrine, 178

  types of ballistic missiles, 177

O

objective research, 24, 27

oceans, freedom of, 133, 140

oil crises, 208–209

oligarchy, 50, 227

one-party systems, 101

Orban, Victor, 261

organizational structure of interest groups, 111

Organski, A. F. K., 122

Outer Space Treaty, 139

overextension, 125

P

Pan Am Flight 103, 190

paradigms, 22

Pareto, Vilfredo, 14

parliamentary democracies

  executives in, 80–81

  in Great Britain, 88–89

  minority governments, 81

  overview, 51, 69

  versus presidential system, 80–81

  vote of no confidence, 81

parochial political culture, 37, 38–39

participant political culture, 38–39

partisan identification, 97, 98, 104

partisanship, 36

Party Government (Schattschneider), 99

party in electorate, 100

party platforms, 105

party systems, types of, 101

patriotism, 40

peace

  democracy and, 28, 186–187

  global humanism and, 129

  idealism and, 128

peacekeepers, U.N., 153, 157–158

peacemakers, U.N., 157–158

About the Author

Marcus A. Stadelmann is a professor of political science and chair of the Department of Political Science and History at the University of Texas at Tyler. Dr. Stadelmann received his PhD from the University of California at Riverside in 1990 and has subsequently taught at universities in California, Utah, and Texas.

He presently teaches classes on American government, international relations, and comparative politics. In addition, he has given many public and academic presentations on American presidential elections and international topics, such as the collapse of the Soviet Union, German unification, the rise of populism in Europe, and the politics of Russia and Ukraine.

Dr. Stadelmann's other publications include *The Dependent Ally — German Foreign Policy from 1949 to 1990*, *The Quest for Power — An Introduction to World Politics in the 21st Century*, and *U.S. Presidents For Dummies*. In addition, Dr. Stadelmann has contributed chapters to many books and has published numerous academic articles.

Dedication

This book is dedicated to the people who had the most impact on my life: my parents, Wolfgang and Heidi, and my two daughters, Katarina and Holly.

Author's Acknowledgments

Special thanks go to my parents and my two daughters, Katarina and Holly. They kept me on track for the last months, supported me in this endeavor, and patiently waited until my work was done. Without their support, this work would not have been possible.

I would also like to express my gratitude to my editor, Linda Brandon, who did an excellent job working with me on this book. Without her input, this book would not have become what it is today.

Publisher's Acknowledgments

Acquisitions Editor: Lindsay Lefevere
Development Editor: Linda Brandon
Copy Editor: Jennette ElNaggar
Technical Editor: Dr. Milind Thakar
Proofreader: Debbye Butler

Production Editor: Siddique Shaik
Cover Image: © TommL/Getty Images